ANALYSIS OF DIS/AGREEMENT –
with particular reference to Law and Legal Theory

Law and Philosophy Library

VOLUME 66

ANALYSIS OF DIS/AGREEMENT – with particular reference to Law and Legal Theory

by

SVEIN ENG

Professor of the Philosophy of Law,
University of Oslo

KLUWER ACADEMIC PUBLISHERS
DORDRECHT / BOSTON / LONDON

A C.I.P. Catalogue record for this book is available from the Library of Congress.

ISBN 978-1-4020-1490-1

Published by Kluwer Academic Publishers,
P.O. Box 17, 3300 AA Dordrecht, The Netherlands.

Sold and distributed in North, Central and South America
by Kluwer Academic Publishers,
101 Philip Drive, Norwell, MA 02061, U.S.A.

In all other countries, sold and distributed
by Kluwer Academic Publishers,
P.O. Box 322, 3300 AH Dordrecht, The Netherlands.

Printed on acid-free paper

For

Lisbeth

Svein Gustav and Ida

Preface to the English edition

This book is a translation of *U/enighetsanalyse – med særlig sikte på jus og allmenn rettsteori* (Oslo 1996, mimeographed; Oslo 1998, Universitetsforlaget/Scandinavian University Press). I have shortened the book to some extent by omitting sections II B 3.3.5 og IV 4. A few references to the literature have been deleted or added. In other respects this English edition is identical to the Norwegian edition.

The task of translating the Norwegian text into English gave rise to many challenges. The very act of going from a dense Germanic language like Norwegian to a grammatically more flexible language like English in itself raises many problems. But also on account of the content of the work, the translation of *U/enighetsanalyse* was very demanding. In the first place it is a matter of a work that has language itself as its subject; the work presents certain general structures in our concrete use of language, and builds the presentation up as a close interplay between the level of theory and concept on the one hand and the level of examples of language usage on the other. Secondly it is a matter of a work that had itself to establish and justify its perspective; one aspect of this was that to a considerable extent there was a need for innovation with respect to concepts and terms.

The fact that these difficulties have shown themselves to be surmountable is to a great extent thanks to the exceptional obligingness and commitment on the part of my colleague Patrick Chaffey in the Department of British and American Studies. Throughout the years 1999-2003 we co-operated very closely on this translation. In the main the work consisted in his writing first drafts of translations of parts of the book, drafts which I reworked, and which we then discussed, word for word, until we had gone through the whole manuscript; after this I went through the manuscript in several rounds and in so doing discussed innumerable questions with him. For long periods of time we had lengthy discussions on a daily basis. Without his help I do not know whether I would have managed to see the translation safely completed, and it would in any event most certainly have been less faithful to the original. It is with great pleasure and gratitude that I look back on our co-operation.

At different stages of the work on the translation I received valuable help from colleagues in Norway and abroad in solving different problems that the work occasioned. I should like to thank Zenon Bankowski, Ronald Craig, Dagfinn

Føllesdal, Neil MacCormick, Stanley L. Paulson, Robert S. Summers and Stuart Toddington.

I also want to thank Arnt Myrstad, Aleksander Peczenik and Eivind Smith for their encouragement and valuable support along the way.

Finally I should like to express my gratitude to my closest family for their encouragement and patience; the English edition is, like the Norwegian edition, dedicated to them.

The Norwegian Research Council, Lovsamlingsfondet (the Statute Collection Fund) and Anders Jahre's Fund provided financial support for the work on the translation.

Parts of section II F appeared earlier in (2000) 13 *Ratio Juris*, and section III 3 appeared earlier in (1999) 18 *Law and Philosophy*.

Oslo, March 2003

Svein Eng

Preface to the Norwegian edition

My thinking concerning the perspective and topic of the present work started in the mid seventies. In the main the work was written in the period from 1983 to 1995.

The work had itself to establish and justify its perspective; this is not present in a well delimited form within existing research traditions.

My main motive for writing this work lay in a combination of two factors: On the one hand, I have a strong and enduring interest in epistemology. On the other hand, I discovered that language and argumentation phenomena that I consider interesting and significant, had not been systematically treated in the literature, but had been dealt with piecemeal, overlooked or denied. Two examples are definition activity formulated in everyday language (with appurtenant boundary between analytically un/true and other propositions) and fusion of descriptive and normative propositions. More generally it is the case that the literature has not captured the wealth of nuances, the internal coherence (system character and dynamics), the independence and the factual significance that all characterise the critically reflexive form that constitutes the perspective and topic of the present work. Thus the literature has to a great extent related blindly to important parts of our power of judgement mediated in and through everyday language, including important parts of lawyers' power of judgement.

Through my work on legal topics it became clear to me that a close connection exists between on the one hand the critically reflexive form brought into focus in the present work, and on the other hand lawyers' language and argumentation. Parallel to and in interplay with my other works in law and the philosophy of law, the present work took shape, and publication became the aim. This was a stepwise and lengthy process. For one thing, it took me a long time to conceptualise, as well as to collect and present evidence for, the wealth of nuances, internal coherence and factual significance that characterise the critically reflexive form. For another, it took me a long time to cognise and conceptualise the independence of the critically reflexive form, including the fact that the perspective and topic of the present work is not reducible to particular -isms on the level of fundamental philosophical positions, or in other ways situated in any univocal relationship to this level.

For comments on a version of 1994–1995 I wish to thank Associate Professor Øyvind Baune, Professor Jes Bjarup, Professor Jørgen Dalberg-Larsen, Professor Åke Frändberg, Associate Professor Arnt Myrstad, Professor Aleksander Peczenik and Professor Jon Wetlesen. My thanks also go to the late Professor Torstein Eckhoff for comments on an earlier work which later grew to become Chapter V.

The present work was defended for the Doctorate in Law in December 1996. In relation to the version used for the disputation I have brought the bibliography up to date and amplified and clarified some points, but I have not made any material changes.

I wish to thank the Faculty of Law Library at the University of Oslo for efficient help with the provision of literature.

For assistance with getting the manuscript ready for printing, I wish to thank in particular Lisbeth Markussen Eng. She provided extensive help in checking the language, verifying quotations and reading the proofs. I further want to thank the students of law Alf Petter Høgberg, who commented on punctuation and in co-operation with me set up a draft for running heads, Karl Kristian Lofstad, who assisted with proof-reading, and Vidar Helgesen, who checked quotations from judgments.

For financial support for printing I wish to thank Anders Jahre's Fund, Lovsamlingsfondet (the Statute Collection Fund) and the Department of Public and International Law at the University of Oslo.

Oslo, April 1998

Svein Eng

Contents

An asterisk after an item means that the section concerned is introduced with a table of contents of its own

II SOME FUNDAMENTAL TYPES OF PROPOSITION ABOUT WHAT SOMETHING IS

IV SOME FORMS OF LANGUAGE AND ARGUMENTATION THAT OFTEN MAKE IT UNCLEAR WHICH TYPE OF PROPOSITION ONE IS CONFRONTED WITH; IN PARTICULAR ON THE FLIGHT FROM THE NORMATIVE PROPOSITION

V RECONSTRUCTION AND REDEFINITION: A DISTINCT AND WIDESPREAD COMBINATION OF THE FUNDAMENTAL PROPOSITION TYPES

Some symbols and conventions used in the text

‘ ’ [single quotation marks]
In addition to their normal uses otherwise, I use single quotation marks to signify that I am talking about linguistic meaning entities (criteria, concepts, propositions).

“ ” [double quotation marks]
In addition to their normal uses otherwise, I use double quotation marks to signify that I am talking about linguistic entities (words, phrases, sentences).

– [dash]
In addition to its normal use otherwise, I use the dash to signify a logical division of the text on the level between the sentence and the paragraph.

↔ [two-way arrow]
I use the two-way arrow to signify that the subsequent text refers back to the area of text indicated by the relata of the arrow. For example, “(a)↔(c)” signifies that the subsequent text refers back to items (a), (b) and (c) in the preceding discussion.

cf.
In addition to its standard use in references to literature I use “cf.” in the general sense of ‘see, in illumination of this, ...’, where the dots may be replaced by reference to e.g. a fact, an argument, or a definition. An example would be: “Decision propositions are common in the case of definitions, cf. the frequency of forms of expression such as “in what follows I shall use the word “x” of …” ”. While “cf.” in this usage has an area in common with “compare”, I typically use “cf.” in cases of more direct evidence and “compare” in cases of more mediated evidence relationships.

Rt.
“Rt.” is an abbreviation for “Norsk Retstidende”, the title of the leading general law report series in Norway. This series contains all the decisions of the Norwegian Supreme Court, either in full or in the form of a short summary. References

to this series are given in the following form: year, slash, and number of the first page of the decision in question, e.g. Rt. 1973/433.

Indented paragraphs in small print

Indented paragraphs in small print are quotations when they are enclosed in quotation marks and my own explanatory remarks on the main text when they are not. The main text may be read independently of these explanatory remarks, which expand on, but are not necessary to understand the argument of, the main text.

Titles in square brackets

In the case of all titles in Scandinavian to which I refer, I have put a literal English translation in square brackets after the original title. To mark the fact that the reference is to a work in Scandinavian, I use only small letters in the translation (except in the case of proper nouns and after full stops).

I

Introduction

1. First formulation of major aims and main threads

In order to determine whether two participants in a discussion are in real *dis/agreement* one must *compare* their propositions. Comparison presupposes common yardsticks and common features: Just as the comparison of two phenomena with respect to length presupposes that one has concepts of units of length and that these concepts are applicable to both phenomena, so the comparison of propositions with respect to dis/agreement will presuppose that one has concepts of types of proposition and that these concepts are applicable to both sets of propositions. – If one has no concepts of proposition types, or if one applies them to propositions in relation to which they are out of place, then the comparison will be only an apparent one (pseudo-discussion) and the result a misunderstanding (pseudo dis/agreement).

A major aim of the present work is to describe and to clarify certain *yardsticks for the comparison of and choice between propositions*, and to demonstrate the area of origin and application of, as well as a certain independence characterising, these yardsticks. It is at the same time an aim *not* to take a standpoint on the *tenability of the propositions themselves*: in particular not to take a standpoint on controversial philosophical, moral, legal, political or similar questions (section 6 below).

The *description and clarification* of the yardsticks (certain proposition types and patterns, criteria and interests) have determined the systematic structuring of this work: from the simple to the complex (section 5.1 below, with further references).

In the parallel demonstration of the *area of origin and application* of the yardsticks, I often return to propositions about legal phenomena, including lawyers' propositions about what the law is. – Seen from the point of view of the yardsticks, it is true that lawyers' language and argumentation is *only one instantiation*: The area of origin and application of the yardsticks is everyday language, in everyday life as well as in academic subjects, science and philosophy, i.e. much wider than lawyers' language and argumentation (section 5.1 below). – However, seen from the point of view of lawyers, the yardsticks are *constitutive of their legal power of judgement*: The work will demonstrate the fact that, and the way in which, unity and continuity in lawyers' language and argumentation are created in and through the yardsticks (sections 5.1–5.2 below, with further references).

The *independence* of the yardsticks cannot in the same way as their area of origin and application be demonstrated continuously. Towards the end of the present introduction I shall give an account of what I mean by "independence" in the preceding sentence and in what way this property of the yardsticks appears from the work (section 6 below).

In and through the yardsticks (the proposition types and patterns, criteria and interests of which the work gives an account) significant acts take place, but these have not been systematically and concretely mapped in earlier literature. In this resides the *value of the work* (section 7 below).

As a concrete point of entry into the perspective and topic of the work I shall continue the present introduction by taking as a starting point one of the most common forms of proposition in everyday language: the form *'what something is'* (section 2 below). After this I shall point to four *main yardsticks* for comparison of and choice between propositions of this form (section 3 below); and then I shall situate these main yardsticks, with specifications and combinations, in the *perspective of the work* (sections 4–6 below).

2. Propositions about what something is

In what follows some examples are presented of questions or propositions about what something is; these examples are intended to illustrate the fact that such questions and propositions are *omnipresent*, but have otherwise been randomly chosen:

> "[A] *legal duty* so called is nothing but a prediction that if a man does or omits certain things he will be made to suffer in this or that way by judgment of the court; and so of a *legal right*" (my italics).[1]
>
> "A *precedent* is a judgment of the Supreme Court ..." (my italics).[2]
>
> "The *case documents of the public administration* are documents which are drawn up by an administrative agency as well as documents which have been received by or submitted to such an agency" (my italics).[3]
>
> "*[P]olitics* is a process of popular education – the task of adjusting the conflicting interests of diverse groups in the community, and bending the hostility and suspicion and ignorance engendered by group interests toward a comprehension of mutual understanding" (my italics);[4] "Politics is the will to achieve something."[5]
>
> "So sehen wir also, daß *der Krieg* nicht bloß ein politischer Akt, sondern ein wahres politisches instrument ist, eine Fortsetzung des politischen Verkehrs, ein Durchführen desselben mit anderen Mitteln" (my italics);[6] "*War* is not part of politics, but the negation of politics, a parasitic growth upon political life" (my italics).[7]
>
> "What is ... a *national state?* Put simply, it is a state in which the population forms a cultural community" (my italics);[8] "A national state is a state that gives expression to a national community."[9]
>
> "*Courage* is a moral quality; it is not a chance gift of nature like an aptitude for games. It is a cold choice between two alternatives, the fixed resolve not

1 Holmes, 'The Path of the Law', p. 169.
2 Peter Wessel Zapffe. Here quoted from Andenæs, *Innføring i rettsstudiet* [introduction to the study of law], p. 113.
3 Freedom of Information Act (Act No. 69 of 19 June 1970), section 3 first paragraph.
4 Frankfurter, *The Public and Its Government*, p. 161.
5 Palme, *Politikk – det er å ville noe* [politics – that is the will to achieve something].
6 Clausewitz, *Vom Kriege*, p. 34.
7 Collingwood, 'Modern Politics', p. 179.
8 Østerud, 'Er nasjonalstaten foreldet?' [is the national state a thing of the past?], p. 352.
9 Østerud, *Hva er nasjonalisme?* [what is nationalism?], pp. 102 et seq.

to quit; an act of renunciation which must be made not once but many times by the power of the will. Courage is will power" (my italics).[10]

"What is *philosophy?*" (my italics).[11]

"What is the *world?* Is it spiritual or material? Or both? What is the relationship in which mind stands to matter? What is *man?* Where does he come from, where does he go? What is the *purpose of life?* What is the *greatest good*? These and similar questions are ones that human beings ask themselves over and over again. In spite of thousands of years of searching in vain for the final answer, each new generation always asks them again" (my italics; Schjelderup's italics omitted).[12]

---

10 Lord Moran, *The Anatomy of Courage*, p. 67

11 Various articles with this title in Stigen (ed.), *Generasjoner i norsk filosofi* [generations of Norwegian philosophy]; Deleuze/ Guattari, *Qu'est-ce que la philosophie?*

12 Schjelderup, 'Filosofiens vesen' [the essence of philosophy], p. 48.

3. Fundamental proposition-types and ambiguities

Propositions about what something is (section 2 above) may be seen as (actual or possible) answers to questions of the form *"What is x?"*. Just as great as the diversity of directions in which this form of question points, is the diversity of proposition types about what something is, with which we operate.[1]

(1) One fundamental ambiguity of propositions about what something is, arises between, on the one hand, propositions that contribute to determining the meanings of words (contribute to determining concepts), and on the other hand, propositions that presuppose this topic and thematise other topics. – In relation to the standard forms of expression "What is x?" and "X is ...", the ambiguity is a question of whether "x" refers to the word (the concept) or to the phenomena that the word designates (the concept covers). For example, do the propositions quoted in section 2 above say something about the meanings of the words and expressions "legal duty", "legal right", "precedent", "case documents of the public administration", "politics", "Krieg", "war", "national state", "courage", "philosophy", "world", "man", "purpose of life", "greatest good"? Or do these propositions say that the phenomena that are designated by these words and expressions have certain properties? In the terminology that is introduced in what follows: Are they *definitions* or *characterisations*?

The distinction between definitions and characterisations is important because *different facts are relevant in the assessment of their tenability*: – If the sentence "a precedent is a judgment of the Supreme Court"[2] is interpreted as expressing a descriptive definition, then the tenability of the proposition must be checked by comparing the proposition with actual language use (the way in which the word "precedent" is actually used). – If this sentence is interpreted as expressing a descriptive characterisation, then the tenability of the proposition must be checked by comparing the proposition with reality other than language use (with the properties of those phenomena that are designated by the word "precedent").

In my subsequent discussion of definitions one main thread consists in mapping different aspects of language use to which definitions relate (sec-

---

1 Robinson, *Plato's Earlier Dialectic*, p. 59: "[Questions of the What-is-x? form] is, perhaps, when unsupported by a context, *the vaguest of all forms of question except an inarticulate grunt.* It indicates less determinately than any other the sort of information the questioner wants" (my italics). – See also same writer, *Definition*, pp. 190, 192.

2 In accordance with normal language usage among lawyers I use the spelling "judgment" for a type of decision of the court. In all other cases I use the spelling "judgement".

tions II B 4–7 below; cf. section II A 2 (1) below, which gives a survey of my discussion of definitions).

(2) Another fundamental ambiguity of propositions about what something is, arises between *descriptive propositions* and *normative propositions.* – In relation to the standard forms of expression "What is x?" and "X is ...", the ambiguity is a question of whether the word "is" means 'is' or whether it means 'ought to be', 'shall be', or the like. When it is taken in isolation, one will certainly say that the word "is" has the descriptive meaning. However, as an element in contexts of concrete language use, a closer analysis often shows that the word "is" has a normative meaning, see for example many possible and reasonable interpretations of the quotations in section 2 above. – Questions or propositions about what something is, consequently often conceal disagreement about what something ought to be, shall be, or the like. This applies whether the propositions are definitions or characterisations. One thread in this work will be to give a more nuanced account of some techniques of language use by which one conceals one's evaluations and choices (Chapter IV below).

The distinction between descriptive and normative propositions is important because one *uses different criteria when assessing their tenability*: – If the sentence "a precedent is a judgment of the Supreme Court" is interpreted as expressing a descriptive proposition, then the tenability of the proposition must be checked by comparing the proposition with reality (in the case of a descriptive definition: by comparing the proposition with the use of the word "precedent"; and in the case of a descriptive characterisation: by comparing the proposition with the properties of those phenomena that are designated by the word "precedent"). – If this sentence is interpreted as expressing a normative proposition, then the tenability of the proposition must be checked by testing the proposition against those arguments that are deemed relevant for justification and criticism of normative propositions (in the case of a normative definition: by testing the proposition against arguments for and against using the word "precedent" only of judgments from the Supreme Court, and not of judgments from the lower courts; and in the case of a normative characterisation: by testing the proposition against arguments for and against using only judgments from the Supreme Court, and not judgments from the lower courts, as binding arguments in later cases).

(1)↔(2) Definitions and characterisations, and descriptive and normative propositions, are important examples of what I call "fundamental types of proposition".[3]

[3] I use the word *"fundamental"* relative to the purpose and structuring of the present work. – A more complete survey of fundamental types of proposition is given in section II A below.

4. A critically reflexive mode of questioning as a remedy. – Language users' implementation of a relatively well-delimited critically reflexive form: the fundamental types of proposition with further nuancing and combinations. – The existence level of the critically reflexive form: the aspect of discussion and decision in language and argumentation

Indeterminacy with respect to the fundamental types of proposition leads to *pseudo dis/agreement*; participants in language and argumentation declare themselves in agreement with or challenge standpoints that other participants in language and argumentation do not have.

As a remedy against pseudo dis/agreement language users implement in different forms and degrees a *critically reflexive mode of questioning*, i.e. thought turning back on itself ("reflexive") and asking for facts and criteria relevant in assessing the tenability of its own propositions ("critical"). – *My concepts of the fundamental proposition types* are laid down in this perspective. They bring into focus *loci for clarifying* facts (section 3 (1) above) and criteria (section 3 (2) above) relevant in tenability assessment. More particularly, they bring into focus loci that experience has shown to be *"essential"*, in the sense that clarifying these loci often has crucial significance for the further development of the argument. – The experience mentioned is particularly clear when it comes to the distinctions between definitions and characterisations, and between descriptive and normative propositions, cf. above. There are graduated transitions to less essential loci. With this proviso the *justification for the other parts of this work is the same*: The concepts of proposition types and of combinations of proposition types presented there, bring into focus loci in actually occurring language and argumentation which experience has shown it to be important to determine when one takes a standpoint with respect to what one dis/agrees on.

Within the perspective now outlined, this work aims to *demonstrate, and to create an awareness of*, the factual significance of a critically reflexive mode of questioning. As part of this, and more particularly, the work aims to demonstrate, and to create an awareness of, the existence, content and factual significance of a *relatively well-delimited critically reflexive form* in language and argumentation; and thereby, it aims to demonstrate, and to create an awareness of, the factual significance of analysis of dis/agreement on the basis of this critically reflexive form (sections 5–6 below).

> I use the word "reflexive", not "reflective", because I wish to draw attention to the importance of thought *also* turning back *on itself* ("reflexive"), even though the immediate topic of thought is a different one, for example the law. The point is not that the critical attitude involves thought (in which case "reflective" would be more appropriate); this is presupposed as a matter of course.
>
> I use the word "form", not "level", since the formulation "critically reflexive level" would have signalled partly a hierarchy and partly that the proposition types and patterns, criteria and interests that the work maps, were only to be found on a particular level in the hierarchy. This would have been misleading terminology, since these proposition types and patterns, criteria and interests are found, inter alia, at *all levels of abstraction* in language and argumentation: from discussions in everyday life, across academic subjects and science, to philosophy (section 5.1 below).
>
> Some people may perhaps associate the word "form" with a Platonic level of existence. To the same extent as this happens, the word "form" is also misleading, cf. the main text after the present indent and the work in its entirety. However, the said association runs so clearly counter to the main threads in the work (the present Chapter I), and the word "form" is used in such a diversity of ways and has thus in itself such an indeterminate meaning, that possible occurrences of the said association are not a decisive argument against the use of the word "form".

The perspective of the present work brings into focus the *interaction between language users*, including the individual language user's interaction with himself; in this reality aspect lies the *reality basis* of the work. – I use here widespread and immediately comprehensible concepts of 'language', 'language users' and 'interaction'. I say "immediately comprehensible", because these concepts bring into focus elements in an activity in which we all continually participate and of which we are all continually able to give examples: such as conversation with ourselves, the reader's imaginary conversation with the author (for example here and now), discussion of a political or moral issue with others, or lawyers' discussions with one another of what the law is. – The critically reflexive form that the present work maps, *exists in and through* interaction between language users: Through their decisions in the continual process of language and argumentation, language users implement inter alia the distinctions between definitions and characterisations; and between descriptive and normative propositions; both with a diversity of further nuancing, as the work will demonstrate. – If one *abstracts* from the language users and their decisions, i.e. if one relates to language as an abstractum, then one at the same time abstracts from the identity criteria for the fundamental proposition types with further nuancing, i.e. one is not able to capture the acts that the present work maps.

The reality aspect to which the present work relates: interaction between language users, in the sense now outlined, I term in shorthand form the *"discussion and decision aspect"* of language and argumentation; and the work's corresponding perspective on language and argumentation, I term in shorthand form a *"discussion and decision perspective"*. The word *"discussion"* is used to indicate that the emphasis is on language and argumentation in the case of which it is deemed relevant to raise the issue of dis/agreement, cf. the title of the present work. The word *"decision"* is used to indicate the continual interplay in language and argumentation between demands for clarification of and decisions with respect to what one means.[1] – When in the present work I use the word "language", I am referring to the discussion and decision aspect, not language as an abstractum. The theoretical and philosophical significance of the discussion and decision perspective will reveal itself through the work as a whole.

In what I have said about the fact that language users implement a critically reflexive mode of questioning in various forms and degrees, and about the fact that the present work is to give a demonstration of the existence, content and factual significance of a relatively well-delimited critically reflexive form, it is not implied that a critically reflexive mode of questioning is omnipresent or that the consequences of this mode of questioning are the same in all areas. The absence of a critically reflexive mode of questioning makes itself felt in philosophy, science, academic subjects and everyday life, and the consequences of such a mode of questioning may vary with the areas.

Philosophy, including the philosophy of law, has historically speaking not contented itself with describing and working within the rationality frames of everyday life. It has purported to discover or to elucidate being ("ontology"); what we can know ("theory of knowledge", "epistemology"); reason ("theory of rationality"); or other aspects that it has claimed to be particularly fundamental. Yet with what right? Philosophy must itself demonstrate whether, and if so in what way, what it does makes any sense, so long as this does not obviously follow on the basis of the rationality frames of everyday life. In this lies inter alia a requirement for a critically reflexive mode of questioning. – The consequences of this mode of questioning can be dramatic; it is a well-known phenomenon that philosophers declare large areas of traditional philosophy or other thinking "meaningless", "without any value", or the like.

> Let us take a look at an example from the philosophy of law: an example partly of dramatic consequences in the form of large areas of traditional philosophy and other thinking being declared "meaningless" etc., partly of lacking implementation of the critically reflexive mode of questioning. – In his main work on legal philosophy, *Om ret og retfærdighed*, 1953 (English

[1] More precisely I could thus have used the formulation "the perspective of problem discussion and language decision", but that would have been too cumbersome.

> edition: *On Law and Justice*, 1958), Ross denies the existence of any tenability criteria other than empirical un/truth, i.e. dis/agreement with sense-experience, which we use to decide the tenability of empirical assertions; and analytic un/truth, i.e. un/truth in the light of presupposed definitions (compare "all spouses are un/married"), which according to Ross we use to decide the tenability of, inter alia, propositions in logic and mathematics.[2] – However, what sort of status do these propositions about the existence of tenability criteria have? Their tenability can obviously not be determined through dis/agreement with sense-experience, nor through un/truth in the light of presupposed definitions; i.e. Ross' propositions are neither empirically nor analytically un/true. Consequently, they cannot according to themselves be subjected to a rational discussion. Ross' rationality theory is thus according to itself (applied to itself) "meaningless", "metaphysical", "unscientific", or the like, as Ross said (about the propositions of others when he applied his rationality theory to these).[3] – My point in this connection is not to declare myself in agreement or disagreement with Ross' view with respect to what we have rational criteria to discuss. My point is the lack of any systematic critically reflexive mode of questioning in Ross.[4] And this lack becomes all the more striking when in addition to the paradox above one sees how categorically he rejects other rationality criteria than his own; precisely in the case of such sharp disagreement there is reason to demand a reflexive justification for choice of tenability criteria.

Within the individual academic subjects, for example in law, the consequences of a critically reflexive mode of questioning are less dramatic than in philosophy. This is the case, because the individual subjects must presuppose certain traditionally accepted rationality frames, so that the task of the members of the community in the subject is to place their propositions in relation to these frames. Some of these frames are specific to the individual subjects, such as the lawyers' doctrine of the sources of law. Others are common to several or most subjects, such as the distinction between definitions and characterisations and the distinction between descriptive and normative propositions.

---

2 Ross, *On Law and Justice*, e.g. p. 39 final paragraph.

3 I shall be returning in more detail to the said propositions in Ross in sections II B 5.2 (5)(b)(ii), 7.3.2 (1); C 2.1 (1), 2.1 (2)(a)(i), 2.3, 3.1 (2); and III 2.2.2 (3).

4 Compare also section III 2.2.2 (3)(c) below, at and in notes 43–45, where in another connection I mention some other writers' answers to a critically reflexive mode of questioning concerning propositions about "what meaning is".

5. Survey. Guidance for the reader

5.1. Survey of the content of the work. The generality of the critically reflexive form

The present work brings into focus a critically reflexive form in *everyday language*. – I use "everyday language" in contrast to "artificial languages", including in particular logic and mathematics.

The term "natural language" is often used with the same meaning as "everyday language" here. In my experience, however, the term "everyday language" gives more apposite associations in relation to matters which I consider to be essential and which constitute the perspective and topic of the present work.

I do not, however, use "everyday language" in contrast to "academic", "scientific" or "philosophical" forms of language and argumentation. Many academic subjects, many sciences and much philosophy are wholly or mainly formulated in forms of language and argumentation which by degrees, and sometimes only to a small degree, differ from those we use in everyday life.[1] This applies, for example, to law and large areas of legal theory.[2] – The area of application of everyday language thus overlaps but far from coincides with everyday life: Everyday language has a *general area of application*, from everyday life, across academic subjects and sciences, to philosophy. And the critically reflexive form that this work maps, has a *corresponding generality*.[3]

On the *conceptual and theoretical level*, the present work is, therefore, not in general limited to propositions within certain areas of life, within certain academic subjects, sciences, or the like. – In its *concrete demonstration* of the reality basis of my concepts and of the tenability of my theory, my presentation is first and foremost directed at *propositions about social phenomena*: be they propositions within morals, politics, law, psychology, history, sociology, or the like.

[1] In the text at the present note and throughout this work I use the term "academic subject" in the broad sense of the Scandinavian "fag" and the German "Fach", i.e. I use it of crafts, professional subjects and academic disciplines. Further, I use the term "science" (1) in the broad sense of the Scandinavian "vitenskap" and the German "Wissenschaft", i.e. to cover natural, social and human sciences, and (2) as an abbreviation for "activity one traditionally terms "science" in this broad sense" – that is, I neither presuppose nor lay down anything contentious through this concept of 'science'.

[2] I use the formulation "legal theory" in a broad sense, also of discussions that are traditionally designated "legal philosophy".

[3] Concerning the everyday-language orientation, see in addition e.g. sections II B 1 (3); 2; and III 1.

And among such propositions, a main emphasis is on *propositions about legal phenomena*, and within these again, on lawyers' propositions about what the law is: lawyers' "propositions de lege lata" (section 5.2 below).

This concrete demonstration has been designed with the intention that, seen as a whole, it is to give an approximately *representative* picture of the generality of the critically reflexive form. – The picture in itself can never be exhaustive. But part of the evidence for the generality of the criticially reflexive form consists in the instantiations of the critically reflexive form given in this work awakening *recognition* in the reader, in his capacity of himself being a participant in language and argumentation; and in the instantiations of the critically reflexive form given in this work thus initiating in the reader, in relation to the reader's own acts of language and argumentation, a process towards the cognition of the generality of the criticially reflexive form.[4]

In *Chapter II*, I give an account of the fundamental types of proposition. Section *II A* provides a survey, and sections *II B–D* deal in more detail with, respectively, descriptive and normative definitions, descriptive and normative characterisations, and analytically un/true propositions. The main emphasis is on definitions: a nuanced and coherent conceptual model for mapping the modalities, functions and means of this proposition type (section II B). Section *II E* gives an account of some common ways of deciding whether one is confronted by one or another type of proposition in the individual instance. In section *II F*, I argue that the distinction between descriptive and normative propositions ought to be seen as a graduated distinction: Lawyers' propositions de lege lata often lie roughly in the middle of the graduated dimension, i.e. lawyers' propositions de lege lata are fusions of descriptive and normative propositions, the two extreme points on the dimension.

In *Chapter III*, I take up two topics from tenability assessment which in my opinion deserve greater attention than they are normally given: In section *III 2* criteria used in the setting up of and choice between normative definitions are refined and systematised. In section *III 3*, I map the factual significance of other criteria than the truth criterion in the setting up of and choice between descriptive characterisations.

In *Chapter IV* an account is given of a practically central phenomenon: the strong tendency to use language in such a manner that it becomes unclear, to oneself or[5] to others, what proposition type one is confronted with in the individual instance. More particularly, an account is given of a distinct tendency in the case of evaluations and choices: the tendency to use language that is polysemous between the descriptive, logical and normative, or that is one-sidedly descriptive or logical.

---

[4] On the relationship between the presentation given in this work and the reader's own reality, see further a retrospective treatment in-depth in Chapter I↔V.

[5] The word "or" I use throughout in the broad sense 'either the one alternative, or the other alternative, or both alternatives'.

In *Chapter V*, I discuss a distinct and widespread combination of the fundamental proposition types, which I term "reconstruction and redefinition": I establish the concept of this mode of analysis. And I put forward and provide evidence for a hypothesis that this mode of analysis can be traced in a large number of propositions about what something is, inter alia in lawyers' propositions de lege lata (sections V 2.4, partly also 2.2–2.3) and in legal theory (sections V 1.1(1), 2.5–2.6, partly also 2.2–2.3). – The diffusion of this mode of analysis calls for a causal explanation; this is the topic of section V 4.2.

At the same time as the work proceeds from the simple (Chapter II) to the complex (Chapter V), I have put emphasis on writing the work in such a way that the individual chapters can *be read on their own*. However, Chapter II lays much of the conceptual foundation for subsequent discussions. For those who do not wish to go in depth into the details in Chapter II, I have provided an introductory survey of this chapter (section II A) which should be adequate with a view to the subsequent discussions.

5.2. Guidance for the reader with a view to law and legal theory. The fundamental significance of the critically reflexive form for lawyers' power of judgement

The aim of *describing and clarifying* a certain actually occurring critically reflexive form has determined the systematic structuring of the present work (sections 1 cf. 5.1, above). – Readers who are particularly interested in this main thread in the work can go directly to the detailed table of contents.

The demonstration of the *area of origin and application* of the critically reflexive tools does not come out equally adequately in the table of contents, and more specifically, nor does the demonstration of the applicability of these tools in analyses of *language and argumentation about legal phenomena.* – I refer readers who are particularly interested in this applicability partly to what does appear from the table of contents, partly to the subject index, and partly to the references that have already been given.[6] By way of supplementation, in what follows I shall emphasise certain points.

Lawyers' propositions de lege lata

Among propositions about legal phenomena, lawyers' propositions about what the law is, lawyers' *"propositions de lege lata"*, are of those that have been most

6 See section 5.1 above concerning sections II F (fused descriptive and normative propositions) and V (reconstructions and redefinitions).

discussed from a critically reflexive angle: "Exactly what kind of propositions are lawyers' propositions about what the law is?"

Lawyers' propositions de lege lata lie throughout in the area of application of the systematic conceptual apparatus of the present work: The critically reflexive form that the work will describe and clarify, is *also* the form of lawyers' power of judgement; and the work will demonstrate that and in what way the critically reflexive form *constitutes* this power of judgement. – In relation to lawyers' propositions de lege lata, the conceptualisations and discussions in the work may be likened to a set of *filters*: For an *apt picture* of lawyers' propositions de lege lata, in contrast to an understanding of the individual aspects, one must look through several of these filters *at the same time*. When we proceed from the fundamental proposition types to lawyers' propositions de lege lata, a recurrent theme in the work will be that the latter in various ways *build on* the former.

Lawyers' propositions de lege lata build on the fundamental proposition types in three main ways: *fusion* of descriptive propositions and normative propositions (section II F); *alternation* between definitions and characterisations (section IV 3.3.3); and *combination* of all four proposition types (sections V 2.4, partly also 2.2–2.3). – Thus the *tenability assessment* becomes correspondingly complex (section III 4, with further references).

Definition theory

The definition theory in the present work has also been influenced by law and legal theory: partly in the form of concepts for the definition theory, and partly in the form of actually occurring definition activity for which a definition theory of analysis and argumentation[7] formulated in everyday language ought to be able to account. I refer to the more detailed account with further references in section II B 2.1 (2)(c) below.

---

[7] Unless more special definition is explicitly stated or is clear from the context, I use "analysis and argumentation" as a derived variant of "language and argumentation". There are two reasons for my use of this variant. First, I wish to point to a practically important specification: In relation to the broad area designated "language and argumentation", "analysis" points to the sub-area of more reflected activity. Secondly, there is the consideration for effective communication of a major feature of the perspective and topic of the present work, namely the focusing of and on everyday language in contrast to artificial languages, including in particular logic and mathematics (section 5.1 above, introductory remarks, cf. the present section 5 in its entirety): To remind the reader of this major feature of the perspective and topic of the work, in a number of places I bring in the qualifier "formulated in everyday language". Even though strictly speaking one might justify the formulation "language and argumentation formulated in everyday language", such a formulation may at first glance provoke resistance ("language ... formulated in ... language" may at first glance look like three terms for the same thing) and may thus get in the way of comprehension. Therefore I link the qualifier "formulated in everyday language" to the formulation "analysis and argumentation".

The question of dispositivity

By the *"question of dispositivity"* I mean the question of transition from the stage of preliminaries to that of being legally bound in the case of stipulated normative propositions: be it in the case of statutes, administrative decisions, judgments, contracts, wills, covenants, or other species of stipulated normative propositions.

Language and argumentation in connection with the question of dispositivity lies in a number of contexts in the area of application of the systematic conceptual apparatus of the present work. Here I want to point in particular to the *analysis of lawyers' argumentation in the question of dispositivity in respect of contracts*: the typically relevant arguments in lawyers' discussions of this question (section IV 2.2 (6)(b)); their ways of using these arguments (sections IV 2.2 (6)(b) and 3.3.1 (3)(b)(ii)); historical continuity with respect to the relevance of and ways of using these arguments (section IV 3.3.1 (3)(b)(ii), concluding remarks); and the pattern of reconstruction and redefinition in their discussions (sections V 2.2 and 2.4).

The flight from the normative proposition

The tendency, in the case of evaluations and choices, to use language that is polysemous between the descriptive, logical and normative, or that is one-sidedly descriptive or logical, extends far beyond lawyers' language and argumentation de lege lata; see Chapter IV. However, lawyers' language and argumentation de lege lata bears strong, and in its linguistic form often distinctive, witness to this tendency (see, for example, sections IV 2.2 (6)(b) and 3.3).

6. The status of the present work's own propositions. The independence of the critically reflexive form

I have pointed to the significance of a *critically reflexive mode of questioning*, i.e. thought (also) turning back on itself and asking for facts and criteria relevant in assessing the tenability of its own propositions. In the light of the fundamental elements in this work presented above, the main aim of the work can now be stated as follows: to demonstrate, and to create an awareness of, the existence, content and factual significance of a relatively well-delimited critically reflexive form (section 4) in the discussion and decision aspect (section 4) of analysis and argumentation formulated in everyday language (section 5); and thereby, to demonstrate, and to create an awareness of, the factual significance of analysis of dis/agreement on the basis of this critically reflexive form. – In this perspective one is logically led to ask what is the *status of the work's own propositions*. This question requires answers in two directions.

The relationship to the conceptual apparatus of the present work

The topic of the work is a critically reflexive form in analysis and argumentation formulated in everyday language. At the same time the propositions advanced in the work are themselves formulated in everyday language. Consequently, the propositions in the work can be determined with respect to their kind and assessed with respect to their tenability in the same *dimensions* of which the work will give an account and demonstrate the applicability.

That the propositions and analyses in the work can be determined in kind and assessed for tenability in the same dimensions of which the work gives an account, does not mean that the *individual concepts* the work establishes necessarily apply. For example, in the modality dimension I shall distinguish between descriptive, normative and fused propositions (sections II A 5; F). In this dimension the propositions in the work are descriptive or normative, never fused, cf. section II F concerning the content and presuppositions of fused modality.[1]

There is thus no difference in principle between the method of the present work and the practices that the work maps. It is this relationship to which I am referring when in a number of instances I designate the critically reflexive form *"the per-*

[1] As the work proceeds, it will provide a basis for a retrospective treatment in-depth of the paragraph containing the present note, see Chapter I↔V, in the second indent.

spective and topic of the work". Likewise, it is this relationship to which I am referring when in a number of instances I use the formulation "the critically reflexive form that the work *brings into focus*"; "brings into focus" is here to be interpreted both in the meaning of 'placing in the centre' (compare "topic", compare also "focusing on") and in the meaning of 'making sharper' (compare "perspective", compare also "focusing of").

The relationship to other perspectives on analysis and argumentation occurring in fact and formulated in everyday language: the independence of the critically reflexive form

My discussions will demonstrate the actual existence of certain types and patterns of proposition with their accompanying tenability criteria and motivating interests. Considered as a unit, the types and patterns of proposition, the criteria and the interests constitute a critically reflexive form with a *certain independence*.

First, there is "independence" in relation to higher levels of abstraction, including in particular the level of fundamental philosophical positions, i.e. the level of ontological, epistemological or other positions of a presumed fundamental nature: There is "independence", partly in the sense that the critically reflexive form is not constituted through deductive argumentation from higher levels, but through such constellations of propositions, modes of analysis, tenability criteria and interests as will be demonstrated in the present work. And there is "independence", partly in the sense that the critically reflexive form according to its own content does not claim to be or not to be a fundamental and exhaustive rationality structure, i.e. does not claim to be or not to be a competing position on the level of fundamental philosophical positions. – Signs that one is *outside* the perspective and topic of the present work, will in the light of this be that one starts seeking the standpoint of the work on philosophical schools.[2]

Secondly, there is "independence" in relation to standpoints on (other) controversial questions: be they of a moral, legal, political or similar nature.[3] The present work will demonstrate the existence and content of a critically reflexive form, not set up theses from which one can derive standpoints on controversial questions. – Signs that one is *outside* the perspective and topic of the present work, will in the light of this be that one starts seeking the standpoint of the work on "what is x?"-questions, when by "x" one is asking about something other than the elements of the critically reflexive form or the meanings of words (concepts) concerning these elements.[4]

One might imagine that the outlined independence of the critically reflexive form could be *justified via a "theory"*: a concept frame within which one could

---

2 "Is the author a realist?"

3 Of a philosophical nature too, if one uses the designation "applied philosophy".

4 "What does the author believe science is?"

say "this is how it must be". This is *not* the perspective and topic of the present work. – The independence of the critically reflexive form will *be demonstrated as a fact*: as an aspect of the work's discussions, seen as a whole, of the existence and more detailed content of the critically reflexive form.

In the light of this, I have for two reasons sought to the greatest possible extent to *avoid taking any standpoint* on conflict between fundamental philosophical positions, or on (other) controversial questions, be they of a moral, legal, political or similar nature. – I shall specify these reasons especially in relation to *fundamental philosophical positions*, since the danger of failing to appreciate the status of the work is greatest in this relation (sections 7 and II A 8, below).

First, the absence of certain univocal (cf. fourth preceding paragraph) connections between the critically reflexive form and the level of fundamental philosophical positions entails that to the same extent (as this absence) it *is not necessary to* take any standpoint on conflict between fundamental philosophical positions.

Secondly, the way in which I shall demonstrate the independence of the critically reflexive form (cf. third preceding paragraph) – as a fact, or more precisely, as an aspect of the present work's discussions, seen as whole, of the existence and more detailed content of this form – entails that to the greatest possible extent it *is necessary not to* take any standpoint on conflict between fundamental philosophical positions. Partly such standpoints may overshadow the demonstration of the independence of the form, and partly they may deceive the reader into placing the critically reflexive form on the level of fundamental philosophical positions.

> Standpoints on fundamental philosophical positions can show themselves through the concepts one uses, through one's definitions; one defines for example 'normative proposition' as propositions with truth value. Or the standpoints can show themselves through views one asserts in other questions than questions of definition, through one's characterisations; one asserts for example that only normative propositions that are in harmony with a certain fundamental ethical position, deserve to be followed. – What has just been said about taking standpoints on conflict between fundamental philosophical positions, applies to both forms of appearance of standpoints: Both in conceptualisations and in assertions of views otherwise it is (to the extent outlined and for the reasons outlined) both not necessary to take and necessary not to take any standpoint on conflict between fundamental philosophical positions.

After the mapping of the critically reflexive form has been carried out, I shall point out that the absence of certain univocal connections does not mean the absence of any connection whatsoever; the work *also* represents a challenge on the level of fundamental philosophical positions (Chapter I↔V).[5]

---

[5] On the theme of independence, see further in section 7 below; a brief specification in section II A 8 below; and a retrospective treatment in-depth, with further references, in Chapter I↔V.

It should after this be clear that the fact that to the greatest possible extent I seek to avoid taking any standpoint on conflict between fundamental philosophical positions, is not an expression of caution in a philosophical sense, as an alternative position on the level of fundamental philosophical positions (compare "scepticism", "fallibilism", etc.). On the contrary, the point is precisely, as has been mentioned, to demonstrate that the critically reflexive form that the work brings into focus, has a certain independence, i.e. to demonstrate the absence of certain univocal connections between the critically reflexive form and the level of fundamental philosophical positions. The work neither claims nor denies caution on the level of fundamental philosophical positions.

7. The shadow existence, in theoretical respects, of the critically reflexive form. The value of the present work

In and through the critically reflexive form that constitutes the perspective and topic of the present work, *significant acts* take place. But neither in literature within general or legal philosophy, nor in any other literature, have I been able to find any analysis of this form along the lines presented above: no nuanced and coherent conceptual model for mapping the critically reflexive form, with accompanying demonstration of – the reality basis of the concepts – the internal coherence of the form (its system character and dynamics) – the independence of the form – and the factual significance of the form: what acts take place, and in what connections and for what language users these acts are significant. In *theoretical respects* the critically reflexive form leads a *shadow existence.*

> Accordingly, the feature of the work that to the greatest possible extent I seek to avoid taking any standpoint on conflict between fundamental philosophical positions (section 6 above, before the penultimate indent) does not express any particular caution in a research-strategic, methodological, psychological, or other sense, either (compare section 6 above, in the final indent, on caution in a philosophical sense). On the contrary, since the critically reflexive form has not previously been systematically treated in the literature, the work has not been able to fit into any tradition and is thus both in its consistency on the level of theory, and in the way it mediates throughout between this level and our linguistic practice, the opposite of a cautious work.

Especially in relation to philosophical literature I assume that one *cause* of this shadow existence is the combination of (i) the independence of the critically reflexive form, i.e. the absence of certain (section 6 above) univocal connections between this form and particular philosophical positions that have traditionally been deemed fundamental, often also mutually exclusive, and (ii) the fact that in general philosophy and the philosophy of law one traditionally relates one's discussions to conflict between such positions. – To take the philosophy of law as an example: Concepts formed with an eye to conflict between positions that legal philosophers traditionally deem fundamental, often also mutually exclusive, for example "natural law", "positivism", "hermeneutics", "coherence theory", etc., have shown themselves incapable of capturing the wealth of nuances, the internal coherence (system character and dynamics), the independence and the factual significance that all characterise the critically reflexive form that the present work brings into focus. Through legal philosophers' traditionally relating their discussions to conflict between such positions, legal philosophy to a great extent relates *blindly* to important parts of our power of judgement mediated in and through everyday language, including important parts of lawyers' power of judgement.[1]

This background (a system of significant acts, in theoretical respects leading a shadow existence) gives value to the present work. After I have demonstrated the wealth of nuances, the internal coherence (system character and dynamics), the independence and the factual significance of the critically reflexive form, I shall by way of summary point back to those threads in the work that I consider to a particularly high degree supplement and represent a challenge to other theoretical work on language and argumentation (Chapter I↔V).

[1] To take general philosophy as an example, and especially in relation to definition theory: Concepts formed on the basis of "falsificationism" (Popper) or "physicalism" (Quine) show themselves incapable of capturing the wealth of nuances, the internal coherence (system character and dynamics), the independence and the factual significance of the definition field of everyday language; see respectively sections II B 1 (4) and G 2, below.

8. Summary of the main aim of the present work

At the beginning of the present introduction I formulated a major aim of this work in the following way: "to describe and to clarify certain yardsticks for the comparison of and choice between propositions, and to demonstrate the area of origin and application of, as well as a certain independence characterising, these yardsticks". In the light of the presentation in the present introduction of fundamental elements of the work, the formulation quoted may now be supplemented and elaborated as follows:

The *superordinate perspective and topic* of the work is a relatively well-delimited critically reflexive form (section 4), in the discussion and decision aspect (section 4) of analysis and argumentation formulated in everyday language (section 5), and with a certain independence (section 6).

There is no difference in principle between the method of the work and the practices that the work maps. It is this relationship to which I am referring when I designate the critically reflexive form "the perspective and topic of the work" and when I use the formulation "the critically reflexive form that the work brings into focus" (section 6).

The *main aim* of the work is to demonstrate, and to create an awareness of, the existence, content and factual significance of the outlined critically reflexive form; and thereby, to demonstrate, and to create an awareness of, the factual significance of analysis of dis/agreement on the basis of this critically reflexive form.

In fact there are close connections partly between demonstrating and creating an awareness, and partly between on the one hand the existence, content and factual significance of the critically reflexive form and on the other the factual significance of dis/agreement analysis on the basis of the same form. In the light of this, I use for the sake of simplicity the singular form "the main aim". – When in certain contexts I use the formulation "a major aim of the work", it is with reference to parts of the main aim now outlined (see, for example, the first sentence of the present section 8). I use the formulations "the purposes/ aims of the work" as common designations for the main aim and aims derived from the main aim; see the accounts linked to my individual discussions.

II

Some fundamental types of proposition about what something is

A Survey

1. Introduction

As mentioned by way of introduction (section I 3): The diversity of directions in which questions of the form "What is x?" point, shows the diversity of types of proposition about what something is, with which we operate. – In the present Chapter II, I shall discuss and establish concepts about types of proposition, taking as a starting point the main aim of the work (Chapter I above): the aim of demonstrating, and creating an awareness of, the existence, content and factual significance of a specific critically reflexive form (I 4–6); and thereby, of demonstrating, and creating an awareness of, the factual significance of analysis of dis/agreement on the basis of this critically reflexive form.

In relation to this aim, the *in-depth discussions* in sections B–G below are important in themselves. In addition, they lay much of the conceptual foundation for subsequent discussions. To assist readers wishing to go straight to one or more of the topics in Chapters III–V, I shall outline in the rest of the present section A the *main part* of the conceptual foundation that is subsequently presupposed. In addition, the present section A serves as an *introduction* to sections B–G; see the schematic survey in section 7 below.

2. Definitions; analytically un/true propositions; characterisations. Possibility and desirability of distinguishing. – "What is meaning?"

(1) Definitions

The word *"definition"* I use of propositions that contribute to determining the meanings of linguistic entities (contribute to determining concepts). Consequently, I use it for example of the proposition expressed in the preceding sentence: a proposition that contributes to determining the meaning of the word "definition" (contributes to determining the concept of 'definition') in the present work.

The rest of the present item (1) makes the connection between the individual elements in the definition just presented and the topics that are to be discussed in the work's definition theory. As part of this I shall explain why the individual elements in the definition are formulated as they are.

The formulation "the meanings of linguistic entities (... concepts)" signals two questions on which definitions can take a standpoint. First, there is the question of how the world is to be *structured* in thought: "meanings (... concepts)". Secondly, there is the question of how these areas-in-thought are to be *named*: "linguistic entities". – One part of the work's definition theory will consist in a more detailed mapping of the structuring function and naming function of definitions (section 3 below).

Another matter is whether definitions are formulated in *concept terminology*[1] ("the concept of 'law' covers ...", "Kant's concept of 'law' covers ...") or in *word terminology*[2] ("the word "law" is used of ...", "Kant used the word "Recht" of ..."). There will be seen to be only a weak connection between, on the one hand, whether definitions are formulated in concept terminology or in word terminology, and on the other hand, the occurrence of structuring function or naming function (sections B 4.4.1–4.4.2 below). – My including "concepts" as an *alternative* to "the meanings of linguistic entities" in my definition is to signal that the work's definition concept covers both definitions formulated in concept terminology and definitions formulated in word terminology.

---

1 By "concept terminology" I mean words like "concept", "conception", "notion", "idea" and their derivatives (or their equivalents in other languages).

2 By "word terminology" I mean words like "word", "term", "expression" and their derivatives (or their equivalents in other languages).

The formulation "the meanings of linguistic entities (... concepts)" covers both propositions about the *connotation* of words or concepts and propositions about the *denotation* of words or concepts (section 4 below). A feature of the work's definition theory will be to bring into focus specifications of denotation on a par with specifications of connotation, in their capacity of means of definition (section 4 below).

> In some contexts it is more common to use *"meaning content"* than "meaning"; see for example the final paragraph of the present item (1) and otherwise numerous places in the present work. To attempt to reform language usage on this point would no doubt simply lead to confusion. I shall therefore stick to the customary use of "meaning content" and state herewith that in this use there does *not* lie any delimitation against the denotation of words or concepts.

The formulation "propositions that contribute to determining" refers to *descriptive* propositions, *normative* propositions, and *fused* descriptive and normative propositions (section 5 below). Further, "to determining" signals a delimitation *against* propositions about the *origins or effects* of concepts (present section 2, item (4) below).

In addition to the features now outlined of my concept of 'definition', features which will be discussed in the present section A, before being treated in depth as part of my definition theory in section B, I shall mention certain other features of my concepts of 'definition' and 'concept', features which will be established and justified in more detail in the definition theory:

- The concept of 'definition' in the present work has been established out of a desire for insight into analysis and argumentation *occurring in fact and formulated in everyday language*. An aim of my definition theory is to map the diversity of modalities, functions and means within the definition field of everyday language, and to show the system character and dynamics of this definition field (section B in its entirety, with further references to other parts of the work: see in particular sections F and III 2).

- My concept of 'concept' is not a separate topic but an auxiliary concept in the definition theory (section B 4.1 (6)).

- My concepts of 'definition' and 'concept' are corresponding concepts (section B 4.1 (1)↔(2)).

- I do *not* lay down *determinacy* as a definitional requirement in my concepts of 'definition' and 'concept' (sections B 2.2 cf. 2.1; 3.2.2; and 4.1 (3), (6)). This is signalled by my writing "contribute to determining" and not simply "determine" in the definition of 'definition'.[3]

[3] I use the formulation "the definition of 'x' ", e.g. "the definition of 'definition' " (in contrast to "the definition of "x" ", e.g. "the definition of "definition" ") when the main emphasis is on the structuring

The features now mentioned are not suited to more detailed presentation in a survey section such as the present section A, but have been mentioned briefly to create clarity on a *central point*: The present work *departs from* and *justifies why* it departs from a widespread feature in common of logicians', philosophers' and science theorists' concepts of 'definition'/ 'concept', namely that definitions/ concepts are determinate (see the same places as referred to in the preceding parenthesis).

Above it was mentioned that definitions can be descriptive or normative or fused. – One thread in the definition theory in this work will be to demonstrate that the traditional distinction between descriptive and normative definitions is too simple. The alternative adduced, "fusion", signals nuancing in one direction (section 5 (4) below). In addition comes nuancing in several other directions (sections B 3.4 and 8 cf. 3–6, below). To give an example: The definition of "definition" given above is itself *normative*. However, this does *not* say anything about whether, and if so in what way or to what degree, the concept of 'definition' in this work departs from other concepts of 'definition' (section B 3.3.4 below). Concerning the *relationship between the language usage in this work and other language usage* I refer to what was said immediately above about the fact that determinacy is not laid down as a definitional requirement here, and otherwise to the systematic presentation of my definition theory (section B below).

By way of conclusion in this survey of the concept of 'definition' in the present work, I mention that some definitions are *formulated*, like the definition of "definition" above, but that I do not lay down the property of being formulated as a concept criterion:

Definitions are a type of proposition. And by "proposition" I mean meaning content to which we can relate in many ways, also in other ways than through linguistic formulations: I consider it fruitful to bring in the fact that we *also* build on cognitive perceptions and normative attitudes that we have *not formulated* or of which we are *not even conscious*. Most important in the context of definition are the "custom-based normative definitions" (section B 3.3.2 below). The link with language, and thereby the justification for extending the word "proposition" also to include these phenomena, consists in the fact that our perceptions and attitudes *can* in any event be expressed linguistically.[4]

---

function of the definition (in contrast to its naming function or language-use function). On the functions of definitions, see section 3 below.

[4] Compare Searle, *Speech Acts*, pp. 19–21; MacCormick/ Weinberger, *An Institutional Theory of Law*, p. 115.

(2) Analytically un/true propositions

(a) Concept and terminology

By *"analytically un/true propositions"* I mean propositions the truth value of which can be decided on the basis of their meaning content alone, i.e. propositions that are true or untrue *by definition*. – In the case of analytically un/true propositions one thus needs only the proposition formulation itself plus definitions of the words and expressions of which the formulation consists, to decide the truth value of the proposition. There is no necessity for any checking against a reality otherwise.[5]

Examples of proposition formulations expressing an analytically true proposition are: "This circle is round" and "A cup is white or a cup is not white". And examples of proposition formulations expressing an analytically untrue proposition are: "This circle is square" and "A cup is white and a cup is not white".

> The exemplary formulations concerning the circle *also* communicate an existence proposition (this is so, whether one would say that this communication takes place through presupposition or explicitly), namely that one is confronted with a phenomenon that is subsumable under the concept of 'circle'. This existence proposition is not analytic. – One can choose exemplary formulations that do not communicate an existence proposition, e.g. "a circle is round". But then it is often more reasonable than in the circle examples in the main text to say that the formulation is indeterminate between definition and analytically true proposition. – In order to illustrate clearly what is analytic in contrast to what is definitional, I have presented exemplary formulations of the form "this x is ..." (the circle examples in the main text). Further, in order to illustrate the diversity of forms in which what is analytic appears, I have in addition presented exemplary formulations of the form "an x is ..." (the cup examples in the main text), and will later present exemplary formulations inter alia of the forms "(all) x are ..." (item (b)(ii) below) and "if x is ..., then x is ..." (section D 4 (2)(a) below).

As is apparent from the examples, analytically un/true propositions (also) fall into the following two groups: – The one consists of propositions the truth value of which is decided by analysis of *non-logical words*, cf. the circle examples. The sentence "this circle is round" does not ascribe to the phenomenon any property beyond those we already know that the phenomenon has by definition, by virtue of the fact that we call it a "circle"; and the sentence "this circle is square" denies the phenomenon a property that the phenomenon has by definition, again by

---

5 In conformity with the superordinate perspective and topic of the present work I do not adopt any standpoint on philosophically controversial questions concerning the relationship between language (thought) and reality (Chapter I above and section 8 below). When in the text at the present note (the sentence containing the present note together with the preceding sentence) I contrast "the proposition" and "a reality otherwise", I am therefore using "reality" in a formal sense: as an open reference to whatever one finds reason to suppose exists. The same applies in the case of subsequent occurrences of the same contrast.

virtue of the fact that we call it a "circle". – In the other group of analytically un/true propositions the truth value is decided by analysis of *logical words*, cf. the cup examples. By "logical words" I mean first and foremost "not", "and", "or", "if", "only if", "all", "some" and "none".[6] For example, when we are to decide the truth value of "a cup is white or a cup is not white", it is sufficient to know the meaning of "or" and the meaning of "not". We do not need to know the meanings of the remaining, non-logical words; it is sufficient to register the repetition of the same physical sequence of words (and to presuppose that the words mean the same each time they occur).

The *terminology* in the case of analytically un/true propositions varies. In relation to the main aim of the present work (Chapter I above) it is on the whole not necessary to relate to this variation; the term "analytically un/true propositions" in the sense now established will suffice.[7]

There may, however, be particular reason to point to one aspect of the terminology: As is apparent, the *basis* for saying that a proposition is "un/true" is *different* in the case of respectively analytically un/true propositions and propositions the truth value of which depends on a reality otherwise (beyond the proposition) against which the proposition is to be checked; in the first case the basis is relationships between thoughts ('circle', 'round', 'square'), in the second case the basis is a relationship between a thought ('Peter drew the circle with a green crayon') and a fact (the colour of the circle Peter drew). This might be a ground for not using the *words "un/true" in both cases*. However, out of consideration for normal language usage and for the sake of simplicity I use these words in both cases.

(b) The critical force of the concept

For two reasons the *critical force* of the concept of 'analytically un/true proposition' is *greatest* in relation to non-logical words with meanings relatively remote from sense-experience: since (i) one does not get any external signal in these cases, and (ii) there is often great uncertainty in these cases about what definitions are presupposed.

(i) It is relatively easy to discover propositions that are un/true by virtue of definitions of logical words. Here the *repetition* of the non-logical words will function as an external signal that "something is wrong" with thought and proposition; cf. the cup examples (item (a) above). – This is different with propositions that are un/true by virtue of definitions of non-logical words. Here one does *not*, neither sender nor recipient, get any such external signal as lies in repetitions of words; cf. the circle examples (item (a) above).

---

6 On logical words and their role in logic, see e.g. von Wright, 'Form and Content in Logic', pp. 1–6; Strawson, *Introduction to Logical Theory*, pp. 40–58 (47–49); Quine, *Mathematical Logic*, pp. 1–3; Føllesdal/ Walløe/ Elster, *Argumentasjonsteori, språk og vitenskapsfilosofi* [argumentation theory, language and the philosophy of science], pp. 220–26.

7 As a background I shall later provide a brief survey of some main words and expressions (section D 4).

(ii) There may well often be uncertainty about the meanings in which logical words are being used.[8] Most people, however, have an intuitive and shared perception of a limited number of relevant meaning alternatives: For example, in the case of sentences of the form "if a, then b" it is often required that we choose between the meaning 'only if a, then b' (necessary and sufficient condition) and the meaning 'also if a, then b' (sufficient but not necessary condition); or in the case of sentences of the form "a or b" it is often required that we choose between the meaning 'either a or b' and the meaning 'either a or b, or both'. – In the case of non-logical words the uncertainty is far greater. This is partly because it is *more indeterminate which* meaning alternatives are relevant; and partly because more often, on account of *differences in their experience and interests*, it is reasonable to believe that one language user uses the words in *other* meanings than other language users.

The uncertainty concerning which definitions of non-logical words a person adopts will typically increase the more remote the use of the words becomes from sense-experience. Compare the difference between, on the one hand, our presuppositions about the meaning of the word "circle", and on the other hand, our presuppositions about the meanings of words and expressions like "law", "legal system", "legal rule" or "proper rule". In relation to these latter-mentioned words and expressions there are to a greater degree differences between, or indeterminacy in, our intuitive presuppositions. See as examples the sentences "the Norwegian legal system promotes the rule of law", "(all) legal systems promote the rule of law". Whether these sentences express an analytically true proposition depends on what definition of "legal system" is presupposed: If it is a criterion in the presupposed concept of 'legal system' that legal systems promote the rule of law, then these sentences express analytically true propositions; otherwise they do not. Both concepts of 'legal system' are widespread in actual language usage.

(i)↔(ii) In analysis of actually occurring analysis and argumentation, it is particularly in relation to examples like the last one (non-logical words, relatively remote from sense-experience) that the concept of 'analytically un/true proposition' has value: In relation to sentences that ostensibly express great and significant truths about reality, it is of interest to be informed whether these sentences do say anything about reality at all, or on the contrary are true by virtue of certain, more or less well-founded/ arbitrary, definitions; or, as the case may be, to be informed that the sender of the sentence has not taken any standpoint on which definitions he[9] presupposes (what he means by the words in the sentence), so that

8 Strawson, *Introduction to Logical Theory*, pp. 78–93; cf. 35–38.

9 I use the word "he", not only of a male person, but also as a reference word to a person irrespective of natural gender. Seen in isolation the latter use is not satisfactory, but is probably the best option ("she" does not fit the bill any better and is more uncommon; "he or she" is too long-winded if this use is adopted throughout; the Norwegian "haun", the English "s/he", or similar constructions, raise a problem of co-ordinating (compare section B 4.2 (5)(d)(iii) below); and "person concerned" or the like cannot always be used and would, moreover, in some cases be in disharmony with the style of language otherwise in the work).

it is indeterminate what criteria are relevant to tenability assessment of the proposition.

Some writers choose not to mention analytically un/true propositions in their accounts of fundamental types of proposition.[10] Others mention one or more types of analytically un/true proposition, but give this proposition type as a whole an inconspicuous place in their presentation.[11] – The fact that I here place analytically un/true propositions on a par with definitions and characterisations is because of what has been said in the main text above about the critical force of the concept.

(3) *Characterisations*

I use the word *"characterisation"* of propositions that are neither definitions nor analytically un/true, i.e. of propositions which do not contribute to determining the meanings of linguistic entities (do not contribute to determining concepts), but which presuppose this topic (in contrast to definitions, which thematise it), and say something beyond what lies in the concept criteria (in contrast to analytically un/true propositions). Examples of characterisations are: "Peter drew the circle with a green crayon", "Peter, draw a circle with a pencil!". – As is apparent, characterisations may, like definitions, be descriptive or normative; and as I shall be demonstrating later, they may, like definitions, have a fused descriptive and normative modality (section 5 below).

As is also apparent, I have distinguished both definitions and characterisations from analytically un/true propositions, i.e. neither definitions nor characterisations can be ascertained to be un/true on the basis of how the words of the proposition formulations are defined. Thus, and in so far as one wishes to say that definitions and characterisations can be "un/true" (something many people will not say if they are normative, compare section 5 (2)(b) below), definitions and characterisations will in much language usage fall under a concept of 'synthetic proposition'. However, a concept of 'synthetic proposition' is not necessary for the present work, so I shall not go any further into this.

(4) *On the relationship between definitions and characterisations in more detail*

(a) Characterisations *presuppose* the meanings of linguistic entities (presuppose concepts): for example the concept of what is characterised ('the circle that Peter drew'), or the concept of the property that is ascribed to the phenomenon through the characterisation ('having been drawn with a green crayon').

---

10 See e.g. Ofstad, 'Om deskriptive definisjoner av begrepet rettsregel' [on descriptive definitions of the concept of 'legal rule'], pp. 39–40; Eckhoff, *Rettsvesen og rettsvitenskap i U.S.A.* [legal system and legal science in the U.S.A.], pp. 279–80.

11 See e.g. Næss, *Interpretation and Preciseness*. "True by definition" and "analyticity" are dealt with on pp. 167–68.

Definitions *thematise* what characterisations presuppose: linguistic entities' meanings (concepts). – The definition's thematising of meaning can consist in a *constitution* of language usage (normative definition). This constitution may take place through custom-based definitions; or it may take place through definitions stipulated for the occasion (e.g. "the verb "to draw" I shall also use of production of figures via a computer"). – Or the definition's thematising of meaning can consist in a *description or prediction* of language usage (descriptive definition, e.g. "the verb "to draw" is used of written production of other figures than letters of the alphabet").

Definitions can in the light of this be characterised as a proposition type with a typically *constituting and preparatory stamp*: Definitions *make possible* characterisations (most importantly, through custom-based definitions; section B 3.3.2 below), and definitions *clarify* characterisations (typically, through explicitly stipulated definitions in the individual instance; section B 3.3.1 below).

(b) Characterisations can also be *about* the meanings of linguistic entities (*about* concepts). It is true that characterisations cannot be about what linguistic entities' meanings (concepts) are or should or shall (or other types of modality) be; in that case the propositions are definitions. But propositions can be about the meanings of linguistic entities (about concepts) *in other ways*:

First, we have *descriptive characterisations* of the *origins or effects* of meanings. Examples would be a description of how children learn to use the words "right" and "wrong", or of what effects it has that they learn this distinction, e.g. what difference it makes to their behaviour; or a description of how Marx formed his concept of 'law' in opposition to Hegel, or of what effects it had that many people adopted this concept, e.g. what difference it made to the labour movement's view of the state and the law. – As long as these proposition examples presuppose one meaning or another of the words "right" and "wrong" and of the word "Recht" in Marx, and do not themselves describe these meanings, then these propositions do not contribute to determining the meanings, and are therefore by definition not definitions but descriptive characterisations of the meanings.

Secondly, we have *normative propositions* about the meanings of linguistic entities (about concepts), which *do not reproduce* these meanings. An example would be: "The Supreme Court has determined the concept of 'ship' in section 422 of the Norwegian Criminal Justice Act in a satisfactory manner." – When a normative proposition thus talks about the meaning but does not reproduce it, the proposition does not contribute to determining the meaning, and is therefore by definition not a definition but a *normative characterisation* of the meaning.

We can change the example in such a way that the Supreme Court's definition *is reproduced*: "The Supreme Court's determining of the concept of 'ship' in section 422 of the Norwegian Criminal Justice Act to include pleasure craft down to a length of 10 feet provides a satisfactory demarcation." – One question is whether this formulation *communicates* a proposition that contributes to determining the meanings of linguistic entities (contributes to determining concepts), i.e. whether this formulation communicates a definition. If the formulation, and the word "communicate", are understood on the basis of normal language usage, it is reasonable to answer the question in the affirmative. – Another question is whether the formulation communicates the definition *through presupposition or explicitly*, and in connection with this, whether the formulation *also* communicates a characterisation. The boundary between what is explicitly stated and what is presupposed is often indeterminate in actually occurring language and argumentation (section B 3.3.1 (4)(a)↔(b) below); this is also the case here. And a formulation will often communicate several propositions (section B 3.3.1 (4)(c) below) On the basis of the perspective and topic of the present work the essentials are partly the indeterminacy, and partly the discussion and decision aspect of language and argumentation (section I 4 above).

(5) The possibility of, and practice concerning, distinguishing between definitions, analytically un/true propositions and characterisations

The distinction between definitions and characterisations presupposes and builds on a distinction between *linguistic meaning* and *other sources of knowledge*: One thing is that everything that falls under a concept satisfies one or more of the concept criteria ("by definition it is the case that cups are for drinking out of"). Another thing is how what falls under the concept is otherwise constituted. This is something about which the concept does not say anything; it must be investigated via experience or other sources of knowledge.

Thus the distinction between definitions and characterisations is potentially exposed to *criticism* that is raised against the distinction between linguistic meaning on the one hand and experience or other sources of knowledge on the other hand: for example, potentially exposed to the criticism that Quine has raised against the distinction between analytically un/true propositions and synthetically un/true propositions, on the basis that the distinguishing criterion, linguistic meaning versus other sources of knowledge, has in his opinion no reality.

However, Quine's criticism is not apt in relation to the perspective and topic of the present work: Quine *abstracts from* the discussion and decision aspect of language and argumentation. Thus he abstracts from the existence level of the critically reflexive form that constitutes the perspective and topic of the present work (section G 2 (4)(c) below, cf. section I 4 above). – To put this in more general terms: Neither Quine nor others have presented tenable arguments for its being impossible that participants in language and argumentation can at any stage decide a boundary between linguistic meaning and other sources of knowledge. Such a boundary *is drawn and deemed legitimate to be required to be drawn* in actually occurring language and argumentation. In the present work I substantiate and map a diversity of ways in which this boundary is drawn and the factual significance of this boundary (section B below, cf. the work in its entirety).

(6) "What is meaning?"

"What is (linguistic) meaning?" has been one of the most controversial "what is"-questions in philosophy during the last hundred years. Quine's discussions, mentioned in item (5) above, are among the most well known, but otherwise only a part of a great diversity. – To the greatest possible extent I aim at neutrality in relation to fundamental philosophical controversies about this question (section 6 (2) below). In so far as I do adopt any position on it, I see it in the same way *as other "what is"-questions*, i.e. I analyse it by means of the concepts of the fundamental types of proposition: Is one asking for a definition of the word "meaning", or is one after a characterisation of those phenomena that fall under a presupposed definition of this word? Is one talking about what language usage or the phenomena are like, or about what language usage or the phenomena should or shall (or other types of modality) be like?

After the present survey of the proposition types (the present section 2 and the following sections 3–5) I shall be saying a little about the way in which the *words* "(linguistic) meaning" and "interpretation" are used in this work (section 6 (2), with further references). – Later, as a step in the in-depth discussion of definitions, I shall be dealing with *persuasive definitions* of the word "meaning" (sections B 7.3.2 (3) cf. III 2.2.2 (3)), and further, with a central *part* of the area of meaning: some ways of using the *word "concept"* (sections B 3.2.2 and 4.1).

3. The structuring function and naming function of definitions

A definition can answer *two questions*:

First, a definition can answer the question of how the world is or should[1] be divided up in thought: for example how many kinds of snow one should operate with, or whether one should distinguish between law and morals. – I call this question the *"structuring question"*. In so far as a definition answers the structuring question, I shall say that it has a *"structuring function"* (section B 4.1 below).

Secondly, a definition can answer the question of which linguistic entities are used or should be used of a *given* area-in-thought with which one is operating: for example whether one should speak of "wet snow" or "sticky snow", or whether one should use the word "morals", the word "ethics" or the word "virtue". – I call this question the *"naming question"*. In so far as a definition answers the naming question, I shall say that it has a *"naming function"* (section B 4.2 below).

In the definition theory here definitions have a structuring function by definition. On the other hand, whether definitions also have a naming function is according to this theory a question of fact and can consequently only be answered by looking at the individual definition (section B 4.3.1 below, with further references).

In literature on definitions, writers often presuppose that both what is being defined and what is defining are linguistic entities, and term these respectively "definiendum" and "definiens". I do not use these terms, but the formulations "what is being defined", "what is defining", and variations on these. My grounds are as follows:

In the definition theory here, what is being defined is not necessarily a linguistic entity, cf. what has just been said about the structuring function of definitions. Nor is what does the defining necessarily a linguistic entity: In actually occurring language and argumentation, the structuring of the world into areas-in-thought takes place by a multiplicity of means (section 4 below, cf. sections B 5–6 below), including the non-linguistic means of pointing to an object (section B 5.2 (5)). – One can of course choose not to define the words "definiendum" and "definiens" so that they are by definition linked to the linguistic level, and define them more neutrally as respectively 'what is being defined' and 'what is defining'. In that case too, however, occurrences of "definiendum" and "definiens" will no doubt often be read as if they referred to the linguistic level, because the neutral definition is overlooked or

[1] For the sake of brevity the word "should" is used in the present section 3 as the representative of normative modality expressions, and the fusion alternative is not given special mention (section 5 (4) below).

forgotten. – Irrespective of how one defines them there is in addition the fact that the words "definiendum" and "definiens" are poorly suited to leading thought towards the reality with which we are concerned.

This question of terminology is incidentally of no great practical significance in the present work, either in the definition theory or in the other parts, cf. the more detailed discussions.

I use the terms *"use of language", "language use" and "language usage"*, sometimes also the term *"language"* itself, with their derivatives and collocations ("... question", "... function"), of the unity of the structuring dimension and the naming dimension.

4. Specification of connotation and specification of denotation

In logic and semantics it is common to make a tripartite division between sentences (propositions); general words and expressions (concepts); and singular words and expressions, i.e. proper nouns, definite descriptions or other words and expressions that function as proper nouns. One draws these distinctions first and foremost to be able to explain what is meant by "logical form" and "logically valid arguments".[1] This reason does not apply in the present work. However, I shall presuppose the tripartite division outlined as I draw a *distinction in particular in relation to general words and expressions (concepts)*:

Let us take as given a general word, for example the word "cup". Two *main ways of defining* are the following: – First, to specify what properties[2] something must have for the word to be able to be used of it, e.g. 'objects that are made for drinking out of'. The individual property viewed in this perspective ('object', 'for drinking out of', etc.) I call a "definitional criterion", sometimes for the sake of brevity "criterion", often more specifically "language use criterion" if it is linked to the word and "concept criterion" if it is linked to the concept. Taken together I call the criteria the *"connotation"* (of the word or of the concept), and definitions by means of criteria I call *"specifications of connotation"* (section B 5.1 below).[3] –The second main way of defining is to specify individual phenomena or types of individual phenomenon of which the word is used. Such individual phenomena or types of individual phenomenon I call the *"denotation"* (of the word or of the concept), and definitions by means of these I call *"specifications of denotation"* (section B 5.2 below).

> The class of those individual phenomena of which general words and expressions are used has been given *different designations* by different writers: "denotation",[4] "extension"[5] and "omfang" [extent].[6] The criteria that specify

[1] See e.g. Føllesdal/ Walløe/ Elster, *Argumentasjonsteori, språk og vitenskapsfilosofi* [argumentation theory, language and the philosophy of science], pp. 220–21, cf. 194–95.

[2] Here and in a number of cases otherwise I use "properties" in a very broad sense, inter alia also of relations.

[3] In relation to the perspective and topic of the present work it may in some connections be expedient to extend the concept of 'connotation specification' also to cover specification of the relations of the word to the more comprehensive linguistic context of which the word is a part (with concomitant extension of the concepts of 'connotation' and 'definitional criterion'); see in more detail in section B 5.5 (3) below.

[4] Mill, *A System of Logic*, Book I (Of names and propositions), especially Chapter II (Of names), Section 5 (Connotative and Non-connotative).

[5] Carnap, *Meaning and Necessity*, Chapter 1.

[6] Næss, *Logikk og metodelære* [logic and methodology], pp. 101–08.

under what circumstances general words and expressions are used of a given phenomenon are then usually designated respectively "connotation", "intension" and "innhold" [content].

One weighty reason to avoid the word-pair "extension" and "intension" is the strong and philosophically relevant polysemy in the case of the words "intension/al" in spoken English, and of corresponding words in other languages ("intensjon/al", "Intention/al", etc.), be it in the spoken language or in writing: (1) = meaning of linguistic entities; (2) = directedness of mind; (3) = purpose. (In some languages one does not have this polysemy in the written language, cf. for example the English distinction between "intension" = (1), and "intention" = (2) or (3)).

The word-pair "extent" and "content" has the disadvantage that these words may seem too much part of the everyday language. It may therefore be psychologically difficult to attach a permanent and more technical association to them.

Against using the word "connotation" it has been objected that this is first and foremost used of "the associations [which a word or phrase] has in the minds of the people who use it. Thus the word "snake" … connotes (to most people, at any rate) the characteristics of being slimy and revolting."[7] This objection does not, irrespective of its weight otherwise, carry great weight in this context since the English meaning of the word "connotation" just quoted is not a permanent and dominant meaning of "connotation".

In logic and semantics one draws distinctions parallel to the distinction now outlined between 'connotation' and 'denotation' also in the case of sentences and singular words and expressions.[8] In relation to a major aim of the present work, dis/agreement analysis (Chapter I above), such an extension of the distinction is of less interest. In most of the connections that are discussed here *singular words and expressions* will be sufficiently effective means of communication: be they proper nouns ("Mary", "Norway", "The Sale of Goods Act"), definite descriptions ("the woman who entered into the contract with Peter", "the northernmost country in NATO", "the Act that was passed on 13 May 1988 as No. 27") or other words and expressions that function as proper nouns ("I", "you", "here", "there", "now", "then", etc.). Communication problems that are connected with *sentences (propositions)* are on the other hand central to the work; but here it is the case that little light can be shed on the problems I shall be discussing, through an extended application of the distinction 'connotation'– 'denotation' that I have outlined above in relation to general words and expressions (concepts).

---

7 Hospers, *An Introduction to Philosophical Analysis*, p. 48 at and in note 14 (Hospers' italics omitted).

8 See e.g. Føllesdal/ Walløe/ Elster, *Argumentasjonsteori, språk og vitenskapsfilosofi* [argumentation theory, language and the philosophy of science], pp. 194–95. – Of the writers mentioned above in connection with the terminology question (notes 4–6 above) Mill and Næss draw their distinctions only in relation to general words and expressions, while Carnap draws his distinction also in relation to sentences and singular words and expressions. The extended use of the distinction goes back to Frege: 'Connotation' is a parallel to Frege's concept of 'Sinn', and 'denotation' is a parallel to his concept of 'Bedeutung'; compare 'On Sense and Meaning', pp. 57–58, 62–63.

5. Descriptive propositions; normative propositions; fusions. In particular on the broad meaning of the term "normative proposition"

(1) Descriptive propositions

By *"descriptive propositions"* I mean propositions of which one can say that they are true or untrue, and which purport to say something about a reality otherwise (beyond the proposition). They may be propositions in the past, present or future tense; about what exists; about what properties something has; or about how existence or properties can be explained, including propositions about causes or effects.

Descriptive propositions can contribute to determining the meanings of linguistic entities (contribute to determining concepts), i.e. be descriptive *definitions* (section B 3.2 below); or they can have another topic, i.e. be descriptive *characterisations* (section C below).

To decide the truth value of descriptive propositions one needs the proposition itself, plus a reality otherwise, which the proposition purports to say something about and against which the proposition can be checked. This is in contrast to analytically un/true propositions, where to decide the truth value it is not necessary to have any checking against a reality otherwise (section 2 (2) above).

(2) Normative propositions

(a) The broad meaning of the term "normative proposition" in this work

I use the term "normative proposition", first, in a *normal and narrow sense*: of propositions that command, prohibit or exempt from commands or prohibitions (duty propositions); of propositions that recommend; of propositions that confer or delimit competence (competence propositions); and of propositions that qualify something as something else (qualification propositions, for example 'fundamental breach of contract is to be reckoned as a ground for termination of the contract').

I do not lay down any further requirement that normative propositions in the narrow sense (duty, recommendation, competence or qualification propositions) must be *stipulated*;[1] must be psychologically *internalised* tout court,[2] or more particularly, as the case may be, by judges,[3] the public at large,[4] or others; must be *justifiable* according to norms of argumentation that are themselves internalised;[5] or must be anything else. – Such requirements are normal when defining in legal theory the concept of 'legal norm', see the preceding notes. One reason for this is no doubt normal language usage; cf. the fact that most people will not say that there is a norm if the normative proposition lacks a fairly tangible and permanent anchorage in reality (delimitation against jokes, thought experiments, proposals, an order given by a bank robber, and the like). However, the present work centres on language and argumentation behaviour, i.e. on propositions and their linguistic expression, not on the behaviour that propositions prescribe. This being so, such further requirements as mentioned, are beside the point.

Secondly, I use the term "normative proposition" of *value propositions*; i.e. of propositions that, for example, say that an action is good, that a work of art is beautiful, or that one dish tastes better than another.

Finally, I also use the term "normative proposition" of *decision propositions*; i.e. of propositions that express a decision about something. – Decision propositions are common in the case of definitions, cf. the frequency of forms of expression such as "in what follows I shall use the word "x" of ..." (section B 3.3.1 (2) below).

All language use, like all action otherwise, *presupposes* intention: in the case of language use, the intention to formulate words, to communicate meaning, to influence others. But only decision propositions *express* intention.

---

1 Austin, *The Province of Jurisprudence Determined*, p. 134 et passim (legal norms as "commands of the sovereign"); Kelsen, *Reine Rechtslehre*, pp. 200 et seq.

2 Hart, *The Concept of Law*, 1st ed. pp. 55–56, 83, 86–88, 96, 99; 2nd ed. pp. 56–57, 85, 88–91, 98–99, 102–03; Sundby, *Om normer* [on norms], pp. 118–48, 160–64; Eckhoff/ Sundby, *Rettssystemer* [legal systems], 1st ed. pp. 108–25; 2nd ed. pp. 52–56; *Rechtssysteme*, pp. 48–51; MacCormick, *Legal Reasoning and Legal Theory*, p. 289 (pp. 275–92); MacCormick/ Weinberger, *An Institutional Theory of Law*, pp. 6, 15.

3 Holmes, 'The Path of the Law', pp. 167–69, 173; Chipman Gray, *The Nature and Sources of the Law*, pp. 84–85; Cardozo, 'The Growth of the Law', pp. 204–05, 207; Frank, *Law and the Modern Mind*, pp. 137, 140–42; Ross, *On Law and Justice*, Chapter 2; *Directives and Norms*, pp. 90–92. – The feature in common mentioned in the text at the present note is not affected by the fact that the writers declare themselves to be in mutual disagreement about the motivating force of normative propositions in the application of the law (compare on the one hand Frank, who argues against Gray's belief in the motivating force of normative propositions: *Law and the Modern Mind*, pp. 131–33, and on the other hand Ross, who postulates that judges are motivated by a common set of normative propositions: *On Law and Justice*, pp. 36, 44, 72).

4 Illum, *Lov og ret* [law and justice], pp. 53–64; Petersen, *Informel ret på kvindearbejdspladser* [informal law in women's workplaces], pp. 65–66.

5 Hart, *The Concept of Law*, 1st ed. pp. 105 (bottom)–06 (top); 2nd ed. pp. 108 (bottom)–09 (top); Augdahl, *Rettskilder* [sources of law], pp. 26–27; Ussing, *Obligationsretten, almindelig del* [the law of obligations, general part], p. 2 (top); Arnholm, 'Fra rettens grunnproblemer' [on some fundamental problems of law], p. 162; Sundby, *Om normer* [on norms], pp. 265, cf. 258–68, 145–46; Eisenberg, *The Nature of the Common Law*, pp. 154–56, cf. 146, 197.

> Many decision propositions may in a different perspective be viewed as promises, i.e. impositions of duty addressed to oneself (normative propositions in the narrow sense). And many promises may in a different perspective be viewed as decision propositions. For example, in many connections it will be possible to understand the sentence "in what follows I shall use the word "x" of ..." both as a decision proposition and as a promise. The fact that I nevertheless lay down decision propositions as a separate type of normative proposition is partly because actually occurring language use is *not* so determinate that one can say that there *is* in this use a univocal connection both ways; and partly because, even if in an instance-type there should be a univocal connection both ways, it may be of *interest* to focus on the *aspect* of 'expressing a decision about something' instead of the aspect of 'impositions of duty addressed to oneself'.

As is apparent from the examples, normative propositions can contribute to determining the meanings of linguistic entities (contribute to determining concepts), i.e. they can be normative *definitions* (section B 3.3 below); or they can have another topic, i.e. be normative *characterisations* (section C below).

The distinctions between normative propositions in the narrow sense, value propositions and decision propositions are *exhaustive* with respect to the area of use of the term "normative proposition" in this work.

(b) I keep the question of whether normative propositions can be un/true out of the definition

For the purposes of this work the now outlined exhaustive and tripartite specification of denotation is basically an adequate definition of the concept of 'normative proposition'. This is so, since my grounds for the formation of this concept do not lie in the existence of something abstract common to the three main types, but in such similarities and relationships in actually occurring language and argumentation as will be dealt with in the rest of this work.

A feature which is often claimed to be a feature in common, and which is often laid down as a definitional feature, is that normative propositions cannot be said to be *true or untrue*.[6] The question of whether normative propositions can be said to be true or untrue is often seen as amounting to the question of whether there exists any distinct reality level with which normative propositions can be said to be or not to be in conformity (irrespective of what people might think about the propositions or whether they in fact follow them). Understood in this way the truth question leads to controversial ontological and epistemological questions, compare shorthand terms such as "Platonic Existence", "divine precept", "natural law", "the Categorical Imperative", and "human rights".

---

6 Among writers who are central in legal theory and norm theory, see e.g. Hägerström, 'Om moraliska föreställningars sanning' [on the truth of moral notions], pp. 41, 46, 50–52, 55; Kelsen, *Reine Rechtslehre*, pp. 75–76; Olivecrona, *Law as Fact*, 1st ed. pp. 45–46, 104; Ross, *Kritik der sogenannten praktischen Erkenntnis*, p. 435; *On Law and Justice*, pp. 6–9; *Directives and Norms*, pp. 102–04; Sundby, *Om normer* [on norms], pp. 169–70; von Wright, 'Value, Norm, and Action in My Philosophical Writings', pp. 19, 22.

The present work brings into focus a critically reflexive form with a certain *independence* in relation to such controversial fundamental philosophical questions.[7] The way in which I shall demonstrate the independence of the critically reflexive form – as a fact, or more precisely, as an aspect of the work's discussions, seen as a whole, of the existence and more detailed content of this form – entails that to the greatest possible extent it is *necessary not to take any standpoint* on conflict between fundamental philosophical positions. For partly such standpoints may overshadow the demonstration of the independence of the critically reflexive form, and partly they may deceive the reader into placing this form on the level of fundamental philosophical positions (section I 6 above). This is the background to why I *keep outside the definition* of 'normative proposition' whether the proposition has truth value, cf. the intimated connection between the truth question and controversial fundamental philosophical positions.

> Ross argues that the question of whether normative propositions have truth value and the question of whether there exists a distinct reality level with which normative propositions can be said to be in conformity, are questions without any logically necessary connection between the answers: Even if one assumes a distinct reality level for normative propositions, it does not follow that normative propositions acquire truth value. For the proposition that a normative proposition is in conformity with a distinct reality level is itself a descriptive proposition according to Ross.[8] – However, the main text above emphasises that many people see these two questions as one and the same, and that such ideas should be taken into account in the formation of the concept of 'normative proposition'. I am also in doubt whether the two questions are so separate as Ross assumes. This is so because, inter alia, I think Ross uses the pertinent words (for example "un/truth" and "norm") more simply than there is support for in actual language usage: He may be right by definition, as he himself uses these words, but he has not thereby shown that normative propositions cannot be said to be un/true in other, reasonable ways of using the words.[9]

A consequence of this formation of the concept of 'normative proposition' is that the class of normative propositions *may* coincide with the class of descriptive propositions, namely *in so far as* in both cases one finds reason to speak of un/truth in relation to a reality.[10] However, such likeness, if any, lies on another

7 See in more detail in sections I 6 above and 8 below.

8 Ross, *Directives and Norms*, p. 103; probably correspondingly in von Wright, 'Value, Norm, and Action in My Philosophical Writings', p. 19.

9 Næss, 'Do we know that Basic Norms cannot be True or False?', in particular pp. 35, 45; 'We still do [not] know that Norms cannot be True or False', in particular pp. 205–06.

10 Cf. the definition of 'descriptive proposition' in item (1) above. – Coincidence would first and foremost be possible to claim in the case of propositions about fundamental duties, competences and values, i.e. in the case of propositions within the first two groups in the definition of 'normative proposition' in item (a) above. Complete coincidence would hardly be claimed by anyone, inter alia because the concept of 'normative proposition' here also covers decision propositions and many of these have the stamp of arbitrariness.

level than the differences and the forms of interplay in actually occurring language and argumentation which have justified the *above formation of the concept* of 'normative proposition' and which are *topics in the present work.*

Above I have used the words "un/truth" of something other than analytic un/truth. How does the distinction between descriptive and normative propositions relate to *analytically un/true* propositions? There are two considerations that go against applying this distinction to analytically un/true propositions. (i) There is *little need* to apply the distinction between descriptive and normative propositions to analytically un/true propositions: What is interesting in relation to *tenability assessment* is precisely whether a proposition is analytically un/true, i.e. whether the meaning content alone is sufficient to decide the un/truth of the proposition. For example, the sentence "all human beings have a duty to comply with the moral law" expresses an analytically true proposition if one presupposes the definition formulation "the term "human being" is used by definition of beings that have a duty to comply with the moral law". In this connection the distinction between descriptive and normative propositions does not bring anything new to bear on the tenability assessment. (ii) As an extension of the fact that there is little need for the distinction between descriptive and normative propositions in the case of analytically un/true propositions, there is *little to indicate* how one might possibly draw this distinction in this case. One might look at the proposition in isolation (e.g. "all human beings have a duty to comply with the moral law"); or one might look at the presupposed definition (e.g. "the term "human being" is used by definition of beings that have a duty to comply with the moral law"), and let the modality of this definition govern the modality of the analytic proposition. When the aim is insight into actually occurring analysis and argumentation it is in my view more appropriate to see analytically un/true propositions as sui generis in relation to the distinction between descriptive and normative propositions. (i)↔(ii) As a result of these considerations I shall not use "descriptive" or "normative" of analytically un/true propositions.

> Carnap uses "descriptive" of words that refer to reality, in contrast to logical words. By derivation he uses "descriptive" of proposition formulations, e.g. of analytic proposition formulations, when they do not only contain logical words ("p or not p"), but also words that refer to reality ("Peter is lying or Peter is not lying").[11] – Also for the purposes of the present work it is of importance to distinguish between the two types of analytic proposition formulation mentioned (section 2 (2) above). Carnap's terminology, however, is not very suitable, since in the present work it is in addition of importance to distinguish between what I have above called "descriptive propositions" and "normative propositions", and since the term "descriptive" ought not to be used in two meanings that are so different (e.g. all moral and legal norms will be descriptive in the meaning of 'referring to reality').

---

11 Carnap, 'Formal and Factual Science', p. 124.

Others use "descriptive", "deskriptiv", etc., of words in the same way as has just been mentioned, of words that refer to reality, but with emphasis on the contrast with words that express concepts prescribing an evaluation,[12] on the contrast with words that evoke or are evoked by emotions,[13] or on the contrast with words that prescribe a manner of acting.[14] – Also for the purposes of the present work these phenomena are of importance.[15] The said terminology, however, is not appropriate in relation to this work otherwise. This is so partly because words in themselves can neither describe nor not-describe. And it is so partly because there is no univocal connection between the classification of words as "descriptive" or "non-descriptive" and the modality of the propositions that words so classified are used to express.[16] For example: On the one hand, all moral and legal norms will also be formulated in descriptive words, see for instance the words "cross", "light" and "red" in "it is forbidden to cross when the light is red". On the other hand, non-descriptive words in the form of words appealing to emotions, for example "democracy", may be used with an evaluation-free connotation and may thus be used to express descriptive propositions (section B 7.3.3 (2)(c) below).

(3) Descriptive propositions about normative propositions

Outside my use of the term "normative proposition" fall *descriptive propositions about normative propositions* (in the broadest sense of "about"). Common and important *types* are the following:

- Propositions about whether a normative proposition was *made, and if so, with what content* ("what did the legislator mean?", "has the Supreme Court departed from the meaning intended by the legislator?");[17]
- Propositions about *people's opinions about and actions in relation to* a normative proposition ("this I consider to be/ not to be in conformity with people's sense of justice");[18]

---

[12] Robinson, *An Atheist's Values*, p. 25; Engisch, *Einführung in das juristische Denken*, pp. 111 cf. 109.

[13] Hare, *Moral Thinking*, inter alia pp. 67–68 cf. 208; Andersson/ Furberg, *Språk och påverkan* [language and influence], pp. 97–98; compare Stevenson, *Ethics and Language*, pp. 59–67, who does not, however, use "descriptive" (also) of a class of words, but (only) of a feature of words ("descriptive meaning").

[14] Hare, the same places as referred to in the preceding note.

[15] On evaluation prescription in the connotations of concepts, see section B 6.1 below; and on the feature of words that consists in their evoking or being evoked by emotions, see section B 7 below.

[16] Compare Ziff, *Semantic Analysis*, pp. 227–32; Ross, *Directives and Norms*, p. 36.

[17] *Rt. 1975/220* (the housewife judgment) on p. 223: "The travaux préparatoires shed … considerable light on the intentions of the legislator"; p. 226: "The intention was to strengthen the position of the spouse working in the home when it came to the right to an item of property in natura, in the case of dissolution of a matrimonial estate."

[18] The same judgment as referred to in the preceding note, e.g. on p. 223: "development and change in people's sense of justice"; p. 226: "poor conformity with … the general sense of justice".

- One takes as a starting point a particular normative proposition and says something about the *effects* of the proposition's being followed, be it effects that one evaluates positively or negatively. An example is a judge saying something about the effects of a particular determination of the law;[19]
- One takes as a starting point a normative proposition in the form of a decision proposition ("I will bake a cake", "the Norwegian government will reduce inflation/ unemployment/ crime") and says something about *means to the presupposedly desired end*. Examples are recipes in a cookery book or experts' investigations of how lower inflation, unemployment or crime can be achieved.[20]

In so far as there is a need for a *short common term*, I call descriptive propositions about normative propositions *"spurious"* normative propositions, in contrast to the *"genuine"* normative propositions mentioned in item (2) above.

The words "spurious/ genuine" have been used with different meanings in connection with norms. The most common meaning stems from Hedenius and is closely related to the meaning each of the words has here: What he calls "o/äkta rättssatser" [spurious/ genuine legal propositions] are subgroups of spurious/ genuine normative propositions.[21]

The terms "spurious/ genuine normative propositions" are not quite satisfactory in relation to the present work since the words "spurious/ genuine" are easily associated with an evaluation (compare section B 7 below) and since this is not the intention here. Nevertheless I consider these terms to be the best among known available alternatives (compare the next paragraph), inter alia in view of the fact that these terms are well known in the Nordic countries via Hedenius, that the main threads in the present work should prevent the evaluation misconception (Chapter I above), and that a need for these terms is only rarely actualised in the present work.

This distinction, or subgroups of it, have otherwise been designated in many ways, inter alia by means of the word-pairs "external"–"internal"[22] and "Rechtssatz"–"Rechtsnorm".[23] – Some writers use "utsagn om normer"

---

19 *Rt. 1977/1035* (the medical records judgment), in particular pp. 1044–48, e.g. p. 1048: "I take it ... that it will only be on rather rare occasions that a ... request [for the right of access to one's own medical records] will be made, and in such cases because the patient has a need for better information. I do not feel convinced that such a right will in practice necessarily lead to a revision of the manner in which records are kept."

20 To a great extent the word "norm" and its derivatives (or their equivalents in other languages) have also been used of such propositions; these propositions have inter alia been called "technical norms", "means-end norms", "heterotelic norms", "hypothetical norms" and "conditional norms".

21 Hedenius, *Om rätt och moral* [on law and morals], Chapter II, in particular pp. 66, 86, 89–90 and 98–101.

22 Hart, see the references in section F 2.1 (1)(b)(ii) below, in note 7.

23 Kelsen, *Reine Rechtslehre*, p. 76. – In the three word-pairs now mentioned by way of example (see in the text at the two preceding notes and at the present one) the words on the right ("genuine", "internal" and "...norm) seem to have significant parts of their meanings in common. The words on the left ("spurious", "external" and "...satz") part company however: Hedenius and Hart appear to want to link the truth value of all descriptive propositions about normative propositions to the existence or non-existence of psychological, social or other facts. Kelsen, in contrast, collects under the

[propositions about norms] of spurious normative propositions, and "utsagn i normer" [propositions in norms] of genuine normative propositions.[24] These terms can be misleading since "propositions about norms" purely linguistically also covers genuine normative propositions, for example evaluations of norms ("It is an infelicitous rule in Norwegian law that ...").

(4) Fused descriptive and normative propositions

The distinction between genuine and spurious normative propositions shows itself to be difficult to maintain as a dichotomy: When it comes to interpretation and categorisation of individual proposition formulations, one must sometimes recognise that a proposition belongs in the dimension 'descriptive–normative' (it is not a question, for example), at the same time as the proposition is neither purely descriptive nor purely normative. It is what I shall call a *"fused (descriptive and normative) proposition"*. The paradigm case is lawyers' propositions about what the law is (section F below). – The consequence is that the dimension 'descriptive–normative' is to be considered a graduated dimension (same place).

---

name of "Rechtssätze" a particular type of descriptive proposition about normative propositions, a type of proposition specific to legal science as it should be practised according to Kelsen, a type of proposition in the case of which the truth value is not linked to the existence or non-existence of facts, but to derivability from norms at higher levels, i.e. to his theory of the hierarchical structure of law and his theory of the basic norm.

24 See e.g. Hägerström, 'Om moraliska föreställningars sanning', pp. 55 and 57: "[S]cience ... has [only] to *represent what is true* [my italics] ... [M]oral science [can]not ... be a doctrine in morality, but only a doctrine *about* [Hägerström's italics] morality"; Ross, *On Law and Justice*, p. 76: "norm-*descriptive*, not norm-expressive, ... *about* norms, not in norms" (my italics; translation altered).

6. The distinctions between the types of proposition lie by definition on the level of meaning, in contrast to the level of language. The way the word "meaning" etc. is used in what follows

(1) The distinctions between the types of proposition lie by definition on the level of meaning, in contrast to the level of language

This aspect of my concepts of the types of proposition entails that one cannot infer by logical necessity (by definition) the occurrence of a particular type of proposition from the occurrence of particular words and expressions. Words and expressions are means of interpretation, not concept criteria.

Before I can justify this aspect of my conceptualisations (item (3) below), I must say a little about how I shall be using the word "meaning" etc. in what follows.

(2) The way the word "meaning" etc. is used in what follows

The expression "(linguistic) meaning" is *polysemous*. Before one can take any standpoint on what meaning an individual formulation has, one must therefore clarify what concept of 'meaning', what yardstick for the interpretation, one is going to apply (section E 1.1 below).

Decisions about what concept of 'meaning' one takes as a basis often rest on philosophically *controversial presuppositions* concerning what exists (ontology) and what one can cognise (epistemology). The present work brings into focus a critically reflexive form with a certain *independence* in relation to such controversial fundamental philosophical questions.[1]

The way in which I shall demonstrate the independence of the critically reflexive form – as a fact, or more precisely, as an aspect of the work's discussions, seen as a whole, of the existence and more detailed content of this form – entails that to the greatest possible extent it is *necessary not to take any standpoint* on conflict between fundamental philosophical positions. For partly such standpoints may overshadow the demonstration of the independence of the form, and partly

1 See in more detail in sections I 6 above and 8 below.

they may deceive the reader into placing the critically reflexive form on the level of fundamental philosophical positions (section I 6 above). This is the background to why to the greatest possible extent I have wished to *avoid* implanting, through the concept of 'meaning', controversial premisses in the concepts of the individual types of proposition.

Taking as a point of departure the superordinate perspective and topic of the work (Chapter I above) I adopt what I call, in shorthand form, a *"discussion and decision perspective"* on linguistic meaning (sections I 4 above and B 4.1 (5)(c), E 2.2.5 (1) and G 2 (4)(c), below).

However, when in what follows I use *words like* "meaning" and "interpretation", the reader may content himself with reading these words as *intermediate stations for thought*, in the sense that one reads them as words, the alternative meanings of which one does not for the time being need to choose between. *What* alternative meanings may be relevant will be discussed *after* the treatment of the individual types of proposition (section E below). As will appear from this subsequent discussion, it will not be necessary then either to make any general choice: What yardstick one takes as a basis for an interpretation ought to rest on what one wishes to cognise.

Here I only name the two *main* types of linguistic meaning that will be discussed: "objective meaning" and "subjective meaning" (sections E 2.1 and 2.2). To the extent that this distinction should present itself as relevant before then, it should be sufficient to understand "objective meaning" and "subjective meaning" more intuitively: as respectively normal language usage and particular individuals' language usage, two entities that may part company, but need not do so.

(3) Why I by definition place the distinctions between the types of proposition on the level of meaning

It is undoubtedly in best *conformity with normal language usage* to place the distinctions between the types of proposition on the level of meaning:

On the one hand, it is quite normal to think that the same linguistic entity may express propositions of different types, all according to the context: for example, to think that the sentence "Peter is shutting the door" may be understood as a descriptive proposition in one context, and as a normative proposition (order) in another context. On the other hand, it is quite normal to think that the same proposition may be expressed linguistically in several ways, for example "Peter is shutting the door", "Peter is closing the door", "Peter ferme la porte", etc. – It is consequently not normal to assume a univocal connection in either direction: either from language to meaning or from meaning to language.

Some writers, however, (for their own purposes) place the distinguishing criteria on the *level of language*; or it may be *unclear* whether they place the distinguishing criteria on the level of meaning or on the level of language. I shall mention two examples from Scandinavian literature:

> The following definition in Næss seems to place the distinction on the level of language: "By "norm" we shall mean the same as we mean by "normative sentence", an expression that may be formulated more precisely as follows: "a sentence that says that somebody should, shall or must do something, or that says that something has (negative or positive) value, or is good, bad, better, worse, best or worst"."[2]
>
> Hägerström uses in his definition of 'private declaration of intent' a criterion he calls the "imperative form", and this he says is "certain words or forms of words". However, other interpretation factors suggest that the criterion lies on the level of meaning.[3]

Distinctions on the level of meaning are, however, for two reasons *more difficult to apply* than distinctions on the level of language. First, the term "(linguistic) meaning" is *polysemous* (item (2) above). Secondly, linguistic meaning, be it objective or subjective, *is not considered to be a (completely) empirically perceptible phenomenon*; this is different in the case of words, in that words are not considered to have any level of existence beyond what one can see, hear or feel (sections B 4.1 (5)(a) and E, below).

For the following reasons, in spite of these difficulties, I draw the distinctions between the types of proposition on the level of meaning. First, consideration for the *normal way of thinking and normal language usage* (see the introductory remarks in the present item). Secondly, and more important, drawing these distinctions on the level of language would make it *more laborious or impossible to communicate* analysis of important phenomena, inter alia a phenomenon that will be dealt with later in the present work: *discrepancy* between on the one hand the objective meaning of linguistic entities, and on the other hand the criteria for the use of language that participants in discussion are subjectively motivated by, *especially* the language user's tendency (on the level of objective meaning) to use polysemous, or one-sidedly descriptive or logical modes of expression, in spite of the fact that (on the level of subjective meaning) the criteria that motivate him are normative (Chapter IV below). Lawyers' language and argumentation represents an important instance-type of this tendency. However, the tendency is more general. It seems to occur in most contexts in which one is discussing how one is to act or should have acted.

---

2 Næss, 'Finnes det objektive normer?' [are there objective norms?], pp. 196–97.

3 See the discussion in Eng, '"Hva er en viljeserklæring?"' ["what is a declaration of intent?"], pp. 26–28.

7. Summary of fundamental types of proposition about what something is. The main emphasis of the present work

The distinctions that have now been outlined (sections 2–5 cf. 6, above) form the core of the critically reflexive form that constitutes the perspective and topic of the present work (section 1, cf. Chapter I, above).

The *main emphasis* will be on the distinction between *definitions* and *characterisations*, and the distinction between *descriptive*, *normative* and *fused* propositions; see the top two levels of heading throughout the table of contents for the work as a whole.

In addition there is great emphasis on two distinctions specific to definitions: the distinction between the *structuring function* and the *naming function* of definitions, and the distinction between defining through *specification of connotation* and defining through *specification of denotation*. – Both distinctions demonstrate that the boundary between descriptive and normative definitions is a matter both of dimensions and of degrees (section B 8 below). Further, both distinctions will be necessary when I subsequently come to give a conceptual representation of a widespread mode of analysis of a more complex kind (Chapter V below). – The distinction between the structuring function and the naming function of definitions will furthermore be necessary for a more nuanced mapping of criteria that are used in the setting up of and choice between normative definitions (section III 2 below).

As a delimiting case come *analytically un/true propositions*: These are neither definitions nor characterisations (section 2 above). Nor is it natural to apply to analytically un/true propositions the distinction between descriptive, normative and fused propositions (section 5 (2)(b) above, concluding remarks); nor the distinction between structuring function and naming function; nor the distinction between connotation specification and denotation specification. – The concepts of 'analytically un/true propositions' serve in the first place to bring the other types of proposition *into relief*. Furthermore, the difference between analytically un/true propositions on the one hand and the other types of proposition on the other serves to create awareness of an important critically reflexive question: what *vulnerability* a proposition has. In that analytically un/true propositions are un/true by virtue of the definitions one presupposes, they say nothing about the world; they are thus propositions of the least vulnerable sort.

Bringing these distinctions together provides a set of *fundamental proposition types*. This set may be specified schematically as follows (the circles specify the places in the rest of the present Chapter II where the individual proposition types will be discussed in more detail):

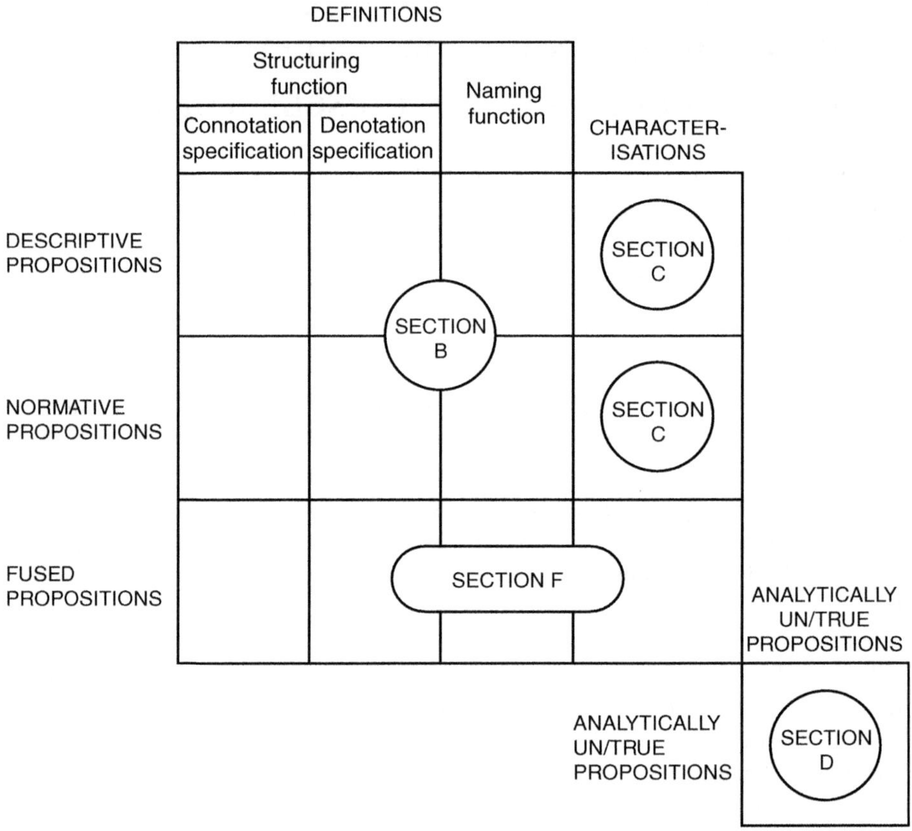

8. Non-empirical propositions

Cutting across the two main distinctions 'definitions–characterisations' and 'descriptive propositions–normative propositions' there runs a distinction between, on the one hand, propositions referring only to empirically perceptible entities, in what follows termed "*empirical* propositions", and on the other hand, propositions that also or only refer to extra-sensory entities, in what follows termed "*non-empirical* propositions".

Examples of propositions that will often be considered to be non-empirical are propositions about gods, about eternal life (after life on earth), about concepts, about linguistic meaning, about natural law, or about the meaning of life.

Non-empirical propositions raise *difficult questions*. They raise such questions directly, concerning the topic of the propositions: What exists, "where", and in what manner? ("ontological questions"). And they raise difficult questions by implication, concerning the relevant tenability criteria: How does one cognise whether an individual non-empirical proposition is tenable or not, and whether one is in real agreement or disagreement? ("epistemological questions").

I do not aim to answer questions about the existence of non-empirical reality levels or about choice of tenability criteria for propositions on these levels. – It is true that in a number of places I shall be dealing with non-empirical propositions. However, the emphasis will then be not on the *tenability* of the propositions themselves, but on *mapping* the existence, content and factual significance of forms of language and argumentation.

As mentioned earlier, this *neutrality* in relation to propositions applies in general: in relation to controversial philosophical, moral, legal, political or similar questions (sections I 1 cf. 6, above). – Nevertheless there may be reason to emphasise the neutrality *particularly* in the case of non-empirical propositions; this is because many fundamental philosophical positions compete in providing answers to the above-mentioned difficult questions, and because it is common for philosophers to relate their discussions to the conflict between these fundamental positions, so common that one expects this.[1]

---

[1] Section I 7 above; Eng, 'Teoristruktur og teorivalg' [theory structure and theory choice], pp. 503–04.

B Definitions

1. Why definition theory?

(1) The concepts in definition theory as means of determining which type of proposition one is confronted with
(2) The individual types of definition as means
(3) To create concepts that are adapted to analysis and argumentation formulated in everyday language
(4) Popper's critique of definitions

(1) The concepts in definition theory as means of determining which type of proposition one is confronted with

One reason for familiarising oneself with definition theory is the significance of such theory for the determination of which type of proposition one is confronted with, both when it comes to propositions that one *sends* and propositions that one *receives*: Is one confronted with a definition, a characterisation, or an analytically un/true proposition?

In relation to the aim of avoiding pseudo dis/agreement concerning proposition type, it is clear that the general concept of 'definition' is relevant; it is through this that one creates an awareness of the *contrast with characterisations and analytically un/true propositions*. But also concepts of different definition types are relevant: Definitions may have different modality (section 3 below) and may, irrespective of modality, concern quite different aspects of the use of language (sections 4–7 and in summarised form in section 8, below).

By characterising a proposition as a definition or a characterisation, one has connected oneself into different sets of relevant facts: certain aspects of the use of words, *in contrast to* other facts (sections I 3 (1) cf. II A 2 (4), above). – Of all the sources of pseudo dis/agreement two are in a special position when it comes to factual significance. One of these is the confusion of definitions and characterisations, or lack of clarity about the relationship between them: The one participant in the discussion speaks about what the meanings of linguistic entities (what the concepts) are or should or shall (or other types of modality) be, while the other participant presupposes this topic and speaks about the properties of things, or it is unclear what the one or the other is speaking about.[1]

> This source of pseudo dis/agreement operates *in discussions of definitions as well.* See, for example, the article under the headword "Definition" in *The Encyclopedia of Philosophy*.[2] There the writer classifies and discusses various other writers' views of definitions,[3] and then puts forward his own view[4] – without defining what he means by "definition". The wording of his discussion seems to suggest that these writers are in disagreement about features of a phenomenon delimited through presupposition and termed "definition"; i.e. that the article discusses different characterisations of one and the same phenomenon. Further examination reveals, however, that *there is no* such common delimitation of a phenomenon through presupposition; the central unity between the propositions that are discussed, seems to be that these propositions were put forward by well-known philosophers *and* that the topic of these propositions has been labelled with the word "definition" or other variants of the Latin original. Nevertheless it *may* be a matter of characterisations, in so far as the writers have linked their discussions to phenomena delimitations that are presupposed but mutually differ. Probably, however, many of the writers who are discussed, and the writer of the article himself, did not (only) intend to characterise phenomena delimitations that are presupposed but (also) to thematise the phenomena delimitation itself, i.e. to define concepts of 'definition'.[5]

(2) The individual types of definition as means

It is one thing to use definition *concepts*, i.e. to use a concept of 'definition' and concepts of different types of definition as means in the determination of one's own propositions and in the interpretation of other people's proposition formulations (item (1) above). It is another thing to use the *definitions themselves*. – On the latter level one may ask which types of definition *most effectively promote* given purposes, for example, language learning, clarity in discussion between people who have learnt the language, or delimitation of the area of application of a statutory provision. It is not to be taken for granted that a type of definition that is suitable for one purpose is also suitable for others. In this connection, definition

---

1 See also section 2.3 (1) below, concluding remarks. – The other source of pseudo dis/agreement in a special position when it comes to factual significance is the confusion of descriptive and normative propositions, or lack of clarity about the relationship between them. Compare section I 3 (1)↔(2) above. – In the sentence at the present note and in some cases otherwise I use the term "thing" in a very wide sense: of what is covered by the meanings of linguistic entities (covered by concepts), without any further delimitations.

2 Abelson, 'Definition'.

3 Op. cit., pp. 314–21.

4 Op. cit., pp. 321–23.

5 In the present context I content myself with the formulation "to define concepts of 'definition' ". For an analysis of what may lie in this formulation, see the present section B in its entirety, and section B 9 for a summary. – On factors that can explain the fact that one understands the definition problem as "the same", see section 4.3.3 (3)(b) below.

theory may contribute by mapping different types of definition and their areas of use, and thus showing what alternative *means* are at our disposal.

(3) To create concepts that are adapted to analysis and argumentation formulated in everyday language

There is a good deal of literature about different types of proposition, including definitions. Nevertheless, when it comes to definitions, I consider there is a *need for a discussion* of features of this type of proposition that is *more oriented towards system, everyday language, and descriptivity*:

"Oriented towards system" in two relations: First, in relation to the theoretical framework and the mapping, in that one establishes a nuanced theoretical framework and actually and in detail carries out a mapping of conceptually possible and actually occurring definition phenomena within the framework. Secondly, in relation to the topic, in that one establishes a theoretical framework suited to demonstrating the system character and dynamics of the definition field of everyday language. – Given a theoretical framework and mapping that is systematic in these two relations, one has a good foundation for taking a standpoint on which aspects of definition phenomena in everyday language one is particularly interested in, and for going conceptually consistently further with analysis of topics that presuppose definition theory (in the present work see particularly the topics discussed in sections III 4, IV 3.3.3–3.3.4 and V, below).

The considerations designated "orientation towards everyday language and descriptivity" relate so closely to my determination of the fundamental concept of 'definition' that I shall treat them in greater depth in this connection (sections 2.1–2.2 below).

(4) Popper's critique of definitions

Popper has formulated certain strongly critical assertions about definitions. Since he is a well-known and widely read writer, since he himself pushes these assertions into the foreground, and since his assertions have a certain representativity both in content and origin, I shall briefly outline my view on the relationship between his assertions and the present work.

Central to Popper is the rejection of *"the Aristotelian method of definition"*, i.e. of "statement[s] describing the essence of a thing".[6] Propositions about the essence of a thing will often be characterisations and thus fall outside the concept of 'definition' in the present work (section 4.1 (5)(b) below; on the concept of 'characterisation' see sections A 2 (3) above, cf. 2.3 below). In addition, it lies outside the perspective and topic of the present work to take any standpoint on the possibility or tenability of propositions about essence (sections I 6 and II A 8, above), including taking any standpoint on Popper's "anti-essentialism".[7]

---

6 Popper, *The Open Society and Its Enemies*, Vol. 2, p. 10.

7 Popper, *Unended Quest*, pp. 17 et seq.

Popper *also* seems to put forward an extremely critical view on propositions that do fall within the concept of 'definition' in the present work:

> "Never let yourself be goaded into taking seriously problems about words and their meanings. What must be taken seriously are questions of fact, and assertions about facts ... [W]orries or quarrels about words and their meanings ... is the surest path to intellectual perdition: the abandonment of real problems for the sake of verbal problems."[8]

The *area of application* for these formulations is not completely clear. – Partly, Popper seems to presuppose that participants in discussions discuss the meanings of words, that they are aware of this, and that they continue a quest for the one and true meaning. As will be apparent in a number of places in what follows, I agree that the belief in one and only one correct linguistic meaning has a certain currency, that it is quite often empirically incorrect, and that definition activity *in so far as* it aims at identifying such unique meaning is then out of place (see particularly section 3.2.2 below). – And partly, the way in which Popper formulates his ideas makes it reasonable to interpret him as being *more generally* an opponent of clarification through definitions and of our acquiring insight into definitions and types of definition.

A norm of this kind lies in its capacity of being a norm outside the perspective and topic of the present work (Chapter I above and sections 2.1–2.2 below). But the norm has interest in its capacity of being a symptom of an *incomplete* picture of the language-and-argumentation reality of which this work is to show the existence:

In philosophical, scientific, academic and other types of discussion formulated in everyday language (moral, political, cultural, etc.), there is an element of definitions that shows that the participants experience a continuous need for clarification. If one follows the present work further into the definition field of everyday language, one meets a diversity of modalities, functions and means, and one meets the system character and dynamics of this field. – Popper does not seem to have an eye for these features of the language and argumentation reality. For example, he claims:

> "[T]he *scientific view* of the definition 'A puppy is a young dog' would be that it is an answer to the question 'What shall we call a young dog?' rather than an answer to the question 'What is a puppy?' ... In modern science, *only* [the first type of question and answer] occur, that is to say, shorthand symbols or labels are introduced in order to cut a long story short" (my italics; Popper's italics omitted).[9] – By "modern science" Popper means the empirical sciences.[10]

---

[8] Op. cit., p. 19 (Popper's italics omitted).

[9] Popper, *The Open Society and Its Enemies*, Vol. 2, p. 14.

[10] Op. cit., p. 12.

The passage quoted overlooks inter alia the factual element and the factual significance of a diversity of custom-based definitions (sections 3.3.2 cf. 4–8, below). To put it more generally: The present work will demonstrate that the definition field of everyday language cannot be captured through such a limited view of definition as Popper outlines (the present section B in its entirety, with further references). Furthermore, it will demonstrate that anybody who participates in analysis and argumentation formulated in everyday language, be it in everyday life, academic subjects, science or philosophy, cannot escape the definition field of everyday language; this field is not linked to one or another area of language and argumentation but is an integral part of the critically reflexive form that this work will show to be an omnipresent aspect of the language and argumentation reality. The view of definition that Popper gives expression to is consequently inadequate as a basis for self-cognition on the part of the participants in language and argumentation; this *also* applies in academic subjects and science.

In the light of this, I consider, first, that Popper does not adequately distinguish between different issues that ought to be kept apart in a discussion of definition activity (the tenability of propositions about essence; advantages and disadvantages of using definitions, in the sense of "definition" that is taken as a basis in the present work; and the significance of reflecting into one's own thinking, concepts of fundamental proposition types, including definitions), and secondly, that he overlooks central aspects of analysis and argumentation occurring in fact and formulated in everyday language.

What explains Popper's narrow approach to actually occurring definition activity seems mainly to be that his approach is only made from and through certain fundamental viewpoints in philosophy and the theory of science. In addition to being made from and through the "anti-essentialism" mentioned by way of introduction, Popper's approach is especially made from and through the fundamental viewpoint that hypotheses must be falsifiable:[11] In the perspective of falsification his impatience with working on concepts can be understood as impatience with all procedures that delay the confrontation of the hypothesis with reality (the falsifiability test).

> However, the diversity of definitions continues to operate even if one relates conceptually blindly to them; this goes in particular for custom-based definitions. Thus, a definition theory along the lines of the present work may contribute to, rather than hinder, "anti-essentialism" and real falsification. It may contribute to "anti-essentialism",[12] in that one relates more soberly to those of one's actions (here, participation in custom-based definition activity and the resulting patterns of meaning) that one has represented conceptually, than

---

[11] On this fundamental viewpoint, see section III 2.2.2 (3)(a) below, with further references.

[12] The quotation marks signal a distance resulting from an indeterminacy in Popper's argumentation, an indeterminacy with respect to what he is arguing against. The causal relationship that is asserted in the text after the present note is, however, a psychological aspect of interest independently of the more determinate content of Popper's critique.

to those of one's actions that, as it were, operate behind one's back. It may contribute to real falsification, in that the custom-based meaning patterns that are formed in and through interaction in the research community are brought to the awareness of those interacting: a condition for identifying dimensions of dis/agreement and thus for identifying tasks for further stipulated definitions.

A simplified picture of actually occurring definition activity, and an attachment to fundamental positions in philosophy and the theory of science underlying this simplification, seem to be a *pattern* in thought cutting across considerable differences otherwise. As I shall demonstrate later, we find the same pattern in Quine (section G 2 below).

2. Introductory remarks on my concept of 'definition'

2.1. Formed out of the desire for insight into analysis and argumentation occurring in fact and formulated in everyday language: including law and legal theory

(1) An everyday language and descriptive orientation
(2) Some consequences for the definition theory
(a) Emphasis
(b) Linguistic, conceptual and systematic innovations
(c) Sources of inspiration

(1) An everyday language and descriptive orientation

I have defined 'definition' as "propositions that contribute to determining the meanings of linguistic entities (contribute to determining concepts)" (section A 2 (1) above).

In the establishment of this concept I have placed particular emphasis on the considerations for (a) an everyday language orientation of definition theory, and (b) a descriptive orientation of definition theory.[1]

(a) An *everyday language orientation* means that one aims at features of meaning determinations that are *also or first and foremost* adequate and interesting in relation to analysis and argumentation formulated in everyday language: be it analysis and argumentation in everyday life, academic subjects, science or philosophy – *not only* adequate and interesting in relation to problem fields in which concepts of 'definition' have been particularly discussed and from which concepts of 'definition' are often taken: such as certain problem fields in philosophy (in a broad sense, including much of what goes under the name of "theory of science"), logic (in a broad sense, including mathematics) and linguistics.

---

[1] The sentence containing the present note and the in-depth treatment in the rest of the present item (1) have their basis in the main aim of the work (Chapter I above): the aim of demonstrating, and creating an awareness of, the existence, content and factual significance of a specific critically reflexive form (I 4–6); and thereby, of demonstrating, and creating an awareness of, the factual significance of analysis of dis/agreement on the basis of this critically reflexive form. – I presuppose, here as elsewhere, what has been said in Chapter I about this.

My impression is that knowledge about definitions and the role they play in fact, is not *so* widespread as the use of words like "definition", "définition", "definisjon", "Definition", etc., might seem to suggest. – I further have the impression that much of the knowledge that is conveyed as *general* knowledge about definitions has been acquired out of cognition interests that more *particularly* make themselves felt in relation to problem fields in philosophy and logic.[2] The latter impression is based on the fact that in my use of everyday language I have come across aspects that I have considered to be interesting, without my having been able to find anything in particular about these aspects within writings in philosophy or logic; or, the other way round: is based on the fact that definition concepts within writings in philosophy and logic are not suited to capturing these aspects (section 2.2 below).

> The fact that academic subjects, science or philosophy are formulated in everyday language, and that the critically reflexive form that constitutes the perspective and topic of the present work has a corresponding generality (section I 5.1 above), thus does not mean that concepts of language and argumentation that are constructed in academic subjects, science or philosophy are necessarily apt in relation to everyday language and the critically reflexive form (section I 7 above). In the extreme case, thought may approach a pragmatic inconsistency, in that thought communicates itself in everyday language and thus presupposes the critically reflexive form and its level of existence, at the same time as thought by virtue of its content denies (whole or significant parts of) the critically reflexive form and its level of existence (compare section G 2 (4)(c)(ii) below, on Quine).

Against this background I have come to the conclusion that there is a need to *supplement* existing thought on definition with a conceptual model more directly aimed at, and with a more direct mapping of, the role of definitions in analysis and argumentation formulated in everyday language.

(b) Furthermore, beside the consideration for everyday language orientation, I have in the establishment of the concept of 'definition' placed particular emphasis on the consideration for *descriptive orientation*: I want first and foremost to contribute to insight into how one *actually proceeds*, when in analysis and argumentation formulated in everyday language one determines the meanings of linguistic entities (determines concepts) – not to argue for what such propositions should, shall or must be like to satisfy a philosophical or logical system (section 2.2 below).

---

[2] Gabriel, *Definitionen und Interessen*, p. 14: "[D]ie Geschichte des Definitionsproblems [ist] eng mit der Geschichte der exakten Wissenschaften verbunden."

(2) Some consequences for the definition theory

I shall briefly outline some consequences for the definition theory of the everyday language and descriptive orientation (item (1) above), and of the interplay with law and legal theory (sections I 1 and 5 above).

(a) Emphasis

The distinction between *descriptive and normative* definitions I have placed centrally in my definition theory. True enough this is a distinction "everybody is aware of". However, partly the distinction between descriptive and normative propositions has received sparse theoretical treatment in relation to definitions (sections 3 cf. 4–8, below); and partly the distinction between descriptive and normative propositions, including definitions, should be understood in a different way from what is customary, provided, that is, that the aim is insight into analysis and argumentation occurring in fact and formulated in everyday language (section F below).

(b) Linguistic, conceptual and systematic innovations

Other distinctions that have a central place in my definition theory may seem more unfamiliar. – At first sight this may be so because of the *terminology*: In certain cases I have found it necessary to introduce new terms; this applies, for example, in the discussion of what is being defined (section 4 below), where I introduce the terms "structuring function" and "naming function". – It is not, however, only or first and foremost the terms that are new. The essentials are the *areas-in-thought* that the terms designate *here* and the *system* these areas are fitted into *here*. I deem it necessary to acquire an awareness of both, *if* one wishes to achieve nuanced cognition of definition activity occurring in fact and formulated in everyday language: for example, *if* one wishes to achieve nuanced cognition of what is being defined (section 4 below), of the means used (sections 5–6 below), of dimensions subject to the distinction between descriptivity and normativity, and of the graduatedness of these dimensions (section 8 below, with further references).

(c) Sources of inspiration

The fact that one must take concepts from *philosophy and logic* also in the case of definition theory with a view to analysis and argumentation formulated in everyday language, is a matter of course and will not be treated in any greater depth here; I refer to the individual discussions. – On the other hand, there may be reason to point briefly to influences along a more unfamiliar path: from *law and legal theory*. One influence consists in concepts for definition theory. Another influence stems from actually occurring definition activity that definition theory ought to be able to account for. Some examples are:

- *Concepts of norms or norm elements* constructed in law and legal theory can contribute to capturing important aspects of definition phenomena (see, for example, section 3.1 (3) below, on the categorisation of the propositional content of definitions into person, situation and action theme; section 3.3.2 below, on custom-based normative definitions; and below in the present item (c), on guidelines).

- Lawyers' thinking through *instance-types* may shed light on the concept of 'definition through specification of denotation' (sections 5.2 cf. 5.4.2, below).
- The element of *evaluations* in lawyers' conceptualisation and subsumption may shed light on the concept of 'definition through connotation specification with evaluation prescription' (section 6.1 below).
- The guidance of lawyers' definitions and subsumptions through a distinct type of norm called *"retningslinjer"* [guidelines] may shed light on the concept of 'definition through connotation specification with factor structure', in contrast to 'definition through connotation specification with condition structure' (section 6.2 below).
- Lawyers' *propositions de lege lata* (propositions about what the law is) are the paradigm case of what I call "fused descriptive and normative propositions" (section F below).

In earlier literature on lawyers' language and argumentation, Astrup Hoel, *Den moderne retsmetode* [the modern legal method] (1925), formulates his ideas in the direction of a definition-theoretical perspective:

Astrup Hoel wishes to "bring forth the general scientific – or more precisely, the philosophical – preconditions for the assessment of the problems specific to legal science".[3] He says in that connection: "In that we ... here are first and foremost confronted with a *concept problem* [Astrup Hoel's italics], we must ... concentrate our interest on *that branch of science that generally regulates precisely the treatment of concepts* [my italics]."[4] – However, it is not reasonable to claim that there is any "branch of science" concerning how one is to define. It is rather the case that such a "branch of science" is waiting to be founded. Astrup Hoel's interests and more detailed discussion proceed in another direction, however. He is most concerned with the role played by "decisions" in lawyers' determining of concepts. And only to a minor extent does he create concepts of types of definition.

---

3 Astrup Hoel, *Den moderne retsmetode* [the modern legal method], p. 19.

4 Loc. cit. Compare also the formulations "the legal concept problem" (p. 18); "how in more detail a logically tenable determination of concepts is to be realised" (p. 42); "the modern concept principles" (p. 46, cf. pp. 43 et seq., 84, 86); "errors that mark the irrational determination of concepts" (pp. 35–39).

2.2. Contrast: Normative cognition interests in philosophy and logic

In philosophical or logical systems, requirements are often put forward for *determinacy* in the case of definitions and concepts, also in the form that determinacy requirements are laid down as a criterion in concepts of 'definition' or of 'concept'.[5] – I use here and often in what follows "determinacy" ("indeterminacy") as a *common term* for the dimensions of *unambiguity* (in contrast to ambiguity and polysemy);[6] of *completeness* (in contrast to incompleteness); of *preciseness* (in contrast to vagueness); and of condition structure of concept criteria, which often means unity in the form of *features in common* (in contrast to factor structure of concept criteria, for example unity in the form of family resemblance).[7]

As I shall later justify in more detail, I do *not* lay down such determinacy requirements as criteria in the concepts of 'definition' or 'concept' (section 4.1 (3) below). The *main reason* is that I first and foremost wish to contribute to insight into how one *actually proceeds*, when in language and argumentation formulated in everyday language one determines the meanings of linguistic entities (determines concepts); I do not wish to argue for what such propositions should, shall or must be like to satisfy a philosophical or logical system. This being the aim, it does not seem particularly appropriate to divide propositions determining the meanings of linguistic entities (determining concepts) into two: those which satisfy the ideal determinacy requirements and those which do not do so. This would mean dividing something which on the basis of the cognition interest here belongs together.

> The fact that I do not lay down determinacy requirements as criteria in the concepts of 'definition' or 'concept' does not mean that my concepts of 'definition' or 'concept' are themselves indeterminate: I want to speak of something actually existing even though this actually existing phenomenon is to a greater or lesser degree indeterminate (namely determinations, formulated in

5 This will be illustrated in the discussion below.

6 Purely linguistically it might have been logical to use the set of terms "univocalness", "equivocalness" and "multivocalness" instead of "unambiguity", "ambiguity" and "polysemy". However, the latter set of terms is standard in linguistics and semantics, see e.g. Lyons, *Semantics*, Vol. 2, pp. 396–409, 550 et seq. I therefore stick to this set.

7 The last-mentioned dimension will later be discussed as a separate topic (see particularly sections 3.2.2 cf. 6.2). – The dimensions of indeterminacy mentioned represent a set of potential problems in the interpretation and application of language in general. These dimensions have relevance in particular in relation to lawyers' language and argumentation, in that interpretation and application of formulations of legal rules systematically confront the lawyer with indeterminacy in these dimensions. – Waismann operates with an indeterminacy dimension that he calls "open texture" ("Porosität der Begriffe"), see 'Verifiability', p. 119. However, I do not consider Waismann's concept so apt in relation to actually occurring language (section 6.2 (3)(a) below), and therefore do not introduce the concept as a separate indeterminacy dimension here. – Out of consideration for readability and normal language usage, I use in some places "lack of clarity" and "clarity" instead of "in/determinacy"; see particularly Chapter IV.

> everyday language, of the meanings of linguistic entities (determinations, formulated in everyday language, of concepts)). To what extent the concepts of this indeterminate phenomenon and its different forms, themselves are or ought to be determinate is another question. The answers to this question are given throughout the definition theory of the present work (see discussions in section A above, and the present section B in its entirety, with further references to other parts of the work: see in particular sections F and III 2, below).

Philosophy and logic have also been the origin of *other* ideal requirements definitions must satisfy than requirements for determinacy.[8] – However, in relation to analysis and argumentation formulated in everyday language, there is reason to pay particular attention to the different ideal requirements for *determinacy*:

Like other ideal requirements, also requirements for determinacy have a tendency to separate propositions that ought to be seen together when the aim is insight into *actually* occurring analysis and argumentation; and thereby they have a tendency to *hinder* fruitful conceptualisation in relation to this cognition aim. – Unlike other ideal requirements, however, requirements for determinacy seem to have a great influence, in that they *stamp many people's concept of 'definition'*: One operates with a dichotomy like the one mentioned, between on the one hand propositions that satisfy the ideal requirements for determinacy, and are thus reckoned as definitions, and on the other hand propositions that do not satisfy these requirements, and are thus deemed to fall outside the concept of 'definition'. – Some *examples* from legal theory will illustrate this:

(i) Requirements for completeness

In the introduction to his discussion of the use of terms relating to rights, Ekelöf says:

> "We shall ... limit our task to finding a more specific expression that can *replace* the term "fordran" [claim] [which Ekelöf uses to exemplify terms relating to rights] ... without this substitution leading to the sentences thereby losing their legal function. Whether the substitute sought after is usable as a definition of the term "rättighet" [right] in general ... lies outside the scope of our investigation. Concerning this question, suffice it to emphasise that one must of course reckon with the possibility that this term may have *different meanings in different contexts* and that, if this is not the case, it has a *more comprehensive signification than the substitute with which we are concerned here*" (my italics; Ekelöf's italics omitted).[9]

---

8 For a general treatment of normative orientation in modern theory of science, including definition theory, see e.g. Essler, *Wissenschaftstheorie I: Definition und Reduktion*, pp. 14–15. For a treatment of some of the particular manifestations, historical and modern, of normative orientation, see Robinson, *Definition*: on the assertion that connotation determines denotation (pp. 114–15); on tendencies to underestimate the significance of ostensive definitions (pp. 122–23); on definition of the concept of 'definition' by means of the concept of 'logical equivalence' (pp. 132–35, cf. 144); on one-sided concentration on some methods of definition at the expense of others (p. 145). I shall come back to actually occurring analysis and argumentation in relation to the first two issues mentioned (in respectively sections 5.1 (3) and 6.1 (2)(c) below, and section 5.2 (6) below).

9 Ekelöf, 'Juridisk slutledning och terminologi' [legal inference and terminology], p. 243.

The passage quoted does not provide any sure guidance concerning Ekelöf's concept of 'definition'. However, I assume that the fact that neither here nor elsewhere in his discussion does he call his own analysis "definisjon"[10] [definition], and the fact that both here and elsewhere in his discussion,[11] he contrasts his own analysis with a more complete analysis and uses the word "definisjon" in this latter connection, are both results of a view that the word "definisjon" is only appropriate in the case of more complete determinations of meaning. – Ekelöf is hardly alone in having such a view of the concept of 'definition' and its relationship to his investigation. In an account of Ekelöf's discussion, Eckhoff says:

> "[Ekelöf] made it clear ... that the meaning ... would be examined by means of a *substitusjonsmetode* [substitution method]. The aim was to find expressions by which the word "fordran" [claim] could be replaced without the sentences losing their legal function" (my italics).[12]

The word "substitusjonsmetode" alone may seem a bit odd; partly because it is not particularly common, and partly because the word "definisjon" would have been natural in this context, at least as something to be mentioned. I assume that the reason that Eckhoff does not use the word "definisjon" of Ekelöf's discussion (or Ross', see note 12) is the same as that for which Ekelöf himself does not do so: They both consider that a definition *requires something more* than what Ekelöf does in his investigation, and that these requirements more precisely refer to aspects of determinacy, here to completeness in particular.

(ii) Requirements for preciseness and brevity

In the introduction to his discussion of the question "What is law?", Hart says:

> "[N]othing *concise* enough to be recognized as a definition could provide a *satisfactory* answer to [this question]. The underlying issues are *too different* from each other and *too fundamental* to be capable of this sort of resolution [i.e. definition]" (my italics).[13]

The same view was central in Llewellyn:

> "The problem of defining law ... The difficulty in framing any concept of 'law' is that there are *so many things to be included*, and the things to be included are *so unbelievably different* from each other" (my italics).[14]

---

10 Since immediately below I shall also be drawing on a Norwegian writer, I shall for the sake of simplicity use the Norwegian term "definisjon" as a common Scandinavian term.

11 Ekelöf, 'Juridisk slutledning och terminologi' [legal inference and terminology], pp. 261 (bottom)–262 (top), 264 second paragraph; see also p. 255 (bottom).

12 Eckhoff, 'Anmeldelse av Ekelöf, Valda skrifter 1942–1990' [review of Ekelöf, selected writings 1942–1990], pp. 187–88. See also p. 189, where Ross' method of analysis of the use of terms relating to rights is likewise designated "substitusjonsmetode".

13 Hart, *The Concept of Law*, 1st ed. p. 16; 2nd ed. loc. cit.

14 Llewellyn, 'A Realistic Jurisprudence – The Next Step', p. 3.

(iii) Requirements for concept criteria to be capable of being expressed as a set of necessary and sufficient conditions

Arnold says: "Obviously, "law" can *never* be defined" (my italics).[15] – The grounds for this proposition may be a requirement for brevity, as in item (ii) above. However, the strong form of expression ("never") suggests that there is more to it, since clearly one cannot rule out the possibility that the word "law" has been or will be used in such simple ways that a brevity requirement will be satisfiable. What comes in addition is probably a requirement that the concept criteria must be expressible as a set of necessary and sufficient conditions. For Arnold places great emphasis on the notion that "the law consists of a *large number* of mutually *contradictory* symbols and ideals" (my italics),[16] and he seems to be of the opinion that such material cannot be delimited through sets of necessary and sufficient conditions.[17] – Posner also claims: " "[L]aw" ... cannot be defined."[18] He bases this on the ground that the word "law" does not have a "fixed intension",[19] which I take to be another way of saying that he deems condition-structuring (compare "fixed") of the concept criteria (compare "intension") to be impossible. This means that he presupposes the possibility and carrying out of condition-structuring as a necessary criterion in the case of the concept of 'definition'.

In his analysis of fundamental legal relations, Hohfeld writes: "The strictly fundamental legal relations are ... *sui generis* [Hohfeld's italics]; and *thus* it is that attempts at *formal* definition are always unsatisfactory, if not altogether useless" (my italics unless otherwise stated).[20] – By "formal definition" Hohfeld probably means here that one specifies the meanings of words (for example, the

---

15 Arnold, *The Symbols of Government*, p. 36.

16 Op. cit., p. 49; cf. pp. 34–36, serving as grounds for the proposition quoted in the text at the preceding note.

17 Arnold uses "contradictory" not only of incompatibility of a formal-logical kind, for example, where the law says that the judge both shall and shall not safeguard consideration for predictability, but also of incompatibility of a practical kind, i.e. where the many "symbols and ideals" of the law indicate different conclusions when they are applied to the same individual instance (for example, where consideration for predictability indicates that the judge should follow a previous judgment, while consideration for concrete reasonableness indicates a different conclusion). – Compare Nietzsche, *Zur Genealogie der Moral*, p. 820: "[D]ie bisherige Geschichte der Strafe überhaupt, die Geschichte ihrer Ausnützung zu den verschiedensten Zwecken, kristallisiert sich zuletzt in eine Art von Einheit, welche schwer löslich, schwer zu analysieren und, was man hervorheben muß, ganz und gar *undefinierbar* ist. (Es ist heute unmöglich, bestimmt zu sagen, warum eigentlich gestraft wird: alle Begriffe, in denen sich ein ganzer Prozeß semiotisch zusammenfaßt, entziehn sich der Definition; definierbar is nur das, was keine Geschichte hat.)" (Nietzsche's italics; his second italics omitted). – Whether it is true that 'law' (cf. Arnold) and 'punishment' (cf. Nietzsche) *cannot* be (descriptively) defined through condition-structuring of the concept criteria, is something on which I do not take any standpoint. The topic here is simply the writers' (presupposed) definition concept: the fact that they presuppose condition-structuring as a necessary criterion in the case of their concepts of 'definition'.

18 Posner, *The Problems of Jurisprudence*, p. 368.

19 Loc. cit.

20 Hohfeld, *Fundamental Legal Conceptions*, p. 36.

meaning of the word "cup") by first subsuming what is covered, under a superordinate category ("thing"), and by then specifying what distinguishes what is covered, from other sub-categories ("for drinking out of"). This is clearly not possible where what is covered is "sui generis", i.e. is not subsumable under a superordinate category. – Definition through category and sub-category is an important instance-type of the form of definition in which the concept criteria are seen as necessary and sufficient conditions (see in more detail in section 3.2.2 (2)(b) below). Even though by adding the qualifier "formal" Hohfeld intimates the use of the word "definition" also in other cases than such condition-structuring of the concept criteria, he actually does not use the word "definition" of his own method.[21] The explanation is probably a view that this word first and foremost belongs to cases in which condition-structuring of the concept criteria is possible and has actually been carried out.

Summers uses the expression "*formal* definition" (directly) of condition-structuring of the concept criteria: "Conceptualization by formal definition – e.g. resort to necessary and sufficient conditions for the use of a word or phrase".[22] – In addition, he mentions five other ways of determining the meanings of linguistic entities (ways of determining concepts) ("synonymous paraphrase", "paradigmatic sample", "examples", "specification of family resemblances", "excluder analysis"). He does not term any of these "definition", however. – Thus, even though Summers, like Hohfeld, by adding the qualifier "formal" intimates the use of the word "definition" also in other cases than condition-structuring of the concept criteria, he too does not use the word "definition" in this way.

(i)↔(iii) Such statements as those that have now been quoted are common. They have two features in common. First, the concept of 'definition' is not explicitly discussed, but *presupposed*. Secondly, this concept seems to consist inter alia in one or more *determinacy requirements*: for example requirements for completeness, preciseness or condition structure (in addition I have above mentioned requirements for brevity, which often presuppose and appear together with the determinacy requirements).

There is reason to ask *why* one shall operate with a concept of 'definition' that does *not* capture actually occurring and practically important ways of determining the meanings of linguistic entities (ways of determining concepts). – In relation to the examples above there is thus reason to ask: Why shall one operate with a concept of 'definition' that does not cover the meaning determinations of Ekelöf, Hart, Llewellyn, Arnold and Hohfeld, or the methods of meaning determination that Summers mentions?

There is much to indicate that *ideal* requirements in philosophy and logic have

---

21 He characterises his own method in immediate continuation of the passage quoted in the text at the preceding note: "Accordingly, the most promising line of procedure seems to consist in exhibiting all of the various relations in a scheme of "opposites" and "correlatives", and then proceeding to exemplify their individual scope and application in concrete cases."

22 Summers, 'The General Duty of Good Faith', pp. 817–18.

seeped out into and coloured a more general, but often simply presupposed, concept of 'definition': partly in such academic contexts as have been quoted, and partly in more general language usage.[23] – As examples may be mentioned ideal requirements in the following three influential writers in philosophy and logic: Frege lays down as a definitional requirement which concepts must satisfy, that they are fully determined, and puts forward the norm that definitions shall determine such concepts, i.e. be correspondingly determined.[24] Carnap lays down as a definitional requirement which definitions must satisfy, that they specify necessary and sufficient conditions for the use of the word (subsumption under the concept) that is being defined.[25] And Næss lays down as a definitional requirement which definitions must satisfy, that they specify person (group of people) and situation ("field of application").[26]

In the light of the *distance* between on the one hand ideal requirements, like those mentioned, for the determinacy of definitions and on the other hand actually occurring propositions that contribute to determining the meanings of linguistic entities (contribute to determining concepts),[27] there may be reason to problematise the use of ideal requirements as criteria in a concept of 'definition'. One should explicitly ask *what* concept of 'definition' one needs for insight into analysis and argumentation occurring *in fact* and formulated in *everyday* language. – This question governs the formation of the concept here.

---

23 *Gyldendals fremmedordbok* [Gyldendal's dictionary of foreign words]: "definere [to define] … nøyaktig [exact] …"; *Norsk riksmålsordbok* [Norwegian Riksmål dictionary]: "definere … i kort og konsis form [in a brief and concise form] … slik at det ikke kan forveksles med andre [so that it cannot be confused with others] … angi det vesentlige [to specify the essential]"; *The Concise Oxford Dictionary*: "define … exact …"; Wahrig, *Deutsches Wörterbuch*: "definieren … genau …".

24 Frege, 'Frege on Definitions – I', p. 139: "A definition of a concept … must unambiguously determine, as regards any object, whether or not it falls under the concept." – In relation to such requirements, the vast majority of actually occurring meaning determinations outside logic and mathematics fall short; see for illustration the present section B in its entirety.

25 Carnap, 'Testability and Meaning', pp. 439–41, 448–50; 'The Methodological Character of Theoretical Concepts', p. 69. – With such a concept of 'definition', many actually occurring meaning determinations outside logic and mathematics fall outside; see for illustration the present section B in its entirety.

26 Næss, *Interpretation and Preciseness*, pp. 147–48 (on normative definitions) and 169–70 cf. 266 (on descriptive definitions). See also *En del elementære logiske emner* [some elementary topics in logic], p. 43; *Logikk og metodelære* [logic and methodology], p. 101. – With such a concept of 'definition', inter alia many meaning determinations in dictionaries fall outside, in that they only specify meaning alternatives, without specification of person or situation; see *Interpretation and Preciseness*, p. 170. – In relation to a general concept of 'rule' many lawyers will probably lay down requirements concerning the specification of person or situation corresponding to those Næss lays down for definitions, cf. Pound, *An Introduction to the Philosophy of Law*, p. 56: "Rules, that is, definite, detailed provisions for definite, detailed states of fact, …"; Llewellyn, *The Common Law Tradition*, p. 343: "The most obvious … is that a "rule" never rises to the full level of a rule, at all, except insofar as its sphere and criteria of application achieve a moderate clarity"; Schauer, *Playing by the Rules*, pp. 118–19: "Rules necessarily specify the scope of their application … the rules of law necessarily specify the people and places to whom their requirements attach …".

27 See remarks in my (first) sentence preceded by a dash in each of the notes 24–26.

2.3. The unity and the diversity in the concept. Terminology

(1) Unity and diversity

My defining 'definition' positively as "propositions that contribute to determining the meanings of linguistic entities (contribute to determining concepts)" at the same time draws a boundary *with* propositions with *another* topic, 'characterisations' (section A 2 above): Definitions thematise what the meanings of linguistic entities (what the concepts) are or should or shall (or other types of modality) be. Characterisations presuppose this topic and thematise other topics.

In a great deal of other literature and discussion, the word "definition" and its derivatives (or their equivalents in other languages) are *also* used of characterisations:[28] in philosophy, inter alia in collocations such as "essential definition" or "real definition",[29] and in psychology and social science, inter alia in collocations such as "defining the situation" or "power to define".

Two illustrations:

Næss uses the designation *"real definition"* of the following characterisations: "[A] certain kind of description [intended to] cover ... *all* denotata of a concept ... already introduced. ... The description should be intended to satisfy the three following requirements: 1) There should be no other class of things to which exactly the same description applies. 2) Other specific or common characteristics of the denotata may be inferred (logically or in the form of well established empirical hypotheses) from the characteristics mentioned in the description. 3) The description as a whole should be short, preferably consisting only of one sentence" (my italics).[30]

When the word "definition" is used in this way, the possible unity that lies in the boundary with characterisations is lost. Therefore Næss must write: "In this work two concepts – or rather two concept families – will be introduced under the names of "normative definition" and "descriptive definition". A term "real definition" will also be introduced ... *There is no assumption whatsoever* that things subsumable under normative, descriptive or real definitions have *common and specific characteristics which warrant the introduction of a more general concept including all*" (my italics).[31]

---

28 *Gyldendals fremmedordbok*: "definere [define] ... beskrive [describe], karakterisere [characterise]"; *Norsk riksmålsordbok*: "definere ... ofte næsten svarende til beskrive, karakterisere [often almost corresponding to describe, characterise]"; *The Concise Oxford Dictionary*: "definition ... a statement of ... the nature of a thing"; Wahrig, *Deutsches Wörterbuch*: "definieren ... erklären".

29 Robinson, *Definition*, pp. 149–92, maps different ways of using the term "real definition". On ways of using this term that include characterisations, see pp. 156–57, 161–70, 171–78, 187.

30 Næss, *Interpretation and Preciseness*, p. 173. The definition quoted is also essentially taken as a basis in *Democracy, Ideology and Objectivity*, supplemented with a further requirement (p. 29): "The characteristics mentioned in the description should be of special importance to the understanding and manipulation of the denotata of the concept."

31 Næss, *Interpretation and Preciseness*, p. 144.

In his analysis of human interaction Goffman takes as his starting point the formulation *"defining the situation"*,[32] and derives formulations like "presenting a definition" (p. 231), "projecting a definition" (p. 20), "division of definitional labour" (p. 21), "conflict of definitions" (p. 21), "definitional claims" (p. 22), "maintaining a definition" (p. 86 in note 6) and "definitional disruptions" (p. 24).

What Goffman wishes to shed light on is the establishment of and competition between different perceptions of everyday situations: the processes through which human beings choose, exclude, emphasise or normatively relate to consciousness of aspects of these situations. – Situations, however, do not have meaning in the same sense as words have, and cannot therefore be defined in the same sense as words can. What Goffman calls "definitions" show themselves on closer examination to be *characterisations*: They may be of a descriptive kind, for example the proposition that there is a superior–subordinate relationship between two people; or they may be of a normative kind, for example the decision proposition from the superior that he now wants the subordinate (also) as a friend. In none of these cases are the meanings of words (concepts) thematised. The meanings are presupposed, in the examples, particularly the meanings of the expressions "superior–subordinate relationship" and "friendship". These presupposed linguistic meanings are used to characterise the situations.

My formation of the concept of 'definition' and my terminology consequently depart from such broad use of language.

However, even if propositions that do not contribute to determining the meanings of linguistic entities (do not contribute to determining concepts) are excluded (section A 2 above), the concept of 'definition' covers propositions *differing from one another*, differences that it is important to be aware of in many discussion contexts; cf. the analyses in what follows of the modalities, functions and means of definitions (sections 3–8). – Why should we then accept the boundary that is being drawn here between definitions and characterisations, as a basis for the *general concept of 'definition'*?

The answer lies in the earlier account of what I wish to achieve through the concepts of the types of proposition: to bring into focus loci in actually occurring language and argumentation which experience has shown it to be important to determine when one is assessing the tenability of propositions, and thus when one is analysing dis/agreement (sections I 4 cf. 2–3 above; and section 1 (1) above). – Central in relation to this aim is precisely the boundary between on the one hand thematising, and on the other hand the presupposition of, what the meanings of linguistic entities (what the concepts) are or should or shall (or other types of modality) be: The unity that lies in the boundary with characterisations, with propositions that do not thematise but presuppose the topic mentioned, plays *such* a central role in the assessment of the tenability of propositions that it justifies my

---

[32] Goffman, *The Presentation of Self in Everyday Life*, pp. 13, 13–27, 246 et passim. The references in parentheses in the rest of the paragraph are to this book.

formation of the general concept of 'definition', and my use of the word "definition" of this and only this area. The more detailed discussions in the present work will provide evidence for this.

> Robinson maintains a related point of departure particularly in relation to philosophers' language and argumentation.[33] The interests that motivated the present work (Chapter I above) have led, however, partly in different directions from Robinson's work, and partly to more nuanced mapping of, and conceptual representation of, aspects of the phenomenon of definition (sections 3–8 below).

(2) Terminology

One may object that one agrees with the importance of the delimitation that lies in my concepts of 'definition' and 'characterisation' but disagrees with my terminology: For example, one says one will use the term *"nominal definition"* of what is here called "definition", and will continue to use the term *"real definition"*, or the like, of briefly formulated characterisations of things (compare Næss' terminology in the quotations in item (1) above).

If one wants a systematic mapping of the modalities, functions and means of definitions, there are several weighty *grounds against* such terminology:

(a) Definitions can do different things: structure areas and name them (sections A 3 above and 4 below). – In the light of this, the term "nominal definition" is misleading, in that the term suggests that definitions simply name and that the areas are lying there ready waiting to be given names. Both notions are wrong (section 4 below; see section 4.3.1 with further references). – Furthermore, the term "nominal definition" is misleading, in that it suggests that definitions do not at any rate structure without at the same time naming. This is also wrong, see, for example, "the concept of 'contract' in English law requires there to be quid pro quo" (same places as in the preceding parenthesis).

(b) There is hardly anything of interest in common between what I call "definitions" and "characterisations". – Of course, one can *say* this; for example, say that the word "definition" is not intended to mean the same in collocations such as "nominal definition" and "real definition".[34] But experience shows that the same word, in this case "definition", will nevertheless be *perceived* by many people as being a common term, and thus lead our thought to seek something in common.

(c) The terms "nominal definition" and "real definition" are used in many different ways, and in the literature the ways in which they are used are often linked

---

33 Robinson, *Definition*, p. 178: "[T]he confusion between the analysis of things and … definition of words has been by far the most damaging error in the theory of definition, and among the most damaging errors in the whole of philosophy."

34 See e.g. Næss, as quoted in item (1) above, in the text at note 31; Ajdukiewicz, 'Three Concepts of Definition', pp. 115–16.

to the individual writer's philosophical system, including the writer's standpoints on controversial philosophical questions.[35]

(a)↔(c) In the light of this, I cannot accept the alternative terminology outlined ("nominal definition", "real definition"). I have difficulty in seeing any advantages to this terminology, and the counter-arguments are strong, *so* strong that it is time for a deliberate break. I assume that terms like "nominal definition" and "real definition" are not just a symptom of, but also a contributory cause of, the fact that the modalities, functions and means of the definition field of everyday language, and the system character and dynamics of this field,[36] have not previously been systematically mapped.

---

35 For a survey of the ways in which the term "real definition" is used, see the reference in item (1) above, in note 29.

36 The present section B in its entirety, with further references to other parts of the work: see in particular sections F and III 2, below.

3. Modality of definitions I: Descriptivity and normativity

3.1. Introduction. Modality and propositional content

(1) The concept of 'modality' and its significance

A *major thread* in the discussion of definitions in what follows is the distinction between *descriptive* definitions and *normative* definitions. For the sake of brevity I call the dimension of this distinction "modality".

In the theory of norms the word "character" (or its equivalent in other languages) has been used of this dimension.[1] I have avoided using this word here, since it is of greater use in the formulation of the distinction between, on the one hand, propositions that contribute to determining the meanings of linguistic entities (contribute to determining concepts) ("definitions"), and on the other hand, propositions that presuppose this topic and thematise other topics ("characterisations"; with its derivatives "to characterise", "characteristic", "character").[2]

A dichotomy between descriptive and normative propositions *does not exhaust* the modality dimension in relation to the perspective and topic of the present work: Analysis and argumentation occurring in fact and formulated in everyday language provides a reality basis for determining the concepts of 'descriptive proposition' and 'normative proposition' as extreme points on a graduated dimension, from the purely descriptive to the purely normative; cf. section F below, which provides a discussion common to definitions and characterisations, of the distinctive modality that arises when the extreme points fuse.

Many writers link their concept of 'definition' to a 'descriptive–normative' dimension, see the references in item (2) below in connection with the question of terminology, as well as references throughout the present discussion of descriptive and normative definitions. No writers, however, appear to have produced a conceptual representation of the phenomenon of fusion. – In the light of this, I both agree and disagree with the literature on definitions. To

1 See e.g. von Wright, *Norm and Action*, pp. 70–71; Sundby, *Om normer* [on norms], p. 29; Eckhoff/Sundby, *Rettssystemer* [legal systems], 1st ed. p. 54.

2 When one wishes to speak about the modality dimension in an international context, one often takes as a starting point Austin's expression "illocutionary force", introduced in *How to do things with Words*, p. 99; further developed in Searle, *Speech Acts*, pp. 30, 70, etc.; 'A Taxonomy of Illocutionary Acts', pp. 1, etc. See further at and in note 5 below.

> give a paradigmatic example: I both agree and disagree with Opsahl when on the basis of, and as a typical representative of, the thinking of Næss, Ofstad and Eckhoff (the "Oslo School"),[3] he writes: "[Definitions] can take one of two forms, which we shall call normative and descriptive. ... These alternatives are exhaustive, according to the conception of definition submitted here. The distinction between them is absolute and essential. It has often been overlooked ... this accounts for much misunderstanding."[4] I agree, in so far as the 'descriptive–normative' dimension is claimed to be central to identifying dis/agreement in actually occurring language and argumentation. I disagree, in so far as the 'descriptive–normative' dimension is conceptualised as a dichotomy and is claimed in this capacity to exhaust the language and argumentation reality.

The descriptive modality and the normative modality ought for many purposes *to be further divided*: the descriptive modality, inter alia into description and prediction; and the normative modality, inter alia into recommendations, promises and impositions of duty. Particularly in the case of the normative modality it may be of significance to keep sight of the variants (section 3.3 below).

Understood in this way (see the preceding two paragraphs of the main text), the distinction between descriptive and normative propositions is central in the critically reflexive form which constitutes the perspective and topic of the present work, and is thus central in dis/agreement analysis on the basis of this critically reflexive form.[5]

The *area of application* of the distinction between descriptive modality and normative modality I specify in the rest of the present section 3 in the main as "definition". However, to gain insight into what there is dis/agreement about, it is often necessary to divide up the definition concept and thus also the points of reference for the distinction between descriptive modality and normative modality (section 3.4 below, with further references).

---

[3] On the "Oslo School", see section 3.3.3 (3)(b)(i) below, with further references.

[4] Opsahl, 'An Inquiry into the Meaning and Function of Legal Definitions', p. 658 (Opsahl's notes omitted).

[5] Other interests than the interest in the perspective and topic of the present work produce other categorisations: via different determinations of or within the categorisation criterion (the modality dimension), or via a crossing of the modality dimension with other categorisation criteria. See e.g. Wittgenstein, *Philosophische Untersuchungen*, Part I, section 23; Austin, *How to do things with Words*, pp. 149 et seq.; Searle, *Speech Acts*, pp. 64 et seq.; 'A Taxonomy of Illocutionary Acts', pp. 12–20; Tugendhat, *Vorlesungen zur Einführung in die sprachanalytische Philosophie*, pp. 505 et seq. – I should remind the reader that my discussion of the concepts of proposition types, including the distinction between descriptive and normative propositions, is divided into two parts. The second part follows in section E below, which provides a discussion common to the different concepts, of how one determines whether they apply to the individual instance of language use ("operationalising" of my concepts of proposition types).

(2) Terminology

Via the influential writings of Arne Næss people in the Nordic countries are quite accustomed to using the word *"definition"* irrespective of the modality of the proposition, i.e. as a *common* term for a group of normative and descriptive propositions. Also outside the Nordic countries this is a normal way of using the word. However, the terminology has not been so firmly established that one can assume this usage: A number of writers, including Næss, to a greater or lesser extent use the word "definition" *only* about what is here designated "normative definition".[6]

The descriptive modality in the case of definitions has been given *other names than "descriptive"*: for example "bruksmåtebeskrivende"[7] [usage-describing] or "lexical"/ "leksikalsk".[8] And the normative modality in the case of definitions has been given *other names than "normative"*: for example "regelgivende"[9] [regulative] or "stipulative"/ "stipulativ".[10]

I prefer the *pair of words "descriptive" and "normative"* for a number of *reasons*:

(a) First, because the distinction between the two types of modality does not only apply in the case of definitions, but also in the case of characterisations; and because the word-pair "descriptive" and "normative" is then the terminology that best both leads one's thought in the right direction and harmonises with normal

---

6 See e.g. Næss, 'Elementære analytiske undersøkelser' [elementary analytical investigations], p. 6; *En del elementære logiske emner* [some elementary topics in logic], p. 43; *Logikk og metodelære* [logic and methodology], p. 66; Ofstad, *Alf Ross's begrepsbestemmelse av begrepet 'rettsregel'* [Alf Ross' determination of the concept of 'legal rule'], p. 1; Aubert, 'Logisk analyse og sosiologi i rettsvitenskapen' [logical analysis and sociology in legal science], p. 527; Ross, *Lærebog i folkeret* [textbook of international law], p. 11: "A definition is a declaration of what the speaker means by a certain word. A definition is therefore not true or false but more or less expedient ..."; Whitehead/ Russell, *Principia Mathematica*, Vol. I, p. 11; Cohen, 'Transcendental Nonsense and the Functional Approach', pp. 835–36: "A definition ... is useful or useless. It is not true or false, any more than a New Year's resolution or an insurance policy."

7 See e.g. Næss, *En del elementære logiske emner* [some elementary topics in logic], p. 43; *Logikk og metodelære* [logic and methodology], p. 66; Føllesdal/ Walløe/ Elster, *Argumentasjonsteori, språk og vitenskapsfilosofi* [argumentation theory, language and the philosophy of science] p. 243.

8 See e.g. Robinson, *Definition*, p. 19, cf. Chapter III; Jareborg, *Begrepp och brottbeskrivning* [concepts and the description of criminal offences], pp. 64–65.

9 See e.g. Næss and Føllesdal/ Walløe/ Elster, in both cases in the same places as referred to in note 7 above.

10 See e.g. Robinson, *Definition*, p. 19, cf. Chapter IV; Andersson/ Furberg, *Språk och påverkan* [language and influence], pp. 162–63; Jareborg, *Begrepp och brottbeskrivning* [concepts and the description of criminal offences], p. 64. – See further Robinson, *Definition*, p. 61, on *other* designations that have been used in literature in English: "imposition"; "institution"; "original definition", "legislative definition", "propositive definition", "invitatory definition" and "imperative definition". – Stipulated normative definitions directed at one's own language usage (see section 3.3.1 (2) below on this type of normative definition) have also been designated "Terminologidefinition" [terminology definition] and "nominal definition", see respectively Lassen, 'Nogle Bemærkninger om Definitioner i Retsliteraturen' [some remarks on definitions in legal literature], p. 60, and Patterson, *Jurisprudence*, p. 69.

language usage. – Transferring one of the word-pairs mentioned above ("usage-describing" and "regulative", or "lexical" and "stipulative") to characterisations as well, would be misleading almost to the point of self-contradiction; one would in that case be designating descriptive characterisations "usage-describing" or "lexical", at the same time as characterisations are by definition propositions with another topic than determining the meanings of linguistic entities (than determining concepts). Furthermore, this would be in direct conflict with normal language usage. – The use of the word-pair "descriptive" and "normative" in the case of characterisations and of another word-pair in the case of definitions, would be misleading by suggesting that characterisations and definitions are different also in the modality dimension.

(b) Secondly, I use the word-pair "descriptive" and "normative" more particularly out of consideration for those phenomena that are covered by the concept of 'normative definition': partly stipulated definitions (section 3.3.1 below) and partly custom-based definitions (section 3.3.2 below). To designate the latter "stipulative" would be misleading almost to the point of self-contradiction; one would in that case be designating customs by a word that one-sidedly leads one's thought towards arbitrary determination. The same applies, albeit to a lesser degree, to many of the other above-mentioned designations that have been used of normative definitions (see at and in note 10 above).

(c) Finally, I use the word-pair "descriptive" and "normative" because the word "normative" provides a tangible connection with general norm theory, a connection which, as mentioned, I consider it will be fruitful to develop (section 2.1 (2)(c) above); and because "descriptive" is then the natural other designation.

(d) There is no language usage so firmly established that one ought for that reason to set aside the considerations mentioned in items (a), (b) and (c).[11]

(3) The propositional content of definitions

Between normative and descriptive definitions it is only the modality that by definition is *different*; the propositional content may be *the same*.[12] Compare, for example, on the one hand "the lecturer uses the term "the law" also of norms that the courts do not apply" (descriptive modality, cf. "uses") and on the other hand the same sentence except that "uses" is replaced by "ought to use/ ought not to use" (normative modality).

I categorise the propositional content of definitions through the concepts of 'person', 'situation' and 'action theme'.

---

11 See the present item (2) in its entirety (including notes).

12 Compare Wittgenstein, *Philosophische Untersuchungen*, Part I, sections 6, 22, 26, 49, 291, and the bottom text on p. 27; Hare, *The Language of Morals*, pp. 17–18, 188–89; Austin, *How to do things with Words*, p. 98; Searle, *Speech Acts*, pp. 22–24, 29–30; Tugendhat, *Vorlesungen zur Einführung in die sprachanalytische Philosophie*, p. 74.

This categorisation originates from discussions of duty norms. There it has been usual to divide the propositional content into the subject of the norm (those to whom the norm is addressed); the situation (the conditions that must be satisfied for the norm to be applicable); and the action theme (what the subject of the norm has a duty to do when the situation conditions are satisfied).[13] – I have earlier argued that these concepts ought also to be used in the structuring of the propositional content of competence norms.[14]

Here I shall in addition use these concepts in the structuring of normative definitions. – With the modification that the concept of 'subject of the norm' is replaced by the concept of 'person', I shall also use this categorisation in the case of descriptive definitions.

Here I shall content myself with briefly specifying what lies in my categorisation, and how it relates to the further discussion:

"Person" designates in the case of descriptive definitions the person who uses the defined linguistic entity (the defined concept), and in the case of normative definitions the person who should or shall (or other types of normative modality) use the linguistic entity (the concept). In the example above, 'the lecturer'.

"Situation" designates circumstances surrounding and having relevance to the use of the linguistic entity (the concept). In the example above, 'in the lecture'. As the example shows, it is not a matter of course that the definition elements are given independent linguistic expression, even if the definition is formulated linguistically, cf. the fact that the specifications of person and situation were merged there.

All definitions are based on presuppositions about how the world is constituted and what meanings attach to other words and expressions than that which is being defined, for example, in the case of the definition of 'chair', the fact that chairs cannot speak. Presuppositions of *this* kind cannot be exhaustively specified, since the only limit lies in the principle of contradiction. I shall later give an account of the fact that, and the reasons why, I keep such presuppositions outside the concept of 'definition' (section 6.2 (3)(a) below).

"Action theme" designates the way of using a linguistic entity (designates the concept) that the definition determines, descriptively or normatively. The subsequent analysis of the propositional content of definitions will in the main be analyses of the action theme: what is being defined (section 4), and how (sections 5–6).

There may be reason to state more precisely the *status* of the categorisation that has now been outlined: – I do not lay down this categorisation as definitional for

13 Bentham, *Of Laws in General*, pp. 34–71, puts forward slightly different and crossing categorisations, which are however related to the categorisation outlined here: "subjects of a law" (pp. 34–40) and "parties which may be affected by a law" (pp. 53–71) cover inter alia the area of person here; "acts" (pp. 41–52) cover the action theme here; and "circumstances" (pp. 41–52) cover inter alia the area of situation here. From more recent literature see e.g. von Wright, *Norm and Action*, pp. 70 et seq.

14 Eng, 'Begrepene 'kompetanse' og 'gyldighet' i juridisk argumentasjon' [the concepts of 'competence' and 'validity' in legal argumentation], pp. 635–51 (636–37).

definitions, cf. the account of the fact that, and the reasons for which, I do not lay down particular determinacy requirements as criteria in the concept of 'definition', and as part of this, the fact that, and the reasons for which, I do not lay down the categorisation into person, situation and action theme as a criterion (sections 2.2 above, cf. 4.1 (3) below). – Nor do I claim that the categorisation into person, situation and action theme represents a stable pattern in actually occurring definition activity. In thought, in the linguistic formulation, or in both, these definition elements may be merged, cf. the discussion of "situation" above. Or the elements may be omitted, cf. dictionary definitions which only specify meaning alternatives, without any specification of person or situation. – On the other hand, I do claim that the categorisation of the propositional content of definitions into person, situation and action theme serves *heuristic considerations*:[15]

First, the categorisation into person, situation and action theme can make definitions easier to *comprehend, recall and apply*. In relation to the perspective and topic of the present work, I mention in particular that the categorisation into person, situation and action theme leads thought towards aspects of the use of language that are typically deemed relevant when one is assessing tenability and analysing dis/agreement, in the case of both descriptive and normative definitions.

Secondly, the categorisation into person, situation and action theme can contribute to *concept development and theory formation*, through an interplay between general norm theory and definition theory. – For example, in the case of normative propositions in the form of competence norms, I assume that the categorisation into person, situation and action theme also has significance as a step in more precise theoretical propositions,[16] something which provides support for trying a systematic application of this categorisation also in the case of other types of normative proposition.[17] – Use of this categorisation in the case of normative definitions thus establishes a connection with general norm theory (see at and in notes 12 and 13 above), a connection which provides possibilities for use of, or, by way of feed-back, for supplementation of, the knowledge lying accumulated in the concepts there. – If normative definitions are structured in person, situation and action theme, this in itself gives reason to structure descriptive definitions in the same way.

---

15 On heuristic considerations in general, see sections III 2.2.6 (1)–(2) cf. 2.4.1, below.

16 Eng, 'Begrepene 'kompetanse' og 'gyldighet' i juridisk argumentasjon' [the concepts of 'competence' and 'validity' in legal argumentation], pp. 646–51 (649–51).

17 Næss uses the expression "marginal references" of specifications of person and situation; see *Interpretation and Preciseness*, pp. 10 (on synonymity sentences), 148 (on normative definition sentences), 169–170 (on descriptive definition sentences). See further pp. 12–20 on some major categorisations of specifications of person and situation. – In my opinion Næss ascribes too little significance to this conceptualisation when he says "[n]o theoretical importance is attached to it"; *Interpretation and Preciseness*, p. 11.

3.2. Descriptive definitions

3.2.1. Definition and types

I have defined 'definition' as "propositions that contribute to determining the meanings of linguistic entities (contribute to determining concepts)" (section A 2 (1) above). In relation to this general concept of 'definition', what is *specific* to descriptive definitions is that the "determining" takes the form of *description or prediction* of actual use of language. The *tenability criterion* in the case of descriptive definitions is thus whether the definition conforms or does not conform with actual use of language (un/truth).

Concerning the *propositional content* an important question in the light of this is whether descriptive definitions are built up in such ways that they are capable of capturing actual language use. Before I go into this question more concretely (section 3.2.2 below), I shall briefly outline some *main elements* of the propositional content.

The *specification of situation* in the case of propositions about *particular persons'* use of language may be an individual situation, for example an individual statement or book. Or the specification of situation may be the use of language more generally of the person(s) concerned, for example: "Francis Hagerup used the term "rettsregel" [legal rule] of norms that had been psychologically internalised by persons in positions of public authority or, as the case may be, by the citizens as well."

The specification of situation in the case of propositions about the language use of a generally specified *group of persons* will typically refer to language use more generally, for example: "Lawyers mainly use the terms "rettsregel", "legal rule", "Rechtsnorm", etc., of propositions with fused descriptive and normative modality."

Irrespective of how specific the specification of situation is otherwise, the propositions may be directed (only or also) towards the *past*, cf. the example with Hagerup, or (only or also) towards the *future*, cf. the example with lawyers.

Different descriptive definitions of the same linguistic entity *may all be true*, namely in so far as the definitions have different specifications of person or situation. This provides one important reason for distinguishing between person, situation and action theme in the case of descriptive definitions: This categorisation leads thought towards aspects of the use of language that are typically deemed relevant when one is assessing tenability and analysing dis/agreement (section 3.1 (3) above, last paragraph but one).

Robinson limits his discussion of descriptive definitions ("lexical definition") to propositions about language use in the past, without its being clear whether this limitation is intended to apply by definition. See for example: "Lexical definition is a form of history. It refers to the real past. It tells what certain persons meant by a certain word at a certain less or more specified time and place",[18] and "Lexical definitions are historical statements".[19] – I cannot see any reason to introduce any such temporal limitation, either in the concept of 'descriptive definition' or as a restriction in one's actual discussion of descriptive definitions.

The word "hypothesis" used of descriptive definitions is most reasonably interpreted as pointing towards the future. However, influential writers like Næss and Ofstad use the word both of definitions in the form of descriptions of the past and in the form of predictions.[20] Thus they use the word to draw a boundary in another dimension than time, probably in a dimension of certainty: The use of the word "hypothesis" draws a boundary with propositions that purport to be certain.[21]

3.2.2. The presupposed concept of 'concept'. Condition concept. Factor concept; especially on family resemblance. Consequences for the method of definition

(1) Survey

(2) Features in common

- **(a) Usual points of departure**
- **(b) The method of definition "through category and sub-category"**
- **(c) Limitations**

(3) Family resemblance

- **(a) Wittgenstein on family resemblance**
- **(b) The concept of 'family resemblance' here. Consequences for the definition method resulting from there being family resemblance**

(4) Placing Wittgenstein's family resemblance analysis in relation to some central concepts in the present work (a–b). The area of application of family resemblance analysis (c–d)

- **(a) Normative or descriptive analysis?**
- **(b) Definitions or characterisations?**
- **(c) The actual area of application of family resemblance analysis**
- **(d) The applicability of family resemblance analysis in science**

(5) Variants of unity: The relationship of family resemblance analysis to concepts of 'concept' (a–c). "Condition concept"; "factor concept", including "family resemblance concept" (d)

- **(a) Arbitrary collection**
- **(b) Family resemblance**

---

[18] Robinson, *Definition*, p. 35.

[19] Op. cit., p. 52; correspondingly on p. 39.

[20] Næss, *Interpretation and Preciseness*, pp. 169–71; Ofstad, 'The Descriptive Definition of the Concept 'Legal Norm' proposed by Hans Kelsen', p. 119; 'Om deskriptive definisjoner av begrepet rettsregel' [on descriptive definitions of the concept of 'legal rule'], in particular pp. 41–46.

[21] A delimitation that is central in Næss' works in "empirical semantics"; see section 3.3.3 (3)(b)(i) below.

(c) Features in common

(d) "Condition concept"; "factor concept", including "family resemblance concept"

(6) The diversity of relationships between the phenomena ("concept types") necessitates openness with respect to method in the case of descriptive definitions

(1) Survey

A commonly held view is that the psychological reason (the motive) for the use of the same word about individually different phenomena lies in the individual phenomena's having a set of *features in common* (items (2) cf. (5)(c)).

It is not always the case, however, that the premiss that there is a set of features in common is correct: When observing the phenomena of which the word is used, one finds (only) a *family resemblance* between the phenomena (items (3)–(4)).

There may thus be *differences* in the types and the degrees of relationship between individual phenomena of which a word is used. It may be of *significance* to be conscious of such differences:

To the different types and degrees of relationship between individual phenomena of which a word is used, correspond differences in *method of definition*; this provides grounds for consciously being open to the differences in the relationships between the phenomena (item (3)(b)).

The differences in types and degrees of relationship between individual phenomena of which a word is used, go a long way towards having a counterpart in the diversity of use of the *word "concept"*; and these differences show that the definite article in this context, "the concept of ...", may be rather misleading (item (5)). – A remedy is to nuance the concept terminology. I distinguish between *"condition concepts"* (the relationship between the phenomena consists in features in common) and *"factor concepts"* (the relationship does not consist in features in common but, for example, in family resemblance) (item (5)(d)).

A major aim of the discussions in the present section 3.2.2 is to shed light on how *method in the case of descriptive definitions must depend on the nature of the use of language* with which one is confronted (items (6) cf. (3)(b)). The reason I here draw a distinction between condition concept and factor concept is to shed light on this matter, not to provide an independent treatment of the question "why does one call different individual phenomena by the same name?" or, expressed in concept terminology, not to provide an independent treatment of the question "what is a concept?". – Furthermore, it is an aim of these discussions to lay a foundation for subsequent discussions (item (5)(d), with further references).

(2) Features in common

(a) Usual points of departure

(i) A commonly held view is that different individual phenomena that we collect together in thought, *must* have a set of features *in common, beyond* the fact that they are usually designated by the same linguistic expression, for example beyond the fact that they are designated "game" or "rett" [Recht, law, right]. – To the extent that relevant differences are found between the phenomena, it is assumed that the phenomena have something in common in another dimension than the dimension of the differences.

That the phenomena must have a set of features in common, we perceive virtually as something we observe when we "look" at our own thought: In thought we collect and separate individual phenomena in ways we perceive as *rule-bound*, in contrast to what we perceive as *arbitrary* collection; and the perception that actions take place in a rule-bound fashion implies precisely that they have something in common, namely that the conditions of the rule are present when the rule is followed.

(ii) Further it is a commonly held view that the features in common of the phenomena are the cause of our collecting the phenomena in our thought and of our using the same word of these phenomena. The physical unity of the word is consequently seen as a *strong indication* of the existence of features common to the phenomena of which the word is used.

(i)↔(ii) The *task* of anybody wishing to give a *descriptive* definition then becomes to find and to describe the common set of features: to describe them through a corresponding set of concept criteria. The *correspondence* will lie in the concept criteria's being fitted into *condition structure*.

(b) The method of definition "through category and sub-category"

The assumption of unity in the form of features in common across the diversity of individual phenomena finds *expression* in an extremely common *method of definition*: "through category and sub-category".[22] – By this expression I mean condition-structuring of the concept criteria through the following two steps: First one groups the things under a more comprehensive *category* ("genus"). One then specifies what is specific to the things, i.e. what distinguishes them from other things under the category, by distinguishing between *sub-categories* ("species", "types", "kinds", or the like). – An example would be to define 'chair' as 'a piece of furniture' (category), 'for sitting on' (sub-category; in contrast to other furniture, like table, cupboard, etc.), 'for one person' (sub-category; in contrast to

---

22 The expression "definition per genus (proximum) et differentiam (specificam)" is used of propositions with the same basic structure, cf. the parentheses in the main text after the present note. However, these propositions are often about the things ("real definition", much of what is called "vesensdefinisjon", "Wesensdefinition", "essential definition", "essence definition", or the like), not about the meanings of words (not about concepts); i.e. are not definitions in the sense of this work (cf. section 2.3 above).

bench, sofa, etc.) and 'with a back' (sub-category; in contrast to, for example, stool).

Definition through category and sub-categories most often seems to be based on a presupposition of the *strongest form of unity*: that the features common to the phenomena are *both necessary and sufficient.* For example, in relation to occurrences of the definition of 'chair' just given, it may be reasonable to assume that the sender holds that the criteria 'a piece of furniture', 'for sitting on', 'for one person' and 'with a back' are each necessary and together sufficient.[23]

(c) Limitations

Another example of definition through category and sub-category would be to define 'law' as 'a system of norms' (category) 'sanctioned through publicly monopolised force' (sub-category; in contrast to other norm systems like morals, custom and etiquette, etc.). Such a definition, however, would not be a true descriptive definition in relation to widespread language usage, in that inter alia international law would fall outside the definition (most rules that are termed "international law" are not sanctioned by internationally monopolised force). – Altogether, definition through category and sub-category, and to put it more generally: through condition-structuring of the concept criteria, has shown itself to be *not very suitable for generating true* descriptive definitions of the concept of *'law'* or of *fundamental legal concepts* like 'right', 'claim' or 'duty'. This is something which Bentham and later Hart pointed out in several works.

> Bentham emphasised that definition through category and sub-category ("per genus et differentiam") was only one of many ways of defining.[24] He further emphasised that definition through category and sub-category was unusable in the case of words without any (clear) genus, inter alia in the case of fundamental moral and legal words like "right", "duty" and "obligation".[25]
>
> Correspondingly, Hart points to the fact that in relation to the use of the word "law" there is no clear genus or anything else in common.[26] – In relation to the word "contract" Hart claims that one may well specify necessary criteria, but that specification of sufficient criteria will veil actual language usage, in that any purportedly sufficient criterion (set of criteria) may be met with a number of objections.[27] – A problematisation of method of definition also lies in Hart's pointing out, in agreement with Bentham, that the words "right" and "duty" are not used for designating, but for joining together other

---

23 The question of the sufficiency of the criteria will be problematised in section 6.2 (3) below.

24 Bentham, *Essay on Logic*, pp. 242–53. Also in *The Theory of Fictions*, pp. 75–104.

25 Bentham, *Essay on Logic*, pp. 245–48, also in *The Theory of Fictions*, pp. 84–91; *A Fragment on Government*, p. 106 in note 1; *Of Laws in General*, pp. 294–95.

26 Hart, 'Definition and Theory in Jurisprudence', particularly pp. 38 and 46; *The Concept of Law*, 1st ed. particularly pp. 14–15; 2nd ed. particularly pp. 15–16.

27 Hart, 'The Ascription of Responsibility and Rights', pp. 148–52; see in more detail in item (5) (c)(iii) below, concluding remarks.

elements of language, and consequently cannot be defined in isolation (compare words like "and", "or", "because", etc.).[28]

Bentham's discussions were ahead of, and Hart's discussions are part of, a *current in modern analytical philosophy* that criticises the assumption that general concepts must be definable through condition-structuring of the concept criteria.[29] The *perspective here* is a somewhat different one, namely the connection between concept type and definition method. Propositions about the existence and diffusion of different concept types then become more of a background. To a certain extent it is, however, necessary to go into this background. For if our language is actually constituted in such a way that all concepts only capture phenomena with features in common, so that condition-structuring of the concept criteria is always possible, then the connection between concept type and definition method becomes less interesting. In this perspective I shall in particular look at one alternative to features in common and condition-structuring: unity in the form of family resemblance (items (3) cf. (4)–(5)) and definition methods which might then be of interest (items (3)(b) cf. (6)).

(3) Family resemblance

(a) Wittgenstein on family resemblance

Under the name of "family resemblance" ("Familienähnlichkeit") Wittgenstein gave expression to a supplementary view of the unity that may exist between individual phenomena and lead to our designating them with the same linguistic expression.[30] – I write a *"supplementary"* and not an "alternative" view, for Wittgenstein hardly held that family resemblance was the only form of unity between phenomena we designate by the same linguistic expression; nor is there reason to suppose that this is so (item (4)(c) below).

Wittgenstein considered it *dogmatic* to assume that individual phenomena that we designate by the same linguistic expression and treat as a unit *must* have a set

---

28 Hart, 'Definition and Theory in Jurisprudence', particularly pp. 38–39, 45–49 cf. 41–45. – Compare section 5.5 below, on structuring via a more comprehensive linguistic context; and section IV 3.3 below, on lawyers' use of linking-terms.

29 Weitz, 'Open Concepts', uses the term "open concept" of concepts that are not definable through necessary *and* sufficient concept criteria (pp. 86, 95), and discusses a number of propositions about concepts' being to a greater or lesser extent open in *this* sense; inter alia propositions advanced by Popper, Stevenson, Waismann, Hart and Wittgenstein. – In German methodological discussion, including such discussion in legal theory, concepts with the openness mentioned are to a great extent discussed under the name of "Typus"; see section 5.4.2 (1)(a)(vi) below, with further references. – In the perspective here (on this perspective, see the main text after the present note) the drawing of a different boundary will show itself to be more important; see item (5)(d) below.

30 Wittgenstein, *Philosophische Untersuchungen*, particularly Part I, sections 65–88. – A contemporary writer who discussed the same thing was Austin, see item (6) below. – Several earlier writers put forward points of view related to Wittgenstein's; e.g. Mill, who again built further on other writers; see the references in item (4)(c) below, in note 51. See also note 34 below, on some other writers' use of the image of family resemblance.

of features in common: "dogmatic" in the sense that this assumption is not grounded on any exact investigation of what our language use is actually like.

> "Betrachte z.B. einmal die Vorgänge, die wir "Spiele" nennen. Ich meine Brettspiele, Kartenspiele, Ballspiel, Kampfspiele, usw. Was ist allen diesen gemeinsam? – Sag nicht: "Es *muß* ihnen etwas gemeinsam sein, sonst hießen sie nicht 'Spiele' " – sondern *schau*, ob ihnen allen etwas gemeinsam ist" (Wittgenstein's italics).[31]

He claims that there is not just one, but that there are *many sorts* of relationship between the individual instances.

> In connection with his analysis of language, including nuancing through the introduction of a number of objects of comparison he calls "language games" ("Sprachspiele"), he writes: "[M]an könnte mir einwenden: "Du machst dir's leicht! Du redest von allen möglichen Sprachspielen, hast aber nirgends gesagt, was denn das Wesentliche des Sprachspiels, und also der Sprache, ist. Was allen diesen Vorgängen gemeinsam ist und sie zur Sprache, oder zu Teilen der Sprache macht. ..."
>
> Und das ist wahr. – Statt etwas anzugeben, was allem, was wir Sprache nennen, gemeinsam ist, sage ich, es ist diesen Erscheinungen garnicht Eines gemeinsam, weswegen wir für alle das gleiche Wort verwenden, – sondern sie sind miteinander in vielen verschiedenen Weisen *verwandt*. Und dieser Verwandtschaft, oder dieser Verwandtschaften wegen nennen wir sie alle "Sprachen"" (Wittgenstein's italics).[32]

The diversity of possible relationships between the phenomena in assumedly unitary concept scopes is illustrated by Wittgenstein through inter alia an analysis of those phenomena we call "games".

> "[W]enn du [die Spielen] anschaust, wirst du zwar nicht etwas sehen, was *allen* [Wittgenstein's italics] gemeinsam wäre, aber du wirst Ähnlichkeiten, Verwandtschaften, sehen, und zwar eine ganze Reihe. Wie gesagt: denk nicht, sondern schau! – Schau z.B. die Brettspiele an, mit ihren mannigfachen Verwandtschaften. Nun geh zu den Kartenspielen über: hier findest du viele Entsprechungen mit jener ersten Klasse, aber viele gemeinsame Züge verschwinden, andere treten auf. Wenn wir nun zu den Ballspielen übergehen, so bleibt manches Gemeinsame erhalten, aber vieles geht verloren. – Sind sie alle *'unterhaltend'*? [Wittgenstein's italics] Vergleiche Schach mit dem Mühlfahren. Oder gibt es überall ein *Gewinnen und Verlieren*, oder eine *Konkurrenz* der Spielenden? Denk an die Patiencen. In den Ballspielen gibt es Gewinnen und Verlieren; aber wenn ein Kind den Ball an die Wand wirft und wieder auffängt, so ist dieser Zug verschwunden. Schau, welche Rolle *Geschick und Glück* spielen. Und wie verschieden ist Geschick im Schachspiel und Geschick im Tennisspiel. Denk nun an die Reigenspiele: Hier ist das Element der Unterhaltung, aber wie viele der anderen Charakter-

---

31 Wittgenstein, *Philosophische Untersuchungen*, Part I, section 66.

32 Op. cit., Part I, section 65.

züge sind verschwunden! Und so können wir durch die vielen, vielen anderen Gruppen von Spielen gehen, Ähnlichkeiten auftauchen und verschwinden sehen.

Und das Ergebnis dieser Betrachtung lautet nun: Wir sehen ein kompliziertes Netz von *Ähnlichkeiten, die einander übergreifen und kreuzen.* Ähnlichkeiten im Großen und Kleinen" (my italics unless otherwise stated).[33]

Wittgenstein compares the relationships between individual phenomena that we designate by the same linguistic expression and treat as a unit, with the *resemblance between a family's different individual members.*

> "Ich kann diese Ähnlichkeiten nicht besser charakterisieren als durch das Wort "Familienähnlichkeiten"; denn so übergreifen und kreuzen sich die verschiedenen Ähnlichkeiten, die zwischen den Gliedern einer Familie bestehen: Wuchs, Gesichtszüge, Augenfarbe, Gang, Temperament, etc. etc. – Und ich werde sagen: die 'Spiele' bilden eine Familie."[34]

Another image he uses, is the *relationship between the individual fibres in a thread and the thread itself.*

> "Und ebenso bilden z.B. die Zahlenarten eine Familie. Warum nennen wir etwas "Zahl"? Nun, etwa, weil es eine – direkte – Verwandtschaft mit manchem hat, was man bisher Zahl genannt hat; und dadurch, kann man sagen, erhält es eine indirekte Verwandtschaft zu anderem, was wir auch *so* nennen. Und wir dehnen unseren Begriff der Zahl aus, wie wir beim Spinnen eines Fadens Faser an Faser drehen. Und die Stärke des Fadens liegt nicht darin, daß irgend eine Faser durch seine ganze Länge läuft, sondern darin, daß viele Fasern einander übergreifen.
>
> Wenn aber Einer sagen wollte: "Also ist allen diesen Gebilden etwas gemeinsam, – nämlich die Disjunktion aller dieser Gemeinsamkeiten" – so würde ich antworten: hier spielst du nur mit einem Wort. Ebenso könnte man

---

33 Op. cit., Part I, section 66.

34 Op. cit., Part I, section 67. – Wittgenstein was *not alone* in this use of the analogy with resemblance in a family. In 1930 Llewellyn used a similar image to illuminate the usage of the term "common law" and the unity between the legal systems of the American states, see *The Bramble Bush*, p. 51: "What we have is fifteen states deciding one way, one state deciding another way and thirty states whose law is still uncertain. Yet in these circumstances, we *do speak of "common law"*, and for this *reason*: True though it is that each state sticks, in the main, to its own authorities, when it has them, yet common to all the states is a large fundamental body of institutions which show at least a *brother-and-sister type of likeness* ..." (my italics; Llewellyn's italics omitted). – Other writers have used the analogy with resemblance in a family, and the term "family resemblance" (or its equivalent in other languages), in the *opposite way*: of the type of unity which Wittgenstein distinguishes from, i.e. of features in common. See e.g. Freud, *Die Traumdeutung*, p. 295: "[I]ch habe das Verfahren eingeschlagen, nach welchem Galton seine Familienporträts [op. cit., p. 155: Familienähnlichkeiten] erzeugt, nämlich beide Bilder aufeinanderprojiziert, wobei die *gemeinsamen Züge verstärkt* hervortreten, die *nicht zusammenstimmenden einander auslöschen* und im Bilde undeutlich werden" (my italics); Bentzon, *Retskilderne* [the sources of law], p. 305: "One can establish a *type*, e.g. of a family's facial features, by means of "mass photography" of its members' profiles, the one picture on top of the other on the same plate. *Like* such a photograph, a word can specify an *average resemblance* of the related phenomena" (my italics).

> sagen: es läuft ein Etwas durch den ganzen Faden, – nämlich das lückenlose Übergreifen dieser Fasern" (Wittgenstein's italics).[35]

(b) The concept of 'family resemblance' here. Consequences for the definition method resulting from there being family resemblance

In what follows I use "family resemblance" of cases in which, between the individual phenomena of which a word is used, there is *not* unity in the form of features in common, but such partial and overlapping resemblances as in the examples and images quoted above.

By "features in common" I mean features that correspond to necessary or exhaustive and surveyable sufficient criteria for the use of the word. – I shall later give a more detailed account of the meaning of "features in common" (item (5)(c) below). Here I content myself with the above when it comes to the delimitation of the concept of 'family resemblance'.[36]

For example our use of the word "game" *cannot* be described through necessary criteria (and consequently not through any set of necessary or sufficient criteria either), for example not through such things as enjoyment effect, victory or loss, competition, skill or luck, being necessary (see the third quotation in item (a) above): Other sides of the phenomena too can justify the use of the word "game". – *Nor* can our use of the word "game" be described through exhaustive and surveyable specification of sufficient criteria. True enough, in the case of this word, as with most words otherwise, one will be able to specify criteria that are sufficient;[37] one will be able to do so by specifying the criteria for the use of the word "game" in instance-types, for example the criteria for 'chess', 'bridge', etc. However, it is not possible to specify in an exhaustive and surveyable way the different alternative and sufficient (sets of) criteria.

The concept of 'family resemblance' has a *critical sting*, in that it undermines the precondition for the method of definition through category and sub-category, namely the precondition that the unity between phenomena that are designated by the same name consists in a set of features in common (items (2) above, cf. (5)(c) below). A family resemblance analysis of the usage of a word thus has conse-

---

35 Wittgenstein, *Philosophische Untersuchungen*, Part I, section 67.

36 This concept has been formed on the basis of the purposes here. I assume that my conceptualisation is adequate in relation to much of what Wittgenstein writes about family resemblance, but I do not aim at capturing or continuing his usage in detail.

37 It might be reasonable to say that in the case of *all* words (*all* concepts) one must be able to specify criteria that are sufficient, because anything else seems to have to mean one of two things: either (i) that the individual instance of language use cannot be generalised to an instance-type; this means that the difference between the individual and the general disappears, and *then* it is reasonable to say that by definition there is no word (no concept), only sound, signs on a page, or the like; or (ii) that one can never know whether the word (the concept) has been correctly used, and *then* one has no use for it; compare Urmson, 'Polymorphous Concepts', p. 255. – For the present discussion, however, the weaker assumption in the main text will suffice: namely that in the case of *most* words (*most* concepts) one will be able to specify sufficient criteria.

quences for *how to proceed in the case of a descriptive definition*: If the person wishing to provide a descriptive definition builds on the premiss of the common set of features, and the aim of the definition is consequently assumed to be to describe this set of features, then there is a great risk that the description of the language usage will be incomplete or directly wrong. In such a case one is pressing the language usage into a *definition schema that does not fit.*

Possible *alternative ways of defining* may be:

(i) to name individual phenomena or types of individual phenomena of which the word is used;
(ii) to divide up the area of which the word is used and see whether the sub-areas have sets of features in common;
(iii) to describe the overlapping resemblances and differences.[38]

Against this background there is reason to be open to, and to work tentatively on the basis of, what one may call *"a methodical family resemblance principle"*: a systematic assumption that there are different types and degrees of relationship between phenomena one speaks of with the same word. I write "reason to", because it is most often better to have an assumption of diversity confuted than to build on misleading descriptive definitions. And I write "tentatively", because the fruitfulness of such a methodological principle must be assessed in relation to the individual language and argumentation areas.

In *law and legal theory* I assume analyses and discussions will have much to gain from the use of a methodical family resemblance principle, cf. the multifarious use of central words and expressions like "law", "right", "justice", "rule", "norm", "principle", "precedent", "contract", etc. – Clarity about the diversity has, here as elsewhere in analysis of language usage, two consequences that I evaluate positively: first, insight into reality; secondly, awareness of the fact that if one intends to work with unitary concepts, then this unity must based on one's own decisions (normative definitions).

---

38 These and other ways of defining I shall be discussing later in a more general perspective (sections 5–6): (i) represents *specification of denotation* (sections 5.2, 5.3–5.4); (ii) represents *connotation specification through condition-structuring* of the concept criteria (sections 5.1, 5.3–5.4, cf. 6.2); and (iii) represents *connotation specification through factor-structuring* of the concept criteria (same places as in the preceding parenthesis).

(4) Placing Wittgenstein's family resemblance analysis in relation to some central concepts in the present work (a–b). The area of application of family resemblance analysis (c–d)

(a) Normative or descriptive analysis?

I assume that Wittgenstein's discussion of family resemblance must be considered to be descriptive, that he intended to analyse our language use as it actually is.[39]

(b) Definitions or characterisations?

In relation to the distinction between definitions and characterisations the categorisation is different for the different elements in family resemblance analyses:

First, we have those propositions through which Wittgenstein establishes the concept of 'family resemblance'. These propositions represent a normative definition.[40]

Secondly, we have propositions which, given a concept of 'family resemblance', say something about concrete family resemblances, for example between those phenomena that are called "games". Here a distinction should be made between two modes of use:

To the extent that such propositions claim that the resemblances that are brought out are actually used or on further reflection will be used by others in their determinations of the meaning of the linguistic entity, then these propositions will be descriptive definitions. For example, there are no doubt many who have used or on further reflection might imagine using one or more of the limited resemblances Wittgenstein points out between phenomena that are called "games", as criteria in explanations of what the word "game" means (enjoyment, victory or loss, competition, skill or luck; see the quotation in item (3)(a) above, in the text at note 33). A reasonable interpretation of Wittgenstein's sentences about the limited resemblances between phenomena that are called "games", is that these sentences express descriptive definitions in relation to this practice.

To the extent that those resemblances that are brought out are not (or not only) thus claimed to enter into meaning explanations but only (or also) to function as causes of language usage, the propositions about resemblances will (also) be descriptive characterisations of this language usage (section A 2 (4)(b) above).

The same two modes of use are also to be found of propositions which, given a concept of 'family resemblance', call the unity between the phenomena that par-

---

39 See the quotations in item (3)(a) above; see also references and quotation in section 3.3.3 (3)(a) below, in note 95. – My standpoint in the main text at the present note presupposes and builds on a non-metaphysical interpretation of Wittgenstein's family resemblance analysis in relation to the question of the area of application of his analysis (item (c) below).

40 See e.g. the quotation in item (3)(a) above, in the text at note 34.

ticular words or expressions are used of, "family resemblance", but without saying anything about what the family resemblances more concretely consist in.[41]

(c) The actual area of application of family resemblance analysis

Partly one may ask whether Wittgenstein holds that, and partly whether it is the case that, family resemblance analysis applies to *some* linguistic expressions, to *particular types* of linguistic expression, or to *all* linguistic expressions.

- The first two alternatives ("some", "particular types") harmonise best with seeing family resemblance analysis in Wittgenstein as an *empirical* approach to the question: One investigates the use of the individual linguistic expressions and can only afterwards answer the question of what unity exists between the individual phenomena of which the expression is used, cf. "Sag nicht: "Es *muß* ihnen etwas gemeinsam sein, sonst hießen sie nicht 'Spiele' " – sondern *schau*, ob ihnen allen etwas gemeinsam ist."[42]
- The last alternative ("all") has a *metaphysical* touch, and therefore harmonises best with seeing the analysis in Wittgenstein as specifically philosophical argumentation, for example as an attempt at a transcendental-philosophically grounded concept of 'concept'.

Wittgenstein himself does not say anything explicitly about this, as far as I can see. What one can establish is that in addition to games, he also analyses a number of other phenomena by means of the family resemblance image: *language*,[43] *mathematics*,[44] *ethics*,[45] *aesthetics*,[46] *reading*,[47] and *deriving*.[48] – I cannot, however, find any basis in his writings for the said "metaphysical interpretation" of Wittgenstein.[49]

Nor have I been able to find any basis for claiming that all or particular groups of our concepts "must" have a family resemblance structure.[50] – Interpreted as empirical, propositions that claim this must (at least) build on very extensive

---

41 See e.g. the quotation in item (3)(a) above, in the text at note 35 (on the use of the word "number").

42 See item (3)(a) above, at and in note 31.

43 Wittgenstein, *Philosophische Untersuchungen*, Part I, section 65, cf. section 23.

44 Op. cit., Part I, section 67.

45 Op. cit., Part I, section 77.

46 Loc. cit.

47 Op. cit., Part I, section 164.

48 Loc. cit.

49 Correspondingly Pears, *Wittgenstein*, pp. 107–08; Fogelin, *Wittgenstein*, p. 136; Baker/ Hacker, *Wittgenstein: Meaning and Understanding*, pp. 201 et seq. Probably correspondingly in McGinn, *Wittgenstein on Meaning*, p. 58 in the note. Conversely Bambrough, 'Universals and Family Resemblances' (passim, but see in particular pp. 191–92, cf. 194–95).

50 Bambrough (same places as in the preceding note) and Bloor, *Wittgenstein: A Social Theory of Knowledge*, pp. 33 et seq., appear to claim that all concepts have a family resemblance structure; and Lakoff/ Johnson, *Metaphors We Live by*, pp. 125, cf. 123 (119–24), that all concepts of experience have such a structure.

investigations of how (main types of) concept designations are actually used. I am not aware of any such investigations. Another matter is that on the basis of more limited investigations one sets up as a working hypothesis that many words are used of phenomena that do not have any set of features in common; at the same time as one lets it be indeterminate what area the generalisation covers, and what unity positively exists between the phenomena.[51] – Interpreted as analytically true, propositions that claim that all or particular groups of our concepts "must" have a family resemblance structure, will build on a normative definition of the concept of 'concept' (and, as the case may be, other key or auxiliary concepts) whereby family resemblance is laid down as a necessary concept criterion. Such a definition is not in itself a basis for cognition, but simply a postulation of the conclusion. – If such propositions are interpreted as metaphysical, the sender must demonstrate another cognition basis than empirical evidence or definition. I do not know of any such cognition basis for all concepts' having to be family resemblance concepts.

> The arguments advanced by Bambrough and Bloor (note 50 above) are not in my opinion convincing. – Bambrough's argument appears to be that one can always demonstrate differences between numerically different phenomena that are conceptually collected together.[52] I am in agreement with this (I assume that it follows by definition from certain presupposed concepts, like inter alia 'numerical difference' and 'resemblance with respect to category' ("resemblance in kind")). It does not show, however, that the language users must lay down or actually do lay down such open-ended series of dis/similarities as concept criteria. – Bloor's argument seems to be an inference from "the conventional character of concept application" to family resemblance structure of concepts.[53] However, it is not clear what he bases this inference on.

---

[51] See e.g. Mill, *A System of Logic*, pp. 24, 99–100, 442–44, 449: "[A] name not unfrequently passes by successive links of resemblance from one object to another, until it becomes applied to things having *nothing in common* with the first things to which the name was given" (p. 99; my italics); Ogden/ Richards, *The Meaning of Meaning*, pp. 128–31: "The slightest study of the way in which words in ordinary speech gain occasional derivative and supernumerary uses through metaphorical shifts of all degrees of subtlety, and through what can be called linguistic accidents, is enough to show that for a *common element* of any interest or importance to run through all the respectable uses of a word is *most unlikely*. Each single metaphorical shift does, of course, depend upon some common element ... [b]ut ... there is no reason to expect that any word at all rich in context will always be borrowed on the strength of the same similarity or overlap" (pp. 128–29; my italics). – See also item (3)(b) above on "methodical family resemblance principle".

[52] Bambrough, 'Universals and Family Resemblances', p. 204: "The realist talks of properties and qualities until, when properties and qualities have been explained in terms of other properties and other qualities, he can *at last* do nothing but point to the resemblances between the objects that are said to be characterised by such and such a property or quality" (my italics; Bambrough's italics omitted).

[53] Bloor, *Wittgenstein: A Social Theory of Knowledge*, pp. 33, 37, 39, 41.

(d) The applicability of family resemblance analysis in science

What place can family resemblance analysis have in activity one traditionally terms "science"?[54] – In answering this question, we ought to draw a distinction between descriptive and normative definitions. The latter I shall take up later (section 3.3.5).

In the case of *descriptive definitions* I consider that the concept of 'family resemblance' has at any rate two *merits*. First, the concept contributes to creating an awareness of a *problem*: What actually occurring relationships are present that motivate the use of the same word of certain given phenomena? Secondly, the concept contributes to creating an awareness of a possible *openness in investigation methods and in answers*. This openness is important to preserve when one is pressurised by theories of how the concepts and the things "must" be: Mapping different actually occurring relationships between the phenomena may partly serve to free one from vainly searching for "das Wesen", "the essence", or the like, of the phenomena; and partly provide a basis for fruitful reflections: for example on connections between motives, or on the different functions of language apart from designating and describing (compare section 4.1 (1)(c) below).

The merits of the concept of 'family resemblance' now mentioned make themselves felt in the case of *all* descriptive definitions of words and expressions in everyday language, whether they be used in everyday life, academic subjects, science or philosophy. Two instance-types should be mentioned in particular. First, there is descriptive definition of *apparently homogeneous* use of language, which on closer analysis dissolves into a diversity of resemblances, differences and relationships, as illustrated in the examples quoted or referred to above. Secondly, there is descriptive definition of the use of words which, alone or in compounds and collocations, express *apparently completely separate* concepts. A good example is the Scandinavian family of words "rett", "ret" and "rätt", and the German "Recht", cf. the uses of these words in connections such as straight line, just, a right, the law, legal rule, legal system, court. Reflection on these uses arouses intuitions about connections from and between mathematics; ethics, religion, politics; and legal phenomena.

> The merits of the concept of 'family resemblance' mentioned above consist in the concept's serving as a means to cognition of family resemblance structure in the *language use that is being investigated*: in the "object language". They do not imply that one lays down family resemblance structure in the *means of cognition*: in the "meta-language". For example, the concept of 'family resemblance' as it is defined here (item (3)(b) above), does not itself have family resemblance structure.

---

54 I should remind the reader that I use the term "science" (1) in the broad sense of the Scandinavian "vitenskap" and the German "Wissenschaft", i.e. to cover natural, social and human sciences, and (2) as an abbreviation for "activity one traditionally terms "science" in this broad sense" – that is, I neither presuppose nor lay down anything contentious through this concept of 'science' (cf. section I 5.1 above, in note 1).

Whether the means of cognition (the "meta-language") have or ought to have family resemblance structure is discussed most aptly as part of the question of normative definitions and family resemblance (section 3.3.5 below).

(5) Variants of unity: The relationship of family resemblance analysis to concepts of 'concept' (a–c). "Condition concept"; "factor concept", including "family resemblance concept" (d)

To such words as *"concept", "begrep", "Begriff", etc.*, as they are normally used, are linked notions and expectations of a certain *unity* between the phenomena a concept covers. Out of consideration for established language usage it is therefore reasonable to lay down requirements for a certain degree of unity before one speaks of "concept", "begrep", "Begriff", etc. (for example, before one speaks of "the game concept" or "rettsbegrepet").[55] – In the light of this, one may ask whether it is reasonable to say that a word expresses a "concept" when there are no features common to the phenomena of which the word is used, but (only) a *family resemblance* between the phenomena.

The question outlined divides on closer examination into two:

First, into a *concept question*: Is one to lay down particular unity requirements as a *criterion in a concept of 'concept'*?

Secondly, into an *individuation question*: Given that one does not lay down particular unity requirements as a concept criterion, for example that one says that a word expresses a "concept" even if the phenomena of which the word is used have no features in common, then, according to what criteria does one decide whether one is confronted by *one* concept or *several* concepts?

In this work, I shall not be saying anything in particular about the individuation question. – The concept of 'concept', however, I shall return to in more detail and in a more general perspective, in its capacity of being one possible answer to the question of what is being defined (section 4 below). I shall then give grounds for why I do not consider it expedient to lay down requirements for determinacy, including requirements for unity in the form of something in common, as a criterion in the concept of 'concept' in this work (section 4.1, in particular item (3)).

Different from the concept question and the individuation question is the *identity question*: According to what criteria does one determine whether a concept has changed so much that one is no longer confronted with the same

55 In the sentence containing the present note, idiom is used that links "speaks of" to linguistic entities (here "concept", "begrep", "Begriff", "the game concept", "rettsbegrepet") and gives "speaks of" the meaning 'uses' (in contrast to 'thematises'). In the present item (5) and in a number of instances otherwise I use such idiom since it is well established (with correspondingly little risk of misunderstandings), and since it simplifies and makes more readable the presentation of the crucial points.

concept? – This question I return to in my discussion of the relationship between old and new in normative definitions (section 4.3.3 (3)(b) below).

However, in the present context, a discussion of family resemblance, the most important thing is not the concept question, but the surveying of certain *facts*: seeing and keeping apart different *types and degrees of relationship between the phenomena*. – Taking as a point of departure the aims of the discussion (item (1) above) and what has been said about family resemblance (items (3)–(4) above), I shall outline relevant categories (items (a)–(d) below).

(a) Arbitrary collection

In some cases the same word[56] is used in different meanings, at the same time as it is *difficult to see any connection* between these meanings. For example the word "banks": "They were fishing on the river banks", "Norwegian banks lent out less money this year than last", "The plane banks steeply to the left". Gathering these phenomena has the character of *arbitrary collection*.

In these cases it would be misleading to use the singular form with the definite article, "the concept of …" ("the concept of bank"). It would arouse expectations of a minimum of unity, which is not to be found. Often it would also be misleading to use the plural forms "concepts of …/ the concepts of …" ("concepts of bank/ the concepts of bank"). For this may lead towards thinking that the individual concepts are types ("species") of a superordinate unity in common ("genus"), or that there is in some other way a unity beyond the concept designation.

Such notions of unity in meaning are out of place in these instances. The only unity lies in the use of the same word.

(b) Family resemblance

In other instances the same word is used in different meanings and it seems to be a fruitful working hypothesis that there are *partial and overlapping resemblances and differences* between these meanings, so that there is *family resemblance*, in the sense in which I use the term "family resemblance" (item (3)(b) above): for example as in the case of "game" (items (3)(a), (b) above), or "rett"/ "Recht" (item (4)(d) above).

In these instances it may vary how helpful it is to speak of "the concept of …":

In some instances it is virtually a matter of taste whether one wishes to say that a sufficient degree of unity exists, or whether one wishes to divide up the area of which the word is used before one speaks of "the concept of …". – The word "game" I take to be such a borderline case.[57]

In other instances it seems that the most reasonable thing is to avoid concept terminology in relation to the total area of which the word is used.[58] – This I take

56 As an identity criterion of words I use here the written image and that alone.

57 Wittgenstein speaks for his part of "der Begriff des Spiels", see *Philosophische Untersuchungen*, Part I, section 68.

58 I should remind the reader that by "concept terminology" I mean words like "concept", "concep-

to apply for example in the case of the words "rett"/ "Recht": By the formulations "begrepet rett"/ "der Begriff des Rechts" one will in practice mean parts of the area that has been outlined (item (4)(d) above), not the whole area (which parts, however, is often unclear.)

> Austin says he is only interested in "good reasons [for calling] different things by the same name", not in "mere equivocation".[59] – This may be misunderstood, since the proposition itself and the footnote form might suggest that the distinction between "good reasons" and "mere equivocation" is a simple side-issue. But I perceive this distinction as the often difficult main issue (and I do not believe that Austin would disagree with this).[60] Indeed, it is inter alia precisely the boundary between "good reasons" (the present item (b)) and "mere equivocation" (item (a) above) one is after, when one asks whether there are any, and if so what, relationships between apparently separate phenomena, that may explain that we use the same word of these phenomena, cf. the example "rett"/ "Recht".

(c) Features in common

Further one has those cases in which there seems to be a *higher degree of unity* between the phenomena of which the word is used: One can identify a set of features in common. – The formulation *"features in common"* is used of *varying degrees of unity*, and this is also my usage here. I shall take a look at three main instances.[61]

(i) The *strongest* form of unity is where the features in common are *both necessary and sufficient*. I have earlier pointed to how the mode of definition through category and sub-category most often presupposes such unity (item (2)(b) above): This mode of definition is most often intended as a structuring of the concept in a set of necessary and sufficient criteria, with a presupposition that the things that are covered have a corresponding set of features in common. – An example would be a definition of 'chair' as 'a piece of furniture, for sitting on, for one person and with a back'.

(ii) A *weaker* form of unity is where what are called "features in common" consist in (sets of) features that are individually *sufficient, but not necessary*, and where the *alternative* (sets of) features can be *specified exhaustively*. – An exam-

---

tion", "notion", "idea" and their derivatives (or their equivalents in other languages) (cf. section A 2 (1) above, in note 1).

59 Austin, 'The Meaning of a Word', p. 38 including note 1.

60 Compare Ullmann, *The Principles of Semantics*, pp. 114–37; Lyons, *Semantics*, Vol. 2, pp. 550–54; *Language and Linguistics*, pp. 146–48; Lakoff/ Johnson, *Metaphors We Live By*, pp. 106–14; Ziff, *Semantic Analysis*, pp. 176–81; Lewis, *Studies in Words*, pp. 109–10, cf. the discussions in the book in their entirety (semantic history leading up to and arousing awareness of the present semantic ramifications of words); von Wright, *The Varieties of Goodness*, pp. 8–18; *Norm and Action*, pp. 1–16; Wittgenstein, *Philosophische Untersuchungen*, Part I, sections 561–62: "[561:] Man möchte sagen … die Personalunion durch das gleiche Wort sei ein unwesentlicher Zufall. [562:] Aber wie kann ich entscheiden, welches ein wesentlicher und welches ein unwesentlicher, zufälliger Zug der Notation ist?"

61 On the status of the examples in what follows, see item (d) below, in the final indent, with further reference.

ple would be a definition of 'divorce' as 'dissolution of marriage by administrative decision or court judgment'. In this definition the criteria 'dissolution of marriage by administrative decision' and 'dissolution of marriage by court judgment' are laid down as being individually sufficient. At the same time the definition is *exhaustive* in relation to the Norwegian legal system; Norwegian law has no other paths to divorce. Thus one can say with a certain degree of reasonableness that an *enumeration* of the alternative and sufficient criteria specifies a set of "features *in common*": "Divorces have in common that marriage is dissolved either by administrative decision or by court judgment."

(iii) To be able to speak with any reasonableness of "features in common", one must thus demand that any *alternative* (sets of) criteria can be specified exhaustively (item (ii) above). It is, however, also natural to demand that any alternative (sets of) criteria can be specified with a certain degree of *surveyability*, as in the case of the concept of 'divorce'.

Problems of surveying alternative (sets of) criteria may be illustrated by contrasting the unity in the concept of 'divorce' with the unity in a *legal concept of 'valid contract'*. The unity in this latter concept serves at the same time as an example of the third main instance of features in common: a weaker form of unity in which the features in common are *necessary, but not sufficient.*

A concept of 'valid contract', which is widespread among Nordic lawyers, has as necessary criteria 'two parties' and 'mutually corresponding dispositive propositions addressed to the other party'.[62] However, these criteria are not considered as sufficient: Various features of the exercise of contractual competence or of the development subsequent to stipulation of the contractual norm, may lead to dispositive propositions between two parties not having effect in accordance with their content.[63] – One might imagine formulating the absence of these features as a necessary criterion in the concept of 'valid contract', and this criterion in combination with the first-mentioned two positive criteria, as a set of necessary and sufficient criteria. Thus: "Legally valid contracts have in common that there are two parties who have addressed to each other mutually corresponding dispositive propositions, and that there is not a or b or c … or n."

---

62 See the respective Nordic contracts Acts, chapter one; see further e.g. *Utkast til lov om avtaler og andre retshandler paa formuerettens omraade* [draft of an Act concerning contracts and other juristic acts in the area of law relating to obligations and property], avgit av de norske delegerte ved det skandinaviske obligationsretsarbeide [submitted by the Norwegian delegates participating in the Scandinavian work on the law of obligations], p. 22; Almén/ Eklund, *Lagen om avtal och andra rättshandlingar på förmögenhetsrättens område* [the Act concerning contracts and other juristic acts in the area of law relating to obligations and property] [Swedish], p. 10; Ussing, *Aftaler* [contracts] [Danish], p. 9; Wrede, *Lagen om rättshandlingar på förmögenhetsrättens område* [the Act concerning juristic acts in the area of law relating to obligations and property] [Finnish], pp. 15–16.

63 Eng, 'Begrepene 'kompetanse' og 'gyldighet' i juridisk argumentasjon' [the concepts of 'competence' and 'validity' in legal argumentation], sections 5.2.3 and 5.2.4, provides a more general survey of respectively exercise norms and development norms in lawyers' argumentation concerning the binding force of stipulated norms.

The alternative circumstances that may lead to a contract's not having effect in accordance with its content are, however, *so* many, varied and value-loaded that it is *not natural to speak of a set of "features in common"*: One must take into account, in the first place, coercion, deceit, usury, whether it will be unreasonable or contrary to good business practice to enforce the contract, frustration, etc.; then, mandatory legal provisions of the most different kinds concerning the content of the contract, such as price controls or provisions relating to consumer protection; furthermore, provisions in public law concerning concessions, grants, permits, etc.; and a great deal more. – The *relevant difference* from the unity in the concept of 'divorce' lies in the fact that the alternative criteria in the latter concept are *surveyable* in a way in which the alternative criteria in the concept of 'valid contract' are not.

On the other hand it is not a relevant difference that the alternative criteria in the concept of 'divorce' refer to circumstances that must be present, while the alternative criteria in the concept of 'valid contract' refer to circumstances that must not be present. – Nor is there any relevant difference in whether the alternative criteria can be specified exhaustively: I cannot see that it would be logically impossible to provide an exhaustive enumeration of alternative grounds of invalidity in contract law at any given time.

Even though it is possible to formulate a definition of the concept of 'valid contract' as a set of assumedly necessary and sufficient criteria, it is thus not very natural to say that such a set represents "features in common" of valid contracts. It is, however, reasonable to say that the first-mentioned and assumedly necessary criteria, 'two parties' and 'mutually corresponding dispositive propositions addressed to the other party', do represent "features in common". The *unity* in lawyers' use of the term "valid [binding, effective, or the like] contract" therefore lies first and foremost in features in common that are assumed necessary, but not sufficient.

In an analysis of the concept of 'valid contract' in English law, Hart comes to the same conclusion concerning the unity in the concept.[64] However, his grounds seem unclear: As far as I can see, Hart does not claim that it would be impossible for *logical reasons* to specify all the alternative circumstances that must not be present. And he says explicitly that it is possible to *formulate* a descriptive definition of the concept of 'valid contract' on the model of necessary and sufficient criteria.[65] However, he asserts that such a formulation would "obscure" the distinctiveness of the concept and be "vacuous".[66] Hart seems to hold that in some way or another it follows from *reality itself* that a formulation by means of necessary and sufficient criteria is misleading. – I cannot grasp Hart's argumentation here. As argued for in

---

64 Hart, 'The Ascription of Responsibility and Rights', pp. 148–52. In the light of this, Hart designates the concept of 'valid contract' a "defeasible" concept, see op. cit., p. 148.

65 Op. cit., pp. 150, 152 in note 1.

66 Loc. cit.

the main text above, the point is in my view a *linguistic* one: It does not harmonise well with normal language usage to use the designation "features in common" of such a complex set of alternative circumstances as we must bring in if we wish to define 'valid contract' descriptively through the form of necessary and sufficient criteria.

(d) "Condition concept"; "factor concept", including "family resemblance concept"

Concept terminology is used more, the less unity there is in what is being investigated: One seldom speaks of "the concept of a chair", "the concept of a cup", or the like. But one often speaks of "the concept of rationality", "the concept of law", or the like.

In the light of this fact and, more generally, in the light of the varying degrees of unity in what the expression "the concept of ..." is used of (items (b)–(c) above), there is a need in relation to the perspective and topic of the present work to *nuance concept terminology* in the following way:

I use the term *"condition concept"* of those cases in which it is reasonable to designate the unity between the phenomena "features in common"; i.e. in which the unity can be specified as necessary features or as exhaustive and surveyable (sets of) sufficient features (item (c)(i)–(iii) above). Further, I use the term *"factor concept"* of the other cases; i.e. in which the unity cannot be specified as necessary features or as exhaustive and surveyable (sets of) sufficient features. *"Family resemblance concept"* designates the group of factor concepts in which the unity in the phenomena consists in family resemblance (item (b) above).

Another group of factor concepts is made up of a large proportion of what I designate *"concepts with evaluation prescription in their connotation"*. These I shall take up in section 6.2 (1) below. – After this I shall look in section 6.2 (2) at *similarities and differences* between the two groups of factor concepts.

It follows from the definitions that a concept is either a condition concept or a factor concept, never both. Another matter is that the status of a concept can change over time: from factor concept to condition concept (sections 3.3.5, and 5.4.2 (1)(d) concluding remarks, below), or from condition concept to factor concept (section 3.3.5 below).

I shall later look at certain arguments that might possibly be advanced against the reality basis of the distinction between condition concepts and factor concepts (section 6.2 (3) below). In so doing, I shall make use of the examples of condition concepts just given (items (c)(i)–(iii) above); the examples have been chosen also with the later discussion in mind and thus have a tentative status. – As I shall justify in more detail in the later discussion, I have not been able to find tenable arguments against the reality basis of the distinction between condition concepts and factor concepts: I consider that this distinction is logically possible; and I consider that in actually occurring language and argumentation one can find both condition concepts and factor concepts.

(6) The diversity of relationships between the phenomena ("concept types") necessitates openness with respect to method in the case of descriptive definitions

A main aim of the discussion in the present section 3.2.2 has been to demonstrate the necessity of openness with respect to method in the case of descriptive definitions: the necessity of not tying definitions to one method, for example through category and sub-category (item (2) above), but of being open in the individual instance to method sui generis. In concept terminology: *The definition method must be adapted to the concept type*:

- The point of departure is that the tenability criterion of a descriptive definition is whether the definition provides a true description of actually occurring language use.
- Even a limited investigation of actually occurring language use shows a multiplicity of relationships between different phenomena that are designated by the same linguistic entity, and a corresponding multiplicity of concept types: I have distinguished between on the one hand condition concepts and on the other hand factor concepts, including family resemblance concepts, according to the criterion of whether or not it is natural to designate the unity between the phenomena "features in common" (items (5)(d) cf. (c), above).

In the *illustration* of the connection between definition method and concept type, it was natural to place the *main weight* on family resemblance concepts (items (3)(b) cf. (a), above), since the risk of wrong definition method is greater there than in the case of condition concepts (item (2) above).

This illustration, with its accompanying conceptualisations, demonstrates *part of the practical significance* of the maxim that the definition method must be adapted to the concept type. In order to demonstrate the whole practical significance of this maxim, one would have to map exhaustively the relationships between phenomena we call by the same linguistic entity (exhaustively map concept types). – This lies outside the purpose here. But to put the maxim about connection between definition method and concept type in perspective, I shall by way of conclusion emphasise the *diversity of relationships* between the phenomena.

Even the very concept of 'condition concept' covers *fairly different logical relationships* between concept criteria: Features in common of the phenomena may, as mentioned, be necessary and sufficient; sufficient but not necessary; or necessary but not sufficient (item (5)(c) above). – The combination that by definition is excluded is features that are neither necessary nor elements in an exhaustive and surveyable specification of (sets of) sufficient features; i.e. the factor structure (item (5)(b) above) or the arbitrary collection (item (5)(a) above).

Further, although it is true that the distinction between condition concepts and factor concepts is exhaustive, what one perceives as *interesting* about a concept type cannot always be captured by means of the concepts of 'necessary feature', 'sufficient feature' and 'factor'; one may be interested in aspects that require other concepts.

In a survey of relationships Austin mentioned inter alia the following:[67] – The phenomena can stand in different relationships to a central usage: for example "healthy body" (central usage), "healthy complexion" (sign), "healthy exercise" (cause). – The phenomena may stand in analogous relationships: for example "human foot", "foot of the hill", "foot of the lamp". – The phenomena may represent different determinations of something one considers to be the same aspect: for example "red", "green", "blue", etc., in relation to the aspect of colour. – Or the phenomena may represent different parts of a complex activity: for example "football", "goal", "penalty area", "corner", etc., in relation to the game of soccer.

Later in this work I shall deal with the connecting function, substituting function and excluding function of words (section 4.1 (1)(c)).

The list of conceptualisations can be made longer: The topic 'concept types' covers much of what goes under the name of "analytical philosophy". A major aim of many works under that name is precisely to identify different ways in which language is used. – What has been said is, however, sufficient for the *present purpose*: to show that by understanding the concept of 'concept' in contrast to 'arbitrary collection', one has not said anything about the internal structure of the concept; that this internal structure is of extremely diverse kinds; and that in the case of descriptive definition one must therefore be open to the possibility that one's familiar method of definition is not apt in relation to the concept type with which one is confronted (openness for definition method sui generis).

3.3. Normative definitions

I have defined 'definition' as "propositions that contribute to determining the meanings of linguistic entities (contribute to determining concepts)" (section A 2 (1) above). In relation to this general concept of 'definition', what is *specific* to normative definitions is that the "determining" has a *normative modality*.

One thread in the following discussion is to show some major types of normative modality in actually occurring definition activity. My point of departure is more general concepts of normative modality, taken particularly from law and legal theory: concepts that have been formed with a view to normative regulation of any actions whatsoever (section A 5 (2)(a) above). The question is how the normative modality *concretely manifests itself when* the action theme more particularly is the use of language (the formation of concepts).

---

67 Austin, 'The Meaning of a Word', pp. 39–42. See also Hart, *The Concept of Law*, 1st ed. pp. 15–16, 2nd ed. loc. cit., who seems to build directly on Austin's account.

The question of *tenability criteria* is more complex in the case of normative definitions than in the case of descriptive ones, and will not be discussed until the foundation has been laid for the necessary nuancing (section III 2 below).

3.3.1. Stipulated normative definitions

(1) Concept. Different normative modalities
(2) Normative regulation of one's own use of language
(3) Normative regulation of other people's use of language
(4) The relationship between normative regulation of one's own and other people's use of language
(5) Situation criteria

(1) Concept. Different normative modalities

By "*stipulated* definitions" I mean the proposition aspect of individual proposition formulations in so far as the proposition contributes to normatively determining the meanings of linguistic entities (contributes to normatively determining concepts). An example would be the proposition expressed by: "In what follows I shall use the word "x" of ..."; or by: "In this Act ... "party" means any person at whom a decision is directed or whom the case otherwise directly concerns".[68] – The latter proposition formulation provides at the same time an example of the subgroup of stipulated definitions that lawyers call "statutory definitions". Statutory definitions have some distinctive features that will be discussed later, as the necessary parts of the definition-theoretical foundation are being laid (see section 3.3.6 below, with further references).

> Most stipulated definitions are directed at the *future*, for example "In this lecture I shall use the word "x" to mean ...". However, the term "normative definition" ought to be extended also to cover certain propositions concerning *past* language usage, for example "I ought to have used the word "x" to mean ...".

Stipulated definitions are by definition *normative*.[69] For the understanding of the role of stipulated definitions it is too simple, however, to conceive of the normative modality as (only) *unitary*. I shall *distinguish between* recommendations, promises and impositions of duty (apart from promises).[70]

---

68 Section 2 of the Public Administration Act (10 February 1967).

69 The same goes for the custom-based definitions, so that the word "normative" is by definition unnecessary in the formulations "stipulated normative definitions" and "custom-based normative definitions". For the sake of clarity, I nevertheless use the formulations mentioned, partly in the headings of the present section 3.3.1 and the following section 3.3.2, and partly in a number of instances in the text.

70 On an aspect of qualification modality, see section 3.3.2 (1) below.

There is a close relationship between the normative modality types mentioned and a normative definition's *person connection*, both on the sender's side and on the recipient's side: It is true that one can address recommendations both to oneself and to others. However, by definition a promise binds only the sender, i.e. the person who advances the normative definition; and by definition impositions of duty (apart from promises) do not bind the definer but others. – In the more detailed presentation of some main types of stipulated definition I have therefore found it most clarificatory to take the person connection as a point of departure (items 2–3 below).[71]

> One can have *norm stipulation* without *sending*, for example where a promise is written without being sent. And lawyers discuss what rules concerning the norm stipulator's being bound by the promise, and, as the case may be, concerning liability for damages, shall apply where the written word was sent without the norm stipulator's intent.[72] – In the case of normative definitions, however, the distinction between stipulation and sending has less interest.

(2) Normative regulation of one's own use of language

(a) Propositions that normatively regulate one's own use of language will linguistically often appear *simply as* descriptions of, or announcements about, a decision that the definer has taken earlier; i.e. appear as "spurious decision propositions" (section A 5 (3) above). They may, for example, appear through formulations of the form: "I *have found* it most appropriate to use the word "x" of ...".

However, in a definition context such formulations will most often *also serve the same function as* propositions that directly express decision; i.e. the same function as "genuine decision propositions". Compare the fact that the formulation just cited will most often serve the same function as the formulation: "In what follows I shall use the word "x" of ...".

Further, the (genuine) decision-proposition function can in another perspective often be seen as a promise, i.e. as an imposition of duty addressed to oneself (section A 5 (2)(a) above, in the last indent).

In the light of this, in definition contexts it is often reasonable to interpret decision formulations as also having a meaning element of *self-imposed duty*; in

---

71 Hospers, *An Introduction to Philosophical Analysis*, pp. 32–33, lets the dimensions 'modality type' and 'person connection' coincide, so that by definition normative definitions are addressed to oneself, while by definition descriptive definitions describe other people's use of language. – This conceptualisation in Hospers is not very expedient when the aim is the mapping of actually occurring language and argumentation. As is apparent from the main text in what follows, it is both conceivable and practical that one describes one's own use of language or normatively regulates other people's.

72 See Arnholm, *Alminnelig avtalerett* [general law of contract], pp. 268–72; *Privatrett II: Avtaler* [private law II: contracts], pp. 284–87; *Lærebok i avtalerett* [textbook of contract law], pp. 227–28.

and by the formulation one *promises*[73] a particular use of words: either tacitly, in that we infer the promise from the context, as in the first exemplary formulation above (what would be the point of simply announcing to one's listeners or readers the fact that at a certain point in time in the past one made a decision concerning the meaning of a linguistic expression?), or we consider that the promise is explicitly given, as in the second exemplary formulation above.

(b) In the case of normative regulation in the form of promises addressed to others, one is oneself both the sender of, and the subject in, the stipulated norm (self-imposed duty), while the *addressee* of the norm is one or more other people (the person to whom the promise is addressed, for example a reader).

However, one can also address stipulated norms to oneself, i.e. one is *oneself* the addressee, in addition to being sender and norm subject: One reflects on the various alternatives for conceptualisation and choice of words, and addresses a norm to oneself, and only to oneself, to use one of the alternatives. – The norm may have *promise modality* ("From now on I shall remember this definition and use it consistently!"), or the norm may have *recommendation modality* ("I think I had better stick to this narrower definition, since the broad alternative covers too many different things and may thus confuse the reader").

(c) Like other norm stipulation, normative regulation of the use of language presupposes *competence*, i.e. a normatively constituted capacity to stipulate new norms (in contrast to physical, intellectual, artistic or other capacities to produce actual effects).[74]

Most people consider that all language users have competence to regulate their own language usage normatively: "*autonomous* competence to define", and that this is so from the moment they begin to use language, even though the language user is only gradually able to exercise this competence, as his language skills are developed. – Autonomous defining competence is thus different from autonomous competence otherwise: One can only legally bind person and property on reaching a particular age, and on condition of a certain minimum of intellectual capacity and accountability. Corresponding norms are found in morals and religion. – The cause of this difference is probably that the exercise of autonomous defining competence is perceived as less potentially dangerous for the exerciser, recipient(s) and society otherwise than the exercise of autonomous competence with respect to person or property.

(d) On some occasions the *promise aspect is the only normative element* in the definition; one does not claim that the normative definition has value beyond the individual spoken or textual context in which it occurs. Beside the promise aspect, the definition has on those occasions a purely factual and *limited end-*

---

73 Austin, *How to do Things with Words*, p. 136.

74 The concept of 'competence' is defined in more detail in Eng, 'Begrepene 'kompetanse' og 'gyldighet' i juridisk argumentasjon' [the concepts of 'competence' and 'validity' in legal argumentation]. Here the criteria mentioned in the text at the present note will suffice.

means aspect: "If the reader wants to understand the *following speech/ text*, then the word "x" must be taken to mean ...".

On other occasions the sender of the definition has greater pretensions. The definition has a *more comprehensive end-means aspect* than making comprehensible the individual spoken or textual context in which it occurs: "If the reader wants to understand *this topic*, then the word "x" must be taken to mean ...". – Such definitions, with a more comprehensive end-means aspect, lead on to a treatment of normative regulation of other people's use of language, in that these definitions most often also have aspects of normative regulation of this kind.

(3) Normative regulation of other people's use of language

The competence to regulate other people's use of language normatively: "heteronomous defining competence", is not perceived as so intuitively a matter of course as autonomous defining competence. However, there are some practically important instance-types. According to the modality we can distinguish between command or prohibition (item (a) below), and recommendation (item (b) below).

(a) A presupposing of heteronomous defining competence in the form of competence to stipulate *commands* or *prohibitions* can be found in the relationship, for example, between parents and child, between teacher and pupil, between therapist and patient, or between the governing bodies of an organisation and its members. In these relationships both the sender and the recipient of a definition will often consider that the sender has the right to dictate how language shall be used: It may be a parent, teacher, or behavioural therapist who dictates what a word shall or shall not mean. Or it may be the governing bodies of an organisation that define in articles, rules of the game, or the like, who shall be considered to be a member, what shall be considered to be checkmate, off-side, etc., and in the case of which the members must accept these definitions if they want to participate in the organisation or its activity.

Further one finds important instances of heteronomous defining competence in the *legal system*. Legislator, public administrative authorities, courts, and contracting parties can have legal competence to lay down with effect for others that words and expressions have a particular meaning:

The legislator's competence shows itself in stipulated definitions in statutory form: "statutory definitions" (section 3.3.6 below).

The heteronomous defining competence of the public administrative authorities and the courts shows itself when in the individual instance they interpret and apply the law with final effect. As a main rule the decisions made by the public administrative authorities may be reviewed by the courts, i.e. it is the courts that have the final defining competence. In some cases, however, the legislator has given the public administrative authorities the last word. This is the case for example with section 5 first paragraph of the Public Administration Act (10 February 1967), which delegates statutory defining competence to the Government, or with section 16 second paragraph of the Hotels Act (Act No. 52 of 3 June 1983), which gives the Ministry defining competence in the individual instance.[75]

The heteronomous defining competence of a contracting party shows itself when he can demand to have his understanding of the words of the contract taken as a basis, for example because the disputed clause was composed by the opposing party, who is accordingly considered the more obvious party to bear the liability for the lack of clarity (interpretation "contra proferentem").[76]

Common to the instances mentioned is that any person who ventures into the preserves of the statute or the contract must accept that other people's understanding of the words of the statute or the contract is taken as a basis.

(b) *Recommendation* is a normal meaning aspect of definitions in more comprehensive or thorough analysis and argumentation. Partly recommendation is an explicitly advanced meaning aspect, cf. formulations such as "I recommend", "one should", and the like; and partly recommendation is a presupposed meaning aspect, in that the person arguing implies that the definitions he applies have a value *beyond* serving as a means to understanding the concrete speech or text in which the definition occurs (cf. item (2)(d) above, on the latter-mentioned, more limited, end-means aspect).

Most people will probably consider that heteronomous defining competence in the form of recommending competence *is to be acknowledged in all* individuals with normal language knowledge plus a certain minimum of knowledge of the topic that the recommended definition refers to. This is in contrast to heteronomous defining competence in the form of competence to command or prohibit, which is considered to require a more tangible basis of an extra-legal or legal kind (item (a) above).

(4) The relationship between normative regulation of one's own and other people's use of language

(a) Definitions that *directly* appear as normative regulation of *other people's* use of language will often be perceived as *also* having normative consequences for the sender's *own* language usage.

One instance-type is that a recommendation or a command/ prohibition relating to other people's use of language is perceived as presupposing a promise: If the sender were in the same argumentation situation, then he would himself follow the normative proposition he is now addressing to the other person.

Another instance-type of normative consequence for the sender is that participants in the legal system are bound by their definitions addressed to others. For example, both the Supreme Court and the public administrative authorities are by virtue of the doctrine of the sources of law to a certain extent bound in future

75 See in general Eckhoff/ Smith, *Forvaltningsrett* [administrative law], pp. 642–44.

76 Huser, *Avtaletolking* [interpretation of contracts], pp. 555–57.

cases by their decisions with respect to how the letter of the law is to be understood. This is in contrast to the legislator, who is not considered to any extent at all to be bound by his decisions on this point (statutory definitions may be freely changed by the legislator by means of a new statute).

(b) From promises with respect to one's *own* language usage one cannot unreservedly infer corresponding normative regulation of *other people's* use of language. It may be that the definer has no other aim with the definition than to make a particular speech or text comprehensible for the recipient (item (2)(d) above).

Sometimes, however, promises with respect to one's own language usage will be perceived as resulting from the view that this language usage is to be recommended for *everybody* who wants to reflect on the topic concerned: The promise is perceived as presupposing and originating from the same grounds as a general recommendation.

(a)↔(b) Several of the inferences that have now been mentioned build on a boundary between what is explicitly *said* and what is *presupposed*. In actually occurring language and argumentation, this boundary is often indeterminate.[77] On the general level one cannot therefore get any further than mapping and illustrating certain typical relationships, such as those mentioned.

(c) One can *express several* independent (i.e. mutually not logically derivable) propositions at the same time through the *same definition formulation*: There are no logical problems with this, and purely factually there is often reason to interpret definition formulations so that they express a multiplicity of propositions.[78]

---

77 Aspects of this boundary are illuminated inter alia in Rommetveit, *Språk, tanke og kommunikasjon* [language, thought and communication], pp. 120–53; Lemmon, 'Sentences, Statements and Propositions', at and in notes 3 and 6, cf. pp. 105–07; Cavell, 'Must We Mean What We Say?', pp. 8 et seq., 31; Searle, 'Indirect Speech Acts', passim. – Concerning this boundary in the case of texts of statutes, see e.g. section 3.3.6 (1) below, in the indent; Eckhoff, *Rettskildelære* [doctrine of the sources of law], pp. 40–41; compare also op. cit. 1st ed. pp. 119–23. – In the case of contracts, wills and other dispositive acts in private law, the indeterminacy of this boundary is reflected in indeterminacy of several other distinctions, e.g. (i) indeterminacy of a methodological distinction between "tolking" and "utfylling" [interpretation and implication]; as far as contracts are concerned, compare Knoph, 'Nogen ord om dommerens stilling til kutymene' [some words on the position and attitude of the judge in relation to usages in trade], pp. 306–08; Stang, *Innledning til formueretten* [introduction to the law of obligations and property], pp. 447–49; Arnholm, *Lærebok i avtalerett* [textbook of contract law], pp. 32–33; Huser, *Avtaletolking* [interpretation of contracts], pp. 121–34; Hov, *Avtalerett* [law of contract], pp. 71–72; Selvig, *Kontraktsretten* [law of contract], pp. 576–77; Krüger, *Norsk kontraktsrett* [Norwegian law of contract], p. 506; (ii) indeterminacy of a distinction between explicit and tacit dispositive acts; as far as contracts are concerned, compare Karlgren, 'Några spörsmål i anslutning till 8 § Avtalslagen' [some questions in connection with section 8 of the Contracts Act] [Swedish], pp. 17–21.

78 Eckhoff/ Sundby use the words "meningskumulasjon" [meaning cumulation]/ "Bedeutungskumulation" of the fact that the same formulation expresses two or more independent propositions, see *Rettssystemer* [legal systems], p. 139; *Rechtssysteme*, p. 117. In the same works, respectively pp. 139–41 and 117–19, they point to some common forms of meaning cumulation in the case of formulations concerning legal questions (definitions are not mentioned).

For example, the formulation "I have found it most expedient to use the word "x" to mean ..." can express an announcement of an earlier decision concerning the meaning of a linguistic entity; a promise actually to implement this decision in relation to the present speech or text; as well as a recommendation to others to use the word to mean the same thing in discussion of the same question.

(5) Situation criteria

In *academic subjects* the situation criteria of stipulated definitions often delimit in one or both of two ways. They delimit through the linking of the definition to a particular *subject* or to a particular *academic systematisation or problem context*: for example to law in contrast to sociology.[79] Or they delimit through the linking of the definition to *individual points in space and time*: for example to a particular book or a particular conversation. – If situation criteria of this kind are not explicitly specified, they are often implied by senders and inferred by recipients.

In *everyday life* broad or even seemingly unlimited situation criteria are more common. The reason is that many of the stipulated definitions in everyday life are intended as instantiations of custom-based definitions and thus *take on* the situation criteria of the latter kind of definition, criteria which are often of the broad or seemingly unlimited kind (section 3.3.2 (3) below). Important instance-types of such instantiation are parents teaching their children language, and language users who clarify what they mean by explicitly adhering to a custom-based meaning.

3.3.2. Custom-based normative definitions

(1) Concept. The qualification modality
(2) The relationship to the fundamental concept of 'definition'
(3) Person criteria and situation criteria. The constitutive role of custom-based definitions

(1) Concept. The qualification modality

By "*custom-based* definitions" I mean propositions which contribute to normatively determining the meanings of linguistic entities (contribute to normatively determining concepts) and which are formed in the course of time through linguistic interaction between a number of people.

The custom-based definitions are often termed "language rules" or "language norms" – or simply "language", as in the sentence "he is not familiar with their language".

Custom-based definitions have a *qualification modality*; they qualify what *is to be regarded as correct* use of the words and expressions of the language,

79 Weber, 'Über einige Kategorien der verstehenden Soziologie', pp. 439–40; Aubert, *Rettens sosiale funksjon* [the social function of law], pp. 15–16; 'Om relationerna mellan juridiska och sociologiska begrepp' [on the relations between legal and social concepts], passim (on inter alia the concepts of 'felony', 'right of ownership', 'contract', 'causality' and 'sanction').

including what situations the individual words and expressions can be used in and which words and expressions can replace one another.[80]

The qualification modality is in these respects also an aspect of many stipulated definitions, both general, for example statutory definitions, and particular, for example "I shall/ you must ... use the word "x" of ...". In both instances the proposition provides *inter alia* a yardstick that one can apply to the subsequent use of language.[81] – In the case of stipulated definitions, however, I consider that other aspects have greater *interest*: recommendation aspect, promise aspect, command/ prohibition aspect, and a factual end-means aspect ("if you want to understand this, then the word "x" must be taken to mean ...").[82]

There is little room for *command* or *prohibition* in the case of custom-based definitions: If one violates a custom-based definition, one risks not being understood, but one does not meet the "you must/ must not" that expresses the duty modality. Another matter is that violating a custom-based definition can be the cause of a normative definition with duty modality being stipulated; for example, parents seeing that their child again and again uses a word wrongly, consider it

---

80 On the qualification modality, see T. Strömberg, *Inledning till den allmänna rättsläran* [introduction to legal theory], pp. 80–86, 92–97; *Rättsordningens byggstenar* [the building bricks of the legal system], pp. 42–49, 57–75; 'Hur gick det för kvalifikationsnormerna?' [what happened to the qualification norms?]; Sundby, *Om normer* [on norms], pp. 34–37, 77–117; Eckhoff/ Sundby, *Rettssystemer* [legal systems], 1st ed. pp. 84–93; 2nd ed. pp. 50, 53–54, 100–07; *Rechtssysteme*, pp. 46, 49–50, 85–89; Peczenik, *Rättsnormer* [legal norms], pp. 26–32. – Even though custom-based definitions have a qualification modality, they are not automatically qualification norms in the terminology of the said writers; see Eng, *U/enighetsanalyse – med særlig sikte på jus og allmenn rettsteori* [analysis of dis/ agreement – with particular reference to law and legal theory], pp. 117–19.

81 Compare Sundby, *Om normer* [on norms], pp. 105–07 ("a completely general concept of 'category membership' "; "duty norms provide criteria for what is to count as mandatory etc. .... a special instance under a broader concept of 'qualification norm' "); p. 80 ("the competence norms ... serve as ... a model for the other qualification norms"). Correspondingly Eckhoff/ Sundby, *Rettssystemer* [legal systems], 1st ed. pp. 91–92; 2nd ed. pp. 100–01 ("all norms could thus be characterised as qualification norms"); Peczenik, *Vad är rätt?* [what is law?], pp. 440, 684. See also Weber, 'R. Stammlers "Überwindung" der materialistischen Geschichtsauffassung', pp. 340 ("solche Vorgänge, welche, vom Gesichtspunkt einer ... "Skatregel" ... aus gesehen, als relevant gelten, charakterisieren uns einen Komplex von Hantierungen als "Skatspiel"" (Weber's italics omitted); "Dienst des Normbegriffs bei der Klassifikation und Objekt-Abgrenzung"), 342, 351; Kelsen, *Reine Rechtslehre*, 1st ed. pp. 4–5(7); 2nd ed. pp. 3–4 ("die Norm als Deutungsschema"); Goffman, *Stigma*, p. 15 ("By definition ... we believe the person with a stigma is not quite human") taken together with the work in its entirety (this shows how many norms also touch on and run together in a socially mediated definition of 'normal person').

82 See sections 3.3.1 above and 3.3.6 below, on these types of modality in the case of stipulated definitions. – In his (otherwise inspiring and informative) discussion of qualification norms, Sundby does not in my opinion distinguish sufficiently clearly between the question of the concept of 'qualification norm' and the question of whether the aspects the concept brings out are of interest (see *Om normer* [on norms], Chapter 4, e.g. pp. 99–114), with the consequence that both questions seem more obscure than necessary. As I understand it, the essentials are that the concept of 'qualification norm' has a very wide area of application (see the preceding note); that the concept in many instances points to an aspect that is of interest; but that the latter area is considerably smaller than the first (see e.g. the main text between the preceding note and the present one).

necessary to command the child to adopt the usage that is customarily correct (see section 3.3.1 (3) above on heteronomous defining competence).

Perhaps one might lay down qualification modality as a *criterion* in the concept of 'custom-based definition' *without* losing any of the definitions that otherwise fall under this concept. The definition via the criterion 'mode of coming into being' that was given by way of introduction above, seems, however, to provide an adequate delimitation of the phenomena I wish to collect and to contrast with stipulated definitions. My keeping the concept open in the modality dimension is therefore more to simplify the concept than because I expect to find examples of customary definitions with duty modality.

(2) The relationship to the fundamental concept of 'definition'

It is not usual to subsume the normative structures I call "custom-based definitions" under concepts of 'definition'.

For example Robinson, *Definition*, and Næss, *Interpretation and Preciseness*, determine the concept of 'normative definition' in such a way that it only covers stipulated definitions. In Robinson this happens through his definitionally determining normative definitions as "explicit and selfconscious" (p. 59) and "deliberate [and] arbitrary" (p. 60). Næss says in its consequences the same by definitionally determining normative definitions as a type of sentence (p. 147). – See also the incomplete pictures of definition phenomena, including the role of custom-based definitions, that can be the result when one approaches analysis and argumentation formulated in everyday language from and through certain fundamental philosophical viewpoints: see section 1 (4) above on Popper and section G 2 below on Quine.

The *main reason* I bring in custom-based definitions is that the stipulated definitions alone give a very incomplete picture of the normative structures we comply with in our own language or invoke when analysing and evaluating the language of others: *It is custom-based definitions we mainly build on when we communicate.*

I have earlier defined the *fundamental concept of 'definition'* as "*propositions* that contribute to determining the meanings of linguistic entities (contribute to determining concepts)" (section A 2 (1) above). – My subsuming custom-based definitions under the concept of 'definition' means that I am using the word "proposition" in a *broad* sense: not only of the meaning content in explicit linguistic formulations, but also of cognitive perceptions and normative attitudes that we *have not formulated,* or of which we *are not even conscious* (section A 2 (1) above, concluding remarks).

(3) Person criteria and situation criteria (a). The constitutive role of custom-based definitions (b)

(a) The *person criterion* in custom-based definitions may be completely or almost unlimited, that is to say that the definitions are common to all or most languages; cf. for example the structurings we express in English by "I", "you", "this", "here", "there", "now", "then", "and", "or", "not". – In other cases the person criterion is more limited, a symptom that the definition is linked to varying social and cultural interests; cf. for example Eskimos' more nuanced concepts of the phenomenon that we speak of undifferentiatedly as "snow".[83]

Whether the person criterion is broad or narrow, the *situation criteria* are often broad or seemingly unlimited. We see this not only in the case of such determinations of person, place and time, and such joining words, as just mentioned, but also in the case of words for the things of everyday life, such as "chair", "table", "cup", and the like. Here we see a contrast with the situation criteria of many stipulated definitions in academic subjects ("this book/ conversation", "this lecture", "this academic context"; see section 3.3.1 (5) above).

(b) The custom-based definitions confront the individual as *given* entities. They *make it possible* for the individual to communicate. Or, the other way round: They *set limits* to what the individual can communicate as long as the individual does not create other definitions. For example, they set limits to what aspects of the things one can factually speak about; and thus limits to what characterisations one can put forward; and thus limits to what truths one can purely factually cognise and what normative propositions one can purely factually assert.[84] – For example, Eskimos with their nuanced concepts of snow and types of snow can speak about *aspects of the phenomenon of snow* that we cannot speak about in our everyday language, and thus cognise truths concerning the phenomenon that we cannot cognise. Or, with respect to the same individual: A law student acquires during his course of study a new set of custom-based definitions, the legal language tradition. Thus, on completion of his studies, he can speak about and cognise *aspects of social phenomena* that he could not have been aware of at the beginning of his course of study.

With a view to the constitutive role custom-based definitions play, it gives more correct proportions to seek examples of linguistic entities *without*, than with, a customarily established meaning. – The *feature in common* of linguistic entities without or with little customarily established meaning is that for one

83 Whorf, *Language, Thought, and Reality*, p. 216; Lyons, *Language and Linguistics*, pp. 306, 311. The word "interest" I use in a broad sense, compare Geertz, 'Common Sense as a Cultural System', p. 88: "In an environment populated with conifers, or snakes, or leaf-eating bats it is practical to know a good deal about conifers, snakes, or leaf-eating bats, whether or not what one knows is in any strict sense materially useful, because it is of such knowledge that "practicalness" is there composed."

84 Mead, *Mind, Self, and Society*, pp. 77–80, 129–33; Whorf, *Language, Thought, and Reality*, in particular pp. 207–20, 233–45, 246–70; Lyons, *Language and Linguistics*, pp. 303–24.

reason or another they are *unfamiliar*. This feature is partly a matter of degree and partly relative to what language group one is speaking about:

Unfamiliar linguistic entities can be words and expressions which are little used in everyday life and which have not (yet) established themselves in academic, scientific or philosophical contexts. Examples are the word "retningslinje" [guideline] before Sundby defined it,[85] or the expression "dispositivt utsagn" [dispositive proposition] before Arnholm defined it.[86]

Or unfamiliar linguistic entities can be foreign words and expressions. Examples in relation to English are the Norwegian word and the Norwegian expression just mentioned, or in relation to English and Norwegian, the Swedish word "tumregel" [rule of thumb] as Jareborg introduces it (together with "dogmatisk regel" [dogmatic rule]), as an alternative to the word "retningslinje".[87]

Or unfamiliar linguistic entities can be linguistic entities that the definer himself invents or puts together. Examples are the Norwegian expression "relevans- og vektnormer" [relevance and weight norms] used of the norms Sundby designated "retningslinjer",[88] or the Norwegian word "tvilsrisikoen" [the bearing of the risk of doubt] used of what one otherwise designates "(den objektive) bevisbyrde" [the burden of proof].[89]

3.3.3. Hybrid forms of and interplay between stipulations and customs

(1) Hybrid forms
(2) Counteraction and co-action in actually occurring communication
(3) As ingredients in the ways philosophers proceed

(1) Hybrid forms

One hybrid form of custom-based and stipulated definitions arises when *custom-based definitions are codified*: as when private or public language councils collect data on the use of language, revise the data according to superordinate principles that are considered to be *worthy of recommendation*, and publish the resulting systems of the use of language in dictionaries;[90] or as when dictionaries are laid down as content in *duty norms*.[91]

---

85 Sundby, *Om normer* [on norms], Part 2.

86 Arnholm, 'Omkring rettshandelsteorien' [concerning the theory of juristic acts], in particular pp. 410–12.

87 Jareborg, 'Regler och riktlinjer – en replik' [rules and guidelines – a rejoinder], p. 440; cf. 'Regler och riktlinjer' [rules and guidelines], pp. 388–89 including note 4, 396–97, 407–08, 409.

88 Eng, 'Sondringen mellom regler og retningslinjer' [the distinction between rules and guidelines], pp. 476, cf. 482.

89 Eckhoff, *Tvilsrisikoen* [the bearing of the risk of doubt], in particular pp. 14–21.

90 Concerning the general use of language, see e.g. Bokmålsordboka [dictionary of the Bokmål form of Norwegian] and Nynorskordboka [dictionary of the Nynorsk form of Norwegian] produced by the Department of Norwegian Lexicography (now the Section for Lexicography) at the University of Oslo

Another hybrid form arises when the *courts decide how a particular formulation of a legal rule is to be understood.* Directly the decision binds only the parties to the case. However, through the unwritten principles constituting judgments as a source of law, the decision has the "force of precedent", i.e. an effect beyond the individual case. The general legal norms to which judgments thus give rise, appear as *something between* on the one hand explicitly stipulated general norms with authoritative wording, as statutes are an example of; and on the other hand customs. In so far as general legal norms are concerned, one may in the light of this speak of a *"semi-competence"* for the courts and of *"semi-stipulations"* on their part.

Propositions in the travaux préparatoires of statutes represent a corresponding intermediate form: The authors of travaux préparatoires do not have the competence to stipulate general norms explicitly, at the same time as it is clear that statements in the travaux préparatoires are ascribed weight in the determination of the content of the rules of statute law. As in the case of judgments it is, however, systematically undetermined what text units will be ascribed weight, and in the event, in what way.[92]

(2) Counteraction and co-action in actually occurring communication

The psychological difficulty of keeping to *new stipulated* definitions indicates the *weight of the customary* element. – One can point to certain *factors* that are typically of significance for the possibility of getting the recipient to go along with a revision of custom-based use of language:

The more *unfamiliar* the linguistic entity being defined is (section 3.3.2 (3) above), the less any associations with the custom-based definitions will get in the way: It is, for example, easier to communicate a stipulated meaning content for the word "retningslinje" [guideline] than for the word "regel" [rule].

In the case of linguistic entities that are not markedly technical, the more *limited* the *situation specification* of the definition is, the easier it is to bring about successful communication: If one gives a commonly used word a new meaning

---

and the Norwegian Language Council. – Concerning particular areas of the use of language, see e.g. dictionaries from the Norwegian Council for Technical Terminology, established in 1938 for the purpose of "working for clarity, unambiguity and uniformity in Norwegian technical terminology"; see Lydersen/ Dahlø, 'Refleksjoner over arbeid med teknisk terminologi' [reflections on work on technical terminology], p. 97.

91 For some general information on duty norms from the Government, the ministries and the Norwegian Language Council, see *St.meld. No. 100 1980–81* [report to the Storting], pp. 4–5. As an example, see the same report, pp. 6–7 with appendices, cf. *S.tid. 1980–81* [reports of parliamentary proceedings], pp. 3772–91, with the consent of the Storting [national assembly] to the proposed duty norms concerning use of language in school textbooks and in the Civil Service.

92 On semi-stipulation through travaux préparatoires and judgments, see Eckhoff/ Sundby, *Rettssystemer* [legal systems], 1st ed. pp. 221–23; 2nd ed. pp. 173–76; *Rechtssysteme*, pp. 146–48. See also Sundby, *Om normer* [on norms], p. 351.

content, the probability that the recipient keeps to (remembers) the definition will be greater where the definition is laid down as applying for a lecture or an article than where the definition is laid down as applying for a thick book.

Words like *"law", "right", "power", "rationality"* and *"reality"* are examples of words that often give rise to unsuccessful communication in the way outlined: Different writers often stipulate different definitions of these words. And often they construct major theories around precisely these definitions. At the same time these words have their *custom-based* and *elusive* meanings. Thus there is a great risk that the reader will interpret these theories on the basis of his preferences among the custom-based meaning variants.

As an *example* we can look at Olivecrona's statements that right and duty do not exist, but are simply an illusion, for example "pure imagination without correspondence in objective reality".[93] – Intuitively it may be tempting to brush aside his propositions as nonsense. However, if one takes as a basis Olivecrona's definitions of "right", "duty" and "exist", then his propositions are not unreasonable, but relate to a real problem. And taking his definitions as a basis will not be arbitrary in relation to custom-based definitions:

- He first demonstrates how we *cannot* reduce the custom-based meanings of "right", "duty" and "binding" to sanctions, feelings of being bound, or other empirically existing phenomena, and how these words customarily understood on the contrary presuppose and refer to a specific validity that is independent of what exists empirically.[94]
- He then presupposes in a number of instances a use of language according to which words like "fact", "existence", "reality", and the like, are *only* used of empirically existing phenomena.

Seen in isolation both these steps in his argumentation are probably in good conformity with widely held views. Together, however, they of logical necessity result in the formulation: "Right and duty do not exist."

Olivecrona's analysis thus clarifies a dilemma and an ambivalence in widely held views.

(3) As ingredients in the ways philosophers proceed

Analyses that go under the name of "analytical philosophy" may be grouped according to *how* and to what *degree* the analyses build on custom-based definitions or stipulated definitions.

(a) *Everyday language philosophy* in a broad sense ("ordinary language philosophy", large areas of "speech act theory") justifies itself, as a direction of its own in philosophy, with the custom-based definitions: Criteria for the tenability of its own propositions are taken from "what we can say and what we cannot say". And

93 Olivecrona, *Law as Fact*, 1st ed. p. 77.

94 Op. cit., pp. 9–17(12–15).

the criteria for this again, are taken from the normative *intuitions* about the meanings of words that the custom-based definitions give rise to. – This applies for example to (the later) Wittgenstein,[95] Austin,[96] Ryle,[97] Searle[98] and Hare.[99]

The present work builds to a great extent on the same foundation: The critically reflexive form in actually occurring language and argumentation that is the topic of the work, I have access to and knowledge of first and foremost by virtue of being a participant in the language and argumentation *practice* "we all" (all normally competent language users) participate *in.* Another matter is the fact that the interests that motivated the present work led to another theoretical perspective on and thereby other *conceptualisations of* language and argumentation than those found in the writers just mentioned (Chapter I above).

(b) Others are less interested in the information that can be obtained from intuitions to which custom-based definitions give rise. They consider this information uncertain, incomplete or irrelevant.

(i) One approach upholds the relevance of custom-based definitions to philosophical questions, but wants to replace intuitions about the customary meanings of words by *scientific investigations of actual use of language.*[100] With this point of departure Næss founded "empirical semantics". He inspired a number of others

---

95 Wittgenstein, *Philosophische Untersuchungen*, e.g. Part I, sections 109, 122–33. – "Die Philosophie darf den tatsächlichen Gebrauch der Sprache in keiner Weise antasten, sie kan ihn am Ende also nur beschreiben. Denn sie kann ihn auch nicht begründen. Sie läßt alles, wie es ist" (section 124).

96 Austin, 'A Plea for Excuses', pp. 129–34. – "[W]e are to proceed from 'ordinary language', that is, by examining what we should say when, and so why and what we should mean by it" (p. 129; Austin's italics omitted). "[O]rdinary language is not the last word: in principle it can everywhere be supplemented and improved upon and superseded. Only remember, it is the first word" (p. 133; Austin's italics omitted). – Correspondingly in *Sense and Sensibilia*, p. 63. See also *How to do Things with Words*, p. 122.

97 Ryle, 'Ordinary Language', passim. – "Philosophers often have to try to describe the stock ... manner ... of employing an expression. ... [This] does not require and is not usually helped by information about the prevalence or unprevalence of this way of employing it. For the philosopher, like other folk, has long since learned how to employ or handle it, and what he is trying to describe is what he himself has learned" (p. 310). – Correspondingly in 'Philosophical Arguments', p. 210.

98 Searle, *Speech Acts*, pp. 12–15. – "By reflecting on linguistic elements I can offer linguistic characterizations which do not record particular utterances but have a general character, deriving from the fact that the elements are governed by rules. The 'justification' I have for my linguistic intuitions as expressed in my linguistic characterizations is simply that I am a native speaker of a certain dialect of English and consequently have mastered the rules of that dialect ..." (p. 13).

99 Hare, *Moral Thinking*, pp. 8–10, 115–16. – "How ... do we establish that any word has any logical property? ... [W]e can tell when people are contradicting themselves because we know the language they are speaking. ... [T]here are linguistic 'intuitions', and the disciplines of logic and linguistics rely on them" (pp. 8–9; Hare's italics omitted).

100 Næss, *Interpretation and Preciseness*, Foreword and Introduction. – "Very roughly, one may distinguish a deductive, an intuitionistic and an empirical component in the writings of analytical philosophers. ... If empirical studies are neglected, we shall see much intelligent debate along intuitionistic lines, but less of that process which many of us find so inspiring in the history of philosophy and science: the development of new branches of reliable knowledge as a result of combined philosophical and scientific efforts" (p. X).

to adopt a corresponding approach; one speaks of the "Oslo School" in analytical philosophy.[101]

> The philosophical relevance of empirical semantics is disputed.[102] In his early works Næss seems to see connection with science qua cumulative knowledge, as a sufficient criterion of relevance.[103] In later works he emphasises that the question of relevance is complicated.[104] – The main merit of Næss' empirical semantics is in my view the critically reflexive stimulus: the fact that it takes seriously propositions that purport to be empirical (propositions with reference to "ordinary language", "everyday speech", and so forth), by carrying out investigations for checking these propositions (for example for checking propositions about the meaning of the word "truth"), and thus forces the producers of such propositions (for example the producers of "theories of truth") to reflect on the basis and status of their propositions. I am, however, not so sceptical as Næss (in his early works) of the information about linguistic meaning that the individual by virtue of being a language user can obtain from his intuitions; cf. the intersubjective character of the custom-based definitions that give rise to these intuitions.[105]

(ii) Another approach places less weight on custom-based definitions and greater weight on *stipulated definitions and formalisation*, with the particular aim that the conceptual apparatuses shall illuminate and assist scientific theories, especially in the natural sciences, and logic/ mathematics. This applies for example to many of the participants in the "Vienna Circle", in the international school of thought the circle gave rise to ("logical positivism"), and in subsequent offshoots from it.[106]

---

[101] Gullvåg, 'Arne Næss og Oslo-skolen i norsk filosofi' [Arne Næss and the Oslo School in Norwegian Philosophy], pp. 110–13, 115–19. Næss' main work in empirical semantics is *Interpretation and Preciseness* (1953). In the foreword he provides a survey of central works from the Oslo School.

[102] See e.g. Jareborg, *Begrepp och brottbeskrivning* [concepts and the description of criminal offences], p. 21.

[103] Næss, *"Truth" as Conceived by Those who are not Professional Philosophers*, p. 174: "Partial solutions, working hypotheses or discussions of "minor" problems ... are worthy: they can be formulated so as to be controllable and there can be hope to verify them by means of prosaic methods. The necessary foundation for progress is thus provided."

[104] Næss, *An Empirical Study of the Expressions "True", "Perfectly Certain" and "Extremely Probable"*, p. 37.

[105] On this intersubjective character, see section 3.3.2 (3) above, with further references; second paragraph of the present item (3), with further references; Cavell, 'Must We Mean What We Say?', pp. 4–8, 12 et seq., 32 et seq.

[106] Carnap, 'Intellectual Biography', pp. 28 et seq.; Feigl, 'The Wiener Kreis in America', pp. 639, 648–49, 658; Ayer, 'Logical Positivism, Editor's Introduction', pp. 7–8. – I shall later, as a step in my treatment of criteria that are used in the setting up of and choice between normative definitions, give an account of the logical positivists' emphasis on operationalisability as a criterion, including their use of persuasive definitions of words like "meaning" and "science" to promote the criterion (sections 7.3.2 (3) cf. III 2.2.2 (3), below). – Further, as a step in the establishment of the concept of an actually occurring pattern of analysis, I shall give an account of the mode of definition Carnap calls "explication", and which he formed with a view to developed conceptual systems in natural science and logic/ mathematics (section V 3.3.1 (2)(c) below).

(c) Common to the approaches mentioned in items (a)–(b) is their essential reliance on a distinction between *linguistic meaning*, on the one hand, and other sources of knowledge, on the other. A further approach in analytical philosophy is characterised by its *rejection* of this distinction.[107] The fundamental argumentation for such "logical nihilism" and "holism" has been formulated by Quine. The present work, however, does build on this distinction.[108]

3.3.4. Normative-traditional and normative-innovative definitions

The concept of 'normative definition' says nothing about the relationship to other language usage. In particular: That a definition is normative does not mean that it departs from the way in which language is actually used. – All according to whether a normative definition *keeps to* or *departs from* a given language usage, I shall designate the definition respectively *"normative-traditional"* and *"normative-innovative"*.

Custom-based definitions are by definition normative-traditional in relation to established language usage.

In the case of *stipulated* definitions it is an empirical question whether the definition is normative-traditional or normative-innovative, in relation to established or any other language usage with which a comparison is made.

I shall content myself here with drawing attention to the main relationships mentioned. The more detailed analysis and use of the concepts of 'normative-traditional' and 'normative-innovative' I shall postpone until the concept of 'definition' has been broken down into the relevant elements (section 4.3.3 cf. sections 4.1–4.2, below).

> More unreflectingly many seem to use "normative definition" (or other names for definitions with normative modality; see section 3.1 (2) above) synonymously with what I designate "normative-innovative definition". I consider, however, that such terminology cannot stand up to closer reflection, but must give way to "normative definition" as a common term for what I designate "normative-traditional" and "normative-innovative" definitions (section 4.3.3 cf. sections 4.1–4.2, below).[109]
>
> In the light of this, categorising a definition as 'normative' *may* be less interesting than one immediately supposes, namely in so far as one is first and foremost interested in the relationship to other language usage.

---

107 Davidson, 'A Nice Derangement of Epitaphs', p. 446: "[T]here is no such thing as a language ... We must give up the idea of a clearly defined shared structure which language-users acquire and then apply to cases"; quoted, with concurrence, by Rorty, 'Two Retrospective Essays', p. 373.

108 See section G below, where I situate the present work in relation to Quine's critique.

109 Differently in Andersson/ Furberg, *Språk och påverkan* [language and influencing], pp. 163–65; Peczenik, *Vad är rätt?* [what is law?], pp. 150 (bottom)–151 (top).

3.3.5. Normative definitions and family resemblance

The unity between phenomena we designate with the same words and expressions may consist in *family resemblance* (section 3.2.2 (3)(b) cf. (5)(b), above). In mapping the relationship between normative definitions and family resemblance one ought to distinguish between custom-based definitions and stipulated definitions.

Among actually occurring *custom-based* definitions one can find definitions which both have (may be understood and expressed in) the form of pure connotation specification[110] and prescribe family resemblance, cf. use of words according to such partial and overlapping resemblances between phenomena as illustrated earlier (section 3.2.2 (3)–(5) above).

Among actually occurring *stipulated* definitions it is unusual to find definitions which are both given the form of *pure connotation specification* and according to *their content* prescribe family resemblance. The reason is probably that family resemblance is perceived as an indeterminacy which ought to be avoided, or which one at any rate does not need. This applies particularly in scientific contexts, but also otherwise. To the extent that, according to their content, stipulated definitions in the form of pure connotation specification relate to family resemblance, it is therefore most often in order to *counteract* family resemblance.

The need for counteracting family resemblance through stipulated definition will typically be perceived to be *stronger, the stronger the family resemblance is.* For example, a writer who wants to use the Norwegian word "rett" or the German word "Recht" in the sense of 'the law as it is found in the positive sources of law' will, in order to avoid misunderstandings, perhaps find it necessary to draw boundaries with rights and with natural law, but hardly necessary to draw a boundary with the sense 'straight' as in "vannrett linje"/ "waagerechte Linie" [horizontal line].

For a stipulated definition to be able to achieve the purpose of removing family resemblance, the definition must establish a *condition concept*: One specifies that one will use the word only of a part of the family resemblance area, and this part is specified by means of necessary conditions or exhaustive and surveyable sufficient conditions for use of the word (section 3.2.2 (5)(d) above). One specifies, for example, that one intends to use the word "law" of abstract law, and "abstract law" is then defined as the system of general norms applied by the courts.

Something else than the unusualness of cases in which, according to their content, stipulated definitions in the form of pure connotation specification prescribe family resemblance, is that the *practising* of stipulated definitions in the form of pure connotation specification without family resemblance structure can *result in* family resemblance: A stipulated definition can no more than a custom-based definition provide answers to all questions of delimitation that in practice crop up.

---

110 On the concepts of 'connotation specification' and 'denotation specification', see section A 4 above. The definitions given there should be adequate here. The main discussion of the two modes of definition and their interplay will be presented in section 5 below.

And the answers which the individual language user chooses over time, or which different language users choose independently of one another, may in the course of time turn out to establish a family resemblance pattern.

That the practising of the stipulated definition may lead to family resemblance applies to an even greater extent if the stipulated definition only, or also, takes the form of *denotation specification* that calls for *comparison*. An important variant is specification of a paradigmatic object of comparison: "*This* is what I mean by a human being!", combined, as the case may be, with a more or less informative connotation specification: "These and other beings with whom we can talk are human beings!" (section 5.4.1(1) below).

3.3.6. Statutory definitions

(1) Concept
(2) Modalities and norm subjects
(3) The specification of situation
(4) The action theme

(1) Concept

By "statutory definition" I mean a *stipulated* definition (section 3.3.1 above) in *statutory form* (in the broad sense of "statutory", which covers inter alia (in practice most important) constitutions, statutes and regulations).

The fact that a definition is stipulated in statutory form means in practice that its specifications of person and situation are *general*, in the sense that they cover more than an individual instance of language use (items (2)–(3) below).

Most often it is clear *when* the wording of a statute can be read as a definition; it will be clear through the occurrence of the word "definition" (or its equivalent in other languages),[111] or through the text otherwise, for example "[m]ed "forbrukerkjøp" menes ["consumer purchase" means] ...".[112] – In some instances, however, the interpretation of the wording as a definition may require conscious reflection. This applies inter alia when the statute formulates a rule and at some distance from this formulation says something about "what the world is like". For example, section 4–2, first and second paragraphs, of the Estate Agency Act (Act No. 53 of 16 June 1989) ties the estate agent's entitlement to commission to whether any transaction has come into being. And in the fourth paragraph it says: "A transaction has come into being when the parties are finally bound." If one goes to the travaux préparatoires, one gets confirmation that the fourth paragraph

[111] E.g. section 2 of the Public Administration Act (10 February 1967).

[112] Section 4, second paragraph, of the Sale of Goods Act (Act No. 27 of 13 May 1988). – Here and in other discussions of this example in what follows, I speak of "consumer purchase", since this is the literal translation of the term in the Norwegian statute and since the perspective of the present work is primarily linguistic and philosophical, not legal. In a great deal of recent Anglo-American law the term "consumer sale" would be more likely.

is meant to be a definition of the expression "a transaction has come into being".[113] – The wording of a statute may *mistakenly* suggest a definition. For example, the second part of the Criminal Procedure Act (Act No. 25 of 22 May 1981) has the heading "[p]artene" [the parties] and contains the chapter headings "[p]åtalemyndigheten" [the prosecuting authority], "[p]åtalen" [prosecution], "[s]iktede" [the person charged], "[f]orsvareren" [defence counsel] and "[f]ornærmedes rett til advokat" [the aggrieved person's right to an advocate]. At first glance it is therefore tempting to assume that all four categories of person mentioned are to be considered as parties within the meaning of the Act. It is, however, clear that the defence counsel is never, and the aggrieved person is most often not, to be considered a party within the meaning of the Act,[114] i.e. the set of headings quoted does not express a statutory definition.

The wording of a statute can communicate a definition through *presupposition.* For example, section 48, first paragraph, of the Inheritance Act (Act No. 5 of 3 March 1972) states: "Any person who has reached the age of 18 years may by last will and testament determine what shall be done with what he leaves when he dies." – Explicitly this wording communicates a competence norm. At the same time the wording communicates through presupposition a definition of the key concept of 'dispositio mortis causa' (beside "dødsdisposisjon" [mortis causa disposition] often called "testamentarisk disposisjon" [testamentary disposition] or "materielt testament" [material testament]), namely that the concept is delimited through the criterion 'to determine what shall be done with what one leaves when one dies'.[115] Such communication of a definition through presupposition may provide useful information and is thus important to be aware of. However, the instances of a definition through presupposition play a less important role than the instances in which a definition is the only or the central proposition that the wording of the statute communicates, cf. the examples at and in notes 111–113 above. In the present work I therefore restrict myself to the latter-mentioned instances of statutory definition.

(2) Modalities and norm subjects

Statutory definitions have a *promise* aspect, in so far as it is natural to read statutory definitions as meaning that the legislators[116] promise to use the word defined

[113] *NOU 1987: 14* [Norwegian official reports], Eiendomsmegling [estate agency], p. 83, cf. *Ot.prp. No. 59 1988–89* [proposal from the Government], p. 48. – Other examples of the same definition technique are to be found inter alia in section 8 of the Copyright Act (Act No. 2 of 12 May 1961) ("a literary, scientific or artistic work is issued when ...", "a literary, scientific or artistic work is published when ..."); sections 13–16 of the Sale of Goods Act (Act No. 27 of 13 May 1988) ("the bearing of the risk passes/ does not pass to the purchaser when ...").

[114] Andenæs, *Norsk straffeprosess* [Norwegian criminal procedure], Vol. 1, pp. 69, 83, 85.

[115] Arnholm, *Arveretten* [law of succession], p. 107; Augdahl/ Hambro, *Arveloven med kommentarer* [the Inheritance Act with commentary], p. 172.

[116] In the case of all constitutions and statutes, and in the case of most regulations, a number of people are involved in the drafting of the text and its passing into law.

in the meaning defined throughout the statute otherwise (or, as the case may be, throughout a narrower or broader area of text to which the definition states that it applies). – This promise aspect holds good in relation to everybody who reads the statute, irrespective of whether any of the other normative modalities apply.

Further, I consider that statutory definitions have a *command* aspect, and that this is so in several relations. First, statutory definitions have a command aspect in relation to public servants who are obliged to apply the law, in practice particularly judges and civil servants. Secondly, statutory definitions have a command aspect in relation to citizens who are subjects in duty norms to which the statutory definitions link themselves. This applies particularly in so far as any breach of the norms is punishable, gives rise to liability in tort, or leads to other sanctions; cf. the fact that ignorance of the law, including ignorance of the existence or content of the definition, does not as a general rule exempt any person from sanctions. Thirdly, statutory definitions have a command aspect in relation to advocates or others providing legal support, who in return for payment or on any other basis of duty make statements about what the law is or give advice that presupposes insight into what the law is.

In addition to the aspects of promise and command comes an *end-means* aspect: If one wishes to understand the statute, then one must take the word defined in the meaning defined. – This factual aspect holds good in relation to everybody who reads the statute, irrespective of whether any of the normative modalities apply.

Furthermore, I consider that statutory definitions have an aspect of *recommendation* in relation to the subjects in in/validity norms to which the definitions link themselves.[117] If these subjects, for example those entering into contracts, do not know the relevant definitions, then there is a danger that the validity norms will be broken, so that the stipulated norm is considered invalid. Since breach of validity norms is not in itself prohibited,[118] the concept of 'duty' is not applicable here; and since a statute is considered to do more than provide information about factual end-means relationships, the descriptive modality does not seem to be fully adequate. The concept of 'recommendation' captures the further modality aspect here.[119]

---

117 On in/validity norms, see Eng, 'Begrepene 'kompetanse' og 'gyldighet' i juridisk argumentasjon' [the concepts of 'competence' and 'validity' in legal argumentation], pp. 653–64.

118 Prohibition may, however, result from supplementary regulation in the duty dimension, see Eng, 'Begrepene 'kompetanse' og 'gyldighet' i juridisk argumentasjon' [the concepts of 'competence' and 'validity' in legal argumentation], pp. 658, 664.

119 Sundby, *Om normer* [on norms], sees statutory definitions as propositions with qualification modality (pp. 115 and 344). Concerning this modality I refer to section 3.3.2 (1) above. As mentioned there, I agree that qualification modality is one aspect of stipulated definitions, but consider that the recommendation, promise, command/ prohibition and end-means aspects are of greater interest in the case of such definitions.

(3) The specification of situation

Most statutory definitions determine their situation area *explicitly*, typically by means of the formulation "In this Act "x" means ...".[120] – If this is not done,[121] one can fall back on two quite weighty guidelines for *filling the gap*. First, the definition applies in relation to all provisions in the statute concerned in which the defined linguistic expression occurs, i.e. there is prima facie no question of relativising the meaning of the expression.[122] Secondly, the definition does not apply in relation to the texts of other statutes or in relation to formulations in non-statute law, in which the same linguistic expression occurs.[123]

In lawyers' language and argumentation the first guideline is crossed by the following relationship and consideration: The more extensive the situation specification of the definition is, the more strongly one will experience a need to relativise the definition; for the more extensive the situation specification of the definition is, the greater the probability that one will meet individual instances with respect to which the application of the concept determination provided in the definition is deemed to be poorly justified.[124]

(4) The action theme

The action theme of statutory definitions has certain *distinctive features* in relation to other definitions formulated in everyday language. Since these features can only be explained as elements in the following discussion of the action theme of definitions, I shall here content myself here with mentioning them: Statutory definitions use to a great extent word terminology (in contrast to concept terminology); they have to a great extent a total (in contrast to partial) naming function; they have a high frequency of denotation specification (in contrast to connotation specification); and they are often inventorial and extensive. – For more detail on these distinctive features see sections 4.2 (4)(f) cf. (a)–(e), and 5.4.2 (2), below.

---

120 See e.g. section 2 of the Public Administration Act (10 February 1967).

121 See e.g. section 4, second paragraph, of the Sale of Goods Act (Act No. 27 of 13 May 1988).

122 Eckhoff/ Smith, *Forvaltningsrett* [administrative law], p. 471.

123 Eckhoff, *Rettskildelære* [doctrine of the sources of law], 1st ed. p. 86.

124 Sometimes a need for relativising is stated explicitly; e.g. in Frihagen, *Forvaltningsloven – kommentarutgave* [the Public Administration Act – a commentary], Vol. 1, p. 64, in relation to the definition of "part" [party] in section 2 (e) of the Public Administration Act (10 February 1967). More often such a need shows itself by presupposition; e.g. in Eckhoff's use of the definition of "enkeltvedtak" [individual decision] in section 2(b) cf. (a) of the Public Administration Act, when on the one hand he claims that contracts concerning the exercise of public authority are individual decisions, see Eckhoff, *Forvaltningsrett* [administrative law], 4th ed. pp. 483–84, and on the other hand claims that the reversal rules in section 35 of the Public Administration Act, which undoubtedly apply to individual decisions, do not apply to such contracts, see op. cit. same ed. p. 551.

3.4. The distinction dimensions in what follows (sections 4–6) are (also) means for stating more precisely the area of application of the distinction between descriptivity and normativity in the case of definitions

The distinction between descriptive and normative definitions was discussed above under the heading *"Modality of definitions I"*. In the course of this discussion something was said about what is being defined (definition objects) and in what manner (definition means).[125] But in the main I have presupposed intuitive understanding on these points, in that I have linked my discussion to the fundamental concept of 'definition'.

To gain insight into what there is dis/agreement about, it is, however, often necessary to see the concept of 'definition' as an intermediate station for thought, in the sense that one sees that and in what manner this concept ought to be made more precise in relation to a multiplicity of objects and means.

As, in the light of this, I turn in what follows to a discussion of the questions of what is being defined (section 4 below) and in what manner (sections 5–6 below), the result is *also* – viewed in the perspective of the present section 3 – new means for stating more precisely the area of application of the distinction between descriptivity and normativity in the case of definitions. For a closer focus on this aspect I shall by way of conclusion in the presentation of my definition theory return to the modality theme, in a *"Modality of definitions II"* (section 8 below).

---

125 See e.g. section 3.2.2 above, on the presupposed concept of 'concept'.

4. The propositional content of definitions: What is being defined

In section 3 above I drew a distinction between the modality of definitions and the propositional content of definitions (section 3.1 (3) cf. (1)). Further I divided the propositional content into person specification, situation specification and action theme (section 3.1 (3)). The emphasis in the discussions in section 3 was placed on the modality. – In what follows I shall look at the propositional content of definitions, or more specifically, at a question concerning the action theme of definitions: the question of *what* is being defined. To shed light on this question, I draw a distinction between the structuring function of definitions (section 4.1) and the naming function of definitions (section 4.2).

4.1. The structuring function of definitions. More on the presupposed concept of 'concept'

(1) The concept of 'the structuring function of definitions'. Terminology
(2) To what extent is it logically (by definition) necessary that a definition structures?
(1)↔(2) In the conceptual framework here the concepts of 'definition' and 'concept' will mutually imply each other. The relationship to other conceptual frameworks
(3) I do not lay down determinacy as a definitional criterion in the case of my concepts of 'definition' or 'concept'
- **(a) Why I do not lay down determinacy as a definitional criterion**
  - **(i) The descriptive purpose of my definition theory**
  - **(ii) My desire to avoid persuasive definitions**
  - **(i)↔(ii) Why the considerations now mentioned have not won through in the thinking on definitions**
- **(b) What requirements for determinacy it is possible to lay down**

(4) Empirical and non-empirical concepts
(5) To what extent is the concept of 'concept' now presented (items (1)–(3) above) empirical or non-empirical (item (4) above)?
(6) The concept of 'concept' as an auxiliary concept in my definition theory. Summary of some aspects of my concept of 'concept' and the corresponding sides of my concept of 'definition'

(1) The concept of 'the structuring function of definitions'. Terminology

(a) I should briefly remind the reader of the concept of *'the structuring function of definitions'* (section A 3 above). This covers delimitation in thought of areas: partly the activity of dividing the world up in thought and partly the result that the world is divided up in thought. – I use the word *"concept"* of those, and only those, areas-in-thought that are thus the result of definitions.

The structuring function of definitions may be *descriptive* or *normative* – all according to whether the definition says something about how an area is delimited, or something about how an area should or shall (or other normative types of modality) be delimited (item 4.3.2 below).

In what follows I shall *go more deeply into the concept of* 'the structuring function of definitions' (items (b)–(c)). By way of conclusion I shall give a summary and lay down a *terminology* (item (d)).

(b) What lies in the "delimitation in thought of an area" may be illustrated by comparison with a concrete phenomenon: One can imagine a certain number of posts being driven vertically at irregular intervals into the bed of a river, so that together they form a figure. In relation to delimitation in thought of an area, the individual post can be seen as corresponding to a concept criterion; the posts taken together, as corresponding to the connotation of the concept; and the volume of water that is delimited by the posts at a particular point in time, as corresponding to the denotation of the concept.[1]

This phenomenon illustrates the possible *interest of a concept of* 'physical delimitation of an area', which does *not only* consist in the concept of the individual physical marking of a boundary, not only in the concept of the sum of the boundary markings, and not only in the concept of the volume that is delimited by the boundary markings at particular points in time, *but in contrast also in the concept of the unity* of these elements in the physical delimiting process.

Correspondingly it may be of interest to have a concept of 'delimitation in thought of an area', which *does not only* consist in the concept of the individual criterion, not only in the concept of the sum of the criteria (the connotation), and not only in the concept of what at a particular (all)[2] point(s) in time is delimited by the criteria (the denotation), *but in contrast also in the concept of the unity* of these elements in the process of delimiting in thought. The concept of 'the structuring function of definitions' aims at capturing this unity.

---

[1] The concept of 'denotation' may be laid down so that it covers those phenomena that are delimited by the criteria at a particular point in time (Næss, *Interpretation and Preciseness*, pp. 73–74); or so that it covers those phenomena which in the past, present and future were, are and will be delimited by the criteria (Hospers, *An Introduction to Philosophical Analysis*, p. 40). – Where this difference is of significance in the present work, the context should provide information about what is intended. I do not consider it necessary to draw a general definitional boundary in this dimension.

[2] See the preceding note.

(c) The word "area" and the picture that was drawn by way of introduction in item (b) above, first and foremost leads our thought towards *concepts of physical objects*. Such concepts are characterised by the fact that one can make a positive physical collection corresponding to the delimitation in thought. One can for example physically collect the objects that fall under a concept of 'cup'.

The concept of 'the structuring function of definitions' and its accompanying result-concept of 'area-in-thought' ("concept") are, however, entirely general concepts. They are meant to cover *all the ways in which one's thought structures the world when one is defining*, i.e. when one contributes to determining the meanings of linguistic entities (contributes to determining concepts). – To illustrate the diversity I shall outline some practically important forms of structuring, in the case of which one *cannot* in the same way (as obviously or directly) as in the case of physical objects speak of a positive collection corresponding to the delimitation in thought.

(i) Words that are used of non-empirical elements

A subgroup here is widespread ways of using words like *"thought", "(linguistic) meaning"* and *"concept"*. – The reason that in these instances one does not in the same way (as obviously or directly) as in the case of words for physical objects speak of a positive collection corresponding to the area delimited in thought is that what falls under the area is to a greater or lesser extent considered not to be empirical (in shorthand form: *"non-empirical denotation"*): One does not collect concepts, for example, in the same way as cups. – I shall later place the use of the word "concept" in the present work more precisely in relation to this complex of problems (items (4)–(5) below; see in particular item (5)(c) on the "discussion and decision perspective" of the work).

In other instances the reason is that the area delimited in thought is altogether not of such a kind that one says, in the same way (as obviously or directly) as in the case of words for physical objects, that something "falls under" the area (in shorthand form: *"no denotation"*). – I shall outline three instance-types of such structuring (items (ii)–(iv)).

(ii) Words with connecting function

A subgroup here is conjunctions like *"and"* and *"or"*. Another subgroup is *linking-terms* in norm systems. The latter I shall be discussing in greater detail in another context (sections IV 3.3.3–3.3.4 below).

(iii) Words with substituting function

A subgroup here is words for one's inner phenomena. An example is words for *pain*, with respect to which I consider that Wittgenstein's descriptive definition has a lot to be said for it:

> "Wie *beziehen* [Wittgenstein's italics] sich Wörter auf Empfindungen? – Darin scheint kein Problem zu liegen; denn reden wir nicht täglich von Empfindungen, und benennen sie? Aber wie wird die Verbindung des Namens mit dem Benannten hergestellt? Die Frage ist die gleiche wie die:

> wie lernt ein Mensch die Bedeutung der Namen von Empfindungen? Z.B. des Wortes *"Schmerz"*. Dies ist eine Möglichkeit: Es werden Worte mit dem ursprünglichen, natürlichen, Ausdruck der Empfindung verbunden und *an dessen Stelle gesetzt*. Ein Kind hat sich verletzt, es schreit; und nun sprechen ihm die Erwachsenen zu und bringen ihm Ausrufe und später Sätze bei. Sie lehren das Kind ein neues Schmerzbenehmen.
>
> "So sagst du also, daß das Wort 'Schmerz' eigentlich das Schreien bedeute?" – Im Gegenteil; der Wortausdruck des Schmerzes *ersetzt* das Schreien und *beschreibt* es nicht" (my italics unless otherwise stated).[3]

I assume substitution analysis is apt in the case of *decision propositions* too. This kind of analysis is apt in the case of decision propositions in general, i.e. in the case of propositions of the form "I wish ...", "I intend ...", or the like. And this kind of analysis is apt in law, inter alia in the case of what lawyers call *"private declarations of intent"* (promises, impositions, notices of default, granting of power of attorney, etc.): Corresponding to the quoted analysis of the use of the word "pain", one can in the case of "declarations of intent" ask whether the declaration describes (communicates) a person's intent, or whether it expresses the intent, in that it takes the place of more "primitive" expressions, such as a child's screams, blows and kicks, or the like, when the child encounters something that gets in the way of its decision.[4]

(iv) Words with excluding function

Some words seem to have their foremost function in excluding something, not in designating phenomena that are positively present.[5] – Some examples may illustrate this, proceeding from analysis of words with a more general area of application, across analysis of the words "justice" and "right", to analysis of terms in legal dogmatics.

Austin describes the use of the English word *"real"* as an excluding function, which also seems adequate in the case of Norwegian words like *"virkelig"* [real], *"ordentlig"* [proper], *"egentlig"* [actual], and so forth:

> "[A] definite sense attaches to the assertion that something is real, a real such-and-such, *only* in the light of a specific way in which it might be ... not real. 'A real duck' differs from the simple 'a duck' only in that it is used to *exclude* various ways of being not a real duck – but a dummy, a toy, a picture, a decoy, &c.; and moreover I don't know just how to take the assertion

---

3 Wittgenstein, *Philosophische Untersuchungen*, Part I, section 244.

4 Eng, ' "Hva er en viljeserklæring?" ' ["what is a declaration of intent?"], pp. 31–32. – In the case of propositions of the form "I wish ...", "I intend ...", or the like, the substituting function is total, intersubjectively cognisable, and linked to individual words ("wish"). In other instances it is partial, concealed, or linked to longer formulations. A metaphor, for example, will, in addition to saying something relevant in the situation, often replace the individual's early/ earlier pattern-creating experiences and emotion constellations; compare Sharpe, 'Psycho-Physical Problems Revealed in Language: an Examination of Metaphor', pp. 159 et seq.

5 Concerning the *word* "excluding", compare the occurrences of "exclude" in the quotations in the main text in what follows, and Hall's term "excluders" in his article with the same title.

> that it's a real duck unless I know just what, on that particular occasion, the speaker has it in mind to exclude. This, of course, is why the attempt to find a characteristic common to all things that are or could be called 'real' is doomed to failure; the function of 'real' is not to contribute positively to the characterization of anything, but to exclude possible ways of being not real – and these ways are both numerous for particular kinds of things, and liable to be quite different for things of different kinds" (my italics; Austin's italics omitted).[6]

He further gives an exclusion analysis of philosophers' use of the words *"free"* and *"freedom"*:

> "While it has been the tradition to present [the problem of freedom] as the 'positive' term requiring elucidation, there is little doubt that to say we acted 'freely' (in the philosopher's use, which is only faintly related to the everyday use) is to say *only* that we acted *not un-freely*, in one or another of the many heterogeneous ways of so acting (under duress, or what not). ... ['F]ree' is *only* used to *rule out* the suggestion of some or all of its recognized antitheses" (my italics).[7]

A number of writers have to a greater or lesser extent analysed *"justice"* and *"right"* as words with an excluding function:

> "Mere justice is, upon most occasions, but a *negative* virtue ... The man who barely abstains from violating either the person, or the estate, or the reputation of his neighbours, has surely very little positive merit. He fulfils, however, all the rules of what is peculiarly called justice" (my italics).[8]
>
> "Wer von der vorgefaßten Meinung, daß der Begriff des Rechts ein positiver seyn müsse, ausgeht und nun ihn zu definiren unternimmt, wird nicht damit zu Stande kommen: denn er will einen Schatten greifen, verfolgt ein Gespenst, sucht ein Nonens [Nichtseiendes]. Der Begriff des Rechts ist ... ein *negativer*: sein Inhalt ist eine blosse Negation. Der Begriff des *Unrechts* ist der positive ..." (Schopenhauer's italics; his other italics omitted).[9]

On the model of Austin's analyses, Hart describes how practising lawyers in the English legal system use the word *"voluntary"* in criminal law:

> "[W]hat is meant by the mental element in criminal liability (mens rea) is only to be understood by considering certain defences or exceptions ... [I]n pursuit of the will-o'-the-wisp of a general formula, legal theorists have sought to impose a spurious unity ... upon these heterogeneous defences and exceptions, suggesting that they are admitted as merely evidence of the absence of some single element ('intention') or, in more recent theory, two elements ('foresight' and 'voluntariness') universally required as necessary conditions of criminal responsibility. ... [Words like 'voluntary'] are treated in such definitions as words having positive force, yet ... the word

---

6 Austin, *Sense and Sensibilia*, p. 70; correspondingly in 'Other Minds', pp. 55–56.

7 Austin, 'A Plea for Excuses', p. 128.

8 Smith, *The Theory of Moral Sentiments*, p. 82.

9 Schopenhauer, 'Zur Rechtslehre und Politik', p. 262 (§ 121).

'voluntary' in fact serves to *exclude* a heterogeneous range of cases such as physical compulsion, coercion by threats, accidents, mistakes, etc., and not to designate a mental element or state; nor does 'involuntary' signify the absence of this mental element or state" (my italics).[10]

This description I consider adequate (also) in relation to Norwegian lawyers' use of words like *"fri"* [free], *"frivillig"* [voluntary], *"tilregnelig"* [of sound mind]. In their use of the said words lawyers do not seem first and foremost to *designate* mental states, processes, etc., in the perpetrator, but to *express the absence* of external or internal coercion, of severe mental retardation, of unconsciousness, or of other subjective circumstances accepted as excluding criminal responsibility; cf. also, as a probable symptom and reinforcing cause, the fact that both in Norway and in other countries criminal law contents itself with specifying the various subjective circumstances that exclude criminal responsibility.[11]

Summers has used the mode of definition in Austin and Hart as a model for an exclusion analysis of requirements for *"good faith"* in American contract law:[12]

> "In my view, good faith in the general requirement of good faith in ordinary moral dealings, and in the general case law of contract up to the late 1960s, was most felicitously conceptualized as an "excluder". That is, it was not appropriately formulable in terms of some general positive meaning ... rather, it functioned ... to rule out a wide range of heterogeneous forms of bad faith."[13]
>
> "[T]he section 205 requirement of good faith [in the Second Restatement of Contracts] [e]xcludes a variety of types of conduct characterized as involving [b]ad fait[h], including evasion of the spirit of the bargain, lack of diligence and slacking off, abuse of a power to specify terms, conjuring up a dispute to force a settlement or modification, wilfully failing to mitigate damages, and so on."[14/15]

(d) As is apparent from the above (particularly item (b)), the concept of 'the structuring function of definitions' covers a *complex phenomenon*. First, it covers a *process*: namely the activity of dividing the world up in thought into areas. Secondly, it covers *products*: namely the areas-in-thought (concepts). And thirdly, it covers *means* in the process leading to the products: namely specification of connotation or specification of denotation.

However, in the present section 4, I consider the structuring function of definitions as a unitary entity. For here the main emphasis is on the distinction

---

10 Hart, 'The Ascription of Responsibility and Rights', pp. 152–53.

11 Andenæs, *Alminnelig strafferett* [general criminal law], pp. 264–65.

12 Summers, '"Good Faith" in General Contract Law and the Sales Provisions of the Uniform Commercial Code', in particular pp. 196, cf. 200–07; 'The General Duty of Good Faith – its Recognition and Conceptualization', in particular pp. 816–21.

13 Summers, 'The General Duty of Good Faith – its Recognition and Conceptualization', p. 819.

14 Op. cit., p. 820.

15 Concerning the excluding function of words, see also the analysis of lawyers' use of the term "valid [binding, effective, or the like] contract" in section 3.2.2 (5)(c)(iii) above.

between the structuring function of definitions and the naming function of definitions.

The discussion of the structuring function of definitions in the present section 4 will provide the *main perspective on the subsequent sections 5–6*: There the elements will be separated and the discussion will focus on the different roles of, and the interaction between, the elements.

When in the present section 4 or later in the work I wish to emphasise the *action aspect*, namely that it is the language users' acts that determine the structuring function of definitions, I often use the formulation "[the language user's] *exercise* of the structuring function". – When the emphasis is on *other* aspects, I sometimes use *for the sake of brevity* simply *"structuring"*, instead of "the structuring function of the definition"/ "[the language user's] exercise of the structuring function".

(2) To what extent is it logically (by definition) necessary that a definition structures?

All definitions have by definition a structuring function, i.e. they relate to the level of meaning ("concepts"); cf. my definition of 'definition' as "propositions that contribute to determining the meanings of linguistic entities (contribute to determining concepts)" (section A 2 (1) above).

Arguments "by definition" do not in themselves show anything but how somebody has decided to use the word defined (what concept somebody has decided on): here, how I have decided to use the word "definition" (what concept of 'definition' I have decided on).

The structuring function as an element in the definition of "definition" I do, however, consider to be absolutely central. As a test one can let the concept of 'definition' remain open with respect to structuring function, and ask whether there are related and interesting propositions *without* structuring function. – I have not been able to find examples of this.

(1)↔(2) In the conceptual framework here the concepts of 'definition' and 'concept' will mutually imply each other. The relationship to other conceptual frameworks

From the above it follows that the concepts of 'definition' and 'concept' in the present work mutually imply each other: – Wherever there is a definition, descriptive or normative, then in the conceptual framework here there will be a concept. – And wherever there is a concept, then in the conceptual framework here there will be a normative definition: It is the normative definitions, first and foremost those that are custom-based, that constitute the language users' concepts (section 3.3 above).

In what follows I shall look at some aspects of the *relationship to other conceptual frameworks* (items (a)–(c)).

(a) In *actual language usage* there is seldom claimed to be a mutually definitional connection between the concepts of 'concept' and 'definition', as here.[16] – This is not an objection, however, since the definitions here do not pretend to be normative-traditional (section 3.3.4 above) in all dimensions.

I shall look at two possible *causes* of the fact that one does not assume a mutually definitional connection between the concepts of 'concept' and 'definition' (items (i)–(ii)).

(i) One cause may be that the existence of what may reasonably be called "concepts" is considered to a greater or lesser degree to be *independent of* norms for use of the words and expressions of a language. Plato's ideas, concepts as one saw them within radical realism in the mediaeval conflict over the status of universals, Kant's transcendental categories, Frege's Begriffe – these are examples of entities claimed to have existence independently of actual language use, and which through functional similarities, among themselves and with other concepts of linguistic meaning, may reasonably be called "concepts".

With such ontological points of departure and an extended use of the term "concept", or words or expressions presumed to have the same meaning as "concept", one can say that human beings have access to concepts *without* these concepts' necessarily finding expression in language, for example because the language users have not, or have only incompletely, cognised the concepts.

> "What is known as the history of concepts is really a history either of our knowledge of concepts or of the meanings of words. Often it is only after immense intellectual effort, which may have continued over centuries, that humanity at last succeeds in achieving knowledge of a concept in its pure form, in stripping off the irrelevant accretions which veil it from the eyes of the mind."[17]
>
> "[C]oncepts may ... be conceived as real objects, namely ... as the properties and relations of things existing independently of our definitions and constructions. It seems to me that the assumption of such objects is quite as legitimate as the assumption of physical bodies and there is quite as much reason to believe in their existence. They are in the same sense necessary to obtain a satisfactory system of mathematics as physical bodies are necessary for a satisfactory theory of our sense perceptions ...".[18]

---

16 For example, one treats concepts and definitions beside each other, pretty much without mediation between the two categories; as examples, see Næss, *Logikk og metodelære* [logic and methodology], Chapter 5 ("Presisering og definisjon" [clarification and definition]) compared with Chapter 6 ("Begrepslære" [doctrine of concepts]); Hospers, *An Introduction to Philosophical Analysis*, Chapter 1 ("Meaning and Definition") compared with Chapter 2 ("Knowledge", including discussion of "Concepts").

17 Frege, *The Foundations of Arithmetic*, p. VII.

18 Gödel, 'Russell's Mathematical Logic', p. 137.

Cognition of concepts (in the extended sense outlined) can often be seen as a *discovery with the character of recognition*, since one is presupposed to be able to become conscious of them only by thinking – about *unchanging* features of one's *own* cognition, thought, existence, or the like.

> For example, it would not be an argument against Kant's transcendental deduction of the categories that one can register that language users do not have words for or conscious thoughts about a necessary causal relationship in nature. Kant could say that his deduction represents a discovery with the character of recognition: Not until this was science able to become *psychologically* conscious of its transcendental-logical basis, which however with transcendental-logical necessity has *always* lain, and will lie, immanent in any cognition of an objective world. – Correspondingly Kant could say of the categorical imperative that it is no argument against the validity of this that one can register that language users do not formulate the imperative or are not conscious of it. Kant could say that not until his philosophy were human beings able to become psychologically conscious of the correct and transcendental-logically necessary relationship between the existence of man as a natural being, subject to the law of causality, and the existence of man as an acting and free being, subject to the moral law.

To the extent that one uses the term "concept", or words or expressions presumed to have the same meaning as "concept", of something that is considered to be independent of definitions of the words and expressions of any language, then propositions that determine concepts will not be definitions, but characterisations, in the *conceptual framework here* (section C below). – In many *other conceptual frameworks*, however, the connection is preserved between concepts in the extended sense outlined and definitions: Propositions determining concepts in this extended sense are brought under an extended concept of 'definition', for example under the name of "real definition" (section 2.3 (1) above) or "essential definition" (section C 2.3 below).

It lies outside the perspective and topic of the present work (Chapter I and section II A 8, above) to take any standpoint on ontological and epistemological questions in the case of such entities as mentioned (Plato's ideas, concepts as one saw them within radical realism in the mediaeval conflict over the status of universals, Kant's transcendental categories, Frege's Begriffe, and the like). Here the emphasis is on the fact that they all illustrate entities which, *if* one accepts their existence *and* wishes to focus on them, *may or must* lead to a different stipulation of the concept of 'concept', and thereby to a different relationship to the concept of 'definition', than I have chosen on the basis of the perspective and topic of the present work.

(ii) Another cause of not assuming any mutually definitional connection between the concepts of 'concept' and 'definition' may be that one lays down *different requirements for determinacy* (unambiguity, completeness, preciseness, features in common) in the case of the two concepts:

It may be that one says that particular requirements for the delimitation of the area must be satisfied before one is willing to call the area a "concept" (section 3.2.2 (5) above), so that there is thus a good possibility that one will call the delimiting proposition a *"definition"* – *without* wishing to call the area being delimited a "concept".

Or the situation may be the reverse, namely that one says that particular requirements for the guidance a proposition provides, must be satisfied before one is willing to call the proposition a "definition" (section 2.2 above), so that there is a good possibility that one will call the area being delimited a *"concept"* – *without* wishing to call the delimiting proposition a "definition".

(b) Even though the *mutually* definitional connection between the concepts of 'concept' and 'definition' is not so common, *elements* of this connection are central to a number of writers, perhaps most importantly assumptions of a connection between the *concept of 'concept'* and *norms*: I wish as mentioned to say that where there is a concept, then there will by definition be a normative definition. Others speak of the connection between the concept of 'concept' and norms in a more general rule terminology.[19] Two important examples are Kant and Wittgenstein. Both often use a rule terminology seemingly synonymously with a concept terminology.[20] What types of norm they mean by their rule terminology and what sort(s) of connection they assume between the concept of 'concept' and norms, one cannot decide, however, without going into comprehensive areas of their thinking.

> Kant's terminology and perspective may be illustrated by the following quotation: "Wir haben den *Verstand* oben auf mancherlei Weise erklärt: durch eine Spontaneität der Erkenntnis, (im Gegensatz der Rezeptivität der Sinnlichkeit) durch ein Vermögen zu denken, oder auch ein Vermögen der *Begriffe* oder auch der Urteile, welche Erklärungen, wenn man sie beim Lichten besieht, auf eins hinauslaufen. Jetzt können wir ihn als das V e r m ö g e n d e r *R e g e l n* charakterisieren. Dieses Kennzeichen ist fruchtbarer und tritt dem Wesen desselben näher. Sinnlichkeit gibt uns Formen, (der Anschauung) der Verstand aber Regeln. Dieser ist jederzeit geschäftig, die Erscheinungen in der Absicht durchzuspähen, um an ihnen irgend eine Regel aufzufinden. Regeln, so fern sie objektiv sind, (mithin der Erkenntnis des Gegenstandes notwendig anhängen) heißen *Gesetze*" (Kant's spacing; my italics).[21]

---

19 By "rule terminology" I mean words like "rule", "norm", "law" and their derivatives (or their equivalents in other languages).

20 I should remind the reader that by "concept terminology" I mean words like "concept", "conception", "notion", "idea" and their derivatives (or their equivalents in other languages) (cf. section A 2 (1) above, in note 1).

21 Kant, *Kritik der reinen Vernuft*, A 126. – Kant's sharp distinction between the sense element of experience (Rezeptivität der Sinnlichkeit) and the concept element of experience (Verstand, Begriffe, Regeln, Gesetze) is an important difference in relation to Hume, *A Treatise of Human Nature*, who saw concepts ("ideas") as a *weaker form of sense impression* ("faint images of [impressions]"), see p. 1.

Wittgenstein's view of the relationship between the concept of 'concept' and norms will be taken up in item (5) below.

T. Strömberg, and later Sundby, Eckhoff, Peczenik, and other writers, use concepts of 'qualification norm' which to some extent coincide with the concept of 'normative definition' here.[22] As far as I can see, they do not, however, establish any definitional connection between qualification norms and concepts.

(c) Against a mutually definitional connection between the concepts of 'concept' and 'definition' one might imagine objecting that many *animals* act in such a way, including using and reacting to signs, that one might well imagine saying that they "have concepts", but not that they "can define".[23]

However, the mutually definitional connection does not necessarily become unreasonable in the case of one's also bringing in animal behaviour and use of signs: In these instances one is at the periphery of the concept of 'concept'. And along the graduated transitions one may say correspondingly that one is at the periphery of the concept of 'custom-based definition'. For even though it may not be very natural to say that animals "*stipulate* definitions", it may, to the same extent as it is reasonable to say that they have concepts, be reasonable to say that they "follow *custom-based* definitions". – The essential thing is to see the factual similarities and differences between human and animal behaviour/ use of signs that may suggest the one or the other conceptual framework. Choice of conceptual framework ought then to rest on what aspects one wishes concretely to direct one's thought at. In relation to the perspective and topic of the present work (Chapter I above) there is, however, no need to draw conceptual boundaries among and between these instances.

(3) I do not lay down determinacy as a definitional criterion in the case of my concepts of 'definition' or 'concept'

In the definition of 'definition' as "propositions that *contribute to* determining the meanings of linguistic entities (contribute to determining concepts)" (section A 2 (1) above) lies the fact that I do not lay down particularly strict determinacy requirements that the delimitation of area must satisfy.[24] It is sufficient that the proposition says *something* about the boundaries of the area.

---

22 See Eng, *U/enighetsanalyse – med særlig sikte på jus og allmenn rettsteori* [analysis of dis/agreement – with particular reference to law and legal theory], pp. 117–19.

23 Compare Kenny, *Will, Freedom and Power*, p. 51, see also pp. 5, 19–21; Chomsky, *Rules and Representations*, pp. 55, 57; Searle, *The Construction of Social Reality*, pp. 61–62.

24 I should remind the reader (cf. section 2.2 above, introductory remarks) that I use "determinacy" as a common term for the dimensions of unambiguity (in contrast to ambiguity and polysemy); of completeness (in contrast to incompleteness); of preciseness (in contrast to vagueness); and of condition structure of concept criteria, which often means unity in the form of features in common (in contrast to factor structure of concept criteria, for example unity in the form of family resemblance).

This applies correspondingly in relation to my concept of *'concept'*: It is sufficient that the concept *to a certain extent* delimits in *one or another* direction.

> This determination of the concept of 'concept' was presupposed in my discussion of family resemblance. I pointed out there that it depends on an evaluation in the individual instance whether concept terminology is used when the area delimitation more closely analysed seems to be based on family resemblance (section 3.2.2 (5)(b) above). And with a view to the perspective and topic of the present work, I drew a distinction between 'condition concept' and 'factor concept' (section 3.2.2 (5)(d) above).

It is quite usual to presuppose or lay down requirements for determinacy as criteria in concepts of 'definition'. I have earlier given examples of writers within legal theory, as well as philosophy and logic, who presuppose or lay down such requirements (section 2.2 above). – In what follows I shall (a) give grounds for *why* I do not lay down particular determinacy requirements as concept criteria, and (b) say something about what requirements it is *possible* to lay down.

(a) Why I do not lay down determinacy as a definitional criterion

I have not been able to find any tenable grounds for why the concept of 'concept' or the concept of 'definition' *must* satisfy determinacy requirements. – I establish these concepts out of the following *considerations* (items (i)–(ii)):

(i) The descriptive purpose of my definition theory

Determinacy requirements will often be considered relevant when participants in language and argumentation reflect on which of several meaning determinations is to be preferred. For example, one takes into account whether a descriptive definition is *so* determinate that it can be tested, or whether a normative definition is *so* determinate that it may have an action-guiding effect. Thus, views about determinacy requirements must be taken into consideration in description of language and argumentation. However, two points should be added here. First, the *determinacy requirement itself* ("what requirements ought to be laid down?") does not belong as a criterion in a concept formed with a descriptive aim: here, with the aim of mapping how one in fact proceeds when in analysis and argumentation formulated in everyday language one determines the meanings of linguistic entities (determines concepts). Secondly, *views* about determinacy requirements can and ought to be taken into consideration without being laid down as a criterion in concepts of 'definition' or 'concept'. I refer to the descriptive aim mentioned. Provided it is clear that the sender of the proposition intended to contribute to determining the meanings of linguistic entities (contribute to determining concepts), or that his formulation of the proposition can reasonably be understood in this way, then, on the basis of the descriptive aim, there is *reason* to take his proposition into account, *even if* the proposition is otherwise indeterminate.

(ii) My desire to avoid persuasive definitions

The desire to avoid language that *conceals evaluations* and provides room for *rhetorical manipulation* goes against bringing particular determinacy requirements into the concepts of 'concept' and 'definition':

When the determinacy criterion is kept out of these concepts, one can say *: "Your concept of 'contract' is vague, please define it", "This is a polysemous definition, please make it more determinate".

When the determinacy criterion is brought into these concepts, one must say **: "You have no concept of 'contract' ", "This is not a definition".

The latter form of expression (**) easily leads to a situation in which evaluations concerning what determinacy requirements *ought* to be demanded, are discussed in *seemingly descriptive* (i.e. in concealing) linguistic forms: "This is not a concept/ a definition", "What exactly is a concept/ a definition?". – The first form of expression (*) provides a more open specification of the topic, with correspondingly less room for misunderstandings and for rhetorical manipulation.[25]

(i)↔(ii) Why the considerations now mentioned have not won through in the thinking on definitions

Considerations (i) and (ii) have been advanced as arguments against laying down moral requirements that the content of rules must satisfy, as criteria in the concept of 'law' in legal theory; see for example Hart's argumentation.[26] – Of interest in the present connection is that Hart can have a clear view of the weight of considerations (i) and (ii) in relation to the concept of 'law', at the same time as he uses a concept of 'definition' according to which definitions must satisfy determinacy requirements.[27] I assume one reason for this weaker critical reflection in the case of the concept of 'definition' than in the case of the concept of 'law' is that evaluations are experienced more weakly in the case of the concept of 'definition' (no parallel to dramatic questions like "Are Hitler's race laws to be considered as law?"), so that one is to a lesser degree forced to reflect on what one wants to achieve by the conceptualisation. Consequently there is little or no resistance to ideal requirements from philosophy and logic stamping a more general concept of 'definition' (section 2.2 (i)↔(iii) above).

---

25 Compare Zapffe, *Indføring i litterær Dramaturgi* [introduction to literary dramaturgy], p. 256: "[I]t will involve hopeless confusion if one also includes quality requirements in the determination of genre ("this is not a tragedy, this is balderdash")"; Goodman, 'When Is Art?', p. 66: "The literature of aesthetics is littered with desperate attempts to answer the question "What is art?" … [a] question … often hopelessly confused with the question "What is good art?""; Myrdal, *The Political Element in the Development of Economic Theory*, p. 192: "[E]conomic reasoning is often obscured by the fact that normative principles are not introduced explicitly, but in the shape of general 'concepts'. … The perpetual game of hide-and-seek in economics consists in concealing the norm in the concept." – Compare section 7 below, on persuasive definitions.

26 Hart, *The Concept of Law*, 1st ed. pp. 203–07; 2nd ed. pp. 207–12.

27 Op. cit., 1st ed. p. 16; 2nd ed. loc. cit. See in more detail in section 2.2 (ii) above.

(b) What requirements for determinacy it is possible to lay down

One may ask whether it is at all possible that a normative definition is determinate, in the sense that the definition decides *all* the cases of doubt about the delimitation of the area that one might imagine arising, and that the concept that the definition constitutes is correspondingly determinate.

In relation to concepts covering phenomena of experience, such determinacy will require that one can survey *future development*. – Further, both in relation to these concepts and in relation to concepts covering other phenomena than those of experience, one might always imagine the *application* of the definition giving rise to doubt (even though it will of course not always do so in fact). A determinacy requirement understood as a requirement to clear away the possibility of *this* doubt goes against concept criteria generally assumed in the case of normative propositions, including normative definitions: the criteria that normative propositions do not apply themselves but must be applied, and that one may always imagine them being applied wrongly ("the rule is broken"). This means that it is always a question of fact whether there is a need for new definitions.

Against this background the most one can achieve in the way of determinacy seems to be a determinacy *relative to concrete persons and situations*, that is to say, seems to be that a definition and the resulting concept clear away all the doubt that on closer examination is in fact found to exist. (However, there is in my view no reason to require any such determinacy either; see item (a) above).

Wittgenstein makes a number of pertinent remarks partly on the arbitrariness and partly on the incoherence of laying down determinacy in the delimitation as a necessary condition for calling something a "concept" ("area"). These remarks are relevant in relation to definitions as well, as the word "definition" is used here; cf. my seeing concept and definition as two sides of the same coin (item (1)↔(2) above).

Concerning *arbitrariness* Wittgenstein says inter alia:

"Man kann sagen, der Begriff 'Spiel' ist ein Begriff mit verschwommenen Rändern. – "Aber ist ein verschwommener Begriff überhaupt ein *Begriff*?" – Ist eine unscharfe Photographie überhaupt ein Bild eines Menschen? Ja, kann man ein unscharfes Bild immer mit Vorteil durch ein scharfes ersetzen? Ist das unscharfe nicht oft gerade das, was wir brauchen?

Frege vergleicht den Begriff mit einem Bezirk und sagt: einen unklar begrenzten Bezirk könne man überhaupt keinen Bezirk nennen. Das heißt wohl, wir können mit ihm nichts anfangen. – Aber ist es sinnlos zu sagen: "Halte dich ungefähr hier auf!"?"[28]

"Wenn ich Einem sage "Halte dich ungefähr hier auf!" – kann denn diese Erklärung nicht vollkommen *funktionieren*? Und kann jede andere nicht auch *versagen*?

"Aber ist die Erklärung nicht doch unexakt?" – Doch; warum soll man sie nicht "unexakt" nennen? Verstehen wir aber nur, was *"unexakt"* bedeutet! Denn es bedeutet nun nicht *"unbrauchbar"*. Und überlegen wir uns doch,

---

28 Wittgenstein, *Philosophische Untersuchungen*, Part 1, section 71 (Wittgenstein's italics).

was wir, im Gegensatz zu dieser Erklärung eine "exakte" Erklärung nennen! Etwa das Abgrenzen eines Bezirks durch einen Kreidestrich? Da fällt uns gleich ein, daß der Strich eine Breite hat. Exakt wäre also eine Farbgrenze. Aber hat denn diese *Exaktheit* hier noch eine *Funktion*; läuft sie nicht *leer*? Und wir haben ja auch noch nicht bestimmt, was als Überschreiten dieser scharfen Grenze gelten soll; wie, mit welchen Instrumenten, es festzustellen ist. Usw." (my italics).[29]

Concerning the *incoherence* in notions of perfect determinacy in rules (definitions and concepts), Wittgenstein refers to the argument in the main text above: that rules do not apply themselves, and that there may always be doubt in their application, so that there is a need for new rules.[30]

Against this background he says more generally of definitions: "Man könnte sagen: Eine Erklärung dient dazu, ein Mißverständnis zu beseitigen, oder zu verhüten – also *eines, das* ohne die Erklärung eintreten würde; aber *nicht: jedes*, welches ich mir vorstellen kann" (my italics).[31]

(4) Empirical and non-empirical concepts

One can speak respectively of "empirical" and "non-empirical" concepts, all according to whether the denotation of the concept only covers phenomena that are empirically perceptible, or also or only covers phenomena that are not empirically perceptible.

Examples of empirical concepts are 'cup', 'chair' and 'persons who have advanced concepts of 'law' according to which the norms must satisfy certain minimum ethical requirements'.

Examples of non-empirical concepts are the said concepts of 'law' themselves, Kant's concept of 'pure intuition' and his categories.

(5) To what extent is the concept of 'concept' now presented (items (1)–(3) above) empirical or non-empirical (item (4) above)?

(a) My definition of the concept of 'concept' above is *normative*, in that it expresses decision, promise and recommendation with respect to the use of the word "concept" in relation to the perspective and topic of the present work, and within this and in particular, in relation to my definition theory.[32] – At the same time significant parts of the content of my definition may be used as part of a *descriptive* definition, in that the content is meant to cover certain widespread intuitions.[33] This goes in particular for the intuition that the *connotations of*

---

29 Op. cit., Part I, section 88. – See also Part I, section 99.

30 Op. cit., Part I, e.g. sections 29, 84–87, 141.

31 Op. cit., Part I, section 87.

32 See the next note.

33 When the presentation of my definition theory has been completed, I shall give some critically reflexive characterisations that are more nuanced, by applying the theory to the definitions in the theory (section 9 below). – At the present stage of the presentation there is not an adequate basis for

concepts are not (fully) empirically perceptible, irrespective of whether the denotation of the concept covers empirical objects: For example, the concept of 'cup' covers empirical objects, but I do not for that reason consider the connotation of the concept of 'cup' as (fully) empirically perceptible. One might possibly object that part of the connotation is constituted by the property that cups are for drinking out of, and that this property is empirical. This is correct, but it does not represent a counter-example. For cognition of the fact that something is for drinking out of presupposes that one has a concept 'for drinking out of'. What is (fully) empirical is thus again the denotation of the concept, in this instance the things that have the property that they are for drinking out of. The connotation of the concept, the criterion 'for drinking out of', is, in contrast, no more here than elsewhere itself (fully) empirically perceptible (items (i)–(ii)):

(i) That the connotations of concepts cannot be identified with purely *linguistic entities* is considered to be clear: It is a fundamental feature of our way of talking about language that language and meaning are two different things, cf. the assumptions that the same meaning may be formulated in different ways and that the same formulation may have different meanings (section A 6 (3) above). – According to widespread intuitions it is also considered clear that the connotations of concepts cannot be identified with *other purely physical (spatio-temporal) features* of our use of language: be it features of persons, situations, actions, or anything else, typically involved in the use of language.

(ii) One might think it more doubtful whether the connotations of concepts could be identified with *certain empirically perceptible phenomena of a psychological kind*: to put it more precisely, whether the connotations of concepts could be identified with the stream of mental images, or with more enduring images in the memory, which both *spontaneously* accompany the use of language; or identified with a *cognitively worked out* mental image of what one considers to be the typical denotatum, for example, of what one considers to be the typical cup. – However, any such identification will also be inadequate in relation to widespread intuitions. First, one uses formulations like "to have the same concept", "to mean the same thing", "to understand the same thing", and so on, even though one cannot have one another's psychological phenomena of the kind mentioned:[34] In the way in which we speak, the psychological phenomena that the reader can observe in himself when he reads this text "can only be the reader's, not mine". In the way in which we speak, the meaning content that the text has for the reader can, however, be "the same" as the meaning content that the text has for me. Secondly, one uses formulations like "to have a concept of", or the like, not only in connection with for example cups in contrast to chairs, but also in connection with for example geometrical figures with a thousand and one sides in contrast to those with a thousand and two sides, even though one neither spon-

---

the same richness of nuances, nor is such richness of nuances necessary; the two critically reflexive sentences that introduce the present item (a) are sufficient for the purpose here.

34 Frege, 'On Sense and Meaning', p. 60; Wittgenstein, *Zettel*, section 96.

taneously gets nor through the exercise of will is capable of producing psychological phenomena of the kind mentioned, specific to figures with a thousand and one sides in relation to figures with a thousand and two sides.

(b) Such conceptual intuitions as have now been outlined (items (a)(i)–(ii) above) can contribute to explaining why many people seem to assume a *non-empirical world*, independent of actual language use, in which *concepts are already existing objects* that can be found and cognised on a par with physical objects in the empirical world. A picture of this kind often lies more or less clearly behind a quest for the "true", "real", "essential", or suchlike concept, for example of law.

> Some variants of this picture were mentioned above (item (1)↔(2)(a)(i)): Plato's ideas, concepts as one saw them within radical realism in the mediaeval conflict over the status of universals, Kant's transcendental categories, and Frege's Begriffe.

Propositions with such pretensions *can* in some instances be interpreted as definitions. However, such an interpretation does not capture what is *interesting and problematic about these propositions*: Is it true that a non-empirical reality exists? (the ontological question). How can we cognise this non-empirical reality? (the epistemological question). – Propositions that take on the task of answering *these* questions will not be definitions, but characterisations in the conceptual framework presented in the present work (section C, particularly C 2, below).

(c) As has earlier been demonstrated (section I 6 above): Taking as a point of departure the superordinate perspective and topic of the present work it is not only to a certain extent unnecessary to take any standpoint on, but to the greatest extent possible, necessary not to take any standpoint on such questions as mentioned in item (b) above, by way of conclusion. – In what follows I shall apply the *"discussion and decision perspective"* of the work (section I 4 above) in particular to linguistic meaning. This is a perspective that *does not* construe our intuitions concerning linguistic meaning (items (a)(i)–(ii) above) to mean that concepts exist in a separate world (item (b) above). *Nor*, however, does it deny such an interpretation. This perspective is a constituent in the superordinate perspective and topic of the work (Chapter I above): a relatively well-delimited critically reflexive form (I 4), in the discussion and decision aspect (I 4) of analysis and argumentation formulated in everyday language (I 5), and with a certain independence (I 6).

I take as a point of departure the picture according to which linguistic meaning (criteria, concepts, propositions) is a matter of the *content of norms for use of the words and expressions of a language*. – The norms in question here will in large measure be what I have called "custom-based normative definitions" (section 3.3.2 above).

> Wittgenstein has given a fuller account of such a view of linguistic meaning: "Wir reden von dem räumlichen und zeitlichen Phänomen der Sprache; nicht

> von einem unräumlichen und unzeitlichen Unding. ... Aber wir reden von ihr so, wie von den Figuren des Schachspiels, indem wir Spielregeln für sie angeben, nicht ihre physikalischen Eigenschaften beschreiben. Die Frage "Was ist eigentlich ein Wort?" ist analog der "Was ist eine Schachfigur?" "[35]

Such more general points of departure do not solve problems of the kind mentioned in item (b) above, by way of conclusion. Such points of departure indicate rather how one prefers to *speak* of the things. For this reason I (also) use the term *"picture"*.

> In particular in relation to the quotation in the text at note 35 above one should note the tension between on the one hand "räumlichen und zeitlichen Phänomen der Sprache", and on the other hand "Spielregeln ... nicht ... physikalischen Eigenschaften": The tension between the level of experience and the level of meaning *is reformulated*, but *does not disappear.*

In this picture of linguistic meaning, as the content of norms for use of the words and expressions of a language, one can see it as being the case that the more detailed content of the norms (content of the concepts) is constituted in the language users' *application of the words and expressions of the language in the individual instance*, in the language users' decisions and actions concerning the applicability of the words and expressions of the language: *"decision"*, here not (only or first and foremost) used of conscious deliberation, but (also and first and foremost) of *routine* application.

> "[E]s [gibt] eine Auffassung einer Regel ..., die nicht eine Deutung ist; sondern sich, von Fall zu Fall der Anwendung, in dem äußert, was wir "der Regel folgen", und was wir "ihr entgegenhandeln" nennen."[36]
>
> "Zur Verständigung durch die Sprache gehört nicht nur eine Übereinstimmung in den Definitionen, sondern ... eine Übereinstimmung in den Urteilen."[37]
>
> "[I]n der Sprache stimmen die Menschen überein. Dies ist keine Übereinstimmung der Meinungen, sondern der Lebensform."[38]

In *this* aspect and in *this* sense, namely continual decisions and actions, one can say that linguistic meaning is *"empirical"*, and, as the case may be, *"psychological" – without* breaking with widespread intuitions concerning linguistic meaning (items (a)(i)–(ii) above).

---

35 Wittgenstein, *Philosophische Untersuchungen*, Part I, section 108. – See also item (1)↔(2)(b) above.

36 Op. cit., Part I, section 201 (Wittgenstein's italics omitted).

37 Op. cit., Part I, section 242. – Here one can read "Definitionen" as custom-based normative definitions; and "Urteilen" as characterisations, in which the custom-based normative definitions are presupposed and applied.

38 Op. cit., Part I, section 241 (Wittgenstein's italics omitted).

(6) *The concept of 'concept' as an auxiliary concept in my definition theory. Summary of some aspects of my concept of 'concept' and the corresponding sides of my concept of 'definition'*

The direct topic of the present section B is definitions, not concepts. The word "concept" is often used, however, in connection with definitions. For this reason it has been necessary to bring in the word "concept"; it has been necessary partly to say what considerations I consider ought to govern the use of this word, and partly to say how I in fact use the word in relation to a number of dimensions that have been discussed. – On account of the multifarious connections in which the word "concept" crops up, I shall give a brief summary.

(a) I use the word "concept" as a name for the areas-in-thought that are the result of the structuring function of definitions (item (1)(a) above). This is the *only* function that the word "concept" has in the present work. To use concept terminology: The concept of 'concept' is here an *auxiliary concept* for the understanding of the proposition type 'definition'. – I see the relationship between the two concepts in this way, because in my experience it is the *concept of 'definition' that is the more important* when one seeks insight into the perspective and topic of the present work (Chapter I above).

(b) Further, I have established the definitional premiss that wherever there is a concept, then there is a normative definition; this may be a stipulated definition or a custom-based definition (item (1)↔(2) above).

(c) Given the said mutually definitional connection between 'concept' and 'definition' (items (a)–(b) above), then the establishment of the concept of 'concept' will *also* illuminate the concept of 'definition' (items (i)–(ii)):

(i) Concerning the *concept of 'concept'* I should remind the reader of the following conclusions:

I do not lay down as a necessary criterion in the case of 'concept' that the individual phenomena that a concept covers share a set of features in common. – Bearing in mind the diversity of relationships between the individual phenomena of which the same word is used, one can distinguish between different types of concept. In relation to the perspective and topic of the present work I distinguish between 'condition concepts' and 'factor concepts' (section 3.2.2 (5)(d) above).

Nor do I lay down as a necessary criterion in the case of 'concept' that a concept is unambiguous, complete or precise (items (1)↔(2) and (3) above).

I say that words express "concepts" not only where words have a collecting function, but also where they have a connecting function, substituting function or excluding function (item (1)(c) above). Consequently, nor do I lay down as a necessary criterion in the case of 'concept' that a concept gathers; the contribution of the concept can also consist in connecting, substituting or excluding.

(ii) In the said aspects of my concept of 'concept' (item (i) above) lies a *corresponding determination of my concept of 'definition'*: I do not lay down as a necessary criterion in the case of 'definition' that a defined concept is a condition concept; that it is complete, unambiguous, precise or in other ways determinately delimited; or that it has a collecting function.

4.2. The naming function of definitions

(1) The concept of 'the naming function of definitions' (see further in item (3) below). Terminology
(2) When is it usual to give names to areas?
(3) To what extent is it logically (by definition) necessary that a definition gives names to the areas-in-thought that are being delimited? – Survey of discussion and conclusions in the present item (3) and the next item (4)
(4) To what extent is it in fact so, that definitions give names to the areas-in-thought that are being delimited; and what clues do definitions usually provide in this respect?
(5) What factors can explain what name an area acquires and whether the area gains ground or is impeded because of the name?
  (a) Properties of the name itself
  (b) The capacity of the name to lead mental representations, thoughts and feelings
  (c) What structurings the name is encumbered with from before
  (d) The naming's degree of correspondence with or departure from earlier language usage
  (e) Authority
  (a)↔(e) The above-mentioned factors may work consciously or unconsciously

(1) The concept of 'the naming function of definitions' (see further in item (3) below). Terminology

(a) I should briefly remind the reader of the concept of *'the naming function of definitions'* (section A 3 above): It covers the activity of giving a name, and the result that a name is given, to a particular area within the partitioning that is the result of the structuring function of definitions.

The naming function of definitions may be *descriptive* or *normative* – all according to whether the definition says something about what name an area has, or something about what name an area should or shall (or other normative types of modality) be given (section 4.3.2 below).

The name that is thus given to a particular area one can, in consequence of the designation "naming function", call "name"; or one can relate directly to the structuring function by calling the name of the area "concept designation"; or one can more loosely call it "designation", "term", "word", "expression", "formulation", or the like. On this point I use the terminology that is best suited to the context. – Neither in my consistent use of "naming function" nor in my use at times of "name" do I wish to suggest that the words are *new*: Just as the name of a person may be and often is in use of other persons, the name of an area-in-thought may be *in use* of other areas-in-thought (section 4.3.3 below).

When in the present section 4 or later in the work I wish to emphasise the *action aspect*, namely that it is the language users' acts that determine the naming function of definitions, I often use the formulation "[the language user's] *exercise* of the naming function". – When the emphasis is on *other* aspects, I sometimes use *for the sake of brevity* simply *"naming"*, instead of "the naming function of the definition"/ "[the language user's] exercise of the naming function".

(b) Between area (concept) and name (concept designation) there is *no univocal relationship in either direction.*

On the one hand, the same concept will often be designated by different linguistic entities. This is so, not only from language to language, but also in the same language. For example, for many people the words "cup" and "mug" will in many contexts designate essentially the same concept, or "right to" and "freedom to" in the formulations "right to walk in the Royal Park" and "freedom to walk in the Royal Park".

On the other hand, the same linguistic entity will often be used as the designation for different concepts, that is to say, the linguistic entity is polysemous. For example, the word "right" is not only used of freedom, as in the example above, but also of privilege, power and immunity, cf. Hohfeld's analysis.[39] Further, the word "right" is used of combinations of these basic elements (freedom, privilege, power, immunity) into more complex legal positions, such as "right of ownership", "civil right", and the like.

The now outlined undetermined and will-dependent nature of the *relationship between area-in-thought and name*[40] stands in contrast to what one considers as the determined and will-independent nature of *causal relationships*. The use of language exhibits *both* relationships. – The relationship between words and areas-in-thought we can call *"conventional sign relation"*; and the relationship between words and their causes or effects we can call *"natural sign relation"*.[41]

---

39 Hohfeld, *Fundamental Legal Conceptions*, in particular pp. 36 et seq., cf. p. 65.

40 Ogden/ Richards, *The Meaning of Meaning*, p. 123; Mead, *Mind, Self and Society*, p. 97; Robinson, *Definition*, pp. 66, 72–73; Hospers, *An Introduction to Philosophical Analysis*, pp. 5–7; Rommetveit, *Språk, tanke og kommunikasjon* [language, thought and communication], pp. 51–52; Lyons, *Language and Linguistics*, pp. 19(–23), 55. – See also section A 6 (3) above, on the corresponding relationship between proposition and language.

41 Some writers call the sign respectively "symbol" and "sign/al", according to whether it is part of a conventional or natural sign relation; see e.g. Parkinson, 'Introduction', p. 1; Andersson/ Furberg, *Språk och påverkan* [language and persuasion], p. 100. It is more usual to use "sign" as the common term ("the theory of signs"). However, the use of "symbol" and "sign/al" varies in several dimensions

The conventional sign relation provides room inter alia for customary and graduated changes in the meanings of words; for stipulated definitions; for understatement, irony and metaphors; and for the use of analogy as a form of argumentation. The element in common is that the word may well carry with it an area-in-thought, but that through stipulated definition of the word or in its application we can change the area in accordance with the definition itself or the application itself. In contrast, the natural sign relation, for example the appeal of words to emotions, lies outside the definition itself or the application itself, and consequently cannot be changed in the same way.[42]

The conventional and the natural sign relations may relate to each other in co-action ("I am happy", uttered in a joyful voice), in counteraction (the same sentence uttered in a monotonous and mournful voice), or neutrally (the same sentence uttered without the voice giving any information about state of mind).[43]

Awareness of the *conventional relationship* between area-in-thought and name leads inter alia to *such questions* as I shall be looking at more closely in what follows.

(2) When is it usual to give names to areas?

There are some areas there is reason to have an awareness of and therefore also *reason to have separate names for*. – For example, the concept of 'cup' delimits a set of physical objects that serve for drinking out of. Since this is an important function for human beings, there is reason in different connections to have an awareness of the area that cups constitute: for example, when we are thirsty and look around for a cup, when we ask others whether they have a cup to sell or to lend, or when we ask somebody to put cups on the table. And there is thus also a need for, and it is thus usual to have, a name of its own for this area: in Norwegian the word "kopp", in English the word "cup", and so forth.

There are other areas there is little or no reason to have an awareness of. – For example, the concept of 'trees with seven branches and a height of 197 cm' delimits an area without any specific role for human beings. And then there is *consequently no* need for, *nor* is it usual to have, a name of its own for this area.

(also) among influential writers; see e.g. Langer, *Philosophy in a New Key*, pp. 29 et seq., 57 et seq.; Alston, *Philosophy of Language*, pp. 50–61; Lyons, *Semantics*, Vol. 1, pp. 95–109. – In the present work it is not necessary to use these terms.

42 On how stipulated definitions are used to change the appeal of words to emotions, see sections 7.3.2 (2)(b) cf. 7.3.1 (4), below.

43 Compare Rommetveit, *Språk, tanke og kommunikasjon* [language, thought and communication], pp. 39–40.

(3) To what extent is it logically (by definition) necessary that a definition gives names to the areas-in-thought that are being delimited? – Survey of discussion and conclusions in the present item (3) and the next item (4)

In the present item (3) I shall look at the logical (definitional) aspect and in the next item (4) the factual aspect concerning when a definition names the areas-in-thought that it delimits. To give an overview and to guide the reader I shall first specify the main conclusions schematically and specify where in items (3)–(4) one will find the more detailed discussion.

To what extent a definition logically ("by definition"; the present item (3)) or in fact ("empirical question"; item (4) below) gives names to the areas it delimits:

			THE AREA THAT IS BEING POSITIVELY DELIMITED	AREA(S) AGAINST WHICH A BOUNDARY IS BEING DRAWN
WORD TERMINOLOGY (DEFINITION OF WORDS)	SAME LANGUAGE		By definition see (3)(b)	Empirical question see (4)(b)
	DIFFERENT LANGUAGE	NOT TRANSLATED	By definition see (3)(b)	
		TRANSLATED	Empirical question see (4)(d)	
CONCEPT TERMINOLOGY (DEFINITION OF CONCEPTS)	SAME LANGUAGE		Empirical question see (4)(e)(i)	Empirical question see (4)(b)
	DIFFERENT LANGUAGE		Empirical question see (4)(e)(ii)	

(a) It may be reasonable to say that communication and discussion of thoughts presuppose by definition that areas-in-thought are *specified linguistically*. For we do not have access to other people's thoughts (concepts) except through their signs, and among actually existing sets of signs, language has the greatest communicative power; only language can convey such nuancing as lies in even simple discussions and at such a speed as one finds even in such instances.

On the other hand I do not wish to say that it is by definition necessary that the area be named. Among linguistic specifications, I thus distinguish a *subgroup* I call *"name"/ "naming"*. The classification criterion is first and foremost whether the given linguistic entity has been formulated with a view to *repeated use*, or is in fact used repeatedly, of the area: in which case it functions as a name – or whether the linguistic entity is only formulated with a view to use on a single or just a few occasions and is in fact not used more often: in which case it functions as linguistic specification of another kind.

The boundary is *relative*: A linguistic entity, which in one person's language usage or in one connection functions as respectively name/ other linguistic specification, may in another person's language usage or in another connection function as respectively other linguistic specification/ name. For example, Peter says: "To understand legal argumentation it is important to be aware of the role weighing and balancing plays, and how weighing and balancing is governed by norms that say something about what arguments one shall, shall not, or may place weight on in the weighing and balancing, and, as the case may be, say something about what weight the arguments have or in what directions they pull"; and Mary replies: "Yes, I agree that guidelines are important." – For Mary the word "guidelines" presumably functions as a name, and the formulation "norms that say something about ... [etc.]" as other linguistic specification of the area; for if she is to speak of the area, she will presumably on the whole use the word "guidelines". If Peter takes over the word "guidelines" of the area, the same will apply for him. If, on the other hand, he continues to talk about the area and to use the long formulation as linguistic specification of the area, then this formulation will be the name of the area in his language usage.

As is apparent, the boundary between names and other linguistic specifications of areas-in-thought is vague, cf. the distinguishing criterion 'repeated use' versus 'use on a single or just a few occasions'. However, for the purposes here it is not necessary to draw any more precise boundary. *What is important* is awareness of the difference between on the one hand linguistic specification pure and simple, which is necessary if one wishes to communicate an area-in-thought, and on the other hand the more determinate linguistic baptism with a view to repeated mention of the area, which is not necessary for communication of the area. The *reason* for calling attention to this distinction in a discussion of *definitions* is that even though definitions always structure (section 4.1 (2) above), and even though they always provide a linguistic specification of the area (the present item), definitions do not always give names to all the areas that are delimited (item (b) cf. item (4), below).

(b) Is it logically (by definition) necessary for a definition to have a naming function? Or, to put it in another way: Is it logically (by definition) possible for a definition to be *completely without* naming function?

In the case of *normative* definitions of *words*[44] the definition will with logical (definitional) necessity have a naming function; cf. for example the definition: "I

[44] I use "definition of words" instead of the complete formulation "definition of the usage/ meaning/ [or the like] ... of a word". I do so, partly for the sake of brevity, and partly because the abbreviated

shall use the word "competence" of ...". – This is because the words that are defined are in this case established as names in and by the definition.

For the same reason *descriptive* definitions of words will by definition have a naming function, provided, that is, that the words that are being defined *have not been translated*. They may be words in the same language that the definition is formulated in, for example: "The word "law" is used inter alia of ...". Or they may be words in another language that are cited directly, for example: "Kant used the word "Recht" of ...".

In the case of descriptive definitions of *translated words*, on the other hand, the definition no longer has a naming function by definition, since in and through the translation an indeterminacy is brought about in respect of the name; cf. for example the definition: "Kant used the word "right" of ...".

Nor in the case of definitions of *concepts* does the definition have a naming function by definition, whether the definition be descriptive or normative.

As I now turn to the discussion of the factual aspect, I shall also return in more detail to the two last-mentioned instance-types (see respectively item (4)(d) on definition of translated words, and item (4)(e) on definition of concepts).

> Many statements about definitions say explicitly or presuppose as a seeming matter of course that all definitions have a naming function.[45] Inter alia for this reason one loses the possibility of focus on and mapping of such aspects of meaning determinations occurring in fact and formulated in everyday language as outlined in the present item (3) and in the following item (4).

---

form isolates what in this context is the essential: that the definition formulation (also) speaks of words, not (only) concepts.

45 See e.g. Mill, *A System of Logic*, p. 86 ("[t]he simplest and most correct notion of a Definition is, a proposition declaratory of the meaning of a word"); Whitehead/ Russell, *Principia Mathematica*, Vol. I, p. 11 ("A definition is a declaration that a certain newly-introduced symbol or combination of symbols is to mean the same as a certain other combination of symbols"); Ogden/ Richards, *The Meaning of Meaning*, p. 118 ("the naming relation is involved in ... every definition"); Carnap, *Der logische Aufbau der Welt*, pp. 70, 159 ("eine Definition ... gibt an, daß ein bestimmtes Zeichen ... in allen Aussagen ersetzt werden darf durch ein anderes ... Zeichen"); Quine, 'Truth by Convention', p. 78 ("[a] definition, strictly, is a convention of notational abbreviation"); 'Two Dogmas of Empiricism', pp. 24–27; 'Carnap and Logical Truth', pp. 394–95 ("[l]egislative definition introduces a notation ... [d]iscursive definition ... sets forth a preëxisting relation ... between notations"); Robinson, *Definition*, p. 191 ("I propose ... that by 'definition' we always mean a process ... either of equating two symbols or of reporting or proposing a meaning for a symbol"); Næss, *Interpretation and Preciseness*, p. 147 ("normative definition [shall mean the same as] sentence which announces that a certain expression ... shall be interpreted or used synonymously with a certain other expression"); p. 169 ("descriptive definition [shall mean the same as] sentence [which] states that a certain expression ... is used synonymously with a certain other expression"); Weinberger, *Rechtslogik*, p. 358 ("[u]nter einer Definition werden wir – annähernd gesagt – die Bestimmung der Bedeutung oder/ und Anwendungsweise eines sprachlichen Ausdrucks mittels anderer sprachlicher Ausdrücke verstehen").

(4) To what extent is it in fact so, that definitions give names to the areas-in-thought that are being delimited; and what clues do definitions usually provide in this respect?

As outlined above it is only in one instance-type logically (by definition) necessary that a definition has a naming function, namely in the case of definition of words that have not been translated (item (3)(b)). – Apart from this the element of naming function in a definition is an empirical question.

In the present section, I shall look more closely at the *extent to which definitions in fact name* the areas-in-thought that are delimited (items (a)–(e)). In so doing, I shall also look at *interpretation* of some major types of definition formulation, with a view to mapping *what clues* they typically provide in the naming question (items (c)–(e)). Finally, against the background of the discussions mentioned, I shall give a brief characterisation of statutory definitions (item (f)).

(a) A definition may have a *total* naming function in relation to its structuring function, that is to say that all areas that are delimited are also given names.

Most simply and most perspicuously this happens where the definition delimits one and only one area. – For example, the definition formulation "the word "cup" is used of things for drinking out of" specifies one and only one area ('things for drinking out of') and its name ("cup").

(b) It is quite usual for definitions to have a *partial* naming function in relation to their structuring function: As a step in the delimitation of the area that is positively brought into focus, the definition specifies one or more other areas against which a boundary is being drawn, *without* these areas being named; that is to say that *the structuring function is more comprehensive than the naming function.* – I shall outline some *variants* for illustration (items (i)–(iii)).

(i) In *language teaching* one may say for example: "No, these things for eating with we do not call "cups"; it is only of these things, which we drink out of, that that word is used." – A boundary is thereby drawn against the area 'things for eating with' without these things being named with words like "knife", "fork", or the like. Naming with "knife", "fork", or the like, can be unhelpful because the person learning the language has for the time being *enough to cope with*, placing the word "cup". Or it can be unnecessary because the person *already has command of* the use of words like "knife" and "fork", so that these are tacitly assumed.

(ii) In the course of his discussion of the definition of "dispositive proposition" Arnholm states: "[O]ne [should] quite certainly restrict the area to propositions within the sphere of private law ...; otherwise the material will not be sufficiently homogeneous."[46] – Arnholm thereby draws a boundary with propositions within public law, for example statutes, judgments and administrative decisions, but without giving these areas one or more separate names. Such naming was neither

46 Arnholm, 'Omkring rettshandelsteorien' [concerning the theory of juristic acts], p. 413.

necessary nor natural, since he precisely did not wish to treat the said areas in his further discussion.

This points to a more *general pattern*: As a step in the definition process it may be expedient to *draw a boundary with one or more neighbouring areas*; one often understands (even) better what area one is concerned with by getting to know a little about what falls outside the area. However, since one wishes precisely to draw a boundary with these areas, there is *no need for naming*. – The difference shows itself in that a linguistic specification of an area that may be expedient when the purpose is delimitation against this area, may be quite unsuitable as a name for the area when one wishes to treat this positively (item (5) below). The linguistic specification of the area may be unsuitable, for example because it does not in the way one wishes lead mental representations, thoughts or feelings towards features of the area (see for example Arnholm's discussion mentioned above, in which the area is only specified as "not propositions within the sphere of private law"). Or the linguistic specification of the area may be unsuitable because it is too elaborate.

(iii) With a view to a more precise placing of one's own topic, one often starts out with a descriptive *mapping of the meanings of polysemous key words*, for example a mapping of meanings of the word "rett" [Recht, law, right]. One delimits several of the areas of which the polysemous key word is used: first and foremost those areas which are most closely related to the area one intends to deal with, because it is in these cases that the danger of a mix-up is greatest. However, this delimiting is done *without* one's holding that the polysemous word itself shall serve as a name; this is something one wishes to avoid because of the polysemy. And this delimiting is done *without* one's holding that the words in the specification of the individual areas shall serve as names; one points out, for example, that the word "right" is often used of a capacity to stipulate norms which, judged by validity norms, can come to be regarded as valid,[47] an area specification that is obviously not suitable as a name.

After such a more or less comprehensive mapping one then gives a name to the area on which one wishes to concentrate the attention: for example "competence" as a name for the capacity to stipulate norms – while one lets the naming question remain open as far as the other areas are concerned.

(c) The naming is clearest where the definition explicitly relates to the *actual words used*: "Stang used the term "viljeserklæring" [declaration of intent] differently from Hagerup, namely of …", "By the formulation "valid law" I shall mean in what follows …"

When the definition relates to *something other than* the actual words used, the uncertainty surrounding the naming immediately becomes greater. Two instance-

47 Compare Eng, 'Begrepene 'kompetanse' og 'gyldighet' i juridisk argumentasjon' [the concepts of 'competence' and 'validity' in legal argumentation], pp. 628 (paragraph in small print) cf. 627 (bottom).

types are definition of translated words (item (d) below) and definition of concepts (item (e) below).

(d) Definition of *translated words* occurs in the case of *descriptive definitions* of the usage of speakers of other languages: "Kant used the word "right" of …".

In such instances one can quite often act on the assumption that the definer has in mind the translation that is most common at the moment of his producing his definition: in the example, the translation between "Recht" and "right". – However, one can easily imagine that the recipient of the definition may have reason to be uncertain on this point. The person whose usage is being described perhaps uses special terminology ("did Kant use any Latin words?"). Or the usage being described goes back in time, so that the usage may have changed ("did Kant write in Latin?", "did Germans use the word "Recht" in the 18th century too?"). Or the translation is uncertain also when it comes to standard usage at the moment of the definer's producing his definition, so that the recipient has no "most common translation" to resort to ("which words in language X come closest to the meanings of our word "right"?").

In the case of *normative definitions* it is not very practical that translation is a source of uncertainty about the designation of the concept.[48] One does not say for example "I shall use the word "Recht" of …", if it is the word "right" one intends to use. Nor does one say "I shall use the English word that corresponds to "Recht" of …"; one will use the word "right" directly. – What one can experience, on the other hand, is statements like "I shall use the corresponding English word of …". But most often it will in such cases be explicitly stated or be clear from the context what the corresponding English word is.

(e) *Concept terminology* makes it possible to formulate definitions on the level of meaning alone, to formulate a definition as delimitation of a concept.[49]

That definitions are formulated in concept terminology is common *in the case of both descriptive and normative definitions*, cf. for example: "Stang has another concept of 'declaration of intent' than Hagerup, in so far as …", "My concept of 'law' covers …". – Furthermore, concept terminology is common *both within the same language*, see the examples in the preceding sentence, *and between different languages*, cf. for example: "Kant's concept of 'law' covers …".

One might think that such definitions had *only* a structuring function, cf. the fact that the definition formulations speak directly only of "concept" and not of any linguistic designation for the concept. – It is *logically possible* for such definitions to have only a structuring function (item (3)(b) above). However, structuring function alone is extremely *rare within the same language* (item (i) below). The occurrence of structuring function alone is *most practical in the case of*

48 See, however, item (f) below, on statutory definitions.

49 I should remind the reader that by "concept terminology" I mean words like "concept", "conception", "notion", "idea" and their derivatives (or their equivalents in other languages) (cf. section A 2 (1) above, in note 1).

descriptive definitions of the usage of speakers of *another language* (item (ii) below).

(i) In the case of concept definitions *within the same language* one can most often take it as given that the linguistic entity used as a designation in the definition formulation is *also* intended as a standpoint through presupposition on the naming question in relation to the area that is being positively delimited:

If we look at the examples by way of introduction in the present item (e) ("Stang has another concept of 'declaration of intent' than Hagerup, in so far as ...", "My concept of 'law' covers ..."), it is extremely unusual for anybody to speak in this way without also intending to use the term "declaration of intent" as the designation of the concept of 'declaration of intent' that is being described, or without also intending to use the word "law" of the concept of 'law' that is being normatively regulated. – And the same seems to apply in general in the case of definitions within the same language which according to their formulation relate to the level of meaning alone: It is unusual that such definitions are not also *by presupposition* intended as a standpoint on the naming of the area one is positively delimiting.

The reason is that it is on the whole *pointless* to structure without at the same time naming the area one is positively delimiting: – In the case of descriptive definitions this would mean that the recipient of the definition did not get to know what linguistic expressions it was, whose use was being described: in the example above, did not get to know what linguistic expressions in Stang and Hagerup it was, whose use was being compared. – In the case of normative definitions this would mean putting effort into delimiting an area one did not intend to use. For if one uses the area several times, the linguistic specification of the area will by definition function as a name.

> In more comprehensive discussions of which normative definitions are to be preferred, it may be expedient *linguistically (presentationally) to divide the definition discussion*, especially into the following three elements: outlines of and comparisons between different concepts that have been proposed or used; an account of one's own decision in the structuring question; and an account of one's own decision in the naming question. Examples of concept discussions along such dividing lines are Eckhoff's discussion of the concept of 'burden of proof',[50] Arnholm's discussion of the concept of 'juristic act',[51] and my own discussion of the concepts of 'competence' and 'validity' in legal argumentation.[52] – Still, it is common to see the elements as steps in *one and the same definition*, that is to say that one does not see the propositions that concern the structuring alone as a separate definition.

50 Eckhoff, *Tvilsrisikoen* [the bearing of the risk of doubt], especially pp. 9–21.

51 Arnholm, 'Omkring rettshandelsteorien' [concerning the theory of juristic acts].

52 Eng, 'Begrepene 'kompetanse' og 'gyldighet' i juridisk argumentasjon' [the concepts of 'competence' and 'validity' in legal argumentation].

What has now been claimed to be uncommon is that the area that the definition *positively delimits* is not at the same time given a name, either in the same or in another part of the definition formulation. I should remind the reader that it is, on the other hand, not uncommon for the structuring function of definitions, as a step in the specification of the area that is being positively delimited, also to delimit one or more *other areas against which a boundary is being drawn*, and for these areas not to be named (item (b) above); that is to say that the structuring function is more comprehensive than the naming function.

(ii) In the case of concept definitions *between different languages*, in practice that is to say in the case of descriptive definitions of the usage of speakers of another language than the language in which the definition is formulated, one cannot infer with equal certainty *from* the linguistic entity used as a designation in the definition formulation *to* a standpoint by presupposition on the naming question in relation to the area that is being positively delimited; for example, one cannot infer with equal certainty from "Kant's concept of 'right' " to "Kant's use of the word "Recht" ". – The reason is that the *source of uncertainty* that lies in concept terminology *is cumulated with* the source of uncertainty that lies in translation (on translation as a source of uncertainty, see item (d) above).

(f) *Statutory definitions* seldom call what is defined "concept" (compare item (e) above), *word terminology* is the usual thing; see the examples given in my main discussions of statutory definitions (sections 3.3.6 above and 5.4.2 (2) below).

In the case of other normative definitions than statutory definitions it is not very practical that *translation* gives rise to uncertainty about the naming (compare item (d) above). When a text passed in the course of international co-operation on legislation becomes national law in translated form, the same applies to statutory definitions in the translated text. However, if the text becomes national law without being translated, especially where reference is made in national law to a foreign-language convention,[53] we are confronted with an example of the fact that the definer (the legislators) addresses a normative definition to others (see section 3.3.6 (2) above on norm subjects in the case of statutory definitions) without determinately naming the defined area: Is one to use the foreign-language name or a name in the national language, and if the latter, what name in the national language?

Most statutory definitions have a *total* naming function in relation to their structuring function, that is to say that all areas that are delimited are also given names (compare item (a) above); I refer to the examples in my main discussions of statutory definitions (sections 3.3.6 above and 5.4.2 (2) below).

53 See e.g. section 3 of the Norwegian Rail Transport Act (Act No. 74 of 15 June 1984).

(5) What factors can explain what name an area acquires and whether the area gains ground or is impeded because of the name?

(a) Properties of the name itself

Features of the concept designation like its *length, spelling* and *pronunciation* have consequences for how easy it is to write, say or remember the designation. And it is reasonable to assume that the easier it is to write, say or remember the designation, the easier it is for the designation to gain ground.

(b) The capacity of the name to lead mental representations, thoughts and feelings

Words evoke and lead mental representations, thoughts and feelings. – Our words can *evoke and lead more or less well* in relation to what is intended to be expressed. I assume that the definer has, and is more or less consciously influenced by, views about such relationships when naming an area-in-thought (item (i)–(iii)).

(i) That the concept designation leads to *mental representations* can be an advantage. For example, the Norwegian word "besittelse" [Besitz, possession] is so strange to non-lawyers that being shown the connection with the concrete action of "å sitte på en fysisk gjenstand" [auf einem physischen Gegenstand sitzen; sitting on a physical object] can make it easier to remember the word. Mental representations can also be a disadvantage, however. The image of a person sitting on a physical object may be more of an obstacle than an aid when one is to go more deeply into the areas-in-thought that the word "besittelse" covers in law.[54]

(ii) Further, the concept designation can lead *more abstract thought.* Perhaps the best way of illustrating the influence from this relation on naming is to point to instances in which the influence has been small, i.e. in which the designation leads less well in relation to what is intended to be expressed. Reflection on such instances creates an awareness that words *normally* lead better and that one *expects* precisely this. – Here are some examples:

The designation *"internasjonal privatrett"* [private international law] leads our thought towards rules which are common to many countries ("international") and which concern matters of private law. Both are misleading, since the rules concerned are national (vary from country to country)[55] and since they also decide

---

[54] Compare Hohfeld, *Fundamental Legal Conceptions*, p. 30: "Much of the difficulty, as regards legal terminology, arises from the fact that many of our words were originally applicable only to physical things; so that their use in connection with legal relations is, strictly speaking, figurative or fictional" (Hohfeld's footnote omitted); Stang, *Innledning til formueretten* [introduction to the law of obligations and property], p. 8.

[55] Gaarder, *Innføring i internasjonal privatrett* [introduction to international private law], p. 22; Philip, *Dansk international privat- og processret* [Danish international private and procedural law], pp. 3–4; Eckhoff, *Rettskildelære* [doctrine of the sources of law], 1st–3rd eds. respectively pp. 257, 258, 254.

other legal questions than those one traditionally says relate to "private law".[56] – A more apt designation would be "lovvalgsregler" [choice of law rules] or "interlegal rett" [interlegal law].[57]

The designation *"bevisbyrderegler"* [burden of proof rules] leads our thought towards notions of a high degree of certainty ("proof"), which is misleading, since the rules often require only a modest degree of preponderance of probability. Further, the term "burden of proof" makes it difficult to express what is often the main rule in a legal system (except in the case of the criminal law issue of the accused's guilt), namely that it is the most probable fact that shall be taken as established. To say "the parties share the burden of proof", "have half the burden of proof each", or the like, sounds artificial. And to say "the main rule in the burden of proof doctrine is that neither of the parties has the burden of proof" is infelicitous since the main rule thereby falls outside the area covered by the name one gives to the problem. – In the light of inter alia such considerations, Eckhoff proposed instead the word "tvilsrisikoen" [the bearing of the risk of doubt].[58]

A central and controversial family of legal area-designations is the German term *"Rechtsgeschäft"* and the corresponding Scandinavian *translations* "rettshandel" [Norwegian], "retshandel" [Danish] and "rättshandling" [Swedish]. Both when the word "rettshandel" [literally: juristic transaction] was introduced into Norwegian legal language around 1850 and subsequently, one could object that "rettshandling" [juristic act] would be a more apt specification of the area delimitation that was intended. This word, however, was already in use as a name for other areas.[59] Later there arose in addition the disadvantage of the word "rettshandel" that different writers linked the word to different structurings.[60] – In the light of inter alia these matters, Arnholm suggested instead the designation "dispositivt utsagn" [dispositive proposition].[61]

(iii) Many words evoke and lead *feelings*. Views about this will often influence the naming: If one wants to counteract what falls within the area, then one chooses words that one assumes will arouse negative feelings in the recipients (oneself included). And if one wants to promote what falls within the area, then one chooses words that one assumes will arouse positive feelings. – This technique for influencing people I shall later discuss under the name of "persuasive definitions" (section 7). Here I mention it only briefly in its capacity of being a causal factor behind choice of name.

---

56 Gaarder and Eckhoff, same places as referred to in the preceding note. – Philip avoids much of this misleadingness by separating out procedural decisions and rules under the name of "international procedural law"; see the same work as referred to in the preceding note, pp. 7–8.

57 Same places as referred to in note 55 above.

58 Eckhoff, *Tvilsrisikoen* [the bearing of the risk of doubt], pp. 14–21.

59 Arnholm, 'Omkring rettshandelsteorien' [concerning the theory of juristic acts], pp. 371–72.

60 Op. cit., pp. 376–89.

61 Op. cit., p. 412. – See also section 4.3.3 below, where analyses of the juristic act serve to illustrate alternation between old and new in the structuring function and naming function of definitions.

(c) What structurings the name is encumbered with from before

The lot of the word "rettshandel" (item (b)(ii) above, at and in notes 60 and 61), illustrates how the possibility of linking a concept designation to a particular area is also connected with what structurings the designation is encumbered with from before: Other things being equal, the coupling of a designation to a *particular* area will the more easily gain ground, the fewer the customary or stipulated structurings the designation has already been linked to. For the more such structurings, the more *polysemous* the designation, and the more difficult it is to keep to the new coupling of name and area.

I refer in this connection also to the earlier discussion of the relationship between custom-based and stipulated definitions, and the pointing out there by way of example of how difficult it is to link words like "law", "right", "power", "rationality" and "reality" to particular areas (section 3.3.3 (2) above). – In the earlier discussion the problem lay in the *encumbrance from custom.* In the case of "rettshandel" the problem lies in the *encumbrance from the many stipulated definitions.* The element *in common* is the risk that the recipient of sentences in which the words are used, interprets these words on the basis of *his* preferences or habits in relation to the many structurings the words have been linked to, in spite of the *sender's* more or less explicit structuring.

(d) The naming's degree of correspondence with or departure from earlier language usage

The consideration for unambiguity (for keeping to the coupling of name and a particular area) may thus be an argument for using completely new names when one is delimiting an area-in-thought (item (c) above). – Such a strategy can, however, lead to consequences that are evaluated negatively: The degree of *attention to thoughts* often seems to become smaller, the more the *naming departs from earlier language usage* (items (i)–(iii)).

(i) One reason is that completely new names can give the impression that there are more new thoughts than is in fact the case, and thereby that greater *attention and effort to familiarise oneself with the material* are necessary than is in fact the case.

(ii) Another reason is the *force of tradition and habit.* Once a terminology has taken root, it costs the individual language user so much *attention and effort to establish new word habits* that even very well-reasoned proposals for change do not win through; see the examples in item (b)(ii) above of traditional and misleading designations in lawyers' language usage ("private international law", "burden of proof").

(iii) In the two causal lines now outlined (items (i)–(ii) above) the *language user's motive* was limited to his *own situation*, to what degree of attention and effort new language usage on his part seemed to demand of him.

In another causal line the language user's motive also incorporates assumptions he makes about *other people's behaviour*: To be left standing alone represents the worst alternative, and the fear of this alternative blocks the way for an innovation in language usage that everybody wants. – The reason that changes in language usage do not win through lies in these cases in a *problem of co-ordination.*

In the case of other forms of behaviour than the use of language, co-ordination problems are resolved through agreements, through organisations or, in relation to the most comprehensive co-ordination problems, through a legal system and a state. In the case of language, the solutions to co-ordination problems are less differentiated and less used; production and distribution of areas-in-thought and names take place to a much greater extent without competition-regulatory agreements and without central control.

> Agreements are often impractical, for example in relation to lawyers as a group within the individual language community. – Central control presupposes competence to decide over major groups of other people, something which is less common in the case of the use of language than in the case of other forms of behaviour (section 3.3.1 (3) above). And exercise of the heteronomous competence there might be is often impractical: for example, the use of legislation to regulate lawyers' use of language.

Changes in language usage are thereby to a large extent left to the *individual language user's initiative.* – This being so, from the individual language user's point of view the question will be *whether* he shall follow the convincing grounds for changing his language usage, with a risk of being left standing alone and in that event with the responsibility for uncertainty and misunderstandings that may arise (the alternative most people will rank lowest); *or whether* he shall follow traditional language usage (the alternative most people will rank as the middle one: better than standing alone on new language usage, but not so good as everybody following new language usage). – In such a motive situation, it is psychologically natural that many language users choose to follow traditional language usage: for example that advocates, judges, civil service lawyers and legal writers continue to use the term "private international law", even though they take the view that the term is unsatisfactory.

> The co-ordination problem outlined is reminiscent of co-ordination problems in society that have been discussed under the name of "game theory".[62] – A difference is that the co-ordination problem in the case of language *does not include the action alternative "I receive, but I give nothing"* (I am an egoist and everybody else shows solidarity). People's actions suggest that this alternative has great motivational force in many connections. An example of this is the payment of tax: The best alternative is that everybody else pays tax, but not I. The second best is that everybody pays. The third best is that nobody pays. And the worst alternative is that I alone pay. – As demon-

62 Johansen, 'Spillteori som grunnlag for samfunnsanalyse' [game theory as a basis for analysis of society]; Elster, *Forklaring og dialektikk* [explanation and dialectics], in particular pp. 74–86, cf. 181–90; Føllesdal/ Walløe/ Elster, *Argumentasjonsteori, språk og vitenskapsfilosofi* [argumentation theory, language and the philosophy of science], pp. 296–301.

strated in the main text above, one finds in the case of language parallels to the last three action alternatives: The best is that everybody changes his language usage; the second best is that everybody follows traditional language usage; and the worst is that only I change my language usage. However, one does not find any parallel to the most egoistic alternative: It is not very meaningful to prefer that everybody else follows the good grounds and changes his language usage, but not I.

(e) Authority

The greater the authority of the person who *suggests* a name or *follows* a naming suggestion from others, the greater the probability that those who are influenced by this authority will see the choice of name as an example to be followed (for example, in the case of scholarly authority), or as something one follows as a matter of course (for example, in the case of authority between parents and small children). And the *more* who follow the choice of name and the *more often*, the greater the probability that the name takes root. – There often arises a self-reinforcing reciprocal action between, on the one hand, the language usage of authorities or actual language usage otherwise, and on the other hand, normative views of what is "natural language usage", "good language usage", or the like.

Here, as in the work's mappings otherwise of causal factors (or of considerations), I imply an *"other things being equal"-proviso*: There are many examples of people with great authority having proposed concept designations that have not caught on. As examples relating to scholarly authority it may be mentioned that neither Eckhoff's proposal for the introduction of the term "tvilsrisiko" [the bearing of the risk of doubt] nor Arnholm's proposal for the introduction of the term "dispositivt utsagn" [dispositive proposition] has won general support (see item (b)(ii) above on the two proposals). Particularly Eckhoff's proposal has had problems getting a foothold in actual language usage among lawyers. One cause is probably the force of tradition and habit (item (d)(ii) above): The word "tvilsrisiko" does not only deviate from consistent and widespread language usage in the Nordic countries ("bevisbyrde", "bevisbörda"), but from consistent and widespread usage in major languages ("burden of proof", "Beweislast").

(a)↔(e) The above-mentioned factors may work consciously or unconsciously

The factors that have been outlined may work as conscious or unconscious motives: be it on the part of the *person defining*, when he gives a name, or on the part of *other language users*, when they are making up their minds about whether they shall follow the definer's choice of name; be it in the case of *stipulated definitions today*, or in the case of stipulated definitions *that in their time gave rise to custom-based definitions.* – However, in the case of stipulated definitions that in their time gave rise to custom-based definitions, the norm stipulator's identity and his motives will often lie back in a past that has gone without trace: "Who used the words "right", "Recht", "rett", for the first time?" What language users can cognise today about the origin of custom-based parts of language is simply that they are confronted with customary language norms that couple word and area.

4.3. The significance of the distinction between the structuring function and the naming function of definitions

In what follows I shall demonstrate how the distinction between the structuring function and naming function of definitions can contribute to more nuanced cognition of *what one is in fact doing when one is defining*.

4.3.1. Whether, and if so to what extent, definitions have the one, the other or both functions. Interplay

The question of whether, and if so to what extent, definitions have a structuring function, a naming function or both has been answered as part of the discussions above: – In my definition theory all definitions have a structuring function *by definition* (section 4.1 (2) above), while it is to a great extent an *empirical question* whether definitions have a naming function (see the schema in section 4.2 (3) above, with further references). – As was apparent from my more detailed discussions (section 4.2 (3)–(4) above), definitions in the case of which the existence of the naming function is an empirical question, *often* have purely factually a naming function.

On closer examination, actually occurring analysis and argumentation often shows an *interplay* between structuring and naming. The words taken as a starting point in the case of a topic specification, for example "law", are considered indeterminate, for example polysemous. Different areas are specified of which the word is used (structuring). Even if the specifications of the individual areas are brief, they will often be comprehensive enough for them to be considered impractical as concept designations. When one focuses on the area that is to be discussed more closely, one therefore gives it a brief designation (naming, for example: "natural law", "legal order", "the legal profession", "the study of law", "valid law", "common law", "statute", "legal precept", "legal", "valid", etc.). In the further analysis a number of distinctions are pointed to within the area that are claimed to be of interest (structuring). In any more detailed discussion of these sub-areas, these are given, for the same reason as mentioned above, a brief designation (naming, for example in relation to the validity area: "void", "voidable", "ex nunc", "ex tunc"). And so forth.

4.3.2. Whether the functions are exercised descriptively or normatively

Both the naming function of the definition and its structuring function can be exercised descriptively or normatively. The functions can be exercised in the same way (items (1)–(2) below). But they cannot be exercised in different ways; that is pointless (item (3) below) or logically impossible (item (4) below).

(1) One possible combination is that *both* the naming function *and* the structuring function are exercised *descriptively.* The person defining in this case takes his point of departure in an actually occurring linguistic entity and says in the definition something about how this linguistic entity is actually used. Or he takes his point of departure in an actually occurring structuring and says in the definition something about what this structuring is actually like and about what linguistic entity or entities are actually used in the naming of the structuring.

(2) Another possible combination is that *both* the naming function *and* the structuring function are exercised *normatively.* The person defining will in this case in purely practical terms often proceed as in the case of descriptive definitions, that is to say, delimit an area and pinpoint a particular linguistic entity as the name of the area. The difference is that the definer now says that he will use the combination of this area and this name, or that one should or shall (or other types of normative modality) use this combination.

The area and the name may be taken from existing language usage (normative-traditional exercise of the definition functions), or they may to a greater or lesser degree be new and unusual (normative-innovative exercise of the definition functions) (section 4.3.3 below).

(3) Can a definition be normative in its structuring function and descriptive in its naming function?

This combination is *logically possible.* An example would be: The definer delimits an area and says that he will use this structuring in his presentation; thus the structuring function is normatively exercised. In addition, the definer says something about what linguistic entities are actually used of the specified area, but he does not say anything about what linguistic entity he himself will use; in such a case the naming function is descriptively exercised.

However, as one can see from the example described, such a combination of the normative and the descriptive will be extremely *impractical.* It is difficult to find any situation in which this combination will serve any purpose. The only logically possible way of implementing the combination seems to be to *introduce the area, but not to use it* (repeatedly). For if the area is to be used (repeatedly), it will in practice be given a name (section 4.2 (3)(a) above), and this will be done normatively, as the definer's decision/ promise (section 3.3.1 (2) above). Another matter is that the giving of the name often takes place tacitly: The definer will consider it unnecessary explicitly to announce his decision in the naming question, because the decision is apparent from the exercise of the structuring function or from the continuation (of the conversation, lecture, book, etc.).

(4) Can a definition be descriptive in its structuring function and normative in its naming function?

This combination is *logically impossible.* A purported example could be: The definer delimits an area and says that this area is actually used by certain people in certain situations. These propositions are descriptive. The definer then says that he will use a particular linguistic entity of the area. This proposition is normative. – However, in the definer's decision concerning the naming there is from a logical point of view *also* a decision concerning the structuring. The reason is that naming is always *relative to* an area: One uses the linguistic entities *of* something, or *in* a particular linguistic connection. That the definer does not actually use the linguistic entity later is not decisive. What is decisive is that *if* the linguistic entity is used, *then* by definition an area is used too. And this necessary connection also applies on the definition level, in the relationship between the naming function of the definition and its structuring function. – The example outlined applies to decision propositions. But the necessary connection also applies to the other normative definition modalities, like imposition of duty or recommendation: If one acts normatively in the exercise of the naming function, then one *also* acts normatively in the exercise of the structuring function.

4.3.3. Whether the functions are exercised normative-traditionally or normative-innovatively. Criteria for "the same definition question"

(1) The problem. Purpose
(2) Comparison with language usage at large
(3) Comparison with particular other definitions
- **(a) Mapping of some possible combinations. 'Juristic act' as an example**
  - **(i) Traditional structuring – Traditional naming**
  - **(ii) Innovative structuring – Traditional naming**
  - **(iii) Innovative structuring – Innovative naming**
  - **(iv) Traditional structuring – Innovative naming**
- **(b) Alternation. Fixed points. Criteria for "the same definition question"**

(4) The graduation in the concepts of 'traditional/ innovative exercise of the definition functions'

(1) The problem. Purpose

In the course of my discussion of normative definitions I pointed out that the concept of 'normative' does not entail that the definition departs from normal language usage; and I introduced the terms "normative-traditional" and "normative-innovative" as names of definitions that respectively keep to and depart from a given language usage (section 3.3.4 above).

Further, I stated that *custom-based* definitions are by definition normative-traditional in relation to normal language usage. This proposition may now be stated more precisely thus: Custom-based definitions are normative-traditional both in their structuring function and in their naming function.

What about *stipulated definitions*? In the earlier discussion I simply said that it is an empirical question whether stipulated definitions are normative-traditional or normative-innovative. In what follows I shall examine more closely the *relationship between old and new in the case of stipulated definitions.*

The *purpose* of my discussion is *not* to take a standpoint on details concerning the *application* of the concepts of 'traditional/ innovative exercise of the definition functions':[63] The concepts of 'traditional/ innovative exercise of the structuring function' are related to many concepts of 'same/ different meaning'. Næss has demonstrated how much work is required to link propositions about the same/ different meaning to experience so that they become intersubjectively testable.[64] – The present discussion lies on a level *prior to* such problems of application: Before one discusses the application, one must know what it is one wants to apply. The present discussion is meant to contribute to the *clarification and mapping* of some main threads in what I assume to be widespread *intuitions about "old" and "new"* concerning concepts and the use of words. The discussion may in so doing contribute to the clarification and mapping of what one might possibly be talking about, inter alia when one uses the expressions "same/ different meaning".

(2) Comparison with language usage at large

The concepts of 'traditional/ innovative exercise of the definition functions' can be used for comparing a given definition with *language usage at large*, in contrast to comparing it with particular other definitions.

That a definition has a *normative-innovative naming function* means, when one compares with language usage at large, that the definition makes use of a completely new word ("neologism"). Examples are the introduction of the word "rettshandel" [juristic act] into Norwegian law by the Insolvency Act of 1863,[65] or Eckhoff's introduction of the word "tvilsrisiko" [the bearing of the risk of doubt].[66]

---

63 For the sake of brevity I use in a number of places "traditional/ innovative exercise of the definition functions" as a common term for the two distinction dimensions 'normative-traditional exercise–normative-innovative exercise' and 'structuring function–naming function'.

64 Næss' major work on this is *Interpretation and Preciseness* (1953). But a number of his other works are also concerned with these problems; see e.g. *"Truth" as Conceived by Those who are not Professional Philosophers* (1938). – See also section 3.3.3 (3)(b)(i) above).

65 Arnholm, 'Fra avtalerettens arbeidsområder' [from the research areas of the law of contract], p. 322; 'Omkring rettshandelsteorien' [concerning the theory of juristic acts], pp. 373–74.

66 Eckhoff, *Tvilsrisikoen* [the bearing of the risk of doubt], pp. 14–21.

That a definition has a *normative-innovative structuring function* means, when one compares with language usage at large, that the definition delimits an area that has not previously been seen on its own. – The innovation may lie in seeing traditional areas *together* ("synthesis", "generalisation"). An example is Sundby's concept of 'guideline' which brings together norms that very few, if any, Norwegian lawyers had previously seen together: sources-of-law principles, sentencing principles, norms about what are relevant considerations in the case of statutes that prescribe weighing and balancing, etc.[67] – Or the innovation may lie in *dividing up* traditional areas ("analysis", "specification"). An example is my model of lawyers' discussion of the binding force of stipulated norms.[68] In relation to traditional use of terms like "kompetansenorm", "competence norm", "power conferring rule" and "Ermächtigungsnorm", I suggest separating out exercise norms (pp. 637–44) and in/validity norms (pp. 664–69). Further, what has in Scandinavian legal theory traditionally been called "materielle kompetansebetingelser" [material competence-conditions], I suggest dividing up into situation conditions and content specifications (pp. 644–51).

Often it will be natural to compare the given definition with one or more *particular other definitions*, for example to compare definitions of 'juristic act', 'the bearing of the risk of doubt', 'guideline' or 'competence norm' with related conceptualisations. This is the topic of the following item (3).

(3) Comparison with particular other definitions

(a) Mapping of some possible combinations. 'Juristic act' as an example

If one combines the distinction dimension 'structuring–naming' and the distinction dimension 'traditional–innovative', four alternatives are provided (items (i)–(iv) below).

As an example to illustrate these alternatives, I shall use a number of definitions of 'juristic act' in Norwegian legal literature. Among these I place Hagerup's definition as a starting point.

Hagerup structures through the formulation "a declaration of intent, aimed at producing legal effects", and he names through the word "rettshandel" [juristic act].[69] – Hagerup's structuring brings together the declarations of intent in the case of which there is an intention to produce legal effects, irrespective of whether or not the legal effect occurs. For example, a promise that is invalid on the ground of having been made by a minor, is grouped together with valid promises, provided the minor intended to bind himself. Further, declarations of

---

67 Sundby, *Om normer* [on norms], pp. 190 et seq.

68 Eng, 'Begrepene 'kompetanse' og 'gyldighet' i juridisk argumentasjon' [the concepts of 'competence' and 'validity' in legal argumentation]. The references in parentheses in the rest of the paragraph are to this article.

69 Hagerup, *Retsencyclopædi* [encyclopaedia of law], pp. 56, 59.

intent are brought together irrespective of area of law: from international law, constitutional law, administrative law, procedural law, private law, etc.[70]

(i) Traditional structuring – Traditional naming

When a definition is adopted and continued by others, both definition functions will be exercised in a traditional way; both structuring and naming will in these instances (by definition) coincide with the language usage with which comparison is being made. – For example, this is the case when lawyers used (or use) the same juristic-act definition as Hagerup.

(ii) Innovative structuring – Traditional naming

In other cases the naming is stuck to, while the structuring is changed. – *Stang* structures through the formulation "private declarations of intent, to which the legal order attaches the consequence that what the declaration states shall be complied with".[71] – Compared with Hagerup's definition, Stang's definition has a normative-innovative structuring function: Stang excludes declarations of intent that do not have effect in accordance with their content, for example on account of invalidity. And he excludes declarations of intent in other areas of law than private law. – Stang's naming, on the other hand, is normative-traditional: He chooses to use the same term as Hagerup.

(iii) Innovative structuring – Innovative naming

Further, one has the instances in which both structuring and naming are changed.

Arnholm's naming is normative-innovative in relation to Hagerup and Stang, in that he chooses the term "dispositivt utsagn" [dispositive proposition] instead of the terms "rettshandel" [juristic act] and "viljeserklæring" [declaration of intent].[72] – Arnholm's structuring too is normative-innovative in relation to Hagerup and Stang, in that he brings in new criteria. Arnholm delimits his area, first, as imperative propositions in contradistinction to indicative propositions, and secondly, as those imperative propositions in the case of which "what is to happen according to the proposition is a change in the legal position of the sender or recipient",[73] "consequently that the proposition immediately purports to realise a legal imperative".[74]

Hov's naming is normative-innovative in relation to Hagerup and Stang (but normative-traditional in relation to Arnholm), in that he adopts Arnholm's basic term "dispositivt utsagn" [dispositive proposition].[75] – Hov's structuring too is normative-innovative in relation to Hagerup and Stang, and in addition in relation

70 Op. cit., p. 59. See also same writer, 'Anmeldelse av Fredrik Stang, Innledning til formueretten' [review of Fredrik Stang, introduction to the law of obligations and property], pp. 189–90.

71 Stang, *Innledning til formueretten* [introduction to the law of obligations and property], p. 210.

72 Arnholm, 'Omkring rettshandelsteorien' [concerning the theory of juristic acts], p. 412.

73 Op. cit., p. 410.

74 Op. cit., p. 411.

75 Hov, *Avtalerett* [law of contract], Chapter 2 ("Det dispositive utsagn" [the dispositive proposition]), cf. the following chapters in the same work.

to Arnholm, in that Hov brings in new criteria in relation to all three writers mentioned: "The central thing about the dispositive propositions is, first, that they purport to create duty, freedom or competence. Secondly, their validity rests – as is the case with statutes and administrative decisions – on their being issued pursuant to a particular competence. ... What thus distinguishes the dispositive propositions from other acts of laying down a norm is that their validity rests on their being made pursuant to the competence that the legal system ascribes to private subjects having legal personality (pursuant to private autonomy), while the validity of, for example, statutes and administrative decisions rests on their being issued pursuant to public-law competence."[76]

(iv) Traditional structuring – Innovative naming

We are left with instances in which the structuring is stuck to, but is given a new name. – *Aarbakke* returns to the word "rettshandel" [juristic act];[77] he thus presupposes a definition that is normative-innovative in its naming dimension, in relation to Arnholm and Hov (and normative-traditional in the same dimension, in relation to Stang and Hagerup). Concerning the structuring, Aarbakke does not say anything beyond what is directly his topic, namely that subscription of shares is a juristic act; however, in connection with the instance-type that is the theme of the present item (iv), traditional structuring – innovative naming, one can point to the possibility of normative-traditional structuring in relation to Arnholm.

(b) Alternation. Fixed points. Criteria for "the same definition question"

The discussion in item (a) above illustrates a *characteristic alternation* in a great deal of analysis and argumentation occurring in fact and formulated in everyday language: an alternation between normative-traditional and normative-innovative exercise of the definition functions, be it of the structuring function, the naming function or both.

Wherein then does the (temporarily) *fixed point* lie that makes it possible *and* interesting to apply the concepts of 'traditional/ innovative exercise of the definition functions'? For it is indeed possible, but hardly interesting, to say that a definition of 'cup' is normative-innovative in relation to Hagerup's definition of 'juristic act', both in structuring function and in naming function. There are no connections between definitions of 'cup' and definitions of 'juristic act' that make such a comparison interesting. Our interest in the concepts of 'traditional/ innovative exercise of the definition functions' thus *presupposes* that we perceive the *definition question* to be *"the same"*.[78]

---

76 Op. cit., p. 26 (Hov's italics omitted).

77 Aarbakke, 'Aksjetegning. Ugyldighet, mislighold og ansvar' [subscription of shares. Invalidity, breach of contract and liability], passim.

78 On questions of identity more generally, see Ekelöf, *Processuella grundbegrepp och allmänna processprinciper* [fundamental procedural concepts and general procedural principles], pp. 39–45. See also section 3.2.2 (5) above, introductory remarks.

There is no single factor that functions as a criterion for "the same definition question". See for illustration the example 'juristic act' in item (a) above and what has been said in general about alternation by way of introduction in the present item (b): Through graduated changes of structuring and naming one can obviously get far away from the starting point, for example from Hagerup's juristic-act definition. – Perceptions of identity in this connection seem to rest on *several factors*:

One connecting factor is that the writers *[i] refer to one another.* – Another connecting factor is that the writers speak in *[ii] the singular with the definite article* of "*the* definition of .../ *the* concept of ..." ("the definition of 'juristic act'/ the concept of 'juristic act' "). – A third connecting factor, which may also explain occurrences of the first two, is *[iii] overlappings in the structuring function*: Changes in the structuring from writer to writer are not perceived as *so* great that the topic changes identity (as it does in the relationship between definitions of 'cup' and 'juristic act', cf. above). Small graduated changes correspond with large graduated overlappings: Different writers' structurings can form chains in which hardly noticeable differences are admittedly cumulated into larger differences, but in which the correspondence may be just as clear, or in which the differences are annulled by one's returning to the starting point at regular intervals. However, the differences may also be more marked; schools of thought may reveal themselves in different structurings.

In what has now been said about connecting factors I have presupposed that both structuring and naming vary between the writers. A commonly occurring case is, however, that *[iv] the name remains fixed* while the exercise of the structuring function varies. An example is definitions of "definition", where the common Latin original provides an easily recognisable unity in much naming, across national languages. The central unity in encyclopaedia articles under the entry "Definition" or the like seems to be that the propositions that are discussed were put forward by well-known philosophers *and* that the topic of these propositions has been *labelled* "definition" or the like (section 1 (1) above, concluding remarks).

It is not possible to specify briefly *how* great are the changes in the structuring function that are actually tolerated before one designates the definition question as "a new/ a different" one. However, one can see that the degree of tolerance is in many cases quite considerable.

With a view to the identity question it is important, first, to be aware that the concept of *'structuring function of definitions'* covers a *complex* phenomenon (even though the phenomenon has for the time being been treated as a unity, in order that the contrast with the naming function of definitions should be brought into focus). And it is important, secondly, to be aware of what *dimensions* this concept has (sections 4.1 (1) above, cf. 5–6 and 8, below): Correspondence or difference in these dimensions contributes to governing our intuitions about whether we are confronted with "the same" definition question. – When one relates discussions of old and new to the *individual* dimensions in the structuring function, there is *especially reason to ask* whether the answer will be the same in relation to criteria (connotation) as in relation to the individual phenomena that are delimited through application of the criteria in the individual instance (denotation).

Thus, an important question in practice is whether a *difference in connotation* corresponds to a *difference in denotation*. – To take an example: The structuring function in Arnholm's and Hov's definitions of 'juristic act' is different in that Arnholm puts the criterion 'imperative' in the centre, while Hov chooses the criterion 'made pursuant to private competence'. However, is the structuring function also different in relation to the application of the criteria in the individual instance; or will their application show that (in the main) it is the same individual phenomena that fall under the different areas-in-thought? – This question will be at the centre of the focus in the concluding Chapter V; there I shall demonstrate that in central parts of actually occurring language and argumentation we meet the pattern "agreement about the denotation, but disagreement about the connotation (criteria)". In the perspective here the emphasis is on the fact that *[v] correspondence in denotation* can contribute to explaining that a definition question is perceived to be the same, across great differences in connotation.

> Another question is whether *correspondence in connotation formulations or connotation* is matched by *correspondence in denotation*. – In using juristic act as an example in item (a) above, out of consideration for the presentation of the main points there, I took such matching as a basis; I considered likeness in connotation formulation or connotation to be a criterion of normative-traditional exercise of the structuring function as a whole. That was a simplification: First, one may agree about a connotation formulation, for example concur with Arnholm's formulation concerning juristic act, but disagree about the denotation; cf. indeterminacy of words and concepts. These are important, but at the same time well-known problems, which with one exception I do not discuss in the present work.[79] Secondly, one may agree about the connotation but disagree about the denotation, in cases in which the connotation prescribes an evaluation (section 6.1 (2)(c) below, cf. section 6.1 in its entirety on this connotation type).

The identity of the definition question is not affected by the number of language users with whose usage comparison is made. The fact that in item (a) above I compared a given definition of 'juristic act' (e.g. Arnholm's) with the definition provided by an *individual language user* (e.g. Hagerup or Stang) was out of consideration for the simplest possible illustration of the application of the concepts of 'traditional/ innovative exercise of the definition functions'. Such limitation to comparison with the usage of individual language users is not part of the presup-

---

79 See section 2.2 above, at and in note 7, on different dimensions of indeterminacy. The exception is factor-structuring of concept criteria, including family resemblance, see the reference in the said note 7.

position that the definition question must be considered to be "the same". It may well be considered to be the same even if one compares with a *group of language users*: for example, as when one asks whether an existing definition of 'juristic act' is normative-traditional or normative-innovative in relation to definitions of 'juristic act' among Norwegian lawyers, lawyers in Scandinavia, or members of other groups.

(4) The graduation in the concepts of 'traditional/ innovative exercise of the definition functions'

In the case of comparison in the *structuring dimension*, the structuring function of the given definition may in several *dimensions* (connotation specification, denotation specification, denotation) be to a greater or lesser extent different from the structuring function with which comparison is being made. – In the case of comparison with groups of language users, whether it be their language usage at large ("language usage among lawyers", compare item (2) above) or their use of particular definitions ("lawyers' definition of 'juristic act' ", compare item (3)(b) above, concluding remarks), there are in addition partly the graduation that lies in the *number of people* whose exercise of the structuring function is correspondent or different, and partly the graduation that lies in the *frequency* of their correspondent or different exercise.

The same applies when in the *naming dimension* one compares with groups of language users: One graduation lies in the *number of people* whose exercise of the naming function is correspondent or different. Another graduation lies in the *frequency* of their correspondent or different exercise. – Also when one compares a single person's language usage with a single person's language usage (with the usage of the same person or of another person), a graduation will lie in the *frequency* of correspondent or different exercise of the naming function on the part of the person with whom comparison is being made. – On the other hand, if one compares a single person's language usage on one particular occasion with a single person's language usage (the usage of the same person or of another person) on another particular occasion, the 'usage frequency' graduation will not come into play. Nor will any other clear 'usage intensity' graduation: *Either* the person whose usage is being compared uses the same words as in the situation with which comparison is being made, *or* the person whose usage is being compared uses other words.[80]

80 True enough, one operates with notions of graduated differences between words too. The criteria that motivate here are, however, partly vague and partly infiltrated with criteria concerning difference in meaning.

4.3.4. Other connections in which the distinction is of significance

In addition to the now demonstrated ways of using the distinction between the structuring function and naming function of definitions as a means of speaking more precisely (sections 4.3.1–4.3.3 above, with further references), I shall later use this distinction as a means of speaking more precisely inter alia in the following connections:

In my discussion of means of definition (how definition takes place) I shall concentrate on means to structuring (sections 5–6).

In my discussion of normative definitions as a means to influencing action, I shall distinguish between, on the one hand, influence on action through exercise of the structuring function (sections 7.1 (1) cf. III 2.2.5), and on the other hand, influence on action through interplay between exercise of structuring function and naming function, particularly through "persuasive definitions" (sections 7 cf. III 2.2.2 (3) and 2.4.2).

In mapping criteria that are used in the setting up of and choice between normative definitions, I shall classify the criteria according to whether they particularly concern the structuring, the naming or the coupling of area and name (section III 2).

4.4. The significance of definitions' mode of formulation

In the discussion above I have in several places touched on variations in the way definitions are formulated: particularly whether they are formulated as definitions of the *way words are used* or as definitions of *concepts*.

Since the topic of the present section 4 is *what is being defined*, and since the said difference in mode of formulation seems to say something directly about this, I shall in what follows define more precisely the concepts of the modes of formulation (section 4.4.1 (1)–(2)), and then look at what significance the use of the one or the other mode may have (sections 4.4.1 (3) and 4.4.2–4.4.4).

4.4.1. Two main modes: Word terminology and concept terminology. Survey of the significance of the mode of formulation

(1) One main way of formulating definitions is in *word terminology*. – By "definitions (formulated) in word terminology" I mean definitions the formulation of which links the delimitation to linguistic entities *and* the formulation of which does not use words that directly refer to the level of meaning, especially not "meaning", "sense", "concept", or their equivalents in other languages. It may be a matter of definitions that explicitly use designations for linguistic entities: "By the word "x" I mean ...". Or it may be a matter of definitions that bring in linguistic entities through presupposition: "By x I mean ...". – For the sake of brevity, I shall in some cases call definitions in word terminology simply "definitions of words".

Definitions formulated in word terminology *imply* that it is a matter of definition of the way the word is used, in its capacity of bearer of linguistic meaning. I refer to the account of the picture according to which linguistic meaning (criteria, concepts, propositions) is seen as a question of the content of norms for use of the words and expressions of a language (section 4.1 (5)(c) above). – If one takes away the meaning aspect, one is left with the word in its capacity of physical object (print in various forms and colours, sound waves, and the like). This can of course also be delimited. But then it is a matter of physical (spatio-temporal) delimitations: One writes particular shapes, at particular distances, in particular places; one speaks with particular pauses; and so forth. Such delimitations have never been called "definitions", as far as I know.

(2) Another main way of formulating definitions is in *concept terminology*. – By "definitions (formulated) in concept terminology" I mean definitions the formulation of which uses the term "concept" (or its equivalent in other languages), or words or expressions presumed to have the same meaning as "concept", like "conception", "notion", "idea", etc. (or their equivalents in other languages), of what is being delimited: "The concept of 'x' covers ...". – In the preceding sentence I presuppose that the term "concept", or the words or expressions presumed to have the same meaning as "concept", is used of entities on the level of meaning, not of words.[81] – For the sake of brevity, I shall in some cases call definitions in concept terminology simply "definitions of concepts".

(1)↔(2) Word terminology and concept terminology can be *combined*, see for example the forms of expression "The word "law" means ...", "I use the word "law" in the sense of ...", "The word "law" expresses a concept of ...". As the examples illustrate, combinations commonly occur (section 4.4.2 (3) below).

(3) *What significance* has the distinction between definitions of words and definitions of concepts?

---

81 The use of the word "concept" of words is common in everyday speech and occurs quite often in academic literature as well; see e.g. Knoph, *Hensiktens betydning for grensen mellem rett og urett* [the significance of intent for the boundary between the lawful and the unlawful], p. 42 ("The concept of unlawfulness ... in the mouth of the lawyer"); Hov, *Avtalerett* [law of contract], p. 24 ("[T]he concept of juristic act ... is an expression that was much used earlier"); Sharpe, 'A Note on "the Magic of Names"', p. 107 (""Good" and "Bad" are the magical words of propaganda by which mass psychology is manipulated. The repetition of scientific concepts such as "Oedipus Complex" could never acquire the power of an incantation"); Larenz, *Methodenlehre der Rechtswissenschaft*, p. 370 ("Der Begriff der "Gesetzlücke" bezeichnet ..."); Stolleis, 'Gemeinschaft und Volksgemeinschaft', passim, e.g. p. 110 ("die Versuche, den Begriff "Gemeinschaft" als neuen Terminus in die Rechtssprache einzuführen").

The main significance seems to lie in the fact that concept terminology gives the impression of greater *unity and objectivity* than word terminology (section 4.4.3 below), and further in the fact that concept terminology is *more difficult to put to the test* than word terminology (section 4.4.4 below).

In contrast, there is only a weak connection between, on the one hand, whether definitions are formulated as definitions of concepts or as definitions of words, and on the other hand, the *occurrence of structuring function and naming function*. This means that the difference between definitions of concepts and definitions of words provides only *weak guidance on what is being defined*. I treat this negative result first (section 4.4.2 below): partly because the lacking connection is interesting in itself, and partly because the question of what is being defined was the reason for the difference in mode of formulation's being taken up here.

Otherwise there is, in the first place, no connection between, on the one hand, whether definitions are formulated as definitions of concepts or as definitions of words, and on the other, whether the definition is *descriptive* or *normative*: Logically (definitionally) definitions in both modes of formulation can be descriptive or normative; and purely factually too there does not appear to be any connection between mode of formulation and modality.

In the second place, when it comes to normative definitions in particular, there does not appear to be any connection between, on the one hand, the mode of formulation, and on the other, the distinction between *stipulated* and *custom-based* definitions (I am thinking here of cases in which the custom-based definition is invoked; custom in itself is by definition not formulated): Logically (definitionally) definitions in both modes of formulation can be stipulated or custom-based; and purely factually too there does not appear to be any connection between mode of formulation and mode of coming into being.

4.4.2. The modes of formulation are in practice often used to express the same definition-functional content

What connection is there between on the one hand whether definitions are formulated as definitions of concepts or as definitions of words, and on the other hand the *occurrence of structuring function and naming function*?

(1) All definitions have by definition a structuring function, whether they are formulated in word terminology or in concept terminology (section 4.1 (2) above). – In the case of *definitions in concept terminology* one might ask whether the definition *only* has structuring function, cf. the fact that in these instances the definition formulation by definition directly only speaks of "concept", or words or expressions presumed to have the same meaning as "concept", not of linguistic designation for the concept. However, as demonstrated earlier, it is not the case that definitions formulated in concept terminology, by definition or most often purely factually, only have a structuring function (section 4.2 (4)(e) above).

(2) In the case of *definitions in word terminology* one might ask whether *all* such definitions have naming function, cf. the fact that in these instances the definition formulation by definition directly only speaks of words. – In the case of definitions of words that have not been translated, the definition has by definition a naming function (section 4.2 (3)(b) above). In the case of definitions of words that have been translated, it is an empirical question whether the definition has a naming function (section 4.2 (4)(d) above).

In the case of definitions in word terminology one might also ask whether there is not a *self-contradiction* in on the one hand saying that all definitions by definition have a structuring function (section 4.1 (2) above), and on the other hand calling definitions in word terminology "definitions". For definitions in word terminology speak by definition directly only of words and not of "meaning", "sense" or "concept", so that it might be reasonable to believe that the definition in these cases *only* has a naming function and never or seldom a structuring function. See for example the definition formulation "Stang used the word "rettshandel" [juristic act] in a different way from Hagerup, namely of ...".

However, definitions in word terminology too have structuring function. If one looks at the definition formulation just quoted, then one will see that the definition *in that* it says what the word is used of, *also* specifies an area: namely the area of which the word is used. – This applies *in general* to definitions in word terminology:

True enough there is a difference in *formulation* between definitions in concept terminology and word terminology. But this difference in mode of formulation does *not* correspond with a difference between structuring and not structuring. In both instances the definition specifies a delimitation on the level of meaning. The difference is that in the case of definitions in concept terminology the delimitation on the level of meaning takes place directly and explicitly; while in the case of definitions in word terminology the delimitation on the level of meaning takes place partly indirectly, via the link with words, and partly more implicitly, via presupposed but not explicitly mentioned norms for use of words. – I again refer to the earlier account of the picture according to which linguistic meaning (criteria, concepts, propositions) is seen as a question of the content of norms for use of the words and expressions of a language (section 4.1 (5)(c) above). And I further refer to what has been said about the difference between, on the one hand, such meaning delimitations as it is a matter of in the case of definitions, and on the other hand, delimitations of words in their capacity of physical objects (section 4.4.1 (1) above).

Thus it is not the case that definitions formulated in word terminology, in and through this mode of formulation, by definition or most often purely factually, only have a naming function. Here as elsewhere it is the case that definitions by definition also have a structuring function.

(3) To sum up, it is the case that there is only a *weak connection* between on the one hand whether definitions are formulated as definitions of concepts or as definitions of words, and on the other hand the occurrence of structuring function and naming function:

Logically (by definition) there is, as mentioned, only one connection, namely that definitions of words that have not been translated always have a naming function. But this function can also be filled by definitions in concept terminology. Thus there is in logical terms *no exclusive connection in either direction* (either from mode of formulation to definition function, or from definition function to mode of formulation).

Nor in *actual use of language* does there seem to be any clear connection between on the one hand mode of formulation and on the other hand occurrence of structuring function and naming function. A main impression is that one *often uses interchangeably three formulation alternatives concerning what is being defined*: definition of words, definition of concepts, or combinations. – To illustrate the multiplicity one can ask in what contexts it will be perceived as reasonable interpretation to use the differences between the following formulations as a basis for assuming differences in the definition-functional content: "The concept of 'cup' covers ..." (an instance of concept terminology); "The word "cup" is used of ..." (an instance of word terminology); "The word "cup" means .../ expresses the concept of ..." (instances of combination). I believe there are few contexts in which such interpretation as mentioned will be perceived as reasonable.

If one wants to cognise nuances and connections in definition activity occurring in fact and formulated in everyday language, it is important to distinguish between the structuring function and the naming function of definitions (sections 4.3 cf. 4.1–4.2, above). Some possibility of expressing the distinction between the definition functions lies in making use of, first, the linguistically intuitive connection between concept terminology and structuring, and secondly, the linguistically intuitive connection between word terminology and naming, so that one adds the term "concept", or words or expressions presumed to have the same meaning as "concept", when one wants to speak about the structuring ("the concept of 'cup' "), and adds the term "word", or words or expressions presumed to have the same meaning as "word", when one wants to speak about the naming of an area within the structuring ("the word "cup""). Even if this alternative should be used deliberately (as in the present work), it is, however, manifestly inadequate in relation to nuances and connections in definition activity occurring in fact and formulated in everyday language. An advanced alternative is to construct a nuanced and systematic conceptual model, as in the present work.

> Rickert distinguishes between Begriffsbestimmung (determination of concepts)[82] and Worterklärung (determination of the meanings of linguistic expressions).[83] The basis of this distinction seems, however, indeterminate in relation to categorisations used here: The basis seems partly to be thought

82 Rickert, *Zur Lehre von der Definition*, in particular pp. 20 et seq., 46–47, 62.

83 Op. cit., in particular pp. 17–20, 46–47, 62.

process versus linguistically formulated product, partly structuring function versus naming function, and partly concept terminology versus word terminology.[84]

The explanation of the indeterminacy may be that Rickert's main purpose is a traditionally epistemological one (compare section I 7 above).[85] Further, the explanation may be that he designs the definition part of his work as a polemic[86] against the view that only Worterklärung "is definition"; in so doing he endeavours to give a persuasive definition of "Definition" so that Worterklärung falls outside.[87] – Both the said features of his work, its main purpose and its polemic design, are in contrast to what is one aim of my definition theory: the construction of a nuanced and systematic conceptual model for the mapping of actually occurring definition activity.

4.4.3. Concept terminology gives the impression of greater unity and objectivity than word terminology

(1) Concept terminology tends to give the *impression of unity*, not least when the definite article is used, "the concept". An example would be: "Mary is in my opinion wrong in keeping the concept of law separate from morality. In my opinion it lies in the concept that ...". Here the term "the concept" gives the impression that one is speaking of something well delimited. – I have earlier discussed relationships that in fact exist between phenomena of which one uses the same word (section 3.2.2 above). As was apparent, there is often no basis for such notions of unity as a lot of concept terminology seems to presuppose.

Word terminology to a greater extent leads our thought towards the *changing and often indeterminate quality of the meaning content.* This can be illustrated by reformulating the example above, as follows: "Mary is in my opinion wrong in keeping the way the word "law" is used separate from morality (free from moral features). In my opinion it lies in the norms for the use of the word that ...". Through this mode of formulation one is led to look at words: something in space and time. And most people then become more unsure than when it is concepts that are being spoken of. For most people have themselves experienced *"wrestling with words"*: It may be that one does not understand what meaning others put into words; that one must conclude that nor do the others have a clear picture of this; that one must realise that one does not oneself have any clear picture of what meaning one puts into words oneself; that other people put another meaning into words than one puts into them oneself; that one searches for words; that words change their meanings over time; or other consequences of the fact that there is not a natural, but a conventional relationship between word and meaning (section

[84] Op. cit., the same places as referred to in the two preceding notes.

[85] Op. cit., pp. IX–X.

[86] Op. cit., pp. 15 et seq., compare p. V.

[87] Op. cit., pp. 21 ("die eigentliche Definition"); 22 ("ihr logisches Wesen"); 62 ("das logisch Wesentliche"). – On persuasive definitions, see section 7.3 below.

4.2 (1)(b) above). By relating to words one is therefore not so easily seduced into notions of unity without any basis in actual use of language.

(2) To what one calls "concepts" one often connects notions of *something already existing, and existing independently of language (objectivity)* (section 4.1 (5)(b) above). Expressions such as "the concept of law" seem on the part of many people to be connected with the notion of something that exists independently of the actual use of the word "law". – There is less room for such objectivity notions when one sees concepts as linguistic meaning, and linguistic meaning as a question of the content of norms for use of the words and expressions of a language (section 4.1 (5)(c) above). One must then in that event make oneself aware of the fact that one is using the word "concept" of two such different things as linguistic meaning on the one hand, and something already existing and independent of language on the other.

Notions of objectivity linked to concept terminology (notions of something already existing, and existing independently) have important *consequences* for actually occurring language and argumentation:

First, lack of clarity often arises with respect to whether propositions formulated in concept terminology express *definition or characterisation*: Does a proposition formulation that uses the expression "the concept of law" refer to the use of words like "law", "rett", "Recht", etc. (definition); or is this topic presupposed and is something being said about the phenomena that are thereby delimited (characterisation)?

Secondly, a tendency arises to understand propositions in concept terminology as *descriptive* to a greater extent than there is any basis for: for example, understanding a proposition formulation that uses the expression "the concept of law", as a description of properties of a phenomenon delimited through presupposition (a descriptive characterisation of natural, rational, religious or other law), *also* in instances in which the sender gives expression to what he himself considers reasonable and just (a normative characterisation).

Word terminology is suited to counteracting both the said consequences: Word terminology makes it clear that one is confronted with a *definition.* And word terminology makes it easier for one to catch sight of the changing and indeterminate quality of the meaning content (item (1) above), and makes it easier for one to catch sight of the fact that this changing and indeterminate quality, as well as determinations of the indeterminate, often rests on the individual language user's *evaluations and choices.*

That concept terminology and word terminology trigger different interpretation tendencies in relation to the distinctions between definitions and characterisations and between descriptive and normative propositions may also be illustrated by returning to the *examples in item (1) above.* It is very natural to formulate the example in word terminology more precisely as "Mary is in my opinion wrong in keeping *her* way of using the word "law" separate from morality (free from moral features) ...". It seems almost odd if the word "her" is not present. It is *not* equally natural to reformulate the example in concept terminology as "Mary is in my opinion wrong in keeping *her* concept of law separate from morality". The cause of such intuitive differences I assume to be the outlined notions of objectivity linked to a lot of concept terminology, with the outlined accompanying propensity to interpret propositions in concept terminology as descriptive.

(1)↔(2) Thus, in a lot of concept terminology there lies a *double shift*: *from* the changing and indeterminate, *to* the unitary (item (1) above); and *from* the individual language user's evaluation and choice of language, *to* description of something already existing, and existing independently of language (item (2) above).

I shall later point to some forms of expression that are related to concept terminology in that they often conceal the language user's evaluations and choices (sections IV 2–3 below).

4.4.4. Concept terminology is more difficult to put to the test than word terminology

Descriptive definitions in word terminology are *easier to put to the test* than descriptive definitions in concept terminology:

In the case of *descriptive definitions in word terminology* the question is whether the words in question are used as the definition specifies.

In the case of *descriptive definitions in concept terminology* there is often considerably greater uncertainty about what factors are relevant to the testing of the tenability of the definition:

One uncertainty lies in *what is the concept designation*, and thus what words one is to link the testing to. I refer to what has been said earlier about this (section 4.2 (4)(e) above).

Another uncertainty lies in *whether one is confronted by a definition at all*, cf. the consequence of concept terminology just discussed: the consequence that a lack of clarity often arises as to whether concept terminology expresses a definition or a characterisation (section 4.4.3 (2) above). – The fact that a proposition is formulated in concept terminology *may* indicate that the sender of the proposition is referring to *something else than* describing areas in actual language usage, i.e. to something else than defining. This applies particularly if the phenomenon in question is considered to have great philosophical, moral, political, or suchlike significance. For example, in the case of occurrences of the expression "the concept of law", if one asks the sender whether he is thereby referring to the use of words like "law", "rett", "Recht", etc., I assume that one will quite often get an uncertain or negative answer. The sender has other pretensions: often to give expression to what he considers reasonable and just (normative characterisation), and, as the case may be, also to maintain that this has an objective existence (descriptive characterisation).

5. Means of structuring I

All definitions have by definition a structuring function (section 4.1 (2) above). Hitherto the structuring function has been seen as a *unity*, since the emphasis has been on the contrast to and interplay with the naming function (section 4 above). In what follows I shall *split up* the structuring function and look more closely at the *means aspect*.

The means aspect can more precisely be *placed as follows*: One aspect of the structuring function is the *process*, the activity of dividing the world up in thought into areas. Another aspect is the *products*, the areas-in-thought themselves (the concepts). A third aspect concerns the *means*: What means enter into the process leading to the products? Or, expressed in the terminology of the definition perspective: How, more precisely, do definitions constitute the areas-in-thought (the concepts)? This is the topic of the present section and the next (sections 5–6).

In the discussion of the question of means of structuring I take my *point of departure* in the distinction between connotation and denotation: The ways of structuring are systematised according to whether they employ connotation specification, denotation specification or combinations as means.

The naming function is exercised independently of whether the way of structuring consists in the one or the other of the means that are treated in what follows. Thus the discussion could throughout have used the word "structuring" instead of "definition". However, for stylistic reasons and in order not to impede understanding through more technical language than necessary, in what follows I use the word "defining" also in many places where the more specific word "structuring" could have been used.

5.1. Connotation specification

(1) The concept of 'connotation specification'

By structuring through *connotation specification* I mean structuring through specification of *criteria* for the delimitation of the area-in-thought (section A 4 above). – An example is the following part of the definition of "enkeltvedtak" [individual decision] in section 2 (a) and (b) of the Public Administration Act (10 February 1967):

"In this Act individual decision means any decision which is made under the exercise of public authority and which is generally or concretely determinative of rights or obligations of [one or more specific] private persons ...".

(2) *What does a connotation specification say about the denotation?*

Defining through connotation specification will always (by definition) *at the same time say something about the denotation*, namely that the concept criteria are to a greater or lesser degree found again in the individual things that the concept covers. – The things thus have "*definitional* properties".

Many connotation specifications have *condition structure*, which most often means that the concept criteria specify a *set of features common* to the phenomena in the denotation (section 3.2.2 (5)(c) above). For example, the definition of "individual decision" quoted in item (1) above entails that all decisions that fall under this concept of 'individual decision' have one of the alternative sets of necessary and sufficient features expressed in the definition.

However, I do not wish to say that by definition connotation specifications have condition structure. That would mean that concepts *without* condition structure, for example family resemblance concepts, could not be said to be defined by connotation specification. This I consider to be rather inexpedient use of language: For, once one uses the word "concept", as is often the case, not only of areas-in-thought in the case of which the delimitation criteria have condition structure, but also of areas-in-thought in the case of which the criteria have another structure, for example family resemblance structure (section 3.2.2 (5)(b) above), then it will be in poor harmony with this usage not to employ the word "connotation" of the delimitation criteria. For the distinction between connotation and denotation is usually linked to concepts pure and simple. I keep to this usage, and consequently use the word "connotation specification" also of specification of criteria without condition structure.

> Robinson comes close to defining 'connotation' via the criterion 'condition structure': "[B]y the 'connotation' of a word I usually mean roughly the *common* characteristic or sort or class in virtue of which the word is applied to *these and only these* things" (my italics).[1]

The individual things that fall under an area-in-thought have of course *other* properties than the definitional ones. However, these are properties the connotation specification (by definition) does *not* say anything about.

In three instances in particular there may be a *need to supplement* the information the connotation specification provides about the denotation:

(i) The linguistic formulation of the connotation specification or the connotation specification itself may be *indeterminate*. These are important, but at the same time well-known problems, which with one exception I do not discuss in the present work.[2]

---

1 Robinson, *Definition*, p. 109.

2 See section 2.2 above, at and in note 7, on different dimensions of indeterminacy of words or concepts. The exception is factor-structuring of concept criteria, including family resemblance, see the reference in the said note 7.

(ii) The connotation specification can *prescribe an evaluation*, which in actually occurring language and argumentation is often considered as a delegation to the language user of competence to lay down the denotation (section 6.1 (2)(c) below).

(iii) Even if we suppose that both the linguistic formulation of the connotation specification and the connotation specification itself are determinate (compare item (i) above), and even if we suppose that the connotation specification is without evaluation prescription (compare item (ii) above), there may be a need to supplement the information the connotation specification provides about the denotation: This need arises in so far as the language users *do not follow* the connotation specification; see the following item (3).

(3) Discrepancy between connotation specification and denotation

One thing is that defining through connotation specification by definition *says* something about the denotation (item (2) above). Another thing is the empirical question of whether what the connotation specification says *conforms with* actual language usage.

Quite often one may see that the individual things that are subsumed under concepts do not conform very well with given connotations.[3] – In the case of *normative* connotation specifications this is a variant of the well-known fact that normative propositions are not always followed, whether it be the person normatively regulating who does not follow the normative propositions he addresses to himself, or others who do not follow his normative propositions addressed to them.[4] – In the case of *descriptive* connotation specifications the definition can be true in spite of discrepancy between connotation specification and denotation, in so far as the definition only aims to describe the connotations that the language users *put forward*, irrespective of whether they follow them or not. If on the other hand the descriptive connotation specification is not meant as a description of a connotation that the language users put forward, but as a hypothesis about an *actually governing* connotation, formed on the basis of observation of the individual things the language users subsume under the area, i.e. on the basis of observation of the denotation, then a discrepancy between connotation specification and denotation will be an objection to the tenability of the definition.

---

[3] Robinson, *Definition*, pp. 114–16.

[4] For *causes*, see sections 3.3.3 (2) and 4.2 (5)(c), above; and section 5.4.3 (1) below, concluding remarks (at and in note 107).

5.2. Denotation specification

(1) The concept of 'denotation specification'

By structuring of areas-in-thought through *denotation specification* I mean structuring through specification of *individual* things or *types* of thing that the areas cover: specification of individual things particularly through proper nouns or definite descriptions, and specification of types of thing particularly through common nouns (see item (2) below, on means to denotation specification).

The *difference* between connotation specification and denotation specification can be illustrated by comparing the connotation specification in the definition of "individual decision" in the Public Administration Act, quoted in section 5.1 (1) above, with the immediately following denotation specifications in the same definition, see section 2, second and third paragraphs, of the Public Administration Act:

> "Any decision concerning appointment, notice of dismissal, suspension, summary dismissal or transfer of a public official shall be deemed to be an individual decision. The same shall apply to any decision to impose a disciplinary penalty on a public official or to grant him a pension. ... Any decision concerning dismissal of a case or use of special enforcement measures to have an individual decision implemented shall also be deemed to be an individual decision."

Even though connotation specification always (by definition) says something about properties of the things that the areas cover (section 5.1 (2) above), they never (by definition) specify what individual things the areas cover. Denotation specification through *specification of individual things* is therefore a distinct way of structuring in relation to connotation specification.

Type specification, in contrast, stands in a *position between* on the one hand specification of individual things and on the other hand specification of general criteria.[5] – The similarity with specification of individual things and the definition-functional contrast with general criteria is apparent from the example "individual decision" quoted above. – The similarity with general criteria shows itself in that a type specification can be rewritten as a general criterion-formulation; for example the type specification "appointment" can be rewritten as the general criterion-formulation "decision that has the property of being appointment". This logical possibility of rewriting, and its accompanying cases of doubt with respect to how it is natural to express oneself, are not decisive arguments for grouping type specification together with specification of general criteria. The decisive factor in relation to the perspective and topic of the present work has been that type specification in many and indeed interesting cases in definition activity occurring in fact and formulated in everyday language, for instance in the example "individual decision" above, is ascribed the same definition-functional role as specification of individual things. – The specific evidence for my claiming that the distinction between type specification and general criterion-formulation is implementable, and that the grouping of type specification together with specification of individual things is of definition-theoretical interest, lies in my individual discussions.

(2) Means to denotation specification

The *means* to denotation specification can be *linguistic*: common nouns ("appointment", "notice of dismissal", "summary dismissal"), proper nouns ("Peter", "Mary", personal identity number, business registration number), definite descriptions ("the blue thing to the right of you"), or other linguistic items ("me", "you", "him", "her", "here", "there", "now", "then", etc.). – Or the means can be *extra-linguistic*: Most important is pointing at the things to which one is referring, a specification method that is often called "ostensive definition" (item (5) below).

(3) Complete and incomplete denotation specification

Complete and positive denotation specification occurs particularly in the form of *enumeration of types*. An example would be the lawyer who explains: "By the term "vedtak" [administrative decision] the Public Administration Act means individual decisions and regulations."[6]

---

5 In the conceptual framework of this work, criteria are by definition general (sections 5.1 (1) cf. A 4, above). The fact that in the sentence containing the present note and in a number of instances in what follows I nevertheless use the formulation "general criteria", is because I want to emphasise, and remind the reader of, the contrast with denotation specification in the form of specification of individual things.

6 In the case of statutory definitions, complete enumeration of types is a practical alternative to connotation specification, see section 5.4.2 (2)(a) below.

Complete and positive denotation specification does, however, also occur in the form of *enumeration of individual phenomena*: via proper nouns, definite descriptions, pointing gestures or other ways of individualising. The occurrences of completeness fall here in practice into two main groups: – One consists of instances in which the denotation covers so few exemplars that they can be perceived collectively. An example would be the concept of a species that is dying out, which can be defined by pointing to all the (known) exemplars; or the concept of 'logical word', which can be defined by enumeration, as follows: "not", "and", "or", "if", "only if", "all", "some", "none", "=" (is identical with) and "∈" (is a member of).[7] – The other main group consists of instances in which the denotation may well cover so many or scattered individual things that they cannot be perceived collectively, but in which every exemplar has a name or a definite description, for example a number in a computer-based registration system. The denotation can then be specified by means of an inventory of the names of all individuals existing at a particular point in time, for example by taking a print-out of the computer data base (personal identity number, car registration number, or the like).

A *complete and negative* denotation specification is *conceivable*, in the sense that the thought is not self-contradictory. It is for example not self-contradictory to suppose that the following negative denotation specification, given as part of the statutory definition of "forbrukerkjøp" [consumer purchase] in section 4 of the Sale of Goods Act (Act No. 27 of 13 May 1988), is complete: ""Consumer purchase" means … [connotation specification]. Purchase of claims and rights is *not* considered to be consumer purchase" (my italics).

However, supposition that a negative denotation specification is complete will *in practice seldom cover the sender's meaning*: The sender will most often be thinking of a more limited area than it is possible to delimit by means of a negative denotation specification. This means that the sender either at the time of his specifying the denotation took the standpoint that the specification was not complete, or now would probably take that standpoint if he were to reflect on the question.[8] – This is particularly clear in the case of negative denotation specification in the form of *specification of individual things*. We can for example imagine the negative denotation specification in the statutory definition of "consumer purchase" reformulated as: "The contract of 1 March 1989 between John Brown and Mary Smith is not considered as consumer purchase." – Negative denotation specification in the form of *type specification* will more easily be capable of placing the boundary closer to the area the sender is thinking of, because a type specification will most often be conceived within and along particular dimensions; for example the negative denotation specification in the statutory definition of "consumer purchase" was obviously conceived within the dimension 'purchase' and

---

7 Føllesdal/ Walløe/ Elster, *Argumentasjonsteori, språk og vitenskapsfilosofi* [argumentation theory, language and the philosophy of science], pp. 221, 242.

8 On actual subjective meaning and hypothetical subjective meaning, see section E 2.2.3 below.

probably along the dimension 'according to the nature of the object to be purchased'. However, also in the case of negative denotation specification in the form of type specification there will most often be discrepancy between the area the sender is referring to and the area the denotation specification is capable of delimiting; for example the type specification in the statutory definition of "consumer purchase" lets there remain an infinity of types of purchase contract according to the nature of the object, of which many are clearly intended to fall outside the denotation.

Further, defining may take place through *incomplete* denotation specification. One specifies some, but not all, types or individual instances of which one wishes to use the expression; or one specifies some, but not all, types or individual instances of which one does not wish to use the expression. Both the *positive* variant and the *negative* variant are common. – In some instances incomplete denotation specification stands *alone*. See for example the travaux préparatoires of Article 110 c of the Norwegian Constitution, which in defining "Menneskerettighederne" [human rights] refrain from connotation specification and instead bring in an incomplete and positive specification of individual instances (enumeration of conventions that are considered to be about human rights).[9] – More commonly incomplete denotation specification is *combined with connotation specification*: See for example the positive denotation specification which is part of the definition of "individual decision" as provided by the Public Administration Act, quoted in item (1) above; or the negative denotation specification which is part of the definition of "consumer purchase" as provided by the Sale of Goods Act, quoted above in the present item; or the combination of positive and negative denotation specification, when a person who is to give a lecture on democracy starts with a connotation specification of the concept, and adds that he includes states A, B, and C but not states F, G and H.

(4) What does a denotation specification say about the connotation?

Denotation specification provides a *basis for inferences* about the connotation, but according to its own content *does not say* anything about the connotation. For example, a definition of 'human being' by means of a print-out from a data base containing proper nouns or definite descriptions referring to all individuals existing at a particular point in time, will not say anything about whether there is any basis, and if so what, for conceiving of the individual entities referred to, as a unity, in contrast to an arbitrary collection.

---

9 *NOU 1993: 18* [Norwegian official reports], Lovgivning om menneskerettigheter [legislation on human rights], pp. 158, cf. 29–33. – The defining takes place more specifically in relation to the first paragraph of the Article, which reads: "It is incumbent upon the state authorities to respect and safeguard human rights."

(5) *Ostensive definitions*

(a) The concept of 'ostensive definition'

The most pervasive feature of actual use of the term "ostensive definition" (or its equivalent in other languages) appears to be denotation specification *by extralinguistic means*; i.e. by pointing gestures, nods, or the like, the definer directs other people's attention to a denotatum that is present. An example would be that the definer explains the meaning of the word "cup" to the child by pointing at a cup.

I lay down denotation specification by extralinguistic means as a necessary and sufficient criterion of the concept of 'ostensive definition' here, with the addition that in the present context I use the term "denotation specification" in a certain extended sense: also of pointing, or the like, to a picture of an exemplar, to a globe, or the like.

(b) Ostensive definitions seen as the bridge from language to a prelinguistic and absolute basis; the significance of this point of view for Ross' theory of valid law

Wittgenstein writes a good deal about ostensive definitions ("hinweisende Definitionen"), in that he is concerned with rejecting the notion that they can establish a connection between language and a *prelinguistically* constituted reality.[10] – I shall say a little about Wittgenstein's argumentation (item (i)), because it criticises a view of reality, language and science that *Ross* was strongly influenced by when he formed his influential theory of valid law (item (ii)).

(i) Wittgenstein does not claim that ostensive definitions *say something about* connotations. On the other hand he does claim that ostensive definitions *presuppose* a certain knowledge of connotations and that they thus presuppose that one is already within language:

> "Man könnte also sagen: Die hinweisende Definition erklärt den Gebrauch – die Bedeutung – des Wortes, *wenn es schon klar ist*, welche Rolle das Wort in der Sprache überhaupt spielen soll. Wenn ich also weiß, daß Einer mir ein Farbwort erklären will, so wird mir die hinweisende Erklärung "Das heißt 'Sepia' " zum Verständnis des Wortes verhelfen. ... Man muß schon etwas wissen (oder können), um nach der Benennung fragen zu können" (my italics).[11]

He justifies these assertions inter alia with the following observations:

> "Vielleicht sagt man: die Zwei kann nur *so* hinweisend definiert werden: "Diese *Zahl* heißt 'zwei' ". Denn das Wort "Zahl" zeigt hier an, an welchen *Platz* der Sprache, der Grammatik, wir das Wort setzen. Das heißt aber, es muß das Wort "Zahl" erklärt sein, ehe jene hinweisende Definition verstanden werden kann. – Das Wort "Zahl" in der Definition zeigt allerdings diesen Platz an; den Posten, an den wir das Wort stellen. Und wir können so

10 Wittgenstein, *Philosophische Untersuchungen*, particularly Part I, sections 27–36.

11 Op. cit., Part I, section 30.

> Mißverständnissen vorbeugen, indem wir sagen: "Diese *Farbe* heißt so und so", "Diese *Länge* heißt so und so", usw. Das heißt: Mißverständnisse werden manchmal so vermieden. Aber läßt sich denn das Wort "Farbe", oder "Länge" nur so auffassen? – Nun, wir müssen sie eben erklären. – Also erklären durch andere Wörter! Und wie ist es mit der letzten Erklärung in dieser Kette? (Sag nicht "Es gibt keine 'letzte' Erklärung". Das ist gerade so, als wolltest du sagen: "Es gibt kein letztes Haus in dieser Straße; man kann immer noch eines dazubauen.")" (Wittgenstein's italics).[12]

Wittgenstein's argumentation is directed *in general* against the notion of an ontological and epistemological foundation *outside* language. – More particularly his argumentation may be seen as directed against elements in a lot of empiricism, from Locke and Hume and up to the present day: viz. supposition of certain smallest possible constituents of reality, which are present to us independently of language, which we have access to through sense-experience, and which via our ostensive definitions can or must be thought to provide an ontological and epistemological foundation.

A number of the elements mentioned are found again in "the early" Wittgenstein, who in the *Tractatus*[13] claimed that meaningful language (apart from logic and mathematics) consisted in combinations of names of the world's simple constituents[14] – precisely the model of language that he later argued against. Under the influence of inter alia the *Tractatus* this model was taken up and further elaborated in the Vienna Circle and Logical Positivism[15] of the inter-war period. There too, this took the form of propositions about language and meaning: – Those, and only those, linguistic formulations (apart from logic and mathematics) were *meaningful* that could be shown, directly or through logical analysis, to refer to independent, simple and immediately experienceable elements of reality.[16] – In addition came the logical positivists' emphasis on science: Only those propositions could be *scientific* that had such meaning as mentioned.

---

[12] Op. cit., Part I, section 29.

[13] Wittgenstein, *Tractatus Logico-Philosophicus*, London 1922 (original German edition 1921).

[14] Stenius, *Wittgenstein's Tractatus*, pp. 61–65, 118–26; Baker/ Hacker, *Wittgenstein: Meaning and Understanding*, pp. 1–27 (25–27); Ayer, *Wittgenstein*, pp. 17 et seq.; Pears, *The False Prison*, Vol. 1, pp. 63 et seq.

[15] Neurath/ Hahn/ Carnap, *Wissenschaftliche Weltauffassung: der Wiener Kreis*, p. 309; Carnap, 'Intellectual Autobiography', p. 57.

[16] In the light of progress in formal logic, attempts were made to carry out the relevant logical analysis as formal-logical analysis, see Carnap, *Der logische Aufbau der Welt* (1928); 'Intellectual Autobiography', pp. 16–17. In this perspective definition theory went a long way to being part of formal-logical theory, see Dubislav, *Die Definition* (1931), p. 147 ("[D]ie Methoden d[er] Begriffs- oder besser Zeichenreduktionen [sind] keine anderen als diejenigen, welche wir bei der Behandlung der Definitionen ... kennengelernt haben"), cf. the work in its entirety. – As a programme, the coupling of the model of language outlined in the main text here and the progress in formal logic had been formulated earlier, see Russell, *Our Knowledge of the External World* (1914), pp. 11, 72, 109, 119, 128–29; 'The Relation of Sense-data to Physics' (1914), pp. 149–52 (p. 149: "The supreme maxim in scientific philosophising is this: Wherever possible, logical constructions are to be substituted for inferred entities"; p. 151: "A complete application of [this] method ... would exhibit matter wholly in

A constantly recurring problem in the thinking outlined is what the extralinguistic basis is to be thought to consist in. Wittgenstein's *Tractatus* did not provide any answer.[17] Among the logical positivists the problem manifested itself in discussions about what was to be considered to be the experiential basis for the most fundamental sentences ("atomic sentences", "elementary sentences", "protocol sentences"): the individual's states of consciousness ("phenomenological language", "private language") or spatial things, properties, events, or the like ("physicalistic language").[18] – However, in relation to the present topic, the role of ostensive definitions, the thinking outlined, in which the nature of the extralinguistic basis is open, is sufficient.[19]

(ii) One reason for lawyers to take note of the outlined model of the relationship between language and reality is that the model structures Ross' theory of valid law as the theory is presented in his main work *Om ret og retfærdighed*, 1953 (English edition: *On Law and Justice*, 1958). There one finds a distinct idea that through sense-experience we have access to a prelinguistic and absolute basis. There one also finds a distinct idea that a necessary condition (outside logic and mathematics) of both the meaningfulness of sentences and of scientificity is that *through pointing one can correlate* linguistic entities with the prelinguistic and absolute basis:

"If the statements of legal science are to be understood as empirico-*scientific* assertions about a social reality – and thus not as metaphysical postulates about a validity outside experience – the same must apply to them as to all other reality propositions, namely that their *logical meaning content* is identical with the *immediate experiences* through which it is tested whether or not the proposition is true. ...

Any meaningful assertion about something real must thus directly concern or imply *elementary*, immediate experiences. If I say for example, "this thing is made of chalk", this assertion implies – in connection with a set of other assertions – inter alia that if I place the object under a microscope, I shall make particular observations; that if I pour acid over it, I shall observe cer-

---

terms of sense-data, and even, we may add, of the sense-data of a single person, since the sense-data of others cannot be known without some element of inference"); cf. both works in their entirety. Russell's formal-logical works and his programme for "scientific philosophising" were also (beside inter alia Wittgenstein's *Tractatus*, cf. the main text here) an important source of influence, see Carnap, *Der logische Aufbau der Welt*, pp. 1, 3–4; Vorwort zur 2. Aufl. (1961, the reference here is to 3. Aufl. 1966), p. XI; 'Intellectual Autobiography', pp. 11, 12–14, 16.

17 Wittgenstein, *Tractatus Logico-Philosophicus*, section 5.557; see also the works and places referred to in note 14 above.

18 Carnap, *Der logische Aufbau der Welt*, pp. 83 et seq.; 'Testability and Meaning', pp. 9–14; 'Intellectual Autobiography', pp. 16–18, 23, 50–53; Ayer, 'Logical Positivism, Editor's Introduction', pp. 13, 17–21; Gullvåg, 'Carnap, Innledning' [Carnap, introduction], pp. 16–19, 59–64.

19 Later I shall discuss emphasis on the consideration for operationalisability more generally (in contrast to ostensive definitions in particular) (section III 2.2.2). In so doing, I shall give an account of how this consideration has been disguised in persuasive definitions of "meaning" and "science" (sections III 2.2.2 (3) cf. II B 7.3).

tain chemical reactions; that if I rub it against a blackboard, I shall observe the production of a stroke; and so forth. ...

In the same way a juridico-scientific assertion too ..., if it is to be interpreted as a *meaningful* proposition about reality, *must* imply assertions about certain elementary, immediate experiences ... which define the real content of the juridico-scientific sentence.

... [T]he real content of [juridico-scientific assertions] refers to the way the courts act ..." (my italics).[20]

(6) Denotation specification and concepts of 'definition'

(a) Denotation specification falls under the concept of 'definition' here

Denotation specification does not say anything about what is the basis for conceiving of the specified individual things or types of thing as a unity (items (1) and (4) above). On the basis of the perspective and topic of the present work it is not expedient to lay down criteria in the concept of 'definition' that rule out denotation specification, including the criterion that definitions must specify what is the basis for conceiving of specified individual things or types of thing as a unity:

I place emphasis on the *functional similarity* between denotation specification and connotation specification, that both proposition types, each in its own way, can contribute to determining the meanings of linguistic entities (contribute to determining concepts). This similarity indicates *joint treatment* when the aim is insight into analysis and argumentation occurring in fact and formulated in everyday language (on this aim, see section 2.1, cf. Chapter I, above).

(b) The relationship of denotation specifications to other concepts of 'definition'

In the literature, concepts of 'definition' have been laid down both in such a way that denotation specifications *are covered* and in such a way that they *fall outside*. It may be illuminating to distinguish between three main approaches.

(i) Robinson can stand as the representative of a definitional approach that brings denotation specifications *at large under* the concept of 'definition'.[21]

(ii) Other writers lay down their concepts of 'definition' more or less clearly so that denotation specifications *fall completely outside*. For example Næss, Ofstad and Føllesdal seem to represent this definition alternative.

Næss defines 'normative definition' as "sentence which announces that a certain expression within a certain field shall be interpreted or used *synony-*

---

20 Ross, *Om ret og retfærdighed* [on law and justice], pp. 52–53. The passages quoted were translated by me. In the English edition parts of the passages quoted were omitted or rewritten, see *On Law and Justice*, pp. 39–40.

21 Robinson, *Definition*, Chapter V §§5–6.

mously with a certain other expression" (my italics);[22] "announcement that a certain designation or formulation, T, within a certain context, or in any context, shall be *interpreted in the same way as* a certain other designation or formulation, U" (my italics).[23] – And he defines 'descriptive definition' as "sentence [which] states that a certain expression ... is used *synonymously* with a certain other expression ... within a certain class of situations" (my italics);[24] "statement that a certain designation or formulation, T, in a certain context, or in any context, in fact *expresses the same as* a certain designation or formulation, U" (my italics; Næss' italics omitted).[25]

Næss does not determinately relate these definitions of 'definition' to the distinction between connotation specification and denotation specification. However, since what defines is in Næss by definition limited to linguistic entities, denotation specification in the form of ostensive definition falls outside. And the fact that the relations between the linguistic expressions that are defined and those that define are termed "synonymity", "interpreted in the same way as" and "expresses the same as", probably means that also denotation specification through exclusively linguistic means falls outside, where the denotation specification is incomplete or negative. Whether denotation specification through exclusively linguistic means falls outside where the denotation specification is complete and positive, depends on precisely what concept of 'synonymity' is taken as a basis.[26]

In a discussion of descriptive definitions of the concept of 'legal rule' *Ofstad* seems to keep denotation specifications outside his concept of 'definition'. True enough, he operates, like many others, with what he calls "denotasjonsanalyse" [denotation analysis] and "konnotasjonsanalyse" [connotation analysis].[27] However, this designates two ways of *checking* descriptive definitions (testing the truth value of descriptive definitions), not two ways of

---

22 Næss, *Interpretation and Preciseness*, p. 147.

23 Næss, *Logikk og metodelære* [logic and methodology], p. 66; correspondingly in *En del elementære logiske emner* [some elementary topics in logic], p. 43.

24 Næss, *Interpretation and Preciseness*, p. 169.

25 Næss, *Logikk og metodelære* [logic and methodology], p. 69.

26 Næss, *Interpretation and Preciseness*, pp. 350 et seq. – In *Interpretation and Preciseness*, pp. 144–45, Næss introduces the term "genus definition" of large parts of what is here termed "denotation specification" (ostensive definitions probably fall outside). However, he keeps genus definitions separate from descriptive and normative definitions, and does not discuss them further. (Incidentally, Næss explicitly rejects placing the different definition concepts under a general concept of 'definition'; see op. cit., p. 144.) – It is generally the case that concepts of 'definition' defined by means of a criterion *'synonymity'* will often be, to a great degree or totally, incapable of capturing main groups of actually occurring propositions that contribute to determining the meanings of linguistic entities (contribute to determining concepts): first, propositions with a structuring function alone, without any naming function (section 4.2 (3)(b) cf. (4), above); secondly, denotation specifications where they have the form of an ostensive definition, other denotation specifications where they are incomplete or negative, often also other denotation specifications even if they are complete and positive (the present item (ii)); and finally connotation specifications where they are incomplete or negative (compare section 2.2 above and the account of actually occurring connotation specifications in section 5.1 above and sections 5.3–5.5 and 6, below).

27 Ofstad, 'Om deskriptive definisjoner av begrepet rettsregel' [on descriptive definitions of the concept of 'legal rule'], pp. 49–51.

defining: The presupposition seems the whole time to be that definitions must have an element of connotation specification, so that a denotation mapping simply becomes a means for testing whether the connotation specification is correct.[28]

In a discussion of what distinguishes a logically valid argument, *Føllesdal* writes: "... could not give any definition of 'logical word', but ... had to rely on enumerating them".[29] Here the word "definition" is obviously used of connotation specification in contrast to denotation specification.

(iii) A third definitional approach brings *some, but not all* denotation specifications under the concept of 'definition'. A common method of selection is to require that what defines be linguistic entities, and to apply the criterion in such a way that *ostensive definitions are excluded.* – For example Williams builds on such a concept of 'definition' when he writes: "[T]he names of colours remain indefinable throughout life. Most words, however, admit of being replaced by groups of other words. This process is called definition."[30]

Williams supports his concept of 'definition' on the following statement in Ogden and Richards: "When we define words we take another set of words which may be used with the same referent as the first, i.e., we substitute a symbol which will be better understood in a given situation."[31] – However, Ogden and Richards do not use a concept of 'definition' that ostensive definitions fall outside. From their further discussion of definitions it is apparent that what defines can also be pointing gestures and things: "If we are asked what 'orange' refers to, we may take some object which is orange and say " 'Orange' is a symbol which stands for This." "[32] Thus Ogden and Richards do not consider "[that] the names of colours remain indefinable throughout life", as Williams for his part claims.[33]

---

28 Op. cit., pp. 39–49.

29 Føllesdal/ Walløe/ Elster, *Argumentasjonsteori, språk og vitenskapsfilosofi* [argumentation theory, language and the philosophy of science], p. 221.

30 Williams, 'Language and the Law', p. 388.

31 Ogden/ Richards, *The Meaning of Meaning*, p. 110 (their italics omitted).

32 Op. cit., p. 117.

33 See also op. cit., p. 118. – In the quotation in the text at note 31 above Ogden and Richards are concerned with arguing that it is words and not things that are the object of definition, that is to say, they discuss what is *being* defined, not what is defin*ing*. Even though the formulation in this quotation *can* be understood also as a standpoint on the latter question, it should be clearly apparent from the quotation in the text at note 32 above that this is not what they mean: First, they hardly require that words must be part of the constituent that is defining. Even though the example ("orange") makes use of words in the constituent that is defining, this appears as secondary; to derive any benefit from the definition one must know that it is a colour that is being defined, and thus a pure pointing gesture at an orange thing would have sufficed. Secondly, they at any rate recognise pointing gestures and things as important elements in definitions.

(c) Causes of the fact that denotation specification is kept out of concepts of 'definition'

What can *explain* the outlined tendencies (items (b)(ii)–(iii) above) to keep denotation specification outside concepts of 'definition'?

(i) One reason is no doubt the fact that denotation specification *does not say anything about the basis* for conceiving of the specified individual things or types of thing as a unity.

(ii) I assume that another reason is the fact that definitions have first and foremost been discussed within, and with a view to problem areas in, *philosophy, logic and science*, in contrast to their being discussed within, or with a view to problem areas in, for example, the upbringing of children, legislation, or other regulatory or conflict-resolving roles (public administration, adjudicating activity, the drafting of contracts, etc.). – In logic and much philosophy and science, various forms of *determinacy in thinking* stand as ideals to a particularly high degree: unambiguity; completeness; preciseness; and condition structure of concept criteria, which often means unity in the form of features in common (section 2.2 above). In relation to the causal question discussed in the present item (c), it is relevant to emphasise, first, the great weight that one places on *system*, and secondly, the great weight that one places on an element derived from this desire for system, namely *complete and mutually exclusive categorisations*.

In *such* a system perspective, connotation specifications often appear as the *better* method of definition: Denotation specifications will by comparison often be incomplete. Partly the denotation specification itself will often be incomplete. And partly the sender's aim will often be to clarify a particular delimitation problem, not a set of delimitation problems. To put this metaphorically: Denotation specifications often place a line on *one side or another* of an individual instance, they do not draw a *closed figure*. – Thus denotation specifications cannot be used for complete and mutually exclusive categorisations, and for this reason they are no doubt viewed as being quite unsuitable in system construction. *Given* the system purpose, it is in the light of this natural to reserve the word "definition" for those determinations of meaning that are more suitable, i.e. for connotation specifications.

However, the determinacy requirements should *not* govern the formation of the concept *when* the aim is insight into analysis and argumentation occurring in fact and formulated in everyday language, either by laying down determinacy as a criterion in the concept of 'definition' (sections 2.2 and 4.1 (3), above), or by more particularly excluding denotation specifications because they are too indeterminate (the present section).

Robinson and Austin point to tendencies to underestimate the significance of denotation specifications, more particularly ostensive definitions.[34] In so doing, Robinson maintains: "[T]he tendency to belittle ostensive definition

[34] Robinson, *Definition*, pp. 122–23; Austin, *Sense and Sensibilia*, p. 123 in note 1.

or change its nature is an aberration of those who are bewitched by the fairy-land of symbolic systems detached from experience."[35] – As is apparent from the main text above, I consider it more apt to focus attention on difference in *interests*, with resulting difference in *perspective and topic*. "[T]o belittle ostensive definition" *may* be right on the basis of the interests of philosophers, logicians or others. *Whether* this is right cannot be decided in general. – In my opinion the problem is not, as the quotation from Robinson seems to say, that philosophers, logicians or others form definition concepts on the basis of their interests. It is rather that those who have their interests directed at everyday language have not constructed conceptual models corresponding to their interests, but have more or less unreflectingly adopted concepts formed on the basis of interests in certain philosophical or logical issues (sections 2.1 (1) cf. 2.2, above).

(a)↔(c) Facts and concept formation

Whether or not one lays down the concept of 'definition' so that denotation specification falls outside, it is important that one sees and agrees on the different *ways that are in fact used*, be it in the connotation dimension, in the denotation dimension or through combined forms, to establish areas-in-thought or to remove uncertainty about their delimitation.

5.3. Combination

As has already been apparent, actually occurring definition activity often consists in combination of connotation specification and denotation specification. – *Usual* forms of combination are connotation specification and denotation specification as co-ordinate;[36] denotation specification linked to the whole of the connotation specification,[37] or to a part of this;[38] and connotation specification linked to the whole of the denotation specification.[39]

---

35 Robinson, *Definition*, p. 123.

36 See e.g. section 1-5 of the Creditors' Right of Recovery Act (Act No. 59 of 8 June 1984): "In the present Act those who are deemed to be closely related to one another are … spouses, unmarried cohabitants, engaged parties, relatives in ascending and descending line, siblings, the said persons' spouses and others *who* stand in a particularly close personal relationship to one another …" (my italics).

37 See e.g. section 3 of the Acquisition of Business Activity Act (Act No. 79 of 23 December 1994): "In the present Act … acquisition means: any form of transfer *including* purchase, barter, gratuitous transfer, lease, acquisition by inheritance or distribution of an estate, forced sale and expropriation" (my italics). See further the statutory definitions quoted above of "enkeltvedtak" [individual decision] (sections 5.1 (1) cf. 5.2 (1)) and "forbrukerkjøp" [consumer purchase] (section 5.2 (3)).

38 See e.g. section 1 of the Travel Guarantee Act (Act No. 72 of 12 June 1981): "In the present Act "travel operator" means any person who in return for any consideration organises travel with appurtenant provision of services, *including* transport and accommodation, and who …" (my italics).

39 See e.g. section 3 of the Regulations concerning animal health conditions for the importation and exportation of live poultry and eggs for hatching within the EEA (23 June 1994 No. 695; Norwegian Law Gazette, Part 1, p. 1076): "In the present Regulations poultry means: chickens, turkeys, geese, ducks, grouse, quails, pheasants, guinea hens and pigeons *that* are reared or kept in captivity for the

A borderline case under the last-mentioned form of combination is that one specifies types or points to exemplars, with a verbal addition that "this *and the like*" are called by the expression defined; that is to say, without its being stated *which* points of similarity are of significance.

I say "borderline case" because the element of connotation specification becomes so diluted that it might be reasonable to see the definition as pure denotation specification.

Again, as in the case of the word "definition" (section 5.2 (6) above), one should distinguish between the questions of fact and the question of language: – What is interesting in a definition perspective is the *difference in fact* between on the one hand "and the like"-combinations and on the other hand denotation specifications that simply consist in the enumeration of types or the pointing out of individual instances. For the expression "and the like" refers to a similarity in kind. It is thus a reference to a connotation specification, *albeit* a reference in blank, so that it is left to the recipient of the proposition to fill in the relevant connotations. – Whether one is to *term* such a way of defining "denotation specification" or "combined connotation and denotation specification" is of less importance.

The distinction between complete and incomplete denotation specification generates new forms of combination, of which some show themselves to be *unusual.* This applies particularly to complete denotation specification linked to the whole of the connotation specification.[40] Inter alia in the case of statutory definitions a complete denotation specification is most often without connotation specification.[41] The reason is probably that, if one is first able to specify the denotation completely, then it is considered unnecessary, or even an obstacle to understanding, to specify a connotation in addition; it is considered an obstacle to understanding, inter alia in instances in which the phenomena one collects through the denotation specification do not have any external features in common, so that a connotation specification in relation to these phenomena would have to consist in alternative sets of criteria, something which would easily be considered unsurveyable (section 5.4.2 (2) below).

---

purposes of breeding, production of meat or eggs for consumption, or the supply of game to be let loose" (my italics).

40 In all the examples mentioned above of denotation specification linked to the whole connotation specification (see note 37), the denotation specification is incomplete.

41 See e.g. section 2(a) of the Trade in Fertilisers Act (Act No. 83 of 4 December 1970): "In the present Act producing means: making, processing, mixing, packing and marking"; section 2 of the Register of Legal Entities Act (Act No. 15 of 3 June 1994): "In this Act affiliated register means: 1. The employers section of the register of employers/ employees ... 2. Register of Business Enterprises ... 3. The county governors' registers of foundations ... 4. [etc.]".

5.4. The role of the means in relation to one another in actually occurring definition activity

Taking my point of departure in the distinction between connotation and denotation, I have now given an account of a number of *different means of structuring* (sections 5.1–5.3 above): connotation specification (general criteria); denotation specification (specification of individual things or specification of types of things, be it through proper nouns, definite descriptions, pronouns, adverbs, pointing gestures, common nouns, etc.); and combinations. – The question in what follows is what *roles in relation to one another* are ascribed to these means by language users in actually occurring definition activity. This question cannot be answered both precisely and in general. The *purpose of what follows* is partly to point to and to illustrate some dividing lines that I consider to be significant in answering this question. And the purpose is partly, and more particularly, to discuss the role of denotation specifications in lawyers' language and argumentation.

Bentham terms denotation specification *"subsidiary"*,[42] more precisely subsidiary to definition through category and sub-category (see section 3.2.2 (2)(b)–(c) above on this method of definition), and subsidiary to definition through paraphrasing a linguistic context of which the linguistic entity to be defined is a part (see section 5.5 below on this method of definition). – Bentham does not say explicitly what he means by the term "subsidiary". Perhaps he means to claim that denotation specification is a *less effective means* of creating clarity than definition through category and sub-category or through paraphrase. I am *not* able to find any basis for such an assertion: What is suited to creating clarity depends on what is experienced as unclear. As has already become apparent from examples (sections 5.2–5.3 above) and as is to be more systematically demonstrated in what follows (the present section 5.4 in its entirety), denotation specifications are often used, both outside and in academic contexts. This must mean that language users often consider that denotation specification is a suitable means of relieving experienced lack of clarity. With increased awareness of different means of structuring, language users can of course change their minds about which means is most effective. However, general sentences about the one or the other means of structuring being supplanted in this way, seem to be unfounded (see the same places as referred to in the two preceding parentheses). – A *normative proposition* that denotation specification is in any event "inferior", "ought to be avoided", or the like, can be a cause of denotation specification's being kept out of the concept of 'definition'. In its capacity of being such a cause, this type of proposition is of interest for the discussion in the present work (compare section 5.2 (6)(c) above). Otherwise, however, this type of proposition lies *outside* the perspective and topic of the work (Chapter I above).

---

42 Bentham, *Essay on Logic*, p. 248 (also in *The Theory of Fictions*, pp. 91–93), in which denotation specification is touched on under the names of "exemplification" and "enumeration".

5.4.1. The definition product

(1) Connotation specifications; combination; paradigmatic denotation specifications
(2) Factors that may pull in the direction of pure denotation specification
  (a) Connotation specification is considered impossible or difficult
  (b) Specification of features in common is considered impossible or difficult
  (c) Effective information and discussion
  (d) Factors more specific to law; see section 5.4.2 (1)(d) and (2)(a), below
(3) Factors that may pull in the direction of pure connotation specification

(1) Connotation specifications; combination; paradigmatic denotation specifications

The definition product will often consist in more or less carefully considered specification of general criteria: *connotation specification* – as the case may be, *combined* with more or less comprehensive specification of instances that fall inside or outside: positive or negative denotation specification.

In actually occurring definition activity the *relationship* between connotation specification and denotation specification may *vary* greatly. According to the area of language and argumentation one can distinguish between certain main tendencies:

In many of the *situations in which language is used in everyday life*, denotation specification plays an important role at the same time as the connotation specification may be fairly diluted. – A frequently occurring instance-type is denotation specifications combined with propositions that *"this and the like"* are called by the expression being defined. A central example is our answers to the child's "What is …"-questions, such as "What is a cup?"; our answer often consists in pointing to a particular individual thing, with verbal additions such as "this/ this and the like/ such things … is/ are called … "a cup/ cups" ".

The *cause* of the use of denotation specifications combined with the "this and the like"-formulation may be that the definer considers it *unnecessary* on the basis of his purposes to specify the connotation; that the definer considers the connotation to be *obvious*, so that it is unnecessary to specify it; that the definer *cannot be bothered* to think about and formulate the connotation; or that the definer is *unsure about* what ought to be considered as the relevant connotation. – The three last-mentioned causes will often lie behind occurrences of "this and the like"-combinations in relation to children. And together with the first-mentioned cause they may contribute to explaining the widespread occurrence of such definitions otherwise.

In discussion of *moral and aesthetic* subsumption questions ("When does the foetus become a human being?", "Is this art?"), one often takes one's point of departure in an *individual instance or instance-type* that one clearly considers to fall under the controversial concept: The individual instance or the instance-type acquires a definitional status by virtue of being used as a *paradigmatic object of comparison and yardstick.* – One frequently occurring cause of this approach is the last of the causes mentioned above: One is *unsure about* what ought to be considered as the relevant connotation and assumes that it will be impossible to find or to reach agreement on a connotation that (is so complete that it) covers and provides a satisfactory solution of the subsumption question concerned. Therefore one would rather take one's *point of departure* in an individual instance or instance-type on which there is agreement (in connection with the exemplary questions in the first parenthesis in the present paragraph: one takes for example one's point of departure in respectively the new-born child, and a particular painting or a school within the art of painting), and hopes *to win the day by* pointing out similarities or differences in relation to the controversial instance.

Definitions in *law* tend more towards the middle of the scale: Textbooks, manuals, topical articles on the development of the law, or the like, have a more even distribution of connotation specification and denotation specification than one finds in respectively laymen's discussions of law on the one hand and legal theory's discussions of fundamental problems on the other. – Lawyers too use paradigmatic denotation specifications. They do so, perhaps with somewhat more methodologically conscious analogical thinking than in everyday life. This analogical thinking is partly an aspect of the use of judgments as a source of law.[43] And it is partly a more general aspect of lawyers' language and argumentation: I shall later demonstrate the pervasive occurrence in lawyers' language and argumentation of what I term *"instance-type propositions"*, which inter alia cover paradigmatic denotation specifications (section 5.4.2 (1) below).

In a great deal of *scientific and philosophical literature* the tendency is towards connotation specification, most often in the form of a set of necessary and sufficient concept criteria, and often at a high level of abstraction. Denotation recedes into the background. – However, certain factors may pull in the opposite direction, see item (2) below.

The intimations now given of some quantitative main tendencies are based on the evaluation-free concepts of 'connotation specification' and 'denotation specification' laid down above. These intimations say nothing about the quality of connotation specifications or denotation specifications in the respective areas.

43 Eng, 'The Doctrine of Precedent in English and Norwegian Law', section 2.4.3.3.

(2) *Factors that may pull in the direction of pure denotation specification*

(a) Connotation specification is considered impossible or difficult

One factor that pulls in the direction of pure denotation specification is that connotation specification *is considered* impossible or difficult:

In the case of *learning processes* (cognition of something new) certain parts of new structurings will probably at any time lie on a non-linguistic level, in the sense that we recognise examples, but cannot (yet) specify criteria: one variant of "knowing without being able to say (explain)".[44]

We claim "to know without being able to say (explain)" *also after* the learning process has been completed, that is to say, in relation to more static parts of the system of structurings in thought.[45] – An example from everyday life is provided by the word "colour" or names for the individual colours,[46] for example where the adult is to explain the meanings of the words to the child who asks: Instead of attempting a connotation specification, no doubt most people will define the word "colour" by enumerating the most common colours, and define names for the individual colours by pointing at things of the colour concerned. – An example from an academic language context is provided by the term "logical word" in the formal-logical doctrine of valid arguments; see the previously quoted enumeration of which words are included (section 5.2 (3) above).

Philosophers have discussed whether there are concepts in respect of which connotation specification *is* impossible (in contrast to being considered impossible), so that denotation specification, or, as the case may be, more specifically ostensive definition, is necessary for acquiring the concept.[47] This question is different from the present topic: actual use of the said modes of definition.

In philosophy and academic subjects, reflection on the use of concepts or of language not infrequently leads to focus on phenomena that can reasonably be seen as variants of "knowing without being able to say (explain)". This may be focus on what the philosopher terms "Urteilskraft" or "Praxis", as an aspect of the application of concepts or the application of language, purely generally;[48] or focus on what the lawyer terms "(sound) judgement",

---

44 The everyday experience of the existence of such knowledge has been made clearer in laboratory experiments concerning the ability to discriminate between figures, e.g. Chinese-like characters, see Hull, 'Quantitative Aspects of the Evolution of Concepts', in particular pp. 17 cf. 43, 67, 79–81, 84–85; Rommetveit, *Språk, tanke og kommunikasjon* [language, thought and communication], pp. 239–45, in particular 241 (bottom)–242 (top).

45 Compare Austin, 'Other Minds', pp. 52–53; Wittgenstein, *Philosophische Untersuchungen*, Part I, section 78.

46 Compare Wittgenstein, *Bemerkungen über die Farben*, Part I, section 68, Part III, sections 42, 86, 102, 127.

47 See e.g. Robinson, *Definition*, p. 126; Passmore, *Philosophical Reasoning*, pp. 113 et seq. – See also section 5.2 (5)(b) above.

48 See respectively Kant, *Kritik der reinen Vernunft*, B 171–72, 674, and Wittgenstein, *Philosophische Untersuchungen*, Part I, sections 201–02, 241–42.

"(sound) intuition", "(sound) iudicium", or the like, as an aspect of qualified and trained lawyers' application of legal rules.[49] These phenomena are different from the present topic: They do not represent, like denotation specification, an alternative to connotation specification, but are aspects of the *application* of a presupposed connotation specification.[50]

(b) Specification of features in common is considered impossible or difficult

Another factor that pulls in the direction of pure denotation specification is that connotation specification may well be considered possible, but one considers it impossible or difficult to specify features in common.

I have previously discussed variants of unity that in fact exist between phenomena of which one uses the same word (section 3.2.2 above). There I defined "features in common" as necessary or exhaustive and surveyable (sets of) sufficient features (item (5)(c)). Concepts in the case of which the unity between the phenomena can be specified as features in common, I termed "condition concepts"; and concepts in the case of which the unity *cannot* be specified as features in common, I termed "factor concepts" (item (5)(d)). As one main group of factor concepts I mentioned family resemblance concepts. Examples given of family resemblance concepts were, inter alia, 'spill' [game] and 'rett' [law/ right]. – In the case of these and other instances of family resemblance, *pure denotation specification* can in some cases appear as an *appropriate method of definition* (as the case may be, combined with the expression "and the like", compare item (1) above): One considers it simpler and perhaps also more informative to specify types of game and types of law/ right, than to make an incomplete enumeration of diverse criteria.

(c) Effective information and discussion

Even if connotation specification is considered possible (compare item (a) above), and even if one considers that connotation specification can build on unity in the form of features in common (compare item (b) above), pure denotation specification may nevertheless be chosen:

One reason may be that one considers denotation specification *better suited to providing the intended language information.* An example would be the adult who is to explain to the child that Europe is not a country, and who must therefore explain the difference in meaning between the words "country" and "continent". If they have a map at hand, the difference can be explained by pointing. Otherwise the difference can be explained by listing ("The world consists of

---

[49] See the references in section V 4.2.2 (1) below, in note 5.

[50] Something different from there not being any clear relationship in fact between an assumption that qualified and trained lawyers have a distinctive application intuition and *occurrence of* denotation specification at the expense of connotation specification in these lawyers' application of legal rules, is that assumption of a distinctive application intuition can bring about *respect for* the lawyer's denotation specification. On the latter, see in more detail in section V 4.2.2 (1) below, after note 4.

the continents of...", "The continent of Europe consists of the following countries ...").

Another reason to choose denotation specification rather than connotation specification may be a conscious desire to *reduce the risk of analytically un/true propositions*: If one has made up one's mind what (groups of) phenomena one wishes to discuss and what linguistic expression one wishes to designate them by, it happens that for the reason mentioned one contents oneself with specifying these two things, without laying down existence or non-existence of particular features of the phenomena as definitional for the use of the expression.[51]

(d) Factors more specific to law; see section 5.4.2 (1)(d) and (2)(a), below

(3) Factors that may pull in the direction of pure connotation specification

One factor that may pull in the direction of pure connotation specification is the desire for the *greatest* possible cognition in the *simplest* possible form; I refer to sections 5.2 (6)(c)(ii) above and III 2.2.6 (3) below.

Another factor that may pull in the direction of pure connotation specification is that *denotation specification is considered to be or is impossible*; I refer to section 5.5 (3) cf. (2), below.

5.4.2. In particular on the role of denotation specifications in lawyers' definitions; "instance-type propositions" and statutory definitions

Denotation specification is a method of definition that is particularly and to a high degree characteristic of lawyers' language and argumentation.[52] One important

---

[51] Goffman, *Asylums*, p. 16: "By anchoring the initial definition of total institutions in [these five rough groupings], I hope to be able to discuss the general characteristics of the type without becoming tautological."

[52] Compare Fleischer, *Anvendelse og fortolkning av dommer* [application and interpretation of judgments], pp. 23–24 ("legal interpretation is to a certain extent in a position of its own on this point – that in practice it is the application, or the non-application, to the concrete instance, and not the determination of the proposition's boundaries in general, that is the central thing"); Jareborg, 'Regler och riktlinjer' [rules and guidelines], p. 410 ("[in] all explanation of when a statutory provision is applicable ... [it] is much more usual for one to use a denotative method of definition than an analytical one"); Frändberg, 'Om tolkning och förståelse' [on interpretation and understanding], pp. 15–17 ("the judge's statutory interpretation is an interpretation with a view to application [in contrast to] for example the literary theorist's interpretation of literary works"); Alston, 'No Right to Complain About Being Poor', pp. 91–92, 98 ("the most telling evidence of the jurisprudential value of the complaints procedure is the fact that the collected 'views' of [the Human Rights] Committee based

form is those propositions I call "instance-type propositions". Another form is statutory definitions that collect phenomena that have no externally perceivable features in common. – I have grouped my discussions as follows:

(1) Instance-type propositions
- **(a) Definition**
- **(b) Examples**
- **(c) Strength of instance-type propositions**
- **(d) Causes of lawyers' use of instance-type propositions**

(2) Statutory definitions

(1) Instance-type propositions

(a) Definition

(i) By *"instance-type propositions"* I mean a group of propositions that relate to concepts with *evaluation prescription* in their connotation. – I shall later come back to evaluation prescription as one way of specifying connotation (section 6.1). Here the emphasis is on the fact that, and the way in which, evaluation prescriptions entail *weighing and balancing* (item (ii) below). In the light of this, the definition in the first sentence can be formulated more precisely as follows: By "instance-type propositions" I mean propositions that say something about the *outcome* of the weighing and balancing in relation to a constellation of facts specified in general terms ("the instance-type").

Instance-type propositions are a means of structuring in the form of *denotation specification*, in that these propositions say something about whether the instance-type falls within or outside the concept's denotation.

My definition does not say anything about the *modality* of instance-type propositions; that is a question of fact (item (c) below).

In what follows (items (ii)–(iv)) I shall go more deeply into the language and argumentation context of which instance-type propositions are part, and which provides the concept of 'instance-type proposition' with a reality basis and interest.

(ii) *Weighing and balancing* is a *factually central feature of evaluations*.[53] An example can illustrate this: According to section 2 of the Price Measures Act (Act No. 66 of 11 June 1993) "unreasonable [prices]" are unlawful.[54] In the evaluation of whether a price is unreasonable, one takes into account certain *typically relevant factors*, such as the usual price otherwise, the quality of the goods, the

---

on individual cases are of infinitely greater value in shedding light on the meaning of the various rights formulations than ... the Committee's General Comments").

53 A factually central, but not a definitional feature of the concept formed here.

54 This provision reproduces the essential content of section 18 of the earlier Prices Act (Act No. 4 of 26 June 1953), cf. *Ot.prp. No. 41 1992–93* [proposal from the Government], p. 119; *Rt. 1996/407* on pp. 412 et seq.

existence and extent of any subsidiary benefits, the relative strengths of the parties, etc. These factors must often be *weighed and balanced against one another*, since they often pull in different directions; the price is, for example, clearly higher than usual, which pulls in the direction of unreasonableness, at the same time as the quality of the goods seems higher than usual and the buyer more knowledgeable and wealthy than the seller, which pulls in the opposite direction. In the weighting of the factors that is therefore necessary, one is often led into *more rounds* of mapping typically relevant factors and of weighings and balancings: For the quality of goods, for example, indeed often depends not on any one single property, but on a complex set of properties. And these properties often dissolve into new mappings of factors and weighings and balancings of factors, out of widely different needs. Compare the many needs, properties, and weighings and balancings that may come into play in the case of something so relatively simple as evaluating a car. – Thus an evaluation prescription can often entail a *nuanced thought structure*. If one is to stress one feature rather than others, then the *weighings and balancings* suggest themselves, since it is these that give evaluations much of their distinctiveness.

> The term "weighing and balancing" as it is used in this work does *not* presuppose that what is weighed and balanced is unitary (for example in dimensions such as 'utility', 'value', 'social utility', 'social value', or the like); the relevant factors can on closer reflection be perceived to a greater or lesser degree as being difficult to compare. On this point the term "weighing and balancing" and its derivatives (or their equivalents in other languages) may mislead: Through their leading thought towards the picture of weighing physical objects and thus towards the measurable dimension 'weight of physical objects', one may be led to believe in a greater degree of unity between arguments than one on closer reflection finds there is support for.[55] However, the term "weighing and balancing" and its derivatives (or their equivalents in other languages) are widely used, and I have not been able to find any terminology that is better suited.

(iii) An *instance-type proposition*, i.e. a proposition about the outcome of the weighing and balancing in relation to a constellation of facts specified in general terms (the instance-type), may in relation to the criterion 'unreasonable price' in section 2 of the Price Measures Act be, for example, that where (i.e. the instance-type) a new car is bought, for the buyer's own use, and for non-commercial purposes, then (i.e. the outcome of the weighing and balancing) a price in excess

---

55 Compare Peczenik, *Vad är rätt?* [what is law?], pp. 648 et seq.; Ahlander, *Är juridiken en vetenskap?* [is law a science?], p. 24; Eckhoff, *Rettskildelære* [doctrine of the sources of law], 1st ed. pp. 310–11, 324–26; 3rd ed. pp. 320–22; MacCormick, *Legal Reasoning and Legal Theory*, pp. 112, 155–56, 194; Raz, *The Morality of Freedom*, pp. 321–66; Nagel, *Mortal Questions*, pp. 128–41; Posner, *The Problems of Jurisprudence*, p. 124; Greenawalt, *Law and Objectivity*, p. 152; Thagard, *Coherence in Thought and Action*, pp. 148, 242, 280 (bottom)–281 (top); Habermas, *Faktizität und Geltung*, p. 316 at and in note 33.

of the market price by approximately 20% or more shall be deemed to be unreasonable.[56]

The sketch in item (ii) above of the evaluation of unreasonableness pursuant to section 2 of the Price Measures Act demonstrated that also *another method of definition* than instance-type propositions may suggest itself in relation to concepts with evaluation prescription in their connotation, namely specifying what factors are relevant to the weighing and balancing, and, as the case may be, what weight they have and in what directions they pull; see what has been said about this in item (ii). – Such a method of definition is a means of structuring in the form of connotation specification, more precisely *connotation specification with guideline structure*. A more detailed discussion of this method of definition belongs under the topic of 'ways of specifying the connotation' (section 6.2 (1) below). However, this method of definition must also to a certain extent be brought into the present context: Causes of defining through denotation specification in the form of instance-type propositions must to a certain extent be sought in the fact that language users take the view that there are weaknesses attached to defining through connotation specification with guideline structure (item (d) below).

(iv) Many norms contain concepts with evaluation prescription in their connotation, see for example section 2 of the Price Measures Act. In so far as the evaluation prescription is understood and practised in such a way that it entails weighing and balancing,[57] I term such norms *"weighing and balancing norms"*.[58]

Weighing and balancing norms are very common in law; this will be apparent partly from examples (item (b) below), and partly from my pointing out certain more general features of lawyers' language and argumentation (section F 3.2.2 (1) below).

> Sundby uses the term *"avveiningsmarkør"* [weighing and balancing marker] of words that call for weighing and balancing when one interprets or applies them.[59] Many rules of law that prescribe an evaluation are, however, formulated in such a way that the evaluation prescription is not apparent; the evaluation prescription is a *feature of the connotations* of concepts in the rule, but is *hidden* behind evaluation-free language attire. Sundby is of course aware of this, and he introduces the term "skjult avveiningsmarkør" [hidden weighing and balancing marker] to capture these instances.[60]

---

56 Compare item (b)(iii) below, at and in note 75.

57 Compare note 53 above.

58 I thus define my concept of 'weighing and balancing norm' via my concept of 'concepts with evaluation prescription in their connotation'. Compare in contrast the concept formed in Sundby, *Om normer* [on norms], Part 2 (p. 200 et passim); Eckhoff/ Sundby, *Rettssystemer* [legal systems], Chapter 7 (p. 108 et passim). – The difference is due to the definition perspective here: Only against the background of the concept of 'concepts with evaluation prescription in their connotation' can one cognise instance-type propositions as a distinct definition method.

59 Sundby, *Om normer* [on norms], pp. 200–01.

60 Op. cit., p. 201.

However, the term "hidden weighing and balancing marker" mixes meaning level and word level, and virtually expresses a self-contradiction; that weighing and balancing is necessary, shall both be hidden and particularly clearly visible. As a term for the fact that the proposition, in contradistinction to the formulation of the proposition, prescribes an evaluation, I use instead "evaluation prescription".

(i)↔(iv) I have *now outlined* the following language and argumentation context: (i) concepts with evaluation prescription in their connotation; (ii) with their accompanying weighings and balancings; (iii) and with different definition methods, in particular denotation specification in the form of instance-type propositions versus connotation specification with guideline structure; (iv) outside or within law. In relation to this language and argumentation context the *focus in what follows is on* instance-type propositions in lawyers' language and argumentation.

(v) By analogy with the concept of 'instance-type proposition' a concept of *'individual instance proposition'* may be defined, the only conceptual difference being that instance-type propositions lay down the denotation through general terms, while individual instance propositions lay down the denotation through singular terms (proper nouns, definite descriptions or other words and expressions that function as proper nouns). – However, with a view to insight into lawyers' language and argumentation, *in particular* with a view to shedding light on lawyers' relationship to *weighing and balancing* in the subsumption process, it is instance-type propositions that have the greater interest. This will become more evident when in item (b) below I go over to looking at actually occurring use of instance-type propositions, and in item (d) below at causes of the use of such propositions.

(vi) In German legal theory one distinguishes between Begriff and Typus.[61] *"Begriff"* is used of concepts defined through necessary and sufficient conditions,[62] and *"Typus"* of other things (see at and in note 67 below). *Common* to discussions relating to this distinction and the discussion in what follows, is the premiss that it is important to analyse the application of linguistic entities/ concepts.[63] – The more detailed content of the discussions

61 Engisch, *Die Idee der Konkretisierung in Recht und Rechtswissenschaft unserer Zeit*, pp. 237–94, 308–12; Larenz, *Methodenlehre der Rechtswissenschaft*, pp. 216–24, 291–94, 461 et seq.; Kaufmann, *Analogie und "Natur der Sache"*, pp. 47–54, 74–76. – For a survey of the diversity of statements about "Typus" from different writers in different subjects, see in particular Engisch, *Die Idee der Konkretisierung in Recht und Rechtswissenschaft unserer Zeit*, pp. 237–62.

62 Kaufmann, *Analogie und "Natur der Sache"*, pp. 47–48: "Der Begriff ... ist geschlossen, der Typus ist offen"; Larenz, *Methodenlehre der Rechtswissenschaft*, pp. 216–22: "Von einem "Begriff" im strengen Sinn läßt sich nur da sprechen, wo es möglich ist, ihn durch die vollständige Angabe der ihn kennzeichnenden Merkmale eindeutig zu definieren" (p. 216); "Ein Begriff ist durch seine Definition in der Weise festgelegt, daß er auf einen konkreten Vorgang oder Sachverhalt "nur dann und immer dann" anzuwenden ist, wenn in ihm sämtliche Merkmale der Definition anzutreffen sind. Für den Typus gilt dieser Satz nicht" (p. 221).

63 "Concept" here used in its sense in this work (sections 3.2.2 (5)(d) and 4.1 (3), above), not limited in the way "Begriff" is (preceding note).

is, however, *different*. First, discussions relating to the distinction between 'Begriff' and 'Typus' are so abstract that what is put forward is hardly specific to lawyers' language and argumentation, but applies to concept application at large.[64] And secondly, in so far as these discussions become more concrete, no clear distinction is made between those elements in lawyers' language and argumentation that in the present model[65] are distinguished from one another and studied in their interplay.[66] An aspect of the latter is that it remains indeterminate what basic terms such as "Typus", "type", "type concept", "typological method", and the like, *stand for*: It remains indeterminate whether the basic terms stand for concepts that have not been defined through necessary and sufficient conditions; concepts with evaluation prescription in their connotation; linguistic entities for evaluation prescriptions; factors to be weighed and balanced, and the nature and strength of the factors; the weighing and balancing itself (the exercise of discretion); inferences from similarity (analogy); inferences from purpose (teleology); a representative individual instance, or, as the case may be, a psychological representation of such an instance (paradigmatic denotation specification); many individual instances, or, as the case may be, a psychological representation of such instances (casuistry); other things, including instance-type propositions in the sense outlined above and to be treated in depth in what follows – *or* whether the basic terms stand for combinations of these or other alternatives.[67]

(b) Examples

The following examples aim, first, to illustrate the distinctive nature of instance-type propositions: the fact that, and the way in which, they specify denotation in the case of concepts with evaluation prescription in their connotation; and thus, secondly, to illustrate the structuring function of instance-type propositions: the fact that through the specification of denotation they contribute to delimitation in thought of an area. – I take a standpoint only on the examples' (formal) property of being instance-type propositions, not on their tenability (according to their content).

A number of the examples are situated in contexts in which they are combined with other definitional propositions: combined partly with other instance-type propositions into more comprehensive denotation specifications, and combined partly with connotation specifications. Here, however, the focus is solely on that part of the definition activity that takes the form of instance-type propositions.

---

64 This applies to e.g. the discussion in Kaufmann, *Analogie und "Natur der Sache"*, pp. 47–54, 75–76.

65 Immediately, in the present section 5.4.2 (1), and further, in the present section B in its entirety.

66 This applies to e.g. the discussion in Larenz, *Methodenlehre der Rechtswissenschaft*, pp. 218–24, 464–73.

67 In addition to the places referred to in notes 64 and 66 above, see Jørgensen, 'Typologi og realisme' [typology and realism], pp. 147–56, who under the basic terms includes large parts of legal methodology; Engisch, *Einführung in das juristische Denken*, p. 256 ("Es gibt unendlich viele Aspekte, unter denen der Typus rechtstheoretisch Verwendung finden kann").

(i) In the law of obligations one has from times of old operated with a non-statutory rule concerning variation or cessation of obligations on account of what in Norwegian law has been called *"bristende forutsetninger"* [subsequently failed contractual assumptions]. Today there is agreement that this rule must be seen as a weighing and balancing norm.[68] No sure formulation of the rule has taken root, but key words in any formulation will have to be *"reasonableness"* and *"justice"*.[69] – Augdahl advances (inter alia) the following instance-type propositions in his structuring of the rule's area of application:

> "It may certainly be set up as an almost exception-free rule that *lack of money* ought not to be relevant. ... An exception must apply in the case of purely or essentially benevolent promises – for example, a promise of a *gift of money*, of an *interest-free loan*" (my italics).[70]
>
> "The advantages in terms of "legal practicality" that are connected with a virtually exception-free rule that a *rise in prices* or a *fall in prices* is not relevant, are so great that the rule is no doubt to be preferred even though it may in some cases seem heavy-handed" (my italics; Augdahl's italics omitted).[71]

(ii) According to *section 33 of the Contracts Act* (Act No. 4 of 31 May 1918) it is a necessary condition for a declaration of intent in the law of obligations and property to be enforceable, that enforcement will not be "contrary to honesty or good faith". – In his structuring of the area of application of the *criterion 'honesty'*, Arnholm says:

> "[I]t happens that a contract is entered into on the basis of reliance on incorrect information that the one party gives to the other in good faith ... [E]ven if he had had every reason to believe that the information was correct, it seems clear that he could not take advantage of the fact that as a result of his own incorrect information he had made a cheaper purchase than the seller would otherwise have granted him."[72]

I interpret Arnholm as advancing the following instance-type proposition: "It will be "contrary to honesty or good faith" within the meaning of the Act to enforce a declaration of intent *brought about by the recipient through incorrect information* that purports to be exact and that has motivated the sender."

(iii) The examples above represent a normal degree of preciseness in the case of legal instance-type propositions. More uncommon are propositions that *put*

---

68 In contrast to earlier, when one attempted to attach the rule to a limited set of legally operative facts, e.g. whether the assumption was visible or not, general or individual, what the parties would have contracted on the issue, etc.; see Augdahl, *Obligasjonsrett* [law of obligations], pp. 146–47.

69 Op. cit., p. 147; *Ot.prp. No. 5 1982–83* [proposal from the Government] (on section 36 of the Contracts Act), p. 35, second column.

70 Augdahl, *Obligasjonsrett* [law of obligations], p. 151.

71 Op. cit., p. 152.

72 Arnholm, *Alminnelig avtalerett* [general law of contract], p. 310. Correspondingly in *Privatrett II: Avtaler* [private law II: contracts], p. 322; *Lærebok i avtalerett* [textbook in the law of contract], pp. 257–58.

figures on the boundaries of the concepts. However, with a view to an adequate picture of the role of instance-type propositions I shall also mention some examples of using figures.

According to *section 36 of the Contracts Act* it is a necessary condition for contracts to be enforceable that enforcement will not be "unreasonable or contrary to good business practice". – In his structuring of the area of application of the *criterion 'unreasonableness'*, Huser says:

> "[T]here [must] be said to be a fairly solid basis for applying section 36 for revision of long-term contracts, including the sum to be paid in such contracts. However, as a point of departure it will probably have to be taken as a basis that the criterion 'unreasonableness' will be stricter here than when it comes to original imbalance, so that it is required that the imbalance on account of changed circumstances has become significant before one will say that it will be unreasonable to enforce the contract. Even though a concrete evaluation will have to be made of what will be significant in this connection, it is safe to assume that it will at any rate as a rule be significant – and therefore unreasonable – when there has arisen a *difference between the sum to be paid and the market price of 50–100%*" (my italics; Huser's italics omitted).[73]

M. Andenæs makes similar use of figures in connection with the prohibition against unreasonable prices in section 18 of the earlier Prices Act.[74/75]

In deciding whether the master of a vessel shall be deemed to be "beruset" [intoxicated] within the meaning of *section 422, second paragraph, of the Criminal Justice Act* (Act No. 10 of 22 May 1902), the courts practise "a concrete evaluation of whether the influence of alcohol has affected his fitness to perform service on board".[76] – In its structuring of the area of application of the *criterion 'fitness'*, the Supreme Court has taken as a basis that the master of a vessel with an *alcohol concentration in his blood of approximately 1.5 milligrams per millilitre* "must ... normally be deemed to be intoxicated within the meaning of the provision".[77]

(iv) In a discussion of the concepts of 'competence' and 'validity' in legal argumentation, I have recommended dividing the concept of *'material competence-condition'* into two: partly into the concept of *'situation condition'*, which covers that element in competence norms that says when (in what situation) the

---

73 Huser, *Avtalesensur* [policing contracts], p. 49.

74 On this provision see item (a) above, in note 54.

75 M. Andenæs, 'Tolking av lover med både strafferettslige og sivilrettslige sanksjoner – belyst ved tre av dem' [interpretation of statutes with both criminal law and civil law sanctions – illuminated by three of them], p. 183: "[T]here is a sort of normal limit to what is to count as a lawful price, going at 15–20% in excess of the reasonable price."

76 *Rt. 1991/739* on p. 740; *Rt. 1990/801* on p. 801.

77 *Rt. 1985/727* on p. 727; see also the judgments mentioned in the preceding note, same places as mentioned there. – In relation to the main topic of the present work, language and argumentation, I designate the decisions of the courts by the common term "judgment", irrespective of whether they are procedurally called "judgment", "order", "ruling", "decision", or something else (for example the decisions mentioned in the preceding note are orders in procedural terms).

competence is present; and partly into the concept of *'content specification'*, which covers that element in competence norms that says what one has competence to lay down.[78]

One reason that I recommend the said nuancing is that I assume it has significance for the in/validity question, for example in the case of public administrative individual decisions: The main rule is that material breach of competence causes an individual decision to be invalid, even if a certain time has elapsed before the conflict comes up, and even if a private individual has in good faith acted in reliance on the decision. Any exceptions must rest on an evaluation, in which one takes into account inter alia how serious the breach of competence is, how much time has elapsed, and the extent to which the private individual has acted in reliance on the decision. *How serious* the breach of competence is, again itself rests on an evaluation. In the case of this evaluation I assume there is reason to advance the following instance-type proposition: "Breach of content specifications will often represent a more serious breach of competence than breach of situation conditions, and thus to a correspondingly greater degree suggest invalidity." For in the case of breach of content specifications the public administrative authorities have purported to have a competence they never possess, while in the case of breach of situation conditions it is a question of the wrong point in time (wrong situation).[79]

(v) The instance-type propositions above relate to the *individual legal rules*, partly in private law (items (i)–(iii)) and partly in public law (item (iv)). If one goes to lawyers' propositions about the *tenability criteria for lawyers' argumentation de lege lata* ("the doctrine of the sources of law"), then one finds instance-type propositions on this level too.

I assume that many central aspects of lawyers' argumentation de lege lata can be described starting from a hypothesis that lawyers have accepted the following *basic weighing and balancing norm*: "The lawyer shall seek the conclusion that, all things considered, including statutes, previous judgments and other forms of practice, has the best grounds to support it."[80] – In relation to this weighing and balancing norm some propositions in the doctrine of the sources of law can be seen as *instance-type propositions* for determining the denotation of the formulation *"the best grounds"*. An example is:

> "That precedents are often invoked does not necessarily mean that they are ascribed great weight. For it may well be that one would have arrived at the same conclusion also without support in court practice. There is much to

---

[78] Eng, 'Begrepene 'kompetanse' og 'gyldighet' i juridisk argumentasjon' [the concepts of 'competence' and 'validity' in legal argumentation], pp. 644–51.

[79] Op. cit., pp. 650–51. There I also give an example for illustration.

[80] This formulation is built on the pattern of Augdahl, *Rettskilder* [sources of law], p. 27. – I emphasise "described": In conformity with the superordinate perspective and topic of the present work (Chapter I above) I neither justify nor criticise lawyers' argumentation de lege lata. – Concerning "many central aspects", but not all central aspects, that is, see section F below.

suggest, however, that references to court practice are not only of frequent occurrence but are also weighty arguments. At any rate the *Supreme Court's precedents are considered to be something approaching absolutely binding on all others than the Supreme Court itself*. Lower courts and administrative bodies may perhaps happen to make decisions contrary to previous Supreme Court judgments that they have overlooked or interpreted differently from the way in which the Supreme Court itself does. However, it is extremely rare for a lower court or an administrative body to depart deliberately from a Supreme Court precedent" (my italics).[81]

(vi) In law, instance-type propositions are often formulated by *writers* on the basis of analyses of *court practice*; this applies inter alia to all the examples from legal literature in items (i)–(v) above. – Writers' or judges' propositions about "instance-types", "the typical instance", "the typical thing", "casuistry" [la casuistique, die Kasuistik], "the usual", "as a general rule", or the like, will often be instance-type propositions.

The *public administrative authorities* too formulate instance-type propositions. – For one thing this happens through administrative bodies' *self-determined practice*: for example practice in public health administration that replaces criteria such as 'most entitled', 'greatest need', and the like, by propositions that persons over a certain age never come into consideration in the distribution of a certain health benefit.[82] – For another thing it happens in the form of *instructions* to subordinates, laying down that the subordinates shall to a greater or lesser degree replace the concrete discretion that a definition prescribes, by instance-type propositions: for example replace the criterion 'best suited' in appointment proceedings by a proposition that persons over a certain age do not come into consideration for a particular type of post.[83] – Furthermore, the public administrative authorities formulate instance-type propositions in the form of *regulations*. In practice one will virtually without exception interpret power to issue a regulation in such a way that it confers competence to lay down instance-type propositions in relation to concepts in the regulation itself. Statutory power to issue regulations may say explicitly that the public administrative authorities have competence to lay down instance-type propositions in relation to concepts in the statute, such as in section 5 of the Public Administration Act: "The King may in the event of

---

81 Eckhoff, *Rettskildelære* [doctrine of the sources of law], 1st ed. pp. 152–53; essentially the same in 3rd ed. p. 135. – I should remind the reader (compare the present item (b), introductory remarks) that I take a standpoint solely on the examples' (formal) property of being instance-type propositions, not on their tenability (according to their content). As I shall later come back to, I assume that in the doctrine of the sources of law there is less of a basis for instance-type propositions than is usually supposed (section III 2.2.6 (4)(b) below).

82 *NOU 1987: 23* [Norwegian official reports], Retningslinjer for prioriteringer innen norsk helsetjeneste [guidelines for priorities within Norwegian health care], p. 77; *NOU 1997: 18*, Prioritering på ny. Gjennomgang av retningslinjer for prioriteringer innen norsk helsetjeneste [priorities again. Examination of guidelines for priorities within Norwegian health care], p. 94. For other examples, see item (d) below, concluding remarks (at and in notes 98 and 99).

83 *Rt. 1964/502.*

doubt determine how the definitions in section 2 first paragraph shall be applied within a particular area of administrative business." Even if it is not explicitly stated in this way, one will no doubt often interpret statutory power to issue a regulation in such a way that it confers competence to lay down instance-type propositions in relation to concepts in the statute too.

(c) Strength of instance-type propositions[84]

In the *modality dimension* instance-type propositions may be *purely descriptive*, i.e. be propositions about how weighings and balancings actually turn out, given a set of facts of a particular type and its accompanying argument constellation.

Further, instance-type propositions may be *purely normative*. An example is where superiors in public administration forbid, order or recommend subordinates by means of instructions to arrive at a particular conclusion in the case of the weighing and balancing in a particular instance-type (item (b)(vi) above).

Instance-type propositions in lawyers' argumentation de lege lata are often neither purely descriptive nor purely normative, but have a *fused descriptive and normative modality*. This I assume to be the case inter alia in the cited examples from legal literature (items (b)(i)–(iv) above). – Fused modality is not a feature peculiar to instance-type propositions de lege lata, but a general feature of lawyers' propositions de lege lata, and will later be analysed on its own (section F below).

In the *situation dimension* instance-type propositions can be formulated *deterministically*, by one's specifying the situation criterion as all instances of the instance-type; or *statistically*, by one's specifying the situation criterion as "usually", "often", "as a rule", "as a general rule", "typically", or the like.

Different combinations of the modality dimension and the situation dimension may, and often will, *be understood in the same way*. This goes for example for the combinations "in all instances of the instance-type one ought to ..." and "usually in the instance-type one shall ...".

> The first combination is an example of the norms Jareborg calls "tumregler"[85] [rules of thumb], and the second combination is an example of the norms Malt calls "gyldigsynlighetsnormer"[86] [Gültigscheinlichkeitsnormen; untranslatable into English]. – What is common to them is that even if the

---

[84] By the *"strength"* of instance-type propositions I do not mean any deeper unitary property, but those features which are mentioned in the main text in what follows, and which have in common that, with more or less determinate views on the part of language users as a starting point, they provide language users with a basis for ranking instance-type propositions. – *Analysis of dis/agreement* can be a reason for seeing these features in relation to one another: Formulations that show disagreement in one strength dimension can show agreement in another strength dimension or when several strength dimensions are seen in relation to one another (see the example at the end of the main text in the present item (c)).

[85] Jareborg, 'Regler och riktlinjer' [rules and guidelines], pp. 388–89 including note 4, with further references.

[86] Malt, 'Svake normer' [weak norms], pp. 175–79.

instance-type is instantiated, one can act in another way than that specified in the action specification in the instance-type proposition *without* one's for that reason being liable to be said not to be following the proposition.[87]

(d) Causes of lawyers' use of instance-type propositions

Connotation specification means that one specifies *criteria* for the ways of using words (concept criteria). In the case of legal weighing and balancing norms this means in practice that one maps what arguments one may, shall or shall not place weight on in the weighing and balancing, and, as the case may be, what weight the arguments typically have and in what directions they pull: The connotation specification has a *guideline structure*.[88] – However, connotation specification with guideline structure is considered by many lawyers to be *inadequate*. They introduce a further type of argument in the form of instance-type propositions. Why is this?

In the earlier general account of the definition product I pointed to some situations with a tendency in the direction of denotation specification (section 5.4.1 (2) above): situations in which connotation specification is considered impossible or difficult; situations in which specification of features in common is considered impossible or difficult; and situations in which connotation specification, even if considered possible and capable of being built on unity in the form of features in common, is considered less suitable as a means for information and discussion. – In what follows I shall supplement the said causes with causes more specific to lawyers and their professional roles.

One cause is the need to *save time and effort in the application of the law*: in the courts, in public administration, in negotiations conducted against a legal background, etc. – In relation to this need, instance-type propositions will most often be preferable to the underlying weighing and balancing norm with its accompanying guidelines, since instance-type propositions mean simplifications both in the deliberation prior to, and in the justification addressed to others for, the determination of concepts: Instance-type propositions mean partly a purely quantitative simplification, in that they reduce the number of relevant criteria, and thereby also the number of sides of the case that are relevant; and they mean partly a simplification of a more qualitative nature, in that they often replace less cognisable criteria in the weighing and balancing norm, and their accompanying guidelines, by criteria easier to cognise. – For example, 'unreasonable' as a criterion in cases concerning revision of contracts makes relevant a virtual infinity of sub-criteria, evidential themes and evidential facts. A strong instance-type proposition to the effect that a rise in prices or a fall in prices in itself can extremely

---

87 Jareborg, 'Regler och riktlinjer' [rules and guidelines], p. 389 in note 4: "exceptions are possible without reformulation of the rule"; Malt, 'Svake normer' [weak norms], p. 177: "a form of delegation ... in that ... the person applying the norm himself makes a decision with respect to whether or not a given instance shall be regulated by the norm consequence".

88 I shall come back to the guideline structure of connotation specifications in section 6.2 (1) below.

seldom or never justify revision,[89] eases the pressure for argumentation on the person applying the law.[90]

A related cause is the need to *save time and effort in learning and mentally storing the rules*. – In relation to this need too, instance-type propositions most often make things easier, for students and for lawyers trying to keep up to date with new rules: Instance-type propositions provide concrete and more fixed points for thought to hold on to. In this respect they serve as *intermediaries* between on the one hand the unstructured masses of guidelines, which point out relevant arguments and, as the case may be, say something about their weight and in what directions they pull, and on the other hand the often rather vacuous weighing and balancing norm.

A further cause of the use of instance-type propositions as arguments is the need of the person applying the law to *reduce the uncertainty and doubt* that legal weighing and balancing norms often lead to,[91] and further, in relation to the parties to the case and outsiders, his need to *justify his decision by means of something more certain* than the considerations concerning expediency, reasonableness, justice, etc., which the guidelines point out as relevant.[92] – In relation to these needs too, instance-type propositions will most often be preferable to the underlying weighing and balancing norm with its accompanying guidelines: The criteria in instance-type propositions will most often to a lesser degree prescribe evaluations, or they may be evaluation-free, and so contribute to toning down the room for choice open to the person applying the law, and consequently contribute to diminishing his vulnerability to criticism. This takes place both in relation to the law applier's own view of the situation and in relation to the parties to the case and outsiders, albeit not necessarily in the same way and to the same degree in the different relations.

Hitherto I have presupposed that the lawyer *of his own motion* makes use of instance-type propositions. In addition come instance-type propositions with *duty modality*: Superiors in public administration instruct subordinates through instance-type propositions, and the Supreme Court's instance-type propositions are regarded as binding by and on other courts and lawyers.[93] – In these instances all the causes of regulation in the public administrative hierarchy or by the

---

89 See the last quotation in item (b)(i) above.

90 In the practice of the Supreme Court there is a certain development in the direction of weaker instance-type propositions in the case of rises and falls in prices; cf. *Rt. 1988/276*, that ascribes to a general rise in prices the effect of being a ground for revision (plenary session judgment concerning upward regulation of rent for leasehold property, in relation to a contract from 1899 that could not be terminated by the lessor; 11–6 decision). See further *Rt. 1988/295, 1992/1387, 1992/1397, 1995/674*. The discussions in these judgments are linked to the criterion 'unreasonableness' in section 36 of the Contracts Act, which in the practice of the courts seems to have gone a long way towards replacing the criterion 'unreasonableness' in the doctrine of subsequently failed contractual assumptions.

91 Compare Eng, *Uenighetsanalyse – med særlig sikte på jus og allmenn rettsteori* [analysis of dis/agreement – with particular reference to law and legal theory], section IV 4.6.

92 Compare op. cit., sections IV 4.2–4.3.

93 Compare op. cit., section IV 4.5.

Supreme Court may be causes of instance-type propositions: party-politically controversial goals or traditional goals of lawyers like avoiding "uncertainty, disputes, and the risk of inequality before the law".[94]

Irrespective of what the underlying causes may be, it is the case that experiencing a need for instance-type propositions provokes *production* of such propositions; and their production may *in itself provoke* the use of these propositions or *reinforce* the needs: Once one has grown accustomed to thinking by means of instance-type propositions, it may require an extra effort to carry out a real and many-sided weighing and balancing.

The causes now mentioned most often lead to instance-type propositions linked to a *limited type of fact*: for example linked to lack of money, or to a rise in prices or a fall in prices, in relation to the criterion 'unreasonableness' in cases concerning revision of contracts (see these and other examples of limited types of fact in item (b) above). – Sometimes, however, instance-type propositions may *totally usurp the weighing and balancing*. An example is an instance-type proposition that the child's best interest is to be with the mother, pronounced as a denotation determination of the criterion 'the best interest of the child' in cases concerning the distribution of child custody between parents:[95] Such an instance-type proposition does not refer to a delimited fact constellation, but replaces the weighing and balancing criterion.[96] In the practice of some administrative bodies one can trace a development according to this pattern:[97] The administrative body's determination of the concepts in the weighing and balancing norm changes completely through practice, *from* many-sided weighing and balancing, *to* one and only one instance-type proposition: for example, from granting a taxi licence according to concrete discretion,[98] to allocation according to seniority alone.[99]

---

94 *Rt. 1990/284* on pp. 293–94, cf. pp. 298–99: The Supreme Court in plenary session, referring to the considerations quoted, instructed courts and other lawyers on the denotation of the expression "reasonable price" in the case of a lessor's claim that the lessee purchase the property leased (more precisely it instructed that in relation to any increase in real value in areas where property was in ever increasing demand the said expression only covered half the increase).

95 Section 34, third paragraph, fourth sentence, cf. section 35, third paragraph, of the Children Act (Act No. 7 of 8 April 1981): "The decision shall first and foremost be guided by what is in the best interest of the child."

96 So broad an instance-type proposition cannot be advanced de lege lata in relation to the criterion in the Children Act (preceding note). However, more narrowly it says in *Innst. O. No. 30 1980–1981* [recommendation from the parliamentary committee], p. 14: "The Committee wishes to stress that in ... the interpretation and application [of the criterion 'in the best interest of the child'] significant weight must be placed on who has the stronger emotional contact with and has in fact had the care of the child. This will entail that the *mother will in most cases continue to be given a prior right to a small child, when she has in actual fact had the main care of the child*" (my italics). Such an instance-type proposition probably to a great extent corresponds to the conclusions of actual weighings and balancings from those applying the law, expert witnesses, and others carrying out weighings and balancings in child custody cases.

97 Eckhoff/ Smith, *Forvaltningsrett* [administrative law], pp. 306–10.

98 *Rt. 1954/1156* on p. 1159; *1955/1162* on pp. 1165–66.

99 *Rt. 1959/733* on p. 735.

(2) *Statutory definitions*

I have earlier given an account of statutory definitions more generally (section 3.3.6 above). Here the topic is the fact that, and the reasons why, the legislators choose denotation specification as a method of definition (item (a)), and the distinctiveness this choice gives to statutory definitions (item (b)).[100]

(a) An important situation-type for statutory definition in the form of denotation specification is where the legislators wish out of an *evaluation based on legislative policy* to collect phenomena that do *not have any externally perceivable features in common.* – It may be a group of *decisions* that are collected; as is the case when the legislator wishes that some, but not all decisions relating to public employment contracts shall be treated according to the rules concerning individual decisions in the Public Administration Act (10 December 1967): "Any decision concerning appointment, notice of dismissal, suspension, summary dismissal or transfer of a public official shall be deemed to be an individual decision. The same shall apply to any decision to impose a disciplinary penalty on a public official or to grant him a pension" (section 2, second paragraph).[101] – Or it may be a group of *persons* that are collected; as is the case in the definition of "nogens nærmeste" [a person's closest relatives] in section 5 of the Criminal Justice Act (Act No. 10 of 22 May 1902): "Where the present Act uses the expression "a person's closest relatives", this includes his spouse, relatives in direct line of ascent or descent, siblings and those equally closely related by marriage, foster-parents and foster-children and his fiancée. ... The spouse of any person related by marriage is also considered to be related by marriage."[102] – Or it may be a group of *actions* that are collected; as is the case when the legislator wishes that certain actions shall require permission, see for example the definition of "byggetillatelse" [building permission] in section 93 of the Planning and Building Act (Act No. 77 of 14 June 1985), as it read until 5 May 1995: permission for inter alia "constructing a building ... altering a facade ... demolishing a building ... use ... for another purpose than presupposed when permission was granted".[103] – Or it may be *other* phenomena that the legislators wish to collect.[104]

---

100 I should remind the reader that I use the term "statutory" in a broad sense: of constitutions, statutes and regulations; and further that I use the plural form "legislators": because in the case of all constitutions and statutes, and in the case of most regulations, a number of people are involved in the drafting of the text and its passing into law.

101 This denotation specification is intended to be complete in relation to decisions relating to public employment contracts, cf. *Ot.prp. No. 27 1968–69* [proposal from the Government], pp. 11–13, 17, 32. Outside fall decisions concerning e.g. additional pay, grants, leave of absence, and schooling or courses as part of the contract of employment; see op. cit., pp. 11–13.

102 In *Rt. 1994/1405* the denotation was extended in that a cohabitant was equated with a spouse in the use of the definition in relation to the rules concerning criminal liability for false statements.

103 Compare *Innstilling av 1960 fra komitéen til revisjon av bygningsloven* [report of 1960 from the committee appointed to revise the Building Act], p. 174: "Although some of the types of work that have been enumerated ... are not really construction work (e.g. ... demolishing ...), the committee has found it justifiable and expedient to use the term "building permission" as a practical common term

Whether the phenomena the legislators wish to collect do not have any externally perceivable features in common, or the legislators are uncertain about which features these are, or the legislators consider them not very informative, the choice of denotation specification will often be caused by, and be justifiable through, the fact that it is *simpler and more enlightening* to specify the individual phenomena or types of phenomenon that are intended to be collected, than simply to specify a connotation. – In addition, the use of denotation specification in statutory definitions is influenced by *more specifically legal considerations*:

First, specifically legal considerations make themselves felt in the form of considerations *internal to procedure*, i.e. considerations relating to implementation of the rule: partly the consideration that it shall be as simple as possible to decide whether the rule applies in the individual instance, and partly the consideration for avoiding evasion of the rule. – Both considerations suggest that the legislators choose the method of definition that gives *fewest evidence problems*. This will often suggest complete denotation specification rather than connotation specification, see the examples above. And it will nearly always suggest that a connotation specification, if any, be combined with a denotation specification.

Secondly, specifically legal considerations make themselves felt in the form of considerations *external to procedure*. A desire for a reasonable and just outcome in the individual instance will often go against complete denotation specification, since such specification provides less leeway for evaluations by the person applying the law than connotation specification does. A desire for legal safeguards, and more especially *predictability*, will on the other hand precisely for the reason mentioned go in favour of complete denotation specification, see again the examples above. – The considerations external to procedure will therefore often be best taken care of through the legislators' combining connotation specification and incomplete denotation specification: The latter can by virtue of being a collection of examples provide the citizens with a considerable amount of information, at the same time as, by virtue of being incomplete, it does not bind too strongly the person applying the law.[105] – If, on the other hand, the legislators place the greatest weight on limiting freedom of evaluation on the part of the person applying the law, because they give priority to predictability, because they are unsure of or disagree with evaluations made in the past by persons applying the law, or for

---

for those forms of permission this Chapter deals with." – By Act No. 20 of 5 May 1995, to amend the Planning and Building Act, the term "building permission" was removed from the Act, see *Ot.prp. No. 39 1993–94* [proposal from the Government], p. 110.

104 See e.g. the next two notes (respectively events and animals); and section 5.3 above, note 41 (actions and registers).

105 See e.g. section 4 of the Natural Damage Act (Act No. 7 of 25 March 1994): "By natural damage is meant damage directly arising from any natural disaster *such as* landslide, storm, flood, storm surge, earthquake, volcanic eruption or the like" (my italics). See also the definitions mentioned in item (b) below; and the definitions quoted or mentioned in section 5.3 above, in notes 37 and 38.

other reasons, then a complete denotation specification that is specified as much as possible is the best means.[106]

(b) The legislators' use of denotation specifications give statutory definitions taken together a couple of *distinctive features*: Statutory definitions are for one thing more *catalogue-like* and for another more *comprehensive* than definitions formulated in everyday language otherwise.

> Neither of these features is definitionally linked to denotation specification; connotation specification too can assume catalogue form and we can easily imagine its becoming more and more comprehensive. In actual fact, however, these features are far more common in the case of denotation specification.

See, for example, from the legislation of 1994 the denotation specification of *"serious aviation incident"* in the Regulations concerning the duty to notify and report to Havarikommisjonen for sivil luftfart [accidents commission for civil aviation] (5 April 1994 No. 304; Norwegian Law Gazette, Part 1, pp. 507 cf. 514–15); the denotation specification of *"cosmetics and/ or toiletries"* in the Regulations for production, importation and retail distribution etc. of cosmetics and toiletries (18 October 1994 No. 940; Norwegian Law Gazette, Part 1, pp. 1703 cf. 1706–07); or the denotation specification of *"waste"* in the Regulations concerning cross-border transport of waste (30 December 1994 No. 1231; Norwegian Law Gazette, Part 1, pp. 2290 et seq.). – *Common* to these three denotation specifications is that they have been provided for clarification of a connotation specification, and that they are explicitly said not to be exhaustive.

> In the last-mentioned example, "waste" has been defined statutorily in that the Regulations provide that EEC Council Regulation 259/93, with the amendments that follow from the EEA Agreement, shall be Norwegian law. This Council Regulation refers in Art. 2 (a) to the definition of waste in Council Directive 75/442. This Council Directive, as amended by Council Directive 91/156, defines 'waste' in Art. 1 (a) first sentence as "any substance or object in the *categories set out in annex I* which the holder discards or intends or is required to discard"; and annex I of the Directive specifies sixteen categories of waste. It says further in Art 1 (a) second sentence of the Directive: "The Commission ... will draw up ... a *list of wastes belonging to the categories* listed in annex I." On 20 December 1993 pursuant to

106 Be it *on its own*: see e.g. section 3 of the Regulations for the combating of Newcastle disease and fowl pest (30 June 1994 No. 705; Norwegian Law Gazette, Part 1, p. 1144): "In these regulations ... poultry means: chickens, turkeys, geese, ducks, grouse, quails, pheasants, guinea hens and pigeons"; see also the examples quoted in section 5.3 above, in note 41. Or be it in *combination* with connotation specification: see the example quoted in section 5.3 above, in note 39, which adds a connotation specification to the denotation specification just quoted. – *However*, even if the legislators have meant a denotation specification to be complete, the Supreme Court considers itself entitled to limit or extend it out of general considerations for reasonableness or justice, see e.g. what is said, at and in note 102 above, about the definition of "a person's closest relatives" in the Criminal Justice Act.

this provision the Commission determined the denotation of the concept of 'waste' in a comprehensive list, commonly referred to as the *"European Waste Catalogue"*. This consists of three hierarchically arranged levels, with respectively 20, 111 and 644 entries. As an example may be mentioned the following thread: The eighth entry on the top level is specified as "wastes from the manufacture, formulation, supply and use (mfsu) of coatings (paints, varnishes and vitreous enamels), adhesive, sealants and printing inks". The third of four entries under the said eighth entry is specified as "waste from mfsu of printing inks". And the ninth and penultimate entry under the said third entry is specified as "waste printing toner (including cartridges)". In addition, here as in many places otherwise on the bottom level, there is a final entry specified as "wastes not otherwise specified".

5.4.3. The psychological process prior to the definition product. Subsequent linguistic practice

(1) In the psychological process that lies *prior* to the definition product, *mental representations of the denotation* play a great part:

In the case of *normative definitions* the starting point is often a mental representation of the denotation: a mental representation of certain phenomena that one wishes through the definition to delimit and name.

In the case of *descriptive definitions* one often has a better picture of the denotation than of the connotation. And it will often be first and foremost the denotation one purports to capture through the definition: We know little about what general criteria guide the language users, unless the language user himself has provided an explicit connotation specification. – This I assume to be one cause of the pattern of analysis I term "reconstruction and redefinition": the pattern that one takes a denotation essentially as given, investigates and characterises the denotation phenomena, and suggests (some of) those properties these characterisations bring out, as a (new) connotation. This pattern of analysis has a certain diffusion, and will be discussed after I have been through the necessary elements for an explanation of it (Chapter V below).

The factual influence that mental representations of the denotation have, shows itself inter alia in the fact that the person defining, normatively or descriptively, will often revise the connotation specification when he becomes (is made) aware of particular facts. The situation is in that case that the definer did not know about or forgot to take into account these instances when specifying the connotation. – Correspondingly, a common *objection* that may be raised against definitions in the form of connotation specifications, both normative and descriptive, is that the connotation specification does not capture those, and only those, individual instances that the definer aims to delimit. The connotation specification is *not sufficiently thought through* in relation to the individual instances it is intended to cover.

That the connotation specification is not sufficiently thought through is one cause of the fact that *discrepancy* not infrequently arises between, on the one hand, normative definition in the form of stipulated connotation specification (and the corresponding intended denotation), and on the other, the definer's *subsequent* linguistic practice (the resulting denotation): In his characterisations the definer uses the word defined of individual instances that are not covered by the connotation specification, or does not use the word of individual instances that are covered by the connotation specification.[107]

(2) To the extent that one *"thinks aloud"* one's definitional deliberation, one to the same extent wipes out the *boundary* between definition product (sections 5.4.1–5.4.2 above) and deliberation prior to the definition product (the present section 5.4.3).

In *written* communication this boundary is nearly always and clearly present. In *spoken* language there is greater *variation*. And in addition, in spoken language one may imagine the *extreme case* in which definition product and deliberation coincide: As the need for definitional determination arises in the conversation/discussion, one points impulsively at an object present (ostensive definition), or mentions the first example that comes to mind (denotation specification other than ostensive definition), or puts forward without reflection those criteria one's thought first seizes on (connotation specification).

107 Another cause of discrepancy may be that one associates *feelings* with words, and that in the subsumption one lets one's feelings override the connotation specification; compare Robinson, *Definition*, pp. 115–16 ("proletarian art", "a native", "realistic art", "propaganda", "money"). Yet another cause may be that one attaches to words religious, philosophical or other *tenets* to which one has an ambivalent relationship; compare Passmore, *Philosophical Reasoning*, pp. 115–18 ("miracle", "sacred", "devil", "free will"). – In philosophy, discrepancy between connotation specification on the one hand and the denotation in linguistic practice on the other (together with other discrepancies between general propositions and individual instances) has led to individual-instance *reminders*' being cultivated as a method of its own: Passmore, *Philosophical Reasoning*, pp. 8–11; even cultivated as *the* (or as something approaching *the*) specifically philosophical method: Moore, 'Hume's Theory Examined', pp. 78 cf. 65, 71–72; 'A Defence of Common Sense', pp. 127–28; 'Proof of an External World', pp. 165–67; 'Certainty', pp. 188 cf. 171; Wittgenstein, *Philosophische Untersuchungen*, Part I, section 127 ("Die Arbeit des Philosophen ist ein Zusammentragen von Erinnerungen zu einem bestimmten Zweck"), cf. more concretely e.g. the first three quotations in section 3.2.2 (3)(a) above; Austin, *Sense and Sensibilia*, pp. 3, 83, 134, cf. more concretely e.g. pp. 8–9, 12–14, 16–19, 22–23, 33–43, 65–77; Wisdom, 'G. E. Moore', p. 51 ("the revival of a particular case is ... part of what in philosophy we aim at, a renewed view of the manifold of particular cases covered by our general terms"). – An example from legal theory of a corresponding approach is Llewellyn, *The Common Law Tradition* ("in all ... matters in this study ... I preach the neglected beauty of the obvious", p. 339, see also pp. 142, 156; see for illustration his mapping of fourteen "steadying factors" in the application of the law, pp. 19–51, and of sixty-four ways of using previous judgments as arguments, pp. 77–91).

5.5. Structuring via a more comprehensive language context

(1) Introduction

The means of structuring that have been mapped above have the *feature in common* that they can structure the area-in-thought "on its own".

If the definition also has a naming function, the said feature of the means of structuring shows itself in the fact that the name of the area can be placed alone on the left side in the definition: for example "the word "law" covers ...".[108] – If the definition does not have a naming function, for example "Kant's concept of 'law' covers ...", this frequently adduced categorisation criterion (see note 108) is not adequate.

I do not use the expression "on its own" in the sense that the area has been structured absolutely (see section 3.1 above, and otherwise throughout in text and examples, concerning the person and situation connections of definitions). Nor do I use this expression in the sense that the area has been structured solely through positive specification (see for example section 5.2 (3) above concerning negative denotation specification). I use the expression *in contrast to* the area's being structured *via a more comprehensive language context of which the name of the area is part* (item (2) below).

Unlike the means of structuring mapped above, the structuring means that are to be mentioned in item (2) are thus by definition linked to definitions that also have a naming function.

---

108 The term "explicit definition" (or its equivalent in other languages) is usually defined through the criterion 'the linguistic entity that is to be defined is placed alone on the left side in the definition'; see Dubislav, *Die Definition*, p. 39; Gullvåg, 'Carnap, Innledning' [Carnap, introduction], p. 53; Marc-Wogau, 'Definisjon' [definition], p. 36; Weinberger, *Rechtslogik*, p. 365. The term is in these cases contrasted with the terminology that is to be mentioned in notes 112 and 113 below. – Many of the definition types that are mapped in the present work are, however, not explicit definitions *even if* they satisfy the said criterion, because they do not satisfy further requirements that are usually made, namely that the formulation that is defining shall be able to replace the linguistic entity that is being defined ("substitutability"); cf. the fact that the definition concept in the present work also covers e.g. incomplete or negative specifications of connotation or denotation. – I have previously pointed to the fact that *synonymity requirements* in relation to a general definition concept often to a high degree or completely render the general concept incapable of capturing main groups of actually occurring propositions that contribute to determining the meanings of linguistic entities (contribute to determining concepts) (section 5.2 (6)(b)(ii) above, in note 26). In the present note, I have pointed to the fact that *substitutability requirements* in relation to a sub-concept defined by means of the starting criterion 'the linguistic entity that is to be defined is placed alone on the left side in the definition', render the sub-concept incapable of capturing main groups of actually occurring propositions that fall under the starting criterion. We can thus conclude that even if synonymity or substitutability should be fitting as concept criteria in relation to *ideal requirements* in philosophy and logic (section 2.2 above), synonymity or substitutability are not fitting as concept criteria when the aim of the conceptualisation is insight into how one *in fact proceeds* when, in analysis and argumentation formulated in everyday language, one determines the meanings of linguistic entities (determines concepts) (section 2.1 above, cf. the present section B in its entirety).

(2) *Two main types*

Structuring via a more comprehensive language context of which the name of the area is part may consist in letting the linguistic entity be undefined except for one's referring to a group of *sentences of which the linguistic entity is part and the role the entity plays in these sentences*. This method of definition is not usual in analysis and argumentation formulated in everyday language; but it is in logic[109], mathematics[110] and formal science.[111/112]

Of greater interest for the perspective and topic of the present work is structuring by the *rewriting* of a language context of which the name of the area is part, so that the name is removed, *at the same time as the meaning is claimed to be the same*. Bentham emphasised this method of definition and termed it "paraphrasis".[113] A good example of the application of the method is provided by linking-term analyses of words and expressions in formulations of legal rules and in lawyers' language and argumentation. In relation to linking-terms in lawyers' language and argumentation, however, the emphasis in the present work is not only on the *method of definition*: contribution to determining the meanings of the terms (contribution to determining the concepts) through rewriting sentences of which the terms are part, but also on aspects of the *use of the terms themselves*: linking-terms as means to flight from the normative proposition. I have chosen to present use of words and expressions as linking-terms in the latter connection and refer to the discussion there (section IV 3.3.3 below, particularly at and in note 72; see also section III 2.2.2 (3)(b)(ii) below, particularly the quotation in the text at note 33).

---

109 E.g. truth-functional definitions of logical words ("not", "and", "or", "if", "only if"): Strawson, *Introduction to Logical Theory*, pp. 66–69; Robinson, *Definition*, p. 117 ("matrix definition"); Næss, *Logikk og metodelære* [logic and methodology], pp. 37 et seq.

110 E.g. definition of the word "point" in geometry by referring to the basic propositions of geometry and the role the word plays in them: Hempel, 'Geometry and Empirical Science', pp. 1640–41.

111 E.g. definition of a theoretical term in empirical science, e.g. names of elementary particles in physics or the term "IQ" in psychology, by referring to the laws of the science concerned and the role the term plays in them: Carnap, 'The Interpretation of Physics', pp. 317–18; 'The Methodological Character of Theoretical Concepts', pp. 45, 48, 49–52, 66 et seq.

112 Terms that have been used of varying parts of the definition area now outlined are "axiomatic definition", "definition by postulates (axioms)", and "implicit definition"; see Dubislav, *Die Definition*, p. 42; Gullvåg, 'Carnap, Innledning' [Carnap, introduction], pp. 57–58; Marc-Wogau, 'Definisjon' [definition], p. 37; Weinberger, *Rechtslogik*, pp. 392–93.

113 Bentham, *Essay on Logic*, pp. 246–48, also in *The Theory of Fictions*, pp. 86–91; *The Theory of Fictions*, pp. 138–39; *A Fragment on Government*, p. 106 in note 1 item (5); *Of Laws in General*, pp. 294–95. – Other terms that have been used of this method of definition are "contextual definition" and "definition in use"; in addition "implicit definition" has been used here too (compare the preceding note); see Dubislav, *Die Definition*, pp. 39–40; Gullvåg, 'Carnap, Innledning' [Carnap, introduction], pp. 54–55; Marc-Wogau, 'Definisjon' [definition], pp. 36–37; Weinberger, *Rechtslogik*, pp. 366–67. – The most well-known example from philosophy of the use of this method of definition is Russell's analysis of definite descriptions, an analysis that commonly goes under the name of "contextual definition". For Russell's discussions, see in particular 'On Denoting', passim, and *Introduction to Mathematical Philosophy*, pp. 167–80.

(3) The relationship to connotation specifications and denotation specifications

Denotation specifications stand in a *more distant relationship* than connotation specifications to the two instance-types of structuring via a more comprehensive language context that have been outlined (item (2) above):

In most cases there will be clear definition-functional *differences* between *denotation specification* and structuring via a more comprehensive language context. The latter-mentioned way of structuring will often be employed in the case of linguistic entities the use of which precisely does not generate any denotation directly: typically in the case of words with a purely systematising role, for example logical words, or linking-terms in lawyers' language and argumentation.

> One might imagine extending the concept of 'denotation specification' also to cover specification of indirectly generated denotations. However, I have not been able to find concepts in that direction suited to bringing into focus interesting features of definition activity occurring in fact and formulated in everyday language.

On the other hand there are clear definition-functional *similarities* between *connotation specification* and structuring via a more comprehensive language context. In both cases *criteria* are specified: in the first case linked to denotata, in the second case linked to the more comprehensive language context. In relation to mapping the role of definitions in actually occurring language and argumentation, I consider the difference in what the criteria are linked to as often less significant than the community existing between these two structuring modes in and through their specification of criteria, and the thereby constituted *common contrast to denotation specifications*. – Thus it might be reasonable to extend the use of the term "connotation specification" also to cover specification of criteria linked to the more comprehensive language context. However, as in earlier discussions of borderline cases in relation to some key terms in my definition theory,[114] one should distinguish between the questions of fact and the question of language. What is interesting in a definition perspective are the factual similarities and differences just mentioned. Whether or not one then terms structurings via the more comprehensive language context "connotation specification" is less important.

---

[114] See e.g. sections 5.2 (6) on "definition" and 5.3 on "connotation specification" and "denotation specification".

6. Means of structuring II: Means of specifying the connotation

6.1. Purely cognitive criteria or evaluation prescription

A connotation specification may determine the connotation through cognitive criteria alone or through evaluation prescription. – I have grouped the discussion of this as follows:

(1) Cognitive criteria
(2) Evaluation prescription
- **(a) Both cognitive criteria and decision with respect to values**
- **(b) The relationship between cognitive criteria and decision with respect to values**
- **(c) The independence of the critically reflexive form**

(3) Evaluation prescriptions, cognitive criteria and the modality of propositions

Something different from these dimensions in the *connotation of the concept* is the *linguistic expressions* for the concept. In particular there is reason to note the following three points. First, evaluation prescriptions are often not expressed linguistically at all, and if they are, it is often in polysemous forms of language and argumentation.[1] Secondly, linguistic expressions that appeal to feelings do not necessarily express concepts that prescribe an evaluation.[2] Finally, the linguistic expression may inform us of evaluation prescription without appealing to feelings; see for example the sentence "the legal concept of 'contract' prescribes an evaluation".[3]

(1) Cognitive criteria

By "cognitive criteria" I mean criteria of which one will say that it is *true or untrue* that they are satisfied in the individual instance. To put this in terms of one standard linguistic form: I mean criteria that can replace the dots in the sentence schema "x is …" so that one gets a proposition that one will say is true or false,

---

1 See section 7.2 (1) and Chapter IV, below.
2 See sections 7.2 (1) and 7.3.3 (2)(c), below.
3 On the concept of 'contract', see sections IV 2.2 (6)(b) and 3.3.1 (3)(b), below. In general on concepts in legal rules, see the next note.

all according to what one replaces "x" by. Examples of criteria that are usually considered to be cognitive, and are normally used in practice as being so, are 'colour', 'form', 'weight', 'age', 'sex', 'address', 'income', 'education', 'occupation', 'knowledge'.

(2) Evaluation prescription

By "evaluation prescription" I mean criteria that prescribe an evaluation. Examples are 'un/just', 'un/reasonable', 'un/lawful',[4] 'good', 'bad', 'beautiful', 'ugly', and the like. – With a view to insight into the critically reflexive form that constitutes the perspective and topic of the present work (item (c) below), I lay down the concept of 'evaluation prescription' in such a way that *two elements* must by definition be present: partly cognitive criteria and partly decision with respect to values (item (a) below). However, the actual *combination* of the elements may vary (item (b) below).

(a) Both cognitive criteria and decision with respect to values

(i) An evaluation prescription is on the one hand by definition distinct *from feelings per se*. More precisely this is so in the following way:

Feelings are expressed through the body, for example through laughter, tears, movement. Given language, feelings can also be expressed verbally. This may take place through pure expressions of emotion, for example through the exclamations "ouch" or "hurrah". Or it may take place through expressions for decisions, for example through the sentence schema "I wish ...", "I intend ...", or the like. – The verbal expressions may be seen as a substitute for the bodily expressions: They do not designate them, but take their place.[5]

In the light of this substitution perspective, one can further adopt the following perspective: Just as the bodily expressions do not involve any thought activity but occur spontaneously, the same goes for the verbal expressions that replace them.

This is different in the case of evaluation prescriptions; these require by definition a decision with respect to values, a decision which by definition *presupposes* thought activity, i.e. use of *cognitive criteria*. The reason I lay down by definition this relationship between evaluation prescriptions and cognitive criteria is the fact that neither in law nor in everyday life would one accept for example spontaneous use of the words "un/reasonable" as being in conformity with the concepts of 'un/reasonable'; these concepts prescribe a minimum of thought activity as a basis for the use of these words. See for example what has been said in connection with the criterion 'unreasonableness' in section 2 of the Price Measures Act, about how thought alternates between the mapping of relevant arguments and the

---

4 I shall later show that evaluation prescription in the connotation is a systematic feature of concepts in legal rules; see sections F 3.2.2 (1)(a)(i)↔(ii) cf. 2.1 (2), below.

5 See section 4.1 (1)(c)(iii) above on this substitution perspective. There I quote Wittgenstein's use of this perspective in the case of terms relating to pain, and outline how I myself used this perspective in analysing the concept of 'declaration of intent'.

weighing and balancing of values, often on several levels (section 5.4.2 (1)(a)(ii) above).

(ii) An evaluation prescription is on the other hand factually distinct *from purely cognitive criteria*. More precisely this is so in the following way:

That evaluation prescriptions by definition require a *decision* with respect to *values* leads in *actually occurring* language and argumentation to an element of personal choice that one does not find in the case of purely cognitive criteria.[6] – What is crucial is not whether in the individual instance a decision with respect to values is in fact *made*, but that the connotation of the concept in question *prescribes* that such a decision shall be made. In this lies the difference from various dimensions of indeterminacy that are linked to cognitive criteria: incompleteness, vagueness or family resemblance. For example, in applying the word "game" the language user may in the case of doubt choose to bring in a decision with respect to values as the basis for his standpoint on the subsumption ("what considerations support or go against my calling this "game", and what standpoint is suggested by these considerations?"). However, it does not lie in the everyday-language concept of 'game' that such a decision with respect to values shall be made. The language user could in the case of doubt have drawn lots with respect to subsumption standpoint without anybody's being for that reason entitled to say that he applied the concept of 'game' wrongly (that he did not understand the concept).

(i)↔(ii) What has now been outlined provides a more general background to and an elaboration of the definition of "evaluation prescription" presented by way of introduction in the present item (2): prescription of a combination of cognitive criteria and decision with respect to values. – Later I shall treat in greater depth the particular feature of actually occurring language and argumentation that the cognitive criteria often operate as weighing and balancing factors, that is to say that the role of the decision consists in carrying out the weighing and balancing in the individual instance (section 6.2 (1)–(2) below).

(b) The relationship between cognitive criteria and decision with respect to values

Actually occurring forms of language and argumentation may be *ranked* according to the degree to which they permit or require respectively cognitive criteria and decision with respect to values. The greater the degree of cognitive criteria that is required, the less acceptance there will be for "I wish ...", "I intend ...", or the like, as sufficient justification in themselves. – By way of illustration I shall outline certain main relationships between language and argumentation in law, morals, aesthetics and in the choice of food and drink.

---

6 In actually occurring language and argumentation, but not definitionally in the conceptualisation here. – I should remind the reader that I do not operate with any definitional difference between descriptive propositions and normative propositions with respect to truth value; see section A 5 (2)(b) above, at and in note 10, compared with item (c) below.

In *propositions de lege lata* (propositions about what the law is), quite a large element of cognitive criteria is often advanced in the interpretation of and subsumption under evaluation prescriptions. For example, in the application of the prohibition against charging an unreasonable price in section 2 of the Price Measures Act (Act No. 66 of 11 June 1993), in relation to "unreasonable" one takes into account the relative strengths of the parties, for example their age, education, occupation and knowledge, all of these being criteria which, if they are inserted into the sentence schema "the party is/ has ...", will produce propositions that are considered to be true or untrue. And this applies correspondingly in the case of other legal evaluation prescriptions: In the interplay between legislators, courts and legal writers, one can often observe the crystallisation of quite fixed norms for what considerations one shall or may take into account, and for how one shall resolve instance-types.[7]

At the other end of the scale one finds language and argumentation in the case of evaluation prescriptions concerning *food and drink*. Such evaluation prescriptions are considered to be literally "matters of taste"; one accepts decision propositions ("I prefer ...") with little support from cognitive criteria. – In these instances too we say "I dis/agree!", but in such cases we do so without seriously purporting that the other speaker is wrong and that consequently there is something to discuss.[8]

In an intermediate position there is language and argumentation in the case of evaluation prescriptions concerning *morally relevant actions*, for example "care" in the sentence "take care of your children!". At the same time as very few people will accept a decision proposition alone ("I do not wish to be with my child any more today"), many will accept a certain element of decision in the interpretation of and subsumption under the said sentence.

In language and argumentation in the case of evaluation prescriptions in *aesthetic propositions*, cognitive criteria are put forward, but not to such a great degree as in the case of evaluation prescriptions in morals and law. On the other hand those criteria that are put forward cause the room for decision propositions to be less here than in the case of evaluation prescriptions concerning food and drink.[9]

---

7 Sundby, 'Kritisk juss: hva er det?' [critical law: what is that?], pp. 119–20: "[L]egal method [is] ... practical argumentation ... with one's hands tied" (compare same writer, *Om normer* [on norms], p. 259); MacCormick, *Legal Reasoning and Legal Theory*, p. 272: "[L]egal reasoning is a special, highly institutionalized and formalized, type of moral reasoning." We find basically the same, but developed in a perspective different from the perspective in the present work, in Alexy, *Theorie der Juristischen Argumentation*, pp. 261 et seq.; Aarnio/ Alexy/ Peczenik, 'The Foundation of Legal Reasoning', p. 260.

8 Foot, 'Morality and Art', p. 134: " 'Disagree' is ... 'a light word'. If you find ... some food delicious and I do not we can say 'how we disagree'."

9 Scruton, *Art and Imagination*, pp. 137–38, points to the ranking relationship between propositions relating to morals, aesthetics, and food and drink. See also Lovibond, *Realism and Imagination in Ethics*, pp. 66–68.

One can easily find borderline cases or exceptions to the main relationships outlined. For example, it may be considered legitimate to adduce a number of (purported) cognitive criteria when choosing between the more expensive wines ("fruitiness", "fullness", "bouquet", "style", "concentration", "balance", etc.). Or it may be considered to be playing to the gallery to adduce anything beyond one's personal decision when choosing between cheap reproductions. – Within *lawyers'* language and argumentation there seem to be *greater variations* in the relationship between cognitive criteria and decisions than is usual in the other proposition areas. It may be a matter of variations at a *given point in time*: between legal rules,[10] between levels of legal rules[11] or between legal areas;[12] or between legal systems or between lawyer cultures dominant in or cutting across systems.[13] Or it may be a matter of variations *over time*: be it in the individual legal rule, on the individual level of legal rule or in the individual legal area;[14] or be it in the legal system or in a lawyer culture dominant in or cutting across systems.[15]

The above is a ranking of common *forms of language and argumentation* (forms of expression).[16] Another question is whether a language and argumentation form provides an adequate representation of the grounds which in fact make themselves felt in the *deliberation* of a participant in the language and argumentation. – I shall later demonstrate that and how lawyers' propositions de lege lata, including their definitions of concepts in legal rules, do not have *such* a secure anchorage in cognitive criteria as widespread forms of language and argu-

---

10 Cf. "discretionary provisions", "discretionary law", "flexible rules", "legal standards", "Generalklauseln" [general clauses, blanket clauses] versus norms formulated through the use of figures; see Sundby, *Om normer* [on norms], pp. 201–22, 231–54.

11 Cf. a basic evaluation prescription in the doctrine of the sources of law versus evaluation prescriptions specific to the individual legal rules; see section 5.4.2 (1)(b)(v) above.

12 Cf. interpretation in areas in which statutory authority is required versus interpretation in areas in which this is not a requirement (in/ outside "the area of the principle of legality"); see Thornstedt, 'Legalitet och teleologisk metod i straffrätten' [legality and teleological method in criminal law]; Eckhoff, *Rettskildelære* [doctrine of the sources of law], pp. 107–11; Røstad, 'Lovprinsippet i strafferetten' [the principle of statutory authority in criminal law].

13 Cf. the brief and syllogistic ways of giving grounds in French judgments versus the literary style of English and American judgments; see Goutal, 'Characteristics of Judicial Style in France, Britain and the U.S.A.', pp. 45–51, 59–65; Wells, 'French and American Judicial Opinions', pp. 85–99; MacCormick/ Summers (eds.), *Interpreting Precedents: A Comparative Study*, pp. 106–08, 318–20, 360–61, 448–50.

14 On the origins and effects of the principle of legality in criminal law (compare note 12 above), see Honkasalo, 'Nulla Poena Sine Lege', in particular pp. 1–36, 57 et seq.

15 Strömholm, *Rätt, rättskällor och rättstillämpning* [law, sources of law and application of the law], p. 426: "If one looks at the discussion about different methods of applying the law in a historical perspective, one finds that the pendulum has swung between two poles. ... At one end of the scale one finds the Age of Enlightenment's and the early 19th century codifications' dream of a body of legislation that was so clear and complete that the application of the law would be purely mechanical. ... At the other extreme of the scale one finds the free law school flourishing at the beginning of the 20th century, which wished to leave it to the courts to decide the individual instances virtually unfettered."

16 More detail on the terminology, section IV 1 below, in the first indent.

mentation may indicate, that is to say that decisions play a correspondingly greater role (section F 4 and Chapter IV, below).

> Yet another question is whether the outlined differences in forms of language and argumentation (forms of expression) correspond to differences in ontology, cognition, reason, or the like: for example whether lawyers' language and argumentation de lege lata "really" is "more rational" than language and argumentation in aesthetics or relating to food and drink. This question lies outside the perspective and topic of the present work (Chapter I and section A 8, above).

The above is, however, sufficient to show that if the *aim* is nuanced insight, be it into actually occurring language and argumentation or into any deliberation different from the language and argumentation, then a dichotomy between purely cognitive criteria and evaluation prescriptions will only be the first *step in a descriptive definition*. The next step will be to ask for the *more precise constellation* of cognitive criteria and decisions in the particular concept with evaluation prescription in its connotation.

(c) The independence of the critically reflexive form

My conceptualisation above aims inter alia to capture the following two experiences: The first is that the phenomenon of connotation in the form of evaluation prescription is widespread. The second is that one may *agree about* the cognitive criteria in the evaluation prescription (what arguments are relevant and, as the case may be, what weight they typically have or in what directions they typically pull; section 6.2 (1) below), *at the same time as* one *disagrees about* the denotation (the decision about how the weighing and balancing shall be carried out in the individual instance; section 6.2 (1) below).

> A generally asserted proposition is that two words cannot have the same connotation and different denotations. This proposition does not necessarily conflict with my conceptualisation and description here: "agreement about connotation, disagreement about denotation". For the generally asserted proposition is only tenable provided one implicitly adds "... unless the connotation by virtue of its own content delegates to the language user competence with respect to laying down the denotation". And in actually occurring language and argumentation, evaluation prescriptions are often perceived precisely as such delegation; cf. item (b) above).

My conceptualisation and description above involves *no* standpoint on how values exist and their cognisability. This conceptualisation and description is compatible with both assumption and rejection of values' "objective existence and cognisability" or the like. The conceptualisation and description does not relate to this question, but is a step in the presentation of the superordinate perspective and topic of the present work (Chapter I above): a relatively well-delimited critically reflexive form (I 4), in the discussion and decision aspect (I 4) of analysis and argumentation formulated in everyday language (I 5), and with a certain independence (I 6), inter alia from controversial fundamental philosophical questions (I 6, II A 8): here, from questions about the ontological status and cognisability of values.

(3) Evaluation prescriptions, cognitive criteria and the modality of propositions

(a) A proposition that contains an *evaluation prescription* is by definition a *normative proposition*. But not all normative propositions contain an evaluation prescription:[17]

Value propositions contain by definition an evaluation prescription. *The other two main groups* of normative propositions (duty, competence or qualification propositions; and decision propositions) in fact often contain evaluation prescriptions, but do not stand, in the way that the concepts have been laid down here, in a definitional relationship with evaluation prescriptions. For example, the sentence "one must not cross when the light is red" may be used to express a duty proposition *without* concepts with evaluation prescription; or the sentence "I do not intend to cross when the light is red" may be used to express a decision proposition *without* concepts with evaluation prescription.

(b) A descriptive proposition consists by definition only of *cognitive criteria*. Cognitive criteria are *not specific to descriptive propositions*, however. Normative propositions too consist to a greater or lesser degree of cognitive criteria. This applies in the case of normative propositions with evaluation prescription; cf. item (2) above. And it applies in the case of normative propositions without evaluation prescriptions; cf. the examples in item (a) above.

(a)↔(b) In the present section B, I distinguish between evaluation prescriptions, cognitive criteria and propositions, out of the desire for insight into definition activity occurring in fact and formulated in everyday language. – Later I shall point to a distinctive fusion of descriptive and normative modality in lawyers' propositions about what the law is (section F below), a phenomenon that does not lend itself to being conceptualised without a distinction being drawn between evaluation prescriptions, cognitive criteria and propositions (section F 3.2.2 in its entirety; see for a brief illustration item (3)(a) of that section).

---

17 In this connection I should remind the reader that I use the term "normative proposition" of three main groups of propositions: first, of duty, competence or qualification propositions; secondly, of value propositions; and finally, of decision propositions (section A 5 (2)(a) above).

6.2. Factors or conditions

I have previously defined the pair of concepts 'condition concept' and 'factor concept' according to the criterion of whether or not it is natural to term the unity between the phenomena "features in common" (section 3.2.2 (5)(d) above). In so doing, I drew a distinction between two practically important subgroups of factor concepts: (a large proportion of) concepts with evaluation prescription in their connotation, and family resemblance concepts. – Here I shall use the said concept types in a discussion of the role of factors and conditions in connotation specifications, as follows:

(1) Evaluation prescriptions; weighing and balancing factors
(2) Family resemblance concepts; factors that are not used in weighing and balancing. Comparison of the roles of factors in the case of family resemblance concepts and evaluation prescriptions
(3) Will condition concepts on closer reflection dissolve into factor concepts?
  (a) Open texture
  (b) Family resemblance
  (c) Evaluations and choices in lawyers' language and argumentation de lege lata

(1) Evaluation prescriptions; weighing and balancing factors

With respect to *definition of concepts with evaluation prescription*, I have previously pointed out that and why lawyers often perceive connotation specification as an inadequate means of structuring in the case of these concepts. The emphasis in the previous discussion was on a usual alternative and supplement: denotation specification in the form of instance-type propositions (section 5.4.2 (1) above). – Here, however, it is the connotation specification that is the topic.

An evaluation prescription prescribes by definition partly cognitive criteria and partly decision with respect to values (section 6.1 (2) above). – When the connotation specification has pointed to the decision element, there is no more to be said about this in itself. Any closer definition will have to consist in an exposition of the *cognitive criteria.*

Concepts with evaluation prescription in their connotation will often be *factor concepts,*[18] in that the cognitive criteria cannot be structured as necessary conditions or as exhaustive and surveyable sufficient conditions (section 3.2.2 (5)(d) cf. (c), above). – True enough one often operates in the actual use of language with *sufficient conditions*; cf. the fact that in the case of evaluation prescriptions one often supplements the connotation specification with *instance-type propositions* (section 5.4.2 (1) above). For example, in the case of the concept of 'subsequently failed contractual assumption' one may imagine supplementing the connotation

[18] Often, but not definitionally in the conceptualisation here.

specification with the proposition that this concept, in relation to questions of revision of commercial contracts, never covers a general rise in prices; that is to say that the criteria 'commercial contract' and 'general rise in prices' are reckoned to constitute a sufficient condition for a set of facts to fall outside the concept of 'subsequently failed contractual assumption'. However, an exhaustive and surveyable specification of such alternative and sufficient (sets of) criteria is seldom considered to be possible.

In correspondence with the term "factor concept", I term the concept criteria *"factors"*. – In actually occurring language and argumentation there are certain interesting differences between those factors that are weighing-and-balancing factors and those that are not (item (2) below). Therefore this distinction should be included in the definition theory. Consequently, the fact that the concept criteria in the case of evaluation prescriptions are often factors (see above) does not entail that they are at the same time by definition weighing-and-balancing factors. The latter is an empirical question (see the rest of the present item (1) as well as item (2) below):

In lawyers' language and argumentation there is seldom any basis for *such* strong instance-type propositions as just used as an example in relation to the concept of 'subsequently failed contractual assumption', cf. the occurrence of the word *"never"* in the example (the penultimate sentence in the last preceding paragraph but one). Nor is there probably any basis for such strong instance-type propositions in relation to the concept of 'subsequently failed contractual assumption'. What one can say is that the concept of 'subsequently failed contractual assumption' in relation to questions of revision of commercial contracts *"seldom"* covers a general rise in prices (compare section 5.4.2 (1)(d) above, at and in notes 89 and 90). – To put this in *general* terms: Instance-type propositions in law are *constantly exposed to being tried against underlying weighings and balancings* (item (2)(b)↔(c) below).

As weighings and balancings thus play an important role, the connotation specification will often consist in a determination of what arguments one may, shall or shall not place weight on in the weighing and balancing, and also, as the case may be, in a determination of what weight the arguments typically have and in what directions they pull. The cognitive concept criteria are in such instances *weighing-and-balancing factors*. The prescribed *decision's role* then consists in carrying out the weighing and balancing with a view to the individual instance. See for illustration the outlined example concerning the prohibition against "unreasonable prices" in section 2 of the Price Measures Act (section 5.4.2 (1)(a)(ii) above).

Sundby's dissertation *Om normer* [on norms] contains important contributions to the illumination of the role and distinctive character of weighings and balancings, in particular in lawyers' language and argumentation.[19] Under

19 Sundby, *Om normer* [on norms], Part 2.

the designation *"retningslinje"* [guideline] Sundby collects those norms that govern the weighing and balancing processes.[20] Sundby was able to build further on insights inter alia in Dworkin, who under the designation "principle" discusses many of the same norms and touches on some central features.[21] – A number of writers have subsequently discussed what would be the best way of laying down a concept of 'guideline'.[22] Eckhoff has most recently laid down the concept as follows: "[T]he feature common to guidelines that we use as a conceptual feature is ... that they specify (or presuppose) what are to be reckoned as relevant (or irrelevant) factors in a weighing and balancing. ... Some guidelines also say something about the direction in which a factor pulls, what weight it has, and whether it is necessary to take it into account or whether one has a free hand in this respect."[23]

In the terminology of a guideline perspective one may thus say that the *connotation specification* in the case of evaluation prescriptions often has a *guideline structure*. To put this more precisely: To the extent that the connotation specification is normative, it takes the form of guidelines, and to the extent that it is descriptive, it takes the form of description of those guidelines that language usage follows.

(2) Family resemblance concepts; factors that are not used in weighing and balancing. Comparison of the roles of factors in the case of family resemblance concepts and evaluation prescriptions

Another main area of connotation specification through factors is *family resemblance concepts*. I refer in this connection to my earlier pointing out, by way of example, of concepts with a family resemblance structure, as well as my establishment of a concept of 'family resemblance'[24] (section 3.2.2 (3)(a)–(b) above).

Evaluation prescriptions and family resemblance concepts have a central feature *in common*: In the case of evaluation prescriptions there is a widespread assumption that it is impossible to specify the connotation in the form of necessary conditions or in the form of exhaustive and surveyable sufficient conditions (item (1)) above). In the case of family resemblance concepts the same impossibility applies by definition (section 3.3.2 (3)(b) above). – True enough one operates in

---

20 Loc. cit.

21 Dworkin, 'The Model of Rules I', pp. 22, 24–28; 'The Model of Rules II', pp. 71–74.

22 Eckhoff/ Sundby, *Rettssystemer* [legal systems], Chapter 7; *Rechtssysteme*, Chapter 6; Eng, 'Sondringen mellom regler og retningslinjer' [the distinction between rules and guidelines]; both with further references. See further Alexy, *Theorie der Grundrechte*, pp. 71–99; 'On the Structure of Legal Principles'; Hart, *The Concept of Law*, 2nd ed. (Postscript), pp. 259–63.

23 Eckhoff/ Sundby, *Rettssystemer* [legal systems], p. 109 (I have reversed the order of the two sentences in the quotation). – Eckhoff's determination of the concept essentially corresponds with what I had concluded in Eng, 'Sondringen mellom regler og retningslinjer' [the distinction between rules and guidelines], p. 482.

24 With its accompanying concepts of 'family resemblance concept' and 'family resemblance word'.

the case of family resemblance concepts, as in the case of evaluation prescriptions, with sufficient conditions in the form of instance-type propositions. For example, in relation to the concept of 'game' one operates with instance-type propositions concerning board games, card games, etc.; or more concretely, concerning chess, bridge, etc., that is to say that the criteria for 'chess', 'bridge', etc., are reckoned as sufficient conditions for a set of facts to fall within the concept of 'game'. However, in the case of family resemblance concepts it is by definition, as in the case of evaluation prescriptions it is according to widespread assumption, not possible to specify such alternative and sufficient (sets of) criteria in an exhaustive and surveyable way. Family resemblance concepts are by definition, as evaluation prescriptions are according to widespread assumption, factor concepts.

There are however certain *differences* in the roles of the factors in the case of family resemblance concepts and evaluation prescriptions.

(a) One difference is that the criteria of family resemblance concepts *are not weighing-and-balancing factors*:

In the case of evaluation prescriptions, one takes a standpoint on sets of facts that do not fall under established instance-types, by *going back to the connotation*, i.e. to factors relevant to the weighing and balancing, and by *carrying out a weighing and balancing* with a particular view to the instance at hand. One gets a *reciprocal action* between weighings and balancings of conceptual factors, and instance-types.

In the case of family resemblance, one does *not* solve the parallel question by going back to the connotation and carrying out a weighing and balancing. – In the first place it does not lie in the connotation of family resemblance concepts that a weighing and balancing shall take place at all. For example, in the case of the concept of 'game' the language user can in cases of doubt draw lots with respect to subsumption standpoint without our for that reason being entitled to say that he applied the concept of 'game' wrongly (that he did not understand the concept). – In the second place, provided that the language user does in fact carry out a weighing and balancing, it will not be a weighing and balancing of the connotation factors; for example in the case of 'game', it will not be a weighing and balancing of the factors 'enjoyment effect', 'victory or loss', 'competition element', 'skill or luck', etc. True enough the connotation factors will play a part, in that a likeness consideration is most often considered relevant. However, the decisive weighing and balancing factors will be *taken from outside the connotation*. One factor may be the cognition interest: for example whether the determination of the area of the word "game" that is being considered, provides new insight. Another factor may be the interest in exerting influence. I shall later give a more general account of considerations that play a part in the setting up of and choice between normative definitions (section III 2). For the purpose here, it is sufficient to point out that a carefully considered application of family resemblance structures in the case of doubt about subsumption is not first and foremost governed by going back from instance-types to the factors of the connotation, but by considerations taken from outside the connotation.

The concept criteria in the case of family resemblance concepts are thus factors, in that they are neither necessary nor exhaustive and surveyable sufficient criteria. However, they are not weighing-and-balancing factors: They are not used as such in the one situation in which it could have been relevant, namely in the case of those weighings and balancings one carries out when one reflects on the boundaries of the family.

(b) In the case of family resemblance concepts it may in certain instances seem as if the connotation factors are *not psychologically effective*; they are not so much motives in the use of language as patterns one reconstructs *after* the language usage has established itself in the one or other direction: One calls an activity "game" not on the basis of a mapping of, and deliberation by means of, the connotation factors, but on the basis of a more or less *arbitrary* decision. Politics, the relationship between teacher and pupil, the relationship between the passengers on a bus, the relationship between light and shade – all these things and many more one can imagine calling "games", without one's reflecting on criteria and without being liable to criticism for unreasonable use of language.

(c) Even if the criteria in the case of family resemblance concepts should be psychologically effective, so that decisions about the scope of the concept are in this respect not arbitrary, it may often seem as if the criteria are *not effective in the capacity of factors*. In a given language situation one has perhaps only one criterion or a limited selection of criteria in mind, and one considers the instance at hand on the basis of its likeness in this relation. *For the language user* in the individual situation the concept may therefore be more or less intuitively perceived as a *condition concept*. Only *for the observer*, who takes examples of language usage from many areas and reflects on them, does the *family resemblance pattern* become a psychological reality, in that he sees the pattern and thereby the concept criteria's status of being factors. Such a difference in the perception of the concept is possible because family resemblance patterns most often have a customary basis, in that they are formed over time through linguistic interaction between many people (sections 3.3.5 cf. 3.2.2 (3)–(5), above); and in the case of customary phenomena it is quite possible that the actor perspective and the observer perspective may generate different content.

(b)↔(c) In both the last-mentioned dimensions there is a difference from legal evaluation prescriptions: In the case of legal evaluation prescriptions, the connotation factors function, first, to a greater degree as psychological *motives* (compare item (b)), and secondly, to a greater degree as *factors* (compare item (c)), more precisely as weighing and balancing factors. Both differences result from the fact that in the case of legal evaluation prescriptions one *actually carries out* a weighing and balancing.

In many legal contexts it is true that there are strong tendencies to apply a limited selection of weighing and balancing factors, or, as the case may be, to replace the weighing and balancing with instance-type propositions (section 5.4.2 (1) above). A counter force lies, however, in the fact that lawyers' language and argumentation is used for conflict resolution through *adversary procedure*: Partly the language user's (the lawyer's) desire for a realistic view of the possibility of winning (in court, in public administrative proceedings, or in private conflict resolution where the opposing party too has legal assistance) leads to his seeking a *comprehensive* selection of relevant factors, also those that go against the interest of his own client. And partly the language users' (the lawyers') definitional propositions seen together bring out *most of* the relevant factors.

I assume that *the same* applies to many evaluation prescriptions in moral, political and other normative contexts: Differences of interest and the resulting conflicts *activate the connotation factors in other ways and to a greater degree* in the case of evaluation prescriptions than in the case of family resemblance concepts.

(3) Will condition concepts on closer reflection dissolve into factor concepts?

In what follows I shall look at certain arguments one might imagine advancing against the basis in reality of the distinction between condition concepts and factor concepts.

(a) Open texture

(i) In an earlier example of condition concept, 'chair' was defined through the criteria 'a piece of furniture', 'for sitting on', 'for one person' and 'with a back' (section 3.2.2 (2)(b) above). I said in that connection that it was reasonable to see the specified features as necessary and sufficient. – In what follows I shall look at certain arguments one might imagine advancing *against* the features' being *sufficient*, and, as an extension of this, against the distinction between condition concept and factor concept.

To call something "chair" one will lay down size requirements; the thing must at least be large enough for a small child, and not so large that an adult disappears. Further, one will lay down requirements that the material must satisfy; the thing must stand up to a normal load. And so forth. – And it is only the imagination that sets limits if one seeks to identify properties that must *not* be present for one to be willing to call something a "chair"; the thing must not for example suddenly begin to speak.

Against this background one might ask whether it is not the case that many connotations which seem to have an exhaustive and surveyable condition structure will on closer reflection dissolve into a factor structure. For in the case of many empirical concepts one *can* of course imagine a *host* of properties which, if they were present, would create doubt with respect to what kind of phenomenon one was confronted with ("what if the chair begins to speak?"). And whether these properties are present in the individual instance one will often not know or not have the time or methods to ascertain. Therefore, to the extent that one thinks over the possibilities, is it not so that one will have to "undertake a weighing and balancing"/ "make an evaluation" before one decides whether or not to apply the concept? – However, in relation to *actually occurring language* neither the element of "weighing and balancing"/ "evaluation" (item (ii) below) nor the potential number of criteria (item (iii) below) entails that the distinction between condition concept and factor concept disappears.

(ii) The terms *"weighing and balancing"* and *"evaluation"* are both ambiguous between the descriptive modality and the normative modality. In relation to the problem here (see item (i) above, concluding remarks) the terms refer to the *descriptive* plane: What one weighs and balances is in the event evidential factors concerning the *probability* that the phenomenon one is to categorise has the one or the other property ("how probable is it that the chair will begin to speak?"). The existence of such deliberation in the language user's interpretation and subsumption does not entail that the connotation loses any exhaustive and surveyable condition structure it might have.

(iii) Nor does the fact that the *number of concept criteria becomes high* mean that the concept changes character from condition concept to factor concept – as long as the concept criteria can be specified exhaustively and surveyably.

It is another matter if the *number of criteria becomes unsurveyably large, in the extreme instance infinite.* – An infinity of criteria seems to be the result if, like Waismann, one presupposes that *all* dimensions that are not self-contradictory are potential parts of the connotations of empirical concepts (something he terms "open texture"/ "Porosität" of empirical concepts).[25] For example, the dimension 'speaks–does not speak' then becomes a potential part of the connotation of the concept 'chair'.

I suppose that this is taking arguments from what one "may imagine" too far. In actually occurring use of language we are not willing to look at all eventualities that are not self-contradictory, as potential parts of the connotation of the concept. We operate with a *boundary*, albeit intuitive and more or less indeterminate, between on the one hand dimensions of the situation which we *presuppose* to be constituted in a particular way, and on the other hand dimensions which we *thematise* as potential parts of the connotation of the concept, and which we through our definitions (stipulated or custom-based) to a greater or lesser degree actualise as parts of the connotation.[26]

---

25 Waismann, 'Verifiability', in particular pp. 119–23.

26 Wittgenstein, *Philosophische Untersuchungen*, Part I, sections 142 cf. 80; *Zettel*, section 350; Austin, 'Other Minds', pp. 56–57; *Sense and Sensibilia*, pp. 122–23; Searle, 'Metaphor', pp. 79–80; 'Literal Meaning', in particular pp. 120–29; Andersson/ Furberg, *Språk och påverkan* [language and influence], pp. 119–20. – Waismann, 'Verifiability', pp. 120 (bottom)–121 (top), says that open texture is not a feature of all empirical concepts. I cannot, however, see that he gives any examples of empirical concepts without open texture, nor can I find any example myself.

How the boundary between these two groups of dimensions is more precisely drawn of course depends on what empirical concept it is that is being problematised. – For example, in the case of defining 'chair' it would hardly occur to many people to thematise the dimension 'speaks–does not speak'. We would simply *presuppose* this dimension, in that without being conscious of it we would build on physical objects' not speaking. This presupposition would in the event of closer reflection be found partly to relate to reality (apart from use of language); chairs lack organs that make sounds possible, and they lack language. And partly the presupposition would be found to relate to concepts; should something resembling language emanate from an exemplar of what we today call "chair", it is uncertain[27] whether we would extend our present concepts of 'to speak' or 'furniture' to such a fact.

To put this more *generally*: In actual use of language, concepts are problematised and defined only within a presupposed frame of beliefs and other concepts. – Arguments from what one "may imagine" that ignore the presupposed frames have little weight when the aim is insight into actual use of language.[28]

The boundary between dimensions that are presupposed and dimensions that are seen as potential parts of the connotation is, as mentioned, intuitive and more or less indeterminate in actually occurring use of language. However, this does not mean that the boundary is not there. And this boundary *makes it possible* for one to imagine and practise exhaustive and surveyable connotation specification, i.e. a sufficient criterion for condition concept; see for example the definition of 'chair' as 'a piece of furniture, for sitting on, for one person and with a back'.

(b) Family resemblance

The question of the area of application of family resemblance analysis is by definition at the same time a question of the diffusion of condition concepts, since a family resemblance concept is by definition a factor concept, never a condition concept (section 3.2.2 (5)(d) above). – Concerning the area of application of family resemblance analysis I refer to section 3.2.2 (4)(c) above.

(c) Evaluations and choices in lawyers' language and argumentation de lege lata

Evaluations are in fact a systematic element in lawyers' standpoints de lege lata (section F 2.1 (2) below). On the level of language and argumentation the evaluations manifest themselves to a great degree through evaluation prescriptions in

---

[27] See the references in the preceding note to Wittgenstein, Austin ('Other Minds'), Searle, and Andersson/ Furberg; see further Fodor, 'On Knowing What We Would Say', pp. 132–33; Margalit, 'Open Texture', pp. 146–48, 150.

[28] Another matter is what weight arguments from what one "may imagine" which ignore the presupposed frames have on the level of fundamental philosophical positions; for problematisations of this, see e.g. Braithwaite, 'Verbal Ambiguity and Philosophical Analysis', pp. 152–53; Østerberg, *Forståelsesformer* [forms of understanding], pp. 23 et seq., 32–34; Eames, 'A. J. Ayer's Philosophical Method', pp. 169–72. In conformity with the superordinate perspective and topic of the work (Chapter I and section II A 8, above) I do not take any standpoint on this question in the present work.

the connotations of concepts (section F 3.2.2 (1)(a) below). Concepts with evaluation prescription in their connotation will often be factor concepts; and the factors will often be weighing-and-balancing factors (item (1) above, with further references).

That evaluations play a large part and manifest themselves through evaluation prescriptions in the connotations of concepts is no obstacle to a situation in which some concepts in legal rules, or some criteria in a concept in legal rules, are neither implemented as weighing and balancing factors nor as themselves incorporating evaluation prescription that dissolves the criterion concerned into weighing and balancing factors. – As tentative examples of condition concepts I have previously mentioned the concept of 'divorce' and the concept of 'valid contract' (section 3.2.2 (5)(c) above, in items (ii) and (iii) respectively). Presuppositions for the examples to be tenable are that lawyers in the case of the concept of 'divorce' and the criterion 'dissolution of marriage by administrative decision or court judgment' neither implement this criterion as a weighing and balancing factor nor as itself incorporating evaluation prescription that dissolves this criterion into weighing and balancing factors; and that in the case of the concept of 'valid contract' and the criterion 'two parties' they neither implement this criterion as a weighing and balancing factor nor as itself incorporating evaluation prescription that dissolves this criterion into weighing and balancing factors. In the opposite case the concepts of 'divorce' and 'valid contract' will be factor concepts. (In this use of the examples I presuppose that none of the other concept criteria is implemented as a weighing and balancing factor or as itself incorporating evaluation prescription that dissolves the criterion concerned into weighing and balancing factors.)

> I shall give a couple of concrete illustrations of what lies in the notion that a criterion is implemented as itself incorporating evaluation prescription that dissolves the criterion into weighing and balancing factors.
>
> As a necessary criterion in the concept of 'valid contract' I previously mentioned 'mutually corresponding dispositive propositions addressed to the other party' (section 3.2.2 (5)(c)(iii) above). On more detailed analysis this criterion appears to incorporate evaluation prescription that partly, perhaps completely, dissolves the criterion into weighing and balancing factors (section IV 2.2 (6)(b) below).
>
> What Rawls terms "the concept of justice", in contrast to "various conceptions of justice", is formulated as a condition concept.[29] However, the criteria appear to be of a kind that is often implemented as including evaluation prescription that dissolves the criteria into weighing and balancing factors.[30]

---

[29] Rawls, *A Theory of Justice*, 1st ed. p. 5, 2nd ed. loc. cit.: "[I]t seems natural to think of the concept of justice as distinct from the various conceptions of justice and as being specified by the role which ... these different conceptions ... have in common."

[30] Loc. cit.: "Those who hold different conceptions of justice can ... still agree that institutions are just when no arbitrary distinctions are made between persons in [for the present purpose it is sufficient to quote schematically] ... and when the rules determine a proper balance between [as in the preced-

The emphasis here is not on the extent to which the said concrete presuppositions concerning the concept examples 'divorce' and 'valid contract' are adequate (in relation to how many lawyers, in how many situations). The emphasis is on, and the examples are intended to illustrate, the following two more general points: – First, the question of whether criteria are neither implemented as weighing and balancing factors nor as themselves incorporating evaluation prescription that dissolves the criterion concerned into weighing and balancing factors, is an empirical question. I do not know of any basis for claiming that all criteria in all concepts in legal rules "must" be implemented as weighing and balancing factors or as themselves incorporating evaluation prescription that dissolves the criterion concerned into weighing and balancing factors: with the consequence that no concepts in legal rules could be condition concepts. – Secondly, a reasonable working hypothesis is that some criteria are neither implemented as weighing and balancing factors nor as themselves incorporating evaluation prescription that dissolves the criterion concerned into weighing and balancing factors: so that some concepts in legal rules can thus be condition concepts.

(a)↔(c) To sum up, it is the case that none of the now mentioned points of departure (open texture, family resemblance, evaluations and choices in lawyers' language and argumentation de lege lata) provides tenable arguments against the basis in reality (be it in general or in relation to particular areas of language and argumentation) of the distinction between condition concepts and factor concepts. Nor do I know of any other points of departure that can be developed into tenable arguments against the basis in reality of this distinction: I assume that the distinction is logically possible. And I consider it a reasonable working hypothesis that in actually occurring language and argumentation, including lawyers' language and argumentation, one can find both condition concepts and factor concepts.

---

ing parenthesis] ... Men can agree to this description of just institutions since the notions of an arbitrary distinction and of a proper balance, which are included in the concept of justice, are left open for each to interpret according to the principles of justice that he accepts." – The same appears to apply also in the case of other occurrences of the pair of terms "concept"–"conceptions"; see e.g. Dworkin, 'Constitutional Cases', pp. 134–36; 'A Reply to Critics', pp. 351–53; *Law's Empire*, pp. 71, 74, 92–94; Aarnio/ Alexy/ Peczenik, 'The Foundation of Legal Reasoning', p. 267.

7. Normative definitions as means to influencing action; "persuasive definitions"

7.1. Introduction

(1) Normative definitions can influence peoples' attitudes and behaviour along a number of lines:

In the first place, the *structuring function alone* can have a *direct* influencing effect: The structuring leads our *attention* towards particular parts of reality at the expense of others; it is selective, a first condition for commitment and action.[1]

In the second place, the structuring function alone can have a more *indirect* influencing effect, where the defined concept is used *in propositions* one lets oneself be convinced by and therefore takes as a basis for one's actions.[2]

Further, normative definitions can exert influence through *interplay between the structuring function and the naming function.* – This mode of influencing is the topic of what follows.

(2) I use the term *"persuasive definition"* of that interplay between structuring and naming that is to be discussed in more detail in what follows.

Unlike the discussion above, the discussion in what follows will not only move inside the definition, but also shift the focus *out of the definition*, to the relationship between on the one hand the definition and on the other hand the language users' normative attitudes.

By way of introduction I shall outline the central elements: words, emotions and things, and say a little about the interplay between them (section 7.2 below).

This will provide a basis for seeing how normative definitions can be used as *means* to persuasion and influencing action:

First I shall define a concept of 'persuasive definition' (section 7.3.1 item (1)), and schematise a general pattern of proposition types that I want to emphasise (item (2)). After having justified the naming of the concept (item (3)), I shall divide it into two main types (item (4)).

---

1 The selectivity can have different degrees; towards the far end of the scale lies "absolutisation of aspects", see sections 7.3.3 (2)(b) and IV 3.2 (1), below.

2 On influencing action through structuring alone (the paragraph containing the present note, and the preceding paragraph), see section III 2.2.5 below.

To shed light on the general pattern and the two main types I shall go relatively thoroughly through two main examples (section 7.3.2 (1) and (2)). Against this more concrete background I shall by way of conclusion point out some characteristic features of persuasive definitions (section 7.3.3).

The presentation is organised in such a way that it can be read both ways: If one prefers to take one's point of departure in the concrete, one can start with the characteristic features (section 7.3.3), go through the examples (section 7.3.2) and end up with the definition (section 7.3.1).

7.2. Interplay between words, emotions and things

(1) Many words have what I term an *"appeal function"*. By this I mean *a part of* the phenomenon that words tend to evoke or to be evoked by emotions, positive or negative: In a broader perspective all words and word sequences are part of a psychological causal relationship, whether or not that is how the sender and the recipient want it to be.[3] When the superordinate topic is dis/agreement and influencing, the centre lies in the more *undiluted* feelings, attached to an *individual* word or a brief sequence of words: the "appeal function of words".[4]

Some words have (almost) *only* an appeal function: from the very beginning ("ouch", "hurrah") or through changes in language usage.[5] More interesting with a view to analysis of dis/agreement are expressions in the case of which the appeal function is *combined* with purely cognitive criteria or with evaluation prescription.

Evaluation prescriptions are by definition linked to the connotation dimension. Whether a linguistic expression prescribes an evaluation therefore depends on how it is defined, more precisely on the connotation specification (section 6.1 above). – *Words' appeal function* is by definition linked to the language dimension, to the words as physical entities. Whether a linguistic expression appeals to emotions is therefore not a question of the *content of concepts*, but of *actual psychological factors outside concepts*.

How can this be? Words are after all simply words. – Words' appeal to emotions arises through a psychological tendency for those feelings that are attached to the *things* to be transferred to the *words* that are used of the things. – In intellectual terms many have no doubt rejected the belief that by affecting

---

3 Weaver, *The Ethics of Rhetoric*, pp. 115–42 (heading): "Some rhetorical aspects of grammatical categories"; Rycroft, 'An Enquiry into the Function of Words in the Psycho-Analytical Situation', p. 414: "Even language which is designed to avoid imaginative reverberations fails to do so since it evokes a feeling of dryness."

4 The appeal function often constitutes a part of what is discussed under the name of "emotive" function; see Ogden/ Richards, *The Meaning of Meaning*, pp. 149 et seq., cf. pp. 123–26, 223–28; Stevenson, see note 6 below; Rommetveit, *Språk, tanke og kommunikasjon* [language, thought and communication], pp. 74–82.

5 Lewis, *Studies in Words*, pp. 7–8, 222–26.

signs for the things, one also affects the things themselves. However, in psychological terms we are all subject to the said transfer of feelings from the things to the words.

From this it follows that evaluation prescriptions *do not by definition correspond* with appeal function:

On the one hand, there are words whose *meaning content prescribes an evaluation without the word's appealing to emotions.* An important instance-type arises through the fact that words without appeal function and with a meaning content that does not prescribe an evaluation, for example "building", "vehicle" or "ship", by being introduced into the formulation of legal rules, acquire a meaning content that prescribes an evaluation. The cause of this transformation of their meaning content lies in lawyers' argumentation practice. When lawyers take a standpoint on whether something is to be deemed, for example, a 'building', 'vehicle' or 'ship', they take into account the reasonableness and justice, both in the instance-type and in the individual instance, of the legal consequences arising as a result of the one or the other standpoint (section F, in particular 2.1 (2) and 3.2.2 (1)(a), below).

On the other hand, there are words that *appeal to emotions without their meaning content's prescribing an evaluation.* An instance-type is many definitions, in academic subjects, of words which have emotive value in everyday life and in the subject: for example Ross' definition of "(gældende) ret" [(valid) law] and "retsvidenskab" [legal science] (section 7.3.2 (1) below).

> It is infelicitous to use the word *"meaning"* of linguistic expressions' appeal to emotions, since the word will then be used *both* of structuring in thought *and* of psychological causes and effects of naming, and since these topics ought in most contexts to be kept separate from each other. Therefore I *reserve* the word "meaning" for the structuring, and use formulations like "psychological causality" and "appeal function" of words in their capacity of being elements in cause-effect relationships. – Others use the word "meaning" also of words' appeal to emotions, especially in the collocation "emotive meaning". One source of this usage is Stevenson.[6] An important reason for Stevenson's using the word "meaning" in this way is that his superordinate concept of 'meaning' has the same structure as the appeal to emotions, namely a cause-effect structure ("causal theory of meaning").[7]

(2) Since existence, diffusion and intensity of words' appeal to emotions are functions of the *language users' attitudes*, the appeal will *vary* to the same degree as human beings' attitudes are varied and changing:

> "We like and dislike different things. There are those who are of the opinion that *politics* and *politician* are derogatory in certain contexts, but are blissfully unaware that the word *lawyer* is a term of abuse for some people. I find

6 Stevenson, 'The Emotive Meaning of Ethical Terms', in particular pp. 18–22; *Ethics and Language*, pp. 37–80, in particular pp. 59–60.

7 Stevenson, *Ethics and Language*, in particular pp. 41–59.

> it useful in the description of Johan Sverdrup [leader of the Norwegian liberal party, "father" of parliamentarism in Norway, prime minister 1884–89] to compare him with Robespierre. To some people Robespierre was an idol, to others a monster. Collocations with the word *"democracy"* [my italics] normally arouse friendly thoughts today; it is not so long since it sounded derogatory in wide circles. *Words have their emotive ups and downs* [my italics] ..." (Seip's italics unless otherwise stated).[8]

An example from law of variations over time is provided by the changes in *lawyers' views of the tenability of arguments from will,* and the accompanying changes in the emotive associations lawyers connect with the word "will" and its derivatives (or their equivalents in other languages): – From the 18th century and up to the end of the 19th century arguments from will were regarded partly as tenable philosophical justifications for state and law ("the social contract"), and partly as weighty legally operative facts within existing legal systems, in particular within that part of the system which relates to obligations and property ("will theories"). – In the 20th century the trend in legal literature was for writers to distance themselves from will arguments when discussing questions relating to the law of obligations and property. For example, they distanced themselves from such arguments when discussing the interpretation of contracts:[9] The decisive thing is claimed to be what the parties' actions and formulations mean according to an objective interpretation, not what the parties might have meant without this having been objectively expressed.[10] – Inter alia this trend in legal literature has contributed to a change in lawyers' more general attitude, from regarding will arguments as weighty or even decisive, to regarding them as ("of course") being of little or no weight.[11] In parallel with this change in the more general attitude to the tenability of will *arguments* there has been a derived psychological change in the associations that accompany the *word* "will".

(3) The *way the psychological mechanism operates* is *simple* where there is only one expression with appeal function that is used. Further, this mechanism is

---

8 Seip, '"Ekte" og "uekte" vurderinger i historieforskningen' [genuine and spurious evaluations in historical research], p. 187.

9 The interpretation of contracts was a central area for "will theories" and for lawyers' discussions of these. On lines of development in legal dogmatic literature on interpretation of contracts, see Huser, *Avtaletolking* [interpretation of contracts], Chapter 3, in particular pp. 181–220, 241–49, 269–301.

10 Compare Knoph, 'Nogen ord om dommerens stilling til kutymene' [some words on the position and attitude of the judge in relation to usages in trade], p. 307; Stang, *Innledning til formueretten* [introduction to the law of obligations and property], pp. 253, 254, 450; Arnholm, *Alminnelig avtalerett* [general law of contract], pp. 127, 129–30; *Privatrett II: Avtaler* [private law II: contracts], pp. 38–39; *Lærebok i avtalerett* [textbook in the law of contract], pp. 33–34; Hov, *Avtalerett* [law of contract], pp. 74–75; Selvig, *Kontraktsretten* [law of contract], pp. 543–44; Krüger, *Norsk kontraktsrett* [Norwegian law of contract], pp. 508, 511.

11 However, very few go as far as Hägerström, Olivecrona and Ross, who in their discussions of the question of criteria in private law for the transition from preliminaries to dispositive acts claim that it is *logically impossible* for dispositive intent (i.e. intention to enter into legal relations) to be a criterion; see Eng, '"Hva er en viljeserklæring?"' ["what is a declaration of intent"].

simple where there are several expressions that are used, which, in relation to a given audience, all pull in the same direction. An example would be: "The book is irrational and unscientific." Most academics will make a reflex association to the effect that the book should be avoided, irrespective of which of the expressions with appeal function one looks at.

The way the psychological mechanism operates is *more complex* where there are several expressions with appeal function that are used, which, in relation to a given audience, pull in different directions or in uncertain directions, for example: "This rule is a legal rule, and like other legal rules it is a means for the ruling class to oppress the weak." Many people will connect positive associations with the term "legal rule" (civilisation, order, predictability, justice, etc.). The vast majority will connect negative associations with the word "oppress" (brutality, injustice, etc.). Given that the proposition formulation quoted has been produced for the purpose of exerting influence, then the sender is taking a chance: He banks on the one emotive expression's killing the other, and on the victorious expression's giving its colour to the losing expression.

However, it is not easy to find good examples of proposition formulations which have been produced for the purpose of exerting influence and which have been built up with expressions which, in relation to a given audience, make an appeal in different directions or in unpredictable directions. A coarse-meshed causal factor is that human beings *strive for a simplification in cases of contradiction*;[12] in the present context this happens through our establishing standardised psychological reflexes not only connected with individual linguistic expressions, but also with particular combinations of expressions that are used in speaking of commonly occurring situations.

By way of *illustration* I return to lawyers' attitudes connected with the word "will": for example in the sentence "this promissory declaration objectively interpreted does not express the sender's will". Today most lawyers will as a reflex let a legally operative fact formulated as "the promissory declaration objectively interpreted" knock out a legally operative fact formulated as "the sender's will", while a good hundred years ago the situation was the reverse.

Such standardised psychological reflexes connected with situation-types often seem *exaggerated*. If one analyses the problem more closely, the answers are not so obvious as the reflexes suggest. The standardised reflexes are an effect of inter alia the fact that human beings more or less consciously consider that *uncertainty and doubt are something unpleasant that must be removed*, so that thoughts and emotions calm down and so that *choices of action are simplified*.[13]

The aforementioned causal factor, that human beings *strive for a simplification in cases of contradiction* (see the text at note 12), may in the light of what has just

12 Heider, *The Psychology of Interpersonal Relations*, pp. 174–217.

13 See Eng, *U/enighetsanalyse – med særlig sikte på jus og allmenn rettsteori* [analysis of dis/agreement – with particular reference to law and legal theory], section IV 4.6, for a more detailed discussion of the operation of this causal factor in relation to language and argumentation.

been said (see the text at note 13) *be nuanced*: The more closely our reactions and our use of language are connected with choices of action, and the greater the interest we have in the choice, the more our reactions and use of language tend towards the standardised. And the more remote the connection is, and the less our interest, the more we allow contradiction in our emotions to be expressed. – Consider by way of *illustration* the contrast between on the one hand our one-sidedly condemnatory reaction and language directed at a person who offends against us; and on the other hand our partly admiring reaction and way of talking when we are not affected, for example our use of expressions like "gentleman crook", "a true scoundrel", etc., of screen characters.[14] Or consider the contrast between on the one hand the individual's reactions and language in and in relation to situations he meets in the role of person applying the law, exposed to his own and other people's critical evaluation, and on the other hand reactions and language in and in relation to the same situations on the part of one who is not a lawyer and does not have any interest in the situation in any other way either.[15]

7.3. Persuasive definitions

7.3.1. Definition and two main types

(1) Structuring
(2) Schematic specification of the relationship between proposition types involved in the use of persuasive definitions
(3) Naming
(4) Two main types of persuasive definition

(1) Structuring

The appeal of words to emotions provides a *particular basis for influencing other people*:

If one wishes to influence others to *accept a given phenomenon*, a suitable means may be to seize on words with a positive emotive value for the person who is to be influenced, and explicitly or by presupposition to build on normative definitions of these words so that the contentious phenomenon is covered. – For example, if one wants to influence another person to accept a particular way of arguing, and if the other person, like most people, connects a positive emotive value with the word "rational", then his acceptance can be expedited by one's using the word "rational" about the way of arguing and about people who use this way of arguing. Or if one wants to win acceptance for a reorganisation of the

[14] Compare Furberg, *Saying and Meaning*, pp. 68–69, on the use of the positively loaded word "true" together with negatively loaded words and expressions ("true scoundrel").
[15] See in more detail in Chapter IV below. See also section III 2.4.2 (1) below.

public sector, and if those affected connect a positive emotive value with words like "efficiency", "autonomy", "modernisation", etc., then their acceptance can be expedited by one's using these words about the reorganisation.

If one wishes to influence others to *reject* a given phenomenon, one can use the same technique, with the difference that one uses about the phenomenon words with negative emotive value for the person who is to be influenced. Examples would be use of the word "irrational" about a way of arguing that one wants to influence the other person to reject, or use of words and expressions like "old-fashioned", "standing in the way of progress", etc., about those who are sceptical of the relevance of market thinking when it comes to organising the public sector.

Such propositions as have now been mentioned will either themselves fall under, or build on propositions that fall under, the concept of 'persuasive definition' that I shall now lay down. – This concept delimits a language and argumentation pattern that exploits the fact that words with *strong appeal function* are often *indeterminate in their structuring function*. Thus it becomes possible to connect these words and their accompanying appeal function to various phenomena, *all according to* what interests one wishes to promote. – Expressions with positive appeal function therefore often function as "*prizes* which each man seeks to bestow on the qualities of his own choice" (my italics).[16] They are *complimentary words* to whose realisation nobody will declare himself opposed, and whose area of use is delimited depending on interest in exerting influence.

The *definitional features* of the concept of 'persuasive definition', as I lay it down and use it here, may be grouped into two main parts:

(i) In the first place, there is a *normative definition of or by means of words with appeal to emotions*: that is to say, either of words which *already have* appeal to emotions (see the example discussed in section 7.3.2 (1) below), or of words which do not have appeal to emotions, but which through the definition *may acquire* this, namely by being defined by means of words which do have such appeal (see the example discussed in section 7.3.2 (2) below).

(ii) In the second place, the language user applies his usage (his normative definition) of the word to such an extent that the word's emotive appeal is *suited to persuading*.

The seminal discussion of persuasive definitions was provided by *Stevenson*, in particular in his article Persuasive Definitions (1938) and in his book Ethics and Language (1944), Chapter IX. – The concept of 'persuasive definition', as I have delimited it here, corresponds to some extent with the concept Stevenson terms "persuasive definition". In the article mentioned Stevenson gives the following definition: "A "persuasive" definition is one which gives a new conceptual meaning to a familiar word without substantially changing its emotive meaning, and which is used with the conscious or unconscious purpose of changing, by this means, the direction of people's interests" (p. 32). – The most important difference is that Stevenson's concept does not

16 Stevenson, 'Persuasive Definitions', p. 35; *Ethics and Language*, p. 213.

> cover the second of the two main types I shall later distinguish between (item (4) below). Perhaps there is also a difference with respect to whether intention to persuade is a concept criterion (see the first paragraph in the main text after the present indent, including note 17).
>
> One must distinguish between, on the one hand, Stevenson's pointing out of particular features of actually occurring use of language, such as through the concept of 'persuasive definition', and on the other hand, his discussion and general theory of "what meaning is", in which he advances a causal view of meaning (see section 7.2 (1) above, concluding remarks). – It is only the first type of proposition that is a source of inspiration here.

There is one possible misunderstanding there is particular reason to warn against: I do *not* lay down as a conceptual feature of 'persuasive definition' that the language user *aims to "fool"* the other participants in the discussion. Such a conceptualisation would separate language and argumentation phenomena that ought to be treated together because they have the practically important *function in common* of having persuasive effect by virtue of appeal to emotions. This effect does, of course, often occur *independently of* the language user's conscious intention. This can be illustrated inter alia by the fact that one uses language and its appeal to emotions also *in relation to oneself*: in forming one's own identity and in defending oneself against threatening cognitions.[17]

Something else than conscious intention's not being a conceptual feature is that persuasive definitions can *in fact* be used consciously. Words and expressions with meaning aspects in this direction are for example "to be able to judge one's public" and "rhetoric". Persuasive definitions are in such contexts seen as *technique or art*. The point of this art is not the *tenability* of propositions, but the psychological *effects* of proposition formulations: the association-producing capacities, in a given social context, of the sensorily perceptible linguistic entities.[18]

---

[17] Nor does Stevenson in all probability intend to lay down conscious intention as a concept criterion, see the definition quoted in the indent above, and his corresponding statement in *Ethics and Language*, p. 210. – His statements do not, however, seem completely consistent, see 'Persuasive Definitions', p. 38, where conscious intention is, as far as I can see, laid down as a concept criterion.

[18] Cicero, *Brutus*, sections 184–88: "What is right or wrong in a man's speaking I shall be able to judge, provided I have the ability and knowledge to judge; but what sort of an orator a man is can only be recognized from what his oratory effects. ... [W]hether or not the orator succeeds in conveying to his listeners the emotions which he wishes to convey, can only be judged by the assent of the multitude and the approbation of the people. For that reason, as to the question whether an orator is good or bad, there has never been disagreement between experts and the common people. ... [T]he very mark of supreme oratory [is] that the supreme orator is recognized by the people. ... [W]hat the multitude approves must win the approval of experts."

(2) Schematic specification of the relationship between proposition types involved in the use of persuasive definitions

Irrespective of area of language and argumentation one can see a *general pattern* of proposition types involved in the use of persuasive definitions. This pattern can be schematised as follows:

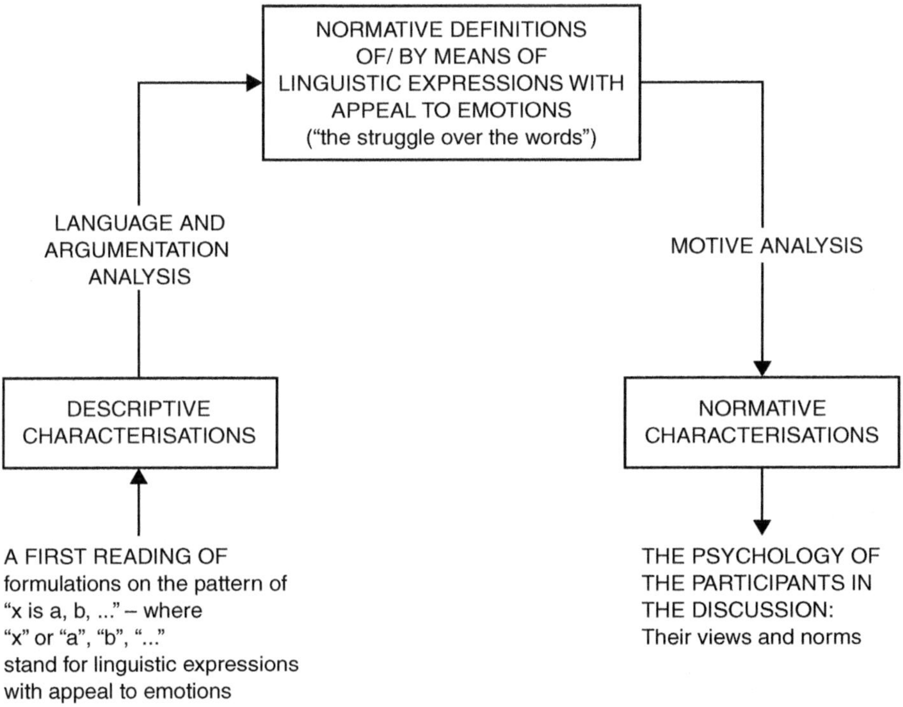

In my experience it is fruitful to have this pattern in mind as a very real possibility, when one is trying to understand discussions. This applies not only to simple discussions, but also to more complex texts; and it applies to philosophy and science as well (compare section 7.3.2 below).

(3) Naming

The language and argumentation pattern delimited in items (1)–(2) above I name *"persuasive definition"*. – This is no obvious choice, since the pattern includes both characterisations and definitions. That I nevertheless choose *"definition"* as part of the name is for two *reasons*. First, Stevenson, who wrote the seminal works on the subject, uses the term "definition" (see item (1) above, in the indent). Secondly, and more importantly, words and the language user's definition of the words are definitionally and factually so *central* in the pattern:

Definitionally speaking, it is the case that the language user employs words with appeal to emotions; and further, that the language user applies his normative definitions of these words to such an extent that the appeal to emotions is suited to persuading. – Factually speaking, it is the case that the means (to persuasion as an effect) is the psychological cause-effect relationships in which the words are situated, and the sender's normative definition of the words as an element in these relationships. – As words and their definition are *so* central, I assume that it produces the most apposite associations to term the language and argumentation pattern "definition".

(4) Two main types of persuasive definition

In section 7.3.2 below I shall *illustrate* the general pattern by looking at persuasive definitions of the linguistic entities "Retts/ Vitenskap" [legal/ science] (item (1)) and "Norm" [norm] (item (2)). Both entities have a central place in law and legal theory, and both have given rise to many and lengthy discussions.

These examples of the basis in reality of the general pattern illustrate at the same time *two main types* of persuasive definition:

The first example ("legal/ science") illustrates persuasive definitions in which the word whose area of application is being normatively regulated, already has an appeal function (the schema's[19] "x" = "science"). – Here the word's area of application is changed, while its appeal function tends to be taken as given, without any further attempt at change.

The second example ("norm") illustrates persuasive definitions in which the word whose area of application is being normatively regulated, prior to the definition appears as neutral (or with appeal in the opposite direction to that which the definer wants), and through the definition is sought to be invested with a particular appeal function (the schema's "x" = "norm") by its being defined by means of words with an already existing and desired appeal (the schema's "a", "b", etc.). – Here *both* the word's area of application *and* its appeal function are thus taken as *variable*.

> Stevenson's concept of 'persuasive definition' does not cover this latter type, only the first, in that he presupposes that the word whose area of application is being normatively regulated, already has an appeal function, and that the appeal function is not changed through the definition.[20] – The two main types are, however, both so frequent in occurrence and so closely related in structure and function (see the schema in item (2) above and my discussions of the examples in what follows),[21] that in relation to the perspective and topic of the present work they ought to be seen together. – A third main type,

19 See item (2) above.

20 Stevenson, 'Persuasive Definitions', pp. 39–40; *Ethics and Language*, p. 210.

21 Compare Stevenson, *Ethics and Language*, pp. 279–81.

the borderline case where the area of application is kept constant and only the appeal function is sought to be changed, is not so important in practice, and will not be specially treated here.[22] Whether one brings it under the concept of 'persuasive definition' is a question of lesser importance. Incidentally, the boundary between this borderline case and the second of the main types mentioned in the main text above is graduated, just like the boundary between the two main types themselves.[23]

7.3.2. Examples

In actually occurring analysis and argumentation, persuasive definitions are not the preserve of demagogues; deliberate playing on emotions is not always looked down on. Nor is this so in professional and academic contexts. Quite the reverse, not seldom it is precisely the *persuasive definitions that are evaluated most highly*. This is also so in professional and academic contexts. – Of the leading Norwegian historian Jens Arup Seip it was said:

> "The lecture which made his name most widely known, was delivered at a meeting arranged by the Student Association in the autumn of 1963. The roof was raised that evening in October when Seip spoke on "Fra embedsmannsstat til ettpartistat" [from senior civil service state to one-party state]. There was jubilation over the perfectly formulated and wittily presented analysis, of course, but also over the liberation of the mind that followed from his *words*. Here was a historian who with authority spoke of *Norway* as a *"one-party state"*, *Arbeiderpartiet* [the labour party] as a *"Stalinist regime"*, the sacrosanct *Gerhardsen* [leading labour party politician, Norwegian prime minister 1945–51, 1955–63, 1963–65] as a *"Caesar"*. I shall never forget the *feeling of illumination* that swept over this country's young academics that evening – after the clammy respect for servile attitudes that the political forms and norms of the 1950s had imposed upon us all. And not only were we changed. Norwegian political life was never quite the same after that evening. *The thinking, the concepts, the form of expression* took a new turn. Not least journalism set out along new paths. We experienced a *change of attitude* of which it may be difficult to sound the depth" (my italics; Dahl's italics omitted).[24]

All according to what area the persuasive definition is used in, one can distinguish between *political, legal, philosophical*, etc., persuasive definitions.

(1) "Legal/ Science"

A distinctive aspect of the words *"true"*, *"rational"* and *"scientific"* is a strong and positive emotive value: Truth, rationality and science are something many people *believe in*, apparently pretty much corresponding to belief in gods. It is

22 On this case, see Stevenson, 'Persuasive Definitions', p. 39; *Ethics and Language*, pp. 277–78.
23 Stevenson, *Ethics and Language*, p. 281.
24 H.F. Dahl, 'Obituary of Jens Arup Seip'.

important to be aware of this when one reads *academic literature*. For there *incantations* with "true", "rational" and "scientific" often lie one after another: There are innumerable discussions of *"What truth is"*, *"What rationality is"* and *"What science is"*.

In what follows I shall take a closer look at some propositions about *"Hva retts/vitenskap er"* [was Rechts/wissenschaft ist, what legal/ science is], with a particular view to demonstrating the three elements in the general pattern (see section 7.3.1 (2) above, on the general): – first, after an immediate reading, the impression that one is confronted with a descriptive characterisation of phenomena that are collected under a presupposed concept of 'legal science'; – secondly, after a more detailed language and argumentation analysis, the identifying of a struggle over the words; – and finally, in the light of assumptions about the psychological basis of persuasive definitions, a hypothesis that the disagreement concerns the discussion participants' norms.

What norms the disagreement concerns may vary. However, my impression is that the examples in what follows are representative, when persuasive definitions of "legal/ science" in these examples are used, or function, as means to changing legal academics' *way of arguing* (items (a), (b), (a)↔(b)); as means to extending legal academics' *subject area* (item (c)(i)); or as means to strengthening legal academics' *self-confidence* (item (c)(ii), cf. also the other examples in the present item (1)).

(a) In *Ross'* theory of "What legal/ science is" one can find again the three elements in the general pattern of persuasive definitions. – I shall begin with a quotation which on first reading may seem to express *descriptive characterisations* of a phenomenon delimited through presupposition and termed "legal science":

> "In this and the following section it will be further investigated how it is tested whether a particular norm is valid (Danish) law, which is ... the same as testing the truth of the corresponding juridico-scientific assertion. ...
>
> The task we are herewith attacking touches the *innermost nerve in the question of the empirical content of legal science*. If the statements of legal science are to be understood as *empirico-scientific assertions* about a social reality – and thus not as *metaphysical postulates* about a validity outside experience – the same must apply to them as to all other reality propositions, namely that their logical meaning content is identical with the immediate experiences through which it is tested whether or not the proposition is true.
>
> It is a *basic proposition in modern empirically oriented logic of science* that an assertion that purports to be a proposition about reality (and not only a logico-mathematical, analytic statement) must directly or indirectly imply that by following a certain procedure under certain conditions, one will have certain immediate experiences. This procedure, which one calls the verification procedure, thus concerns how one is to proceed in order to test the truth of the proposition, and at the same time defines its meaning content. If such a procedure cannot be specified – as is the case, for example, with an assertion that the world is governed by an invisible demon – we are completely at a

> loss when it comes to the question whether the proposition is true or false. Such propositions are said to lack (logical) meaning and are called metaphysical.
>
> Any *meaningful assertion about something real* must thus directly concern or imply elementary, immediate experiences. If I say for example, "this thing is made of chalk", this assertion implies – in connection with a set of other assertions – inter alia that if I place the object under a microscope, I shall make particular observations; that if I pour acid over it, I shall observe certain chemical reactions; that if I rub it against a blackboard, I shall observe the production of a stroke; and so forth. All these verifiable implications constitute the logical meaning or real content of the assertion.
>
> In the same way a juridico-scientific assertion too, for example
>
> P = (section 28 of the Bills of Exchange Act) is valid Danish law,
>
> if it is to be interpreted as a *meaningful proposition about reality*, must imply assertions about certain elementary, immediate experiences which can be tested in a verification procedure, and which define the real content of the juridico-scientific sentence. ...
>
> [T]he real content ... is a prediction that ... the directive to the judge contained in section 28 of the Bills of Exchange Act [will] enter into the grounds of his judgment as an integral component" (my italics; Ross' italics and note omitted).[25]

The quoted passages by themselves give grounds for doubting whether Ross is giving descriptive characterisations of a phenomenon delimited through presupposition and termed "legal science". And in the subsequent text there is much to indicate his intending to give a *normative definition* of the term "legal/ science". This definition functions at the same time as a *persuasive definition*, since the word "science" clearly has a strong emotive value for Ross and probably also for many of those who are his intended readers, and since he does not explicitly at the beginning of his discussion make it clear that it is a normative definition that will follow:

> "The analysis conducted of the concept of 'valid Danish law' aimed to make out the real content of sentences which according to their meaning and intention have the character of scientific assertions that a certain rule is valid Danish law.
>
> Another question is whether legal doctrine, in the form in which it in fact appears in current expositions and treatments of Danish law, is according to its own meaning and intention concerned with presenting and giving grounds for assertions of this kind. It is the *question of whether legal doctrine is and wishes to be a science* [Ross' italics] of valid law *in the sense defined in the preceding discussion* [my italics]."[26]

---

[25] Ross, *Om ret og retfærdighed* [on law and justice], pp. 52–53, and p. 55 (final paragraph of the quotation). The passages quoted were translated by me. In the English edition of 1958, *On Law and Justice*, parts of the passages quoted were omitted or rewritten, see *On Law and Justice*, pp. 39–40.

[26] Ross, *Om ret og retfærdighed* [on law and justice], p. 59. The passages quoted were translated by

From this last quotation it is also apparent that Ross' concept structuring and his choice of the word "science" is not governed by the aim of cognising how lawyers in fact argue. First, it is apparent that Ross' *structuring* is a means in his exposition of what is for him an ideal. Secondly, it is apparent that the *choice of word* partly expresses Ross' support for the ideal, and partly represents a means to getting lawyers to live up to this ideal, to getting them to behave in the way he believes is right, to getting them to comply with his *norms*.

(b) Ross is of course not alone in the persuasive use of the complimentary term "legal/ science". By way of illustration from Norwegian legal theory I shall quote a piece from *Sundby's* argumentation *against Ross*.

Sundby placed great weight on bringing out the pervasive *weighing and balancing character* of lawyers' argumentation. In order to be able to *describe* this weighing and balancing character (more precisely than had previously been usual), he formed the concepts of 'rule' and 'guideline' (section 6.2 (1) above, concluding remarks). Those features of lawyers' argumentation that Sundby singles out in the *following quotation* have therefore a clearer starting point in assumed facts than does Ross' definition. However, the three elements in the general pattern of persuasive definitions do *also* lie in Sundby's argumentation: – Again one gets a strong first impression that the text expresses descriptive characterisations of a phenomenon delimited through presupposition and termed "legal science", cf. inter alia the occurrences of the word "theory". – But again it is reasonable to interpret the disagreement as a struggle over the term "legal/ science": Sundby's *structuring* works not only as a means to cognition of facts, but also as a means in the presentation of an ideal. – And again the use of the *word* "science" serves, albeit not so one-sidedly as in Ross, partly as an expression of support for the ideal and for the norms that can be derived from this, and partly as a means to influencing action:

> "The distinction between rules and guidelines, combined with the systematic weighing-and-balancing view of legal reasoning and the softening up of the concept of 'basic norm', has for me great consequences in the direction of a *fundamental juridico-philosophical view of positive (i.e. actually given) legal systems*.
>
> The so-called "prediction *theory*" – the most outstanding representative of which in the Nordic countries is Alf Ross – has no adherent in me. Viewing juridico-scientific statements de lege lata as predictions of the courts' behaviour *turns the matter upside down* and *means that law is transformed* into a hypothetico-deductive science of social facts. It may be interesting in practice – for example for an advocate – to have a go at predictions about the courts' reactions. But neither he nor the theorist can escape the normative, bound weighing and balancing of arguments that constitutes *the core of law*. It is mastery of the method that makes well-grounded predictions possible.

---

me. In the English edition of 1958, *On Law and Justice*, parts of the passages quoted were omitted or rewritten, see *On Law and Justice*, pp. 45–46.

> The prediction *theory* is inadequate in terms of "Occam's razor". And this *theory* is inadequate – a misunderstood form of "realism" – because it rests on *far too narrow a concept of 'scientificity': Law is* no empirical science in the usual sense, nor is it deductive pseudo-mathematics. There remains a third possibility.
>
> As far as law is concerned, this possibility – argumentation within complicated norm structures – entails limited objectivity, as demonstrated above ... To claim anything else will give a *false picture of legal science*" (my italics; Sundby's italics and note omitted).[27]

(a)↔(b) Both Ross and Sundby clearly place great weight on *monopolising the term* "legal/ science" for the way of arguing that each of them believes is the right one. The cause of this I take to be precisely the *appeal to reflex approval* that the word "science" has, and the corresponding *appeal to reflex rejection* that lies in saying of a given way of arguing that it is "unscientific".

Neither Ross nor Sundby appear to be sufficiently aware of the possibility that they *agree* with others (and in the case of Sundby, with one another) about the way in which lawyers in fact argue; that the *disagreement* there might be, concerns the way in which lawyers ought to argue; and that as a means in this struggle they attempt to acquire the sole right to the positively loaded term "legal/ science".

The quotations from Ross and Sundby illustrate how even the most acute minds can fail to distinguish sufficiently clearly, in relation to analysis of dis/agreement, between the fundamental types of proposition: between definitions and characterisations, and between descriptive and normative propositions. – *Or*, can it be the case that their intellectual acuity is not a hindrance, but rather a causal factor: Can it be that precisely the person who is intellectually sharp and well read can more easily exploit, and thus more easily engages in, the rhetorical possibilities that lie in the "What is"-form and follow from the play on the appealing words?

Irrespective of what the causes of such argumentation are, and irrespective of how one evaluates the goodness of such argumentation, the argumentation can be effective in its capacity of being a psychological means of influencing. Ross' argumentation has no doubt been effective in this capacity: It requires both a capacity for independent thinking and considerable work to penetrate Ross' text and to clarify its relationship to the fundamental types of proposition. To many readers, Ross' text has no doubt appeared as a tenable and compelling argument: "This is how legal dogmatics *must* be conducted. Otherwise it's not *science*!" has appeared as a piece of *reasoning*, instead of as the *persuasive definition* (postulated normative definition) of the term "legal/ science" that Ross' text on closer analysis turns out to function as.

The whole of the long road Ross lays through the term "legal/ science" seems in retrospect to have its *foremost function in the persuasive aspect*: – Ross' discussion cannot be intended as a descriptive characterisation of Danish lawyers'

27 Sundby, *Om normer* [on norms], p. 265.

way of arguing, since such a characterisation is so clearly false (compare the second quotation from Ross in item (a) above). – Nor does Ross' discussion provide any independent justification for the ontological and epistemological premisses from philosophical empiricism on which he builds his definition, but simply reproduces and postulates these controversial premisses (compare the first quotation from Ross in item (a) above).[28] – Nor does Ross' discussion consist in an open presentation and discussion of those norms that he adheres to in the question of how legal dogmaticians ought to proceed: We do not get any mapping and evaluation of the multifarious considerations (factual connections, values and norms) that are relevant in a discussion of this question. – Instead the reader gets Ross' conclusion on this question, his norm, presented in an indirect way: through his discussion of "What legal/ science is", through a complex persuasive definition.

(c) The struggle over the term "legal/ science" does not show any sign of losing any of its force; new participants are constantly enlisting. By way of illustration I shall look at two examples from Nordic literature today.

(i) Hanne Petersen has investigated normative phenomena of a more informal kind than those that legal dogmaticians otherwise usually concern themselves with. Out of her own interests, particularly derived from women's interests, she considers these phenomena to be important.[29] She considers them to be so important that she believes it justified to set up the following *norm* for legal dogmaticians at large:

> "Legal dogmaticians too must recognise that the state norm-system is not in absolute control, and that the state is not the all-deciding frame. It is necessary to describe different norm systems which function within different frames or worlds, and to investigate and describe their reciprocal action in order to understand so-called reality and its normative aspects."[30]

The standpoint that legal dogmaticians ought to take a closer look at more informal norms is one for which I believe many good *grounds* can be given. – Petersen appears, however, to take the view that this standpoint ought not only to be supported by grounds, but that the standpoint also requires that the *use of the word "ret"* [law] be extended to the informal norms.

Petersen invests a lot of work in undertaking such an extension.[31] The result is that the *practical question* of what legal dogmaticians ought to engage in and with what pretensions on behalf of their field, recedes into the background. – This is partly because the question is transformed into and discussed through the polysemous question formulation *"What is law?"*.[32] – And it is partly because

---

28 On some central ontological and epistemological premisses on which Ross builds his definition, see section 5.2 (5)(b)(ii) cf. (i), above.

29 Petersen, *Informel ret på kvindearbejdspladser* [informal law in women's workplaces], pp. 15–16.

30 Op. cit., p. 92.

31 Op. cit., pp. 31–104 (Part I).

32 Loc. cit., cf. also the heading of Part I.

Petersen's discussion circles round and ends up with standpoints on the *use of the word "ret"* [law]. She wishes this word to be used also of:

> "normative notions and considerations, patterns of behaviour and action, which are not based on a clear-cut distinction between law and morals ... [and which] cannot be determined through authoritative written sources, but are [often] acknowledged and communicated ... orally".[33]

With this definition legal dogmaticians are not only spurred on by the grounds that might support their being interested in more informal norms, but also by the *appeal* that lies in the fact that a study of such norms can now be designated by the *term "legal science"*: an appeal that in relation to lawyers consists partly in the fact that the term "legal science" is more *homely and safe* than words like "sociology", "anthropology", "psychology", etc.; partly in the fact that the term "legal science" gives lawyers *an apparent academic and professional competence* which the words "sociology", "anthropology", "psychology", etc., do not give; and partly in the fact that for many lawyers the term "legal science" no doubt signals *something finer and more elevated* than do the words "sociology", "anthropology", "psychology", etc.

(ii) David Doublet and Jan Fridthjof Bernt do not want first and foremost to *change* legal dogmaticians' way of arguing, as Ross to a certain degree wished to do, or to *extend* legal dogmaticians' subject area, as Petersen wishes to do; they want instead to *ensure* that the term "legal/ science" can (at any rate) be used of legal dogmatics in the way it is traditionally understood and conducted.[34]

For this purpose they attack ways of using the *term* "retts/vitenskap" [legal/ science] that lead to legal dogmatics' falling outside:

> "Claiming that legal science is no science[35] is a destructive point of departure" (p. 13).

Further, they present their own way of using the *term* "legal/ science", which in their view leads to legal dogmatics' being covered:

> "[T]he point of departure for our discussion [is] that *legal science is a science*" (pp. 78–79; partly my italics);
>
> "Is it possible by means of hermeneutics to justify the view that *legal science is a science* and to provide apt expression for the requirements for scientificity that must be made of this activity?" (p. 87; my italics);
>
> "[H]ermeneutics [is] a practical method that is learnt by *practical scientific exercise*. ... The new element that hermeneutics may ... bring to legal science is a *scientific creation of awareness* of what takes place in the actual application of the law. ... [I]f legal science is to have any pretensions to being science, it must develop its own methodological self-understanding,

---

33 Op. cit., p. 65.

34 Doublet/ Bernt, *Retten og vitenskapen* [the law and science]. The following quotations are from this work.

35 These are their exact words. – The same comment applies to the following quotations.

> and this presupposes a creation of awareness of methodology, a creation that is possible *for example by means of the hermeneutic principles of interpretation*. Such a creation of awareness will, in our estimation, be necessary for all *scientific further development*" (p. 100; my italics; Doublet and Bernt's italics omitted).

It is not clear to me *why* Doublet and Bernt consider it so important that the *term* "legal/ science" can be used of legal dogmatics; nor can I on any other basis see that it particularly matters. I assume that part of the explanation must lie in the more general notion for which their and others' preoccupation with this term seems to provide a basis: namely that it means a lot for academics' self-confidence to be able to use the term "science" of their own activity.[36]

(2) "Norm"

In the preceding item the controversy was about the term "legal/ science". In the present item, I shall show first how the *same general pattern of argumentation* recurs in discussions of "What is a norm?", "Norms are ..." (item (a)); and then in what way the "norm" example *differs from* the "science" example (item (b)).

(a) I shall first quote a passage from *Sundby's norm definition*, a passage which the following quotations discuss:

> "Thus we now know the semantic content of norms quite well. But we have not yet discussed what it takes for a normative proposition to acquire the status of the meaning content of a real norm. ... [T]he proposition ... must *have a particular connection with the individual or group in question* for us to reckon with the occurrence of a norm.
>
> There are a number of *reasons for laying down this additional requirement*. ... [W]e ought to require a pretty specific way of actualising in order to distinguish norms from normative propositions like [e.g.] pure imperatives, personal wishes, etc. The reason for a difference here is grounded in the motivation-psychological aspect: *Norms* will typically be followed so to speak for their own sake, while *ordinary imperatives* are followed, if at all, out of strategic considerations: fear of the sender's reaction in the case of disobedience. In terms of motivation there may of course be mixed cases and many grey areas. But in principle the distinction is important" (my italics; Sundby's notes omitted).[37]

In two reviews of Sundby's book, Sundby is respectively criticised and praised for laying down the individual-psychological concept of 'internalisation' as a criterion in the concept of 'norm'. – In the *critical* review one immediately runs into the first element in the general pattern: a seeming discussion about properties of a phenomenon delimited through presupposition and termed "norm", about

---

36 Compare Eng, *U/enighetsanalyse – med særlig sikte på jus og allmenn rettsteori* [analysis of dis/ agreement – with particular reference to law and legal theory], section IV 4.4 (7).

37 Sundby, *Om normer* [on norms], pp. 118–19.

human beings' relationship to this phenomenon, etc., that is to say that the propositions seemingly have the status of *descriptive characterisations*:

> "What norms are, Sundby tries to suggest (p. 119): "Norms will typically be followed so to speak for their own sake, while ordinary imperatives are followed, if at all, out of strategic considerations: fear of the sender's reaction in the case of disobedience. In terms of motivation there may of course be mixed cases and many grey areas. But in principle the distinction is important." *This distinction in principle* between "norms" and "imperatives", as he defines it, *strikes me as being pretty fishy*. I cannot see that Sundby gives any *grounds for why it must be so*, but I think that the justification he might give must be that law shall be free from domination: If the norms are internalised by people, and to the extent that law builds on and expresses such norms, then the laws will be followed for their own sake and not because people will risk a "reaction in the case of disobedience". This is a *standpoint that expresses* the morally acceptable, domination-free law. Lawyers speak of norms in this way and thereby make their profession moral, at the same time as the legislators assume that it is not so, and stuff their statutes with penal provisions. There is a danger that either law is not free from domination, and then the penal provisions are coercion, or Sundby's distinction is scholastic and unusable in practice" (my italics; Johnsen's italics omitted).[38]

On more detailed analysis there is, however, little to indicate that we are here faced with a discussion of the phenomenon of norm, that there is disagreement about factual properties of a phenomenon delimited through presupposition and termed "norm". On the other hand, there does seem to be disagreement about the use of the word "norm" in relation to, for example, the word "imperative" (but without this being made into a clear theme of the discussion). This means that the propositions have the status of *definitions*.

The critical reviewer supposes that Sundby wants it to be so that "law *shall* be free from domination", that is to say, the reviewer supposes that through his definition Sundby expresses adherence to an ideal: a situation in which the rulers do not need to use coercion, because their rule is accepted by those who are ruled. The reviewer then glides over to talking about the *fact* that law is *not* free from domination: "Lawyers speak of norms [as the morally acceptable, domination-free law] and thereby make their profession moral, at the same time as the legislators assume that it is not so, and stuff their statutes with penal provisions." The reviewer hardly disagrees with the ideal he ascribes to Sundby, but probably takes the view that it is more important that the *words used comply with reality* than *with the ideal*.

Behind this disagreement there appears to lie a disagreement about politics and legitimacy, about how from a political point of view one was to relate to the legal system as it was in fact in the 1970s, which may have been a disagreement about *norms* (but also about strategies): I assume that on the basis of his political views

---

38 Johnsen, 'Anmeldelse av Sundby, Om normer' [review of Sundby, on norms], p. 168.

(norms) the reviewer considered it more important to bring out (strategies) the oppressive aspects of law than the ideal of law free from domination.

Another review of Sundby's book *approves* of laying down the individual-psychological concept of 'internalisation' as a criterion in the concept of 'norm'. And this approval builds explicitly on political consequences of using the word "norm" in a particular way. In other words, the persuasive functions of concept structuring and choice of words are openly admitted here:

> "[T]he status of being a norm *for* somebody, actual existence as a norm, is acquired by a normative proposition (for example of the type "You shall do x") if it "aktualiseres" [is actualised], as Sundby says, through one of two types of speech act – by *internalisation* or by *stipulation*. ...
>
> *Internalisation* is really a concept taken from psychology. In that field it stands for the speech act by which a norm subject (consciously or unconsciously) "considers" a norm as "obligating". Of the said two kinds of actualisation Sundby reckons internalisation to be the fundamental one, a standpoint which with his starting point is virtually inevitable, but which is also perhaps the better of the alternatives his way of thinking offers us: at any rate better for *one who has democratic and anti-authoritarian preferences* [my italics]" (Tranøy's italics unless otherwise stated).[39]

The definition alternatives (of Sundby, Johnsen and Tranøy) thus seem in part to have the form of persuasive definitions, that is to say, to function, and, as the case may be, also to be intended to function, as *instruments of power*: as appeals to psychological reflexes in the direction of approval or rejection, linked to the term "legal/ norm". But this is not so easy to see as in the example "legal/ science". In the following item (b) I shall therefore show more precisely *where* the persuasive elements lie.

(b) At the same time as both the "norm" example and the "science" example fit into the general pattern of persuasive definitions, there is the following *difference* between them:

Controversies over the word *"science"* can play on the word's *already existing appeal function*. The latter is usually taken as given, and the attention is concentrated on the word's area of application: The participants in the discussion try to structure the word's area of application in such a way that the preferred ways of proceeding are covered, and the rejected ways of proceeding are excluded (item (1) above).

The word *"norm"* does not like the word "science" have an already existing appeal function on which the participants in the discussion can play. But an *appeal function can be created through the definition activity*; it can be created through limiting the word's area of application to phenomena that are evaluated unambiguously positively, and through using words with a positive appeal function of this structuring. The quoted discussion centring around the word "norm" (item (a) above) I see as an example of this second main type of persuasive defi-

---

39 Tranøy, 'Anmeldelse av Sundby, Om normer' [review of Sundby, on norms], p. 477.

nition, i.e. as an example of treating both the word's area of application and its appeal function as variables that can be regulated through the definition:

Sundby wants to link the word "norm" to normative propositions that have been directly or indirectly internalised by the person to whom the proposition is addressed. By means of this definition Sundby does two things: – First, he normatively regulates the area of application of the word "norm", by excluding for example the bank robber's order to the bank clerk. – Secondly, he bestows on the word "norm" a potential positive appeal function. Partly he does so in an indirect way, through the said normative delimitation in itself. And partly he does so in a more direct way, by using the word "internalisation" (with meaning aspects 'approval', 'acceptance', 'consent') of this delimitation: For it is clear that for example commands and prohibitions that one has accepted, are evaluated more positively than commands and prohibitions that are experienced as encroachments.

To emphasise the structure of this second main type of persuasive definition I shall demonstrate it in a further example:

> "*Sexuality* is not a "thing", a technique, but an arena for communication and personal development which two persons who are mutually committed share, in mutual respect and equal worth, for one's own and the other's enjoyment" (my italics; Finstad's italics omitted).[40]

In this proposition about "what sexuality is" we can again see *the general pattern*: The linguistic form of the proposition pulls in the direction of the discussion's being about questions of fact, that is to say that the proposition seemingly has the status of a *descriptive characterisation*; cf. the formulation "[s]exuality *is not ... but [is]*". It is, however, clear that the proposition, in spite of its linguistic form, cannot be intended as a descriptive characterisation. "Everybody knows" that this is not what sexuality in fact and in the statistics *is like*. The formulation does not describe the factual phenomenon of sexuality, but provides a *normative definition* of the word "sexuality": – First, the formulation provides a normative delimitation of the word's area of application, by excluding phenomena that most people evaluate negatively and by linking the word to phenomena that most people evaluate positively. – Secondly, the formulation provides a tentative normative regulation of the word's appeal function. Partly it does so in an indirect way, through the said normative delimitation of the word's area of application. And partly it does so in a more direct way, by using words with an already established appeal function of this area, cf. the words "communication and personal development", "mutually committed", "share", "mutual respect and equal worth", "for one's own and the other's enjoyment".

The last-mentioned phenomenon, the use of words with an already established appeal function in the constituent that defines, is *the specific feature* of the second

---

40 Finstad, 'Forord' [foreword]. – It is apparent from the context that Finstad is advancing this formulation on behalf of another person. Here the formulation is used only in its capacity of being an illustrative example of a way of using language.

main type of persuasive definition within the general pattern: The defining words ("a", "b", etc. in the schema in section 7.3.1 (2) above) *charge up* the defined word ("x" in the same schema). – They charge up x *from a neutral* position (x = "norm"), or *in the opposite direction* of an existing charge (x = "sexuality", a word that arouses in many people an intuitive fear and defensive position). – They charge up x *with a positive* appeal function ("a", "b", etc. arouse positive feelings), or *with a negative* appeal function ("a", "b", etc. arouse negative feelings). The definitions of "norm" and "sexuality" both charge up with a positive appeal function. They play on words for human beings' self-determination etc.; this is most clearly the case in the example "sexuality", cf. the strongly positively loaded words that are used in the delimitation there. These definitions are thereby suited to bringing about the defined word's promotion to expression of an ideal: for example in contrast to "dependence", "oppression", "prostitution", or the like.

(3) "Meaning"

"Meaning", "meaningful", "meaningless" have been central appeal words in philosophy during the last hundred years. – Since one of the most common directions for persuasive definition of "meaning" is 'operationalising in terms of sense-experience', I shall discuss this group of persuasive definitions in connection with operationalising as a criterion in the setting up of and choice between normative definitions (section III 2.2.2 (3) below).

(4) "Law", "right", "rule of law" and "legal safeguards" [Rechtssicherheit]

"Law", "right", "rule of law" and "legal safeguards" [Rechtssicherheit] are central appeal terms both for lawyers and non-lawyers. – Persuasive definitions of these terms I shall discuss in connection with concealed action influencing as a criterion in the setting up of and choice between normative definitions; and I shall do so with emphasis on lawyers' persuasive definitions of the terms (section III 2.4.2 (1) below).

7.3.3. Some characteristic features of persuasive definitions

In the analysis of what is being defined, I drew a distinction between the structuring function and the naming function of definitions.[41] – In what follows I shall briefly characterise persuasive definitions in the light of this distinction and the examples above. The features that will be mentioned are thus not without reservation concept criteria, but follow from the definition seen in connection with fundamental factual circumstances.

---

[41] See section A 3 for an overview of this distinction and section 4 in the present section B for a more thorough discussion.

(1) Interplay between structuring function and naming function

Characteristic of persuasive definitions is the *interplay* between two elements: On the one hand there is the element in the definition that expresses a *normative structuring* (normative way of categorising the phenomena), for example: "Evaluations are not science", "Propositions that have not been internalised are not norms", "Sexuality is not a thing, a technique, but ...". On the other hand there is the element in the definition that consists in the use of *words with a presupposed appeal function* of this structuring: "science"; "internalisation" ("approval", "acceptance", "consent"); "communication and personal development", "mutually committed", "share", "mutual respect and equal worth", "for one's own and the other's enjoyment".

(2) On the structuring in more detail

(a) The topic here has been instances in which the defined word's area of application is taken as a variable, that is to say, in which the normative structuring is more specifically normative-innovative in relation to the recipients. See section 7.3.1 (4) above, concluding remarks (in the indent), where I draw a boundary with the more rarely occurring instances in which the structuring is normative-traditional, that is to say, in which persuasion is sought simply through changing the appeal function of the naming.

(b) Often the normative-innovative structuring will be held up as the *only tenable* structuring,[42] typically through linguistic intensifiers like "actual", "real", "true", or the like;[43] for example "actual/ real/ true ... science, norm, sexuality ... is ...". – Even though such *absolutisation of aspects* of phenomena is common in the case of persuasive defintions,[44] I do not consider it very expedient to lay down absolutisation as a concept criterion.[45]

(c) There is *no* definitional connection between persuasive definitions and *particular means of structuring*. On the one hand, one can define persuasively

---

42 In contrast to cognition and expression of the fact that phenomena can be seen from a logically speaking infinite number of viewpoints, and that the importance of an aspect is relative to the language user's interests; see section III 2.2.4 (3) below.

43 On such intensifiers, see Stevenson, 'Persuasive Definitions', pp. 35–36; Austin, *Sense and Sensibilia*, pp. 68–77; Lakoff/ Johnson, *Metaphors We Live By*, pp. 123–24; Furberg, *Saying and Meaning*, pp. 60(62)–70; Andersson/ Furberg, *Språk och påverkan* [language and influence], pp. 170(171)–75; Zapffe, *Indføring i litterær Dramaturgi* [introduction to literary dramaturgy], p. 24.

44 The combination of persuasive definitions and absolutisation of aspects is a widespread way of linguistically veiling one's evaluations and choices; see section IV 3.2 (1) below.

45 Stevenson, 'Persuasive Definitions', pp. 38–39, seems to lay down absolutisation of aspects as a concept criterion: "[W]hen [the definition] in no way suggests that this is *the one* legitimate sort of classification, then the definition will not be called persuasive" (Stevenson's italics). In *Ethics and Language*, absolutisation of aspects has, on the other hand, the status of an (often occurring) empirical feature; see e.g. pp. 213–14.

through all the means of structuring that have earlier been discussed (sections 5–6 above). On the other hand, there is none of these that must always be an element. *Nor* must evaluation prescription in the connotation of the concept always be an element. An instance-type of persuasive definitions without evaluation prescription in the connotation of the concept is many definitions, in academic subjects, of words which have emotive value in everyday life and in the subject: for example Ross' definition of "(valid) law" and "legal science" (sections 7.2 (1) cf. 7.3.2 (1), above). Another and in and of itself randomly chosen example of persuasive definitions without evaluation prescription is many definitions of "democracy". One associates strong and positive feelings with this word (compare contrasting words like "dictatorship", "despotism", "police state", or the like). In this respect the word is well suited as a point of departure for persuasive definition. At the same time the connotation is frequently determined without evaluation prescription: for example as a system in which citizens over a particular age, irrespective of sex, race, occupation, beliefs, or the like, can at certain specified intervals choose who is to run the state.

> The formulation "essentially contested concepts" has gained a certain currency.[46] This formulation was introduced by Gallie, as a term for "concepts the proper use of which inevitably involves endless disputes about their proper uses on the part of their users".[47] From Gallie's further definition[48] it is apparent that a positive evaluation is a definitional feature;[49] and from his further discussion otherwise it is apparent that many of the concepts to which he refers, are in fact named by means of appeal words.[50] However, it remains unclear what is meant by Gallie's saying that a "concept" is "essentially" contested, and why a "concept" should have this property. One cause of this lack of clarity is that Gallie does not (sufficiently clearly) distinguish between on the one hand the source of dis/agreement that lies in the exercise of any evaluation prescription there might be in the connotation of the concept (sections 6.1, cf. 5.4.2 (1) and 6.2, above); and on the other hand desires to monopolise appealing naming for one's own standpoint, be it a standpoint as an element in the exercise of evaluation prescription or standpoints otherwise (the present section 7).[51] Whether these two features of reality occur

---

46 As examples, see from respectively philosophy, social science, history, and law, Hurley, 'Objectivity and Disagreement', p. 83; Lukes, *Power: A Radical View*, pp. 9, 26; Foner, *The Story of American Freedom*, p. xiv; O'Fallon, 'Adjudication and Contested Concepts: The Case of Equal Protection', pp. 20, cf. 22 et seq.

47 Gallie, 'Essentially Contested Concepts', p. 169.

48 Op. cit., pp. 171–80.

49 Op. cit., p. 171: "[An essentially contested concept] must be appraisive in the sense that it signifies or accredits some kind of valued achievement" (Gallie's italics omitted).

50 Op. cit., pp. 168, cf. 180–87: "work of art", "democracy", "Christian doctrine".

51 See in this connection the fact that Gallie alternates between "concept" and "term" in a way that suggests he does not ascribe to this distinction any significance specific to his conceptualisation. For example he writes (op. cit., p. 168): "We find groups of people disagreeing about the proper use of the concepts, e.g., of art, of democracy, of the Christian tradition. When we examine the different uses of these terms ...". And for example he alternates without further explanation between "appraisive con-

severally or conjointly (section 7.2 (1) above and the present item (c)), an apt picture of actually occurring dis/agreement requires that one has concepts of the two reality features and does not glide theoretically between them.

(3) On the naming in more detail

Exercise of the naming function (choice of linguistic expression for the normative structuring) has by definition and in fact a *central place* in the case of persuasive definitions: It is the kind and strength of the words' appeal to feelings that decide whether, and if so to what degree, the definition has psychological causality in the form of a persuasive effect; that is to say, whether we are confronted with a persuasive definition at all, and if so, how successful it is.

In the case of many other definition types neither naming nor particular features of the naming are definitionally necessary (section 4.2 (3) above). – In actual fact the exercise of the naming function may have a central place also in the case of other definition types: For an area-in-thought to gain ground, the concept designation ought not to be too long, it ought to give the right associations, etc.[52] Nevertheless, in the case of other definition types the exercise of the naming function is not without exception of *such* central importance for whether the definition is to achieve its goal as in the case of persuasive definitions.

(4) The tacit character

Further, persuasive definitions are characterised by the fact that the features now mentioned (the interplay between normative-innovative structuring and the appeal function of the naming) are *not made clear*. For if they were, the persuasive effect would disappear: The person to be persuaded would then become aware that no argument was being presented, only a psychological appeal via choice of words with a potential persuasive effect. – I should remind the reader that there does not need to be persuasive intent, that is to say that "the person to be persuaded" can *also* be the person defining. Language then serves to strengthen the language user's own self (section 7.3.1 (1) above, in the text at note 17; section 7.3.2 (1) (c)(ii) above, at and in note 36). This may contribute to explaining that a proposition's status of being a definition is not made clear in the examples above.

(5) Invocation

Many formulations *do not express persuasive definitions so directly* as the examples above, at the same time as their *relationship to persuasive definitions is very close*. – An example may illustrate this. The sentence schema "My philosophy is ..." has become common in more prosaic contexts too: cf. "management

---

cept" (op. cit., p. 171; see the quotation in note 49 above) and "appraisive term" (op. cit., pp. 180, 182).

52 See section 4.2 (5) above on a number of factors that may explain what name an area acquires, and whether the area gains ground or is impeded because of the name.

philosophy", "purchasing philosophy", "production philosophy", and the like. Directly one then states one's views (on management, purchasing, production, or the like). By presupposition one advances a persuasive definition of "philosophy", through which one partly ascribes certain qualities to one's views: they are well-considered, wise, independent, and the like; and one partly ascribes certain qualities to oneself: one is an intelligent and wise person with integrity.

Such a close relationship between the stated and the presupposed I term *"invocation"*. – Invocation of persuasive definitions involves a *two-step* invocation. First, there is the invocation of the persuasive definition itself. Secondly, there is the invocation of the normative propositions to which the definition by presupposition marks adherence: cf. the "philosophy" example as well as the analysis of the main examples above.[53]

(1)↔(5) Persuasive definitions may in the light of this be characterised as appealing naming of normative-innovative structurings – *without* either the proposition's status of being a definition, or the naming's appeal to presupposed feelings in the recipients, or the structuring's normative-innovative modality being made clear.

53 On invocation of normative propositions *without* going via persuasive definitions, see Sundby, *Om normer* [on norms], pp. 174–76; Eckhoff/ Sundby, *Rettssystemer* [legal systems], pp. 64–65; *Rechtssysteme*, pp. 58–59.

8. The modality of definitions II: Dimensions, degrees, fusion

The question of whether the definition is descriptive or normative is closely connected with certain other central questions. My discussions above in the present section B provide a basis for pointing to two connected central questions (sections 8.1–8.2).

8.1. The distinction between descriptivity and normativity can in the case of definitions relate to different dimensions

One central question is what features of reality the definition describes or normatively regulates. – As is apparent from my discussions, definitions can relate to a number of different *dimensions*:

There is the structuring dimension, i.e. division into areas-in-thought (sections 4.1 cf. 4.3.2, above); and there is the naming dimension, i.e. choice of linguistic expression for the area (sections 4.2 cf. 4.3.2, above).

When it comes to the structuring dimension, the definition can relate to the connotation, in that the definition is given the form of connotation specification (sections 5.1 cf. 5.3–5.5, above); or the definition can relate to the denotation, in that the definition is given the form of denotation specification (sections 5.2 cf. 5.3–5.5, above).

And when it comes to the connotation specification, the criteria can in respect of their content be specified as purely cognitive or as prescribing an evaluation (section 6.1 above); and the criteria can in respect of their strength be specified as factors or as conditions (section 6.2 above).

8.2. The strength of normative definitions; dimensions and degrees

Given that one has determined the definition's modality as normative, then my discussions above make it possible to give a conceptual representation of intuitions about the strength of normative definitions.[1]

(1) The modality
(2) The scope of the specification of person and situation
(3) The mode of use of the concept criteria: Factor or condition
(4) The relationship to other language usage: Normative-traditional or normative-innovative definition

(1) The modality

In the modality dimension one can rank normative definitions along a scale of strength from (weakest) qualification (section 3.3.2 (1) above), across recommendations, further across promises, to commands and prohibitions (section 3.3.1 above).

(2) The scope of the specification of person and situation

When it comes to normative definitions' specification of person and situation, one can rank such definitions along a scale of strength from (weakest) definitions addressed to a single person or situation (see for example section 3.3.1 (2) above on normative regulation of one's own use of language), across a graduated scale of intermediate instances, to definitions addressed to all language users or all situations in which language is used (see for example section 3.3.2 (3) above).

(3) The mode of use of the concept criteria: Factor or condition

When it comes to the mode of use of the concept criteria in interpretation and subsumption, one can rank normative definitions along a scale of strength from (weakest) definitions that lay down criteria in the form of factors, across definitions in which the factors are given increasing weight, to definitions that lay

---

[1] Concerning the use of the word "strength", the same applies here as in the case of definitions in the form of instance-type propositions (section 5.4.2 (1)(c) above): By the *"strength"* of normative definitions I do not mean any deeper unitary property, but those features which are mentioned in the main text in what follows, and which have in common that, with more or less determinate views on the part of language users as a starting point, they provide language users with a basis for ranking instance-type propositions. – *Analysis of dis/agreement* can be a reason for seeing these features in relation to one another: Formulations that show disagreement in one strength dimension can show agreement in another strength dimension or when several strength dimensions are seen in relation to one another.

down criteria in the form of conditions. And the latter can again be ranked along a scale of strength from definitions that lay down necessary conditions, across definitions that lay down sufficient conditions, to definitions that lay down necessary and sufficient conditions (sections 6.2 cf. 3.2.2 (5)(c), above).

(4) The relationship to other language usage: Normative-traditional or normative-innovative definition

On the basis of the definition's relationship to other language usage, one can rank normative definitions from (weakest) normative-traditional, to normative-innovative (section 3.3.4 above). – A realistic mapping requires, however, that in applying this yardstick one distinguish between *different dimensions of the definition*: dimensions with respect to which the yardstick shows sliding scales, and with respect to which the results in one dimension do not necessarily coincide with the results in the other dimensions (section 4.3.3 above).

8.3. The distinction between descriptivity and normativity is itself graduated: See section F on fusion of descriptive and normative propositions

One main conclusion of my discussions above is thus that the *area of application* of the distinction between descriptivity and normativity ought not to be seen as the definition pure and simple, but as a number of different *dimensions* of the definition (sections 8.1 cf. 4–6, above).

Even if this conclusion is accepted, most people will nevertheless probably still presuppose that the individual definition proposition is *either* descriptive *or* normative: The fact that the distinction has a heterogeneous area of application does not entail that it is graduated. And when thought has nothing else to hold on to, it seems to tend naturally towards bipartite division (dichotomy). In addition comes the fact that writers with great authority (academic, scientific and philosophical discussion) often seem to take it for granted that the distinction between descriptive and normative propositions is a dichotomy.

On the basis of *experience of lawyers' language and argumentation*, I shall argue that the distinction between descriptivity and normativity ought to be seen as a *graduated* distinction. As I do not limit this assertion to definitions, but make it also in the case of other propositions that are termed "descriptive"/ "normative", I shall postpone the discussion until after the remaining fundamental proposition types have also been discussed. Thereafter, under the heading "*fusion* (of descriptive and normative propositions)", I shall justify my assertion in more detail (section F below).

9. Taking a critically reflexive turn. The definition theory applied to the definition theory

(1) The definition theory in the present work has a *descriptive purpose* (sections 1–2 above): to provide a systematic survey of, and insight into, features of a particular group of propositions, namely propositions occurring in fact and formulated in everyday language that fall under the fundamental concept of 'definition' in the work. This survey and this insight are at the same time self-cognition: "We all" (all competent language users) take part in analysis and argumentation formulated in everyday language (if not otherwise, at least in conversation with ourselves), and thereby in the critically reflexive form which is the topic of the present work and of which the definition theory maps a part.

The individual concepts in my definition theory have been defined as the work progressed, as steps in the presentation of the theory. These definitions *can themselves be made objects of the definition theory*:

The definitions of the concepts in the definition theory (the table of contents for the present section B shows most of these concepts) all have both a *structuring function* and a *naming function* (section 4 above). They are all *normative* definitions, more precisely *stipulated* normative definitions (section 3.3.1 above). The normative modality has systematically throughout the form of a *promise* with respect to my own language usage (section 3.3.1 (2) above). The promise aspect is systematically throughout combined with *recommendation* with respect to other people's use of language (section 3.3.1 (3)(b) above), *provided that* others share the work's descriptive interest: more immediately, a recommendation provided that others share the descriptive interest in relation to the phenomenon delimited through the fundamental concept of 'definition'; more mediately, a recommendation provided that others share the descriptive interest in relation to the critically reflexive form which is the topic of the work and of which the definition theory maps a part (Chapter I above). – In addition to the said normative modalities, the definitions of the concepts in the definition theory have a purely *factual end-means aspect* (section 3.3.1 (2)(d) above): If one wants to understand the work's definition theory, one must take as a basis the definitions of the theory's concepts and terms presented as the work progressed.

The language usage of my definition theory does not have any one single *relationship to other language usage*; on this point there is no basis for general statements, as there is in relation to the definition dimensions mentioned in the preceding paragraph. – As steps in the presentation of the theory, a good deal has been said about the relationship to other language usage, and there is no occasion for repetition or summary. The illustration begun above of the application of the definition theory to the definitions in the theory itself I shall therefore take further, more particularly in relation to the definition of the fundamental concept of 'definition' (on the fundamental concept, see in particular sections A 2 (1) and B 2, above):

In the *structuring dimension* (section 4.1 above) my definition of 'definition' has the *form* of connotation specification, in contrast to denotation specification (section 5 above); of purely cognitive criteria, in contrast to evaluation prescription (section 6.1 above); of conditions, in contrast to factors (section 6.2 above); and of a surveyable set of necessary and sufficient conditions, in contrast to unsurveyable alternative sets of sufficient conditions (section 3.2.2 (5)(c)(iii) above). – In these formal features, my definition of 'definition' is *normative-traditional* (sections 3.3.4 and 4.3.3, above) in relation to much philosophy and logic.

According to its more specific *content*, however, the connotation specification in my definition of 'definition' is *normative-innovative* in relation to much philosophy and logic; this is so partly in that I exclude characterisations, including characterisations under such names as "essential definition" and "real definition" (section 2.3 (1) above), and partly in that I do not lay down determinacy requirements as a criterion (sections 2.2 and 4.1 (3), above).

In the *naming dimension* (section 4.2 above) my definition is normative-traditional in relation to widespread language usage, be it in analysis and argumentation formulated in everyday language or in formalised science or in logic.

The definition is not suited to being a *persuasive definition*, in that neither the word "definition" nor the words that are used for defining have such appeal to emotions as are then necessary (section 7.3 above).

(2) Now, at the end of the presentation of my definition theory, the necessary basis is at hand for specifying in what respects I consider this theory to be innovative. It is innovative through (a) its (more generally, the present work's) *perspective and topic* (Chapter I above, cf. section II B 1–2 as well as the presentation in section II B in its entirety); (b) normative-innovative features of the *individual* definitions, as outlined by way of example in item (1) above and more comprehensively covered in the systematic presentation; (c) *the systematic whole*: I do not know of any correspondingly nuanced and coherent conceptual model for mapping the modalities, functions and means of definitions occurring in fact and formulated in everyday language.

C Characterisations

1. Introduction; survey of topics concerning characterisations that are discussed in this work

By the word *"characterisation"* I mean, as previously explained (section A 2 (3)–(4) above), propositions that are neither definitions nor analytically un/true; that is to say, propositions which do not contribute to determining the meanings of linguistic entities (do not contribute to determining concepts), but which presuppose this topic (in contrast to definitions, which thematise it), and say something beyond what lies in the concept criteria (in contrast to analytically un/true propositions). What is said beyond the concept criteria may be about non/existence of phenomena that satisfy the concept criteria, or about (presupposedly existing) phenomena's properties beyond the concept criteria. And independently of this, characterisations can have descriptive, normative, or fused descriptive and normative modality.

The discussion of characterisations in the present section C is less comprehensive than the discussion of definitions in section B above. This is so partly because those features of characterisations that are of interest in relation to the perspective and topic of the present work have to a greater extent been discussed by other writers. And it is so partly because much of what it is relevant to bring out will be taken up elsewhere in this work: the *boundary* between characterisations on the one hand and definitions and analytically un/true propositions on the other (sections A above and D and G below); the *modality* of characterisations (section F below); the *tenability criteria* of descriptive characterisations (section III 3 below); the *flight from* normative characterisations, by clothing them in language attire that is polysemous between the descriptive, logical and normative, or that is one-sidedly descriptive or logical (Chapter IV below); the intimate *interplay* between definitions and characterisations in lawyers' language and argumentation de lege lata (section IV 3.3.3 below); and *combinations* of the fundamental proposition types into more complex patterns of analysis (Chapter V below).

In the present section C there is a major emphasis on questions concerning *non-empirical characterisations*, i.e. characterisations that to a greater or lesser degree refer to extra-sensory entities, for example "divine precept/ the law of reason/ the law of Nature". However, as otherwise in the present work, the *aim* is not standpoints on the tenability of such or other actually occurring propositions. What it is (Chapter I above), is that of demonstrating, and creating an awareness of, the existence, content and factual significance of a specific critically reflexive form (I 4–6), with a certain independence in relation to controversial questions of a philosophical, moral, legal, political or similar kind (I 6, II A 8); and thereby, of demonstrating, and creating an awareness of, the factual significance of analysis of dis/agreement on the basis of this critically reflexive form.

2. Non-empirical characterisations

2.1. Descriptive

(1) Concept and instance-types
(2) Problems of justification
(3) Normative function

(1) Concept and instance-types

By *"non-empirical descriptive characterisations"* I mean propositions that assert or deny a non-empirical reality.

A common *area* for non-empirical descriptive characterisations is the setting up of and choice between *concepts of 'concept'*. One uses concepts of 'concept' that presuppose a non-empirical level of reality, so that discussions about these concepts of 'concept' to a great extent take the form of non-empirical characterisations: One asserts or denies the level of reality that the concept of 'concept' in question builds on. For example, one asserts or denies the reality level of Plato's ideas, concepts as one saw them within radical realism in the medieval conflict over the status of universals, Kant's transcendental categories, or Frege's Begriffe (section B 4.1 (1)↔(2)(a)(i) cf. (5), above).

Another common area for non-empirical descriptive characterisations is the setting up of and choice between *criteria for the tenability of normative propositions*. One uses tenability criteria that presuppose a non-empirical level of reality, so that discussions about these criteria to a great extent take the form of non-empirical characterisations: One asserts or denies the level of reality that the criterion in question builds on. For example, one asserts or denies the reality level of divine precept, an absolute law of reason or an eternal law of Nature.

We can distinguish between non-empirical descriptive characterisations according to whether they assert or deny a non-empirical reality:

In the case of the categorical imperative Kant puts forward a *positive* non-empirical characterisation. He asserts the existence of a non-empirical reality: more precisely a moral law of reason independent of all experience.

As a step in his theory of valid law Ross puts forward a *negative* non-empirical characterisation. He denies the existence of other levels of reality (other sources of cognition) than sense-experience, and claims that possible criteria of the tenability of propositions must be taken either from formal logic or from sense-experience: If a proposition is neither analytically un/true nor capable of being tested against sense-experience, then it is not possible to assess its tenability.

The two examples now given (from Kant and Ross) will be used as *recurring examples* in my discussion of non-empirical characterisations in what follows. They have had great influence; they are still relevant; and the contrast between them seems to point to something general, in that similar contrasts often crop up when in the case of disagreement one retraces the steps in the justification.

What justification situation does one meet when one attempts to take a standpoint on and choose between such contradictory characterisations as in the two examples?

(2) Problems of justification

In attempts to survey and reflect on justifications for non-empirical descriptive propositions, one meets inter alia a tension between postulates (item (a)) and transcendental argumentation (item (b)).

(a) By *"postulates"* I mean characterisations that are not given a purportedly serious justification.

The *role* of postulates is different in the case of respectively empirical and non-empirical descriptive characterisations.

In the case of *empirical characterisations* there is wide agreement about the relevant criteria for the assessment of such characterisations: Provided that the propositions are free of contradiction and conform with sense-experience, then they are true. And provided that the propositions are free of contradiction and do not conform with sense-experience, then they are untrue.

> Often one must conclude that one knows little or nothing about the part in question of the world of experience: for example about what effects a particular statute has or about what effects a proposed statute will have if it is passed. But justification for a conclusion of (justification for a characterisation with) little preponderance of probability, or of ignorance, is also a justification. Such characterisations I therefore do not term "postulates".

In the case of *non-empirical characterisations* one does not find any corresponding agreement about the relevant tenability criteria. This leads to some characteristic *differences* from empirical characterisations, with respect to the role of postulates (items (i)–(ii)).

(i) Postulates are considered *more legitimate* in the case of non-empirical characterisations than in the case of empirical ones. One accepts to a greater degree that characterisations of a non-empirical reality refer to faith: "God's existence is a question of faith", or to a special intuition or sense of the non-empirical: "The cognition of the good is a question of beholding the idea of the good", "The capacity for beholding the good/ the beautiful is not given to just anybody", or the like. Most people will not accept such references to faith, intuition or special senses in the case of empirical characterisations.

Problematic postulates are not the preserve of the unschooled. Even the sharpest and most influential writers use them. An example is Alf Ross in his definitive presentation of his theory of valid law.[1] – In this presentation Ross denies the existence of other levels of reality (other sources of cognition) than sense-experience, and thus of other tenability criteria than analytic un/truth and dis/agreement with sense-experience. Propositions the tenability of which cannot be decided in one of these ways are in Ross' language without "representative meaning" (pp. 16–18/ pp. 6–8), "semantic meaning" (p. 16/ p. 6), or "logical meaning" (pp. 16, 52/ p. 40); they are not "scientific" (in particular pp. 19 and 52–53/ pp. 39–40), but on the contrary "metaphysical" (p. 52/ p. 40). – Ross uses strong words of the significance of his denial of non-empirical criteria: "the innermost nerve in the question of the empirical content of legal science" (p. 52/ not in the English edition). However, he does not provide any justification.[2] And this is striking; for if one applies Ross' propositions about tenability criteria to these propositions themselves, then they seem to be without "(logical) meaning" and "metaphysical" (section I 4 above, last indent).

(ii) Another difference between the role of postulates in the case of respectively empirical and non-empirical characterisations is that it is *more difficult to change a proposition's status from a postulate to a justified proposition* in the case of non-empirical characterisations. – In the case of empirical characterisations there is a great degree of agreement about what investigations are appropriate in the individual area to check the tenability of the characterisation. Consequently in the case of empirical characterisations one knows what one must do to meet an objection that one is simply postulating. – This is different in the case of non-empirical characterisations. Given the lack of agreement about what tenability criteria are relevant, then it is relatively speaking more difficult to meet an objection that one is simply postulating:

One possibility of meeting the objection is to refer to faith, intuition, or the like (item (i) above). – Another possibility is that one *constructs one's own mode of justification*. One example is Goodman and Rawls, who lay down concepts of 'reflective equilibrium', and other writers, who lay down more or less related concepts of 'coherence' (sections V 3.4–3.5). Another example is Kant, who lays down a concept of 'transcendental argumentation' (item (b) below); through this concept Kant constitutes a form of argumentation directed against the fundamental rationality structure of empiricism, of which Ross is also a representative.[3]

(b) The term *"transcendental argumentation"* is used of types of justification that can be fairly different from one another. In what follows, building on Kant, I

[1] Ross, *Om ret og retfærdighed*, Chapter II; English edition: *On Law and Justice*, Chapter 2. The references in parentheses in the rest of the paragraph are to this book; the references before the slashes are to the Danish edition, and the references after the slashes are to the English edition. On several of the relevant points the English edition is briefer than the Danish edition. For a translation of some of the relevant sentences omitted or rewritten in the English edition, see section B 7.3.2 (1)(a) above.

[2] Ross' language and argumentation has strong elements of persuasive definitions (section B 7.3.2 (1) above). Persuasive definitions, however, I do not consider to be justifications.

[3] Sections B 5.2 (5)(b) above and III 2.2.2 (3)(a) below.

shall outline those features that I consider most important in relation to the perspective and topic of the present work.[4]

The relationship of the concepts to one another is subject to a distinct form of necessity: the *formal-logical*. The formal-logical necessity shows itself in analytically un/true propositions, i.e. propositions that are un/true by definition, for example "this circle is square/ round". Such formal-logical necessity is considered to be stronger than the necessity to which factual phenomena are subject: *empirical necessity*. Empirical necessity shows itself in empirical characterisations, i.e. propositions in respect of which one must have recourse to sense-experience to check their truth value, for example "this circle has been drawn with a pencil".

A recurring question in philosophy since Kant is whether also the relationship of concepts to empirical reality is subject to a distinct form of necessity, the *transcendental-logical*, which is different from both formal-logical and empirical necessity. It was Kant's main point – in opposition to empiricism, with Hume at the forefront – that one must assume such a transcendental-logical relation between thought (the cognising and acting subject) and reality.

> With Rossvær we can formulate a central assertion on the part of Kant as follows: "[T]he limits for referring to something objective are narrower than the limits for what it is not self-contradictory to deny …".[5] – Compare for example on the one hand the fact that in ordinary language usage it is not blatantly self-contradictory to say that an empirical event does not have any cause, and on the other hand Kant's view of the status of the pair of concepts 'cause–effect', see the main text immediately in what follows.

On the basis of the assumption of such a transcendental-logical relation, Kant argued for the existence of *non-empirical features* of *human cognition and action*: First, the forms of intuition, space and time. Secondly, the categories, i.e. certain fundamental concepts, such as 'cause–effect'. And finally, a moral law of reason, "der kategorische Imperativ": "[H]andle nur nach derjenigen Maxime, durch die du zugleich wollen kannst, daß sie ein allgemeines Gesetz werde."[6]

The transcendental structures' not being empirical means inter alia that they cannot be seen as *innate* properties;[7] nevertheless, many understand Kant to mean

4 These features will be more precisely placed and discussed in relation to the conceptual apparatus of the present work in section 2.3 below; the present item (b) is also a (minimum) basis for the discussion there.

5 Rossvær, 'Transcendentale problemstillinger i moderne filosofi' [transcendental problems in modern philosophy], p. 108.

6 Kant, *Grundlegung zur Metaphysik der Sitten*, p. 42 (Academy edition p. 421). – On some aspects of the relationship between Kant's various formulations of the categorical imperative, see O'Neill, 'Universal Laws and Ends-in-Themselves', passim; Guyer, 'The Possibility of the Categorical Imperative', passim; Storheim, 'Innledning' [introduction], pp. xvi–xxv.

7 Kant, *Von der Form der Sinnen- und Verstandeswelt und ihren Gründen*, § 8, § 15 Zusatz, concluding remarks; *Kritik der reinen Vernunft*, B 91.

the opposite.[8] – At the same time the basis for the transcendental structures is not pure thinking. Thought alone cannot cognise anything but propositions that are true by definition, for example "all bachelors are unmarried". If thought seeks cognition in isolation from human experience, for example cognition of the world as unconditioned and a totality ("the first cause", and the like), it gets into insoluble problems: a "transzendental Dialektik".[9]

Kant thus criticises *pure empiricism*: He argues that our cognition and our morality are only possible given the said transcendental structures. – At the same time, however, he also criticises *pure rationalism*: The transcendental contributions in the processes of cognition and action lie literally there, *in* the processes. They are *immanent*, not transcendent, in relation to our experience and action.[10] – The transcendental contributions are thus not objects of sense perception, but at the same time they are bound to man qua empirical sensory being. They lie in our cognition and action precisely in the respect that this cognition and action *cannot be conceived of in isolation from* our empirical experience.

Transcendentally necessary structures are *features of the already constituted unity* within which our experience and action move: the already constituted unity of cognising subject and a world that can be cognised. Such structures are not constituted through definitions. They exist *independently of* our factual language habits and our factual patterns of analysis and justification: A Kant-inspired philosopher of science would, for example, be able to claim that the causality category came into play as a structuring element in our experience, *irrespective of* changing paradigms in the sciences. And a Kant-inspired moral philosopher would be able to claim that the moral law, formulated in the categorical imperative, applied *irrespective of* man's changing empirical circumstances, of social, economic, or other kinds.

(3) Normative function

Descriptive characterisations of a specifically normative reality seem to be able to fill several of the *same practical functions* as normative characterisations. Compare on the one hand normative characterisations, such as: "You must not kill", "Killing is forbidden", "It is your duty not to kill", and on the other hand descriptive characterisations of a specifically normative reality, such as: "Divine precept is that life is sacrosanct", "According to the law of reason life has absolute value", "Man's place in Nature is sacrosanct". – The said proposition formulations all seem able to be used for inter alia communicating something it is reasonable to call "the same message": for example in teaching children, discussing with other adults or disciplining oneself.

---

8 See e.g. Kelsen, 'Die Entstehung des Kausalgesetzes aus dem Vergeltungsprinzip', pp. 102, 125–26; Madsen, *Psykologiens historie* [history of psychology], pp. 31, 37.

9 Kant, *Kritik der reinen Vernunft*, B 349 et seq.

10 In contrast to concepts of 'the unconditioned' and 'totality'; op. cit., B 383.

If one supposes that the proposition formulations stand in different positions with respect to conditions for acceptance or with respect to the stability or motivational force of the acceptance, one has a starting point for possible *strategic choice* of proposition formulation.[11]

2.2. Normative

Can non-empirical characterisations be normative? The problem intuition behind the question is whether one can imagine *genuine* normative propositions addressed *from* human beings *to* divine beings, reason or other forms of non-empirical order.

The question must clearly enough be answered in the affirmative if by "normative propositions" one means spurious normative propositions, i.e. descriptive propositions about normative propositions; see for example in section 2.1 above, on descriptive characterisations of a specifically normative reality.

It is common for human beings to address normative propositions to *extra-sensory lawmakers, typically gods*. It may be a matter of normative propositions in the form of promises, decision propositions, requests, supplications, or value propositions; but it is seldom a matter of duty propositions, since human beings consider themselves as being in a relationship of subordination to the divinity.

On the other hand it does seem to be uncommon for normative propositions to be addressed to *specifically practical reason*. I do not know of any examples of the same person's *both* justifying a normative proposition as a commandment of reason *and* advancing an incompatible normative proposition addressed to that same reason: for example both accepting Kant's argumentation for the categorical imperative and requesting that it must not apply in an individual instance.

The explanation for this difference is no doubt that one uses the word "reason" of a property of *man* and the word "god" of a subject *separate from* man. There is *then*, by definition or by psychology, little or no room in relation to reason for the interaction between the individual and the divinity (prayer, comfort, or the like) that is usual in a great deal of religion.

However, there seem to be *graduated transitions* from concepts of 'reason' covering properties of man, to religions' concepts of 'god'; and thus to be by

---

11 Compare Næss, 'Ayer on Metaphysics, a Critical Commentary by a Kind of Metaphysician', p. 339: "The sentence 'ultimately all life is one' is obviously intended to have a normative function. Why not transform it into a kind of moral precept about treating non-human life forms decently? Because moral precepts are weak, whereas a changed way of conceiving reality is potentially very strong in its motivational force. If you tend to 'see yourself' in all living beings, decent treatment is quite natural (provided your relation to yourself is good)."; 'Self-realization: An Ecological Approach to Being in the World', p. 236: "I am suggesting ... the supremacy of environmental ontology and realism over environmental ethics as a means of invigorating the environmental movement in the years to come."

> degrees more room for normative propositions from man to "reason". An example can be found in Hegel's system, when he seems to use the word "Vernunft" of a historical necessity, which concretely manifests itself in the laws of the state, and to which the individual must subject himself.[12]

2.3. "Essential definition"

Propositions referring to non-empirical features *can* be definitions in relation to the concept of 'definition' laid down in the present work: This will be the case where the proposition links non-empirical features to the meaning of a linguistic entity (to a concept), for example: "I am not going to use the word "law" of (I lay down the concept of 'law' so that it does not cover) norms contrary to divine precept/ the law of reason/ the law of Nature." – If one does use the term "essential definition" at all, then in my opinion the most reasonable thing is to use the term of such instances of non-empirical criteria for the use of linguistic entities (non-empirical concept criteria).

> I say "the most reasonable thing", because it is difficult to find alternatives. There is hardly reason to use such a pretentious term as "essential definition" of descriptive or normative empirical definitions, of descriptive or normative empirical characterisations, or of analytically un/true propositions.

However, "essential definitions" in this sense do not capture, but only *presuppose*, what is *interesting* about propositions referring to non-empirical features: *To what extent is it correct that a non-empirical reality exists?* (the ontological question). Or: *How can we cognise this non-empirical reality?* (the epistemological question).[13]

For *illustration* we can take our point of departure in *Kant's categorical imperative*, in its capacity of proposition about *morality*. The next question should then be: Does Kant's categorical imperative provide a definition of the concept of 'morality/ moral action', or a characterisation of an already delimited phenomenon of morality/ moral action? – However, the central real problem of the categorical imperative is the ontological and epistemological premisses: How would Kant justify the existence and cognisability of the categorical imperative, and would his justification be tenable? (compare section 2.1 (2)(b) above). – *Given* Kant's answer to the question of justification, then it may seem less important whether one says that the categorical imperative provides a (normative) definition, in so far as it says how Kant lays down a concept of 'morality/ moral action'; or whether one says that the categorical imperative provides a characterisa-

---

[12] Hegel, *Grundlinien der Philosophie des Rechts*, §§ 142 et seq., in particular §§ 144–45 with Additions [Zusätze]; compare the discussion of Kant's concept of 'reason' in Remark and Addition to § 135.

[13] The two questions mentioned can in many connections be seen as two different perspectives on what it is reasonable to call "the same problem", compare Eng, 'Noen synspunkter på en teori om etikk, rett og erkjennelse' [some views on a theory of ethics, law and cognition], p. 294.

tion, in so far as it says something about non-empirical properties of moral thinking and action.[14] – It is, however, not unimportant for the further development of the discussion which perspective one chooses: True enough both perspectives are possible. But the characterisation perspective captures the real problems better than the definition perspective. In the definition perspective it is easy to think: "Kant has his concept of 'morality/ moral action'. We have ours. And that is that." Such a train of thought would be *unjustified trivialisation* of real ontological and epistemological problems.

The point about where our cognition interests lie applies not only in relation to propositions that *assert* a non-empirical reality, like Kant's propositions, but also in relation to propositions that *deny* such a reality. – For illustration we can take our point of departure in *Ross' theory of valid law*. Large parts of Ross' definitive presentation are formulated as discussions in the first place of what it takes for something to be able to be called "science", and in the second place of how legal dogmatics must be conducted to satisfy these criteria for science.[15] The next question should then be: Does Ross' theory of valid law provide a definition of the concept of 'legal/ science', or a characterisation of an already delimited phenomenon of legal/ science? – However, the central real problem of Ross' theory is the ontological and epistemological premisses: How would Ross justify the non-existence, or, as the case may be, the non-cognisability, of non-empirical criteria, that is to say (given Ross' concept of 'the empirical', compare section B 7.3.2 (1)(a) above), how would Ross justify that one is necessarily thrown upon criteria taken from sense-experience, for example judicial behaviour; and would his justification be tenable (compare section 2.1 (2)(a)(i) above)? – *Given* Ross' answer to the question of justification, then it may also here seem less important whether one says that Ross' theory provides a (normative) definition, in so far as it says how Ross lays down a concept of 'legal/ science'; or whether one says that Ross' theory provides a characterisation, in so far as it says something about the impossibility of non-empirical criteria for cognition of norms.[16] – However, as in relation to Kant's categorical imperative, it is not unimportant for the further development of the discussion which perspective one adopts: Both perspectives are no doubt possible. But here too the characterisation perspective captures the real problems better than the definition perspective. In the definition perspective it is easy to think: "Ross has his concept of 'legal/ science'. We have ours. And that is that." Such a train of thought would again be *unjustified trivialisation* of real ontological and epistemological problems.

---

[14] Or whether one says that Kant's propositions form a combination, compare Chapter V below on reconstruction and redefinition.

[15] See the references in the indent below.

[16] Or whether one says that Ross' propositions form a combination, compare Chapter V below on reconstruction and redefinition. – See in this connection Ross' terminology in *On Law and Justice*, pp. 45–46, where he terms his propositions partly "analysis" (p. 45 final paragraph) and partly "definition" (p. 46 first paragraph).

> Ross himself contributes to such trivialisation, in that in the definitive presentation of his theory of valid law he only postulates his standpoint on the ontological and epistemological problems (section 2.1 (2)(a)(i) above) and for the rest gives his argumentation the form of a persuasive definition of "legal/ science" (section B 7.3.2 (1) above).

These examples can be *generalised* and used as a basis for a recommendation concerning how one *ought* to argue in particular situations: In argumentation situations in which one is faced with propositions that build on ontological or epistemological *premisses that are viewed as problematic*, then it is in the first instance these ontological and epistemological premisses themselves that the discussion ought to concentrate on.

Such propositions, which aim to answer ontological or epistemological questions, are not "definitions", but "characterisations" in my terminology. To go back to the examples: Concentrating on the ontological and epistemological premisses for Kant's and Ross' discussions means, first, that in their argumentation one *looks for* characterisations of certain phenomena delimited through presupposition: respectively human action and morality, and the activity of legal dogmatics. And secondly, it means that one *asks for* the tenability criteria for, and the tenability of, these characterisations (section 2.1 (2) above).

3. The strength of characterisations[1]

3.1. The strength of descriptive characterisations

(1) The guideline and instance-type structure of action explanations
(2) Strength dimensions of descriptive characterisations of a non-empirical kind

(1) The guideline and instance-type structure of action explanations

(a) By *"explanations"* I mean characterisations that place what one is talking about *in relation to* other phenomena, in order thereby to provide a better understanding of why what one is talking about exists or not, or why it is as it is. An example is: "Offences of this kind are committed because there is so much to gain from offending, and the risk of detection is so small."

Explanations *presuppose and build on* suppositions about relationships, inter alia causal relationships and motivational relationships. – By *"causal relationship"* I mean partly the strongest form of relationship: "deterministic relationships", and partly weaker forms of relationship: "statistical relationships". By *"motivational relationship"* I mean relationship between motive and action.

In sciences concerning man and society there are *close connections* between suppositions of causal relationships and suppositions of motivational relationships:

First, suppositions of causal relationships will often *build on* suppositions of motivational relationships. For example, supposition of the statistical causal relationship, "the more the individual stands to gain from an offence, the more offences will be committed – other things being equal", builds on supposition of the motivational relationship that people let themselves be motivated by their own gain.

---

[1] Concerning the use of the word "strength", the same applies here as in the case of definitions in the form of instance-type propositions and as in the case of normative definitions (respectively sections B 5.4.2 (1)(c) and 8.2, above): By the *"strength"* of characterisations I do not mean any deeper unitary property, but those features which are mentioned in the main text in what follows, and which have in common that, with more or less determinate views on the part of language users as a starting point, they provide language users with a basis for ranking instance-type propositions. – *Analysis of dis/agreement* can be a reason for seeing these features in relation to one another: Formulations that show disagreement in one strength dimension can show agreement in another strength dimension or when several strength dimensions are seen in relation to one another.

Secondly, propositions about causal relationships will often *refer to* types of motive: in the example just given, consideration for one's own gain.

The said close connections between the two types of relationship do *not* in themselves entail that propositions about motivational relationships are *the same thing as* propositions about causal relationships; compare the example just given of statistical causal relationship with the corresponding proposition about motivational relationship: "In deciding how they shall act, including whether they shall comply with or contravene the provisions of a statute, most people let themselves be motivated by consideration for their own gain."

It is particularly the setting up of general relationships (causal relationships, motivational relationships or others) that seems to distinguish writings in the *sociology of law* from writings in legal dogmatics and writings in the history of law. – In connection with the effects of statutes as a topic, I shall illustrate how the setting up of general causal relationships concerning actions in everyday life typically *builds on* suppositions of general motivational relationships and *refers to* types of motive; and further, illustrate how causal relationships which in this way go via motives are often specified as statistical relationships, or more precisely, how the specification often takes on a *guideline structure* (item (b)) or an *instance-type structure* (item (c)).[2]

> I should remind the reader that in conformity with the main aim of the work (Chapter I and section II A 8, above; cf. section 1 above, concluding remarks) I do *not* take any standpoint on controversial ontological or epistemological questions: here, controversial ontological or epistemological questions concerning motivation, causality or free will.

(b) A great deal of sociology of law thematises *action and motivation*. The discipline's descriptive characterisations will often *content themselves with* pointing to motivational factors that typically come into play, and what circumstances typically influence their motivating force. It is difficult to say anything about the individual motivational factor's impact in the individual instance, because the weight of the factor will vary with which of the other motivational factors come into play.

Descriptive characterisations of legal phenomena will therefore often take on a *guideline structure*. By "guideline structure" I mean that the descriptive characterisations seek to answer the same main questions as the norm type that has been discussed under the name of "retningslinjer" [guidelines]: namely questions of what factors are relevant, in what directions the factors pull and what weight the factors have.[3]

---

[2] The two types of structure are also practically important in the case of definitions, see respectively sections B 6.2 (1) above (guideline structure) and B 5.4.2 (1) above (instance-type structure).

[3] Section B 6.2 (1) above, concluding remarks. – The difference between the descriptive characterisations and the norms is that the former refer to motivational factors and the latter to justificatory factors (criteria). However, this difference is not relevant here.

As an *example* we can look at the question of the effects of statutes. Here descriptive characterisations will typically go via people's motivation, and consist in a mapping of properties of the individuals, their action situations and the more comprehensive social structure, which one assumes are of significance for the effects of a statute.

> On the general deterrent effect of the threat of penal sanctions Andenæs writes: "The general deterrent effect depends both on the severity of the penal sanction and on how great is the risk of detection. In the case of both factors it is not the objective circumstances that are decisive, but how they are *perceived* by the potential offenders" (my italics).[4]
>
> Eckhoff discusses legal rules in general, and writes in this connection: "That a rule is known and understood by those it is addressed to, is not sufficient for it to be complied with. ... In addition to knowledge of rules, *motivation* to follow them is also required" (Eckhoff's italics).[5]

With such a point of departure, part (but not the whole) of the problem of the effects of statutes will consist in mapping individuals' motivation situation in relation to statutory provisions. – For illustration I shall briefly outline some main conclusions relating to relevant features of the motive situation (I presuppose that the statute is addressed to the citizens (in contrast to the public administrative authorities), and that the statute changes the state of the law):

- The point of departure is that the provisions of the statute must be *known* in order to be complied with. In this very fact lies an important variable: ways in which statutory material can be communicated.[6] In this connection may also be mentioned the significance of whether the statute is addressed to or mediated via organisations, firms or other groups, or whether the statute is addressed to individuals and not supported by intermediaries; the first alternative will typically increase the tendency for the statute to be complied with.[7]
- Another obviously important variable is the norm addressees' general *capacity to consider* their actions.

Given these two points of departure, i.e. knowledge of the provisions of the statute and the degree of general capacity to reason, the literature[8] points to a number of other typically relevant variables:

---

4 Andenæs, *Alminnelig strafferett* [general criminal law], p. 81.

5 Eckhoff, *Statens styringsmuligheter, særlig i ressurs- og miljøspørsmål* [the state's possibilities of governing, with special reference to questions of resources and the environment], p. 45.

6 Aubert, *Rettens sosiale funksjon* [the social function of law], pp. 128–35; Eckhoff, *Statens styringsmuligheter, særlig i ressurs- og miljøspørsmål* [the state's possibilities of governing, with special reference to questions of resources and the environment], pp. 36–45.

7 Aubert, *Rettens sosiale funksjon* [the social function of law], p. 135; Eckhoff, 'Juss og samfunnsforskning' [law and social research], pp. 327–29; 'Almenprevensjon og forvaltningslovgivning' [general deterrence and public administrative legislation], pp. 100–01.

8 See inter alia the works mentioned in notes 4–7 above.

- Statutes that prescribe the use of force versus statutes that distribute resources, seen in connection with the norm addressees' views of probabilities: partly how strongly they *fear* detection and reaction in the event of their offending, and partly how strongly they *hope* to receive resources in the event of their complying with the statute.
- The relationship of the statute to *morals, religion and other sets of norms*: reciprocal support or counteraction. Other things being equal, it is reasonable to believe that the more a statutory prohibition coincides with a moral, religious or other prohibition, the more the prohibition will be complied with.
- The relationship between the behaviour specified in the statutory provision and what is *to the advantage or to the disadvantage* of the citizen, quite apart from sanctions in the event of his offending. Other things being equal, it is reasonable to believe that the more disadvantageous a prohibited way of behaving is for the citizen, the more the prohibition will be complied with; and the more advantageous a required way of behaving is for the citizen, the more the requirement will be complied with.

(c) Perhaps on the basis of empirical reseach[9] or "general psychological reasoning"[10] one will venture some more specific hypotheses that for certain *combinations of* features of individuals, action situations or the wider social structure there is a *tendency for* statutes of a particular type to have this or that effect. – The characterisations will in that event have the stamp of *propositions about instance-types* with respect to the individuals' *weighings and balancings* of such motives as were discussed in item (b) above.

(a)↔(c) I have not been able to find examples of descriptive characterisations of statutes' effects that say that *all* statutes of a given type, in the case of a given combination of such features as mentioned in item (b) above, in fact have this or that effect ("deterministic strength"). – I assume the *cause* to be a combination of two factors:

First, our cognition situation being what it in fact is, one believes oneself able to predict *more* about actions in everyday life through general causal relationships that build on suppositions about motivational relationships and refer to types of motive (item (a) above), than through general causal relationships that do not do so; this is so even if it should be difficult to get an overview of all relevant motivational factors (item (b) above, introductory remarks).

Secondly, the more difficult one considers it to be to get an overview of all relevant motivational factors, the more one is forced into a particular form of specifying general causal relationships that build on suppositions about motivational relationships and refer to types of motive, namely specification through a *guide-*

---

9 Aubert, *Rettens sosiale funksjon* [the social function of law], pp. 144–65, gives a survey of some empirical data concerning the effects of statutes.

10 Andenæs, *Alminnelig strafferett* [general criminal law], p. 80.

line or instance-type structure ("statistical strength"); and the effects of statutes is a topic in respect of which it is considered difficult to get an overview of all relevant motivational factors (items (b)–(c) above). – Since explanations take on the strength of the relationships the explanations presuppose and build on, *action explanations* will to a corresponding degree be forced towards a guideline or instance-type structure.

(2) Strength dimensions of descriptive characterisations of a non-empirical kind

Non-empirical descriptive characterisations are often asserted with *great* strength in *several* dimensions. This is the case for example with Ross' denial and Kant's assertion of non-empirical levels of reality (section 2.1 (2) above, respectively items (a)(i) and (b)):

Ross obviously means to apply to all human beings in all cognition situations partly his assertion of analytic un/truth and dis/agreement with sense-experience as the only possible tenability criteria, and partly the underlying denial of other levels of reality (other sources of cognition) than sense-experience.

Kant asserts his categorical imperative vis-à-vis all human beings, in their capacity of beings who act. And he does not allow any exception on the basis of features of the concrete action situation; he thus asserts that the duty to be truthful means that one must tell the murderer the truth when he asks whether our friend is in the next room.[11] – The same applies in the case of the categories (those concepts that according to Kant structure our cognition of sensory reality, for example the concept of 'causality' and the concept of 'thing with properties'). Kant asserts the categories vis-à-vis all human beings, in their capacity of beings with sense-experience. And he does not make any exception on the basis of features of the concrete experiential situation: The categories are not subject to our psychological control, as we are used to in the case of other concepts (compare section III 2 below). The categories are presupposed in all sense-experience, including the individual's experience of himself as an empirical being with psychological will.

Such assertions about what one can roughly term "great strength" seem to be a feature in common of characterisations that assert or deny a non-empirical reality, a feature in common cutting across great differences in other dimensions.

---

11 Kant, 'Über ein vermeintes Recht, aus Menschenliebe zu lügen', pp. 202–03. (According to Kant, a lie will, true enough, not be a wrong done to the murderer, but it will be a wrong done to "[die] Pflicht überhaupt", and will harm "[die] Menschheit überhaupt", in that one will no longer be able to trust other people's propositions and consequently no longer be able to rely on contracts).

3.2. The strength of normative characterisations

In my discussion of normative definitions I pointed out different strength dimensions (see the summary in section B 8.2 above, with further references). The same dimensions apply to normative characterisations: In the first place, the normative *modality*. Secondly, how comprehensive a *person and situation specification* the normative proposition has. Further, whether the normative proposition lays down *conditions* for the normative consequence or points to *factors* that are neither necessary nor sufficient. And finally, to what degree the normative proposition *departs from actually occurring ways of acting*.

In addition may be mentioned two strength dimensions that play the greatest role in the case of normative characterisations. In the first place, *main rule–exception*: the fewer the exceptions, the stronger the proposition. Secondly, *special to decision propositions*: transitions such as the transitions from "yes, perhaps ...", across "I think it best to ...", to "I shall ...", "I intend ...".

D Analytically un/true propositions

1. Introduction

By the term *"analytically un/true proposition"* I mean propositions that are true or untrue by definition. – I refer to the account of the fundamental concept, with examples, in the introductory survey (section A 2 (2) above). I further refer to the account in the same place of the *critical force* of this concept, and thus of why I consider it important to keep analytically un/true propositions separate from both definitions and characterisations. In what follows I shall look more closely at these two boundaries.

2. The boundary with definitions

I determine the relationship between analytically un/true propositions and definitions in two steps.[1]

First, analytically un/true propositions *presuppose a definition*. – The expression "un/true *by* definition" is thus to be taken literally: The presupposed definition *makes possible* analytically un/true propositions, but *is not itself* an analytically un/true proposition.

Secondly, the presupposed definition is a *normative definition*. – It is a concept criterion in the case of analytically un/true propositions that the meaning content is sufficient to decide the truth value. The concept of 'analytically un/true proposition' therefore presupposes an existing meaning content. And words get their meaning content through normative definitions: stipulated (section B 3.3.1 above) or custom-based (section B 3.3.2 above).

> If the definition is descriptive, one can on the basis of the definition *decide whether a person is advancing* an analytically true proposition. For example, given the descriptive definition "John Brown reserves the term "legal rule" for rules he considers just", then on the basis of this definition one can conclude that John Brown is advancing an analytically true proposition when he says "This unjust rule is not a legal rule". – But the analytically true *proposition itself* only becomes possible through John Brown's having accepted the definition as a normative proposition in relation to his own language usage.
>
> A number of accounts subscribe to a conceptual framework according to which analytically un/true propositions presuppose definitions. However, some accounts are indeterminate with respect to whether the presupposed definition must be normative, or whether it can be descriptive, or whether it can be both.[2]

---

1 For a brief but probably in essentials corresponding account, see Næss, *Interpretation and Preciseness*, p. 167.

2 See e.g. Næss, *Logikk og metodelære* [logic and methodology], respectively pp. 117 and 100 ("[A]nalytical propositions of the class we have gone through in this section are closely connected to determinations of concepts … [T]wo main ways [of interpreting a concept determination are] the regulative (normative) and the descriptive"); Sundby, 'Legal Right in Scandinavian Analyses', p. 89 in note 38 ("Definitions are not analytic sentences. The situation is rather this: In order to classify something as an analytic sentence, some sort of definition is presupposed").

3. The boundary with characterisations

(1) Introduction

I shall look at some problematisations of the possibility of drawing a boundary between on the one hand analytically un/true propositions, and on the other hand propositions in the case of which experience or other sources of knowledge different from linguistic meaning are necessary to decide the truth value. The latter-mentioned propositions include both descriptive characterisations and descriptive definitions. For the sake of simplicity I shall speak only of (descriptive) characterisations in this problem context.

I take my point of departure in objections from Wittgenstein and Quine to the distinction between analytically un/true and other propositions. The purpose is to *illustrate and state more precisely the status* of my conceptual framework by relating it to problematisations.

It will, however, be more expedient for *Quine's problematisation* to be discussed *after* I have advanced and given grounds for an assertion that the distinction between descriptive and normative propositions is a graduated distinction (section F below): Quine's views might possibly be taken as support for a *corresponding* graduation in the relationship between definitions, characterisations and analytically un/true propositions. In my view there is *no* parallelism between the two dimensions, in that one finds in the dimension 'descriptive proposition–normative proposition' graduation and fusion of a kind that one does not find in the dimension 'definition–characterisation'; see sections G cf. F, below.

(2) Wittgenstein's problematisation

Wittgenstein points to two important factors in relation to the distinction between analytically un/true and other propositions. First, it depends on the *language users' actions* what are concept criteria and what are not, and thus which propositions are analytically un/true and which are not. Secondly, these actions do not form any simple pattern, but *vary* with the situation in which the language user finds himself, and with what interests come into play; and it can inter alia therefore be indeterminate, or difficult to decide, which features in the individual instance are concept criteria and which are not.

> "Es ist nichts gewöhnlicher, als daß die Bedeutung eines Ausdrucks in der Weise schwankt, daß ein Phänomen bald als Symptom, bald als Kriterium eines Sachverhalts angesehen wird. Und meistens wird dann in einem

> solchen Fall der Wechsel der Bedeutung nicht gemerkt."[1] – "Sätze werden oft an der Grenze von Logik und Empirie gebraucht, so daß ihr Sinn über die Grenze hin und her wechselt und sie bald als Ausdruck einer Norm, bald als Ausdruck einer Erfahrung gelten."[2] – "Das Schwanken wissenschaftlicher Definitionen: Was heute als erfahrungsmäßige Begleiterscheinung des Phänomens A gilt, wird morgen zur Definition von "A" benützt."[3]
>
> "Das Schwanken in der Grammatik zwischen Kriterien und Symptomen läßt den Schein entstehen, als gäbe es überhaupt nur Symptome. Wir sagen etwa: "Die Erfahrung lehrt, daß es regnet, wenn das Barometer fällt, aber sie lehrt auch, daß es regnet, wenn wir bestimmte Gefühle der Nässe und Kälte haben, oder den und den Gesichtseindruck." Als Argument dafür gibt man dann an, daß diese Sinneseindrücke uns täuschen können. Aber man bedenkt dabei nicht, daß die Tatsache, daß sie uns gerade den Regen vortäuschen, auf einer Definition beruht."[4]

I agree that it is important to be aware of such alternations and obscurities as Wittgenstein points to, between features that are made into concept criteria and other features. – One important remedy for obscurities is definitional decisions with respect to concepts/ words that are central in one's propositions/ proposition formulations: Such decisions serve partly as a help for oneself to avoid advancing analytically un/true propositions without being aware of it, and partly as a means to avoiding others' believing that one is advancing analytically un/true propositions when one is in fact not doing so. – Demands for and expectations of such decisions are woven into actually occurring language and argumentation (section G 2 (4) below).

(3) Quine's problematisation

See item (1) above.

---

[1] Wittgenstein, *Zettel*, section 438.

[2] Wittgenstein, *Bemerkungen über die Farben*, Part I, section 32, cf. Part III, section 19.

[3] Wittgenstein, *Philosophische Untersuchungen*, Part I, section 79, concluding remarks (Wittgenstein's parenthesis omitted).

[4] Op. cit., Part I, section 354. See also Part I, sections 104, 392.

4. Excursus on terminology used of analytically un/true propositions

I take as a starting point four proposition formulations which, according to interpretation on the basis of normal English usage, seem to express propositions in the case of which the meaning content is sufficient to decide the truth value:

(i) "The cup is white or the cup is not white."
(ii) "The cup is white and the cup is not white."
(iii) "Some bachelors are unmarried."
(iv) "John is a married bachelor."

It is fairly common to use the term *"analytic proposition"* of all propositions in the case of which the meaning content is sufficient to decide the truth value.[1] According to such terminology, examples (i)–(iv) are all analytic propositions.

(1) One categorisation of analytic propositions goes according to whether the *truth value* is "true" or "untrue":

Analytic propositions with the truth value "true" tend to be called "*positively analytic* propositions"[2] or "*analytically true* propositions". Some people also use the word "tautology" of these cases, but see item (2) below on a more technical use of that word. – Examples (i) and (iii) fall under this set of terms.

Analytic propositions with the truth value "untrue" tend to be called "*negatively analytic* propositions"[3] or "*analytically untrue* propositions". Many people also use the words "(self-)contradiction" of these cases, but here the same applies as to the word "tautology", namely that they are also used in a narrower sense, see item (2) below. – Examples (ii) and (iv) fall under this set of terms.

(2) Another categorisation of analytic propositions goes according to whether the *truth value is decided by analysis of logical or non-logical words* (by "logical words" I mean, as mentioned in section A 2 (2)(a) above, first and foremost "not", "and", "or", "if", "only if", "all", "some" and "none").

(a) Analytic propositions in the case of which the truth value is decided by analysis of *logical words* are sometimes called "logically un/true propositions".[4]

Logically true propositions are often called *"tautologies"*. One example is proposition formulation (i) above. Another example is: "If a legal rule is provided

[1] Quine, 'Two Dogmas of Empiricism', in particular pp. 23–37; Carnap, *Meaning and Necessity*, p. 222; Næss, *Logikk og metodelære* [logic and methodology], p. 115.
[2] Næss, *Logikk og metodelære* [logic and methodology], p. 115.
[3] Loc. cit.
[4] Quine, 'Two Dogmas of Empiricism', p. 22; Carnap, *Meaning and Necessity*, p. 222; Føllesdal/ Walløe/ Elster, *Argumentasjonsteori, språk og vitenskapsfilosofi* [argumentation theory, language and the philosophy of science], pp. 221–22.

by statute and is just, then it is just." Or: "If some legal rules are just, then not all legal rules are unjust ("not just")." This tautology concept was introduced by Wittgenstein in his *Tractatus*.[5] Subsequently the word "tautology" has been used partly in this way, and partly of positively analytic sentences altogether. – Logically true propositions have also been called "identical propositions".[6] But this term is less common than "tautology", and its meaning content tends to be less determinate.[7]

Logically untrue propositions tend to be called *"(self-)contradictions"*.[8] An example is proposition formulation (ii) above. Another example is: "John Brown's complaint has been made too late and it has not been made too late."

(b) In the case of analytic propositions the truth value of which is decided by analysis of *non-logical words*, no corresponding more technical use of terms has developed. Here, all the terms that were mentioned above occur in a looser sense. In addition, in these cases one often uses more everyday or literary words and expressions for intuitions about necessity in thought: for example "vacuous", "saying the same thing twice", "it follows by definition of course", "begging the question" ("petitio principii"), "truism", "pleonasm", and the like. – Two examples of this type of analytic proposition are expressed in proposition formulations (iii) and (iv) above, with respectively the truth values "true" and "untrue".

(3) Analytically true propositions are often called *"necessary"*, in contrast to experiential propositions that are called *"contingent"*. Such terminology does not say so much, since it is polysemous in relation to the fundamental proposition types: The words "necessary" and "contingent" are used, like other modal expressions such as "must", "shall" and "can", in logical, normative and empirical senses (section IV 2.2 (3) below).

For this reason additions like "logical", "normative" or "factual" are often necessary (factually!) to avoid pseudo-disagreement. In my opinion such an addition must (normatively!) therefore often be made. Thus at least a basic clarification has been carried out with respect to what criteria are relevant in the assessment of the tenability of the proposition: criteria for deciding analytic un/truth, criteria for deciding normative in/validity, or criteria for deciding empirical un/truth. – However, the additions "logical", "normative" or "factual" are not strictly necessary (logically!); i.e. one does not get into any self-contradiction if the additions are not there, one "only" runs the risk of lack of clarity, with subsequent pseudo-agreement, or subsequent pseudo-disagreement and fruitless discussions.

---

5 Wittgenstein, *Tractatus Logico-Philosophicus*, London 1922 (original German edition 1921).

6 Bolzano, *Grundlegung der Logik*, pp. 232, 234 ("identische Sätze").

7 As examples of rather indeterminate usage, see Mill, *A System of Logic*, p. viii (the table of contents) cf. pp. 71–73; Scheel, 'Om Rettens Grund som Udgangspunkt for Læren om Retskilderne' [on the foundation of law as a point of departure for the doctrine of the sources of law], p. 255.

8 Næss, *Logikk og metodelære* [logic and methodology], p. 115; Føllesdal/ Walløe/ Elster, *Argumentasjonsteori, språk og vitenskapsfilosofi* [argumentation theory, language and the philosophy of science], p. 222.

E Separating

1. Introduction

1.1. Why is it, in addition to the discussion above, necessary to discuss how one decides which type of proposition one is confronted with in the individual instance?

The topic of the present section E is how one decides which type of proposition one is confronted with in the individual instance: definition or characterisation? normative or descriptive proposition?

Why is it necessary to discuss this question, now that we have discussed the concepts of the fundamental proposition types above? Is it not the concept criteria for the types discussed, that decide which type of proposition one is confronted with in the individual instance? – Basically the answer is in the affirmative. However, for two reasons one gets the outlined *doubling of the problem*:

(i) In the way in which the concepts of the fundamental proposition types have been defined above, they cover *meaning entities*: The concepts of 'definition', 'characterisation', 'descriptive proposition', 'normative proposition' and 'analytically un/true proposition' have meaning entities in their denotations (section A 6 (1) cf. (3), above).

(ii) The word "meaning" is *polysemous* (is used in many different senses) also in the connection just mentioned.

(i)↔(ii) In the light of this, I have found it expedient to divide my discussion of the concepts of the fundamental proposition types into two main stages:

First, the discussion above (sections B–D), which *presupposes and refers to* the meaning plane as the application plane of the concepts.

Secondly, discussion of *what "(linguistic) meaning" in this context means*. This is the topic of the present section E.

Words like "meaning" and "interpretation" have thus hitherto been used as *intermediate stations for thought*, in the sense that one has been able to read them as words, the alternative meanings of which it has for the time being not been necessary to choose between. – A choice between concepts of 'meaning' is, however, *necessary for it to be possible to decide which kind of proposition type one is confronted with* in the individual instance. For one's concept of 'meaning' determines goal and method of the interpretation of proposition formulations, and in so doing, determines goal and method of classification of a proposition as a definition or characterisation, and as descriptive or normative.

The outlined two stages in my discussion of the concepts of the fundamental proposition types are as mentioned only a "main division". The first stage too (sections B–D above) contains discussion of (linguistic) meaning, partly in the form of discussion of a central part of the area of meaning: concepts of 'concept' and types of concept (sections B 3.2.2 and 4.1, above), and partly in the form of establishing what I call a "discussion and decision perspective" on linguistic meaning (section B 4.1 (5)(c) above). To a certain extent it will be relevant and necessary to refer back to these discussions in what follows (see in particular section 2.2.5 (1) below).

1.2. The status of, the main threads in and the purposes of the further discussion

(1) Status

When the proposition types are defined as meaning entities and if one is to explain what lies in this, it may be tempting here, as often in other connections, to resort to the form "What is x?": here *"What is meaning?"*.

"What is meaning?" is, however, *just as polysemous as* "What is x"-questions otherwise (sections I 2–3 above). – The perspective and topic of the present work (Chapter I above) entails in relation to "What is meaning?", as in relation to "What is x"-questions otherwise, application of the distinctions between the fundamental proposition types: The question becomes whether one is after a descriptive or normative definition of ways of using the word "meaning" (descriptive or normative definition of a concept of 'meaning'); or whether one is after descriptive or normative characterisations of the phenomena that fall under a presupposed way of using the word "meaning" (a presupposed concept of 'meaning').

The topic in what follows is a mapping of some alternative major meanings of "meaning" in actual language use, i.e. a *descriptive definition.* The topic is not which meaning alternative one ought to choose (that choice ought to rest on the concrete discussion situation and what one wishes to achieve by using the word there).

This means that I have not found it expedient to build any particular concept of 'meaning' into the concepts of the individual proposition types.[1]

---

[1] Section A 6 (2) above. – An exception applies in the case of the concept of 'fused descriptive and normative proposition', see item (2) below, concluding remarks.

(2) The main threads in and the purposes of the further discussion

I shall look at *two main ways of using* of the word "meaning" in actually occurring language and argumentation: what the proposition formulation means according to widespread linguistic practice, here termed *"objective interpretation/ meaning"* (section 2.1 below); and what the sender of the proposition formulation means or a particular person understands by it, here termed *"subjective interpretation/ meaning"* (section 2.2 below). – After this I shall give a summary of the *relationship* between them (section 2.2.5 (1) below).

My concentrating on these main directions for the operationalising of the concept of 'meaning' aims at the problem that is the topic of the present section E (cf. section 1.1 above). Furthermore it aims, more broadly, at the following:

First: The sender often uses forms of expression which objectively interpreted appear as descriptive, logical or indeterminate, *even though* he is subjectively motivated by normative criteria. – In the perspective of the present section E this linguistic flight from the normative proposition represents an obstacle to determination of subjective meaning; more specifically, it represents an obstacle to determination of subjective meaning with respect to proposition type (section 2.3 below). – In another perspective I shall later show that linguistic flight from the normative proposition is not a technical flaw in language use that may be put right by one's being made aware of it, but a pattern deeply woven into language use (Chapter IV).

Secondly: The argumentation features I wish to emphasise through the concept of 'fused descriptive and normative proposition' indicate that this concept should be linked to subjective meaning (section F below, particularly section F 3.1). What is said in the present section E about subjective meaning thus also provides a foundation for the later discussion of fusion.

2. How does one decide which proposition type one is confronted with in the individual instance?

2.1. Meaning according to widespread linguistic practice, especially according to custom-based normative definitions ("objective interpretation/ meaning")

2.1.1. The concept

By the *"objective"* meaning of a proposition formulation I am referring to its meaning according to widespread linguistic practice.

By definition I use the word *"practice"* of a unity of normative propositions and acts of, and decisions concerning, application of the normative propositions.[1] In the case of linguistic practice the normative propositions are more precisely normative *definitions.*

In everyday life widespread linguistic practices are almost always governed by *custom-based* normative definitions (section B 3.3.2 above). In professional language one can more often find examples of widespread practices that are governed by *stipulated* normative definitions: for example statutory definitions in law[2] or physicians' classification systems for diseases.[3]

> "Governed", but not "determined"; cf. the fact that linguistic practices do not only consist in abstract normative propositions (normative definitions), but in the unity of these and the language user's acts of, and decisions concerning, application (see in more detail in section B 4.1 (5)(c) above).

The *aim* here is not to give an account of objective meaning in itself, but to outline the contrast between objective meaning and subjective meaning in their capacity of being two main directions for the operationalising of the concept of

---

1 See sections A 2 (1) concluding remarks and B 3.3.2 (2), both above, on the broad use of the word "proposition" in this work.

2 See in particular sections B 3.3.6 and 5.4.2 (2), above.

3 See for example *The International Classification of Diseases*, from the World Health Organisation (10th ed. 1992).

'meaning'. Therefore I *confine* myself in the rest of section 2.1 to the most important normative basis for widespread linguistic practices: custom-based normative definitions. For the sake of brevity I term these *"language norms"*.

2.1.2. Some features of custom-based definitions that make possible difference and interplay between objective meaning and subjective meaning

(1) Point of departure: Like other norms, provide answers to something, but not everything

Language norms, like other norms, provide answers to something, but not everything: Legal and other interpretation activity clearly show that in relation to the diversity of delimitation questions that crop up when language is used, language norms are often *indeterminate, and are so in several dimensions*; polysemy, incompleteness, vagueness and factor structure of concept criteria are some of the most important.[4]

Nevertheless there is a widespread belief that language norms *always delimit* (delimit in relation to any question of doubt that might possibly arise) in the individual concrete situation. – The very use of the word "concept", and not least of the definite article, "the concept", often seems to be the result more of a *desire* for unity and certainty than of a well-founded view that what one is talking about *is* unitary and certain. The alternative, speaking of "(norms for) use of words and expressions", to a greater extent leads our thought to its being tied to something empirical, changing and to that extent uncertain (section B 4.4.3 above). – The belief that language norms always delimit, is not only "pre-scientific", but we bring it with us into academic subjects, science and philosophy, and it constantly gives rise to distorted argumentation (see the same places as referred to in note 4 above).

(2) In particular concerning the level of language norms along the dimension 'general–individual'. Polysemy as an example of resulting indeterminacy

The constituting of the meanings of the words and expressions of a language by the language norms takes place on a relatively general *level.*

(a) On the one hand, the person or situation specification of language norms is not empty, i.e. in practice the norms always relate to *one or another context*. For

---

4 I refer to what has been said earlier about the arbitrariness and incoherence of laying down determinacy in the delimitation as a necessary criterion in concepts of 'concept' or 'definition' (section B 4.1 (3)(b), see also section B 2.2, above). – Especially concerning factor structure of concept criteria I refer to my discussions of family resemblance (sections B 3.2.2 and 6.2 (2), above) and my discussions of evaluation prescriptions in the connotations of concepts (sections B 6.1 and 6.2 (1), above).

example, the language norms for the Scandinavian family of words "rett", "ret" and "rätt" (Norwegian, Danish and Swedish, respectively; cf. the German "Recht") relate to such different contexts as food ("matrett", cf. "Gericht"), space ("vannrett", "loddret", cf. "waagerecht", "senkrecht"), tenability assessment ("det rette", cf. "rechte"), and norms and institutions ("moral og rett", cf. "Moral und Recht"). – It is not possible to answer a question about the meaning of "rett" independently of such contexts. To put this in general terms: Language norms do not specify word-meaning "pure and simple", "in and of itself", "as an absolute", or the like.

(b) On the other hand, the person or situation specification of language norms is *not linked to the individual utterance*. True enough, the person or situation specification of language norms can be more specific in relation to some words than to others, but by virtue of their being custom-based, the norms apply by definition to the instance-type, not to the individual instance. For example, even though the meanings of the word "rett" that are constituted through the language norms have not been exhausted by the instance-types mentioned in item (a) above, any further explications of the norms will also move on the level of the instance-type: for example the explication that lawyers' use of the word "rett" in formulations about "hva som er rett" [what the law is], sometimes refers to the norms the sender of the formulation believes other lawyers will take as a basis (descriptive proposition), sometimes to the norms the sender of the formulation considers provide the most reasonable and just outcomes (normative proposition), and often to a fusion of the two (section F below).

(a)↔(b) As language norms in this way constitute different meanings for different types of context, the linguistic entity viewed in isolation becomes *polysemous*. It will often be possible for the polysemy *to be reduced or removed* by placing the linguistic entity in one particular context among those which the language norms are linked to. However, this is not always the case: For example, the said polysemy between descriptivity, normativity and fusion in the case of lawyers' proposition formulations about "what the law is" (item (b) above, concluding remarks) will often *subsist even if* one brings in the most specific person specification of the language norms (e.g. legal writers in the Norwegian legal system today) and their most specific situation specification (e.g. use of formulations about "what the law is" in legal textbooks).

In such cases of polysemy one must conclude that there is *no determinate* linguistic meaning in relation to a given question of delimitation, *if* by "meaning" one is referring to the meaning according to custom-based normative definitions.

If in cases of polysemy or other cases of indeterminacy in language norms (incompleteness, vagueness, factor structure of concept criteria) one *nevertheless* wants to find a *determinate* meaning, it must be meaning in *another* sense of "meaning" than 'meaning according to language norms (custom-based normative definitions)'.

In the following section 2.2, I shall look at an alternative meaning of "meaning" that is often used, and which thus represents, in actually occurring language and argumentation, another main direction for the operationalising of the concept of 'meaning'.

2.2. Sender's meaning or a particular person's understanding ("subjective interpretation/ meaning")

2.2.1. The concept

I shall call the meaning that the individual in the individual instance attaches to words and expressions in the language *"subjective meaning"*.

In my use of "subjective meaning" there is no definitional limitation with respect to *whose* subjective meaning is relevant; the individual concerned may be the sender, the recipient or another person who takes a standpoint on the meaning content of the individual proposition formulation. For the sake of simplicity, however, the following presentation is concentrated on the sender and the recipient.

In doctrines of the sources of law, lawyers most often reserve the terms "subjective interpretation/ meaning" (or corresponding terms) by definition for standpoints on the meaning content on the part of a *limited circle*, namely one or more of those who are involved in the production of the source of law concerned: for example one or both of the contracting parties in relation to the contract as a source of law,[5] or members of the legislative assembly in relation to the text of the statute as a source of law.[6] – In the context of sources of law, this may be a reasonable use of language: If one looks for subjective meaning there, then it is in particular "the parties' meaning" (in the sense outlined) which is relevant according to doctrines of the sources of law. – When, on the other hand, as here, the topic also covers other language use than that of the sources of law, there is no reason to limit the concept of 'subjective meaning' along corresponding lines, which would have meant limiting it to the sender and the recipient of the individual proposition formulation. In relation to the present topic, others who take a *standpoint* on the meaning content will *to that extent* place themselves on the same footing as the sender and the recipient: They contribute to that extent (in that they take a standpoint), in the same way as the sender and the recipient, to a basis in reality for an alternative operationalising of the concept of 'meaning'.

---

5 Huser, *Avtaletolking* [interpretation of contracts], pp. 67–68, 73–78.

6 Eckhoff, *Rettskildelære* [doctrine of the sources of law], pp. 123–25; Augdahl, *Rettskilder* [sources of law], pp. 83–88; von Eyben, *Juridisk grundbog, Bind 1: Retskilderne* [basic manual of law, vol. 1: the sources of law], pp. 27, 28; Cross, *Statutory Interpretation*, pp. 21 et seq.; Larenz, *Methodenlehre der Rechtswissenschaft*, pp. 316–20, 328 et seq.

2.2.2. *May coincide with, innovate, supplement, make more precise, or break with objective meaning*

(1) Subjective meaning may *coincide* with objective meaning. – In the main this *is* how it is, and in linguistic interaction one builds on its being so, cf. the fact that in practical interpretation activity one as a matter of course takes as a starting point the widespread linguistic practices that apply to the particular area of conversation. If there were no such coincidence in the main, conversation would not be possible: Every new definition by means of which one explained to the other party what one subjectively meant, would require a further definition of the words that were used in the explanation, ad infinitum.

(2) The meaning that the individual attaches to words in the individual instance, may be *different from* their meaning according to widespread linguistic practice; and not infrequently this *is* the case:

First, subjective meaning may *give rise to* objective meaning – through first-time structuring, naming, or coupling of area and name.

Secondly, subjective meaning may *supplement* objective meaning or make it *more precise*. For example, a legal writer makes his formulations about "what the law is" more precise by stating that by the word "law" in this context he is referring to the norms he believes the courts will take as a basis.

Further, subjective meaning may *break with* objective meaning. One instance-type is pure misunderstandings (children, foreign speakers, laymen in relation to academic language). Another is metaphorical use of language, indirect forms of expression, irony, or the like. A third is more or less deliberate discrepancies between objective meaning and subjective meaning, created in order to protect oneself against personal responsibility for a decision, in order to exert influence, etc. (section IV 3 below).

2.2.3. *May be actual or hypothetical. In particular on the use of the hypothetical variant*

(1) The concepts
(2) Hypothetical meaning may be the only alternative
(3) What reasons can one have for being interested in hypothetical meaning?

(1) The concepts

Subjective meaning may be a *psychological reality*, in the sense that the sender or recipient in fact makes a *decision* with respect to a particular question of interpretation. For example, the sender takes a standpoint on whether he intends to define the use of a word (define a concept) or to characterise a phenomenon that falls under a presupposed use (a presupposed concept); or whether he intends to describe or normatively regulate.[7]

An alternative to seeking such actual subjective meaning (in what follows simply termed "actual meaning"), may be to seek *hypothetical subjective meaning* (in what follows simply termed "hypothetical meaning"), i.e. what decision a person would have made *if* he had thought about a particular question of meaning, for example if he had thought about the distinction 'definition–characterisation' or the distinction 'descriptive proposition–normative proposition'.

(2) Hypothetical meaning may be the only alternative

Sometimes one *must content oneself with* reflections about *hypothetical* meaning. An important instance-type is (a)+(b):

(a) The sender *did not have any particular notion* of the status of his own propositions. This lay outside the sender's definiteness of intention.[8]

(b) A *subsequent decision cannot replace* the question about hypothetical meaning.

There can be several *reasons* why a subsequent decision "cannot" replace the question about hypothetical meaning:

(i) It may be that a subsequent decision *is not factually possible*: for example in the case of questions about what was meant by a deceased writer.

(ii) Or it may be that a subsequent decision *is not normatively relevant, or is even forbidden*. Two examples may illustrate this.

First, the question of when two potentially contracting parties shall be deemed to have moved from the stage of preliminaries to that of being legally bound, is according to Norwegian court practice a question that rests on a weighing and balancing of a number of different factors (section IV 2.2 (6)(b) below). In proceedings about this, it will inter alia be relevant what the parties to the case would have decided if they had thought the question over at the alleged moment of transition from preliminaries to being bound. On the other hand it is not relevant what they might decide today.

Another example is questions about what the legislator meant. In Norway it has never happened that the national assembly (the Storting) or its legislative divisions (the Odelsting and Lagting) has convened *simply* to pronounce on what they meant by words and expressions in a previously enacted statute. And if this were to be put forward as a possibility, I think many Norwegian lawyers would say that such a subsequent decision was irrelevant in statutory interpretation, perhaps also forbidden: It is integral to the Constitution that when a statute has been enacted, it is the courts that have the final word concerning its interpretation and application.

---

[7] On the psychological aspect, and as part of this, the present work's discussion and decision perspective on linguistic meaning, see further in section 2.2.5 below.

[8] On the concept of 'definiteness of intention', see section 2.2.5 (2) below. Here it is sufficient to understand "definiteness of intention" in the spatio-analogical sense of 'the breadth and depth of what one has thought over'.

If the legislator wishes to put right a weakness in the wording of the statute, there must be a new statute with new wording.

On the other hand it does happen that the Odelsting or Lagting, or the Storting in plenary session, in connection with the transaction of other business *also* make statements about what they meant by words and expressions in a previously enacted statute. There is controversy about what weight ought to be ascribed to such statements in statutory interpretation.[9]

(3) What reasons can one have for being interested in hypothetical meaning?

Questions about the sender's hypothetical meaning do not have any great interest in natural science, nor in a good deal of social science: There the interest does not relate to *what the individual researcher would have said* if he had thought about the question, but to *what the world is like*, and, by derivation from this, to *what evidence the researcher has* for the assertions he in fact advances.

This is different in cases in which the sender's propositions are accorded authority *beyond* their tenability value, as in law. There the word "meaning" is often used in the sense of 'hypothetical meaning'. An important causal factor is that many lawyers must regularly make decisions of great importance for other people, and as a result acquire a strong psychological need to protect themselves against personal responsibility for the decision. One way the lawyer can protect himself is to seek to ground his decision in the meanings of words that others have uttered, in so far as these other people are also recognised as having authority in the question concerned. For example, the lawyer may seek to ground his decision in the legislator's meaning: "the *Act* states that ...", or in the disputants' meaning: "the *contract* states that ...". The legislator's or the contracting parties' actual meaning is, however, often indeterminate. In this situation the lawyer resorts inter alia to propositions about hypothetical meaning (compare section IV 3.3 below).

9 Boe, 'Utvikling i lovers form og innhold' [development in the form and content of statutes], pp. 662 et seq.; 'Fusadommen i forvaltningsrettslig og rettsteoretisk perspektiv' [the Fusa judgment in the perspectives of administrative law and legal theory], pp. 326–29; 'Domstolskontroll med forvaltningen' [judicial review of public administration], pp. 329 et seq.; Eckhoff, *Rettkildelære* [doctrine of the sources of law], pp. 80–84; Fleischer, *Rettskilder* [sources of law], pp. 105–07; Graver, *Materiell forvaltningsrett* [substantive administrative law], pp. 70 et seq.; Kjønstad, *Rett til helsehjelp og sosiale tjenester* [the right to health care and social services], pp. 85–86; *Innføring i trygderett* [introduction to social security law], pp. 195–96.

2.2.4. *May be sought through the language user's propositions about what he means himself or through the language user's behaviour. In particular concerning reaction to phenomena that do not have the property the proposition formulation specifies, as a criterion of proposition type*

(1) Introduction
(2) The language user's propositions about what he means himself
(3) Reaction to phenomena that do not have the property the proposition formulation specifies
  (a) Use as a definitional criterion of proposition type
  (b) A more specified criterion in literature on norms

(1) Introduction

In the search for objective meaning, the choice of words read in the light of suppositions about widespread linguistic practice, is by definition the only interpretation factor (section 2.1 above).

In the search for subjective meaning – whether it be the sender's meaning, the recipient's meaning or the meaning a particular other person attaches to the choice of words; whether it be actual or hypothetical – one also places great weight on the meaning according to widespread linguistic practice (section 2.2.2 (1) above). However, this is no longer, either definitionally or factually, the only interpretation factor: Now the objective meaning is supplemented by other interpretation factors linked to the person with whose meaning one is concerned (items (2)–(3) below). In what follows, for the sake of simplicity I speak mostly of the sender, but what is said applies correspondingly to the recipient or to others whose subjective interpretation is of interest.

(2) The language user's propositions about what he means himself

A widespread and simple way to decide what kind of proposition one is confronted with in the individual instance is to *ask* the sender.

Sometimes, however, this is factually impossible, forbidden or normatively irrelevant; cf. the examples in section 2.2.3 (2)(b) above.

Moreover, even if it is factually possible, permitted and relevant to ask, one may choose not to ask. One reason can be that one assumes that the sender has no concepts of the proposition types and therefore cannot answer. Another reason can be that different response alternatives have different practical consequences for the sender, so that one is in doubt about how reliable an answer will be; for example, the judge or civil servant who grounds his decision against the one party in "legislator's meaning" may, inter alia in order to protect himself against personal responsibility, have an interest in his proposition's being understood as descriptive and leaving no other alternative, not as an expression of the evaluations and choices that in fact played a part (Chapter IV below).

In several of the situations now mentioned an alternative to asking the sender may be to look at the sender's actual language use and accompanying behaviour; see the following item (3).

(3) Reaction to phenomena that do not have the property the proposition formulation specifies

A behavioural element that fairly often seems to be used as a step in the operationalising of the concept of 'subjective meaning' with respect to proposition type, is the sender's *reaction* when he confronts a *phenomenon which does not have the property that the proposition formulation specifies.* – This criterion is general, in that it can contribute to the operationalising of both the boundary between descriptive propositions and normative propositions, and the boundary between definitions and characterisations (item (a) below).

I do not know of any other literature that has formulated the general criterion mentioned. On the other hand, in the literature a more specific criterion has been used for the operationalising of the boundary between the descriptive and the normative (item (b) below).

(a) Use as a definitional criterion of proposition type

As an example for illustration I shall use the proposition formulation "The legal rules provide legal safeguards for everybody". – One may imagine that the sender becomes aware of a rule that he considers to have an unfortunate effect in the perspective of legal safeguards, for example the fact that the accused in criminal cases that are so serious that they go straight to lagmannsrett [the second level in the three-tier Norwegian court system] has the facts of the case in respect of the question of guilt examined only once.[10]

(i) If one experiences that the sender *corrects the proposition*, a reasonable interpretation is that the proposition formulation is intended to express a *descriptive characterisation*. In this case the example is interpreted as a descriptive characterisation of the legal rules: In the light of the said legal rule concerning the examination of facts with respect to the question of guilt, the sender realises that his proposition provides too little nuanced a characterisation of the phenomena that fall under his presupposed concept of 'legal rule'. – "I was wrong."

(ii) If one experiences that the sender *does not correct the proposition, but tries to correct reality*, a reasonable interpretation is that the proposition formulation is intended to express a *normative characterisation*. For in the case of normative

---

[10] This was the rule according to both the Criminal Procedure Act 1887 (Act No. 5 of 1 July) and the Criminal Procedure Act 1981 (Act No. 25 of 22 May). See further next note.

characterisations it is precisely the phenomenon, and not the proposition, that is to be changed in the event of discrepancy between them. In the example it is in this case the said legal rule concerning the examination of facts with respect to the question of guilt that is to be changed. – "This ought to be corrected."[11]

(iii) If one experiences that the proposition, when it is tentatively seen as a characterisation, does not accord with the sender's view of reality; and if one experiences that the sender knows the facts that create discrepancy, and even so *neither corrects the proposition nor tries to correct reality* – then one possible interpretation is that the proposition formulation does not express a characterisation of the phenomenon, but a *definition* of words for the phenomenon, i.e. that *there is no discrepancy* between proposition and reality. In this case the example is interpreted as a definition of the term "legal rule": Confronted with the said rule concerning the examination of facts with respect to the question of guilt, the sender says that this rule does not fall under the use of the term "legal rule" that his formulation defines. – "This is not a legal rule."

> This applies whether the definition is descriptive or normative: A *descriptive* definition says that those whose language use is being described do not use the term "legal rule" of a rule they consider to have an unfortunate effect in a legal-safeguards perspective. And a *normative* definition expresses, for example, that the sender will not use the term "legal rule" of a rule he considers to have an unfortunate effect in a legal-safeguards perspective.

(iv) In the situation outlined in item (iii) above another possible interpretation is that the sender is not sufficiently aware of the distinctions between the fundamental proposition types, i.e. that the sender's proposition is *indeterminate* in these dimensions.

(i)↔(iv) The example demonstrates the fact that, and the way in which, the individual's reaction to phenomena that do not have the property the proposition formulation specifies, may more generally be considered and used as a *definitional criterion* of what kind of *proposition type* one is confronted with in the individual instance.

However, this criterion is *not alone* sufficient for unambiguously determining the proposition type in all relations. In relation to lawyers' propositions about what the law is, that part of the criterion that concerns reaction to discrepancy between proposition and reality (items (i)–(ii) above) is not in itself sufficient for an adequate picture of the occurrence of and relationship between descriptive and normative propositions (section F 1, cf. section F in its entirety, below).

(b) A more specified criterion in literature on norms

In literature on norms a part of the criterion 'reaction to phenomena that do not have the property the proposition formulation specifies' (item (a) above) has been used for operationalising the boundary between the descriptive and the normative:

---

[11] Cf. Act No. 80 of 11 June 1993 concerning amendments to the Criminal Procedure Act, which introduced a system of two instances (in operation from 1 August 1995).

namely the criterion 'reaction to discrepancy between expectation/ proposition and reality' (see the examples in item (a)(i)–(ii) above, for illustration of reaction to this discrepancy). – As mentioned, I do not consider that reaction to discrepancy is alone sufficient for understanding the distinction between descriptive and normative propositions in actually occurring argumentation (item (a) above, concluding remarks, with further references). – Here I shall, however, take a look at another side of the literature's use of the reaction criterion, namely the fact that, and the way in which, the individual's reaction to discrepancy is used to operationalise what are, from a theoretical point of view, different points of departure: a psychological concept of 'expectation' (item (i) below), a semantic concept of 'proposition' (item (ii) below), or combinations (item (iii) below).

(i) In psychological and sociological literature (inter)action and motivation are usual points of departure; and in connection with these, a great deal of work has been done on and with concepts of 'action' and 'expectation'. *Expectations* are usually divided into expectations relating to what will in fact happen ("cognitive expectations"), and expectations relating to what ought to or shall happen ("normative expectations"). – With such points of departure it is natural to use the expectation as a building block for a norm concept.[12]

In operationalising the concepts of 'cognitive expectation' and 'normative expectation', the individual's reaction when he experiences that reality does not accord with expectation is a reasonable criterion: If the individual tries to change reality, it is a criterion of a normative expectation. If the individual changes his expectation, it is a criterion of a cognitive expectation.[13]

(ii) In a good deal of literature the point of departure is not in action and motivation but in *linguistic entities and their meanings*. – With such a point of departure it is not a psychological concept of 'expectation' but a semantic concept of 'proposition', or more exceptionally concepts of purely linguistic entities,[14] that is used as a building block for a norm concept.

In the case of linguistic meaning content too one gets an operationalisation task: How does one decide whether an individual proposition formulation expresses a descriptive or normative proposition? Moreover, in these contexts of linguistic analysis too the individual's reaction to any discrepancy has a tendency to

---

12 Weber, 'Über einige Kategorien der verstehenden Soziologie', p. 440, pp. 441–74 passim; Homans, *The Human Group*, pp. 122–24; Galtung, 'Expectations and Interaction Processes', pp. 214–17; Aubert, *Sosiologi* [sociology] (1964), Chapter 2, in particular pp. 24–33; *Sosiologi* (1979), p. 85; *Rettens sosiale funksjon* [the social function of law], p. 18; Luhmann, *Rechtssoziologie*, pp. 42 et seq., 54; *Soziale Systeme*, pp. 436 et seq.; *Das Recht der Gesellschaft*, pp. 133–34.

13 Galtung, 'Expectations and Interaction Processes', pp. 216–17; Aubert/ Messinger, 'The Criminal and the Sick', pp. 146–47; Luhmann, *Rechtssoziologie*, p. 42; *Soziale Systeme*, p. 437; *Das Recht der Gesellschaft*, pp. 133–34. – A more complex model is provided by Rommetveit, *Social Norms and Roles*, pp. 44–52 (more complex inter alia because Rommetveit seems to lay down cognitive expectations (much of what Rommetveit calls "expectations") as a criterion of normative expectations (much of what Rommetveit calls "pressure")).

14 On purely linguistic criteria of the concept of 'norm', see section A 6 (3) above.

crop up: this time, reaction to discrepancy between proposition and reality, and this time, as a criterion of subjective linguistic meaning with respect to proposition type.[15]

(iii) A *combination* of these two perspectives has also been advanced. An example of this is Sundby's norm definition. He defines the concept of 'norm' as a normative proposition (compare item (ii) above) that is internalised (compare item (i) above).[16]

The individual's reaction would come in here in two ways: partly as a criterion of an individual proposition formulation's expressing a normative proposition at all, and partly as a criterion of the proposition's being internalised. – In practice the two ways will often overlap, since a person who advances a normative proposition according to the criteria for subjective linguistic meaning has often also internalised the proposition. However, this does not always apply. For the concept of 'internalisation' in Sundby covers only the more *enduring and deep-rooted* attitudes. Therefore one may imagine a person's advancing a normative proposition according to the criteria for subjective linguistic meaning, *without* his also having internalised the proposition.

> However, Sundby does not say very much about these matters: The operationalisation problem is discussed thoroughly in the case of the concept of 'internalisation',[17] but almost not at all in the case of the concept of 'normative proposition'.[18] And, as far as I can see, nothing is said about the relationship between the two ways of bringing the individual's reaction into the analyses. – The same applies to the combination of the two perspectives in his co-operation with Eckhoff.[19]

(iv) I assume it need not matter particularly whether one takes one's point of departure in a *psychological concept* of 'normative expectation' or in a *semantic concept* of 'normative proposition':

Neither of the concepts (as they are normally laid down) refers directly to intersubjectively available experiences. And, as shown above, it is reasonable to use, and people have in fact used, the *same experience* in the operationalising of both the concepts: the individual's reaction to discrepancy between expectation or proposition on the one hand and reality on the other.

---

15 Compare Næss, *Interpretation and Preciseness*, pp. 271–72; Anscombe, *Intention*, pp. 56–57; Kenny, *Will, Freedom and Power*, p. 38; Searle, 'A Taxonomy of Illocutionary Acts', pp. 3–4; Eckhoff/ Sundby, *Rettssystemer* [legal systems] p. 51; *Rechtssysteme*, p. 47. – Eckhoff/ Sundby do not distinguish between expectations and propositions, in that those places in Galtung and Luhmann that are mentioned in item (i) above, are said to use the reaction criterion to distinguish between propositions.

16 Sundby, *Om normer* [on norms], Part 1.

17 Op. cit., Chapter 5.

18 Op. cit., pp. 27–28.

19 See Eckhoff/ Sundby, *Rettssystemer* [legal systems], 1st ed., Chapter 6 (pp. 108–17 et passim) on internalisation, and pp. 52–53 on interpretation; 2nd ed., pp. 52–56 on internalisation, and pp. 51–52 on interpretation; *Rechtssysteme*, pp. 48–51 on internalisation, and pp. 47–48 on interpretation.

Any comparison of and any choice between conceptual approaches ought therefore to be linked to the *whole* conceptual apparatus, both to the abstract criteria and to the criteria that bridge the gap over to intersubjectively available experience: Differences that seem great in the light of the abstract criteria alone, may show themselves to be less significant when links with experience are established. For example questions of whether, and if so in what form, the individual's reaction plays a part, and whether the individual's reaction in the one form or the other ought to be brought into the conceptualisation, can be discussed without any distinction's being made between whether the individual's reaction is linked to expectations or propositions.[20]

2.2.5. *In what relations and in what sense is subjective meaning "psychological"? Similarity with and difference from objective meaning. In particular on definiteness of intention*

(1) In what relations and in what sense is subjective meaning "psychological"? Similarity with and difference from objective meaning

I have previously given a more general account of the extent to which, in relation to the perspective and topic of the present work, I see linguistic meaning as something empirical (section B 4.1 (4)–(6) above; see particularly item (5)(c) on the present work's discussion and decision perspective on linguistic meaning). In what follows I shall briefly apply the main points from the earlier account to subjective meaning in particular, and in so doing, emphasise what is the definitional difference from objective meaning.

Like objective meaning, subjective meaning is *not* identical with linguistic entities or other purely physical (spatio-temporal) features of language use (section B 4.1 (5)(a)(i) above). Nor is it identical with certain empirically perceptible phenomena of a psychological kind: to put it more precisely, neither identical with the stream of mental images or with more enduring images in the memory, which both spontaneously accompany the use of language; nor identical with a cognitively worked out mental image of what one considers to be the typical denotatum, for example, of what one considers to be the typical cup. Inter alia one talks of "meaning the same thing", "understanding the same thing", "having

---

20 Compare Hart, *The Concept of Law*, 1st ed. pp. 54–56, 86–88, 112–14; 2nd ed. pp. 55–57, 88–91, 115–17; MacCormick, *Legal Reasoning and Legal Theory*, pp. 139–40, 275–92. – Differently in e.g. Luhmann, *Rechtssoziologie*, pp. 42–43; Sundby, *Om normer* [on norms], pp. 139–41. In the places mentioned both place greater weight on the abstract differences: on the fact that they themselves take their points of departure in respectively expectations in contradistinction to propositions, and propositions in contradistinction to expectations (for Luhmann it is also important that his definition is "funktional", see pp. 42, 60–61 including note 68, but this aspect is not relevant here).

the same concept", or the like, even though different people cannot have one another's psychological phenomena, for example phenomena of the kinds mentioned in the previous sentence (section B 4.1 (5)(a)(ii) above).

The *difference* between the concepts of 'subjective meaning' and 'objective meaning', as the concepts have been established here, consists in subjective meaning's being linked to *individual* instances (individual persons in individual language use situations), while objective meaning is linked to *general* instances (open classes of individuals and situations):

In the light of this, I consider assertions about the objective meanings of *particular words and expressions* to be *generalising propositions*, in the case of which the *data* that provide the basis for the generalisation are perceptions of subjective meaning. – The continual *actions and decisions* (conscious deliberation or routine application) that constitute the subjective meanings of words, and the factual factors that are taken as criteria for these decisions (the language user's propositions about what he means himself or other behaviour than such propositions, see section 2.2.4 above), thus contribute *also* (at the same time) to the constituting of the objective meaning of the word (section B 4.1 (5)(c) above).

Accordingly the definitional difference between subjective meaning and objective meaning does *not* consist in subjective meaning's being *"more psychological"*: I define *all* concepts of linguistic meaning, also the concept of 'objective meaning', as linked to actual individuals and their behaviour – as outlined in the account now given.

> The aspects concerning language use and propositions about language use that my formation of these concepts points to, and the interests that have motivated my formation of these concepts, lie in another plane than the interrogative intuition "how does linguistic meaning arise?", with connected interrogative intuitions like "what comes first, objective meaning or subjective meaning?", "which is the more fundamental?", or the like:[21] Taking as a point of departure the perspective and topic of the present work, it is not only to a certain extent unnecessary to take any standpoint on, but to the greatest extent possible, necessary not to take any standpoint on[22] such interrogative intuitions and their often accompanying "theories of meaning".[23]
>
> Næss has in a number of works emphasised that it is of great importance that assertions about the objective meanings of given words and expressions are linkable to propositions about individual instances of language use, so that the said assertions *allow themselves to be empirically checked*; and he has himself worked a great deal on developing methods for such operationalising.[24] – It is undoubtedly the case that many assertions about objective

---

[21] Compare Stigen, *Betydning og mening, handling og ytring* [signification and meaning, action and utterance] pp. 73 et seq. ("what is primary, signification or meaning" (p. 73); " 'meaning' is a more fundamental concept than 'signification' " (p. 74)).

[22] See section I 6 above; cf. sections A 6 (2) and B 4.1 (5)(c) above, and G 2 (4)(c) below.

[23] See section III 2.2.2 (3)(c) below on such theories.

[24] See in particular Næss, *Interpretation and Preciseness*, Foreword and Introduction, both with further references.

meaning build on few and scattered propositions about subjective meaning, not seldom simply on one's own perceptions of the meaning of the linguistic entity in question. Whether this shall be considered a weakness, rests in the first place on the *degree* to which one considers that the question under discussion depends on an *exact* description of objective meaning, and in the second place on what *confidence* one has in *one's own* ability for (and as part of this, one's own imagination as a means to) representative mapping of different language use situations (section B 3.3.3 (3) above).

(2) In particular on definiteness of intention

An important aspect of the concept of 'subjective meaning' is what Næss calls *"definiteness of intention"*: "The more exactly a person can state what he attached to [his proposition formulation] ..., the greater the definiteness of intention he is said to have had when he uttered [it]."[25]

In relation to the present work the question is particularly whether the sender took a standpoint on *which type of proposition* his proposition formulation was intended to express: a definition or a characterisation?; a descriptive, normative or fused (descriptive and normative) proposition?

2.3. Particular problems as a result of "flight from the normative proposition"

It seems to be a general psychological feature that we tend to want to get away from cognition of or openness about the place uncertainty has in life, *"the flight from uncertainty"*, and thus also to get away from cognition of or openness about the influence of our evaluations and choices on our actions. In relation to this psychological feature the emphasis in the present work is on *symptoms in actually widespread language use*:

Above I have mapped some *alternative concepts of 'meaning'* that are actually in use. – When in the case of individual proposition formulations one is going to use the *subjective alternative* (sender's meaning or a particular person's understanding) as a criterion of which type of proposition one is confronted with, a *particular problem* often arises:

---

25 Næss, *En del elementære logiske emner* [some elementary topics in logic], pp. 31–32. Compare same writer, *Interpretation and Preciseness*, p. 79: A question of meaning lies outside a person's definiteness of intention when "[t]he fundamentum divisionis was unknown and not even indirectly contemplated or applied by him"; *Hvilken verden er den virkelige?* [which world is the real one?], pp. 145–46: "[The concept of] 'definiteness of intention' ... has been adapted to empirical investigative methodology (psychological and phenomenological concepts of 'intention')." – The concept of 'definiteness of intention' was introduced in *Interpretation and Preciseness*, see particularly pp. 79–80. See also Næss, *Scepticism*, pp. 102–04; *The Pluralist and Possibilist Aspect of the Scientific Enterprise*, p. 129. For Næss' more precise definition, see particularly the three places last mentioned.

One runs up against an obscurity or discrepancy in the relationship between linguistic formulation objectively interpreted and subjective meaning: The sender justifies his standpoint with linguistic formulations that objectively interpreted are either polysemous between the descriptive, logical and normative (section IV 2 below), or more one-sidedly descriptive or logical (section IV 3 below). At the same time one often has reason, independently of the linguistic formulation, to believe that the criteria that motivate the sender's standpoint are, to a greater or lesser degree, normative. – The flight from cognition of or openness about uncertainty, evaluations and choices manifests itself *linguistically* as the *flight from the normative proposition.*

F Fusion of descriptive and normative propositions. The concepts of 'descriptive proposition' and 'normative proposition' as concepts of degree

1. Introductory remarks on my concept of 'fusion'. Terminology

In sections B–C above I have pointed to dimensions and degrees in definitions and characterisations. By using the concepts of dimensions and degrees as a basis for questions addressed to (for analysis of) the individual proposition, one can nuance *what the distinction between descriptivity and normativity refers to.*

Yet given answers to such questions, most people still presuppose that *individual propositions are either descriptive or normative.*

This presupposition I consider sometimes to acquire the stamp of *prejudice*: One assumes that if the distinction between descriptive and normative propositions is applicable (for example, one is not confronted with a question), then the proposition *must* be *either* descriptive *or* normative. No third possibility exists.

In what follows I shall point to features of actually occurring argumentation that I consider to be such a third possibility: *a graduation in the descriptivity and normativity themselves*, not in the definitions or characterisations as such, i.e. a graduation that is common to definitions and characterisations:

Descriptive and normative propositions can be *more or less tightly interwoven* so that it is more or less difficult to keep the propositions apart psychologically. In some cases the propositions are *so* tightly interwoven that it is in practice difficult to separate them even if one wants to: The individual utterance, after having been interpreted, can neither be said to express an individual proposition of either descriptive modality or normative modality, nor be said to express several propositions that can be separated and categorised as either descriptive or normative. The utterance expresses propositions that *cannot be categorised as either descriptive or normative.*

Cognition of the sui generis character of these cases calls for a *separate concept*: the concept of 'fusion of descriptive and normative propositions'. To keep in mind the difference, and to facilitate psychologically separation from cases in which the descriptive and normative propositions can be kept apart, I use the *terms* "fusion of/ fused descriptive and normative propositions" instead of "combination of/ combined descriptive and normative propositions".[1] For the sake of simplicity, in a number of cases I use the abbreviated forms "fusion" and "fused propositions".

Fusion of descriptive and normative propositions is by definition, as the concept of 'fusion' is established here, a *feature of subjective meaning*, i.e. a feature of the sender's meaning or of a particular person's understanding (on subjective meaning, see section E 2.2 above). Fusion is not a feature of the objective meaning of linguistic entities, i.e. is not a feature of meaning according to widespread linguistic practice (on objective meaning, see section E 2.1 above).

The concept of 'fusion' can thus be illuminated by going back to one of the criteria for subjective meaning with respect to proposition type of which an account has already been given, namely the *language user's reaction to discrepancy between proposition and reality* (section E 2.2.4 (3)(b) above; in what follows I sometimes speak only of the sender, for the sake of simplicity). To recapitulate briefly: If the sender corrects the proposition, then this is a criterion of his intending to advance a descriptive proposition. If the sender tries to correct reality, then this is a criterion of his intending to advance a normative proposition.

I shall use this reaction criterion for the *operationalising of the concept of 'fusion'*, as follows:

(a) If one does not only look at the individual fused proposition, but at the class of such propositions as a whole, then one sees that the sender does not only use two possibilities with respect to correction, respectively only the proposition or only reality, but that the sender uses all degrees and combinations, thus including partial correction of propositions combined with partial correction of reality.

---

[1] An example of combination is that a descriptive proposition *presupposes* normative definitions: custom-based, and, as the case may be, definitions stipulated for the occasion (section A 2 (4)(a) above). Perhaps normative characterisations too are presupposed, cf. "discourse-ethical" justifications for fundamental norms; see Habermas, 'Wahrheitstheorien', pp. 255–58; 'Diskursethik – Notizen zu einem Begründungsprogramm', pp. 96–103; 'Erläuterungen zur Diskursethik', pp. 132–34, 154–55, 174, 194. – Another example of combination is what Sundby and Eckhoff call *"påkallelser" [invocations]*, for example the car passenger who says "parking is prohibited here", and who thus intends both to describe to the driver the legal situation (descriptive proposition) and to give expression to what the driver ought not to do (normative proposition); see Eckhoff/ Sundby, *Rettssystemer* [legal systems], 1st and 2nd eds., p. 65; *Rechtssysteme*, p. 58; Sundby, *Om normer* [on norms], pp. 174–76; see also von Wright, *Norm and Action*, p. 105.

I shall supplement the reaction criterion with criteria concerning the *language user's deliberation* as follows:

(b) When advancing the proposition the sender lets it remain open whether in the event of subsequent discrepancy between proposition and reality he will correct proposition or reality.

(c) The sender sees any discrepancy as in itself a relevant argument in the consideration of what is to be corrected.

The fact that I add supplementary criteria concerning the language user's deliberation is because the reaction criterion alone is not sufficient *in the individual instance* to distinguish between on the one hand descriptive or normative propositions, and on the other hand fusions. A proposition may in fact have fused modality *even if* the language user in the individual instance only corrects the proposition or only tries to correct reality. For example: A lawyer may decide to correct in full his previous proposition about what the law is, because the Supreme Court has later unanimously and clearly advanced a different view, which according to the criteria for good legal argumentation the lawyer does not consider to be so poorly justified that he can argue against it. Thus the lawyer who prior to 7 April 1973 argued that the formulation "master of any ship ... on duty" in section 422 of the Criminal Justice Act (Act No. 10 of 22 May 1902) did not include drivers of pleasure craft, after this same date corrects his proposition in full in accordance with the unanimous judgment of the Supreme Court of this date according to which drivers of pleasure craft are included.[2] – In spite of this total correction on his part it will most often be misleading to see the lawyer's previous proposition as descriptive. The reason lies in the criteria (b)–(c). These criteria must therefore be taken into account if one is to be able to capture the phenomenon of fusion.

In the further discussion I first show lawyers' propositions de lege lata as the *paradigm case* of fused descriptive and normative propositions (section 2 below). Reflection on and a desire for insight into lawyers' propositions de lege lata have been an important factor behind my establishment of the concept of 'fusion'.

Against this more concrete background I shall return to the delimitation of the concept of 'fusion' (section 3 below). – For a satisfactory definition of the concept it is also necessary to say a good deal about *what the concept does not cover*; for it is an easy matter to *confuse* the phenomenon of fusion with other phenomena that in one or another vague sense may be said to concern the "relationship between the descriptive and the normative" (sections 2.2 and 3.2, below).[3]

---

2 *Rt. 1973/433*. – I should remind the reader that in relation to the main topic of the present work, language and argumentation, I designate the decisions of the courts by the common term "judgment", irrespective of whether they are procedurally called "judgment", "order", "ruling", "decision", or something else (section B 5.4.2 (1)(b)(iii) above, in note 77).

3 The literature contains many statements that might suggest that it was the phenomenon of fusion that was being spoken about. A general problem of interpretation is, however, that a distinction is seldom made to a sufficient degree between different phenomena that in one or another vague sense can be said to concern the "relationship between the descriptive and the normative"; this applies e.g. to the otherwise inspiring survey in Eckhoff/ Sundby, *Rettssystemer* [legal systems], pp. 64–65;

Since fusion is a feature of subjective meaning and not of the objective meaning of linguistic entities, it is a factual question that must be investigated in the individual instance whether, and if so in what way, a fusion has been *given linguistic expression* (section 4 below).

In retrospect, fusion will appear as an apparently *specific feature* of lawyers' propositions de lege lata. Nevertheless I call lawyers' propositions de lege lata the "paradigm *case*", because it is a *factual* question whether fusion is also to be found in other areas of argumentation.

Rechtssysteme, pp. 57–59. – To the extent that the literature is determinable, it contains a good deal about a number of the phenomena with which I draw boundaries in what follows (particularly about "wishful thinking" in the psychological genesis of propositions, section 2.2 below, and about close relationships between the cognitive criteria of evaluation prescriptions and decision with respect to values, section 3.2.2 (3) below). However, I have not found any statements about a concept of 'fusion of descriptive and normative propositions', as established here, or about that feature of lawyers' argumentation which I use here as the paradigm case of the concept. – Concerning the terminology (see in the text at note 1 above) I mention that some writers use the word "sammensmeltning" [fusion] (or the corresponding word in other languages) more by way of suggestion, or use the word of such phenomena as those with which I draw boundaries in what follows; see e.g. Ahlander, *Är juridiken en vetenskap?* [is law a science?], pp. 82–83, 127; Ross, *On Law and Justice*, p. 140 (see in more detail in section 2.2 below); Christensen, 'Kvinnorätten och lagpositivismen' [women's law and legal positivism], p. 86 (see in more detail in section 3.2.2 (3)(a)↔(b) below); Eckhoff/ Sundby, *Rettssystemer*, p. 64; *Rechtssysteme*, p. 57.

2. Lawyers' propositions de lege lata as the paradigm case

By lawyers' *"propositions de lege lata"* I mean lawyers' propositions about what the law is. Lawyers' propositions de lege lata may be general in one or more dimensions, for example the proposition that the formulation "master of any ship ... on duty" in section 422 of the Criminal Justice Act (Act No. 10 of 22 May 1902) includes drivers of pleasure craft and, as the case may be, what types of boat and with what lower limits for the size of boat or motor; or lawyers' propositions de lege lata may relate to the individual instance in one or more dimensions, for example the proposition that the formulation just quoted applies to John Brown's driving of a 17-foot plastic boat with a 115-hp motor.

As the expression "propositions de lege lata" is used here, it is *by definition open* whether the propositions are descriptive, normative or fused. This is an *empirical question.* – I want to emphasise this. I wish to do so because lawyers contrast "propositions de lege lata" with "propositions de lege ferenda", and by the latter expression mean propositions about what the law ought to be. In consequence it might be tempting to believe that propositions de lege lata are by definition considered to be purely descriptive. On this point, the modality, lawyers' use of the expression "propositions de lege lata" is, however, most often indeterminate. – Definitional openness concerning the modality of lawyers' propositions de lege lata is also presupposed here. Thus we can formulate the *topic*: What modality have lawyers' propositions de lege lata in their actually occurring argumentation?[1]

The demonstration in what follows of the existence of the fused modality in lawyers' propositions de lege lata does *not* rest on the one or the other general definitional boundary in relation to the one or the other *border area* of lawyers' use of language (cf. note 1 on relevant terms in lawyers' use of language). I take as a starting point uncontroversial *model examples* of lawyers' propositions de lege lata and link the demonstration of the existence and diffusion of the fused modality to such examples.

Since in a number of places in what follows I refer to the above-mentioned example concerning section 422 of the Criminal Justice Act, I shall briefly

[1] For stylistic reasons I vary in a number of cases between the formulations "propositions de lege lata" and "propositions about what the law is". – The formulations "rettsdogmatiske utsagn" [legal dogmatic propositions] and "utsagn om gjeldende rett" [propositions about valid law] are also much used by lawyers, but here I use these on the whole only where there is a need to remind the reader of the connection with this usage.

outline the background to the example. – The relevant part of section 422 of the Criminal Justice Act says: "The master of any ship … who wilfully or negligently becomes intoxicated while on duty or when about to go on duty, is liable to fines or to imprisonment for a term not exceeding 1 year." – In *Rt. 1973/433* the Supreme Court arrived at the conclusion that the formulation "master of any ship … on duty" included the driver of a 17-foot plastic boat with a 115-hp motor. The accused had in a state of intoxication almost run down a smaller boat with four people in it. – In favour of letting section 422 of the Criminal Justice Act cover drivers of pleasure craft, there was in particular the need for counteracting dangerous behaviour. Further, there was the consideration for consistency in the legal system; compare in particular the fact that the driving of a vehicle in a state of intoxication is punishable under section 22 of the Road Traffic Act (Act No. 4 of 18 June 1965). In favour of the opposite conclusion, the wording of section 422 did not fit drivers of pleasure craft particularly well ("ship", "master … on duty"); cf. in this connection also the requirement in Art. 96 of the Constitution for statutory authority for penal sanctions, and the considerations behind this requirement, in particular that the citizens shall be able to foresee their legal position and that the question of criminal liability shall not depend on the discretion of the individual judge. – The question of what acts are covered by "master of any ship … on duty" has been subsequently discussed in *Rt. 1975/374, 1992/759, 1995/1878*; and later decisions of relevance to the questions of what types of boat are covered, and of lower limits for the size of boat or motor, are to be found in *Rt. 1980/1154, 1982/808, 1986/823, 1995/901, 1995/1734.*

2.1. Fused modality in connection with a general descriptive component: "What opinion other lawyers will probably hold"

(1) The source of the descriptive component
- **(a) What I claim**
- **(b) Stating my position more precisely by drawing some boundaries with what others have claimed**

(2) The source of the normative component

(3) Fusion in concrete argumentation

(1) The source of the descriptive component

(a) What I claim

A relatively tangible source of the descriptive component in lawyers' propositions de lege lata is the possibility that lawyers always have of thematising *what norms motivate those enforcing the law.* For example, legal science or advocates can thematise what norms motivate judges or civil servants. Such propositions are *descriptive*; they are, as it has been put in the literature, "uekte normer" [spurious norms], "om normer" [about norms] or "norm-deskriptive" [norm-descriptive] (section A 5 (3) above).

Propositions about what norms motivate those enforcing the law are considered to be of *interest* for a number of reasons. The most widespread reason is the wish to avoid wasting time, effort and money in actual conflict resolution. For this purpose one wants to know what those with power, inter alia those enforcing the law, will say: The client wants the advocate's view on what possibilities he has of succeeding through a lawsuit or legal remedies in civil or criminal proceedings; and the advocate wants legal writers to lay the ground for such views.[2] Another reason, which is fairly widespread, is the desire to be scientific, using language in a way in which only descriptive propositions are called "scientific".[3]

This first-mentioned and relatively tangible source I see as a special case of a *general feature* of lawyers' argumentation de lege lata, namely that it is always considered relevant to ask *"What will the other lawyers say?"*. For example: "What will the other lawyers say about ... my saying that section 422 of the Criminal Justice Act ... does not cover pleasure craft/ covers pleasure craft – in the latter instance, does not cover boats under 10 feet and with smaller motors than 15 hp.?". "What will they say", partly in the sense 'do they agree?', and partly in the sense 'if not, what in that case is their argumentation and reaction otherwise?'.

As with the lawyer's relationship to those enforcing the law in particular, so too the relationship between lawyers more generally provides the opportunity for descriptive propositions about what are the norms that motivate, in this case propositions about *what are the norms that motivate in communities of lawyers*, be it in the community of *all* lawyers or in *partial* communities. How the individual lawyer more concretely imagines the community or communities of lawyers to which he relates, may vary. But what I take to be common is the ability to adopt the perspective of "the generalised lawyer" (section 2.3 below).

Propositions about what are the norms that motivate in communities of lawyers are relevant in *all* connections de lege lata. Other lawyers' rejection or acceptance of an argument is according to the tenability criteria for lawyers' argumentation de lege lata of *constitutive significance*: If the argument is rejected by other lawyers of sufficient number and repute, then the argument is not only more or less *unpopular*, it is also *untenable* de lege lata; and if the argument is accepted by other lawyers of sufficient number and repute, then the argument is not only more or less *popular*, it is also *tenable* de lege lata.

---

2 Compare Eckhoff, *Rettskildelære* [doctrine of the sources of law], p. 16; Selvig, *Kontraktsretten* [the law of contract], p. 537; Krüger, *Norsk kontraktsrett* [Norwegian law of contract], p. 505 (bottom); Brusiin, *Über das juristische Denken*, pp. 154–55, 156; Hellner, 'Positivism och metod inom rättsvetenskapen' [positivism and method in legal science], p. 358.

3 See in more detail section B 7.3.2 (1) above.

In lawyers' argumentation de lege lata there is thus not an absolute separation but a *mutual justificatory relationship* between what other lawyers *will* probably *assume* and what is *tenable*; between what other lawyers will probably assume to be the law and what is tenable law (item (3) below). – The weight in the present item (1) lies on the omnipresent relevance and weight of what other lawyers will probably assume to be the law.

(b) Stating my position more precisely by drawing some boundaries with what others have claimed

To go into greater depth about what has been said of the descriptive component (item (a) above), I shall point to certain *differences* from, on the one hand, pure prediction analyses, and on the other, criticism of prediction analyses.

(i) The descriptive component outlined *does not exhaust* my analysis of lawyers' propositions about what the law is (items (2)–(3) below). This is in contrast to, for example, the analyses by Holmes and Ross, in which lawyers' propositions about what is the law are subordinated to the prediction.[4]

(ii) My analysis is *not personally limited* (section 2.3 below). For one thing, the descriptive component outlined entails a prediction *of what norms motivate lawyers more generally*, not only of what norms motivate judges or other persons enforcing the law (as in Holmes and Ross). For another, I claim that the element of prediction is *part of propositions about what the law is from all lawyers*: first, that the element of prediction is not only part of propositions about what the law is from, for example, legal writers (which is the starting point in Ross, *On Law and Justice*); and secondly, that the element of prediction is also part of propositions about what the law is from judges and other persons enforcing the law.

There may be reason to emphasise the latter, that the element of prediction is *also* part of propositions de lege lata *from persons enforcing the law*, since a certain amount of criticism of prediction analyses seems to build on the premiss that this is logically impossible. It is true that the proposition de lege lata from a person enforcing the law cannot be interpreted as a prediction of what the person concerned will *himself* conclude concerning what the law is. But there are no logical problems in interpreting the proposition from the person enforcing the law as descriptive with respect to what opinions *other* sections of the legal community hold.[5] And I consider that such a descriptive perspective is just as consti-

---

4 On Holmes' propositions, see sections I 2 above (in the text at note 1) and V 1.1 below; and on Ross' propositions, see sections I 4, II B 7.3.2 (1), C 2.1, 2.3, 3.1 (2) above, and V 2.6 below.

5 This seems to have been overlooked by, for example, Strahl, 'En allmän rättslära' [a general theory of law], p. 293 ("the kitten chasing its tail"); von Eyben, '"Gældende ret"' [valid law], p. 105 (declares himself in agreement with Strahl); Fleischer, *Grunnlovens grenser* [the limits of the Constitution] p. 187; *Rettskilder* [sources of law], p. 50 ("does not make any sense to the judges ... themselves"; "absurdity"); perhaps also by, for example, Arnholm, 'Fra rettens grunnproblemer' [on some fundamental problems of law], pp. 146 (bottom)–147 (top); Aubert, *Om straffens sosiale funksjon* [on the social function of punishment], p. 21; Jørgensen, *Ret og samfund* [law and society], p. 101; Hart, *The Concept of Law*, 1st ed. p. 143; 2nd ed. pp. 146 (bottom)–147 (top); Summers, *Instrumentalism*

tutive of the propositions de lege lata from a person enforcing the law as of other lawyers' propositions de lege lata; cf. item (a) above, and the discussion in what follows.

> Hart therefore gives, in my opinion, a *misleading picture of the basic structure of the application of the law* when, in his argumentation against pure prediction interpretations, he writes (my italics): "[The judge] does *not* look upon the rule as a statement that he and *others are likely to* punish deviations ... The predictive aspect of the rule (though real enough) is *irrelevant to his purposes* ..."[6] and, further, when he categorises lawyers' propositions de lege lata as "*internal* statements", at the same time as he advances a *sharp conceptual and factual distinction* between on the one hand "internal statements" ("internal aspect of rules", "internal point of view") and on the other hand "*external* statements" ("external aspect of rules", "external point of view"), including assumptions about what motivates other lawyers (predictions).[7]
>
> I cannot see that Hart provides any tenable arguments for saying that assumptions about what motivates other lawyers (predictions) cannot logically be included or are not in fact included as *components* in judges' or other lawyers' propositions de lege lata.[8]

(iii) My propositions *do not have the status of descriptive or normative definitions* of the formulations "lawyers' propositions about what the law is"/ "lawyers' propositions de lege lata". – I presuppose the meaning content of these formulations, and the phenomenon that is thereby delimited: lawyers' propositions about what the law is. My propositions are *descriptive characterisations* of this phenomenon, in that they aim to describe an actually occurring feature: fused modal-

---

and American Legal Theory, pp. 131, 144; Harris, *Legal Philosophies*, p. 97. – Another reason why the descriptive component may appear logically impossible is that one puts this into the formulation of the problem, see e.g. Hart, 'Scandinavian Realism', p. 165 (my italics): "[E]ven if in the mouth of the ordinary citizen or lawyer 'this is a valid rule of English law' is a *prediction* of what a judge will do, say or feel, this cannot be its meaning in the mouth of a judge who is *not engaged in predicting* his own or others' behaviour or feelings." The *question* is, however, precisely *whether, and if so in what manner and to what extent*, the lawyer, including the judge, "is engaged in predicting".

6 Hart, *The Concept of Law*, 1st ed. pp. 10 (in the form Hart reproduces a view advanced by others, but it is apparent that he agrees with the passage quoted), 102; 2nd ed. pp. 11, 105.

7 Hart, 'Scandinavian Realism', pp. 165–69; *The Concept of Law*, e.g. 1st ed. pp. 55–56, 83, 86–88, 96, 99; 2nd ed. pp. 56–57, 85, 88–91, 98–99, 102–03. – The only connection Hart seems to see between propositions de lege lata ("internal statements") and assumptions about what motivates other lawyers (predictions) ("external statements") is that propositions de lege lata *presuppose* that the legal system in its entirety is on the whole effective; see 'Scandinavian Realism', p. 168; *The Concept of Law*, 1st ed. pp. 82, 86, 100–01; 2nd ed. pp. 84 (bottom)–85 (top), 88, 103–04. – Neither the advancement of the sharp distinction between "internal" and "external" statements nor of the presupposed connection between them just mentioned, are particular to Hart. The sharp distinction had been advanced in many forms and under many names, see e.g. section A 5 (3) above, concluding remarks; and the presupposed connection mentioned, had been advanced by Kelsen, see *Reine Rechtslehre*, 1st ed. pp. 72–73. Today, however, Hart is the most discussed and influential representative of this concept formation and is quoted here in this capacity.

8 On the logical, see at and in note 5 above.

ity. I do not say that fused modality is or ought to be a criterion for the use of the formulations "lawyers' propositions about what the law is"/ "lawyers' propositions de lege lata".

> This is in contrast to the analyses by Holmes and Ross, in which descriptive characterisations and normative definitions are combined (Chapter V below, sections 1.1 and 2.6 respectively).

(2) The source of the normative component

The normative component in lawyers' propositions de lege lata stems from the fact that lawyers more or less directly resolve conflicts. The parties and the public expect, and the lawyers themselves wish to achieve, what one considers to be *reasonable and just outcomes*, both in the case of general interpretation (i.e. on the level of rules) and in the case of subsumption (i.e. in the individual instance); neither the individual nor society can in the long run live with a picture of himself/ itself as "unreasonable and unjust".[9]

> "The judge will as far as possible understand and interpret the statute ... so that he is able to accept his decision ... also as "just" or "socially desirable" ";[10] "That a solution is found ... to be the reasonable and best one ... is particularly often the decisive factor both for theory and for the practice of the courts";[11] "In this book the significance [of evaluations] in the application of the law has been a recurring theme";[12] "Ethical requirements [are] a significant group of practical fundamental preconditions for all application of the law and interpretation of statutes";[13] "Many lawyers understand the term "legal argumentation" in such a way that the following supposition can be considered reasonable: If decisions are made in a particular area without any consideration whatsoever for justice, it is strange to consider these decisions as being of a legal nature";[14] "Gemeinsamer Nenner bei Richter und "Umwelt" ist ... daß die nach legitimer Verfahrensweise und in korrekter Anwendung juristischer Begriffsbildung und Logik gefundene Lösung ... gerecht und vernünftig sein "müsse" ";[15] "... the importance in the [judicial] deciding process of considerations of sense, decency, policy, wisdom, justice ...".[16] – In particular with legal science in mind: "If all statements on valid law were to be interpreted as predictions of judicial behavior, the legal

---

9 For the sake of brevity I use the formulation "reasonable and just" as the representative of fundamental normative concepts.

10 Ross, *On Law and Justice*, p. 138; see further pp. 99–100, 136–40, 145–47, 151 et seq.

11 Augdahl, *Rettskilder* [sources of law], p. 17.

12 Eckhoff, *Rettskildelære* [doctrine of the sources of law], 1st ed. p. 312; see further Chapters 4 and 12, and 3rd ed. pp. 127–28 and Chapter 14.

13 Strömholm, *Rätt, rättskällor och rättstillämpning* [law, sources of law and application of the law], p. 425.

14 Peczenik, *Vad är rätt?* [what is law?], p. 100.

15 Esser, *Vorverständnis und Methodenwahl in der Rechtsfindung*, p. 24; see further inter alia pp. 69, 118–19, 135, 140, 152.

16 Llewellyn, *The Common Law Tradition*, p. 59; see further inter alia pp. 23–24, 59–61, 121, 238.

> scholar would be bound by an adherence to the status quo, which would be objectionable, both from his own point of view and from that of wider social interests. It would deprive legal thinking of a creative, dynamic element which is probably socially beneficial."[17]
>
> Cognition of the factual element of others' expectations of and one's own wishes for reasonable and just outcomes may also be expressed in a more concealed form: through the proposition that it is not only so, that the conclusion in the individual instance is justified through the rule, but at the same time so, that the rule is justified through the conclusion in the individual instance.[18] "Expressed", if one by the said proposition means a structure in which (i) the conclusion in the individual instance is justified through *that* aspect of the conclusion that it (the conclusion) falls under the linguistic formulation of the rule and contributes, as the case may be, to realising the purpose of the rule; (ii) at the same time as the rule is justified through *that* aspect of the conclusion that it (the conclusion) is considered reasonable and just.

"Reasonable and just" shows itself on closer examination of actual expectations and wishes to be a property of propositions that is *not* reduced to truth, for example that is not reduced to 'conforming with earlier practice', 'conforming with other lawyers' views', 'conforming with widespread moral views', 'conforming with divine precept', or the like. – The factors mentioned are also considered to be relevant to a greater or lesser degree. But in addition come expectations of and wishes for a reasonable and just *decision*, in the light of the specific nature of the instance-type or of the individual instance.[19] For example, in addition come expectations of and wishes for a reasonable and just decision with respect to whether the formulation "master of any ship ... on duty" in section 422 of the Criminal Justice Act covers the drivers of pleasure craft, and if so, what types of boat and with what lower limits for the size of boat or motor. – Such propositions are *normative* in the terminology of this work; they are, as it has been put in the literature, "ekte normer" [genuine norms], "i normer" [in norms] or "norm-ekspressive" [norm-expressive] (section A 5 (3) above).

---

[17] Aubert, 'Predictability in Life and in Science', p. 133.

[18] For occurrences of this proposition, see Hyllested, '"Individualismen"' ["individualism"], p. 246; Cardozo, declaring himself in agreement with Munroe Smith, in the former's 'The Nature of the Judicial Process', p. 114 at and in note 16; Arnholm, 'Noen metodologiske betraktninger' [some methodological considerations], p. 510; Eckhoff/ Sundby, *Rettssystemer* [legal systems], p. 165; *Rechtssysteme*, p. 138; Esser, declaring himself in agreement with Radbruch, in the former's *Vorverständnis und Methodenwahl in der Rechtsfindung*, p. 32 at and in note 2; Luhmann, *Rechtssoziologie*, p. 359. – By virtue of its being (directly) a proposition about reciprocal action, the proposition mentioned is among those that are often expressed through the formulation "hermeneutic circle", see e.g. Kaufmann, 'Über den Zirkelschluß in der Rechtsfindung', pp. 73–76, with further references.

[19] In conformity with the superordinate perspective and topic of the work I do not adopt any standpoint in the present work on whether the use of "reasonable", "just", or the like, *can* be reduced to truth (Chapter I and sections II A 5 (2)(b) and 8, above). What is relevant in relation to the perspective and topic of the work is that lawyers are not expected to undertake and do not in fact undertake such a reduction when they take standpoints de lege lata.

The normative propositions can coincide with a descriptive proposition about what motivates larger or smaller sections of the legal community, i.e. in relation to these other lawyers they can be *normative-traditional* propositions: for example, "it is reasonable and just that the formulation "master of any ship ... on duty" in section 422 of the Criminal Justice Act covers the drivers of pleasure craft". Or the normative propositions can deviate from a descriptive proposition about what motivates larger or smaller sections of the legal community, i.e. in relation to these other lawyers they can be *normative-innovative* propositions: for example, "it is not reasonable and just that the formulation "master of any ship ... on duty" in section 422 of the Criminal Justice Act covers the drivers of pleasure craft" (probably a deviation from the opinion of many other lawyers).[20]

To an adequate picture of the role evaluations and choices play in lawyers' argumentation belongs the fact that others' expectations of and lawyers' wishes for reasonable and just outcomes not only enter into lawyers' propositions de lege lata (the present section F), but also into lawyers' propositions concerning the facts of the individual case (section III 3.2.3 (3) below).

(3) Fusion in concrete argumentation

Even though neither the purely descriptive interpretation nor the purely normative interpretation appears totally unreasonable in the *abstracting perspectives* that have now been outlined (respectively items (1) and (2) above), neither of these interpretations is particularly often apt in relation to lawyers' *concrete argumentation*. There one finds instead that the *fused modality* dominates. – A criterion of this is *how lawyers react in the event of discrepancy* between their propositions about what the law is and a decision from a body enforcing the law, for example a decision from a court:

On the one hand the advocate, the legal writer, the judge, the civil servant, or other lawyers will seldom say quite simply that they made a mistake and exclusively correct their own propositions de lege lata; i.e. they will seldom consider their own propositions as purely descriptive.

The most practical exception is the advocate's proposition about what the law is, in a situation in which he is deliberating whether a lawsuit will succeed. It is less practical that legal writers consider their propositions about what the law is as purely descriptive.[21] And it is least practical that proposi-

[20] The quotation from Aubert at note 17 above is aimed at the normative-innovative propositions. If one is to give an adequate picture of the significance of fused modality, the normative-traditional propositions must, however, also be taken into consideration, see section 3.2.1 below.

[21] One example is the Swedish legal scholar Knut Rodhe, who has consistently stated that he wants to limit himself to descriptive characterisations; see 'Om gränserna för lagstiftarens makt på civilrättens område' [on the limits of the legislator's power in the area of civil law], pp. 96–97 ("necessary that ... from the scientific presentations one takes away all statements about how legislators and courts ought to act and contents oneself with investigating how they actually act"); *Obligationsrätt* [law of obligations], p. III ("The handbook is not intended – in conformity with the writer's fun-

tions about what the law is from judges and civil servants are intended as purely descriptive.

On the other hand the same groups of persons will seldom say quite simply that a decision that does not conform with their own earlier propositions is incorrect, and exclusively criticise the decision; i.e. they will seldom consider their own propositions as purely normative.

Instead one sees, first, a characteristic openness with respect to what ought to be adjusted. Secondly, one sees a desire to go through the earlier arguments behind one's own proposition and to consider them in the light of the discrepancy, before one decides what is to be adjusted.

If one asks the lawyer whether he can *sort* the descriptive from the normative in his proposition de lege lata, the answer will often be negative: The lawyer will say that when making his proposition de lege lata he did *not adopt any standpoint* on what should be adjusted in the event of any subsequent discrepancy.[22] And the lawyer will often add that *nor does he see taking such a standpoint as right or possible*, in the perspective of generally accepted criteria for (good) legal argumentation de lege lata. What is to be adjusted in the event of any subsequent discrepancy depends on the arguments behind the earlier proposition de lege lata considered in the light of the nature and degree of the subsequent discrepancy, all assessed in the light of the criteria for (good) legal argumentation. Lawyers will for example be more inclined to revise a proposition de lege lata if it does not agree with a subsequent unanimous judgment of the Supreme Court,[23] than if it does not agree with a subsequent judgment of the Supreme Court with dissent.[24]

---

damental view of the task of legal science – to give any recommendations to legislators and courts other than in questions of terminology"); 'Beskrivning – prognos – rekommendation[.] En trosbekännelse' [description – prognosis – recommendation. A confession of faith], p. 1 ("a legal writer can and should concern himself with description and prognoses but … should refrain from recommendations"), cf. pp. 3–4. – Rodhe's standpoint has won little support, see inter alia Ekelöf, 'Är den juridiska doktrinen en teknik eller en vetenskap?' [is legal doctrine a technique or a science?], pp. 121–24; Arnholm, 'En håndbok i obligasjonsrett' [a handbook on the law of obligations], pp. 125–26.

22 Andenæs, 'Rettsteori og rettspraksis' [jurisprudence and court practice], pp. 419–20: "If [a legal writer] has expressed his view on the correct solution of a legal issue and he is then asked whether his statement means that the *Supreme Court* will probably resolve the matter in this way, or whether it is the solution *he himself* would choose, he will perhaps be slightly embarrassed and not quite know what to answer" (Andenæs' italics).

23 For example *Rt. 1973/433*, where the Supreme Court unanimously concluded that the formulation "master of any ship … on duty" in section 422 of the Criminal Justice Act covers the drivers of pleasure craft.

24 For example *Rt. 1992/759*, where the Supreme Court concluded with a majority of 3–2 that the formulation "master of any ship … on duty" in section 422 of the Criminal Justice Act also covers passengers aboard pleasure craft who "abruptly and unexpectedly [are] given control of the craft", unless the passenger "has no reasonable possibility of preventing the situation or of limiting the driving by stopping the motor or in any other manner" (p. 761, the majority; the minority wished on account of the abruptness and unexpectedness of the situation not to deem the passenger as being "master of any ship", and could consequently not accept the last quoted and cumulative condition for acquittal).

To put things in more general terms: Lawyers' propositions de lege lata often seem to have the distinctive modality that in section 1 above I have defined and called *"fusion"*. They are often neither purely descriptive nor purely normative: neither "uekte normer" [spurious norms] nor "ekte normer" [genuine norms], neither "om normer" [about norms] nor "i normer" [in norms], neither "norm-deskriptive" [norm-descriptive] nor "norm-ekspressive" [norm-expressive]. Squeezing lawyers' propositions de lege lata into these dichotomies is liable to obscure their *distinctiveness in the modality dimension.*

> I said earlier that in lawyers' argumentation de lege lata there is a mutual justificatory relationship between what other lawyers will probably assume to be the law and what is tenable law (item (1)(a) above, concluding remarks). This proposition can now be made more precise: Often in lawyers' propositions de lege lata, the lawyer's view of what other lawyers will probably assume to be the law (the descriptive proposition) *fuses with* the lawyer's view of what ought to be the law (the normative proposition) *into* the lawyer's view of what is tenable law (the fused descriptive and normative proposition).

2.2. Drawing the boundary with descriptive propositions about particular sources-of-law facts and with "wishful thinking" in the genesis of such propositions

Above I have identified and concentrated on a *general* descriptive component in lawyers' propositions de lege lata: that it is always considered relevant to ask and to take into account "what opinion other lawyers will probably hold".

Lawyers' argumentation de lege lata brings in many other and *particular* sources-of-law facts. In particular, it brings in what the legislator, legal draughtsmen, contracting parties, courts or public administrative authorities have said, and what they have meant by what they have said.

In relation to these topics for descriptive propositions, *fusion-like phenomena* often arise. For example, in connection with judges' propositions about the legislator's intention, Ross points out:

> "[T]he distinction between [the judge's] cognitive and evaluating functions is an artificial one, so far as these two merge in practice, leaving it impossible to say precisely where one ends and the other begins. This is because it is impossible for the judge himself as well as for others to distinguish between those evaluations which are manifestations of the judge's own preferences and those evaluations ascribed to the legislator which are therefore a datum for a purely cognitive interpretation. ... If now ... the judge identifies his

> own evaluations with those of the legislator, in his mind the two types of interpretation will fuse into one."[25]

I keep such phenomena *outside* the concept of 'fusion of descriptive and normative propositions'. They do not satisfy the concept criterion that when advancing the proposition, the sender lets it remain open whether in the event of subsequent discrepancy between proposition and reality he will correct the proposition or reality (section 1 above, criterion (b)). – This may be illustrated by a specification of the situation described by Ross: If it turns out that a lawyer has overlooked a statement in the travaux préparatoires, and this statement shows that his proposition about "what the legislator meant" was untenable, then the lawyer will not be in any doubt that he must correct his proposition. – To put this in general terms: Propositions about the particular sources-of-law facts entail by definition an obligation to revise the proposition if there later turns out to be discrepancy between proposition and reality. Upholding the proposition would not be understood.

Propositions about the particular sources-of-law facts are thus *descriptive.* There is no fusion in the modality of these propositions. However, there is (and *this* is the topic of the quotation from Ross above) often "wishful thinking" in the *psychological genesis of the propositions*:[26] Because one wishes that something shall be so (psychological cause), for example, because the lawyer, on the basis of what he deems reasonable and just, wishes a question of law to be resolved in a particular manner, one believes and says that it is so (psychological effect), for example, the lawyer believes and says, in the absence of any proof to the contrary, that the legislator or a contracting party intended to lay down the solution the lawyer deems reasonable and just ("the legislator's/ contracting party's intention was ...").

Such "wishful thinking" in the genesis of the proposition does not make the proposition into a fused descriptive and normative proposition. If when making the proposition one is asked what one will correct in the event of discrepancy between proposition and reality, no other answer is meaningful but that one will correct the proposition.

This is different in the case of the general descriptive component in lawyers' propositions de lege lata, concerning what motivates the legal community as a whole. Here it makes good sense and is institutionalised practice to say that the question of what is to be revised, is kept open (section 2.1 (3) above): If it turns out that other lawyers judge the question differently, it is not thereby given that the lawyer must revise his proposition 'the rule is .../ the solution of the indi-

---

[25] Ross, *On Law and Justice*, p. 140.

[26] The inverted commas ("wishful thinking") signal that at the same time as widely held views on wishful thinking point our thought in the right direction, the expression has not been defined in a theoretical context and will easily be liable to be too indeterminate in relation to other theoretical purposes. The signpost function is however sufficient here, where the emphasis is not on positive determination of wishful thinking, but on differences in relation to fused modality.

vidual question of law is ...'. The lawyer will go through the earlier arguments behind his own proposition and consider them in the light of the discrepancy before he decides what is to be adjusted.[27]

"Wishful thinking" in the psychological genesis of descriptive propositions is widespread in everyday life, academic subjects, science and philosophy. Fusion in the modality of propositions, as this phenomenon is delimited here, is not equally widespread: Through the further discussion the phenomenon of fusion will appear as an apparently specific feature of lawyers' argumentation.

2.3. The perspective of "the generalised lawyer"

The general descriptive component in lawyers' propositions de lege lata corresponds with the *perspective of "the generalised lawyer"* – in contrast to propositions about particular sources-of-law facts (section 2.2 above), which do not correspond with any specific lawyer perspective.

> The physical and mental facts that form particular sources-of-law facts (what particular individuals or groups have said or intended) are, on the contrary, often more easily accessible to non-lawyers and their working methods. For example, professional opinion researchers are better equipped than lawyers to make statements about what the individuals who constituted the legislative assembly when an Act was passed, meant by the text and what purposes they wished it to promote.

By the perspective of "the generalised lawyer" I mean a *fundamental consciousness perspective* on the part of the individual lawyer:[28] a perspective that cannot be reduced to propositions about what particular individuals, courts or administrative bodies have said or intended; a perspective that seizes on *particular aspects* of the phenomena (in general terms: "legal persons", "right", "duty", etc.; in more concrete terms: "contract", "breach of contract", "building", "duty to obtain a licence", etc.) and which uses a *particular method* (lawyers' language and argumentation) to decide the existence, content and duration of these aspects; a perspective which *is extended in depth* through knowledge of actual exercise of power (in what public bodies/ parts of private firms is what decided) and through

---

27 In the light of this, I am not completely in agreement with Ross when he says that the matter he is discussing in the quotation in the text at note 25 above, is "*parallel to* ... the fluid boundary between legal-theoretical intention and legal-political intention in doctrine", *On Law and Justice*, p. 140 (my italics). "[T]he fluid boundary" between legal dogmatics and legal politics is due *both* to "wishful thinking" in the genesis of descriptive propositions about particular sources-of-law facts *and* to fusion in the modality of the propositions de lege lata; and these matters should, as argued in the main text, be kept apart.

28 In using the term "the generalised lawyer", I have been inspired by Mead, who in his discussions of the constitution of linguistic meaning, self-awareness and society introduces the term "the generalised other"; see *Mind, Self, and Society*, pp. 89–90, 154–55 (152–64), 256 (253–56). – The concept, however, has been formed on the basis of the purposes here.

knowledge of other individual lawyers (who is a judge, public prosecutor, director general in a ministry, company lawyer, etc., and what type of lawyer is the person concerned). – The perspective builds on and generalises from the opinions and actions of other lawyers. Thus it ties the lawyer's foremost loyalty to other lawyers. Loyalty to the legislator or to the people ("the general sense of justice") is only derived.

By virtue of his being a politically and morally motivated individual, the individual lawyer can obviously feel loyalty to the legislator, people or other groups outside the circle of lawyers. But such loyalty does not lie in the basic structure of lawyers' consciousness that is the topic here.

It seems *necessary to assume the existence* of such a consciousness perspective on the part of the individual lawyer. For if this perspective is hypothetically eliminated, then the possibility of the general descriptive component in lawyers' propositions de lege lata also seems to disappear, and thereby the possibility of the fusion modality in these propositions; but I consider the fusion modality in lawyers' propositions de lege lata to be a fact (section 2.1 above, and the discussion in what follows). – Consequently, I consider that the ability to adopt the generalised lawyer's perspective is a necessary condition for transition from lawyer standpoints *learnt by heart* (for example, in the case of the non-lawyer or the law student) to *one's own production* of propositions de lege lata. An important effect of legal education is that it lays the foundation for this ability in the individual lawyer, so that lawyers' propositions de lege lata are passed on as a distinctive type of proposition.

3. More on the concept of 'fusion' and its consequences for the distinction between descriptive and normative propositions

3.1. The concepts of 'descriptive proposition' and 'normative proposition' as concepts of degree

(1) The concepts of degree, and three resting places for thought

The essential *reason* for being conscious of and applying the distinction between descriptive and normative propositions is that the tenability criteria are different. If one is not aware of or if one does not implement the distinction, analyses and argumentation soon become too loose.

However, the concept of 'fusion' reveals a *limit* to the applicability of a dichotomy between descriptive and normative propositions:

The concepts of 'descriptive proposition' and 'normative proposition' I see as *extreme points on a graduated dimension*, from the purely descriptive to the purely normative. In the middle of this dimension there are pure fusions. From the middle towards the extremes there are degrees of preponderance of descriptive or normative elements.

As is apparent from the discussion above: The graduated empirical basis which I here take as a point of departure as a concept criterion is the *sender's reaction* to any discrepancy between proposition and reality. The reaction criterion *is supplemented by the sender's deliberation* at the time of making the proposition (actual or hypothetical deliberation), with respect to how he will react to any future discrepancy (section 1 above). This part of my conceptualisation (sender's reaction, and his deliberation with respect to his own reaction) *is applied against a background of double interest* on the sender's part: interest partly in purely descriptive propositions, and partly in purely normative propositions (section 2.1 above). – The three features of reality mentioned (i.e. sender's reaction, his deliberation with respect to his own reaction, his double interest), in the functional relationship outlined (i.e. reaction as a point of departure, supplemented by deliberation, against a background of interests), constitute the content of my definition of the concepts of 'descriptive proposition' and 'normative proposition' as concepts of degree, and thereby also of my definition of the concept of 'fused descriptive and normative proposition'.

It may seem misleading to say that a fused proposition is *both* descriptive *and* normative: Our thought is then easily led towards a notion that the fused proposition is only a temporary mixture, in which the elements can be separated if one so wishes. However, if that is the case, one is by definition confronted not with a fusion, but with a combination. – It is therefore better to say that fusions lie in the graduated dimension between descriptive and normative propositions, but are themselves *neither* the one *nor* the other (cf. the relationship of the colour grey to white and black). – Thus in the case of fusions it is not a question of anything but *metaphorical estimates* of a certain relationship between the descriptive and the normative.

Against this background I consider it *more appropriate to speak of a tripartite division than a dichotomy in the 'descriptive-normative' dimension*: The concepts of 'descriptive proposition', 'normative proposition' and 'fused proposition' provide three points for our thought, which each allow our thought to rest, and which seen in connection with each other show the graduatedness of the dimension and thereby the necessity of openness of thought.

The concept formation now outlined focuses on features of reality that it is not usual to see in connection with one another (reaction, deliberation with respect to reaction, interests). As is apparent from the discussion above, I consider these features to be in fact active in an interesting way; that it is these which lawyers are intuitively motivated by when lawyers consider it neither possible nor right to call their propositions de lege lata either "descriptive" or "normative" (section 2.1, especially item (3), above; see also section 3.2.4 below). Thus, this concept formation serves to demonstrate a basis in reality for intuitions about fusion, and to clarify this basis.[1]

(2) The concepts of degree refer to the individual proposition, not to systems of propositions

Galtung too emphasises the graduation in the distinction between the descriptive and the normative. However, with reference to, and by analogy with, Quine's criticism of the distinction between analytic and synthetic propositions, Galtung transfers the graduation from the individual proposition to the *system* of propositions.

---

1 I place emphasis on concept formation's having a demonstrable reality basis, in contrast to (i) the simply thinkable; compare e.g. Ofstad, 'The Functions of Moral Philosophy', pp. 48–49, who points to graduatedness in concept formation as possible in thought ("possible conceptual systems", "possible worlds"), not as a feature of actually occurring language and argumentation (Ofstad does not directly discuss the distinction between descriptive and normative propositions); (ii) concept formations that are claimed to cover something real, but where the connection with reality is indeterminate; see Eng, 'Teoristruktur og teorivalg' [theory structure and theory choice], pp. 498–50 (item 5); see also section III 2.2.2 below.

> "[T]he degree of normativity is just as little inherent in the expectation itself as the degree of analyticity, but is rather a function of the structure of attitudes and beliefs held by the individual ... Like Quine, we see no immediate way of translating these ideas into operational devices that could give us, for a given person, a given situation and a given expectation, the degree of normativity."[2]

I do not agree that graduation and fusion are an argument for separating the distinction between descriptivity and normativity from the individual proposition:

First, there is *no definitional connection* between on the one hand dichotomy or graduation with respect to the distinction between descriptive and normative propositions, and on the other hand individual propositions or systems of propositions: Both dichotomy and graduation can refer to both individual propositions and systems of propositions.

Secondly, in section G below, in connection with Quine's criticism, I shall explain why it *is not apt* in relation to actually occurring analysis and argumentation to separate the concepts of 'definition' and 'characterisation' from the individual propositions (section G 2 below). – My argumentation there will apply *correspondingly* in relation to Galtung's statement quoted above and in relation to the concepts of 'descriptive proposition', 'normative proposition' and 'fused descriptive and normative proposition'.

> I shall briefly outline the main points that apply *correspondingly*:
>
> In actually occurring analysis and argumentation one *uses* descriptive, normative and fused propositions, and concepts of these propositions (section 2.1 (3) above, *compare* section G 2 (4)(a) below). Furthermore, one links these concepts to the *individual propositions*, not to whole systems of propositions (section 2.1 (3) above, *compare* section G 2 (4)(b) below).
>
> Often it is indeterminate what, when advancing the proposition, one meant by the words one used, e.g. whether one intended to make a descriptive, normative or fused proposition. However, one accepts a demand that one must make a *decision* with respect to which proposition type one will now understand by the words (section 2.1 (3) above, *compare* section G 2 (4)(a)–(b) below). The legitimacy in actually occurring analysis and argumentation of the demand for such a decision constitutes the *"operational device"* that Galtung is seeking in the quotation above.
>
> Quine, and Galtung in so far as he builds on Quine in the context of the present problem, *abstract from* the discussion and decision aspect of language and argumentation. Thus they abstract from the existence level of the critically reflexive form that constitutes the perspective and topic of the present work (section G 2 (4)(c) below, cf. section I 4 above).

---

2 Galtung, 'Expectations and Interaction Processes', pp. 217–18, cf. 215–16. – As is apparent, Galtung is more precisely speaking of expectations and not of propositions; but since this distinction is not of significance here, I content myself with "proposition" in the main text. On the relationship between proposition and expectation, see section E. 2.2.4 (3)(b) above.

In the light of this, the occurrence of graduation and fusion is *not an argument for separating* the distinction between descriptivity and normativity from the individual propositions. Graduation and fusion are a *decision alternative on the level of proposition*, on a par with descriptive proposition and normative proposition.

3.2. Contrasting of fusion with some other phenomena

In the present section, I shall illuminate the concept of 'fusion of descriptive and normative propositions' by contrasting the phenomenon covered by this concept with a number of other phenomena. These other phenomena have been chosen because they are often confused with fusion of descriptive and normative propositions.

3.2.1. Drawing the boundary with the graduated distinction between normative-traditional and normative-innovative propositions

(1) The distinction between descriptive and normative propositions, and within this the relationship between them in a fused modality, is something else than the distinction between normative-traditional and normative-innovative propositions. The latter distinction is a question of whether, and if so to what degree, a presupposedly normative proposition departs from a practice or opinion in the question that is being normatively regulated.[3]

(a) Fused modality where the normative proposition component is normative-traditional:

On the one hand, lawyers' propositions about what the law is, may have a great deal of support in objectively present sources of law and in equitable considerations that are widespread among lawyers, and thus have a great deal of support in an element of prediction with respect to what courts or other bodies enforcing the law will conclude. This is not, however, the same as such propositions' being purely descriptive. On the contrary, there is probably a tendency in the direction that the greater support of the kind mentioned a proposition has, the greater the number of lawyers who will find that their views of the reasonable and just lead to the same proposition, and the greater the degree to which they will find this; and the less inclined will they consequently be to correct the proposition in the event of any subsequent discrepancy between the proposition and a decision of an authority enforcing the law. – In the light of this, I shall characterise the status of such propositions more precisely as propositions with fused modality where the normative component is normative-traditional.

[3] See sections B 3.3.4 and 4.3.3 above on these concepts applied in particular to definitions.

(b) Fused modality where the normative proposition component is normative-innovative:

On the other hand, lawyers' propositions about what the law is, may have little support in objectively present sources of law and in equitable considerations that are widespread among lawyers, and thus have little support in an element of prediction with respect to what courts or other bodies enforcing the law will conclude. This is not, however, the same as such propositions' being "more normative" than in the case above. The lawyer will in these cases often try to convince other participants in the legal system, inter alia by means of his proposition about what the law is; for example a professor of law may try to convince judges and other persons enforcing the law, by means of his scholarly reputation. Any subsequent discrepancy between the proposition and decisions of authorities enforcing the law will be a sign that the persons enforcing the law have not let themselves be convinced; and the lawyer then most often corrects his proposition, in acknowledgement of this. – The status of such propositions too will most often have to be characterised as propositions with fused modality. For even in extreme cases these propositions will have at least *some* support in objectively present sources of law and in equitable considerations that are widespread among lawyers, so that a descriptive interpretation of the proposition is not totally unreasonable (section 2.1 (1) above). If the propositions do not have such support, they will not be considered at all as propositions about what the law is, but as juridico-political, general-political, moral, or the like, propositions. – In the light of this, I shall characterise the status of lawyers' propositions about what the law is that have little support in objectively present sources of law and in equitable considerations that are widespread among lawyers, more precisely as propositions with fused modality where the normative component is normative-innovative.

(2) *Confusion* of the graduated dimension between normative-traditional and normative-innovative propositions with the graduated dimension between descriptive and normative propositions may be one *cause* of lacking cognition of the existence and diffusion of the phenomenon of fusion. – For example, Ross seems to presuppose that when one can predict the reaction of the courts with great probability, then there is no room for the normative proposition component, only for the descriptive, cf. the first sentence, antithetically, in the quotation below. This would be confusion of normative-traditional propositions with descriptive propositions (compare item (1)(a) above). The consequence is that one does not see that the fused modality is a *systematic* feature of lawyers' propositions de lege lata.

> "In legal problems, *where* it is possible with only a small degree of probability to predict the reaction of the courts, the legal writer can adopt one of the two attitudes. He can *either* ... try ... to surmise the *most probable*

solution. *Or*, he may pursue his own evaluations in order to find the *solution which he himself would arrive at were he in the judge's place*" (my italics).[4]

3.2.2. Drawing the boundary with evaluation prescription in the connotations of concepts and, as the case may be, evaluation-free language attire

(1) Drawing the boundary with evaluation prescription <u>in itself</u>. Lawyers' propositions de lege lata as an example
- **(a) Evaluation prescriptions are factually central even though they are not strictly necessary for the formation of fused descriptive and normative propositions**
- **(b) Evaluation prescription is not sufficient. In addition, it is required that it be possible and interesting to see the decision that is prescribed, as the decision of another person than the language user himself**

(2) Propositions with the concept of 'illness' as an illustration of evaluation prescription's not being sufficient for fusion of descriptive and normative propositions
- **(a) Evaluation prescriptions in the concept of 'illness'**
- **(b) Propositions with the concept of 'illness' contrasted with lawyers' propositions de lege lata**

(3) Drawing the boundary with <u>features of</u> evaluation prescriptions
- **(a) The relationship between the cognitive criteria of the evaluation prescription and its decision element**
- **(b) Evaluation-free language attire**

(1) Drawing the boundary with evaluation prescription in itself. Lawyers' propositions de lege lata as an example

(a) Evaluation prescriptions are factually central even though they are not strictly necessary for the formation of fused descriptive and normative propositions

I have earlier given an account of *evaluation prescription* as a way of establishing the connotation of the concept (section B 6.1 above). Evaluation prescription is characterised by a combination of cognitive criteria and the language user's decision with respect to values (section B 6.1 (2)(a)).

Evaluation prescription in the connotations of concepts is *not* definitionally or factually a *necessary* condition for fusion of descriptive and normative propositions. True enough, it is definitionally necessary that a normative interpretation of the proposition is interesting, and thus (in that sense) possible (section 3.1 (1) above). However, the source of the normative component in the fusion, others'

---

4 Ross, *On Law and Justice*, p. 48.

expectations of and one's own wishes for reasonable and just outcomes (section 2.1 (2) above), *can* be given expression in normative propositions *without* concepts with evaluation prescription in their connotation (section B 6.1 (3)(a) above).

Evaluation prescription in the connotations of concepts is, however, *in fact a central factor* in the formation of the fused modality in lawyers' propositions de lege lata. The cause is that others' expectations of and one's own wishes for reasonable and just outcomes to a great extent seek expression in discussion of interpretation and subsumption in relation to words and concepts in already existing norm formulations:

(i) When the normative component in lawyers' propositions de lege lata is normative-innovative (section 3.2.1 (1)(b) above), the lawyer's views of the reasonable and just will often *not be able to find apt expression in* earlier legal formulations (e.g. statutes or judgments) of duty, competence or qualification norms. The lawyer will therefore not be able to give any satisfactory justification for his normative-innovative standpoint simply by bald agreement with such formulations. In this situation the lawyer will often choose not to let his views of the reasonable and just find public linguistic expression at all (Chapter IV below). However, to the extent that the lawyer does give public expression to them, and when the lawyer discusses with himself, this most often happens in and through discussion of interpretation and subsumption in relation to words and concepts in earlier norm formulations; combined, as the case may be, with decision propositions ("I am of the opinion that .../ my opinion is ..."). Decision propositions alone will *seldom be considered acceptable*, since they will conflict too strongly with the ideology that the lawyer does not create the law, but finds and applies it.

(ii) Even if the normative component is normative-traditional (section 3.2.1 (1) (a) above), so that the lawyer's views of the reasonable and just would be able to find apt expression in earlier legal formulations of duty, competence or qualification norms, bald agreement with earlier formulations will in many situations *not satisfy expectations concerning justification*. And decision propositions ("I am of the opinion that .../ my opinion is ...") will often *be considered out of place*, since the lawyer is agreeing with earlier practice and opinions. Here too the justifications which are actually given therefore most often take the form of discussion of interpretation and subsumption in relation to words and concepts in earlier norm formulations.

(i)↔(ii) Thus, two *characteristic features of lawyers' language and argumentation de lege lata* are constituted:

First, *evaluation prescription* in the connotation is constituted as a *systematic* feature of concepts in legal rules.

That evaluation prescription in the connotation is a systematic feature of concepts in legal rules seems today to be generally recognised in literature on lawyers' language and argumentation (see the references in section 2.1 (2) above). But the way of putting it is different, since a definition and concept perspective is not common. Instead writers refer to deliberation and justification more generally and use in that connection formulations such as "reale hensyn" or "reelle hensyn" [equitable considerations] (Ross, Eckhoff), "pragmatiske faktorer" [pragmatic factors] (Ross), "vurderinger" [evaluations] (Eckhoff), "sakens natur" [the nature of the case] (Augdahl), "etiska krav" [ethical requirements] (Strömholm), "etiska värden" [ethical values] (Peczenik); see the more detailed references in section 2.1 (2) above.

Secondly, discussion of interpretation and subsumption in relation to these evaluation prescriptions are constituted as a *central form* of the normative component in lawyers' propositions de lege lata.

(b) Evaluation prescription is not sufficient. In addition, it is required that it be possible and interesting to see the decision that is prescribed, as the decision of another person than the language user himself

In the light of the central factual role evaluation prescriptions play (item (a) above), I shall briefly relate the general account of the fusion modality in lawyers' propositions de lege lata (section 2 above) to evaluation prescriptions in particular.

Evaluation prescription in the connotation of a concept entails that a proposition with the concept concerned is by definition a normative proposition (section B 6.1 (3)(a) above). And since evaluation prescription in the connotation is a systematic feature of concepts in legal rules (item (a) above), the purely *normative interpretation* of lawyers' propositions about what the law is, will thus seldom be a totally unreasonable interpretation alternative (section 2.1 (2) above).

Evaluation prescription alone, however, is *not sufficient* for fusion. In addition, it is necessary that the decision with respect to values that is prescribed, can reasonably be seen *also as the decision of another person* than the language user himself. *Only then* is the purely *descriptive interpretation* also possible, namely the interpretation that the language user is not expressing his own decision, but describing or predicting the other person's decision. – In lawyers' language and argumentation de lege lata, the decision that is prescribed, can reasonably be seen also as the decision of another person: of judges and civil servants with competence to determine finally and with binding effect the connotations and denotations of concepts. This institutional framework makes possible the interpretation of lawyers' propositions de lege lata that they describe or predict the application of evaluation prescriptions by persons enforcing the law; and more generally, that they describe or predict the application of evaluation prescriptions in communities of lawyers (section 2.1 (1) above). Thus the fusion of the descriptive and normative interpretations is also made possible (section 2.1 (3) above).

The outlined possibility of fusion *is realised* because lawyers have *interests* connected with both the extreme points in the interpretation of their propositions de lege lata: partly with the description and prediction of other lawyers' concept determination (section 2.1 (1) above), and partly with their own evaluations and choices with respect to reasonableness and justice winning through (section 2.1 (2) above).

(2) Propositions with the concept of 'illness' as an illustration of evaluation prescription's not being sufficient for fusion of descriptive and normative propositions

(a) Evaluation prescriptions in the concept of 'illness'

Illness is contrasted inter alia with normality (item (i)), criminality (item (ii)) and self-inflicted harm (item (iii)). These are all drawings of boundaries that when looked at more closely turn out to prescribe evaluations.

(i) Illness requires deviation from the normal.[5] Both the deviation criterion and the normality criterion prescribe that the language user undertake supplementary evaluations. First, only deviation that is *evaluated negatively* is considered to be illness; for illness is something that calls for change, and positive deviations are not something that one wishes to change. Secondly, the *normality criterion itself* prescribes evaluations. This is particularly clear when the criterion is applied to mental phenomena.[6] Supplementary evaluations show themselves to be neces-

---

5 Some writers use concepts of 'illness' in which the criterion is deviation not from the normal but from the ideal. For example, this may occur when one takes as a point of departure, the World Health Organisation's definition of 'health' as "a state of complete physical, mental and social well-being and not merely the absence of disease or infirmity" (in the introduction to the Constitution of WHO of 22 July 1946). According to the wording, the definition establishes a zone between illness and the ideal state of health, but in practice the definition has been understood to mean that the concept of 'illness' is complementary to the ideal concept of 'health'; see e.g. Søgaard/ Førde, 'Jo mer helse, jo mindre trivsel' [the more health, the less enjoyment] ("had a medicalising effect; all of life's minor and major problems are defined as illness"). – The analysis here, however, takes as its point of departure the concept of 'illness' in everyday life, and in that concept the criterion is deviation from the normal.

6 Sapir, 'Cultural Anthropology and Social Psychology', p. 235 ("cultural anthropology ... believes the external form of normal adjustment to be an exceedingly elastic thing ... is constantly rediscovering the normal"); Benedict, *Patterns of Culture*, pp. 232–57; Horney, *The Neurotic Personality of Our Time*, pp. 13–19; *New Ways in Psychoanalysis*, pp. 179–80 ("no simple measuring rod as to what is healthy or not"); Adorno/ Frenkel-Brunswik/ Levinson/ Nevitt Sanford, *The Authoritarian Personality*, p. 7; Szasz, 'The Myth of Mental Illness', pp. 116–18; *The Myth of Mental Illness*, p. 11 ("psychiatric interventions are directed at moral ... problems"), cf. e.g. pp. 32, 243, 255, 269–70; A. Freud, *Normality and Pathology in Childhood*, p. 107 ("the variations of normality [are] innumerable"), p. 177 at and in note 11, p. 178; Drury, *The Danger of Words*, pp. 132–33 ("in our search for a principle of differentiation between madness and religion ... we ... [looked] for the wrong type of answer. ... We did not see ourselves and our own manner of life as intimately involved in the settlement of this question"), cf. pp. 115–37; Zapffe, 'Den sidste Messias' [the last Messiah], pp. 19–28; *Indføring i litterær Dramaturgi* [introduction to literary dramaturgy], pp. 87–90; Sundby, 'Strafferetten og dens begrensninger' [criminal law and its limitations], pp. 67–68, 70–73. – I may add that it is difficult to find literature that directly and clearly deals with the present topic: evaluation prescription in the connotations of concepts of 'mental normality'. In the literature no clear distinction is drawn between on the one hand *this* feature of concepts of 'normality' and on the other hand, partly the fact that normality concepts vary with societal conditions (Sapir, Benedict, Horney, Adorno/ et al.; compare section B 3.3.2 (3) above); partly that normality concepts are indeterminate (A. Freud; compare section B 2.2 above, at the beginning); and partly that many people associate negative feelings with

sary, however, also when the normality criterion is applied to somatic phenomena. This is so whether the somatic facts and relationships are clear, for example in the case of involuntary childlessness, the menopause, small/ large breasts, baldness, or the like; or whether it is a matter of subjectively experienced somatic discomfort that medical experts cannot find any somatic basis for, for example in the case of the sets of symptoms that are discussed under the name of "fibromyalgia". And evaluations come into play in the case of phenomena in which the mental and somatic aspects engage in interplay, for example in the case of intoxicants (from use, via misuse, to dependency) and food (from slimming, to bulimia, anorexia, or the like).

(ii) Illness has a boundary with *criminality*, in so far as illness makes the perpetrator *of unsound mind* in criminal law; insanity is the most important example, cf. section 44 of the Criminal Justice Act (Act No. 10 of 22 May 1902). The drawing of the boundary with criminality is partly coextensive with the drawing of the boundary with normality (item (i) above), in that persons who are deemed to be of unsound mind will also be deemed to deviate from the normal; and partly different from the drawing of the boundary with normality, in that not all persons who are deemed to be of sound mind will be deemed to be on a par with the normal, cf. the fact that soundness of mind is not affected by all mental illnesses.[7]

The drawing of the boundary with criminality raises *separate* questions, which illustrate the evaluation prescription in the connotation of the concept of 'illness', *inter alia* the following dilemma: – The fear of standing alone promotes a picture of humanity as a homogeneous crowd, of which one is oneself an inseparable part. A manifestation of this picture is an inclination to consider the perpetrator as being of unsound mind the more deviant the act is. To consider the perpetrator as being of sound mind may produce an ominous picture of what man is. – Against this need for a normatively acceptable (ideal) picture stands the need for punishment as deterrence; this need supports reckoning the perpetrator as being of sound mind even in the case of the most incomprehensible acts.[8/9]

> An attempt to resolve this dilemma is to reckon with two alternatives to soundness of mind. One does not just reckon with unsoundness of mind, which entails freedom from penal sanctions, but also with fundamental evil:

---

words that are used of what one classifies as mentally abnormal (Sundby; compare section B 7 above). If one is conscious of these distinctions, however, the observations of the writers mentioned can also contribute to illuminating the present topic.

7 Andenæs, *Alminnelig strafferett* [general criminal law], pp. 274–85; *Ot.prp. No. 87 1993–94* [proposal from the Government], pp. 22–36.

8 *Rt. 1988/69* on p. 70: "[W]hat has been stated by the defence about the personal background of the convicted person [is] in my opinion hardly … suited to explaining, or facilitating an understanding of, the acts he has committed. I deem it necessary to react with the most severe penalty allowed by law."

9 Aubert/ Messinger, 'The Criminal and the Sick', compare the concepts of 'illness' and 'criminality', but do not discuss in particular how evaluation prescription is built into the drawing of the boundary. Perhaps, for the purpose of contrasting the concept of 'illness' with the concept of 'criminality', they have gone too far in presenting the concept of 'illness' as evaluation-free, see e.g. p. 140.

evil which is considered incomprehensible and thus beside the distinction between soundness and unsoundness of mind, which does not entail freedom from penal sanctions, and to which one can ascribe the most incomprehensible acts. – An indication that such a way of thinking is widespread, is the resistance Arendt aroused when she portrayed Adolf Eichmann as an ordinary bureaucrat, concerned with following the law and effectively carrying out the administrative tasks he was given:[10] Since unsoundness of mind was not a practical alternative,[11] and since Arendt rejected the concept of 'evil' as an explanatory device, the readers were forced to closer reflection on the difference between themselves and Eichmann.

(iii) Further, illness has a boundary with a person's own *fault* where the person is *himself the cause* of his troubles. Again, this is a drawing of a boundary where the criteria prescribe evaluations and choices: – The fact that a person can be blamed for the *arising* of his negative deviation does not seem to be a particularly strong consideration against the illness characterisation. One considers, for example, lung cancer as illness even if the sick person is a chain smoker and was aware of the positive and strong connection between cancer and the smoking of cigarettes. – The judgement seems to be different if the person claiming to be ill can be blamed for his deviation's *persisting*. As long as one cannot find causes that lie outside the control of the person concerned, typically physical causes, then alcoholism, drug addiction, obesity and depressions, for example, will often be said to be the person's own fault, and therefore be considered to lie outside the concept of 'illness'. – More generally, it is probably the case that suspicions that, and difficulties in disproving that, the person claiming to be ill is himself to blame for the persistence of his negative deviation, is one reason that *mental disorders* are not so easily considered as illness as physical disorders.

Why does one consider that difficulties in checking whether (in disproving that) the person claiming to be ill is to blame, make the use of the word "illness" problematic? And why does one often consider that the person claiming to be ill being himself to blame for the persistence of his negative deviation, excludes the use of the word "illness"?

Here one must take into account the fact that the application of the concept of 'illness' gives the sick person a number of *advantages* in relation to his surroundings:

The sick person is *free* to stay at home from work. If the sick person is infectious, he has a *duty* to do so.

Further, any person suffering from mental disorders has to a certain extent *immunity* against penal sanctions. And irrespective of the nature of the illness, the sick person has the *competence* to demand a certain degree of help and sympathy, if the surroundings do not already provide such things of their own motion.

---

10 Arendt, *Eichmann in Jerusalem – A Report on the Banality of Evil*, inter alia pp. 44–45, 135–50, 276; Young-Bruehl, *Hannah Arendt*, pp. 328–78, in particular pp. 367 et seq.

11 Arendt, *Eichmann in Jerusalem – A Report on the Banality of Evil*, pp. 25–26.

In everyday life the word "illness" is thus also used as a *linking-term*: Provided that at least one of a number of alternative sets of conditions is satisfied (the criteria for the different types of illness), then one is to be termed "ill". And if one is termed "ill", then this triggers a cumulative set of normative consequences, inter alia such freedoms, duties, competences and immunities as those just mentioned.[12]

(i)↔(iii) In the light of this, one can distinguish between *two main sets* of evaluations in the concept of 'illness'.

First, a *misuse evaluation*: The surroundings are, given the outlined advantages for the sick person (item (iii) above), on their guard against people who misuse the sick role, for example by simulating illness, by exaggerating symptoms, or by not doing anything or not doing enough to get better.

Secondly, a *purpose evaluation*: In the determination of the area of application of the concept of 'illness' (including its application in the dimensions (i)–(iii) above), one evaluates whether the normative consequences fit in the individual instance(-type), account being taken of the purpose of letting these consequences arise.

In actual language use both these evaluation sets are built into the connotation of the general concept of 'illness'.

(b) Propositions with the concept of 'illness' contrasted with lawyers' propositions de lege lata

The difference between propositions with the concept of 'illness' and lawyers' propositions de lege lata may be illustrated by analysis of *"presumably"* in the sentence schema "a is presumably x": on the one hand, "John is presumably ill", and on the other, "This rule is presumably law" (general proposition de lege lata) and "John presumably has title to the property" (particular proposition de lege lata).

In these sentences the word "presumably" points in one meaning dimension towards the question of the *normatively tenable* (in what follows called "the question of tenability"), and in another meaning dimension towards the question of the *descriptively probable* (in what follows called "the question of probability"). – Wherein does the difference lie that constitutes fused descriptive and normative modality in propositions de lege lata, but not in propositions with the concept of 'illness'?

In the question of tenability there is the following *similarity* between propositions with the concept of 'illness' and lawyers' propositions de lege lata. On the one hand: How shall one exercise the evaluation that the concept of 'illness' prescribes (item (a) above)? On the other hand: How shall one exercise the evaluation that the legal rules systematically prescribe (item (1)(a) above)? – Al-

12 Compare Parsons, *The Social System*, pp. 436–37, on "institutionalized expectations" that constitute "the sick role"; essentially the same in 'Definitions of Health and Illness in the Light of American Values and Social Structure', pp. 274–76.

ready from this very similarity, it follows that any difference in relation to fused modality cannot stem from this point. As I shall immediately demonstrate, the exercise of these evaluation prescriptions is thus something else than fusion of descriptive and normative propositions (item (3)(a) below).

In the question of probability there is a certain *similarity* between propositions with the concept of 'illness' and lawyers' propositions de lege lata. On the one hand: Is John only saying that he is in pain, or is he actually in pain? On the other hand, in relation to general propositions de lege lata: Has the lawyer now taken into account all relevant arguments, or has he overlooked, for example, a Supreme Court judgment? And in relation to particular propositions de lege lata: Is John only saying that Jane promised him the property, or did this in fact happen? – Again, it follows already from this very similarity that any difference in relation to fused modality cannot stem from this point.

The *difference* stems instead from another interpretation of the probability question. In relation to general propositions de lege lata: How probable is it that the rule will be applied by the courts/ other lawyers? And in relation to particular propositions de lege lata: How probable is it that John will be recognised as the owner by the courts/ other lawyers?

This interpretation is a *necessary condition* for fused descriptive and normative modality in lawyers' propositions de lege lata (section 2 above). The interpretation has an institutional basis in lawyers' conflict-resolving activity (section 2.1 (1) above); and it corresponds with a fundamental consciousness perspective on the part of the individual lawyer (section 2.3 above). – Since propositions with the concept of 'illness' are not part of a corresponding institutional arrangement for final and binding concept determination, these propositions cannot be interpreted as descriptive propositions about a conflict-resolver's application of the concept. Thus, nor will any fusion in relation to *such* a source of descriptive propositions be able to arise. – Conceivably, *other* possibilities might exist for seeing the decision with respect to values that the concept of 'illness' prescribes, as the decision of another person than the language user himself. But I have not been able to find any possibilities that are systematically used.

(3) Drawing the boundary with features of evaluation prescriptions

(a) The relationship between the cognitive criteria of the evaluation prescription and its decision element

I have defined evaluation prescription as a combination of cognitive criteria and the language user's decision with respect to values (section B 6.1 (2)(a) above). The more detailed *relationship* between the cognitive criteria and the decision element can vary (section B 6.1 (2)(b) above). I have the impression that many people's intuitions about, in one sense or another, "fusion of the descriptive and normative" are linked to *this* relationship: (i) Many philosophers' intuitions about particularly close relationships between "is" and "ought", "fact" and "value", or the like, are linked to the relationship between cognitive criteria and decision elements in concepts like 'good', 'ought', 'right', 'honest', 'brave', 'loyal', etc.; and conceptualisations and analyses then part company according to whether one emphasises that cognitive criteria and decision elements can be separated[13] or one emphasises the close relationship.[14] (ii) Many lawyers' corresponding intuitions are linked to the systematic occurrence of evaluation prescriptions in concepts in legal rules (item (1)(a) above), and to the often close relationship between cognitive criteria and decision with respect to values, in the subsumption: Even an experienced and reflective lawyer cannot always or most often keep these elements apart. When the lawyer is to decide whether he is confronted with a building within the meaning of the Planning and Building Act (Act No. 77 of 14 June 1985), he does not first decide whether a set of cognitive criteria have been satisfied and then whether a decision with respect to values indicates an adjustment of the cognitively based subsumption.

> The usual situation is that the lawyer up to a certain limit can point to cognitive criteria that have motivated him, for example the wording of the statute objectively interpreted, or a strong similarity between the instance at hand and another that has earlier been decided by the Supreme Court; and further that the lawyer can point to decisions of his with respect to values that have motivated him, for example a decision with respect to what is just in the instance at hand. However, when it comes to the more nuanced features of the lawyer's deliberation, the distinction between cognitive criteria and decision with respect to values becomes blurred. Cf. for example how the lawyer's decision with respect to what is just may have affected his understanding of the wording of the statute, or affected the similarity he sees with the earlier instance and thus the weight he places on the views of the Supreme Court in its earlier judgment; or how the lawyer's understanding of the wording of the statute or the degree of respect he feels towards the majority in the earlier judgment may have affected his decision with respect to what is just in the instance at hand; and so forth, with interplay between a diversity of cognitive criteria and decisions with respect to values.

More or less close relationships between an evaluation prescription's cognitive criteria and decision with respect to values, be it more generally or in lawyers' language and argumentation, have, however, neither definitional nor factual con-

---

13 For example, Hare distinguishes between the "prescriptive/ evaluative meaning" and the "descriptive meaning" of words. And with the relationship of the meaning elements to each other in mind, he distinguishes between words with only "descriptive meaning", only "prescriptive/ evaluative meaning", and words with both elements. And further, in the case of words with both elements, he distinguishes between whether the one element is "primary" or "secondary" in relation to the other. See *Freedom and Reason*, pp. 21–27.

14 For example, Williams introduces the term "thick concepts" with such an emphasis; see *Ethics and the Limits of Philosophy*, pp. 29–30, 140 et seq. As Williams seems to use the term, it includes the last three concepts mentioned here in the main text ('honest', 'brave', 'loyal'), but probably not the first three mentioned ('good', 'ought', 'right'); see op. cit., p. 152.

nection with fusion of descriptive and normative propositions: Independently of the precise constellation between cognitive criteria and decision, the proposition is *by virtue of* the decision element a normative proposition. – For fusion of propositions to be able to arise, it must *in addition* be possible and interesting to see the decision as another person's (than the language user's). Only then is the purely descriptive interpretation also possible, namely the interpretation that the language user is not expressing his own decision, but describing or predicting the other person's decision. And thus, only then is a fusion of the normative and descriptive interpretation possible (items (1)(b) cf. (2)(b), above).

(b) Evaluation-free language attire

The decision element of the evaluation prescription does not always find linguistic expression. Objectively interpreted the concept designation can appear as the expression of a purely cognitive connotation (Chapter IV below; see also section B 6.1 (2)(b) above).

Nor does evaluation-free language attire, however, have definitional or factual connection with fusion of descriptive and normative propositions: Independently of whether the linguistic expression signals the evaluation prescription, the proposition of which the concept is a part can be fused or not fused. – For example, in propositions with the concept of 'illness', the word "illness" does not signal the evaluation prescription in the connotation of the concept. At the same time propositions outside law and with the concept do not have fused modality (item (2)(b) above), while propositions in law and with the concept often have fused modality (item (1) above).

(a)↔(b) Given a proposition with a concept with evaluation prescription in its connotation: The decision element of the evaluation prescription can thus stand in close relationships to the cognitive criteria of the evaluation prescription (item (a) above), and the decision element can, as the case may be, be clothed in language that lets the uninitiated (e.g. non-lawyers) be in ignorance of the role of the decision element (item (b) above), *without* the proposition's amounting for these reasons to a fused descriptive and normative proposition.

In many analyses these phenomena, in combination, as the case may be, with one or more of the other phenomena with which I draw boundaries in the present section 3.2, are *treated without differentiation.* – For example, Christensen points to the phenomenon of fusion in lawyers' propositions de lege lata, as follows:

> "The normative in law lies not only in the normative form. Law is not only a codifying in normative form of human practice in the way it in fact takes shape. The content of the norm is also influenced by notions that above practice, in the way it in fact takes shape, there are norms that say how it ought to be. One sees this in the very *concept of 'valid law'*. If the norm is not applied, [if] the reality disappears, the norm is no longer valid law. But *the opposite too* applies. Even if the rules of law are in fact applied in a certain manner, it may happen that this is not recognised as valid law, because

> there is conflict with a value that is considered as being superordinate to human practice" (my italics).[15]

Christensen terms this feature of lawyers' propositions de lege lata "*sammansmältning av verklighet och värde*" [fusion of reality and value].[16] Immediately after the passage quoted, using the same term, Christensen turns to examples illustrating that *evaluation prescription* is part of the connotations of concepts in law. And further, she mentions that the evaluation prescription in the pair of concepts 'well'–'ill' is hidden in *value-neutral language attire*.

My experience is that these phenomena ought to be kept *conceptually apart* and studied in their *actual interplay* when the aim is insight into actually occurring language and argumentation.

3.2.3. Drawing the boundary with persuasive definitions

I have previously given an account of persuasive definitions (section B 7.3 above). There too the relationship between descriptive and normative propositions was central. But the concept of 'persuasive definition' and the concept of 'fusion of descriptive and normative propositions' lie in *different planes*:

In that the concept of 'fusion' focuses on the relationship between descriptive and normative propositions, one looks by definition at a relationship *in the meaning plane*. In the case of persuasive definitions, the perspective is widened; one moves one's gaze out of the meaning plane and looks at the appeal to emotions and play on *feelings* that attach to the *words* (see the schema in section B 7.3.1 (2) above).

3.2.4. Drawing the boundary with indeterminacy

A linguistic expression may be indeterminate through polysemy, or its meaning content (be it objective meaning or subjective meaning; compare section E above) may be indeterminate through incompleteness, vagueness or family resemblance.[17]

The concept of 'fusion' cannot be reduced to any of the forms of indeterminacy mentioned:

Fusions lie in another plane than indeterminacy which attaches to *linguistic expressions*, for example in another plane than polysemy; fusion is as shown a feature of linguistic meaning content, more precisely subjective meaning.

> Ahlander points to the fact that lawyers' sentences de lege lata are often ambiguous between the descriptive and the normative proposition when the yardstick is objective meaning, i.e. widespread linguistic practice.[18] This fact

---

15 Christensen, 'Kvinnorätten och lagpositivismen' [women's law and legal positivism], p. 86.

16 Loc. cit.

17 See section B 2.2 above, at and in note 7.

18 Ahlander, *Är juridiken en vetenskap?* [is law a science?], pp. 78, 88, 94–95, 126–27, 130 (on the ambiguity); pp. 89, 93–94 (on the yardstick).

> is of interest in a perspective that later in this work is to be put on language and argumentation, namely 'the flight from the normative proposition' (Chapter IV). However, in the present perspective, 'mapping of actually occurring proposition types', lawyers' sentences and their objective meanings lead attention away from the essential: namely away from how the fused modality in lawyers' thinking is constituted by the different interests that come into play in the production of lawyers' propositions de lege lata[19] and by the institutional surroundings[20] of these propositions. The language attire and its objective meaning is another question (section 4 below).
>
> Ahlander is, however, representative when he omits to analyse the fusion phenomenon because this part of reality does not fit into his presupposed scheme of analysis: the dichotomy between descriptive and normative propositions.[21]

Nor are fusions the same as forms of indeterminacy that may be seen as features of linguistic expressions' *meaning content* (be it objective meaning or subjective meaning), for example not the same as incompleteness, vagueness or family resemblance. There is nothing strikingly incomplete or vague, either about the concept of 'fusion' or about the phenomena that the concept covers, nor is there any family resemblance.

It should be particularly emphasised that fusion is not the same as the *sender's* having no concept of the distinction between descriptive and normative propositions, or as his "having forgotten" the distinction or its significance when he made the fused proposition. The sender may well have reflected on the distinction and be conscious of its significance. The phenomenon of fusion is not constituted through *lack of insight or decision* on the part of the sender, but through the sender's *choice being another* than the extreme points on the graduated scale. Take lawyers' propositions de lege lata in their capacity of serving as the paradigm case: At the time of making the proposition the lawyer takes *the standpoint that he will not take any standpoint* on what is to be adjusted in the event of any subsequent discrepancy between the proposition and the practice of authorities enforcing the law; and this *"third standpoint"* is institutionalised through the legal community's customarily practised norms for good legal argumentation (section 2.1 (3) above).[22]

---

19 See in particular section 2.1 above.

20 See in particular sections 2.1 (1), cf. 3.2.2 (2)(b) concluding remarks, above.

21 Ahlander, *Är juridiken en vetenskap?* [is law a science?], p. 89: "[A]ssertions of the type: it is your duty to .... may often aim both at producing a theoretical view and at arousing a sense of duty. We can therefore confidently conclude that it is not possible to draw any boundary in principle between value sentences and theoretical sentences by examining more closely what the speaker or writer may have intended to express by formulating a given sentence. There then remains nothing else but to study the sentences themselves as free-standing occurrences"; see further, op. cit., pp. 78–100 passim.

22 The words "choice" and "standpoint" are not intended to imply that the lawyer consciously reflects on the distinction between descriptive and normative propositions every time he makes a proposition de lege lata. The words *also* cover what the lawyer would choose *if* he were asked at the time of making the proposition.

The difference between on the one hand lack of insight or decision on the part of the sender with respect to the distinction between descriptive and normative propositions, and on the other hand fusion of such propositions, often seems to be overlooked. – For example, Ross seems to build on the *premiss* that if the language users (the lawyers) only thought more deeply about what they were doing, their propositions would fall into a dichotomy; the language users would be able to, and would in fact, decide that the propositions were either descriptive or normative.

> "[E]ven according to intention it is difficult to draw [any sharp boundary line between cognitive pronouncements concerning valid law and legal-political activity]. ... This difference of attitude, however, will in practice often not be a conscious one, because the jurist – rightly or wrongly – *identifies* his own evaluations with those of the court. He is often *not* even *aware of* the conditional and problematic character of these presuppositions ..." (my italics).[23]

A major point in the present discussion has been that the premiss mentioned does not tally with a great deal of actually occurring argumentation among lawyers.

3.2.5. Drawing the boundary with lack of knowledge on the part of the recipient

Aubert touches on the phenomenon of fusion in the following way:

> "Logical analysis of legal science has inter alia been faced with the major problem of classifying propositions as normative *or* descriptive. ... [T]o find out whether propositions are intended and used descriptively *or* normatively by a particular writer is often extremely difficult. ... Often the *material for analysis will be so poor* that the only reasonable conclusion will be that it is impossible to classify the formulation in either of the categories. Such a conclusion certainly need not be uninteresting. There is much to suggest that precisely such formulations of a rather indeterminate character have important psychological and social functions. Therefore there is no reason to *do violence to the material* and to be hell bent on placing the proposition in one of the two main boxes" (my italics).[24]

Unlike Ross, Aubert does not draw our attention to lack of insight or decision on the part of the sender (section 3.2.4 above), but to lack of knowledge on the part of the recipients with respect to the sender's decisions: If only one knew enough about the sender's subjective meaning, then the sender's propositions would allow themselves to be categorised as either descriptive or normative. – That this

[23] Ross, *On Law and Justice*, p. 48. – There are graduated transitions between lack of insight or decision on the part of the sender with respect to the distinction between descriptive and normative propositions, and "wishful thinking" on the part of the sender with respect to what others have actually said or intended (section 2.2 above).

[24] Aubert, 'Logisk analyse og sosiologi i rettsvitenskapen' [logical analysis and sociology in legal science], pp. 527–28 (the first two sentences in the quotation) and p. 529 (the rest of the quotation).

premiss is not tenable either, follows from what has been said about lawyers' propositions de lege lata (sections 3.2.4 (in the text before note 22) cf. 2.1 (3), above).

3.2.6. Drawing boundaries with structures in language, morals and the relationship between parents and children

In what follows I shall point out that and why the phenomenon of fusion is not found in language qua language, morals and the relationship between parents and children. – For the sake of brevity I use the formulation "is not found". The differences to be pointed out lie, however, in different dimensions, and the individual dimensions are of a graduated nature. The differences may therefore be more or less considerable; see the present section 3.2.6, concluding remarks. – The structures that I shall point to with respect to language qua language, morals and the relationship between parents and children are also of interest, and should also be investigated, on account of their distinctiveness. Here, however, the task will be limited to placing the phenomenon of fusion in relief.

When we use *language*, we build on custom-based normative definitions (section B 3.3.2 above), for the sake of brevity called "language norms" in what follows. One aspect of the fact that these norms are custom-based, is the possibility of using them as a basis for prediction with respect to how other language users will understand and apply the words of the language. Thus there is a normative proposition and the possibility of a descriptive proposition. The fact that the phenomenon of fusion is nevertheless not found in language qua language is inter alia because of the following differences from lawyers' propositions de lege lata: Particularly in relation to the descriptive proposition, it is the case that there is no general institutional context consisting of bodies that have competence to make final and binding decisions concerning interpretation of and subsumption under formulations of language norms (compare section B 3.3.1 (3) above), and accordingly no corresponding interest either, on the part of the language user, in prediction with respect to what such bodies will conclude. Particularly in relation to the normative proposition, it is the case that, for one thing, the norms are not linked to reasonableness and justice (compare section B 3.3.2 (1) above), and that, for another, they are not advanced with the same force as the normative component in lawyers' propositions de lege lata. In the case of disagreement about how words ought to be used, the one's gain is not the other's loss, as is usually so in legally formulated conflicts. If two people discover that they are using a word in different ways, then they have a joint interest in co-ordinating their language usage (compare section B 4.2 (5)(d) above, concluding remarks).

Normative propositions relating to *morals* have greater similarity than language norms with the normative component in lawyers' propositions de lege lata: For one thing, normative propositions relating to morals are linked to reasonableness and justice, and for another, two people who advance incompatible propositions relating to morals will often advance their propositions with (at least) the same force as lawyers advance the normative component in their propositions de lege lata (the one's gain is often the other's loss). However, not in morals either is there any institutional context consisting of bodies that have competence to make final and binding decisions concerning interpretation of and subsumption under norm formulations; and accordingly no corresponding interest either, on the part of the participants in moral argumentation, in prediction with respect to what such bodies will conclude. Therefore, not in morals either is there any fusion.

In the relationship between *parents and children*, the normative propositions are linked to reasonableness and justice, and if parents and their children discover that they are advancing incompatible normative propositions, they often advance their propositions with (at least) the same force as lawyers advance the normative component in their propositions de lege lata (the one's gain is often the other's loss). Furthermore, in the relationship between parents and children there is an institutional context in which one or two people, one or both parents (here there are great cultural variations), have the competence to make final and binding decisions concerning interpretation of and subsumption under norm formulations; and accordingly there is a corresponding interest on the part of the child in prediction with respect to what one or both parents will conclude. That we do not find any fused descriptive and normative modality in the case of the child's propositions either, is inter alia because the descriptive proposition remains particular. It is linked to one or two particular individuals. There is no parallel to the generalised lawyer's perspective, which constitutes special aspects of reality and which employs a special method to decide the existence, content and duration of these aspects. The child qua opposite party to the parents does not assume a position analogous to the lawyer's in relation to other lawyers, but a position analogous to the advocate's client in relation to the judge, after the client has been told which judge is to deal with his case. Therefore, not in the relationship between parents and children either is there fusion.

Generally it is the case that we may perhaps find phenomena that show similarity with the phenomenon of fusion in one or more of the dimensions in which I have now pointed to differences. However, we would only find similarity, in different dimensions and in different degrees. I have not been able to find the same phenomenon outside lawyers' argumentation de lege lata. What is to be reckoned as the 'same phenomenon' depends on the concept formation. If one forms more abstract concepts, i.e. if one renounces distinctions that lie in the concept of 'fusion' as it has been established here, then one will soon reach a level of abstraction on which one finds the same phenomenon also outside lawyers' argumentation de lege lata. Then, however, one will no longer be talking about the phenomenon that has been brought into focus in the present section F.

4. Forms of expression, within the framework of lawyers' language and argumentation de lege lata

4.1. Not direct expression through individual words, but indirect showing through patterns of argumentation

As is apparent from the definition and the examples above, the concept of 'fusion of descriptive and normative propositions' lies on the level of *"meaning" in a subjective sense*, i.e. on the level of the individual language user's deliberation and decision (section E 2.2 above). The concept of 'fusion' does *not* lie on the level of "meaning" in an objective sense, i.e. does not lie on the level of meanings of words and expressions according to widespread linguistic practice (section E 2.1 above). – This entails that fusions *can, but need not find linguistic expression.*

I have cited lawyers' propositions de lege lata as the paradigm case of fusion of descriptive and normative propositions. However, within the framework of *normal legal language usage* there are *few means of expression* for the phenomenon of fusion.

> This is the reason why, in formulating some items in the present section F, namely items that might possibly be read as saying something about the reality basis of the concept of 'fusion', I have not used terms like "language" or "language and argumentation" (in relation to the paradigm case: "lawyers' language", "lawyers' language and argumentation"). Instead I have used terms like "proposition", "argumentation", "analysis and argumentation" and "thinking" (in relation to the paradigm case: "lawyers' propositions de lege lata", "lawyers' argumentation", etc.), i.e. terms that do not imply anything about the composition of the language plane.

First, the *linguistic expressions* are adapted to the presupposition of *dichotomy* between descriptive and normative propositions that I have above argued is dogmatic and untenable in relation to lawyers' propositions de lege lata. – It may well be that lawyers make gradations *internally in respectively* descriptivity and normativity: That a rule is a legal rule, is "more or less probable", or "more or less reasonable". However, the distinction between descriptive and normative propositions *itself* is more seldom graduated. Thus lawyers say that a legal rule either "is" or "ought to be" (valid) law; that a proposition is either "de lege lata" or "de lege ferenda"; that they are engaged in either "legal dogmatics" or "legal politics". Even though the two latter distinctions are not (without reservation) explained as coinciding with the distinction between descriptive and normative propositions, they are not used either to graduate this distinction. By virtue of being dichotomies they actually reinforce the general grip on our way of thinking that dichotomies appear to have (compare sections III 2.2.6 (4)(b) and 2.5.2, below).

Secondly, there is a tendency for fused descriptive and normative propositions, like purely normative propositions, to be formulated in ways that are either *polysemous* between the descriptive, logical and normative, or *one-sidedly descriptive or logical*, at the expense of the purely normative or fused (Chapter IV, respectively sections 2 and 3, below). The consequence is in both cases that the fused modality gets less attention, irrespective of the supply otherwise of means of expression.

If one is to find expression of the phenomenon of fusion among lawyers, one must therefore go from the individual *words and expressions* to the argumentation and the more comprehensive *patterns of expression* to be found there. In stylised form, the relevant expression pattern in cases of subsumption may be specified as follows: "In the light of the facts of the case, an overall consideration of the legally relevant grounds – in particular the wording of statutes, travaux préparatoires, practice, equitable considerations, *and* other lawyers' probable views of what these other grounds indicate – suggests that John Brown has the right/ a duty to ...". And the relevant expression pattern in cases of interpretation may be specified in stylised form as follows: "An overall consideration of the legally relevant grounds – in particular the wording of statutes, travaux préparatoires, practice, equitable considerations, *and* other lawyers' probable views of what these other grounds indicate – suggests the rule that ...".

The phenomenon of fusion is thus something that *indirectly* (via more extensive argumentation patterns) *shows itself*, not something that directly (in particular words for this) is specified. – A symptom of this being the case, may be that many lawyers seem to sense that a dichotomy between 'descriptive propositions' and 'normative propositions' is not well suited to lawyers' propositions about what the law is, at the same time as the phenomenon of fusion is a feature of lawyers' argumentation that has been little treated and understood, cf. inter alia the fact that this phenomenon is confused with other phenomena (section 3.2 above).

4.2. Independent of forms of expression of evaluation prescription

I have drawn a boundary between *fusion* of descriptive and normative propositions and *evaluation prescriptions* in the connotations of concepts: Evaluation prescription is factually central, but is neither necessary nor sufficient for fusion of propositions (section 3.2.2 (1)–(2) above). – This entails that there is no necessary connection between linguistic openness with respect to evaluation prescription and linguistic openness with respect to fusion:

On the one hand, one can have open expression of an evaluation prescription *without* open expression of any fusion of propositions. For example, the formulation "virke urimelig" [have unreasonable effects] in section 36 of the Contracts Act (Act No. 4 of 31 May 1918) gives open expression to an evaluation prescription. Yet this does not solve the question of whether one is confronted with a descriptive, normative or fused proposition when lawyers say: "An increase in prices may according to the unreasonableness criterion in section 36 of the Contracts Act give rise to revision of long-term contracts with fixed prices", or: "Mary Smith is, according to the unreasonableness criterion in section 36 of the Contracts Act, entitled to revision of her contract with John Brown".

On the other hand, an evaluation prescription may be concealed through an evaluation-free linguistic expression *without* linguistic concealment of any fused modality of propositions of which the expression is part. For example, the concept of 'illness' has evaluation prescription in its connotation, although the word "illness" is not usually read in this way (section 3.2.2 (2) above). Yet this does not prevent a lawyer from being able to give expression to the fused modality of a proposition of which the word "illness" is a part: "In the light of the illness caused to the injured party, an overall consideration of the legally relevant grounds – in particular the wording of statutes, travaux préparatoires, practice, equitable considerations, *and* other lawyers' probable views of what these other grounds indicate – suggests that the injured party has the right to ...". In this proposition the illness characterisation is taken as objectively given, but may easily be conceived as concealing evaluations and choices, at the same time as the fused modality of the proposition is given a certain, albeit indirect, expression (on the indirect, see section 4.1 above).

G No corresponding fusion of definitions and characterisations

1. A difference in the use of the 'descriptive proposition–normative proposition' dimension and the 'definition–characterisation' dimension

There is a *difference in the actual use* of the two dimensions of fundamental proposition types, a difference which means that there is no basis in reality for speaking of fusion of definitions and characterisations, as is the case with descriptive and normative propositions:

In the 'descriptive proposition–normative proposition' dimension one can see the existence of language use situations in which the sender considers that *both at the time of formulating the proposition and afterwards, it is impossible* to determine the proposition as either descriptive or normative; and in which it is *logically impossible for a third party* to demand that the sender take such a decision. I return to the paradigm case of fusion of descriptive and normative propositions (section F 2 above):

In the case of lawyers' propositions de lege lata the possibility of, and necessity of, fusion lie in the norms for what is to be reckoned as (good) legal argumentation ("the doctrine of the sources of law"), seen in connection with the situations in which lawyers must in fact pronounce their propositions de lege lata and the interests that these situations in fact actualise: partly interests in a purely descriptive proposition (section F 2.1 (1) above), and partly interests in a purely normative proposition (section F 2.1 (2) above). The lawyer will often say that he does not consider it right or possible on the basis of generally accepted criteria for (good) legal argumentation to determine his propositions de lege lata as either descriptive or normative, be it at the time of formulating the propositions or afterwards (section F 2.1 (3) above). – Further, it is logically impossible for a third party *both* to accept the doctrine of the sources of law, lawyers' decision situations and the interests that these situations in fact actualise, *and* at the same time to demand that the distinction between descriptive and normative propositions be carried out without exception: The latter would mean that one asked the lawyer to do *something else* than advance propositions de lege lata within the factual frames in which these propositions are advanced, i.e. that one did *not* accept the doctrine of the sources of law, lawyers' decision situations and the interests that these situations in fact actualise.

I have not been able to find any corresponding example of the sender's considering that at the time of formulating the proposition or afterwards, it would be impossible to take a decision with respect to whether his proposition formulation is to be reckoned as expressing a definition or a characterisation; or of its afterwards being logically impossible or illegitimate for a third party to demand that the sender take such a decision, where the third party suspects he is participating in a pseudo-discussion caused by different perceptions of what type of proposition one is confronted with.[1] – To be more specific: I have not been able to find either any institutionalised example, such as lawyers' argumentation, or any less institutionalised examples from other analysis and argumentation formulated in everyday language.

I do not exclude the possibility that there may be *one or another* analysis and argumentation situation formulated in everyday language that provides an example of fusion in the 'definition–characterisation' dimension, of the same or similar kind as outlined as specific to the 'descriptive proposition–normative proposition' dimension: Whether such a situation exists, is an empirical question and may consequently only be answered by going through all areas of analysis and argumentation occurring in fact and formulated in everyday language.

However, I consider the present work and the material from analysis and argumentation formulated in everyday language on which it builds, as a sufficient basis for the following *hypothesis*: Within analysis and argumentation formulated in everyday language (section I 5 above) there is no fusion in the 'definition–characterisation' dimension which both (i) is of the *same kind* as the fusion in the 'descriptive proposition–normative proposition' dimension, and (ii) is of *such* great diffusion and practical significance as this fusion, cf. the diffusion and significance of lawyers' propositions de lege lata.

[1] I assume that this discussion and decision aspect of language and argumentation, and as part of this, definitions stipulated at any time and for the individual occasion, play a greater role than Quine appears to assume; see section 2 (3)–(4) below.

2. The relationship between the present work and Quine's critique of distinctions that build on a boundary between linguistic meaning and other sources of knowledge

(1) Introduction

Quine has criticised distinctions that build on the drawing of a boundary between linguistic meaning and other sources of knowledge. Several of the fundamental distinctions in the present work build on the drawing of such a boundary: cf. the fact that I define 'definition' as "propositions that contribute to determining the meanings of linguistic entities (contribute to determining concepts)", and in so doing, contrast definitions with characterisations (section A 2 (1) above, with further references); and cf. the fact that I define a delimiting case 'analytically un/true propositions' as "propositions the truth value of which can be decided on the basis of their meaning content alone, i.e. propositions that are true or untrue by definition" (section A 2 (2) above).

Since Quine has a central place in modern linguistic theory, I shall give a more detailed account of how I see the relationship between his critique and the present work.

The discussion in what follows is concerned partly with the general question of the possibility of a boundary between linguistic meaning and other sources of knowledge; and it is concerned partly with the derived questions of the possibility of boundaries between definitions, characterisations and analytically un/true propositions. In this latter respect the discussion here is a continuation of the discussion in section D 3 above.

I have placed the discussion here for the following reason:

If one supposes that it is not possible to draw a boundary between linguistic meaning and other sources of knowledge, and thus no boundaries either between definitions, characterisations and analytically un/true propositions, then it is tempting to assume graduation and fusion in the 'definition–characterisation' dimension, perhaps in parallel with the graduation and fusion in the 'descriptive proposition–normative proposition' dimension, of which an account has been given in section F above.[1]

As explained in section 1 above, there is in my view *no* such parallel. The following discussion is also an in-depth treatment of this: how the absence of *such* a parallel means that, in the 'definition–characterisation' dimension to a greater degree than in the 'descriptive proposition–normative proposition' dimension, one can maintain a boundary between the proposition types, and in fact does so.[2]

(2) Quine's critique

In 'Two Dogmas of Empiricism' Quine states that he does not accept any *general* distinction between analytically un/true and other propositions. And further he states that he only accepts the distinction in relation to *two types* of proposition, which he again accepts as analytically un/true:

First, propositions the truth value of which rests on logical words and expressions.[3]

Secondly, propositions the truth value of which rests on certain stipulated definitions of non-logical words and expressions.[4]

---

1 For example, Galtung, 'Expectations and Interaction Processes', pp. 215–18, takes Quine's analysis as support for the graduated nature of both dimensions.

2 I emphasise "the absence of *such* a parallel", i.e. in relation to the phenomenon of fusion. As is apparent from the discussion in section F above, I assume that fusion of descriptive and normative propositions is a phenomenon with relatively clearly delimited diffusion, in that this phenomenon appears in actual fact to be specific to lawyers' propositions de lege lata. – Apart from the phenomenon of fusion I do not claim, in relation to the perspective and topic of the present work, that there is any difference with respect to the degree to which the fundamental distinctions in the two proposition dimensions can be maintained (on the other hand, I do claim that there are certain differences with respect to the degree to which they are in fact maintained; see Chapter IV below).

3 Quine, 'Two Dogmas of Empiricism', pp. 22–23; compare same writer, *Word and Object*, p. 65 in note 3. See on this type of analytically un/true proposition, section D 4 (2)(a) above. – In what follows I shall to a great extent concern myself with 'Two Dogmas of Empiricism', because this article directly addresses the present problem (the possibility of distinguishing between analytically un/true and other propositions), because it is very well known, and because, as far as I know, Quine has ever since built on the views he expresses there. On the origin of this article and its ideas, see *Word and Object*, p. 67 in note 7.

4 Quine, 'Two Dogmas of Empiricism', p. 23, cf. pp. 25–26.

With respect to what sort of definitions he is referring to, Quine says: "the explicitly conventional introduction of novel notations for purposes of sheer abbreviation",[5] and further: "[The linguistic entity being defined is] a newly created notation, newly endowed with meaning here and now".[6] – From this it should be apparent that Quine is referring to certain stipulated normative definitions (see section B 3.3.1 above on stipulated normative definitions).

As I shall explain in more detail in item (4) below, definitions stipulated with the individual discussion context in mind have greater significance for the perspective and topic of the present work than Quine ascribes to them for his purposes.

However, Quine's discussion of definitions in their capacity of being a possible basis for analytically un/true propositions, is terse and moreover unclear on essential points. First, it is unclear which stipulated normative definitions in particular Quine is referring to in the statements quoted in the preceding indent; for one thing he offers no example, and for another he terms the relevant type of stipulated definition "an extreme sort of definition".[7] Secondly, it is unclear whether his categorisation of definitions is intended to be exhaustive,[8] which the categorisation ought to be if his argumentation is to be tenable; and it is difficult to check whether the categorisation is exhaustive, since Quine does not give any account of his categorisation criteria.

A feature of Quine's discussion of the distinction between analytically un/true and other propositions, or of related topics, is that his statements on definitions pronounced in that context do not constitute any nuanced and coherent conceptual model for the mapping of definitional activity occurring in fact and formulated in everyday language (compare section B above). For one thing, his statements are terse and unclear, see the preceding paragraph. For another, Quine's interest is closely linked to logic, mathematics and formalised science.[9] This interest leads to Quine's conceptualisations and propositions in a number of cases having a limited area of application, a limitation one can ascertain without going into the tenability of the conceptualisations and propositions in their area. Compare for example his denial of the significance of the distinction between descriptive and normative definitions in formalised systems[10] with sections B 3, 8 and F above and III 2 below.

---

[5] Op. cit., p. 26.

[6] Op. cit., p. 27.

[7] Op. cit., pp. 25 (bottom)–26 (top), 27.

[8] Beside the type of definition that is dealt with in the preceding indent ("the explicitly conventional introduction of novel notations for purposes of sheer abbreviation"), Quine operates with two types of definition, which he terms respectively "reports upon usage" and "what Carnap calls explication"; see op. cit., pp. 24–26, 27.

[9] Quine, 'Truth by Convention', pp. 78 et seq.; 'Two Dogmas of Empiricism', pp. 26–27; 'Carnap and Logical Truth', pp. 394–95; 'Vagaries of Definition', passim.

[10] Quine, 'Carnap and Logical Truth', p. 395: "Increasingly the word 'definition' connotes the formulas of definition which appear in connection with formal systems, signalled by some extra-systematic sign such as '=df'. Such definitions are best looked upon as correlating two systems, two notations, one of which is prized for its economical lexicon and the other for its brevity or familiarity of expression [note with reference to *From a Logical Point of View*, 1953 ed. p. 26f]. Definitions so

> The said limitation of area is in itself important in the assessment of Quine's conceptualisations and propositions. For the assessment of Quine's critique of the distinction between analytically un/true and other propositions it is, however, also important that the area limitation be both kept conceptually separate from and seen in its factual connection with a more fundamental limitation in Quine's critique: his abstraction from the discussion and decision aspect of language and argumentation, his limitation of perspective (see the final sentence of the quotation in note 10 above and the discussion in item (4)(c) below).

Apart from the two instances mentioned above Quine *denies* that it is possible to find any general criterion which would enable us to make the distinction between analytically un/true propositions and other propositions. And his objection is directed inter alia against using reference to presupposed definitions as a criterion, where the definitions are not exceptionally of such a kind as he is willing to accept as a basis for analytically un/true propositions.[11] – Quine thus denies that the distinction between analytically un/true and other propositions can be drawn, precisely in the case of those propositions in relation to which the distinction has in my view *particular significance for a critically reflexive mode of questioning*: namely in the case of propositions the truth value of which rests on definitions of non-logical expressions, and where the relevant expressions have not been explicitly defined earlier in the discussion context concerned.[12]

Having gone through and rejected some other criteria that have been proposed for the distinction between analytically un/true and other propositions, Quine summarises his view as follows:

> "It is obvious that truth in general depends on both language and extralinguistic fact. The statement 'Brutus killed Caesar' would be false if the world had been different in certain ways, but it would also be false if the word 'killed' happened rather to have the sense of 'begat'. Thus one is tempted to suppose in general that the truth of a statement is somehow analyzable into a linguistic component and a factual component. Given this supposition, it next seems reasonable that in some statements the factual component should be null; and these are the analytic statements. But, for all its a priori reasonableness, a boundary between analytic and synthetic statements simply has not been drawn. That there is such a distinction to be drawn at all is an unempirical dogma of empiricists, a metaphysical article of faith."[13]

This rejection of the possibility of distinguishing between analytically un/true and other propositions has been subsequently upheld by Quine, inter alia in one of his

---

used can be either legislative or discursive in their inception. But this distinction is in practice left unindicated, and wisely; for it is a distinction only between particular acts of definition, and not germane to the definition as an enduring channel of intertranslation."

11 Quine, 'Two Dogmas of Empiricism', pp. 24–27. Concerning "exceptionally", see the text at note 7 above.

12 See section A 2 (2)(b)(i)↔(ii) above.

13 Quine, 'Two Dogmas of Empiricism', pp. 36–37. See also pp. 41–42.

principal works, *Word and Object*. In *Word and Object* this rejection is put into a new context in relation to 'Two Dogmas of Empiricism', namely into a discussion of (radical) translation and indeterminacy of translation.[14] However, as I now go over to more detailed discussion of the relationship between Quine's critique and the present work, it will become clear that the *essential thing* for and in this relationship is a feature in common of Quine's criticisms: his abstraction from the discussion and decision aspect of language and argumentation, his limitation of perspective (item (4)(c) below).

(3) Three different dimensions: Ontology, theory, and actually occurring analysis and argumentation

In relation to Quine's critique one ought to distinguish between three (sets of) questions.

First, there is the question of what *exists* ("ontology").

Secondly, there is the question of what presuppositions about what exists *must* be taken into account in *theories* of language. – More particularly with Quine's critique in mind, there is the question of whether propositions in actually occurring analysis and argumentation which seem to presuppose the existence of something else than individual empirical phenomena can be replaced by other propositions that do not presuppose this ("logical reduction"). Can we for example do without concepts of linguistic meaning (understood as concepts of something else than individual empirical phenomena)?

Thirdly, there is the question of what choices *language users* are in fact confronted with with respect to what exists, and of what *decisions* in this respect they are in fact *required to make and do take* when they are discussing.

> In connection with the third question one can also ask what tendencies in actually occurring analysis and argumentation *ought to* be brought to the language user's awareness and strengthened. This normative question falls outside the main thread of the present discussion, but see item (4)(c)(i) below, in the indent.

Quine discusses mostly the first and second questions.[15] His main objection to the distinction between analytically un/true and other propositions is that he cannot find any anchorage in sensory experience for the distinction, and that it is thus impossible to draw the distinction.

Quine's discussion of the third question[16] for his purposes does not bring into focus what is relevant in relation to the perspective and topic of the present work.

---

14 Quine, *Word and Object*, pp. 26–79, compare pp. 65–67.

15 In his article 'On What There Is', particularly pp. 12–19, Quine gives an account of his view of the relationship between the two questions.

16 Quine, 'On What There Is', pp. 16–19; 'Two Dogmas of Empiricism', pp. 44–46; *Word and Object*, pp. 233–76.

In the following item (4) I shall relate the present work to the above-mentioned questions and to Quine's discussions; and in so doing I shall give my grounds for what is said in the previous paragraph.

(4) The distinction between definitions, characterisations and analytically un/true propositions is invoked and applied in actually occurring analysis and argumentation

This work concerns itself with one and only one of the questions mentioned in the preceding item. – The point of departure is *not* the questions: "Do meaning entities (concepts and propositions) exist?" (the first question in the preceding item), or: "What proposition types and tenability criteria is it necessary to operate with in a theory of language?" (the second question in the preceding item), *but*: What proposition types and criteria *are advanced in actually occurring analysis and argumentation*? (the third question in the preceding item).

In relation to *this* question I take my point of departure in two experiences (items (a)–(b) below). As a result, the nature of my question is different from Quine's (item (c) below).

(a) Invocation of concepts of 'meaning' and 'analytically un/true propositions'

When we discuss, we place weight on what proposition types we are confronted with, because we consider that the criteria or facts that are relevant for tenability assessment vary with the type of proposition (sections I 2–4 cf. II A, above): One main distinction goes between on the one hand descriptive propositions, the tenability of which is most often termed "truth" ("probability"), and on the other hand normative propositions, the tenability of which is termed in more varied language, "validity" for example. Another main distinction goes between on the one hand definitions, in the case of which tenability assessment relates to the meanings of linguistic entities (to concepts), and on the other hand characterisations, in the case of which tenability assessment presupposes this topic and relates to other topics. – In both the main distinctions, analytically un/true propositions represent delimiting cases: In the case of analytically un/true propositions there is little need to apply the distinction between descriptive and normative propositions, and, as an extension of this, there is little to indicate how one might possibly draw this distinction (section A 5 (2)(b) above, concluding remarks). And analytically un/true propositions cannot be classified as definitions (section D 2 above) or characterisations (section D 3 above and the present section G 2).[17]

Such distinctions *we do use in fact*; see the present work, throughout, which in detail demonstrates a diversity and system of significant acts that take place in

[17] See also the schematic representation in section A 7 above of the different proposition types and of how analytically un/true propositions come in as a delimiting case.

and through the distinction dimensions. We use these distinctions inter alia in the sense that in actually occurring analysis and argumentation we invoke them. More particularly, with the distinction dimension 'definition–characterisation–analytically un/true proposition' in mind, the following applies:

- We accept being challenged with respect to what we *meant* by the words and expressions we used. In so doing, we accept the possibility that we advanced analytically un/true propositions.
- Often we are *not able to give* any clear answer to what we in certain respects meant by the words and expressions we used: The presupposed custom-based definitions may be indeterminate in a relevant respect, and often we have not provided any explicit definition beforehand, either for others or for ourselves. And even if we have done so, the definition does not always cover the respects in which doubt later manifests itself, for example because other participants in the discussion have presuppositions we did not reckon with. – However, we *do accept having to make* a decision concerning what meaning we will *now* ascribe to the words: In actually occurring analysis and argumentation it is deemed *legitimate to demand* that an explicit definition *be given* afterwards, so that one can *thereby* decide whether a proposition advanced is true by definition, or whether one must have recourse to sense-experience or other sources of knowledge to establish its tenability value.

(b) Application of these concepts in relation to the individual proposition

In the language and argumentation practice that has now been outlined (item (a) above), the distinction between meaning and experience, and the corresponding tenability assessments involved, are linked to the *individual proposition*: Through the concepts of 'definition', 'characterisation' and 'analytically un/true proposition' the focus is placed on the individual proposition, not on the system of propositions.

(c) The difference between the present work and Quine's problematisation: a discussion and decision perspective

(i) In relation to a mapping of proposition types with their accompanying tenability criteria it may thus be concluded that in the case of propositions that one advances oneself and thereby "has responsibility for", one accepts a demand for an answer to whether the proposition is a definition or characterisation or is analytically un/true.

The present work seizes on this *practising* of the distinctions between the fundamental proposition types, with their accompanying tenability criteria.[18]

---

18 Compare Grice/ Strawson, 'In Defense of a Dogma', pp. 142–47, on philosophical and general uses of the distinctions.

> It is true that this practising represents only a *tendency* in actually occurring language and argumentation: In the individual instance the distinctions between the fundamental proposition types may be absent or only fairly indeterminately present, partly in the language user's awareness, partly in the linguistic expression. – I consider, however, that practising the distinctions has *value* in its capacity of providing certain fundamental criteria in linguistic communication: criteria for understanding, for the establishing of agreement and for the resolving of disagreement. Therefore the tendency towards practising the distinctions between the fundamental proposition types ought to be *brought to the language user's awareness and strengthened.*[19]

In the light of this, what is crucial is not whether Quine's critique of concepts of 'meaning' and 'analytically un/true propositions' is *tenable or untenable*, but the fact that his critique concerns *other situations and questions* than those relevant in relation to the perspective and topic of the present work:

Quine *abstracts from* the interaction between language users, from what I by way of introduction termed the "discussion and decision aspect" of language and argumentation (section I 4 above): He links his critique of the distinction between analytically un/true and other propositions to language occurrences *without* the aspect that language users demand of one another answers to what they mean by their words and expressions, and thus without the corresponding answers (item (2) above).[20] – Quine's critique rests on our, in *these* situations, *lacking sense-experience criteria* for drawing the distinctions (item (3) above).

---

[19] Compare Carnap, 'Replies and Systematic Expositions', p. 922 ("I believe that the distinction between analytic and synthetic statements, expressed in whatever terms, is practically indispensable for methodological and philosophical discussions"); Feigl, 'Some Major Issues and Developments in the Philosophy of Science of Logical Empiricism', pp. 6–7 ("The sharp distinction between analytic and synthetic statements is not only fruitful but indispensable ... if for nothing else, then certainly for the sake of mere clarity of thought"); Robinson, *An Atheist's Values*, pp. 73 cf. 81–84 ("There is a virtue of exercising our power to think in good ways ... In seeking to decide which of a pair of contradictories is the true one, the reasonable man asks first whether they are analytic or synthetic statements"); *Definition*, pp. 177–78 (see the quotation in section B 2.3 (1) above, in note 33); Stenius, 'The Concepts 'Analytic' and 'Synthetic' ', p. 58 ("One of the main tasks of philosophical analysis, I think, is to make clear the difference between questions about linguistic convention and questions about ... matters of fact, values, moral norms, and so on. It is as a step in the clarification of this difference that the distinction between 'analytic' and 'synthetic' is important"); see also pp. 75–76. – To avoid any misunderstanding I must mention that the quotations now given are intended *solely* to illustrate the fact that the normative view advanced in the text at the present note has a certain amount of support; neither the quotations nor their authors' fundamental philosophical positions are cited as evidence for the basis in reality of the distinctions between the fundamental proposition types. The evidence for the basis in reality of these distinctions is such features of actually occurring language and argumentation as the present work as a whole demonstrates and systematises, see the main text in what follows.

[20] The abstraction mentioned is an important feature in common of the fundamental discussions in 'Two Dogmas of Empiricism' and *Word and Object*. The same abstraction recurs in Quine's later and more brief discussions too; see 'Epistemology Naturalized', p. 86; *The Roots of Reference*, pp. 78–80; 'Vagaries of Definition', pp. 51–52. – Scattered in Quine's works one can find some statements that perhaps refer to parts of the discussion and decision aspect; see, for example, 'Carnap and Logical Truth', p. 395 (partly quoted in item (2) above, in note 10); 'Reply to Herbert G. Bohnert', p. 94.

The critically reflexive form which constitutes the perspective and topic of the present work, has its *existence* in the discussion and decision aspect from which Quine abstracts (section I 4 above): The work brings into focus the aspect that language users *demand of one another* answers to what they mean by their words and expressions, and that language users in so doing *in fact advance boundaries between* propositions about what they mean (definitions), propositions that are un/true by virtue of the definitions (analytically un/true propositions), and propositions that are neither definitions nor analytically un/true (characterisations) (items (a)–(b) above). – The present work demonstrates that these proposition types with their accompanying tenability criteria exist in *that* sense: as a *continuous interplay between demands for clarification of and decisions with respect to what one means*, in the interaction between language users. Whether the proposition types and the criteria exist in any *other* sense, is *not* a topic in this work.

(ii) The above is an application to an individual problem area in the philosophy of language of the superordinate perspective and topic of the present work (Chapter I above): a relatively well-delimited critically reflexive form (I 4), in the discussion and decision aspect (I 4) of analysis and argumentation formulated in everyday language (I 5), and with a *certain independence*, inter alia from controversial fundamental philosophical questions (I 6, II A 8): here, inter alia from the first two questions mentioned in item (3) above. – A "certain independence" from controversial fundamental philosophical questions means absence of certain univocal connections between the critically reflexive form and the level of fundamental philosophical positions (sections I 6, II A 8). But it does not mean absolute independence. For even though I claim and demonstrate the absence of certain univocal connections between the critically reflexive form that the work brings into focus and the level of fundamental philosophical positions, I neither claim nor demonstrate the absence of any connection whatsoever. For one thing, absence of any connection whatsoever does not follow from the absence of certain univocal connections. For another thing, it is not very reasonable to assume absolute boundaries in thought; I have difficulty in seeing how thought might anywhere be able to escape the critically reflexive form that constitutes the perspective and topic of the present work.

With the present work, and not until this, a *necessary condition* has come into being for discussion of what more nuanced connections might exist between the critically reflexive form that the work brings into focus and the level of fundamental philosophical positions: namely the condition that one *first* systematically maps the critically reflexive form. – A mapping of what *more nuanced* connections might exist between the critically reflexive form and the level of funda-

---

These statements are, however, too terse and unclear for one to be able to deduce anything definite from them concerning the existence and factual significance of the discussion and decision aspect, or concerning Quine's views on these points. And even if one adds information obtained from those of Quine's views that are most fundamental in the present connection, namely Quine's physicalism, a fundamental indeterminacy remains; see item (ii) below.

mental philosophical positions, would however be *another* work: As I justified by way of introduction, given the perspective and topic of the work it is both not necessary to take and necessary not to take any standpoint on conflict between fundamental philosophical positions (section I 6).

Outside the now outlined main thread of the work, but to round off the placing of the work in relation to Quine's critique (the present section 2), I shall clarify the *main* elements of a connection between the critically reflexive form and the level of fundamental philosophical positions: namely *that* it is possible to use the insights of the present work as a basis for an argument on Quine's problem level; the *content* of the argument; and how the argument *tips the scales* in the relationship between Quine and his critics.

The present work demonstrates the existence, content and factual significance of a critically reflexive form in the discussion and decision aspect of language and argumentation. In so doing, the work demonstrates that the distinction between definitions and characterisations has a basis in reality in the discussion and decision aspect; the criteria for the distinction lie in the fact that participants in language and argumentation continually challenge one another and make decisions in and through this distinction. This fact again provides a basis in reality for a derived distinction between analytically un/true and other propositions.

Quine does *not* make this aspect of language, its being implemented by subjects, part of his reflections. In item (i) above I termed this side of Quine's discussions "Quine's abstraction". In the present critical context it is more pertinently termed "Quine's limitation of perspective". For given this side of his discussions, he relates blindly to precisely that feature of the language-use situation which gives the elements of the critically reflexive form their identity criteria: the interaction between participants in language and argumentation, with continual implementing through decisions.

The cause of Quine's not being able to find any criterion for the distinction between analytic and other propositions, is the said limitation of perspective. This limitation is *not possible to justify* if one wishes in general to claim the non-existence of a distinction in language, as Quine claims. For we, including Quine, are at any time situated *in language* when we speak about language, *also* when we deny the existence of a distinction in language. A perspective that looks past the discussion and decision aspect is therefore never a sufficient basis for claiming the non-existence of a distinction in language. The discussion and decision aspect must also be made part of one's reflections before a conclusion can be drawn that a distinction in language does not exist. – Quine's perspective, which consistently looks past the discussion and decision aspect, is therefore only seemingly a general perspective.

As the present work centres on the discussion and decision aspect of language and argumentation, and as the work demonstrates in detail a diversity and system of significant acts that take place there in and through the dimension 'definition–characterisation–analytically un/true proposition', it at the same time provides a basis for the conclusion that Quine's critique has a *limited scope*: Quine's critique is only tenable as critique of an *abstract* view of the distinction between analytically un/true and other propositions, as critique of a view that the distinction can be drawn *independently of* the discussion and decision aspect of language and argumentation. Quine's critique is not tenable as general critique.

Finally I shall relate the conclusions above to those of Quine's views that are most fundamental in the present context. In so doing, I shall point to a fundamental indeterminacy in Quine's position.

Quine's abstraction from the discussion and decision aspect of language and argumentation, Quine's limitation of perspective, is a result of Quine's physicalism. By the formulation *"Quine's physicalism"* I mean the following fundamental views in Quine: first, the view that questions of what exists, are questions for the natural sciences;[21] secondly, the view that everything that happens, has effects on the level of physical theory, and consequently and to that extent, on the basis of these effects, can be expressed in physical theory;[22] finally, the view that physical theory is to be preferred to other kinds of theory when the aim is cognition.[23] – Quine abstracts from the discussion and decision aspect of language and argumentation (and in so doing, he abstracts from the discussion and decision aspect of the language and argumentation of logic, mathematics and physical theory) because this aspect is not thematised in logic, mathematics or physical theory.

> I have previously pointed out (item (2) above, in the second indent) that Quine's interest is closely linked to logic, mathematics and formalised science; that this interest leads to Quine's conceptualisations and propositions in a number of cases having a limited area of application; and that this limitation of area ought both to be kept conceptually separate from and to be seen in its factual connection with a more fundamental limitation in Quine's critique: Quine's limitation of perspective. – The conceptual difference between the limitation of area and the limitation of perspective should be sufficiently apparent from what has been said about the two limitations. The factual connection consists in both limitations' being traceable back to Quine's physicalism: Quine forms his concepts and pronounces his propositions taking his point of departure in logic, mathematics and formalised science (physics) because these are the kinds of theory he prefers; and he abstracts from the

21 Quine, 'Things and Their Place in Theories', p. 21: "[I]t is within science itself, and not in some prior philosophy, that reality is to be identified and described."

22 Quine, 'Goodman's Ways of Worldmaking', p. 98: "[N]othing happens in the world, not the flutter of an eyelid, not the flicker of a thought, without some redistribution of microphysical states. ... If the physicist suspected there was any event that did not consist in a redistribution of the elementary states allowed for by his physical theory, he would seek a way of supplementing his theory. Full coverage in this sense is the very business of physics, and only of physics." – Concerning "to that extent" in the main text at the present note, compare at and in note 24 below.

23 Op. cit., pp. 97–98: "[a] sequence of worlds or versions ... I would end it after the first step: physical theory"; "... my special deference to physical theory as a world version, and to the physical world as the world".

discussion and decision aspect of language and argumentation because this aspect is not thematised in logic, mathematics or physical theory.

Quine's physicalism is, however, problematic. In the present context, this is so especially with the element that expresses his preference for physical theory: partly because it is difficult to find any tenable justification for such a preference; and partly because we have now come to questions concerning the foundations of Quine's position that Quine himself has not discussed. – One might imagine Quine defending his preference by claiming that everything we can say, can be translated into logic, mathematics or (presupposedly all-embracing) physical theory. But Quine explicitly rejects such strong physicalism.[24] What lies in this rejection is not quite clear. On the one hand, Quine would hardly claim that the discussion and decision aspect has no form of existence whatsoever. For one thing such a total denial of existence would be a *pragmatic inconsistency*: While totally denying the existence of the aspect, one is acting in and through it. For another thing a total denial of existence would be in clear *contradiction with demonstrated language and argumentation practice*, cf. the present work in its entirety. On the other hand, Quine seems to see the discussion and decision aspect as an utterly peripheral and volatile form of existence.[25]

In what has now been outlined there is a fundamental *indeterminacy* about Quine's position. On the one hand, Quine attempts to formulate a general theory of language and argumentation on the basis of his physicalist starting point; cf. the generality that Quine ascribes in his works to the consequences he deduces from his physicalist starting point, and in so doing, the generality he ascribes to the consequence that the discussion and decision aspect in that case, with a physicalist starting point, does not exist (is not able to speak up for itself). On the other hand, Quine expresses indeterminate cognition of the fact that in actually occurring language and argumentation we advance interesting propositions that cannot be translated into logic, mathematics or physical theory, and in so doing, he expresses indeterminate cognition of the existence of the discussion and decision aspect: in both cases "indeterminate", because Quine does not give criteria for forms and degrees of respectively interest and existence.

In recent philosophical literature John McDowell has traced the same indeterminacy in Quine, in the form of an *ambiguity* about Quine's terminology concerning experience. – McDowell too argues that Quine's abstraction from the discussion and decision aspect of language and argumentation represents a fundamental problem in Quine's discussions.[26] McDowell demonstrates

---

24 Op. cit., p. 98.

25 See, for example, statements on the volatile status of definitions in Quine, 'Carnap and Logical Truth', p. 395; 'Necessary Truth', p. 75; 'Reply to Herbert G. Bohnert', p. 95; 'Reply to Ulrich Gähde and Wolfgang Stegmüller', p. 138; 'Reply to Geoffrey Hellman', p. 206.

26 McDowell, *Mind and World*, pp. 129–61, in particular pp. 129–39, 156–61. – McDowell terms the discussion and decision aspect of language and argumentation "the order of justification" and (de-

that this abstraction leads to uncertainties and inconsistencies on the level of fundamental philosophical positions, in that the abstraction leads to Quine's ascribing an ambiguous status to his entities of experience: In the way in which Quine speaks of experience, experience is to be both outside and within the discussion and decision aspect, to be both cause and cognitional argument.[27]

Common to the present discussion and McDowell's discussion is the pointing out that it is Quine's abstraction that leads to problems: In the present discussion the emphasis is on the fact that it is Quine's abstraction that leads one to look past the existence and factual significance of the diversity and system of language and argumentation acts which the present work maps. In McDowell's discussion the emphasis is on the fact that it is Quine's abstraction that leads to uncertainties and inconsistencies on the level of fundamental philosophical positions. McDowell's discussion thus provides support for there being certain connections between the discussion and decision aspect and the level of fundamental philosophical positions.

To avoid any misunderstanding I must mention that the present work and McDowell's discussion *in other respects* go in different directions. On the one hand the present work goes beyond McDowell's discussion, in that McDowell treats the discussion and decision aspect as a roughly unitary entity, without differentiation in terms of content: He does not touch on the critically reflexive form that is brought into focus in the present work. This also means that he does not provide evidence for the distinction between definitions and characterisations, and by derivation, between analytically un/true and other propositions, in the way in which evidence is provided descriptively and in detail in the present work.[28] On the other hand I do not take any standpoint on McDowell's more detailed views at the level of fundamental philosophical positions. That would have meant answering the question of what more nuanced connections might exist between the critically reflexive form that is brought into focus in the present work and the level of fundamental philosophical positions: which lies outside the present work, cf. the present item (ii), introductory remarks.

---

claring himself in agreement with Wilfred Sellars) "the space of reasons", see op. cit., e.g. pp. 133–34, compare p. 5 at and in note 4.

27 Op. cit., in particular pp. 133–35, 136–37, 160–61. – "Quine ... impossibly tries to have it both ways – to exploit the idea of experience as a tribunal that stands in judgement over beliefs, while conceiving experience so that it has to stand outside the order of justification" (p. 137; see also pp. 134–35 in note 5).

28 I must mention in this connection that McDowell too does not seem to have an eye for the factual significance in the discussion and decision aspect of the distinction between definitions and characterisations; see op. cit., p. 158.

H Interplay

After discussion of *separation* of the fundamental proposition types (section E above) and of cases of *fusion* (section F above), it might be tempting to imagine *interplay* being the next topic; this would provide a certain verbal aesthetics and ostensibly also a logic with respect to content.

However, a specification of topic as "interplay between the fundamental proposition types" would cover a very great deal of language and argumentation: First, in purely general terms it is the case that custom-based normative definitions make possible a significant amount of actually occurring language and argumentation, in that the custom-based definitions constitute our concepts (sections B 3.3.2 cf. E 2.1 above). Thereby a purely general interplay is established, partly between definitions and characterisations, partly between normative and descriptive propositions. Secondly, as one moves towards more specific areas of language and argumentation, for example to law, one finds an increasing diversity of content-determined types of interplay that may be worthy of interest, partly in relation to aims outside the area concerned, and partly in relation to aims within the area itself.

The thread of my further discussions is therefore not interplay pure and simple, but *selected* forms of interplay. Taking as a point of departure the main aim of the present work (Chapter I above) and views about what more specific topics there may be a particular need to illuminate within this frame, I shall in what follows discuss these types of interplay:

- Normative propositions that motivate in the case of the setting up of and choice between normative definitions; and normative propositions that motivate in the case of the setting up of and choice between descriptive characterisations (Chapter III).
- Use of forms of language and argumentation which objectively interpreted are polysemous between the descriptive, logical and normative, or more one-sidedly descriptive or logical, in cases where, independently of the linguistic formulation, one has reason to believe that the criteria that motivate the language user are normative (Chapter IV).
- Finally, and on the basis of several of the earlier discussions, I shall present a distinct interplay between definitions and characterisations, descriptive and normative (Chapter V).

III

Topics from the assessment of tenability

1. Introduction

By way of introduction I stated that, and gave an outline of the manner in which, I lay down the concepts of the fundamental proposition types *in order to bring into focus* loci in actually occurring language and argumentation which experience has shown it to be important to determine when one is assessing the tenability of propositions, and thus when one is analysing dis/agreement (sections I 4 cf. 2–3, above): It is other facts that are relevant when one is to test the tenability of a definition than when one is to test the tenability of a characterisation; and it is other criteria that are relevant when one is to test the tenability of a descriptive proposition than when one is to test the tenability of a normative proposition.

As is apparent from the account of the fundamental proposition types (sections II A, cf. B–D and F–G, above), this bringing into focus takes place in *two ways*. First, it takes place through a combination of an element *per definitionem*, through the concepts of the fundamental proposition types, *and* an element per actually occurring language and argumentation, through demonstration of the basis in reality of the concepts: Per definitionem other facts are relevant when one is to test the tenability of a definition than when one is to test the tenability of a characterisation, *and* this conceptualisation captures a central feature of actually occurring language and argumentation (sections II A 2 (1), (3) and (4), cf. B, C and G, above).

Secondly, this bringing into focus takes place *per actually occurring* language and argumentation, through demonstration of connections existing there between the fundamental proposition types and essential loci in the tenability assessment: A large part of the question of what criteria are relevant in the tenability assessment, is not answered by the concepts of the fundamental proposition types. One must instead go to actually occurring language and argumentation and see what connections have been established there between the proposition types and tenability criteria. *This* is the subject area of the present Chapter III.

> I have thus defined the concept of 'normative proposition' through a denotation specification and *not* laid down particular criteria for the tenability assessment as concept criteria (section II A 5 (2)(a) above), either positively or negatively; the question of whether normative propositions can be un/true I also keep outside the definition (section II A 5 (2)(b) above). And I have defined the concept of 'descriptive proposition' as "propositions of which one can say that they are true or untrue, and which purport to say something about a reality otherwise (beyond the proposition)" (section II A 5 (1) above); this is *not* an obstacle to also other criteria than the truth criterion in fact being ascribed weight in the setting up of and choice between descriptive propositions.

Within the stated subject area, I shall concentrate on two topics which in my opinion deserve greater attention than they are normally given: In section 2 below some tenability criteria for *normative definitions* are refined and systematised, criteria that in the literature can often only be traced through hints and scattered occurrences. And in section 3 below I map the factual significance of other criteria than the truth criterion in the setting up of and choice between *descriptive characterisations*. – These two discussions also include *lawyers' propositions de lege lata*. In the case of these propositions, however, the tenability assessment is *less surveyable* than in the case of the fundamental proposition types seen by themselves. By way of conclusion I point out causes of this, and how the assessment of tenability in the case of propositions de lege lata requires that one combine the tenability criteria for the individual fundamental proposition types (section 4 below).

The *main aim* is the same as in the work otherwise (Chapter I above): to demonstrate, and to create an awareness of, the existence, content and factual significance of a specific critically reflexive form (I 4–6); and thereby, to demonstrate, and to create an awareness of, the factual significance of analysis of dis/agreement on the basis of this critically reflexive form.

2. Criteria that are used in the setting up of and choice between normative definitions

2.1. Point of departure: A more complex evaluation than in the case of descriptive definitions. Aim: A mapping of certain general features of the motive situation

In the case of descriptive definitions the truth criterion is the dominant criterion.[1] In the case of normative definitions a more complex evaluation is practised: In actually occurring analysis and argumentation it is not one criterion, but a *multiplicity of criteria* that motivate the choice.

Given an informative level of concretisation, space would not permit an account of *all* types of consideration that motivate us in the setting up of and choice between normative definitions. However, it is of importance to the present work to get *farther* than statements that concept determinations are a "question of expediency", or the like (section 2.2.3 below): The setting up of and choice between normative definitions is an action type with a certain inner diversity. Cognition of this diversity contributes to shedding light on the system character and dynamics of definition activity formulated in everyday language, and more generally, of the critically reflexive form that constitutes the perspective and topic of the present work. – This is the background to the following mapping of *certain general features* of the motive situation.

In the more detailed account I shall divide my discussion according to whether the criteria *concern* the structuring, the naming or the coupling of area and name (sections 2.2–2.4).

The diversity of criteria leads to constellations of heterogeneous criteria pulling in different directions. This necessitates weighings and balancings – *in so far as* one consciously reflects on choices of structuring or naming, which is certainly not always the case: *custom and chance* also play a part (section 2.5 below).

Some of the criteria can be termed *"internal"*, because and in the sense that they represent desired ends that the definer can achieve by his own efforts, independently of other people. Examples are desires for freedom from contradiction

---

1 In the case of descriptive characterisations, on the other hand, the truth criterion gets more competition from other criteria, see section 3 below.

(section 2.2.1), operationalisability (section 2.2.2), cognition (section 2.2.4) and aesthetics (section 2.2.6). Other considerations can in contrast be termed *"external"*, because and in the sense that they represent desired ends (also) in the form of effects on other people, and thus something the definer cannot fully achieve by his own efforts. This is in general terms the consideration for influence on action (sections 2.2.5 and 2.4.2); and concretised in one direction, the consideration for heuristics (section 2.4.1).

My discussions are aimed at normative definitions *with a view to characterisations*: be they descriptive, normative or fused characterisations. – Of course, it also happens that one defines with a view to (other) definitions. However, this constellation of proposition types I keep out of my discussions: partly because this constellation is less common than definitions with a view to characterisations, and partly because the constellation does not actualise specific tenability criteria in comparison with definitions with a view to characterisations.

Some of the criteria in what follows are considered relevant in the case of all characterisations (formal-logical criteria, cf. section 2.2.1 below); others are applied more selectively. But common to them all is that they are applied over wide areas, cutting across boundaries between everyday life, academic subjects, science and philosophy, and cutting across boundaries between the individual subjects and between the individual sciences.[2]

2.2. The structuring

2.2.1. (Formal-)logical criteria

(1) Self-contradiction

There seems to be general agreement that the *principle of contradiction* places restrictions on the range of normative definitions one has available to choose from: One does not accept that *one and the same* structuring says both that a property is a criterion and simultaneously is not a criterion of the concept (of the use of the word); or that it says both that an individual phenomenon or a type of phenomenon is covered by and simultaneously is not covered by the concept (by the use of the word).

On the other hand, the principle of contradiction does not provide any delimitation criterion when applied to the *relationship between* different structurings. Here it functions on the contrary as a criterion of real difference and thus as a criterion of what structurings one *ought to take into account* (in

[2] Different from the now outlined mapping of the motive situation are discussions of traditionally received textbook rules for definitions; on these rules, see e.g. Dubislav, *Die Definition*, pp. 130–31; Robinson, *Definition*, pp. 140–48; Abelson, 'Definition', pp. 322–23; Essler, *Wissenschaftstheorie I: Definition und Reduktion*, pp. 50–53.

the use of the criteria in what follows, cf. sections 2.2.2–2.2.6): "Which of two logically incompatible structurings (the property is a criterion/ is not a criterion; the phenomenon is covered/ is not covered) ought I to choose?"

The cause of the use of the principle of contradiction as a restriction is no doubt that from a self-contradictory premiss one can prove anything in a formal-logically valid manner,[3] that one is thus not able to prove anything definite, and that consequently it is difficult to see any point in introducing a self-contradiction.

(a) Contradiction on the basis of the meanings of logical words[4]

Contradiction solely on the basis of an analysis of logical words (first and foremost "not", "and", "or", "if", "only if", "all", "some", "none") is seldom found in the normative definition *itself.* For then the contradiction would most often be obvious. An example would be: "To call a rule a "legal rule" I shall require that it satisfies certain minimum requirements concerning content, and not require that it satisfies certain minimum requirements concerning content."

On the other hand, one can quite often find contradiction solely on the basis of logical words, *in the relationship* between a *definition* and the *actual use* of the linguistic entity being defined. A practical example is that one says that one will use the term "legal rule" neutrally in relation to the content of rules, at the same time as in concrete discussion one keeps the term back or applies it on account of the content of a rule.

(b) Contradiction on the basis of the meanings of non-logical words

In relation to non-logical words one can come across contradiction not only in the relationship between the definition and actual use, but also in the definition itself. – An example from psychology, social science and law is *"unconscious motive", "unconscious presupposition", "unconscious assumption"*, or the like: Here the possible self-contradiction lies in the fact that one ascribes to something both the property of being psychologically known ("motive", "presupposition", "assumption") and not known ("unconscious") to the person acting. An example from the theory of norms is Sundby's term *"skjult avveiningsmarkør"* [hidden weighing and balancing marker] (the definition will be quoted in the indent below): Here the possible self-contradiction lies in the fact that one ascribes to something both the property of being visible ("marker") and not visible ("hidden").

In order to decide whether there is self-contradiction on the basis of non-logical words, the words must be interpreted. Whether there is in fact self-contradiction

---

[3] Compare the fact that the inference $(p \& -p) \rightarrow q$ ("if p and not-p, then q") will be true according to the rules of sentential logic irrespective of the truth value of p and q. See further Popper, 'What is Dialectic?', pp. 317–21.

[4] On the distinction between logical and non-logical words, see sections II A 2 (2) and D 4 (2), above. For the sake of understanding the account here, however, what is said in the present item (a) and in item (b) below should suffice.

depends on what *interpretation criterion* is chosen (section II E above): One thing is that by virtue of custom-based normative definitions (objective meaning), the concept designation leads our thought towards self-contradictory structuring, as has now been illustrated. Another thing is whether the definition's structuring is self-contradictory for the individual language user (subjective meaning). The latter does not follow from the former, since the language user can save himself by normatively regulating the meaning: by saying that he is using the words in a different meaning from the usual one, so that the self-contradiction disappears.

> An example is Sundby's definition of "hidden weighing and balancing marker", from which it is evident that he intends to use the word "marker" *also* of something that does *not* mark. This is an unusual way of speaking, but the self-contradiction according to normal language usage that was outlined above, disappears:
>
> "I call weighing and balancing norms those norms that prescribe that a weighing and balancing shall take place. In many formulations of such norms there are one or more central expressions which directly or *indirectly* prescribe that a weighing and balancing shall be undertaken and which, as the case may be, also provide certain indications as to what the weighing and balancing shall take account of. These expressions *I* am going to call weighing and balancing *markers*. ... The form of expression varies quite strongly, the norm's weighing and balancing marker may be open or hidden ... An open weighing and balancing marker explicitly prescribes that the question shall be resolved according to a weighing and balancing, or consists of expressions the application of which presupposes a weighing and balancing. A *hidden* weighing and balancing marker acquires such a content *by interpretation*. A textbook example is the case of the interpretation of Article 97 of the Constitution [providing that no statute shall be given retroactive effect] in conformity with what is called the standard theory: The expression "tilbakevirkende kraft" [retroactive effect] is interpreted in such a way that it becomes a weighing and balancing marker in my sense" (my italics; Sundby's italics omitted).[5]

Self-contradiction on the basis of the (objective) meanings of non-logical words may be *intended*. Such cases range from linguistic *strangeness* in order to arouse the recipient's attention,[6] to philosophically *significant* formulation placed in the forefront of a system that is claimed to be universally valid.[7] – Or the self-contradiction may be *unintended*. Such cases range from the *odd slip* that can easily be put right when one notices it,[8] to symptoms of *unsolved real problems*. These may be symptoms of unsolved problems concerning facts, concepts, or the

---

5 Sundby, *Om normer* [on norms], pp. 200–01.

6 E.g. as when a work of a musical, literary, filmatic or other kind that a desire is felt to focus on, is termed an "instant classic".

7 E.g. as when a standpoint on how lawyers ought to argue is based on Hegel's system and championed under the key term "konkret-allgemeinen Begriff". On this line of development, see Rüthers, *Die Unbegrenzte Auslegung*, pp. 304 et seq.; *Entartetes Recht*, pp. 78 et seq.

8 The example "hidden weighing and balancing marker" I take to fall in this group.

relationship between them,[9] or symptoms of unsolved problems concerning interests.[10]

(2) Circularity and infinite regress

Circularity and infinite regress are two other tenability criteria of a logical nature that one may quite often find put forward in concept discussions. – An example of the use of these criteria in legal concept-discussion is provided by the objections raised by Hägerström, Ross and Olivecrona against intent as a feature of the legal concept of 'declaration of intent'.[11]

(3) A little on the actual use of the criteria

(a) Logical criteria are generally accepted as arguments with great or decisive *weight* and with a completely general *area of application*: – The self-contradiction argument is ascribed decisive weight, and that is so in all areas. – The circularity and infinite regress arguments are also used in all areas. However, their weight is not so great as the weight of the self-contradiction argument, since there is not general agreement about when circularity or infinite regress create untenable arguments.[12]

(b) Logical arguments provide the possibility of *"achieving much through little"*. First, this provides an *aesthetic* attraction. Secondly, it appeals to desires to exercise *power*; one seems to be able to refute any scholarly authority whomsoever without needing to go into the depths of the subject of the person concerned.[13]

(a)↔(b) The now mentioned features of logical arguments make them *attrac-*

---

9 The example "unconscious motive" I take to fall in this group. From psychology compare Freud, *Die Traumdeutung*, pp. 513 et seq., 559 et seq., 578 et seq. (579–83); 'Das Unbewußte', pp. 125 et seq.; *Abriß der Psychoanalyse*, pp. 18 et seq. From law compare Vahlén, *Formkravet vid fastighetsköp* [the form requirement in the case of the purchase of real estate], pp. 210 et seq.; 'Bör förutsättningsläran avskaffas?' [ought the doctrine of assumptions to be abolished?], pp. 396 et seq.; Christensen, 'Förutsättningar och misstag' [assumptions and mistakes], pp. 324 et seq.; Lehrberg, *Förutsättningsläran* [the doctrine of assumptions], pp. 83–95.

10 The division of managerial responsibility between doctors and nurses in hospital wards has been termed inter alia "enhetlig todelt ledelse" [unitary bilateral management]; see *NOU 1997:2* [Norwegian official reports], Pasienten først! Ledelse og organisering i sykehus [the patient first! management and organisation in hospitals], pp. 40, 56, 104, 106.

11 For a presentation of the individual arguments and an assessment of their tenability, see Eng, '"Hva er en viljeserklæring?"' ["what is a declaration of intent?"].

12 One draws a distinction between virtuous and vicious circles; compare e.g. Goodman, *Fact, Fiction, and Forecast*, pp. 63–64 (quoted in section V 3.4 (1) below); Maus, 'Freiheitsrechte und Volkssouveränität', pp. 523–27; compare also section II F 2.1 (2) above, at and in note 18. And one does not always deem it to be the case that infinite regress in itself makes the definition (the concept) incomprehensible; compare e.g. Eckhoff/ Sundby, 'Om selvrefererende lover' [on self-referring statutes], p. 44.

13 "Only *as* much knowledge of the field, above all of the academic jargon, is required as will enable one to understand the *logical meaning content* of the central propositions of the theory", Sundby, 'Strafferetten og dens begrensninger' [criminal law and its limitations], p. 87 (Sundby's italics).

tive. – In this there may lie a *danger*: The urge for generally accepted, rapid and elegant solution of apparently endless discussions may lead to one's *too* rapidly concluding that other people's views are untenable on account of breach of logical criteria. One interprets other people's statements in a schematic way, overlooking interpretation alternatives that are tenable according to the logical criteria.[14] This includes one's finding a logical flaw, but without being aware that it stems from one's own definitions.

> An example is provided by the assertions of Hägerström, Olivecrona and Ross that it is logically impossible to have intention to enter into legal relations as a conceptual feature of dispositive acts in private law. – In an analysis of their argumentation I said by way of conclusion: "The main purpose of this work has been to examine some formulations in legal theory that seem to assert that it is logically impossible to have intent as a dispositivity criterion [in the case of dispositive acts in private law]. My conclusion is that none of the arguments put forward can justify such an assertion. To the extent that something has been logically impossible, the basis has been the theorist's own presupposed definitions."[15] – As a step in the preceding analysis I showed that Hägerström's, Olivecrona's and Ross' presupposed definitions were neither logically necessary, nor linguistically or psychologically apposite.[16]

2.2.2. *Operationalisability*

(1) Definition

(2) Three sources of operationalisation problems in the case of legal rules

(3) A little on actually occurring argumentation concerning the consideration for operationalisability

- **(a) Absolutising. Persuasive definitions**
- **(b) Relativising. Operationalisability as a graduated property**
- **(c) "Theories of meaning"**

As previously mentioned (section II B 7.3.2 (3)) the discussion here will *also* be a step in the discussion of persuasive definitions, because words like "meaning", "meaningful" and "meaningless" have a strong appeal to emotions and because argumentation for operationalisability as a consideration in the case of conceptualisations often takes the *form* that operationalisability is laid down as a criterion in the arguer's meaning concept (item (3) below).

---

14 Føllesdal, 'Den moderne positivisme og dens kritikere' [modern positivism and its critics], p. 128: "... the first precept in all hermeneutics ... that if a person or text appears so absurd under a given interpretation that it is inconceivable that anybody could have had this view, this is a good sign that it is the interpretation that there is something wrong with."

15 Eng, '"Hva er en viljeserklæring?"' ["what is a declaration of intent?"], p. 38.

16 Op. cit., inter alia pp. 13–17, 25–33. – Also Bentzon noted Ross' tendency to project logical error; see 'Retskildeproblemet' [the sources-of-law problem], p. 530: "... to accuse one's victim of "circular inferences" of which the accused is in reality not guilty", cf. p. 526: "the misuse of purely logical considerations".

(1) Definition

By a concept's *"operationalisability"* I mean the possibility of specification of intersubjectively testable criteria for whether or not something falls under the concept.

Whether or not a concept is operationalisable will often have to be decided by seeing the concept in connection with other concepts, as an element in a proposition or a system of propositions (argumentation in everyday life, court judgment, scientific theory, etc.). The concept's operationalisability will thus be a function of the operationalisability of the proposition or of the system of propositions of which the concept is part (item (3)(b)(ii) below). Inter alia for this reason the concept's operationalisability will often be a *matter of degree*; the concept's connection with intersubjectively testable criteria may be more or less direct, and more or less unambiguous.

Hitherto I have for the sake of brevity spoken of "a concept's" operationalisability. However, operationalisability is advanced as a consideration not only *in the case of* concepts, but also in the case of linguistic entities and propositions, and when it comes to propositions, in the case of both definitions and characterisations. – Most often not much weight seems to be placed on what this consideration is linked to. A quite common way arguments go is to raise the objection to a *characterisation* that one cannot take a standpoint on its tenability because the words and expressions of the formulation of the characterisation are unclear. After having been given one or more *definitions* of the contentious words and expressions, one may uphold the view that the formulation does not express intersubjectively testable criteria. In such a situation one can find occurrences of all the above-mentioned forms of expression: The objection concerning lack of operationalisability is directed against the linguistic expression, against the expression's meaning content (the concept), against the definition of the expression, or against the characterisation of which the expression is part.

(2) Three sources of operationalisation problems in the case of legal rules

(a) By virtue of being *meaning entities* and thus something *general*, criteria in legal rules will share in operationalisation problems common to all conceptualisation: How does one get *from* the meaning entity and the general *to* the empirical and the particular?

These problems are partly of a *factual* kind: The more indeterminate the conceptualisation is, the more difficult it is (by definition) to specify intersubjectively testable criteria for whether or not something falls under the concept. This one may change by forming more determinate concepts.[17] – And partly the problems are of an *ontological and epistemological* kind: "What is a concept? And where is

[17] On the concepts of 'in/determinacy', see section II B. 2.2 above, at and in note 7.

it?" (compare section II B 4.1 (5) above). The ontological and epistemological problems cannot be solved through amended conceptualisations, but are connected with conceptualisation as such.

(b) By virtue of being *elements in normative propositions*, criteria in legal rules will share in two operationalisation problems specific to normative propositions in comparison with descriptive propositions.

In the first place: What is the *yardstick* for the *tenability* of normative propositions, and how does one get *from* the yardstick *to* the normative proposition (the legal rule with its criteria)? – This problem is of an *ontological and epistemological* kind: Are there divine norms, a law of reason, or the like, that can be used to measure the tenability of the legal rule? Or are we left to our own decisions? – The problem is not specific to law, but is an aspect of all argumentation about the tenability of normative propositions, for example in politics, ethics and aesthetics.

In the case of normative propositions with *evaluation prescription* in the concept's connotation, the following operationalisation problem presents itself in addition: How does one get *from* the evaluation prescription *to* the empirical and the particular?[18] – This problem is of a *factual* kind: The smaller the degree of cognitive criteria that is required, the greater the acceptance there will be for "I wish ...", "I intend ...", or the like, as sufficient justification for whether or not something falls under the concept, and the more difficult it will be to specify intersubjectively testable criteria for the subsumption. This one may change by increasing the proportion of cognitive criteria at the expense of the decision element. – This problem is not specific to law either (section II B 6.1 (2)(b) above). But the variations in the relationship between cognitive criteria and decisions appear to be greater in lawyers' language and argumentation than in other proposition areas (same place, at and in notes 10–15).

(c) By virtue of being *elements in lawyers' decision of individual cases*, criteria in legal rules will share in the following operationalisation problem: How does the lawyer get *from* the submission of evidence *to* the facts taken as established in the case?

The application of the law is in the main retrospective. Typically central questions are for example: "How did the parties act?", "What did the parties know?", "What was the situation?". – The main problem concerning the assessment of evidence is the transition from the evidence presented in the case to that description of fact which is taken as a basis for the decision. This problem is first and foremost of a *factual* kind.

True enough, such question formulations as mentioned might suggest a connection between evidence problems in the application of the law and ontological and epistemological issues in philosophy, cf. typically epistemological question formulations as "What can we know?", "How can we

18 On evaluation prescription in the connotation of the concept, see section II B 6.1 above.

know?". But this similarity is only a linguistic similarity in question formulations.

This problem is not completely specific to law either; for example moral judgements of actions are also often retrospective and raise problems concerning the assessment of evidence. But the problem is more specific to law than the two first-mentioned (groups of) problems.

(a)↔(c) The aforementioned sources of operationalisation problems are not individually specific to legal rules. However, much of the *distinctiveness of lawyers' language and argumentation* is formed in a relationship of tension between on the one hand the *combination* of the said sources of operationalisation problems in the *application* of the legal rule, and on the other hand a view of the law as something *certain and predictable*, something that is found, in the double sense of 'already existing' and 'being discovered':

The person applying the law *mediates between* often indeterminate (item (a)) or evaluation-prescribing (item (b)) and always (by definition) general criteria (item (a)), *and* a particular set of facts (item (c)) which in a more limited perspective often appears trivial; he does so *against a background of* more or less controversial criteria for extra-legal legitimising and criticism, be they of a philosophical, moral, political, religious or other kind (item (b)); these are criteria which the person applying the law must always be prepared for the parties to the case or outsiders to measure his decision against, and which he consequently does not escape (section II F 2.1 (2) above). – The person applying the law must be prepared to have to *tackle extreme points* in the outlined dimensions 'indeterminate–determinate', 'evaluation-prescribing–cognitive', 'general–particular', 'existential–trivial', '(philosophically, morally, politically, religiously, or the like) controversial–uncontroversial'; he must be prepared to do so not only in different cases, but in the same case; not only in exceptional cases, but in the application of the law throughout. However, the person applying the law has a constant and powerful *preparedness against loss of control* in institutionalised forms of language and argumentation (sections IV 3.3 cf. 2–3, below).

(3) A little on actually occurring argumentation concerning the consideration for operationalisability

If one wants to investigate the opinions of different writers during the last hundred years on relevance and weight of operationalisability in the case of the formation of concepts, one must in large measure seek the answers in "what is"-discussions and persuasive definitions. In what follows I shall look at a number of otherwise well-known discussions from *this* perspective.[19]

---

19 The topic is in other words not a representative survey of points of view on concepts and definitions, nor is it the tenability of particular points of view.

(a) Absolutising. Persuasive definitions

Many empirically oriented scientists and philosophers have argued that the consideration for operationalisability in terms of sense-experience *ought to have very great weight.*

In the last hundred years, discussions of this view have often been *formulated* through questions like "what is meaning?", "what is science?", "what is rationality?". And the different standpoints have been formulated through persuasive definitions of "meaning", "science", "rationality": Operationalisability in terms of sense-experience has been asserted or denied as a *necessary* condition for the *"meaningfulness"* of linguistic expressions, for the *"scientificity"* of analyses, for the *"rationality"* of thought.

Inspired by "the early" Wittgenstein[20] many *logical positivists* put forward a verification criterion; criticism of this criterion led others to a falsification criterion. The element in common was that only those sentences whose truth or falsehood could in principle be ascertained, were deemed to have meaning or to be scientific.[21] – Verifiable or falsifiable sentences were considered to fall into two main groups: the analytic, i.e. those the truth value of which could be decided on the basis of the meaning content of the words and expressions constituting the sentence (section II D above), and the empirical, i.e. those the truth value of which could not be decided without recourse to sense-experience.[22]

The American physicist *Bridgman* claimed that only that use of language was meaningful in which the language user could specify what particular operations had to be performed to determine whether or not something fell under the linguistic expression:

---

20 Partly by the *Tractatus Logico-Philosophicus*, London 1922 (original German edition 1921), and partly by conversations, see next note.

21 Verifiability as a condition for linguistic meaning was expressed in writing inter alia through the well-known formulation "the meaning of a proposition is the method of its verification"; see Schlick, 'Meaning and Verification', p. 148; Carnap, 'Testability and Meaning', pp. 421–24. This formulation stemmed from Wittgenstein's conversations with the Vienna Circle; see Waismann, *Ludwig Wittgenstein and the Vienna Circle*, p. 47; Monk, *Ludwig Wittgenstein: The Duty of Genius*, pp. 286–87; Carnap, 'Intellectual Autobiography', p. 45. – Falsifiability as a condition for science (apart from logic and mathematics) was advanced by Popper, *Logik der Forschung* (Vienna 1935); English edition, *Logic of Scientific Discovery*, pp. 34, 40–44 including third asterisked note, 54–55, 69–71, 78 et seq., 311–14.

22 One of the most widely read expressions of the fundamental position outlined is Ayer, *Language, Truth and Logic*, 1st ed. London 1936; 2nd ed. London 1946 (Ayer concentrates on linguistic meaning, and in so doing ties in with the verification criterion). – The *Tractatus* (note 20 above), however, was not much read beyond an inner circle of general philosophers and philosophers of science, who on the other hand studied it thoroughly. For example: "In the Vienna Circle, a large part of … *Tractatus* … was read aloud and discussed sentence by sentence", Carnap, 'Intellectual Autobiography', p. 24. – The *Tractatus* turned out to be ambiguous, however; see Janik/ Toulmin, *Wittgenstein's Vienna*, pp. 208–22. And Wittgenstein himself was not willing to go along when philosophy was made into an auxiliary subject for science, and into a judge presiding over ethics and religion; see Monk, *Bertrand Russell: The Spirit of Solitude*, pp. 338–43; Janik/ Toulmin, *Wittgenstein's Vienna*, pp. 208–22; Carnap, 'Intellectual Autobiography', pp. 25–27.

> "[T]he concept of length involves as much as and nothing more than the set of operations by which length is determined. *In general*, we mean by any concept *nothing more than* a set of operations; the concept is synonymous with the corresponding set of operations" (my italics; Bridgman's italics omitted).[23]

This viewpoint Bridgman called "the operational point of view", often simply referred to as "operationism"/ "operationalism". – Bridgman's starting point was the language of physics, for example what actions one performs to determine length, time or simultaneity. But he advanced his point of view completely generally, also for concepts of mental and social phenomena.[24]

Ross transferred the now mentioned fundamental views pretty directly to his thinking on valid law.[25]

Closer analysis of such propositions about meaningfulness, scientificity or rationality often reveals the pattern which I have earlier given an account of and termed *"persuasive definitions"* (section II B 7.3): *Ostensibly descriptive and deep characterisations* of meaningfulness, scientificity or rationality show themselves to be analytically true, by virtue of certain presupposed *normative definitions*. – These normative definitions express the sender's decisions with respect to the use of appeal words like "meaning", "meaningful", "meaningless"; "science", "un/scientific"; "rationality", "ir/rational". Decisions with respect to the use of appeal words are an indirect way of expressing adherence to values and putting forward *normative characterisations*: The sender has taken a decision with respect to how language shall be used ("meaning"), how research shall be conducted ("science"), or what arguments shall be accepted ("rational"): three aspects that overlap or are closely connected.

Such statements as now outlined, from logical positivists and others who were inspired by them, illustrate how even those who place criticism and clarity at the forefront may become entangled in the *illusory depth* that lies in persuasive definitions and analytically true propositions in the light of such definitions.

---

23 Bridgman, *The Logic of Modern Physics*, p. 5.

24 Op. cit., pp. 5, 30–32; same writer, *Reflections of a Physicist*, pp. v–vii, and the individual chapters referred to there; 'The Operational Aspect of Meaning', in particular pp. 252–53.

25 See the quotation in section II B 5.2 (5)(b)(ii) above (the emphasis there was on denotation specification as a means of structuring, more particularly on ostensive definition; in the perspective here, ostensive definition is one way of operationalising concepts). There appears to be a close *connection in thought* between such views as outlined in the main text before the present note, and prediction analyses of valid law: Partly Ross' premisses led him to a prediction analysis. And partly the direction of influence in the 1870s was probably the reverse. At that time the direction was probably *from* Holmes' prediction analysis (later formulated as "the prophecies of what the courts will do in fact, and nothing more pretentious, are what I mean by the law", 'The Path of the Law', p. 173, see also section V 1.1 (1) below) *to* Peirce's meaning analysis ("there is no distinction of meaning so fine as to consist in anything but a possible difference in practice … effects", 'How to Make Our Ideas Clear', pp. 30–31); compare Fisch, 'Justice Holmes, the Prediction Theory of Law, and Pragmatism', p. 94 ("pragmatism was a generalization of the prediction theory of law"); Feigl, 'The Wiener Kreis in America', p. 662 ("one is impressed with how close Peirce came to anticipating the basic positivistic and operationalist outlook"); 'The Origin and Spirit of Logical Positivism', p. 5.

The *real questions*, which such forms of language and argumentation are apt to conceal, are what *grounds* one has for one's decisions concerning *what to base one's views and actions on.* – These questions can be discussed *without* "what is"-questions via appeal words and persuasive definitions of these. Linguistically this may well be rather long-winded, but it will have the advantage that one will more clearly see when one arrives at the point of decision: "I choose to base my views and actions on evidence of type a and not of type b." – Given, for example, the psychologist who says: "Nach langem Zögern und Schwanken haben wir uns entschlossen, nur zwei Grundtriebe anzunehmen, den Eros und den Destruktionstrieb."[26] Or given the legal writer who says: "The main purpose of the following presentation is to give an account of … those rules that in my opinion are for the time being suited to being applied by the authorities enforcing the law."[27] In both cases the viewpoint here suggests an implied presupposition, or if this presupposition fails, a supplementary remark, of the following standard form: "Whether one *calls* my propositions "meaningful", "scientific", "rational", or the like, is of no significance by itself, as long as one keeps this naming question separate from the question of what I *base* or *ought to base* my views and actions on."

(b) Relativising. Operationalisability as a graduated property

The emphasis that the logical positivists placed on criticism and clarity led at an early stage to a number of them seeing problems with such forms of expression as mentioned in item (a) above.[28] They saw, for example, problems that stemmed from *too absolute* an assertion of the consideration for operationalisability. *Relativising* was considered necessary, in several directions.

(i) In the first place, one had to acknowledge that advancing the consideration for operationalisability as a necessary condition for *"meaning altogether"* led to confusing terminology and thereby to much unnecessary discussion. One began to distinguish between different *types of meaning*, and made it clear that lack of operationalisability in terms of sense-experience only led to what one called "*cognitive* meaninglessness".

> "Unfortunately, following Wittgenstein, we formulated our view in the Vienna Circle in the oversimplified version of saying that certain metaphysical theses are "meaningless". This formulation caused much unnecessary opposition, even among some of those philosophers who basically agreed with us. Only later did we see that it is important to distinguish the various meaning components, and therefore said in a more precise way that such theses lack cognitive or theoretical meaning. They often had other meaning

---

[26] Freud, *Abriß der Psychoanalyse*, p. 12 (Freud's italics omitted).

[27] Ussing, *Obligationsretten, almindelig del* [law of obligations, general part], pp. 1 (bottom)–2 (top).

[28] von Wright, *Myten om framsteget* [the myth of progress], p. 155: "Logical positivism contained the seeds of self-criticism perhaps to a higher degree than any other school of philosophy in history"; Føllesdal, 'Den moderne positivisme og dens kritikere' [modern positivism and its critics], pp. 120, cf. 98–99 and 127–28.

components, e.g., emotive or motivative ones, which, although not cognitive, may have strong psychological effects."[29]

(ii) Secondly, it had to be acknowledged that it also led to confusing terminology and thereby to much unnecessary discussion to advance the consideration for operationalisability in relation to *individual words or individual sentences*: be it as a condition for "meaning altogether" or as a condition for "cognitive meaning". It was concluded that operationalising often takes place and ought to take place *indirectly, via more comprehensive proposition systems*.[30]

In relation to *natural science* the logical positivists themselves took the lead in such relativising of the consideration for operationalisability.[31] Also others among the writers mentioned in item (a) above arrived at the same standpoint: "Of course when the ultimate object of the theory is the description of a concrete physical situation, we must demand that the ultimate outcome of the theory be expressible in terms of operations applicable in the concrete physical situation, but I can see no reason why one should not allow himself any latitude whatever in his *intermediate constructions*" (my italics).[32]

In *law* the notion of indirect operationalising has found expression in what we may call *"linking-term analyses"*. These I shall discuss in greater detail in section IV 3.3.3 below. Here I shall use the following quotation from Ross to illustrate that and in what manner the notion of indirect operationalising formed the more general background:

"[W]hat [is the meaning of] the "state" ... as the name of the subject to whom the action is ascribed[?]

This question has in reality no meaning. When it has been specified under what *conditions* propositions of the type "the state has issued a statute", "the state has concluded a treaty", "the state has convicted a person", "the state has granted a licence", "the state has constructed a railway", etc. – that is, *sentences* in which the "state" figures as acting subject – *are applied correctly*, all that can be said has been said. Herewith the meaning of these sentences has been specified – which is precisely the conditions that must be satisfied, the facts that must be present, for it to be possible to hold the sentence to be true. It is thus not possible to pick out an *individual word*, the word "state", in these sentences and to ask what it means or stands for. It is not possible through a substitution method to replace the word "state" by other words, so that one thereby points to a certain substance, event, activity, property, or something else, that "is" the "state". There is no concept of 'state' – contained in the language usage that is being analysed here – that

---

29 Carnap, 'Intellectual Autobiography', pp. 45–46.

30 The perspective here is historical (albeit limited, see at and in note 19 above). For a definition-theoretical perspective, see section II B 5.5 above.

31 Carnap, 'Testability and Meaning', pp. 3, 24–28, 33–35; 'The Methodological Character of Theoretical Concepts', pp. 52–53, 65–66; 'Intellectual Autobiography', pp. 56–59, 77–81; Hempel, 'Empiricist Criteria of Cognitive Significance: Problems and Changes', pp. 102–13; Feigl, 'The Wiener Kreis in America', pp. 654–55, 657; Ayer, 'Logical Positivism, Editor's Introduction', p. 14; Føllesdal, 'Den moderne positivisme og dens kritikere' [modern positivism and its critics], pp. 107–08.

32 Bridgman, *Reflections of a Physicist*, p. 16.

> can be defined according to the formulae: "the state is …" or "by the "state" one understands …". The concept of 'state', if one indeed wishes to speak of such a concept at all, can only be defined implicitly, in the way indicated.
>
> There is nothing strange or unique in this. On the contrary, the same must be presumed to apply to a large number of legal concepts. I have earlier demonstrated in great detail that it applies to the concepts of rights, e.g. the concept of 'right of ownership'. I said at that time that such concepts were meaningless. This way of putting it is unfortunate. *Those sentences in which the term occurs demonstrably have meaning, and thus the term has so too*. It is more correct to say that the term does not "stand for anything" in the sense that its meaning can be defined by means of the substitution method" (my italics; Ross' italics omitted).[33]
>
> In *philosophy (of language)* holism has become an important point of view, particularly through the works of Quine (section G 2 above).

Inter alia on account of such connections with other concepts, the operationalisability of a concept will be a *question of degree*.[34]

(c) "Theories of meaning"

Today too the question of the relevance and weight of operationalisability in the case of the formation of concepts is often formulated through "what is"-questions addressed to appeal words, and standpoints on this question are often formulated through persuasive definitions of appeal words. – For example, Føllesdal puts it this way:

> "[The logical positivists'] central idea [in their rejection of metaphysics and … stressing of argumentation and evidence] is … that everything that it is at all meaningful to assert or to deny, one must be able to argue for or against. Where argumentation is no longer possible, one leaves the meaningful and crosses over into the meaningless. *The problem then becomes* to find out where this dividing line between the meaningful and the meaningless goes, that is to say, to find a *criterion of meaning*. Logical positivism was to a great extent an attempt to solve this problem. It can therefore be regarded in the main as a *theory of meaning*" (my italics).[35]

The first two sentences in this quotation go a long way to expressing what I see as *real questions* (cf. concluding remarks in item (a) above). The reformulation of the problem in the rest of the quotation (after the first italics), by inserting the word "meaning", expresses a *turning towards* "what is"-questions ("what is meaning?") and persuasive definitions ("meaning is …"). – The value of parts of what is called *"theory of meaning"* is in my view diminished by the systematic *polysemy* with respect to the fundamental proposition types that attaches to the

---

33 Ross, 'Om begreberne "stat" og "statsorgan" i statsforfatningsretten' [on the concepts of 'state' and 'state body' in constitutional law] pp. 117–18; correspondingly in *Dansk Statsforfatningsret* [Danish constitutional law], Vol. I, pp. 35–36 including note 14.

34 Hempel, 'A Logical Appraisal of Operationism', pp. 131–32; 'Empiricist Criteria of Cognitive Significance: Problems and Changes', p. 117.

35 Føllesdal, 'Den moderne positivisme og dens kritikere' [modern positivism and its critics], p. 100.

sentence forms "what is meaning?", "meaning is ..." (Chapter I above), and by the *appeal to emotions* which attaches to persuasive definitions and which often takes the place of arguments (section II B 7.3 above):[36]

See partly *answer formulations* proposed, such as "the meaning of a proposition is the method of its verification",[37] "the meaning of a sentence is constituted by the fact, the existence of which makes the sentence true",[38] "the meaning of a definition is found in its consequences",[39] "meaning is use",[40] "meaning ... is the ... response of another organism",[41] "meaning is a difference which makes a difference".[42]

See in addition attempts to determine the *status* of such formulations: Some writers use only the indeterminate form "x is ...".[43] Others provide more elaborate determinations, not always with any corresponding increase in clarity.[44] Yet others relate the formulations to a conceptual apparatus of the same family as the conceptual apparatus of the present work (in particular the distinctions between definitions and characterisations, and between descriptive and normative propositions), and seem to conclude that the formulations are more or less indeterminate in relation to these distinctions.[45]

---

36 In connection with what follows I should remind the reader that the topic here is the way in which the consideration for operationalisability has been promoted – not the diversity of meanings of words like "mening", "meaning", "Bedeutung", in and of itself; on this diversity see e.g. Ogden/ Richards, *The Meaning of Meaning*, pp. 185–208, who reckon with sixteen different meanings of "meaning".

37 See item (a) above, in note 21.

38 Hedenius, *Om rätt och moral* [on law and morals], p. 71.

39 Cohen, 'Transcendental Nonsense and the Functional Approach', p. 838, cf. pp. 825–26, 843, 844.

40 Compare Wittgenstein, *Philosophische Untersuchungen*, Part I, section 43. – Other "meaning is ..."-propositions in Wittgenstein are mentioned in Baker/ Hacker, *Wittgenstein: Meaning and Understanding*, pp. 368–69.

41 Mead, *Mind, Self, and Society*, p. 80, cf. pp. 78, 81, 145, etc.

42 Compare Feigl, 'The Origin and Spirit of Logical Positivism', pp. 5, 7; Bateson, *Steps to an Ecology of Mind*, pp. 271–72, 459, 489.

43 See as an example Hedenius, *Om rätt och moral* [on law and morals], who asks the question "*what* theoretical "meaning" *implies*" (p. 70; my italics), and who says of his own answer formulation, quoted in the text at note 38 above, that it is "obviously inadequate and must be further clarified ... but it does state something essential about *what* the meaning of sentences *is*" (p. 71; my italics).

44 Compare e.g.: "By a *theory of meaning*, we here intend the traditional attempt to lay out an account of meaning – criteria for determining meaningfulness, sameness of meaning, or particular meanings – in an *a priori* fashion. We contrast this approach with that ... where characterizations of meanings, meaningfulness, and synonymy are adjuncts of and outgrowths from a general semantic theory, derived from and grounded in the empirical investigation of languages. Theories of meaning, as we here use the expression, will generally be *reductive* in character and will attempt to give an account of meaning, synonymy, or meaningfulness in nonsemantic terms, or at least in terms that do not themselves belong to this family of concepts", Rosenberg/ Travis, 'Readings in the Philosophy of Language, Editors' Chapter Introduction', pp. 391–92 (their italics).

45 See as an example Ayer, 'Logical Positivism, Editor's Introduction', pp. 15–16. Ayer assumes there that the principle of verification *can* be seen as "an empirical hypothesis about the way in which people actually use the word "meaning", *but* in that case it would appear to be false" (my italics). Further, he assumes that it *can* be seen as metaphysical (meaningless according to itself), as many suppose that Wittgenstein does in the conclusion of his *Tractatus*, "*[b]ut* this is a vain attempt to have

Such indeterminacy in answer formulations and status propositions as now outlined is in my experience a symptom of a *pervasive* indeterminacy in much of what one calls "theories of meaning".

2.2.3. *References to "expediency", "fruitfulness", "the purpose", or the like. The necessity for further specifications*

(1) Diffusion of references to "expediency" or the like

Both in the debates of everyday life and in academic analysis and discussion one often finds discussions about "what something is" that can reasonably be interpreted as *discussions of normative definitions*, but *without* its being clear what difference it makes whether or not one accepts the definition.

To the extent that any justification is given, references to *"expediency", "fruitfulness", "the purpose of the investigation"*, or the like, are among the most common forms of justification.

> Cf. the standard formulation "How the concept is to be laid down is a matter of expediency." – For example, in general terms the following statement has been made: "[A]n important question ... a practical, not a theoretical question ... is the question of whether or not to accept ... new linguistic forms. The acceptance cannot be judged as being either true or false because it is not an assertion. It can only be judged as being more or less *expedient, fruitful, conducive* to the aim for which the language is intended" (my italics).[46] – And, in relation to the question of whether it ought to be laid down as a condition for calling norms "legal" (whether it should be made a feature of the concept of 'legal norm') that these norms satisfy particular requirements concerning content, the following statements have been made:
>
> "[W]hat really is at stake is the comparative merit of a wider and a narrower concept or way of classifying rules, which belong to a system of rules generally effective in social life. If we are to make a reasoned choice between these concepts, it must be because one is superior to the other in the

---

it both ways" (my italics). Ayer assumes that the Vienna Circle tended to ignore this difficulty concerning status, but considers it "fairly clear that what they were in fact doing was to adopt the verification principle as a convention". – Earlier Ayer had referred to the principle as "a definition ... [b]ut ... not an arbitrary [one]. It purports to lay down the conditions which *actually* govern our acceptance, or indeed our understanding, of common sense and scientific statements, the statements which we take as describing the world 'in which we live and move and have our being' ": 'The Vienna Circle', p. 75 (my italics). – Later he termed his own version of the verification principle "a *stipulative* definition": 'Conversation', p. 77 (my italics).

46 Carnap, 'Empiricism, Semantics, and Ontology', p. 214. – The formulation "new linguistic forms" in the passage quoted refers directly to more fundamental linguistic frames, e.g. concepts like 'physical object', 'number', 'proposition' or 'properties'; see op. cit. pp. 206–13. At the same time the passage quoted provides a pointed expression of Carnap's attitude to the setting up of and choice between concepts more generally, and Carnap's attitude in this respect represents a widespread attitude.

way in which it will *assist our theoretical inquiries*, or *advance and clarify our moral deliberations*, or both" (my italics).[47]

"Nun besteht allerdings "Definierfreiheit": Man kann in den Begriff des "garantierten Rechts" alle garantierten Normen einbeziehen. Man kann aber den Terminus "Recht" auch solchen garantierten Normen vorbehalten, die bestimmten ethischen Postulaten genügen; für garantierte Normen, denen dieses zusätzliche Merkmal fehlt, muß man dann eine andere Bezeichnung erfinden. Ob man für den Begriff des Rechts die erste oder die zweite Abgrenzung wählt, ist eine Frage der Zweckmäßigkeit. *Zweckmäßiger* ist aber wohl der erste, merkmalsärmere Begriff; *denn* er besitzt das größere theoretische Auflösungsvermögen und läßt die möglichen Divergenzen oder Konvergenzen zwischen garantiertem "Recht" und ethischen Postulaten in aller Klarheit zutage treten. Ein Begriff hingegen, der die ethischen Kriterien schon unter die Merkmale des garantierten "Rechts" aufnähme, würde diese spannungsreichen Beziehungen zwischen Recht und Sittlichkeit eher verschleiern" (my italics).[48]

"Seen from *our objective* there is no reason ... not to consider something as a legal system simply because it contains norms or practice that go strongly against our own moral views. *We are interested in* studying the interplay between norms and activities in such complex systems as play a central role in government of and by the state and in the relationship between states. Such a study does not lose its interest simply because one finds a system immoral. And it would be of interest even if one considered the moral norms that were violated as having objective validity. In this book we therefore use the term "legal system" in a value-neutral sense" (my italics).[49]

These quotations are among the more reflective. First, the view of the problem as a problem of definition is already an important step: away from the extensive polysemy attaching to propositions of the form "what is x?", "x is ...", and over to the question of tenability criteria for normative definitions. Secondly, certain hints are given about the considerations that lie behind the formation of the concepts, but only briefly and relatively abstractly.

(2) The limited information in references to "expediency" or the like

(a) References to "expediency" or the like do not in themselves say so much. These references say something about the form of the reflections that govern the conceptualisation: namely *that* the conceptualisation is seen as a *means* to achieving ends. Such references do not, however, say anything about the concrete content: either about *what ends* one is seeking to achieve by the conceptualisation, or about *what evaluations and choices* have preceded adherence to the ends.

---

47 Hart, *The Concept of Law*, 1st ed. pp. 204–05; 2nd ed. p. 209.

48 Zippelius, *Das Wesen des Rechts*, p. 47.

49 Eckhoff/ Sundby, *Rettssystemer* [legal systems], 1st ed. p. 243, see also p. 68; 2nd ed. p. 206, see also pp. 68–69; *Rechtssysteme*, p. 181, see also p. 62.

(b) References to "expediency" or the like presuppose that the effect of the conceptualisation is *intended* by the person defining. However, this presupposition does not always prove right. This applies in academic work too. There, specialist communities and customs in the individual subjects often have a strong regulatory effect, consisting inter alia in the individual researcher's taking over and working within a complex of problems with its accompanying conceptual apparatus. In such cases it may not be very pertinent to advance "expediency", or the like, as grounds for the variations that there might be in the concepts formed (compare section 2.5 below).

(3) Causes of the use of references to "expediency" or the like

Formal references to "expediency" or the like may be understood in the light of more general causes of the fact that considerations in the setting up of and choice between normative definitions are not discussed to a greater degree. One cause is that clarification in thought of the basis for the formation of concepts, and linguistic formulation of this basis, may demand a great deal of *effort*. Another cause is that reflection on the basis for the formation of concepts will reveal the role and distinctiveness of normative definitions, and that this distinctiveness will by many people *be perceived as trivialisation of deep thoughts*: One will have to acknowledge that the basis for the formation of the concept is in many cases considerations of a relatively prosaic nature, for example the consideration for influencing action (sections 2.2.5 and 2.4.2, below), aesthetic considerations (section 2.2.6 below), or heuristic considerations (sections 2.2.6 and 2.4.1, below).

Formal references to "expediency" or the like may in such a context fill two functions. In the first place, they may serve as a replacement for, not just as an introduction to, a concrete and nuanced discussion of the considerations in the individual instance, and thereby *save the definer the effort* of such a discussion. Secondly, they may *counteract impressions of trivialisation*, in that by virtue of their wording these references fit well into norms for scientific thinking: When one speaks in terms of expediency alone, one pushes out of the discussion and simply presupposes an indeterminate answer to what is interesting, namely the considerations (the ends), and focuses instead on the fact that different definitions are means to different considerations (ends). One pushes out the evaluations and choices that constitute the perspective and topic of thought, and directs thought at something present and testable (end–means relationships).[50]

(1)↔(3) In the light of this, the next step will be to map what considerations typically motivate under such names as "expediency", "fruitfulness", "the purpose", or the like, in the setting up of and choice between normative definitions.

---

50 We find basically the same on the limitation of expediency considerations, but developed in a perspective different from the perspective in the present work, in Gabriel, *Definitionen und Interessen*, pp. 84–88, 121 in note 14 concluding remarks.

My discussions in the present section 2 can also be seen in this perspective. This applies clearly enough to the considerations for cognition, action influencing, aesthetics and heuristics (see the following sections). But also the considerations for freedom from contradiction, freedom from circularity, freedom from infinite regress, and operationalisability (see the preceding sections) will often fall under the actually widespread and loose use of "expediency" or the like.

2.2.4. Cognition

(1) Introduction

An important motive behind the setting up of and choice between normative definitions is the definer's wish to *cognise certain selected parts of reality*.

With law as an example of the object of investigation, I shall illustrate how normative definitions (language) constitute(s) a diversity of perspectives (item (2)), and how the choice of perspective (normative definition) cannot be justified by logical criteria or the truth criterion, but rests on evaluations and choices (item (3)). – Distinctive features of the diversity in thought can be illustrated through contrasting with polysemy in a drawing (item (4)).

(2) Diversity of perspectives on the same phenomenon

One can approach the *same concrete phenomenon* from *different conceptual viewpoints*, which again causes characterisations of the phenomenon to bring out *different properties*. For example, water can be seen from the viewpoint of 'drink', and be characterised as 'fresh' or 'salt'; or from the viewpoint of 'washing agent', and be characterised as more or less 'hard'.

The same applies to the *denotation of a concept of 'law'* or, as the case may be, to parts of such a denotation. We can take the *right of ownership* as an example: One thing is that from the viewpoint of 'legal argumentation' one characterises the norms concerning the right of ownership as condition side or consequence side of the right of ownership as a linking-term.[51] Another thing is that from the viewpoint of 'social function' one characterises the same norms as elements in social power relationships.[52] Or we can take the *contract of employment*: One thing is that from the viewpoint of 'legal argumentation' one characterises this type of contract as a stipulated norm (a product of the exercise of competence).[53] Another thing is that from the viewpoint of 'social function' one characterises this type of contract as an element in a social reality.[54]

---

51 Section IV 3.3.3 below.

52 Aubert, *Rettens sosiale funksjon* [the social function of law], in particular pp. 81–104.

53 Eng, 'Begrepene 'kompetanse' og 'gyldighet' i juridisk argumentasjon' [the concepts of 'competence' and 'validity' in legal argumentation].

54 Aubert/ Eckhoff/ Sveri, *En lov i søkelyset* [a statute under the searchlight].

(3) Confrontation with evaluations and choices

(a) *Logically* speaking there is *no limit to the number of possible* conceptual viewpoints on the same concrete phenomenon; an infinity is conceivable.[55] And logically speaking there is *no contradiction between* such analyses as outlined in item (2) above: They can all be true, in the sense that all the connotations can in fact be applied to law in its capacity of being a concrete and multifaceted phenomenon.

(b) *Truth* is *not connected to concepts*. It is not connected to them *directly*: One does not say that concepts are "true" or "untrue"; that one says only of propositions. Nor is it connected to them *indirectly*: No conceptualisation can with any right be said to lead to truer cognition than other conceptualisations; the most peculiar conceptualisation provides a basis for true propositions, if for no other proposition, at least for the proposition that no such thing exists as the concept specifies.

The objection will perhaps be raised that some conceptualisations provide a basis for a *greater number* of true propositions than other conceptualisations: for example, that basic concepts in physics or psychology provide a basis for more true propositions than the concept of 'abominable snowman' (for the sake of the example I presuppose that the latter concept only provides a basis for one true proposition, namely that abominable snowmen do not exist). – I assume, however, that most people will on closer reflection on this objection come to the conclusion that it is not based on the number of, but on the interest one has in, those propositions that a conceptualisation provides a basis for. This may be illustrated by one's replacing in the example basic concepts in physics and psychology by empirical concepts which are not of any interest, for example the concept of 'tree with seven branches and a height of 197 cm' (many people will have little interest in true propositions for which this conceptualisation provides a basis, irrespective of number); or by one's replacing in the example the concept of 'abominable snowman' by the concept of 'God' (many people will have more interest in finding out the truth value of the one proposition 'God exists' than the truth value of a wealth of propositions in physics or psychology).

(a)↔(b) Something we may reasonably call the same phenomenon, can thus be referred to through an infinity of different understandings, which are logically compatible and which can all lead to true cognitions.

These different understandings are constituted through our *normative definitions*. – In the setting up of and choice between normative definitions one must thus *seek criteria elsewhere* than in logic or in the consideration for truth.

---

55 In the sentence containing the present note, the terms "the number" and "infinity" have been chosen in contradistinction to the term "all": In conformity with the superordinate perspective and topic of the work (Chapter I and section II A 8, above) I do not adopt any standpoint in the present work on whether all conceptualisations are logically possible (cf. the diversity of meanings of "logically possible" on the level of fundamental philosophical positions).

(c) The setting up of and choice between normative definitions is a function of our *interests* in a broad sense, and of the connection the phenomenon that is to be characterised has with these interests; cf. the examples in item (2) above and in item (b) above.[56]

Especially for law it is the case that it is perceived by many people as having a *central connection with vital and diverse interests in our lives*. This may contribute to explaining the diversity of conceptual approaches.

The relationships between interests, normative definitions (conceptualisations) and characterisations comes out clearly in the following observations concerning law as an object of investigation:

> "The polysemy and the contradictions in the concept of 'law' are connected with the fact that legal rules and the enforcement of the law have *a number of tasks*. Five tasks stand out: 1. The law serves to govern the behaviour of the members of society. 2. It serves as a means to allocating benefits and burdens in society. 3. It ensures expectations. 4. A fourth task is to deal with conflicts and, as the case may be, to contribute to resolving them. 5. The final task consists in the law's expressing ideals and values" (my italics).[57]
>
> "Many of the distinctive features of the law stem from the fact that the legal system is a *meeting place for politics and morals*. Requirements are laid down both for the system to be an effective means for carrying out political objectives, and for it to reflect people's moral attitudes. These requirements sometimes come into conflict with one another. And many divergences within legal philosophy reflect such tensions" (my italics).[58]

The passages quoted are used by their authors as points of departure for closer analyses, but the quotations also have value as shorthand expressions of the *potentially multifaceted character of cognitions* of legal phenomena: All according to which of the said tasks of the law (see the first quotation) an individual is most *concerned with*, and all according to whether the individual is most *oriented towards* a political or a moral viewpoint (see the second quotation), the individual concerned will be able to choose between *different* normative definitions of "law" or of other words for the whole or part of what is usually termed "law" ("legal phenomena"); and all according to which conceptual points of departure are chosen, he will be able to put forward *different* characterisations of the law.

(a)↔(c) Some people will perhaps consider what has now been outlined to be pretty much a matter of course, something I believe may be due to their not having *completely* thought the outlined insights through. Compare the seemingly obvious correctness of, and the matter-of-courseness with which we assert, sentences like "our existing conceptual framework may not have got things right

56 See also section II B 3.3.2 (3) above, at and in notes 83 and 84.

57 Aubert, *Rettssosiologi* [sociology of law], pp. 49–50.

58 Eckhoff/ Sundby, *Rettssystemer* [legal systems], 1st ed. p. 260; 2nd ed. p. 226; *Rechtssysteme*, p. 193. See also Eckhoff, 'Rett, moral og politikk' [law, morals and politics], pp. 9–11.

initially", "a conceptual schema more faithful to the facts is needed".[59] – My impression is that most of us, to a greater or lesser degree and more or less consciously, have the idea that some conceptualisations are "truer" than others (compare also section II B 4.1 (5)(b) above). Among causes of this idea I assume some are connected with the *consequence of rejecting the idea*: The insights that an infinity of conceptualisations is possible, and that no conceptualisation can with any right be said to provide a basis for truer cognition than other conceptualisations, lead to *confrontation with one's own evaluations and choices*: All conceptualisations must be justified with their relation to interests; cf. the present section III 2.

(4) Contrasting with polysemy in a drawing

There are some illustrative similarities and differences between analyses in thought of a phenomenon, for example law, and different aspects of the same drawing, for example Rubin's vase–faces or Wittgenstein's hare–duck:[60]

(a) One difference lies in *where the polysemy is*. In the case of the drawings it is in visual impressions, so that cognition of the relationship between the aspects is partly of a *perceptual psychological kind*. Cognition of different aspects of law, on the other hand, is typically of a more purely *intellectual kind*. One often presupposes that the different sets of criteria that constitute the basis for the conceptualisation have already been acquired through the sociology of law, the psychology of law, the doctrine of the sources of law, purely conceptual analyses, etc.

In the cognition of the ambiguities/ instances of polysemy, there is thus the psychological difference between the drawings and law that lies in alternating between concrete visual impressions versus alternating between already acquired thought content.

[59] Summers, 'Legal Philosophy Today – An Introduction', p. 4.

[60] Gross, *Psychology*, p. 240; Wittgenstein, *Philosophische Untersuchungen*, p. 309.

But once we have cognised the ambiguities/ instances of polysemy, the logical point is the same: that something it is reasonable to call the *same phenomenon* can be referred to through a number of *different understandings*.

(b) Concerning the *degree of aspect diversity*, a difference lies in the fact that the drawings only open the door to *two* aspects, while law, as we have seen, has shown itself to open the door to a *great diversity* of aspects.

(c) As far as the *significance of the interests* is concerned, a difference lies in the fact that on the whole *no* special interests relate to which aspect of the drawings one sees, while many have *placed very great weight on* their choice of one aspect of law rather than other aspects.[61]

2.2.5. *Influencing action*

Interests motivate not only choice of conceptualisation out of a desire for cognition (section 2.2.4 above), but also motivate choice of conceptualisation out of a *desire to influence others*.

The desire to influence shows itself particularly in the case of conceptualisation with a view to *normative characterisations*. It shows itself for example in the case of the legislator's laying down the concepts in the statute, and later in the case of the exposition of these concepts in legal dogmatics and the application of the concepts by the courts and the public administrative authorities: Legislators and lawyers build on the notion that the very fact of whether or not a type of act is placed under the statute is of significance for whether such acts will be performed. Inter alia for this reason a great deal of work is invested in drawing boundaries for the concepts (on means of structuring, see sections II B 5–6 above); and for the same reason, in the drawing of these boundaries great weight is placed on which acts one wishes to encourage and which acts one wishes to prevent.

The desire to influence also makes itself felt in the case of conceptualisations with a view to *descriptive characterisations*: Through the setting up of and choice between normative definitions one can *lead other people's attention* to that aspect of the things that the conceptualisation brings out and that one considers important. – In legal science and the social sciences, the motive for leading other people's attention is often a *desire for social change*: One wants to increase the attention paid to a group's position and to the group's way of seeing things, in order thereby to contribute to empathy with the group's views, and in order thereby again to contribute to changes for the *good of the group* (see the first and second quotations below). – Feminist-oriented research in particular has actualised the same motive constellation in other subjects too, such as medicine (see the third quotation below).

---

61 On absolutisation of aspects, see section IV 3.2 (1) below.

> "[T]he purpose of women's law is to describe, explain and understand the legal position of women, with the specific aim of improving the position of women in law and in society."[62]
>
> "To describe the [mental] patient's situation faithfully is necessarily to present a partisan view. For this ... bias I partly excuse myself by arguing that the imbalance is at least on the right side of the scale, since almost all professional literature on mental patients is written from the point of view of the psychiatrist, and he, socially speaking, is on the other side."[63]
>
> "The Medicine and Health Program wishes to continue its commitment within women's research in medicine. ... The need to strengthen women's health has its source in the fact that parts of medical research are founded on investigations done exclusively on the male sex, and that a number of important aspects of women's health have to a very limited degree been given priority in terms of research. The objective of this commitment is to contribute to equal medical knowledge and practice for women and men, through inter alia generating new knowledge, developing leading-edge competence and making visible the need for a gender perspective generally, in medical research."[64]

Desires for influencing action make themselves felt not only via the structuring and thus openly, as outlined here, but also covertly, via persuasive definitions (section 2.4.2 below).

Whether desires for influencing action are actualised in conceptualisations with a view to normative characterisations or in conceptualisations with a view to descriptive characterisations; and whether these desires are openly communicated or make themselves felt covertly – if one wants to map criteria that are used to justify wishes for particular influences on action, one is led over to *general practical argumentation.* One is, inter alia, led over to arguments from justice: Legislators, lawyers, social scientists, and others, argue for and choose certain structurings rather than other structurings, (also) because the chosen structurings are to a greater degree considered to contribute to equal treatment of what one considers ought to be treated equally. See, for example, in connection with the quotations above, the use of justice argumentation in women's law (re the first quotation),[65] "the imbalance is ... on the right side of the scale" (in the second quotation) and "equal medical knowledge and practice" (in the third quotation).

---

62 Stang Dahl, *Women's Law: An Introduction to Feminist Jurisprudence*, p. 17 (also in 'Kvinnerett – en rettsvitenskapelig fornyelse' [women's law – a renewal of legal science], pp. 67–68). – A corresponding desire to improve the position of the group in question probably motivates lawyers' work with other person-oriented legal disciplines too, e.g. children's law, prisoners' law, immigration law, patients' law or social law (see some examples in section 2.4.2 below). But it is seldom that the objective of influencing is expressed so officially and clearly as in women's law.

63 Goffman, *Asylums*, p. 8 (Goffman's parenthesis omitted).

64 Norwegian Research Council, text of an announcement concerning the Medicine and Health Program, 1996.

65 Stang Dahl, *Women's Law: An Introduction to Feminist Jurisprudence*, pp. 48–51, 87–96.

2.2.6. *Aesthetic and heuristic considerations*

(1) Definitions
(2) Heuristic considerations; including discussion of aesthetic considerations as an instrumental value
(3) Aesthetic considerations as an intrinsic value
  (a) Hohfeld
  (b) The principle of legality
(4) Aesthetic considerations as an obstacle to cognition of what things are like
  (a) Geometrical figures
  (b) Dichotomies

(1) Definitions

By *"aesthetic considerations"* I mean considerations like simplicity, symmetry, consistency, etc.

> In actually occurring language and argumentation there are indeterminate boundaries for what are categorised as 'aesthetic considerations'.[66] For the present discussion it is not necessary to draw determinate boundaries; it is sufficient to focus on some central types of consideration that are considered relevant in the setting up of and choice between normative definitions, cf. the considerations just mentioned.

By *"heuristic considerations"* I mean desires to make an amount of information easier to comprehend, recall and apply. – Having defined the term in this way, I use it partly of aims of a more *passive* kind ("easier to comprehend and recall"), and partly of aims of a more *active* kind ("easier to apply"). As an extension of the more active aims lies the consideration for *creative* thinking; in the formation of concepts, one can aim at opening new perspectives and thereby contribute to concept development and theory formation in directions one considers interesting.

(2) Heuristic considerations; including discussion of aesthetic considerations as an instrumental value

Heuristic considerations I assume motivate partly the structuring (the present item (2)), partly the naming (section 2.3 below), and partly the coupling of the two (section 2.4.1 below). Out of consideration for the interconnections in the material, I shall deal with heuristic considerations as a criterion in the case of the structuring, also in the last-mentioned context (see section 2.4.1 (2)). – Here I shall mention two features of structurings that I assume can be explained inter alia on the basis of the desire to promote heuristic considerations.

---

66 Sheppard, *Aesthetics*, pp. 38–39, 62–63. – See also item (3) below.

First, there is the placing of emphasis on *aesthetic considerations*: We find it *easier to* comprehend, recall and apply something, the simpler, the more symmetrical, the more consistent, or the like, the material is. – Aesthetic considerations become in this role a means to heuristic ends.[67]

Secondly, there is the combination of the aesthetic with a certain *contrast to reality*. – One constructs concepts which are remote from reality in their simplicity, symmetry, consistency, or the like, but which, when they are confronted with reality, provide a schematic contrast intended to facilitate comprehension and synoptic grasp in a particular direction: for example Wittgenstein's greatly simplified language games;[68] or, as the case may be, provide a schematic contrast (also) intended to facilitate further concept development and theory formation: for example Weberian ideal types;[69] or, as the case may be, provide a schematic contrast (also) intended to facilitate comprehension and synoptic grasp of a more indeterminate kind: for example structurings as elements in Carnapian explications or rational reconstructions.[70] – Or one takes over concepts with one or more of the now mentioned properties, from custom-based language: for example the everyday concept of 'democracy', understood as 'government by the people'.[71]

(3) Aesthetic considerations as an intrinsic value

Beside instrumental value (item (2) above) aesthetic considerations are often ascribed an *intrinsic value* in the case of the formation of concepts: One chooses that description, explanation or justification which, *other things being equal*, is the simplest, most symmetrical, most consistent, or the like. And one chooses

---

67 Ihering, *Geist des römischen Rechts*, pp. 340 et seq., 409–12.

68 Wittgenstein, *Philosophische Untersuchungen*, Part I, section 130: "Unsere klaren und einfachen Sprachspiele sind nicht Vorstudien zu einer künftigen Reglementierung der Sprache ... Vielmehr stehen die Sprachspiele da als *Vergleichsobjekte*, die durch Ähnlichkeit und Unähnlichkeit ein Licht in die Verhältnisse unsrer Sprache werfen sollen" (Wittgenstein's italics).

69 Weber, 'Die "Objektivität" sozialwissenschaftlicher und sozialpolitischer Erkenntnis', pp. 189–212; *Wirtschaft und Gesellschaft*, pp. 3, 4–5, 10–11. – "[Der Idealtypus] ist ein Gedankenbild, welches ... die Bedeutung eines rein idealen *Grenz*begriffes hat, an welchem die Wirklichkeit zur Verdeutlichung bestimmter bedeutsamer Bestandteile ihres empirischen Gehaltes *gemessen*, mit dem sie *verglichen* wird" (first-mentioned work, p. 194; Weber's italics); "Die Konstruktion eines streng zweckrationalen Handelns ... dient ... der Soziologie, seiner evidenten Verständlichkeit und seiner ... Eindeutigkeit wegen, als Typus ("Idealtypus"), um das reale, durch Irrationalitäten aller Art (Affekte, Irrtümer) beeinflußte Handeln als *"Abweichung"* ... zu verstehen" (latter-mentioned work, p. 3; my italics; Weber's italics omitted).

70 Sections V 3.3.3 cf. 3.3.1–3.3.2, below. See also Carnap, 'Replies and Systematic Expositions', p. 940; Goodman, 'The Significance of Der logische Aufbau der Welt', pp. 552–54, 555.

71 No state exists in which all citizens (irrespective of age, mental state, criminal record, property, sex, etc.) are involved in all the state's decisions of different kinds (legislative, executive, judicial) at all times (constantly). The said concept of 'democracy' ('government by the people') functions instead as a multi-dimensional (see the preceding parentheses) yardstick that actually occurring states can be placed in relation to. Compare Ross, *Dansk statsforfatningsret* [Danish constitutional law], Vol. I, p. 132; *Hvorfor demokrati?* [why democracy?], pp. 110–17.

description, explanation or justification on the basis of aesthetic considerations *at the expense of* other considerations.[72]

The *psychological causal factors* behind views that aesthetic considerations have intrinsic value, I take to be partly the *pleasantness* of simplicity, symmetry, consistency, or the like,[73] and partly the *feeling of power* it gives to feel that one has mastery of a given problem area.[74]

There may be disagreement about *which* conceptualisation is "most aesthetic". Such disagreement may arise on account of disagreement about what properties shall be covered by the term "aesthetic";[75] it may arise on account of disagreement about what properties shall be covered by terms like "simplicity", "symmetry", "consistency", or the like; or, given that one is in agreement on these points, it may arise on account of disagreement about what weight one shall place on the properties in relation to one another.

> The formulation "most aesthetic" has a positive appeal and is thus simply a name for a decisional outcome: that the conceptualisation in question is aesthetically to be preferred. The formulation is not intended here to refer to a simple aesthetic property: Which conceptualisation is considered best in terms of aesthetic considerations will typically be considered to depend on a *weighing and balancing* of the various more specific properties, like simplicity, symmetry, consistency, and the like.

---

72 Quine, *Word and Object*, pp. 19–20; Goodman, 'Science and Simplicity', p. 346. – Concerning conceptualisations of legal phenomena, see notes 75 and 76 below; items (a)–(b) below; and item (4) below.

73 Heisenberg, *Der Teil und das Ganze: Gespräche im Umkreis der Atomphysik*, p. 99: "Wenn man durch die Natur auf mathematische Formen von großer Einfachheit und Schönheit geführt wird ... auf Formen, die bis dahin noch von niemandem ausgedacht worden sind, so kann man eben nicht umhin zu glauben, daß sie 'wahr' sind, das heißt daß sie einen echten Zug der Natur darstellen. ... Sie können mir vorwerfen, daß ich hier ein ästhetisches Wahrheitskriterium verwende, indem ich von Einfachheit und Schönheit spreche. Aber ich muß zugeben, daß für mich von der Einfachheit und Schönheit des mathematischen Schemas, das uns hier von der Natur suggeriert worden ist, eine ganz große Überzeugungskraft ausgeht."

74 Strawson, *Introduction to Logical Theory*, pp. 60, 61. – The statements referred to in the present note and the preceding note do not concern analysis and argumentation formulated in everyday language (cf. sections 1 and 2.1, and further cf. section I 5, above). However, by virtue of being statements about causes of the fact that aesthetic considerations are perceived as having intrinsic value, I assume that these statements have weight also in relation to analysis and argumentation formulated in everyday language: In the aesthetic aspect (simplicity, symmetry, consistency, and the like), formal languages constitute refinements of features of analysis and argumentation formulated in everyday language.

75 With a view to conceptualisations of legal phenomena, compare Ihering, *Geist des römischen Rechts*, pp. 406–07: "Natürlichkeit, Durchsichtigkeit, Einfachheit, Anschaulichkeit"; Radbruch, *Rechtsphilosophie*, pp. 206–07: "[H]aarscharfen Genauigkeit", "[D]er eleganten Auflösung scheinbar hoffnungslos verworrener juristischer Verknotungen"; Frank, *Law and the Modern Mind*, p. 281: "[S]ymmetry, consistency or logical simplicity"; Llewellyn, 'On the Good, the True, the Beautiful, in Law', pp. 171, 173, 196: "[F]unctional beauty, the beauty of ... turbine ... The c.i.f. construct ... has proved in test after test as surely ... gauged to the work it had to do as any legal engine man has yet designed"; pp. 183–84: "[E]sthetics drove in the direction of cold clarity ... the Formal Style". – See also item (1) above.

Such disagreement as mentioned does not affect the present point: *that* aesthetic considerations are in fact ascribed great intrinsic value.

Many conceptualisations of *legal phenomena* seem to be motivated and evaluated inter alia out of a quest for aesthetics in its own right.[76] I shall mention two examples.

(a) Hohfeld

A well-known conceptualisation which was probably strongly motivated by aesthetic considerations in their own right, is Hohfeld's analysis of ways of using terms relating to rights. Posterity too has in its evaluation of this conceptualisation often adopted an aesthetic viewpoint:

> "Early in our century the American W. N. Hohfeld published the analysis of the concepts of rights (jural relations) which has now become classic and which represents *one of legal theory's most beautiful results*" (my italics).[77]

(b) The principle of legality

In recent Norwegian literature I see the discussions of the principle of legality, and the differences from older literature on this topic, as examples of the significance of aesthetic considerations for the formation of concepts.

The Norwegian term "legalitetsprinsippet" [the principle of legality] is used in the literature on constitutional and administrative law of the norm that the public administrative authorities must in certain cases have authority in statute law to be able to impose duties on the citizens or to perform actual acts to the detriment of the citizens.

For the justification and determination of those cases in which the public administrative authorities need statutory authority, the *traditional presentation* of the principle of legality uses a complex and partly tacitly presupposed line of argumentation:[78]

The point of departure seems to be a *moral* norm investing the individual with a right to self-determination. From this, one more or less intuitively infers a *political* norm, to the effect that the people shall take part in the decision process, when *general* duties are imposed on the people themselves. This political norm

---

[76] For a correct picture of the role played by considerations for simplicity, symmetry, consistency, and the like, in conceptualisations of legal phenomena, it must also be taken into account that among lawyers these considerations often go under names other than "aesthetics"; historically speaking the considerations inter alia go under the name of "elegance", see Stein, 'Elegance in Law', passim; and in more modern discussions, they inter alia go under the name of "logic", see e.g. Cardozo, 'The Nature of the Judicial Process', pp. 117–25.

[77] Frändberg, 'Till frågan om de juridiska begreppens systematik' [on the question of the systematics of legal concepts], p. 91.

[78] Aschehoug, *Norges nuværende Statsforfatning* [the present constitution of Norway], Vol. 2, p. 119, cf. pp. 98 et seq.; Morgenstierne, *Lærebok i den norske statsforfatningsret* [textbook of Norwegian constitutional law], Vol. 2, pp. 86–96, 101–05; Castberg, 'Hvilke statsviljesytringer maa avgives i lovs form?' [which utterances of the will of the state must be issued in statutory form?], pp. 727–28, cf. 725–30; *Norges statsforfatning* [constitution of Norway], Vol. II, pp. 10, cf. 7–11; Andenæs, *Statsforfatningen i Norge* [constitution of Norway], pp. 212–13, cf. 210–17.

then justifies the *legal* norm that material *law* must have authority in statute law, that is to say, be enacted by the popularly elected assembly. – To get from the general norms to the individual norms or individual actual acts, one must next appeal to a *purpose consideration*: If the purpose is to be achieved, it must also be required that the public administrative authorities' *individual* norms and actual acts have authority in statute law. For if the public administrative authorities were free to act against the citizens in individual instances without authority in statute law, the citizens would not get any protection from the norm that material law must have authority in statute law.

The mixture of moral, political and legal evaluations in this reasoning, the use of purpose consideration, and the vagueness in the concept of 'material law', all make this reasoning *vulnerable* in both its main applications: Partly this reasoning is vulnerable in its capacity of *justification*. And partly this reasoning is vulnerable in its capacity of *means to drawing boundaries*, between those cases in which the public administrative authorities must have authority in statute law and those cases in which this is not necessary.

For the justification and determination of those cases in which the public administrative authorities need statutory authority, *recent theory* has formed another set of criteria. As far as *actual acts* are concerned, one uses the principle of lex superior:[79] If an act is prohibited by a particular statutory provision or according to unwritten law, it may only be lawfully performed if it is permitted by (another) specific statutory provision. For example, sections 228 et seq. of the Criminal Justice Act (Act No. 10 of 22 May 1902) make it an offence to use violence against another person, but in a number of cases the public administrative authorities have been given statutory permission to use physical force. As far as *stipulation of norms* is concerned, one uses the principle of legality and gives it a negative formulation.[80] I have in another work given an account of how the content of the negative formulation may in the main be reproduced in the form of *two axioms*:[81]

The first axiom I term the *"competence axiom"*. By this term I mean that competence is as a general rule[82] a necessary condition for any valid stipulation of a norm. This applies whether one imposes duties on oneself or on others. Seen in the critically reflexive perspective conceptualised in the present work, the compe-

---

79 Eckhoff, *Forvaltningsrett* [administrative law], 1st ed. pp. 155–60; Eckhoff/ Smith, *Forvaltningsrett*, pp. 251–57.

80 Eckhoff, *Forvaltningsrett* [administrative law], 1st ed. pp. 139–63, in particular p. 143, cf. pp. 142–47; Eckhoff/ Smith, *Forvaltningsrett*, pp. 235–57, in particular pp. 238, 240, cf. pp. 237–43; E. Smith, 'Legalitetsprinsippets hjemmelskrav og subjekter' [the principle of legality's requirement for legal authority, and its subjects], in particular pp. 669–72. A negative formulation also lies in the extension of the argumentation in Ross, 'Friheds- og ejendomskriteriet' [the freedom and property criterion], pp. 84–90.

81 Eng, 'Begrepene 'kompetanse' og 'gyldighet' i juridisk argumentasjon' [the concepts of 'competence' and 'validity' in legal argumentation], pp. 647–48.

82 Op. cit., pp. 664–69.

tence axiom is an element in a reconstruction and redefinition (Chapter V below). More precisely, this axiom is an element in a reconstruction and redefinition of the individual decisions lawyers typically term "in/valid".[83] The competence axiom thus applies to all parts of the legal system.

The second axiom states that *if the stipulator of a norm does not have any other competence basis, he must have authority in statute law*. This axiom follows from the competence axiom plus an obvious additional premiss that statute law is a possible competence basis in Norwegian law. – Corresponding axioms can be formed for stipulators of norms in all areas of law. For example, in the law of contract this may be done as follows: "If a contracting party does not have any other competence basis for his claim, he must have authority in contract", or in the law of inheritance as follows: "If an heir does not have any other competence basis for his claim, he must have authority in last will and testament", and so forth.

It is reasonable to assume that aesthetic considerations have been a *causal factor* behind the setting up of the principle of legality in recent theory: – As considerations in support of the new formulation of the principle of legality it has been adduced partly that this formulation provides a *better* explanation of the legal basis of the principle, and partly that the formulation provides *better* justifications concerning which decisions need statutory authority.[84] – At the same time the presupposition seems to be that the new formulation generates in the main the same standpoints as traditional theory does, with respect to when the public administrative authorities need statutory authority for their decisions.[85] – In the expressions "better explanation" and "better justification" there probably therefore lies inter alia an evaluation in terms of simplicity, symmetry, consistency, and the like.

At the same time the said aesthetic considerations are undoubtedly considered to be *legitimate grounds*, not only psychological causal factors, in the formation of concepts.[86] And I assume that for many people the said aesthetic considerations have pretty considerable weight: both when seen as means to effective learning, storing and application of central legal rules concerning public administrative authorities (item (2) above), and when seen as values in themselves (the present item).

---

83 Op. cit., p. 627, cf. Eng, *U/enighetsanalyse – med særlig sikte på jus og allmenn rettsteori* [analysis of dis/agreement – with particular reference to law and legal theory], section V 1.1 (4), in note 11.

84 Eckhoff, *Forvaltningsrett* [administrative law], 1st ed. pp. 145–47; Eckhoff/ Smith, *Forvaltningsrett*, pp. 237–38, 241–42.

85 This aspect of the relationship between traditional and recent theory will be treated in greater depth in section V 2.3 below.

86 Compare Bernt, 'Legalitetsprinsippet og andre hjemmelsspørsmål i den offentlige rett – noen prinsipielle betraktninger' [the principle of legality and other authority issues in public law – some considerations of principle], p. 512; Boe, 'Eckhoffs/ Smiths framstilling av lovskravet i forvaltningsretten' [Eckhoff/ Smith's account of the requirement for statutory authority in administrative law], p. 153.

(4) Aesthetic considerations as an obstacle to cognition of what things are like

In law, in legal theory, and also more generally, one sometimes chooses *other* conceptualisations than those that are *best* suited to capturing important features of reality. One factor causing this I assume to be the urge for aesthetics: This urge can, consciously or unconsciously, acquire *such* a strong intrinsic value that the considerations for true description and adequate systematisation of the diversity of facts are set aside. One creates a "Teutonic intellectual style";[87] one creates a style in which "concepts give birth to one another, instead of being born of observation".[88]

I shall illustrate and support this assumption with a couple of instance-types: geometrical figures and dichotomies.

(a) Geometrical figures

On the grip that aesthetic considerations have on thought, Seip says, in a more polemical context within history and social science:

> "There is ... a danger [attached to models, to concepts, indeed to words altogether] that comes ... from within, from our own innate apparatus, preferences in ourselves. There are *thought figures which are immediately attractive to us*, which are attractive to *our aesthetic and logical sense*. Such a figure is the *circle with its centre*. What is more beautiful than a circle and what is more attractive than a centre? – Parenthetically, let me say here that to me models like those constructed by Talcott Parsons or J.-J. Rousseau, represent fiction, they are poetry. It can be read with pleasure, and even, like good poetry, provide piecemeal insight. The same applies to Galtung's and Rokkan's paradigms. They are comely clouds" (my italics).[89]

In relation to conceptualisations of law ("what is law?"), we can as an instance-type of the force of aesthetic considerations mention theories of the *law as a pyramid*. Eckhoff puts it this way:

> "Many legal theorists have imagined the legal system as a pointed *pyramid* where on the top one finds something that gives validity to all the underlying layers of norms. In earlier times one often operated with a personal top point such as the God of natural law or Austin's "Sovereign". But as a result of secularisation and democratisation these have to a great extent had to give way to such impersonal top points as Kelsen's "Grundnorm" and Hart's "Rule of recognition".
>
> It is psychologically understandable that many people have sought for such an anchorage in common for all legal norms. It satisfies *needs for*

87 Galtung, 'Deductive Thinking and Political Practice. An Essay on Teutonic Intellectual Style'.

88 Seip, 'Det 19. århundres norske byråkrati belyst gjennom moderne forvaltningsteori' [the 19th century's Norwegian bureaucracy illuminated through modern administrative theory], p. 169 (Seip's italics omitted).

89 Seip, 'Modellenes tyranni' [the tyranny of models], pp. 225–26.

> *simplicity and for considering the law as a unity*. And one gets a facile way of justifying the validity of legal norms.
>
> But the justifications that are provided by operating with a highest norm common to the legal system are more facile than convincing" (my italics).[90]

A feature in common of the theories that are criticised in the two preceding quotations is that these theories claim that something (respectively society and law) is built up like a *geometrical figure* (respectively the circle and the pyramid): The aesthetic influences concept formation and thinking via the *sense of vision*.

(b) Dichotomies

Another regularity in concept formation in respect of which I assume that inter alia the sense of the aesthetic operates as a causal factor is dichotomies. I agree with the following general and critical observation Seip provides concerning dichotomies:

> "We have a need to think in *pairs, contrasts*, black and white, in terms of God and the devil, periphery and centre, culture and counter-culture ... Primitive dichotomies of this kind mean a mighty simplification of the material of our experience. It is a simplification that is attractive to us because it – seemingly – makes us master of the material. ... I think it is not a very felicitous point of departure to start with a dichotomy. ... It consists of two elements seen in relation to each other, with the weight on the relation. It is more reasonable to take one's point of departure in the individual elements. These can be seen as massifs, as blocks, with more than one side. A salient point is precisely that a block has *more than one side*, that it can have more than one opposite party ..." (my italics).[91]

In this quotation dichotomies are contrasted with the phenomena's many aspects, and the significance of the latter is emphasised (on the diversity of aspects, see section 2.2.4 above). – In relation to *propositions about lawyers' argumentation de lege lata* it is no less important to contrast dichotomies with the *graduated transitions* within the individual aspects, and to emphasise the significance of this graduatedness. I say emphasise, because much legal theory, including much of the theory of the sources of law, assumes dichotomies where in my view there is no basis for doing so. One example is talking about lawyers' argumentation de lege lata through the dichotomy between descriptive and normative propositions (section II F above). Another example is talking about lawyers' argumentation de lege lata through dichotomies in propositions within the doctrine of the sources of law:

---

90 Eckhoff, 'Feed back i rettstenkning og rettssystemer' [feedback in legal thinking and legal systems], p. 78. See also Golding, 'Kelsen and the Concept of 'Legal System' ', pp. 98–99; Simpson, 'The Common Law and Legal Theory', pp. 86–87, 99; Eckhoff/ Sundby, 'The Notion of Basic Norm(s) in Jurisprudence', pp. 136–37, 144.

91 Seip, 'Modellenes tyranni' [the tyranny of models], pp. 226–27. See also same writer, *Utsikt over Norges historie* [survey of Norwegian history], First Part, p. 8.

- One[92] expresses oneself as if some sources of law in general can be said to be more weighty than others, for example "Statutes are the most important source of law."[93]
- One formulates questions about the legal argumentatory significance of a type of argument as a question of whether the type of argument is "binding" or "not binding", "mandatory" or "permissive".[94]
- One expresses oneself as if a statement in the grounds of a judgment is either "obiter dicta" (an unnecessary element in the grounds), and thus not binding; or "ratio decidendi" (a necessary element in the grounds), and thus binding

---

92 The following formulations in the main text are not verbatim quotations, but are intended to formulate meaning content, dichotomies, that one to a greater or lesser degree finds in Norwegian and Nordic lawyers' propositions *about* sources of law (in contrast to their actual use of the sources of law), and in many Norwegian and Nordic presentations of sources of law. – My impression is that these dichotomies also mark lawyers' propositions about sources of law in many other countries. This I base partly on knowledge of the literature and partly on more general reflections on the psychology of decision-makers; on the latter, see Eng, *U/enighetsanalyse – med særlig sikte på jus og allmenn rettsteori* [analysis of dis/agreement – with particular reference to law and legal theory], section IV 4. – The references in the notes in connection with the formulations in the main text do not aim to be either exhaustive or representative; they are intended only as a minimum of exemplification in relation to fundamental tendencies. – The topic here is the occurrence of dichotomies. I do not undertake any tenability assessment of the individual writer's conceptual apparatus and propositions at large: Maintaining such dichotomies as are mentioned in what follows *can* be combined with otherwise descriptively apt propositions.

93 Boe, *Innføring i juss* [introduction to law] (1993), Vol. 1, pp. 176 ("[T]he wording of the statute counts most"), 179; *Innføring i juss* (1996), pp. 184, 195; Peczenik, *Juridikens metodproblem* [the problem of method in law], p. 50 ("The wording of the statute takes precedence over the travaux préparatoires and precedent"); *Vad är rätt?* [what is law?], p. 222 ("In Sweden in principle only statute law is binding"); Peczenik/ Schött, 'Juridisk konservatism' [legal conservatism], p. 725 ("[S]tatute law takes the foremost place. ... Only special reasons can motivate a precedent's being decisive for the interpretation of the statute and the letter of the law's being interpreted away"). – See also note 102 below.

94 Peczenik, *On Law and Reason*, p. 319 ("some sources of the law ... that are and some that are not binding"); *Vad är rätt?*, pp. 218, 222–23; Peczenik et al., *Juridisk argumentation* [legal argumentation], pp. 147–48 ("two kinds of sources of law ... binding and not binding"); Kjønstad/ Syse, *Velferdsrett* [welfare law], p. 190 ("The Constitution provides clear rules concerning how a Bill shall be dealt with in order for it to become a statutory text that is binding ... travaux préparatoires are not binding"); Boe, *Innføring i juss* [introduction to law] (1993), Vol. 1, p. 174 ("The point of departure is that mandatory factors shall have greater weight than permissive factors"); *Innføring i juss* (1996), p. 187. See also Hart, *The Concept of Law*, 1st ed. pp. 246–47; 2nd ed. p. 294 (divides sources of law into "mandatory" and "permissive"). – Aarbakke groups sources of law into "formally binding" and "formally guiding", but it is unclear what significance he ascribes to this distinction, see *Skatt på inntekt* [tax on income], Part 1, pp. 17 et seq., compare pp. 23 et seq. – Malt wants under the name of "hovedkilder" [principal sources] to reintroduce forms of expression from the 19th century, according to which statute and customary law, and only these, are said to be "(absolutely) binding", see 'To glemte linjer i tradisjonell rettsfinningslære' [two forgotten lines in the traditional doctrine of finding law], in particular pp. 62–64, compare p. 59 from which it is apparent that Malt is aware that such a form of expression does not correspond to actual use of the sources of law. – In 'The Doctrine of Precedent in English and Norwegian Law', section 4.1.2, I criticise the dichotomy between "being bound" and "not being bound", in particular with respect to judgments as a source of law.

according to the principles otherwise applying, of the binding force of precedents.[95]

- One expresses oneself as if a judgment is either "prejudikat" [precedent], and thus decisive for the case at hand; or "ikke prejudikat" [not a precedent], and thus without significance.[96]
- One expresses oneself as if practice is either trade usage or customary law, and thus decisive; or not trade usage or customary law, and thus without significance.[97]
- One sets up catalogues of typical constellations of sources of law, with specification of which source of law weighs most heavily:[98] for example with the specification that the wording of statutes in the case of conflict takes precedence over/ does not take precedence over travaux préparatoires, judgments or equitable considerations.

On the whole such dichotomous modes of formulation as have now been mentioned are *inadequate as descriptions* of judges' and other lawyers' use of legally relevant arguments ("sources of law"): The graduated weighting in the light of a diversity of equitable considerations that lawyers perform, cannot without great risk of misunderstandings be described through such dichotomies. – The dichotomous modes of formulation *must be replaced by* concepts with a graduated structure, mappings of factors that influence the weight of arguments, and an emphasising of the pervasive weighing and balancing character of law, *provided* the purpose is description.[99]

---

95 Fleischer, *Rettskilder* [sources of law], pp. 171–72. – In 'The Doctrine of Precedent in English and Norwegian Law', sections 2.3–2.4 and 4.1.1, I discuss some aspects of this distinction in the two systems.

96 Eckhoff, *Rettskildelære* [doctrine of the sources of law], 1st ed. Chapters 6–7, in particular pp. 151 et seq.; 2nd and 3rd eds. Chapter 7 section III contrasted with section IV; Andenæs, *Innføring i rettsstudiet* [introduction to the study of law], Chapter 6 VI contrasted with Chapter 9; see also note 100 below. – In contrast to these kinds of material concepts of precedent, Fleischer wishes to use "precedent" synonymously with "an earlier judicial decision", see *Rettskilder* [sources of law] pp. 160–61. In his more detailed discussions, however, Fleischer too builds on a material and dichotomous concept of 'precedent', see e.g. p. 173: "It must … be an irrefutable conclusion that judgments of lower courts [i.e. other courts than the Supreme Court] cannot be ascribed the role of precedents."

97 However, in Norwegian domestic law pressure for such a form of expression is less today than earlier, since statutes and judgments have taken over as the most often cited sources of law, and the practice of private individuals is seldom cited today. In international law, on the other hand, this form of expression related to customary law still plays an important part, see e.g. Jennings/ Watts (eds.), *Oppenheim's International Law*, pp. 25–31.

98 Boe, *Innføring i juss* [introduction to law] (1993), Vol. 1, pp. 176 et seq.; *Innføring i juss* (1996), pp. 189 et seq.; Helset, 'Innledning til rettskildelæren' [introduction to the doctrine of the sources of law], pp. 282–83; Peczenik, *Juridikens metodproblem* [the problem of method in law], pp. 50–51; *Vad är rätt?* [what is law?], pp. 214–16, 219–20, 281; Peczenik et al., *Juridisk argumentation* [legal argumentation], pp. 144–49.

99 Sundby, *Om normer* [on norms], Part 2 (see e.g. pp. 265–68); Eng, 'The Doctrine of Precedent in English and Norwegian Law', section 4.1. See also MacCormick/ Summers (eds.), *Interpreting Prece-*

For example, in the case of judgments: It is not very pertinent to say that lawyers ask and think along a dichotomy according to which a judgment either is or is not a precedent. It is more pertinent to say that lawyers consider all judgments to be potential arguments, and that the legal argumentatory significance here and now of the judgment is a question of ascribing weight and of weighing and balancing:

Properties of the judgment that have significance for its weight in the individual instance (for the sake of brevity I term these "weight factors") are inter alia at which instance the judgment was pronounced, the occurrence and strength of any dissent, the age of the judgment, the nature of the legal issue, and the goodness of the conclusion.

The weight of the weight factors may itself cause doubt, whereby *new rounds* of weighing and balancing *other* relevant weight factors are necessary. – For example, in the case of doubt about the weight of a dissenting opinion, lawyers look at inter alia the degree of dissent, who dissented, and the professional soundness of the dissenting opinion.

Parallel to and in interplay with identification of relevant features of the judgment and the weighing and balancing of these against one another, on different levels, the lawyer directs his attention to *another* weighing and balancing question: the weight of the judgment in relation to *other* sources of law.[100]

I assume that the same applies in the case of other legally relevant arguments, such as the wording of statutes, travaux préparatoires, public administrative practice, the practice of private persons, international law, etc: The weight of the argument in the individual instance rests on a *weighing and balancing* of certain features of the argument type: partly a weighing and balancing of the *argument-specific features in relation to one another* (see as an example the argument-specific features of judgments mentioned above), and partly a weighing and balancing of these argument-specific features *against the features of the other arguments.*

---

dents: A Comparative Study, pp. 11, 477–79, 533–34, 544–45. – Peczenik says in general terms that he wants both to describe and to be normative; see *On Law and Reason*, p. 313; *Vad är rätt?* [what is law?], p. 213. At the same time he often lets it be indeterminate which modality the individual proposition has (see, however, the two works mentioned, respectively pp. 320 and 222). – Many writers do not say explicitly that they also want to be normative. But their sticking to dichotomies face to face with a graduated reality may in itself be a sign that these dichotomies are intended as normative; see in more detail in section IV 3.2 (2) below. – A particular source of indeterminacy in a writer's doctrine of the sources of law arises when dichotomies and a graduated weight perspective run parallel and are theoretically unmediated in relation to each other, see as an example Boe, *Innføring i juss* [introduction to law] (1993), Vol. 1, pp. 117 et seq.; *Innføring i juss* (1996), pp. 133 et seq.

100 Eng, 'The Doctrine of Precedent in English and Norwegian Law', section 4.1.3; 'Noen synspunkter på en teori om etikk, rett og erkjennelse' [some viewpoints on a theory of ethics, law and cognition], pp. 283–84. – Concerning the relationship to other theory, I do not exclude the possibility that e.g. Eckhoff and Andenæs (note 96 above) might be able to agree with much of the description of lawyers' use of judgments that is put forward here; see e.g. Eckhoff, *Rettskildelære* [doctrine of the sources of law], 3rd ed. pp. 135,145. But this does not come out well in their discussions, since the *dichotomy* 'precedent–not precedent' is placed *in the centre* (see the references in note 96 above).

The consequence is that the different linguistic variations on the model "binding"–"not binding" or on the model "source of law a is more binding than source of law b" is not very adequate as a description of lawyers' argumentation de lege lata. For example, one *cannot* say that the wording of the statute is *always* ascribed the greatest weight in the case of conflict with travaux préparatoires, judgments or equitable considerations. Nor can one say that this is the *usual thing*: On the contrary, given that the said sources of law pull in different directions, which by definition is part of the framing of the issue here,[101] then many Norwegian and Nordic lawyers today adopt an attitude of a "freirechtlich" character, in the sense that they often let the wording of the statute give way, partly to Supreme Court judgments, and partly to purpose considerations, considerations for justice and reasonableness, or other equitable considerations.[102]

2.2.7. Content of structuring and way of structuring

Those criteria of which an account has now been given (sections 2.2.1–2.2.6 above) may be seen as applying to the individual area-in-thought, or in shorthand form, to the *"content of the structuring"*: One considers that the content of the structuring ought not to be self-contradictory or lead to circularity or infinite regress; or that the content of the structuring ought to be operationalisable, provide cognition, influence other people's actions, be aesthetic or heuristic (facilitate comprehension, memory and application).

---

[101] It may seem as if this feature of the framing of the issue is overlooked in a number of cases, which may contribute to explaining statements such as "statute law is the most important source of law", or the like: One perhaps thinks of the wording of the statute as being the source of law that those applying the law most often have a psychologically conscious *feeling of following*, which is probably right, cf. the routine application of the law by e.g. the social security authorities, tax authorities, etc. This fact says nothing, however, about what *weight* the lawyer places on the wording of the statute in the case of *conflict* with other sources of law.

[102] Perhaps it is intuition about this fact that lies behind veiling of the distinction between source of law, and rule, e.g. in von Eyben, *Juridisk grundbog, Bind 1: Retskilderne* [basic manual of law, vol. 1: the sources of law], p. 20: "It is not possible to make a clear ranking order among the sources of law, beyond the fact that a completely clear rule of statute law must of course always take precedence"; Stuer Lauridsen, *Om ret og retsvidenskab* [on law and legal science], p. 106: "The point of departure will always be that the legal norm that is expressed through the statute shall take precedence over conflicting sources of law." – Attaching to the passages quoted is the ambiguity between the source of law 'wording of the statute' and the rule one arrives at after having weighed and balanced the wording of the statute against other sources of law. Neither of the alternatives in the ambiguity, however, leads to a tenable proposition. That it is not the case that the *wording* of the statute "must ... always take precedence" is something I have just given an account of. Whether the *rule* of statute law "must ... always take precedence" is a question it is virtually impossible or uninteresting to answer, because this question has virtually no factual basis: "Rule of statute law" is the name given to the result of a weighing and balancing of the most central sources of law (in particular the wording of the statute, the travaux préparatoires of the statute, judicial practice that interprets or applies the wording of the statute and the travaux préparatoires, and equitable considerations); thus there is most often little or nothing left in relation to which the rule of statute law can be given precedence (I ignore conflict between rules, which is another topic and which the passages quoted do not explicitly deal with).

There is a sliding scale over to more formal features of the area-in-thought, or in shorthand form, to the *"way of structuring"*. – I have previously given an account of some *aspects* of the way of structuring:

First, use of connotation specification, denotation specification or a combination (section II B 5). Secondly, as far as connotation specifications are concerned, use of purely cognitive criteria or evaluation prescription; and use of factors or conditions (section II B 6).[103] Thirdly, use of dichotomies (section 2.2.6 (4)(b) above, with further references).

The reason I here point to the outlined distinction between content of structuring and way of structuring is that the *criteria* of which an account has now been given, are not only applied to the content of the structuring, but in some cases also to the *way of structuring*. – A couple of examples may serve as illustration:

In the course of my discussion of *aesthetic considerations* I pointed out the fact that, and the way in which, aesthetic considerations can lie behind *dichotomies* in the concept structure (section 2.2.6 (4)(b) above).

In the course of my discussion of *denotation specifications* I pointed out in particular lawyers' use of denotation specifications in definitions de lege lata (section II B 5.4.2 (1)), and in so doing, I pointed out some possible causes of this use (same section, item (1)(d)). Some of the causal factors that were mentioned also function as criteria (normative reasons): for example *heuristic considerations* (denotation specifications can contribute to one's saving time and effort in the learning and remembering of the rules).

In these cases it is the way of structuring and not the individual content that is the terminus for one's deliberation.

2.3. The naming

I have earlier given an account of a number of factors that may *causally* explain what name an area acquires and whether the area gains ground or is impeded on account of the name (section II B 4.2 (5) above). – Several of the same factors are *also* used as *elements in normative justifications*: partly as criteria in the case of naming in isolation (the present section), and partly as criteria in the case of the coupling of area and name (section 2.4 below).

> One cannot, however, assume that there is full correspondence between motives that act as causes and motives that are deemed to be able to serve as normative grounds (section 2.4.2 (2) below; see also section 2.5 below).

In their capacity of normative grounds the factors may be viewed as *values in themselves* or specifications of such. – For example, *aesthetics* as an intrinsic

[103] Earlier the focus was on the here mentioned definition features in their capacity of being means to the delimitation of the area-in-thought (see the headings of sections II B 5–6). Here the focus is on their capacity of constituting more formal features of the area-in-thought.

value may be specified inter alia as *simplicity*, which may again be specified in relation to the *name's length, spelling* or *pronunciation* (section II B 4.2 (5)(a) above): The shorter, the simpler to spell and the easier it is to pronounce, the more aesthetically appealing and the more worthy of recommendation the name will often be considered to be.[104]

The factors can also be viewed as *means* to other values. – For example, given a desire to make information easier to comprehend, recall and apply (heuristic considerations), then *simplicity* in the said naming dimensions (length, spelling, pronunciation) may be a means of achieving precisely these ends.

2.4. The coupling of area and name

2.4.1. Heuristic considerations

(1) General remarks

(a) By *"heuristic considerations"* I mean desires to make an amount of information easier to comprehend, recall and apply (for the more detailed definition, see section 2.2.6 (1) above). – Heuristic considerations I assume motivate partly the structuring (section 2.2.6 (2) above), partly the naming (section 2.3 above), and partly the coupling of the two (the present section 2.4.1). What follows also contains a *joint discussion*, in that in item (2) below I look at heuristic considerations as a criterion also in the case of the structuring.

(b) Several features of the coupling of area and name often seem to motivate in a heuristic perspective, features that have previously been discussed in their capacity of causal factors (section II B 4.2 (5) above): *how well the name leads* mental representations, more abstract thoughts, or feelings, in relation to what is intended to be expressed ((5)(b)); *how encumbered the name is* with other structurings ((5)(c)); and the naming's degree of *correspondence with/ departure from* earlier language usage ((5)(d)).

The *significance* of these features in a heuristic perspective is on the whole evident: One ought to choose names which lead well in relation to what is intended to be expressed, which are not greatly encumbered with other structurings, and which do not depart too much from earlier and normal language usage. – For example, when it comes to the relationship to normal language usage, the more the

104 The topic here is the aesthetic impulse *within* the frame of a language. – Langer, *Philosophy in a New Key*, claims that an aesthetic impulse operates as a causal factor in relation to language *altogether*, both in the individual human being and in the human species (pp. 43–44, 116 et seq.): The infant's period of aimlessly formulating and playing with sounds seems to be a necessary step in the process towards the subsequent use of sounds as conventional signs, in that it has shown itself to be difficult to establish sounds as conventional signs in today's species of apes (where the individuals do not have a babbling period) and in "wild children" (where the babbling period has passed without the sounds' receiving any answer). Compare Lyons, *Language and Linguistics*, pp. 249–51, 254–55.

coupling of area and name deviates from normal language usage, the greater is the danger that listeners/ readers will believe that it costs more attention and effort to get into the material than is in fact the case. Or, irrespective of whether listeners/ readers should have a correct view in this respect, the more the coupling deviates from normal language usage, the greater is the danger that it in fact costs so much to get into the material that the sender loses some of the listeners/ readers at whom he is aiming. In both cases, the less worthy of recommendation the coupling will be, given the value 'to make the material easier to comprehend, recall and apply'.

As in their capacity of causes these factors can in their capacity of normative grounds *pull in different directions*, and in their capacity of normative grounds thus necessitate *weighings and balancings*. – For example, the consideration for not alienating possible recipients of new thoughts, goes in favour of not deviating too much from normal language usage, that is to say, *against* choosing completely new words; while the consideration for avoiding names that from earlier on are encumbered with different structurings (polysemy), goes *in favour of* choosing completely new words.[105]

Often an intermediate solution is chosen, in that the name differs from previously used names, at the same time as it contains an element in common that shows the connections that exist between the phenomena. Robinson mentions as an example the name "penicillin" which was introduced in the light of the already existing name "penicillium".[106] The difference marks the fact that one is confronted with a new area, and guards against confusion with the already known area. The likeness signals a connection with the already known ("penicillium" designates a fungus that naturally produces the substance that is medicinally exploited under the name of "penicillin").

Those features of the coupling of area and name that have been mentioned in the main text above are seen there as *means* to comprehending, recalling and applying information. To complete the picture it should be mentioned that these features can also motivate in the capacity of being *values in themselves*:

Aesthetics as an intrinsic value may be specified inter alia as *preciseness*, which can again be specified partly as *how well the name leads* mental representations, more abstract thoughts, or feelings, in relation to what is intended to be expressed, and partly as *how encumbered the name is* with other structurings. Consequently: The better the name leads representations, thoughts and feelings in relation to what is intended to be expressed, and the fewer the other structurings that the name is encumbered with, the more precise is the name, and the more aesthetically appealing, and thus worthy of recommendation, the coupling of area and name may be considered to be.

---

105 Robinson, *Definition*, pp. 87–90, discusses this weighing and balancing problem.

106 Op. cit., p. 90.

(2) Law[107]

Heuristic considerations are important in law, with its unsurveyable and constantly changing mass of legally relevant arguments. But this consideration type, and altogether the question of why lawyers set up and choose the *systematic* concepts they in fact do, is less often discussed today (item (b)) than earlier (item (a)).

(a) The discussions about the *constructive method* around the turn of the last century provide examples of heuristic considerations' also being advanced in justifications of ways of defining that are addressed to others:

> "Thus, I am of the opinion that it is complete self-delusion when one believes that any legal science can do without *abstract legal concepts*. For this reason, nor can any legal science do without a *theory that deals with the determination of these concepts* and *makes it its task to see the legal material in the light of them.* To put it briefly, the significance of such a theory lies in the fact that it shows us the legal rules not in isolation but in their systematic connection with one another, not as a jumbled multitude of heterogeneous, more or less arbitrary precepts, but as applications or variations of certain simple basic forms, which to a certain degree possess universal validity. And we are thereby provided with the *means to* both more complete *mastery* and more secure *application* of them" (my italics);[108] "... facilitates the lawyer's *acquisition and mastery of the legal material*" (my italics).[109]
>
> "The determination of the concept of 'law' ... poses a double task: the logical *summary of the content of law* and the psychological demonstration of the way it works" (my italics).[110]
>
> "Through such [i.e. via legal construction] subsumption of the legal material under a system of relatively few and simple concepts, the *acquisition of it and the mastery of it* is greatly facilitated. ... Through the constructive tracing of general legal norms back to simple concepts, and through the cognition of these concepts' systematic connection with one another, the understanding is gained that here it is in reality a matter of relatively few elements, which it is important to penetrate in order thereby to be able to master a wide range of individual precepts and *with relative ease and speed to be able* to get one's bearings when confronted with new or unfamiliar legal rules. ... With respect to the simplification of the legal material and the facilitation of the acquisition thereof, which the formation of legal concepts brings about, an apt comparison has been made between the formation of legal concepts and the *formation of the alphabet*" (my italics).[111]

---

107 The present item (2) provides a joint discussion, in that I look at heuristic considerations as a criterion also in the case of the structuring (see in more detail in item (1)(a) above).

108 Hagerup, 'Nogle Ord om den nyere Retsvidenskabs Karakter' [some words on the character of recent legal science], p. 38.

109 Op. cit., p. 41.

110 Hagerup, 'Til Retsbegrebets Bestemmelse' [on the determination of the concept of 'law'], pp. 297–98.

111 Hagerup, *Retsencyclopædi* [encyclopaedia of law], pp. 29–30. – The reference to the comparison with the alphabet is almost certainly made with Ihering in mind, see the latter's *Geist des römischen Rechts*, in particular pp. 339 et seq., 363, 372 et seq.

> "In addition to directly producing law, [i.e.] proposing and justifying decisions of new conflicts ..., [legal science] ought also to seek to *summarise* the already existing decisions, as well as the content of those declarations of intent that authoritatively regulate the application of the law. And here, where it is a matter of *making possible the cognition of a multitude of different facts*, it is an absolute methodological necessity to have synthesis, classification under general viewpoints. Legal science is thus here – without seeming to be actually productive – practical, already and precisely through the fact that its generalisations *facilitate the acquisition* of valid law" (my italics).[112]
>
> "The constructive method is what one calls that method in legal science according to which one seeks to *summarise* the norms of positive law in more general propositions with the intention of *cognising the logical coherence* in the legal order, *saving the memory* the labour of retaining an infinity of detailed norms, and – in many people's view – acquiring, in the generalisations set up, means for the resolution of newly arising questions of law" (my italics; Castberg's italics omitted).[113]

Also some writers who argued against a greater or lesser part of what went under the name of "constructive method" praised the method in terms of heuristics:

> "There is no doubt that the constructive school cleared up a great deal. To a great extent it brought with it a *simplification of concepts*, a simplified presentation. I need only recall what the treatment of joint and several liabilities has won in simplicity and clarity through the doctrine that they encompass *as many obligations as there are debtors.* Earlier the traditional teaching was that in the case of joint and several liabilities there was *one obligation with several subjective references.* Through the new construction it was possible to *say in one single sentence almost everything it is necessary to know* about joint and several liabilities. In many areas the constructive school also led to a deeper understanding of the phenomena, because it grouped them differently from previously and thereby placed them in a new light. I need only recall the enrichment that Hagerup's treatment of the law of mortgages provided on many points" (my italics).[114]

(b) An advantage of the debate about the constructive method was that it made clearer the general and important question that is the topic here: *why* one sets up and chooses the normative definitions (the concepts) one actually does.

In *later* discussions of method among *Norwegian* lawyers the said question has passed more into the background, and today there seems to be fairly poor awareness of the question. Often one contents oneself with more general and non-com-

---

112 Hyllested, '"Individualismen"' ["individualism"], p. 216. See also p. 212. – The phrase between the dashes in the last sentence of the quotation in the text at the present note has been translated in accordance with its grammatical form. However, on the basis of the content of the quotation otherwise, one might have expected the phrase to read "without actually functioning productively".

113 Castberg, 'Den konstruktive metode' [the constructive method], p. 294. See also pp. 304 ("facilitates the intellectual mastery of the legal material") and 316 ("urge for logical cognition").

114 Stang, 'Om rettsvidenskap' [on legal science], p. 123.

mittal references to "expediency", "fruitfulness", "the purpose", or the like, when one is to say something about why the formation of a concept turns out as it does (compare section 2.2.3 above).

It is a matter of *tendencies* here. – *Exceptions* are found, individual writers and *broader directions*, in the latter case often with *features in common internationally*. For example, writers with a system-theoretical approach to law seem in a number of cases to be relatively conscious of their concept choices, inter alia in that their choices *are related to* heuristic aims.

> "The whole purpose of dividing legal systems into laws is to create simple small units to *facilitate discourse about and reference to* various parts of the legal system, as well as to *promote the analysis of* law. ... The laws individuated by the principles of individuation should, as far as possible, *make clear important connections* between various parts of a legal system" (my italics).[115]
>
> "To explain [why Sundby and Eckhoff consider the distinction between rules and guidelines to be so significant] it is necessary to say something about the different roles that rules and guidelines play in legal reasoning and about the interplay between them. A central viewpoint in the works of Sundby and myself has been that one must not content oneself with studying the individual *norms* in isolation, but also look at how they *work together*" (my italics).[116]
>
> "[M]acro-morphology [concepts of types of legal rules and relations between them] can be of considerable help in rule specification, i.e. the *collation* of the (fragmentary) provisions that must be combined *in order that* one shall be able to apply the law to a given instance" (my italics).[117]
>
> In the quotations given here from writers with a system-theoretical approach, the conceptualisation is *justified with* heuristic considerations. In other instances of a system-theoretical approach, the conceptualisation is justified through asserted *contrast with* heuristic considerations.[118] – Whether the discussions take the form of adherence or distancing, they provide examples of the fact that, and the ways in which, heuristic considerations are *considered as central* (something one ought to relate to) in the assessment of the tenability of concepts formed.

115 Raz, *The Concept of a Legal System*, respectively p. 143 (the first sentence in the quotation) and p. 145 (second sentence); correspondingly in 'Legal Principles and the Limits of Law', pp. 831–32.

116 Eckhoff, 'Retningslinjer og "tumregler"' [guidelines and "rules of thumb"], p. 154.

117 Frändberg, 'Till frågan om de juridiska begreppens systematik' [on the question of the systematics of legal concepts], p. 105.

118 Canaris, *Systemdenken und Systembegriff in der Jurisprudenz*, pp. 86 et seq., cf. 16–18, 40–60.

2.4.2. *Concealed action influencing*

(1) As a criterion

Action influencing takes place already through the definition's structuring function; through this function thought is led towards certain aspects, at the expense of others (section 2.2.5 above). – However, desires to influence action also make themselves felt covertly, through *persuasive definitions*; here one does not play solely on the structuring, but on the coupling of a normative-innovative structuring with naming that appeals to emotions: One chooses words one presumes will arouse negative feelings in the recipients, if one wants to work against what the area covers; and one chooses words one presumes will arouse positive feelings, if one wants to promote what falls within the area. I refer to the earlier account (section II B 7.3 above), including my pointing out that the playing with words and feelings must operate covertly to have effect (section II B 7.3.3 (4) above).

The influence that the examples accompanying the earlier account illustrated, particularly relates to *analysis and argumentation*: cf. persuasive definitions via the appeal words "science" (section II B 7.3.2 (1) above) and "meaning" (sections II B 7.3.2 (3) cf. III 2.2.2 (3), above). In other instances the desire to influence action takes a *more concrete moral, legal or political direction*: for example via appeal terms with less or more specific connection with law, like "right", or "rule of law" and "legal safeguards" [Rechtssicherheit], or "(valid) law".

The use of the word *"right"* is extended for the purpose of exerting influence to those phenomena one wants to protect.

> For example, it is extended to the foetus at a particular stage of its development, to future generations, to animals, to trees, or to non-animate nature.[119]

With the purpose of improving the situation of prisoners, Eskeland defines the word *"rettssikkerhet"* [rule of law, legal safeguards, Rechtssicherheit] in such a way that it also covers a qualitative minimum standard.

> "In this presentation, my taking as a basis a concept of 'legal safeguards' that is not only of a formal nature, but also contains value components, is due … also to the fact that such a concept of 'legal safeguards' conforms best with

---

119 Rawls, *A Theory of Justice*, 1st ed. pp. 286 et seq.; 2nd ed. pp. 252 et seq.; The World Commission on the Environment and Development, *Our Common Future*, p. 41; Regan, *The Case for Animal Rights*, pp. 266–329; D'Amato/ Chopra, 'Whales: Their Emerging Right to Live', pp. 48–54; Stone, 'Should Trees Have Standing – Toward Legal Rights for Natural Objects', pp. 450–501 (the book with the same title contains the article, an account of how the article was written to influence the Federal Supreme Court in a concrete case, as well as the Federal Supreme Court's decision of the case: Sierra Club v. Morton, 405 U.S. 727 (1972)); Eckhoff, 'Kan elver og skoger ha rettigheter?' [can rivers and forests have rights?], passim; Ariansen, *Miljøfilosofi* [philosophy of the environment], pp. 165–208; Bergman, 'Bör naturen tillerkännas rättigheter?' [ought Nature to be accorded rights?], pp. 22–32; Næss, 'Equality, Sameness, and Rights', passim. – Compare Ross, *On Law and Justice*, pp. 180–83, on the splitting of the subject aspect of the right into interest subject, subject of proceedings, and disposition subject.

> what I deem to be the core of everything that is classified as legal safeguards in legal contexts ... namely human worth."[120]

Scholars in the law relating to health and social welfare "take up arms" against "the dismantling of the Norwegian welfare state", with *combinations of the words "rettighet" [right] and "rettssikkerhet" [rule of law, legal safeguards, Rechtssicherheit]* as one of their most important weapons.

> "Today, the national welfare state is being dismantled. ... A battle between the politically "necessary" and the legally tenable has just about commenced. ... In the years to come, the temperature of this struggle will pretty certainly rise. What makes this battle possible is inter alia that over the past 25 years health and social welfare law has slowly won the status of a legal discipline in which legal-safeguards thinking is central. The development of this discipline has shifted the power relationship between patient and recipient on the one hand and the care apparatus on the other. Patients and recipients ... can [now] ... refer to legal rights that the public authorities are obliged to respect. ... One may well ask whether social welfare law will not come to play a greater role for the course of developments than many of today's politicians and bureaucrats wish. In the longer term we believe that social welfare law will receive much of the honour for the welfare state's not being dismantled more than it will be."[121]

The quotations at and in note 121 illustrate a form of concealed action influencing *peculiar to lawyers' language and argumentation de lege lata*: – One element involves language, in the form of persuasive definitions: In addition to varied use of many other appeal terms (inter alia "right", "rule of law" and "legal safeguards"), lawyers explicitly or by presupposition designate their standpoints by the appeal term *"(valid) law"*. By virtue of their education and professional affiliation lawyers practically have a factual monopoly of this persuasive effect; a non-lawyer who calls his standpoint "(valid) law" will often have difficulty in being taken seriously if he cannot refer to an authority on law. – Another element in-

---

120 Eskeland, *Fangerett* [prisoners' law], p. 103 (Eskeland's italics omitted).

121 Eskeland/ Syse, 'Sosialrett i en innstramningstid' [social welfare law in a time of cut-backs]. See also Boe, 'Utviklingslinjer i forvaltningsretten' [lines of development in administrative law], pp. 57–58; 'Fusadommen i forvaltningsrettslig og rettsteoretisk perspektiv' [the Fusa judgment in the perspective of administrative law and legal theory], p. 333 ("An idea that has been put forward in legal literature over the last few years is that services provided by the public administrative authorities must satisfy a certain minimum standard. The first person on the scene was Eskeland, who saw the requirement for a minimum standard as a legal-safeguards guarantee"); p. 327 ("Thinking in terms of rights is altogether on its way into the health and social welfare sector. Much of the honour for this falls on Kjønstad"); Kjønstad/ Syse, 'Pasientrettigheter i Norge – framvekst og utviklingsmuligheter' [patients' rights in Norway – growth and possibilities for development], pp. 398–99 ("In the 1980s Norwegian research on health law experienced strong growth and established a clearer profile in support of patients' rights and legal safeguards. ... Norwegian research on patients' law ... stands out as one of the most expansive fields in Norwegian legal science"); Kjønstad, 'Pasientrettighetenes framvekst' [the growth of patients' rights], pp. 252–58; p. 258 ("A researcher who adopts the patient perspective and another who adopts the doctor perspective may in some cases come to different conclusions, because to some extent they see different considerations and weight them differently").

volves the relationship in lawyers' argumentation de lege lata, between what other lawyers will probably assume to be the law and what is tenable law (section II F above, in particular section 2.1, items (1)(a) cf. (3), concluding remarks in both): The quotations at and in note 121 above show how even a small group of lawyers, by *referring to one another* (what other lawyers will probably assume) can transform their personal standpoints into law (what is tenable).

In the *combination* of action-influencing as the aim, and persuasive definition of appeal words as the means (the present section 2.4.2 cf. section II B 7.3 above), or, as the case may be, conceptual structuring alone as the means (section 2.2.5 above), there lie *similarities and connections* between on the one hand a great deal of legal and social science, and on the other hand literature, art and philosophy.[122]

(2) Only as a cause

Above it has been demonstrated how factors that have previously been discussed as causes in the naming process (section II B 4.2 (5)) are *also* used as elements in normative justifications: partly as elements in justifications for the naming in isolation (section 2.3 above), and partly as elements in justifications for the coupling of area and name (the present section 2.4).

The motive of action-influencing illustrates, however, that there is not complete correspondence between motives that function as causes and motives that are considered to be fit to serve as normative grounds: I assume that for many people the possibility of influencing that lies in persuasive definitions will *not be considered at all* as a normative ground for coupling of area and name.

The reason is that the possibility of influencing most often only, and at any rate most effectively, realises itself where the possibility is not known, where the recipient is not aware of the playing with words, feelings and normative-innovative structuring (section II B 7.3.3 (4) above). And this goes against a desire among or demand from many people to be told whether, and if so how, other people influence them ("self-determination" as a motive and normative ground).

---

122 Stevenson, 'The Emotive Meaning of Ethical Terms', p. 29; *Ethics and Language*, pp. 144–45, 333–34; Robinson, *Definition*, pp. 75, 76–77, 82; Wisdom, 'Philosophy, Metaphysics and Psycho-Analysis', pp. 263–64; Wilson, *To the Finland Station*, pp. 338–44, 358, 371; Posner, *The Problems of Jurisprudence*, pp. 150–52, 350, 394–95; Stone, *Should Trees Have Standing – Toward Legal Rights for Natural Objects* (for the context and content of this book, see note 119 above), pp. xii–xiii: "[S]ocieties, like human beings, progress through different stages of sensitiveness, and ... in our progress through these stages the law – like art – has a role to play, dramatizing and summoning into the open the changes that are taking place within us. ... I saw at once [that Sierra Club v. Morton (see note 119 above)] was the needed case, a ready-made vehicle to bring to the Court's attention the theory I was developing."

2.5. Limits to the motivational weight of the above-mentioned considerations: Custom. Chance

I have now looked at a number of factors which I assume to a certain degree *motivate* in the case of conceptualisation or naming, and which *are also advanced as normative grounds*.

If one wants to *explain causally* and (in this sense) understand why a conceptualisation or terminology has turned out as it has, such grounds will provide *some* understanding, but seldom a completely satisfactory understanding. One must supplement with *other* motivating factors, *without* the status of normative grounds; in the heading these factors have been hinted at with the keywords "custom" and "chance".

Custom makes itself felt directly, partly in relation to the content of the structuring and of the naming (section 2.5.1), and partly in relation to more formal features: the way of defining (section 2.5.2). In addition, custom plays a part in an indirect way, via the accepted normative grounds (section 2.5.3).

2.5.1. The content of the structuring and of the naming

General customs constitute everyday language (section II B 3.3.2 (3) above). More particular customs constitute inter alia subject-specific variants of analysis and argumentation formulated in everyday language, for example the legal variant (the present work in its entirety). – In so far as participants in language and argumentation keep within these limits, their definitions are *normative-traditional*. To explain causally their structurings and namings, a reference to upbringing within the custom *may* in that case be sufficient. But this is not always so, since a participant in language and argumentation may reflect on the custom and decide to follow it on the basis of such grounds as mapped in sections 2.2–2.4 above.

Normative-innovative definitions by definition introduce something new, and this a custom by definition cannot explain. However, that does *not* mean that any variation in structuring or naming *must* have its cause in the language user's conscious deliberation about the variation, still less that it must have its cause in such factors as mapped in sections 2.2–2.4 above, that is to say, in motivating factors with the status of normative grounds:

Variations in structuring or naming may have their cause in *ignorance* of other people's definitions (this is one instance-type that in the perspective of the present section 2 may be termed "chance").

Further, variations in the structuring in particular may have their cause in the fact that one may well have had knowledge of other people's definitions, but *understood the wording in a different way* from the sender or others. Just as one is seldom able to envisage the consequences of one's non-linguistic acts, one is seldom able to envisage the possible interpretations of what one says. This applies even in oral communication between persons who are of the opinion that they know each other. And it applies all the more if what one says is spread to recipients with presuppositions that are different from one's own and different in relation to one another (this is another instance-type that in the perspective of the present section 2 may be termed "chance").

2.5.2. The way of defining

Custom may also make itself felt in more formal features of structuring or naming, that is to say, *independently of* whether one looks at the one or the other structuring or naming in terms of content.

By way of illustration I return to lawyers' *tendency towards one-sidedly dichotomous thinking* when they reflect on their own argumentation de lege lata. I have pointed out some dichotomies which lawyers make in this connection and which I consider misleading, and partly explained the occurrence of these dichotomies through the *urge for aesthetics* (sections 2.2.6 (4)(b) cf. 2.2.7, above).

The urge for aesthetics is, however, hardly sufficient to explain lawyers' tendency towards dichotomies when they reflect on their own argumentation de lege lata. Among other causal factors I assume that *custom* plays an important part, in that lawyers' language and argumentation de lege lata has dichotomies in its general centre: 'lawful–unlawful', 'guilty–innocent', 'prohibited–permitted', 'mandatory–discretionary', 'competence–incompetence', 'valid–invalid', etc. This gives rise to a *habit in lawyers' thinking* which, together with other causes of dichotomies, leads to dichotomies *also* where these are misleading, inter alia in the case of lawyers' reflection on their own argumentation de lege lata: for example accounts of the weight of judgments as a legal argument through the dichotomy 'precedent–not precedent' or accounts of the weight of statements in judgments through the dichotomy 'ratio decidendi–obiter dicta' (section 2.2.6 (4)(b) above), or accounts of propositions de lege lata through the dichotomy 'descriptive proposition–normative proposition' (section II F above).

2.5.3. The ways in which custom works

Beside such *direct* effect as now outlined (sections 2.5.1–2.5.2 above), custom also has *indirect* effect in the case of the setting up of and choice between normative definitions: Custom exerts influence in the determining of the *more detailed content of the other criteria*. This is so whether the criteria refer to the structuring, the naming, or the coupling of area and name. For example: What shall be reckoned as "virtuous" versus "vicious" circles (section 2.2.1 (1) cf. (3)(a) including note 12); what connection the conceptualisation ought to have with intersubjective criteria (section 2.2.2); what interests ought to be promoted, and thus what is important cognition (section 2.2.4) or action (sections 2.2.5 and 2.4.2); what is considered to be aesthetically more or less attractive (section 2.2.6); what names are considered simple or difficult to manage, and what associations a name produces (section 2.3); what combinations of area and name are considered to facilitate learning and application (section 2.4.1) – in the case of these (and other) aspects of the other criteria, custom exerts influence in the drawing of boundaries.

In addition, beside the now outlined direct and indirect effects, custom has a third role; it is both an accepted reason for and a factual cause of the other criteria's *being considered at all as relevant* normative grounds: When one discusses what is a good definition, one presupposes a customary community in criteria.

3. Criteria that are used in the setting up of and choice between descriptive characterisations

3.1. The topic. Point of departure: The truth criterion. "Thou shalt not lie!"

I have defined the concept of 'descriptive proposition' as "a proposition of which one can say that it is true or untrue, and which purports to say something about a reality otherwise (beyond the proposition)" (section II A 5 (1) above). – That one can say of propositions that they are true or untrue, is not the same as publicly stating them to be either true or untrue. Nor is it the same as the truth criterion's being used, being used as the only criterion, or being used as the most weighty criterion, in private mental deliberations connected with the setting up of and choice between the propositions.

The *topic* of the present section 3 is *actual use* of un/truth as a criterion in the setting up of and choice between descriptive characterisations, whether one uses the criterion in public justifications or in private mental deliberations. My discussions provide descriptive characterisations of un/truth as a criterion in the setting up of and choice between descriptive characterisations. – The topic is *not* "what is truth?", "truth theories", or similar specifications: "similar" in that they have not been determined in relation to the fundamental types of proposition.[1] And given the distinctions between the fundamental types of proposition, the discussions do not define (either descriptively or normatively) concepts of 'truth', and they do not characterise normatively one use or another of un/truth as a criterion. – The topic outlined (actual use of un/truth as a criterion) can be discussed, and will here be discussed, *independently of* standpoints on the questions now mentioned for purposes of setting them aside, questions partly of a philosophically controversial nature.

The truth criterion is the *point of departure* both according to widespread views and in a great deal of actually occurring analysis and argumentation. Religion,

---

[1] The "what is …?"-question and the theory terminology have the same obscurities and much of the same aspect of persuasion in the case of "truth" as in the case of "meaning"; see my earlier discussions of "theories of meaning" (section 2.2.2 above) and of persuasive definitions in general (section II B 7.3 above).

general morality, philosophical and popular attitudes to life, and so forth, say "thou shalt not lie!", or say that one must actively seek the truth.

If one probes more deeply into actually occurring analysis and argumentation, one realises, however, that and in what way in central areas of life the consideration for truth is weighed against other considerations in the setting up of and choice between descriptive characterisations: Un/truth is used in many connections *as a factor to be weighed and balanced, not as an absolute value.*

This weighing and balancing character is to be illuminated in what follows through *examples* from everyday life, politics, law and science. The examples are presented in that order, starting in an area of life in relation to which many people accept that the truth must sometimes give way (everyday life), moving across areas in relation to which this is perceived as increasingly problematic (politics and law), to an area in relation to which many people assume that the truth criterion is paramount (science). – The method is thus casuistic. However, the aim is a certain representativity in relation to the problem aspects.

The weighing-factor character of the truth criterion manifests itself not least in *law*. My impression is that many people assume the opposite: Different national variants of the form *"veritas et ius/ lex"* are used to express not only a normative grouping of two values, but also a belief that they are in fact connected to a particularly high degree. One seems to assume intuitively that *at least* the legal system does not build on propositions that there is reason to believe are not true. Actually it is, however, a normal feature of the legal assessment of evidence that one builds on propositions less probable than other propositions (section 3.2.3 below).

As will appear from the examples in what follows, the *cause* of the weighing and balancing character of the truth criterion lies in the *conflicting interests* that are often involved in the setting up of and choice of one descriptive *characterisation* rather than another.

> In the case of descriptive *definitions*, conflicting interests make themselves felt to a lesser degree, so there the truth criterion has more the character of a necessary and sufficient condition in the assessment of tenability.

Interests thus come into play in *two stages* in the case of descriptive characterisations. First, they enter into the choice of *perspective*. On this choice, see section 2.2.4 above: Neither logical criteria nor the truth criterion can justify choosing one perspective rather than another from which to view the phenomenon. Secondly, interests enter into the choice between logically incompatible characterisations *within* the given perspective: The characterisations refer to the same aspect of the phenomenon, but say different things about what the phenomenon is like in this respect. Here the truth criterion *can* be used as a choice criterion, but in actually occurring analysis and argumentation it meets interests that pull in other directions. *This* choice is the topic of the present section 3.

3.2. Normative propositions that set true characterisations aside or increase the probability of untrue characterisations

3.2.1. Everyday life

One aspect of the use of the truth criterion in everyday life is the distinction most people, more or less consciously, draw between untruths termed *"white lies"* and other untruths. White lies are considered by definition to be innocent and permissible, sometimes perhaps even right and mandatory. – With reference to placebos in medicine and testimonials from schools and employers, Bok shows that the trivial and innocent aspect of an untruth is often only apparent:[2] When the patient does not trust the doctor (placebos), or when the employer does not trust the applicant's testimonial (all people get testimonials stating that they are good workers), the total effect of many people's untruths becomes a destructive *lack of trust*. Or the effect may be that an institution *loses its point*; if the majority of applicants for jobs can produce testimonials stating that the applicant is among the best ten per cent, then these testimonials will no longer serve to discriminate between the applicants, *even if* the employers take them at their word.

Another aspect of the use of the truth criterion in everyday life is the ability and will of human beings to attain truth with regard to *"great questions"*, for example with regard to their own limitations and weaknesses, the needs of others, or pain and death. A number of writers have formulated general and sceptical propositions about the ability and will of human beings in this connection. For example, this is the case with Dostoyevsky, who makes the grand inquisitor put the church in place of God and base this on the ground that human beings cannot bear the truth about themselves; or with Ibsen, who lets demands for truth be met with "Take the saving lie ["livsløgnen", literally: "life lie"] from the average man and you take his happiness away, too"; or with Freud, who believed that the individual's resistance to self-insight was often so strong that only prolonged psychoanalysis could give the person concerned a realistic perspective on himself and his surroundings; or with Zapffe, who considered that the human species only avoids epidemics of madness by refraining from using to the full its faculty of cognition on its own biological-cosmic situation.[3] – It may be difficult to take a standpoint on the tenability of such formulations, since reasonable interpretations require one to take a standpoint on non-empirical phenomena or to make fundamental choices with respect to how life is to be lived, and since one then lacks generally accepted criteria for the resolution of disagreement; thus, discussion of

---

2 Bok, *Lying*, pp. 57–72.

3 Dostoyevsky, *The Brothers Karamazov*, pp. 283-99; Ibsen, *The Wild Duck*, p. 244; Freud, *Vorlesungen zur Einführung in die Psychoanalyse*, pp. 285–99, 415–45; Zapffe, 'Den sidste Messias' [the last Messiah], pp. 17–28; *Indføring i litterær Dramaturgi* [introduction to literary dramaturgy], pp. 86–90.

the empirical question of the ability and will of human beings *to attain* truth, easily glides over into discussion of what *is* true.

3.2.2. Politics

In politics one argued in the 19th century from an ideology according to which popularly elected representatives were responsible only to *the truth and their own consciences*. Consequently, the individual's intellect, knowledge and judiciousness were the most important criteria in public justifications for who ought to be elected.

> "[T]he moral climate of the times ... made a virtue of *independence from public opinion and from other people's views*, and required that the men who participated in political life should lock themselves inside their armour and act "according to their consciences", be "men of character", as one put it" (my italics).[4]

With the formation of parties, a new ideology came into being. In the extreme case, truth and personal conviction were replaced by the party view; and consequently the individual's *loyalty to the party* became the most important criterion for who ought to gain political power. – An example of the extreme case can contrast and shed light on this *graduated aspect of politics through parties*. At the Thirteenth Party Congress of the Communist Party of the Soviet Union in May 1924 Trotsky maintained:

> "None of us wants to be or can be right against his own party. *The party in the last analysis is always right*, because the party is the only historical instrument given to the proletariat to resolve its fundamental tasks. ... I know that it is impossible to be right against the party. One can be right only with the party and through the party, for *history has not created any other way of determining what is right*" (my italics).[5]

Seen from one side, this statement may be understood as a step in the struggle for power in the party during Lenin's illness and after his death (in January 1924).[6] Yet a precondition for this statement to be able to function as a means in the power struggle was that it appealed to actually occurring views. That the statement could be made in public within the party with an appearance of sincerity, is an indication of the great weight that was placed on the party line as a normative criterion. Other indications are that party members carried out the forced collectivisation, and that during Stalin's show trials they confessed to obviously false charges.

---

4 Seip, *Et regime foran undergangen*, p. 64. See also same writer, *Utsikt over Norges historie* [survey of Norwegian history], First Part, pp. 88–115 (in particular 106–10), 117; Second Part, pp. 74, 174–75.

5 Quoted from Medvedev, *Let History Judge – The Origins and Consequences of Stalinism*, p. 127.

6 Op. cit., pp. 127–28.

That leading party members confessed in open court to the most fantastic crimes was something new and called for an explanation. – Koestler made the false confessions a subject of his book Darkness at Noon (1940), in which the main character, Rubashov, is modelled on Nikolai Bukharin.[7] Koestler sees the false confessions as the result of, inter alia, the desire to serve the party. – In a discussion of the book, Orwell formulates the weighing of the consideration for truth against other considerations, as follows: "[T]he whole book centres round one question: Why did Rubashov confess? ... Rubashov ultimately confesses because he cannot find in his own mind any reason for not doing so. Justice and objective truth have long ceased to have any meaning for him. For decades he has been simply the creature of the Party, and what the Party now demands is that he shall confess to non-existent crimes. ... The Czarist officer [who inhabits the next cell and who talks to Rubashov by tapping on the wall] is shocked when he learns that Rubashov intends to capitulate. As he sees it from his 'bourgeois' angle, everyone ought to stick to his guns, even a Bolshevik. Honour, he says, consists in *doing what you think right*. 'Honour is *to be useful without fuss*', Rubashov taps back ... Like Bukharin, Rubashov is 'looking out upon black darkness'. What is there, what code, what loyalty, what notion of good and evil, for the sake of which he can defy the Party and endure further torment?" (my italics).[8] – Later writers have, to varying degrees, seen the confessions also as a result of torture, persecution of the family of the person concerned, or the helpless victim's vacillation between fear of and identification with the almighty persecutor.[9]

Today politicians less often refer to truth and their own consciences or to the party in *such* a pure form as in the two historical occurrences mentioned above. Instead the two sets of criteria seem to function beside each other; politicians' language and argumentation may in one dimension be understood as varying constellations in an alternating interplay (co-action or counteraction) between the two sets of criteria.

---

7 Nikolai Bukharin (1888–1938) held leading positions in the Communist Party of the Soviet Union and the Communist International. He was editor of Pravda 1918–1928, wrote several well-known and influential books on Marxism and communism, and was considered an innovative political writer. Lenin called him the "the favourite of the party" in his so-called "testament" (reproduced, for example, in Medvedev, note 5 above, p. 80). Bukharin was one of the accused at, and was shot immediately after, the third and last of the great show trials in Moscow, in March 1938.

8 Orwell, 'Arthur Koestler', pp. 279–80.

9 Something with which Koestler did not disagree, see inter alia *Darkness at Noon*, p. 201. For a general treatment of the confessions, see Conquest, *The Great Terror*, pp. 123–45. In particular on Bukharin, see Conquest, *The Great Terror*, pp. 126, 135, 391; Cohen, *Bukharin and the Bolshevik Revolution*, p. 375; Solzhenitsyn, *The Gulag Archipelago*, Part I, pp. 412–19; Medvedev, *Nikolai Bukharin – The Last Years*, pp. 142–45; Volkogonov, *Stalin – Triumph and Tragedy*, pp. 299–300; Radzinsky, *Stalin*, pp. 374–84. – Cohen furthermore argues that Bukharin's statements during the show trial were deliberately ambiguous: apparent confessions, but in reality a political message; see *Bukharin and the Bolshevik Revolution*, pp. 372, 376–79, with further references to other writers who have maintained the same understanding. Correspondingly Tucker, *Stalin in Power*, pp. 497–500.

The legal rules too show symptoms of the existence of such a mixed ideology, cf. (1) the fact that the binding force of politicians' promises (party programmes, election manifestos, "I guarantee ..." uttered at a meeting with the employees in a firm, or the like) are assessed according to criteria different from those applying to other promises, perhaps they fall outside legal regulation altogether,[10] and that today the justification for this legal situation would probably assume a mixed character;[11] and (2) the fact that defamation legislation affords less protection within political activity than outside it.[12]

3.2.3. Law

In law there are numerous examples of norms that increase the probability of untrue characterisations' being taken as a basis for the application of the law. In what follows I shall focus on three main groups of such norms (items (1)–(3)). A feature in common is that also considerations other than the consideration for truth in the individual case are ascribed weight.[13] Thus, the norms on which I shall be focusing stand in contrast to norms that exclude claims based on true characterisations (for example, norms that lay down time limits for making a claim).

(1) Exclusion of evidence

For court cases there are rules that exclude the submission of evidence, *even if* the evidence must be deemed capable of shedding light on the facts of the case:

A practically important group is rules concerning the *duty of secrecy*. These are mainly rules of *statute law*.[14] – In the practice of the courts, the submission of evidence has also been excluded in a number of other instances and on a *non-statutory basis*:

In order to protect "the free political exchange of information and confrontation of opinion for which the meetings of the Cabinet form the framework",[15]

---

10 As far as I know, these questions have virtually not been dealt with in Norwegian theory and judicial practice. Compare the terse and general statements in Castberg, *Norges statsforfatning* [constitution of Norway], Vol. I, p. 277; Andenæs, *Statsforfatningen i Norge* [the constitution of Norway], p. 146. An unpublished lower-court judgment was pronounced by Eidsivating lagmannsrett [the High Court of Eidsivating] on 15 October 1982 (the Arne Factories judgment).

11 Historically, a general proposition that politicians' promises to the voters are not binding, is a manifestation of the ideology of truth and independence that was outlined first in the present section 3.2.2. Today, the ideological context of the proposition is *also* virtually the opposite: also a manifestation of the ideology of power and party that was outlined afterwards.

12 See in particular *Rt. 1990/257* (the Hagen judgment) on p. 264; *Rt. 1994/50* (the Holstad judgment) on p. 55.

13 The considerations that positively justify the individual norms are, however, just as different in kind as the considerations behind the legal norms otherwise, cf. my discussions in what follows.

14 Civil Procedure Act (Act No. 6 of 13 August 1915) sections 204 et seq., cf. section 250 first paragraph; Criminal Procedure Act (Act No. 25 of 22 May 1981) sections 117 et seq., cf. section 204 first paragraph.

15 *Rt. 1994/1036* on p. 1044; *Rt. 1996/1101* on p. 1103.

the courts have excluded the submission of evidence concerning *discussions in Cabinet*.[16]

Out of "strong considerations for the protection of privacy" the courts have excluded a *lie detector test* as evidence.[17]

The submission of evidence has in certain instances been excluded if the *evidence has been obtained in an unlawful manner*.[18] The fundamental view in the practice of the courts is that the answer to this question of exclusion depends on a weighing of arguments.[19] On the one hand, there is in particular the consideration for illumination of the case.[20] On the other hand, there is in particular the weight of the interests that have been infringed by the unlawful procurement of the evidence.[21] – The unlawfulness may consist in duress applied to secure a confession,[22] or a confession in response to a promise of amnesty;[23] in the seizure of an

---

16 *Rt. 1980/711* (The Interlocutory Appeals Committee of the Supreme Court; unanimous): the private party could not demand that a minister's notes to Cabinet colleagues be presented; *Rt. 1994/1036* (interlocutory appeal case dealt with by the Supreme Court; unanimous): the private party could not demand that ministers be questioned about the treatment of the case in Cabinet; *Rt. 1996/1101* (Interlocutory Appeals Committee of the Supreme Court; unanimous): the private party was excluded from presenting a Cabinet memorandum in the party's possession.

17 *Rt. 1996/1114* (interlocutory appeal case dealt with by the Supreme Court; unanimous); *Rt. 1997/689* (Interlocutory Appeals Committee of the Supreme Court; unanimous); *Rt. 1997/1145* (Interlocutory Appeals Committee of the Supreme Court; unanimous).

18 The expert committee which prepared the Criminal Procedure Act of 1981 was of the opinion that "it is not possible ... to give any general answer to the question of what effect errors of procedure ought to have on the entitlement to use a piece of evidence. ... One has ... decided to keep the status quo by leaving the solution to theory and practice in the same manner as hitherto": *the Committee's Report of 1969*, p. 197. The committee's standpoint was taken as a basis in the further work on the statute; see *Ot.prp. No. 35 1978–79* [proposal from the Government], p. 139, *Innst. O. No. 37 1980–81* [recommendation from the parliamentary committee], p. 21.

19 This fundamental view has shown itself in several important decisions of the Supreme Court in recent years, cf. the casuistry in what follows. Earlier court practice, on the other hand, is limited and provides little guidance, see Bratholm, 'Den straffeprosessuelle betydning av at et bevis er skaffet til veie på ulovlig måte' [the criminal procedural significance of the fact that a piece of evidence has been obtained in an unlawful manner], pp. 122–27.

20 *Rt. 1992/698* (Interlocutory Appeals Committee of the Supreme Court; unanimous; the Treholt case): "A factor of essential significance in the assessment of whether an unlawfully obtained piece of evidence may be allowed to be submitted is what illegal actions the case concerns. The consideration for illumination of the case manifests itself more strongly in the case of serious offences than in the case of less gross offences" (p. 706).

21 *Rt. 1991/616* (Supreme Court; unanimous): "In the present case it is a question of ... a serious infringement of integrity. To be exposed to secret video surveillance at one's place of work must be experienced by an employee as grossly stigmatising. In my opinion, essential considerations for the protection of privacy indicate that the courts should reject the use of a piece of evidence obtained in this manner. Through such an attitude the courts will counteract this form of infringement" (p. 623).

22 *Rt. 1948/46* (Supreme Court; unanimous): The Supreme Court deemed it to be an error that confessions made during mock executions were permitted to be read out in lagmannsretten [the High Court]. Yet the error was not ascribed any effect with respect to the validity of the judgment of the High Court, since the Supreme Court was of the opinion that the police officers who carried out the "executions" and recorded the confessions, could lawfully testify about the content of the confessions.

object in the course of an unlawful search;[24] in the procurement of testimony given out of court without the accused or his defence counsel's having been notified and given the opportunity to be present;[25] in the procurement of evidence by means of extraordinary methods of investigation (including the use of "agents provocateurs");[26] or in other things.[27]

Even if the evidence has been obtained in lawful manner, exclusion is possible if it is a matter of proving *another issue* than that for which the evidence was originally and lawfully obtained.[28]

The Supreme Court does not give any grounds for why the police officers' testimony was deemed lawful, while the reading out of the written and signed confessions was deemed unlawful.

23 *Rt. 1994/1139* (Supreme Court; unanimous): The Supreme Court "finds it prima facie difficult to accept the possibility of the prosecuting authority's demanding that statements made to the police as a result of a "promise of amnesty" shall be read out ..." (p. 1141). However, the Supreme Court did not find it proven that any promise had been made.

24 *Rt. 1992/698* (Interlocutory Appeals Committee of the Supreme Court; unanimous): The Interlocutory Appeals Committee deemed that the consideration for illumination of the case had such great weight (see note 20 above) that after a weighing of arguments, it should take precedence over the need to react against the deliberate setting aside of rules concerning notification in the case of a search (pp. 705 (bottom)–706). – Andenæs, *Norsk straffeprosess* [Norwegian criminal procedure], Vol. 1, p. 243, puts forward a more categorical rule ("the owner [can]not demand that the evidence be excluded").

25 *Rt. 1991/1096* (Supreme Court; unanimous): The Supreme Court excluded the reading out both of the testimony and of the statements from the police officers who had conducted the interrogation; this latter point was in contrast to *Rt. 1948/46* (note 22 above). – The legal basis for exclusion was Art. 6.3 (d) cf. 6.1 of the European Convention on Human Rights of 4 November 1950. These articles express, first, a combination of a rule of duty and a rule of in/validity addressed to national courts; these courts shall not apply testimony in contravention of Art. 6.3 (d) cf. 6.1, and if they do so, the judgment may be deemed invalid. On the practising of Art. 6.3 (d) cf. 6.1 in this capacity by the Supreme Court, see Aall, *Rettergang og menneskerettigheter* [legal proceedings and human rights], pp. 393 et seq., particularly pp. 404–22; Jebens, 'Opplesning av vitneforklaringer' [the reading out of testimony], pp. 97–106. Secondly, the Supreme Court uses the places mentioned as a basis for rules of duty addressed to the police and prosecuting authority, so that it is thus natural to say that the evidence has been "obtained in an unlawful manner"; cf. the judgment of 1991 on p. 1098 and further *Rt. 1994/1566* on pp. 1569–70 (Supreme Court; 3–2 decision; dissenting opinion).

26 *Rt. 1984/1076, Rt. 1992/1088, Rt. 1994/319* (Supreme Court; unanimous decisions; arguments of the accused rejected); *Rt. 1993/473, Rt. 1998/407* (Supreme Court; unanimous decisions; arguments of the accused accepted). – If the police provoke an act that would not otherwise have been committed, the consequence may be not only that one excludes evidence and thus reduces the possibility of finding the most probable fact, but that one does not classify the act as criminal at all; cf. the judgments of 1992 on p. 1091, 1994 on p. 321 and 1998 on p. 410.

27 *Rt. 1991/616* (Supreme Court; unanimous): With reference to the Working Environment Act (Act No. 4 of 4 February 1977) and considerations for the protection of privacy (note 21 above), the Supreme Court excluded the use of video recordings of an employee in a criminal case concerning embezzlement (compare now, after amendments in Act No. 78 of 11 June 1993, section 390 b of the Criminal Justice Act (Act No. 10 of 22 May 1902) and section 37 a of the Act relating to Personal Data Filing Systems, etc. (Act No. 48 of 9 June 1978)).

28 *Rt. 1990/1008* (Supreme Court; unanimous): The Supreme Court ruled that a photograph taken by a speed camera could be used in evidence in a prosecution for gross theft, not only as proof of exceeding the speed limit.

(2) Burden of proof

Some rules concerning the burden of proof say that among the competing descriptive characterisations being advanced, one shall take as a basis the descriptive characterisation that is most probable: a standard of proof which in Anglo-American law is most commonly expressed as a "balance of probabilities" or a "preponderance of evidence/ probability". Other rules concerning the burden of proof say that *more* than a simple preponderance of probability (more than "more probable than not") is required.[29]

A central frame for rules that require more than a simple preponderance of probability is that an incorrect judgment in one direction is considered worse than an incorrect judgment in another direction: An important *consideration* behind rules requiring more than a simple preponderance of probability is then to reduce the risk of an incorrect judgment in the direction in which it is considered worse to make a mistake; this indicates that one places the burden of proof on the party demanding judgment in that direction. An ideologically important example is criminal cases, in which one says "It is better that ten innocent people go free than that one innocent person is convicted", and in which, on the basis of this view, one places a very strict burden of proof on the prosecution.[30]

> The influence on the rules concerning the burden of proof from the consideration mentioned becomes particularly clear when a given person's burden of proof, with respect to a given descriptive characterisation, varies according as the characterisation is judged in different legal contexts. A practical category is that a person is deemed not to have performed an act in relation to criminal liability, but is deemed to have performed the same act in other legal contexts. It might be that, in proceedings concerning what one sees as a less severe sanction, the person concerned is deemed with (down to) a simple preponderance of probability to have performed the act;[31] or even that, in proceedings in which the interests of others are also at stake, the person

---

29 For a survey of rules concerning the burden of proof in Norwegian law, see Hov, *Rettergang i sivile saker* [legal procedure in civil cases], pp. 431–47; Andenæs, *Alminnelig strafferett* [general criminal law], pp. 96–97; *Norsk straffeprosess* [Norwegian criminal procedure], Vol. 1, pp. 162–63. – Sometimes the term "burden of proof" is used to mean that by definition more than a simple preponderance of probability (that is, more than "more probable than not") is required. If one is to use the term at all (compare section II B 4.2 (5)(b)(ii) above), I consider it most convenient to use it of all possibilities, and to say that the "burden of proof is shared equally" in instances in which a simple preponderance of probability is sufficient for a fact to be taken as established.

30 In Norwegian law this rule is not statutory. However, the rule is considered as being beyond doubt in lawyers' practice. Only seldom is it necessary for the Supreme Court to thematise the rule as a step in its review of decisions of the other courts. An example is provided by *Rt. 1978/884*: "For conviction to be possible, full proof of the facts is required … any reasonable doubt must be treated to the advantage of the accused." See also the statements of principle in *Rt. 1998/1945*.

31 For example, a person who in an earlier criminal case has been acquitted of having himself provoked the circumstances resulting in an insurance claim (insurance fraud) may lose in civil proceedings for recovery of the insurance sum on the grounds that he has provoked the same circumstances, see e.g. *Rt. 1985/211*, *Rt. 1990/1082*.

concerned is deemed to have performed the act because he has not established the probability of the opposite.[32]

In the instances now mentioned, namely requirements for more than a simple preponderance of probability, it is the individual rules concerning the burden of proof that, according to their *own content*, increase the probability of untrue characterisations. In addition the rules concerning the burden of proof contribute to untrue characterisations in a more indirect way: By virtue of their *indeterminacy* they may be used as a means of satisfying one's own wishes for and others' expectations of a concretely reasonable and just outcome, through adjustment of the facts; see the following item (3).

(3) Adjusting the facts on the basis of a norm that one should seek to achieve a concretely reasonable and just outcome

The person applying the law may get into the situation that application of the legally most well-founded rules of law on the most probable fact in a case at hand, will lead to what he considers an unreasonable or unjust outcome in the case. The person applying the law may, in such a situation, make the decision he considers unreasonable or unjust. Or he can attempt legal innovation. Or he can take as a basis a descriptive characterisation of the facts of the case that leads to a reasonable and just outcome under the legal rules, that is, he can take as a basis *another* descriptive characterisation than the most probable one: "adjusting the facts out of a desire for concrete reasonableness and justice".[33]

I assume that in actual application of the law the latter alternative is *used* on a par with the two first-mentioned alternative courses of action. I assume that the *cause* is one's own wishes for and the expectations of the parties and the public of

---

32 *Rt. 1989/320*: A person who had been reported to the police for sexual offences against a stepchild, and who was not indicted because the prosecuting authority did not consider that it could to a sufficient degree establish the probability of the offences, lost in civil proceedings for the daily care of his own children on the grounds that (inter alia) it could not be ruled out that the offences had taken place. "That the prosecuting authority took the view that there was not sufficient proof in a criminal case is not decisive in this case. Particularly in proceedings concerning the care of minors, it may be argued that no risk whatsoever can be taken ..." (p. 326).

33 Adjusting the facts is often not mentioned or only briefly discussed in literature on the application of the law. Of works that take up this topic, may be mentioned Frank, *Law and the Modern Mind*, pp. 144–45; *Courts on Trial*, pp. 168–69; Llewellyn, *The Common Law Tradition*, p. 361; Posner, *Cardozo: A Study in Reputation*, pp. 38–40, 43; Eckhoff, *Rettsvesen og rettsvitenskap i U.S.A.* [legal system and legal science in the USA], pp. 145–46; 'En bok om bevisbyrden' [a book on the burden of proof], pp. 35–37; *Rettskildelære* [doctrine of the sources of law], 1st ed. pp. 29, 107–08, 173–74; 3rd ed. pp. 29, 159; Aarbakke, 'Harmonisering av rettskilder' [harmonisation of sources of law], pp. 516–18; Gaarder, 'Domstolene og den alminnelige rettsutvikling' [the courts and the evolution of the law], p. 230; Andenæs/ Kvamme, 'Om grunner til uenighet om rettsspørsmål' [on grounds for disagreement on questions of law], p. 24. – Eng, 'The Doctrine of Precedent in English and Norwegian Law', section 4.3, discusses the adjusting of facts with particular reference to the situation of precedent, that is, situations in which the legal rule that is deemed to lead to an unreasonable or unjust outcome is based on earlier judgments.

a reasonable and just outcome in the individual case, combined with the fact that adjusting the facts in many situations of applying the law is considered as the better or as a supplementary means of achieving such an outcome (compare section II F 2.1 (2) above, concluding remarks).

> I have in another work pointed to causes of the fact that adjusting the facts may appear as a better means than the second alternative course of action mentioned above (attempting legal innovation):[34] the ideology of the separation of powers, the desire not to be held responsible for the consequences of the decision, and the fact that adjusting the facts demands less work and time than legal innovation – and more specifically for persons applying the law at the lower levels: the possibility that their decision will be appealed against and then deemed to be clearly legally untenable, poor access to the sources-of-law material that may be necessary for convincing legal argumentation, and a feeling of not being professionally up to creating new law.

The adjusting of facts out of the desire for a reasonable and just outcome in the case takes place partly through the determining of what probability *there is* of a descriptive characterisation's being true (assessment of evidence), and partly through the determining of what probability *shall be required* for the descriptive characterisation to be usable as a basis (burden of proof).

> In the latter instance one can also see it as being the case that the law, namely the rules concerning the burden of proof, is adjusted. Yet in the perspective here, norms that increase the probability of untrue characterisations' being taken as a basis in the application of the law, the relevant feature of the thinking is that a norm that one should seek to achieve a concretely reasonable and just outcome governs the determining of the facts of the case, be it via the assessment of evidence or via the burden of proof.

Linguistically, the terminology of the burden of proof is the form that makes it most difficult to ascertain whether any adjusting of facts has taken place. If, for example, the judge deems it more probable that the self-employed man with severe pressure on his liquidity supplied defective goods than that he supplied goods according to contract, but unreasonable that he shall go bankrupt because of the wealthy purchasing company's claim for compensation, the judge may say that he "does not find it sufficiently proven that the defect was present at the time of delivery". This formulation simply says that the probability requirements have not been satisfied with respect to a descriptive characterisation about the defect's being present at the time of delivery; the formulation says nothing about what probability actually attaches to this characterisation, about what requirements have been made, or about what considerations have justified the requirements.

> In literature on current Norwegian law, different views are advanced about whether the consideration for a concretely reasonable and just outcome is

[34] Eng, 'The Doctrine of Precedent in English and Norwegian Law', section 4.3.4.

relevant in the apportionment of the burden of proof.[35] A denial of relevance may, but need not, represent disagreement with the text above: There the topic is only the *actual* motivation of the person applying the law, while propositions about current law often also incorporate the speaker's standpoint (here the standpoints of the writers mentioned in note 35) on what is the *best* motivation (section II F 2 above).

On the indeterminacy of and the evaluation prescription in the legal rules concerning the burden of proof, see further section IV 3.3.1 (3)(b) below; and on similar features in science, see section 3.2.4 (2) below.

3.2.4. Science

In relation to activity one traditionally terms "science" it is often taken for granted that the truth criterion takes precedence over all other considerations.[36] In what follows I shall briefly outline a couple of aspects of the use of the truth criterion which reveal limits to the view mentioned, and which do not receive the attention that their practical importance warrants.

(1) Are the propositions of science categorisable as either descriptive or normative?

I have kept the question whether normative propositions can be un/true outside the definition of the concept of 'normative proposition' (section II A 5 (2)(b) above). In the present item (1), however, I take as a point of departure the *actually* widespread view that only descriptive propositions can be un/true (im/probable). A *precondition* for the implementation of a truth criterion is *then* (i.e. given this view) that one can separate, and in fact has separated, descriptive and normative propositions from one another. – The *possibilities* of separating descriptive and normative propositions, and thus the assumed *latitude* for the truth criterion, seem to vary between different areas of science and discussion; something which may be illustrated by means of a comparison between economics and law.

In *economics* a number of influential writers have placed great weight on one's giving an account of the evaluations and choices that take place at a preparatory stage, *before* models and measurements:

> "It is ... in the *choice of the preconditions that science takes as a foundation* that the evaluative aspect comes in. It is only when this evaluative point of

---

35 See, on the one hand, the negative answers to the question whether one can take into consideration the one party's being weaker than the other, in Eckhoff, *Tvilsrisikoen* [the bearing of the risk of doubt], pp. 135–37; Hov, *Rettergang i sivile saker* [legal procedure in civil cases], p. 439 (concluding remarks in the indented paragraph); and see, on the other hand, the opposite answer to the same question in Bratholm/ Hov, *Sivil rettergang* [civil proceedings], p. 301.

36 I should remind the reader that I use the term "science" (1) in the broad sense of the Scandinavian "vitenskap" and the German "Wissenschaft", i.e. to cover natural, social and human sciences, and (2) as an abbreviation for "activity one traditionally terms "science" in this broad sense" – that is, I neither presuppose nor lay down anything contentious through this concept of 'science' (cf. section I 5.1 above, in note 1).

> departure has been specified that the actual scientific analysis can begin. In the final instance the whole type of scientific analysis one is to obtain, therefore becomes dependent on what non-scientific evaluations one takes as a foundation. ...
>
> Already with respect to the actual description of the phenomena with which economics is concerned, the evaluative aspect comes in. ... A selection must be made. And ... selection, or ... basis of interpretation will not only depend on what in a certain objective sense is "right", but will to a very considerable extent also depend on what the results may possibly be used for, in other words on something evaluative. ...
>
> [T]here are ... presupposition choices in which economics is in a much more difficult position [than the natural sciences]. This applies in particular to the choice of the fundamental principles that have important consequences for which of the economic phenomena are to be considered as "significant", and for the main principles that are to be used in the interpretation. ...
>
> This does not mean, however, that in the case of these questions one must renounce scientific objectivity. It means only that one must always seek to be aware of to what extent the conclusions are *dependent on* the non-scientific presuppositions on which the analysis was based. Not least it is important to be aware of those presuppositions that are apparently "objective", "non-political", etc. In so far as a *clear and deliberate distinction* between what is fact and what is evaluation is successfully carried out, it will be possible to preserve objectivity. Indeed, this is actually the *only way* in which it can be preserved" (my italics; Frisch's italics omitted).[37]
>
> "The final solution of the value problem in economics and in the social sciences generally must ... be to set up a method by which human valuations are rationally and *openly introduced* into theoretical and practical research ..." (my italics).[38]

In sciences concerning man and society other than economics, it is not always possible to make a distinction between description and evaluation as economists purport to do, inter alia as a distinction between (mathematical) models and their normative presuppositions. For example, *lawyers' propositions de lege lata* (propositions about what the law is) often have a fused descriptive and normative modality, cf. the earlier account of the existence and content of this type of modality (section II F above). When, as in this case, one cannot analyse concrete utterances into descriptive and normative propositions, there is correspondingly less room for truth as a tenability criterion in the setting up of and choice between the propositions.

---

37 Frisch, 'Skillet mellom sak og vurdering' [the distinction between fact and evaluation], pp. 8–9; with the support of Haavelmo, *Samfunn, styring og velferd* [society, governance and welfare], p. 9. Compare Bergh/ Hanisch, *Vitenskap og politikk, linjer i norsk sosialøkonomi gjennom 150 år* [science and politics, trends in Norwegian economics over 150 years], p. 151: "Frisch formulated the view of the distinction between fact and evaluation that has since been trend-setting for Norwegian economists' perception of this problem."

38 Myrdal, *Value in Social Theory*, p. 260.

(2) *Burden-of-proof considerations*

Given a division of the propositions of science into descriptive and normative (item (1) above), probably very few people would put into the truth requirement a duty to *seek* the greatest possible number of truths, or a duty to *pass on* all the truths one cognises.[39] A truth criterion as a norm in relation to science seems first and foremost to be understood in the form that one shall not pass on characterisations one considers to be untrue. This entails that *if* one wishes to pass on research results and *if* one has given consideration to several competing descriptive characterisations, then one must *advance that characterisation that one considers to be most probable*.[40]

This normative core may meet *resistance*: from self-interest, identification with the interests of others, prejudices, hopes, dreams, or the like. Not all such resistance is considered objectionable. In the case of theories and in the case of descriptions and existence propositions directed at the future, the truth requirement may meet competition from *burden-of-proof considerations* in a similar way as in law (section 3.2.3 (2)–(3) above): One takes into account which proposition-alternative will entail the most harmful effects if one makes a mistake: for example when one is to take a standpoint on whether a drug or human beings' use of natural energy resources (in what follows called "energy use", for the sake of brevity) has harmful and irreversible side-effects.

The feature *in common* is that one accepts and uses as a basis for actions a descriptive characterisation that *is not necessarily the most probable*: for example the descriptive characterisation *that* the drug causes harmful and irreversible side-effects in human beings, or the descriptive characterisation *that* our energy use leads to harmful and irreversible climatic changes of a global nature (thinning of the ozone layer, greenhouse effect). And one does this *because* one considers it *better* that one mistakenly assumes that the drug has harmful and irreversible side-effects and therefore forbids its use, with the consequence that the pharmaceutical firm loses income or incurs greater expenditure, *than* that one mistakenly

---

39 Tranøy has in several works discussed norms relating to different aspects of scientific activity. Concerning the place of a truth criterion, see in particular *Vitenskapen – samfunnsmakt og livsform* [science – a power in society and a way of life], pp. 145–49, 153–54, 169–70, 174–77. See also 'Vitenskap og etikk, sannheten som verdi' [science and ethics, the truth as a value], pp. 126–27; 'The Foundations of Cognitive Activity: An Historical and Systematic Sketch', pp. 133–34, 138–39, 147; 'The Ideology of Scientific and Scholarly Conduct', pp. 338–41, 347–48.

40 Tranøy uses a slightly different emphasis in the works mentioned in the preceding note, in that he stresses that the truth requirement is first and foremost directed at the individual's *psychological acceptance/ rejection* of descriptive characterisations: One is to accept true assertions and reject untrue assertions. This proposition is an example of what Tranøy calls "unrejectable norms", see ' 'Ought' implies 'Can': A Bridge from Fact to Norm?', p. 129. – In relation to a main objective of the present work, dis/agreement analysis (Chapter I above), criteria for asserting propositions *in relation to other people* have the greatest interest. The same criteria that make inroads on the truth criterion in relation to others, cf. the main text in what follows, may, however, also be relevant to the individual's psychological acceptance/ rejection, and thereby sow doubt about the tenability of the "unrejectable norm" mentioned.

assumes that the drug is harmless, with the result that human beings are harmed. Or one does this *because* one considers it *better* that one mistakenly assumes that our energy use causes irreversible damage to the environment and therefore reduces consumption, with the consequence that production, employment and living standard drop, *than* that one mistakenly assumes that our energy use is harmless, with such consequences as increasing radiation hazards or rising levels of the oceans.

> Politicians and lawyers have in recent years introduced the term *"føre-var prinsippet"/ "the precautionary principle"* of inter alia such burden-of-proof considerations in environmental law. However, the use of this term is fairly indeterminate: In addition to the meaning 'the doubt shall go in favour of the environment', "the precautionary principle" is also used in the meaning of 'prevention'. Between these meanings there is no necessary connection, since preventive measures can be combined with all degrees of probability of connection between the measure and what one wishes to prevent (for example, one does not prevent until a preponderance of probability suggests damage). Furthermore, internationally one seems to use "Vorsorgeprinzip" and "precautionary principle" in other senses as well.[41] – *Burden-of-proof considerations* under the name of "the precautionary principle" are, like burden-of-proof considerations otherwise (see section 3.2.3 (2)–(3) above), often indeterminate, in that nothing more detailed is said about what combinations of types of damage and degree of probability one will or will not accept; see from Norwegian law, for example, the travaux préparatoires of the Genetic Engineering Act (Act No. 38 of 2 April 1993): "The [precautionary] principle means in this connection that where there is doubt whether the use of biotechnology may have negative consequences for the environment, health or other areas, the doubt should go in favour of nature and society."[42] – In international law relating to climatic changes, views on the *legal relevance* of the precautionary principle (in the sense of a burden-of-proof principle) are developing.[43]

---

41 Compare Rehbinder, 'The Precautionary Principle in an International Perspective', passim. – A broad presentation of the precautionary principle is given in NENT (the national committee on research ethics for natural science and technology), *Føre-var prinsippet: mellom forskning og politikk* [the precautionary principle: between research and politics]. However, the report does not provide any overall analysis of different meanings of the term "føre-var prinsippet" (or its equivalent in other languages); and the content and role of burden-of-proof considerations do not come out clearly (see as part of this, statements that are mutually incompatible, p. 29: "The precautionary principle does not first and foremost entail any revision of proof requirements ...", "Generally it may be maintained that the precautionary principle entails a shift in the burden of proof ...").

42 *Ot.prp. No. 8 1992–93* [proposal from the Government], p. 46.

43 Compare, for example, Boyle, 'International Law and the Protection of the Global Atmosphere: Concepts, Categories and Principles', p. 16; Freestone, 'The Precautionary Principle', pp. 36–38; Bugge, 'Rio-konferansen i rettslig lys' [the Rio conference in a legal light], pp. 473, 477; ' "Bærekraftig utvikling" og andre aktuelle perspektiver i miljøretten' ["sustainable development" and other current perspectives in environmental law], p. 496.

4. Lawyers' propositions de lege lata: a complex tenability assessment

Those tenability criteria of which an account has now been given (sections 2–3 above) relate to respectively normative definitions and descriptive characterisations. The impact of the criteria is *less surveyable* in the case of lawyers' propositions de lege lata (propositions about what the law is) than in the case of the fundamental proposition types seen by themselves, i.e. as we saw them above. The cause is that lawyers' propositions de lege lata *cannot be reduced to* the one or the other of the fundamental proposition types, or to any single combination, but in different ways *build on them all.* Thus the tenability assessment becomes correspondingly complex. I shall point to some features of lawyers' propositions de lege lata that contribute to this complex tenability assessment.

(1) Fused descriptive and normative propositions

I refer to my discussion of how lawyers' propositions about what the law is, often have a *fused* descriptive and normative modality (section II F above). – The consequence of the fused modality is that tenability criteria *both* for descriptive propositions *and* for normative propositions are relevant, *but without* its being possible to reduce the tenability assessment to the tenability assessment for descriptive propositions, for normative propositions, or for particular combinations of descriptive and normative propositions: Just as the modality of lawyers' propositions de lege lata is sui generis in relation to a dichotomy between descriptive and normative propositions, the tenability assessment of lawyers' propositions de lege lata is sui generis in relation to the tenability assessment of those propositions that this dichotomy captures.

(2) Linking-terms

The fragmentary nature of legal rules, and the linking-term technique more particularly, make it possible for lawyers to discuss and take a standpoint on normative *characterisations*, through discussing *definitions* (section IV 3.3.3 below). – The consequence is that tenability criteria *both* for characterisations *and* for definitions are relevant.

(3) Reconstructions and redefinitions

Lawyers' analysis and argumentation de lege lata often follows the pattern I term "reconstruction and redefinition", a distinct combination of the fundamental proposition types (Chapter V below). – The consequence is that tenability criteria for *all* the four fundamental proposition types mentioned (descriptive and normative propositions, characterisations and definitions) are relevant (section V 1.1), with the modifications that follow from the fact that lawyers' propositions de lege lata often have a fused descriptive and normative modality: see in particular the fact that the redefinition element, which in the case of reconstructions and redefinitions in other areas has a purely normative modality, in the case of reconstructions and redefinitions de lege lata often assumes a fused modality (sections V 1.1 (3)(b) and 2.4, partly also 2.2–2.3).

(4) Concepts in legal rules and concepts about legal rules

Lawyers' propositions about what the law is, use partly concepts that are *part of* legal rules; and they use partly concepts that are *about* legal rules, typically in order to systematise and summarise the rules (examples will be given in the discussion immediately below). – The consequence is that in the tenability assessment it is relevant to take into account *criteria for definitions, both of* concepts in legal rules *and of* concepts for systematising and summarising legal rules. These criteria are so different that it is important to have a clear picture of which type of conceptualisation is in the individual instance part of the proposition about what the law is: the one, the other or both types.[1]

By the terminological distinction "in"–"about" I mean in this connection whether persons applying the law are *normatively motivated* by the concept, that is to say, view subsumption under the concept as directly or indirectly leading to certain legal consequences rather than others: in which case I shall say that the concept is used "in legal rules"; or whether persons applying the law use the concept to *speak about* concepts that motivate normatively: in which case I shall say that the concept is used "about legal rules".[2]

> This distinction relates to concepts, not propositions. It consequently cuts across the distinctions between the fundamental proposition types: Whether a concept is used in legal rules or about legal rules, a proposition about the concept may be a definition (contribute to determining the concept) or a characterisation (for example, say something about the origin or effects of the concept); and in both cases the proposition may have a descriptive, normative or fused modality. – In particular concerning fused modality it must, however, be added: In relation to the definitional possibilities just mentioned, the interests that pull in the direction of fused modality (section II F 2.1 above) make themselves felt first and foremost in the case of concepts in legal rules, and in such cases in the form of definition of these. Characterisations of the origin or effects of the same concepts, or propositions about

[1] Compare Frändberg, 'Till frågan om de juridiska begreppens systematik' [on the question of the systematics of legal concepts], p. 112.

[2] Frändberg's mapping of legal concept types in the work mentioned in the preceding note is at the same time also a mapping of possible clarifications of the distinction 'in–about'.

concepts about legal rules (be it definitions or characterisations of such concepts), tend to a lesser degree towards fused modality.

One cause of confusion of the distinction here and the distinctions in the modality dimension may be that both have been expressed by means of the keywords "in"–"about", keywords that are, however, misleading in the modality dimension (section II A 5 (3) above, concluding remarks).

The boundary between the normative function and the systematising function is of a *graduated kind.* And the boundary is *relative to the individual decision*, in that what normatively motivates persons applying the law may vary. In certain situations, however, the mode of use is *typically* the one or the other: – On the one hand, one has concepts which clearly enough motivate normatively and which have little systematic interest, for example the concept of 'indecent intercourse' in the Criminal Justice Act (Act No. 10 of 22 May 1902, sections 192 et seq.) and innumerable concepts otherwise that are specific to the individual rules. – On the other hand, one has concepts that are deliberately formed with a view to the systematising and summarising of legal rules, for example a concept of 'competence'.[3] Such concepts will *at the time* of their being launched only be able to have the intended function.

However, a concept can *change* its function: – If, and in the event as, a concept with systematising function comes into common use, it may change to a normative function; see for example on the concept of 'misuse of authority' and its subconcepts, immediately below. – It is more seldom that a concept with normative function changes to a systematising function; if a statutory or non-statutory rule ceases to apply, the concepts in the rule most often die out at the same time.

In the case of *unwritten* law, the function of the concept is often particularly unclear.[4] Is for example a concept of *'misuse of authority'* in administrative law only a concept that summarises other motivating factors, or also a concept that directly motivates those applying the law? If one assumes that the concept on the whole only summarises, one can further ask whether the concepts of what is summarised (in Norwegian law, for example 'irrelevant considerations', 'arbitrariness', 'gross unreasonableness' and 'biased difference in treatment')[5] directly motivate, or whether these concepts too only have a summarising function. And in this way one can continue asking, until one arrives at concepts that clearly enough and generally motivate those applying the law.

If one looks at the categorisation in the parenthesis at note 5 above, the answer may vary. 'Irrelevant considerations', 'gross unreasonableness' and 'biased difference in treatment' seem to have established themselves as concepts that

---

[3] Eng, 'Begrepene 'kompetanse' og 'gyldighet' i juridisk argumentasjon' [the concepts of 'competence' and 'validity' in legal argumentation].

[4] Castberg, *Norges statsforfatning* [constitution of Norway], Vol. I, p. 64: "It can often be doubtful whether in a given instance one is confronted with a juristic construction or a rule of customary law, i.e. a rule that has as its basis a number of actions based on a certain conviction that they are in conformity with the law."

[5] Eckhoff, *Forvaltningsrett* [administrative law], 5th ed. pp. 249–63.

directly motivate those applying the law.[6] 'Arbitrariness', on the other hand, is a concept that for the time being mostly seems to be used as a residual category in the systematisation of the rules: The word "vilkårlighet" [arbitrariness] is used of instances as heterogeneous as, on the one hand, decisions based on pure chance,[7] and on the other, a situation in which "[the public administrative authorities'] decision [leaves] doubt as to whether all relevant considerations were weighed and balanced, even though they were known".[8]

6 See respectively *Rt. 1933/548* (the City Hall Hostel judgment), *Rt. 1951/19* (the Mortvedt judgment), and *Rt. 1956/29* (the judgment of the district court, on p. 33).

7 Such as where a municipality wishes to allocate beer licences by drawing lots; see *S.tid. 1987–88* [reports of parliamentary proceedings], pp. 3166–67.

8 *Rt. 1981/745* (the Isene judgment) on p. 748; cf. Eckhoff/ Smith, *Forvaltningsrett* [administrative law], p. 299, who use the word "vilkårlighet" [arbitrariness] of this. – Incidentally, in a number of instances lawyers use the word "vilkårlighet" even more loosely: They use it partly of the other categories of misuse of authority, e.g. of biased difference in treatment, see the district court judgment referred to in note 6 above; and partly of errors of fact in the exercise of discretion, see *RG 1988/602* on p. 608. ("RG" is an abbreviation for "Rettens Gang", the title of the only general law report series in Norway for decisions from courts other than the Supreme Court.)

IV

Some forms of language and argumentation that often make it unclear which type of proposition one is confronted with; in particular on the flight from the normative proposition

1. Survey

In Chapter II, cf. Chapter I, I gave an account of fundamental proposition types. In the present Chapter IV, I shall be looking at some forms of language and argumentation that often lead to lack of clarity about *which* of these proposition types one is confronted with.

I use the compound term *"form of language and argumentation"* because the forms in question consist partly in particular words and expressions ("language") and partly in connections in which the individual words may vary ("argumentation"). In some contexts I shall for the sake of brevity use only the term *"mode of expression"*. – Variation between "form", "mode", "pattern", or the like, is mostly for stylistic reasons.

The main emphasis in what follows is on forms of language and argumentation that create lack of clarity in the *modality dimension*: between descriptive, logical and normative propositions. But also forms of language and argumentation that create lack of clarity about the relationship between *definitions and characterisations* will be touched upon (see for example sections 3.2 (1) and 3.3.3, below).

A recurring theme will be the *flight from the normative proposition*. In particular the emphasis will be on the tendency to avoid unambiguously evaluative and decisional propositions in the case of evaluations and choices, and instead to use either modes of expression that objectively interpreted are polysemous between the descriptive, logical and normative (section 2 below), or modes of expression that objectively interpreted are one-sidedly descriptive or logical (section 3 below). In both cases there is often the psychological consequence that the evaluations and choices are veiled, so that the supposedly greater intersubjective certainty in criteria and judgement that many connect with descriptive and logical propositions has the field to itself; the proposition gains an imagined authority.

On the use of the word *"normative"*, see section 2.1 (2) below, concluding remarks.

By the formulation "*logical* proposition" ("mode of expression", "argumentation", or the like) I mean in what follows partly analytically true propositions (section II D above); partly proposition patterns built with logical arguments, for example arguments from self-contradiction, circularity or infinite regress (section III 2.2.1 above); and partly language and argumentation which in any other ways or more indeterminately claims particularly strong necessity (see for example section 3.2 (1) below).

2. Use of polysemous modes of expression in the case of evaluations and choices

2.1. The concept. The topic: A factual tendency in the case of evaluations and choices: use of modes of expression that are polysemous between the descriptive, logical and normative

(1) By "*polysemous* use of language" I mean linguistic forms that are commonly used in several meanings, and where there is, at any rate in some contexts, a certain practical interest in keeping these meanings apart (see in more detail in the following item (2) and in section 3.1 (2) below, on some aspects of this concept and the terminology I use).

The *main emphasis* in what follows is on polysemy in the *modality dimension*, and on the tendency to use this polysemy *when one evaluates and chooses*; see section 1 above.

(2) Polysemy is something different from *fusion* of descriptive and normative propositions (section II F above).

Fusion is a feature of the *level of meaning*; it is propositions that may have fused descriptive and normative modality. Polysemy is a feature of *linguistic entities*; it is words, formulations, sentences, etc., that may be polysemous.

Polysemy and lack of clarity are *two sides of the same coin*. – Fusion, however, does *not in itself give rise to any lack of clarity* about what type of proposition one is confronted with: The fact that there is fusion means that one is confronted with a proposition type sui generis, that is to say, propositions that are distinct both from the purely descriptive ones and from the purely normative ones; it does not mean that the proposition type is unclear. Lack of clarity is only the result if one is not conscious of the distinctive nature of fusions and wants to force them into the dichotomy 'descriptive propositions–normative propositions' (section II F 3.2.4 above).

Fusion and polysemy can make themselves felt in *one and the same instance of language use*: Also in the case of lawyers' propositions about what the law is, that is to say, in the paradigm case of fused descriptive and normative propositions (section II F 2 above), there is a tendency towards the use of modes of expression that are polysemous between the descriptive, logical and normative. – Once linguistic formulations are polysemous in the modality dimension, they may therefore possibly be not only three-ways polysemous: between the descriptive, logical and (purely) normative, but also *four-ways*: between the descriptive, logical, (purely) normative, and fused. – The reason for my use of the weak formulation "they *may ... possibly* be" is that actually occurring language among lawyers exhibits few means of expression for the phenomenon of fusion, and as one aspect of this scarcity, exhibits few means of expression that are in fact used in several meanings, of which one meaning connects with fusion (section II F 4 above). Consequently (to the same extent) we lack, as I use the word "polysemous", the factual basis for saying that lawyers' modes of expression are "polysemous" ("four-ways polysemous") between the descriptive, logical, (purely) normative, and fused (section 3.1 (2) below).

In the light of this, and taken together with the fact that in relation to the topic of the present Chapter IV it would be disproportionately complicated to specify the meaning of every single occurrence of "normative" in relation to the phenomenon of fusion, I use the word *"normative"* in two senses in the present Chapter IV and let the particular context show which meaning is the relevant one: the meaning 'purely normative', or the meaning 'purely normative or fused descriptive and normative'. – When I speak of modes of expression that are polysemous between the descriptive, logical and normative, then it is basically the narrow sense of "normative" ('purely normative') that is intended, cf. the preceding paragraph. When I speak of the level of meaning alone (the modality dimension) and lawyers' propositions de lege lata are an instantiation (explicitly adduced by me or possible to adduce), then it is basically the broad sense of "normative" ('purely normative propositions or fused descriptive and normative propositions') that is intended. However, these are simply points of departure. With a view to presenting in their interconnections those forms of language and argumentation, in those connections with the level of meaning, which in the perspective in the present Chapter IV are of the same kind, other linguistic usage may also be expedient. I refer to my individual discussions and the guidance that follows from them, partly from explicit statements and partly from the specific framework of the individual discussion.

2.2. Some modes of expression that are systematically polysemous between the descriptive, logical and normative

I take my point of departure in the modes of expression "What *is* x?", "X *is* ...":

(1) "What is ..."-propositions

After this I shall look at some *combinations* with other word groups that typically appear as polysemous:

(2) Function terminology
(3) Modality terminology
(4) Essence terminology
(5) Theory terminology

Combinations with more specifically legally relevant words and expressions are also an important instance-type: for example combinations with principle terminology. But central parts of lawyers' language in the case of evaluations and choices, including principle terminology, are not only polysemous, but more one-sidedly descriptive or logical; see section 3 below.

Beside "is"-compounds, mention should also be made of *relation terms*, such as "means", "entails", "follows from", "is a consequence of", "reason", "cause":

(6) Relation terminology
- **(a) In general**
- **(b) In lawyers' application of legal rules with intention as a legally operative fact**

Concept terminology also belongs in the perspective here. I refer to my earlier pointing out of the fact that, and the way in which, a great deal of concept terminology involves a double shift: from the changing and indeterminate, to the unitary; and from the individual language user's evaluation and choice of language, to description of something already existing, and existing independently of language:

(7) Concept terminology; see sections II B 4.4.3 cf. 4.1 (5)(b), above.

(1) "What is ..."-propositions

Propositions about what something is, often appear as being open in relation to the distinctions between definitions and characterisations, and between descriptive, logical and normative propositions. I refer to the examples and discussions given by way of introduction (sections I 2–3), and to a number of places otherwise in this work (see for example sections II B 7.3.2 and III 2.2.2 (3)(c), above).

(2) Function terminology

The word "function" is used to express *logical* propositions. This is the case in mathematics and logic: "x is a function of y". And the word "function" is used to express *descriptive* propositions. This is the case for example when it is placed as a key term in the vocabulary of sociology:

> "By "sosial funksjon" [social function] I mean a group of objective effects of an institution. The function of an institution is not necessarily identical with the "purpose" or "aim" of the institution. The originators of the institution may well have been motivated by expectations that are not realised through its objective effects. ... But not all the effects of an institution have to do with its function. Only those effects that in fact contribute to increasing the probability of the institution's continued existence belong among the functions. Effects which reduce the probability of the institution's continued existence are sometimes called "dysfunctions"."[1]

If one goes more closely into the use of function terminology in concrete argumentation contexts in the social sciences and law, one will often also discover *normative* propositions. This is so for example in the case of proposition formulations that make use of the expression "the function of the courts". A typical case would be: *"The function of the courts is to judge, not to legislate."* By many people this formulation will purely linguistically be considered descriptive; and in fact it gives an initial, rough account of what the courts do. At the same time, among lawyers and those who are interested in politics, this formulation will often be ascribed the normative meaning that the courts must be cautious about setting up and following rules that may be contrary to what the legislative branch has laid down or would have laid down if it had thought the question over. Such a norm is widespread and is one side of the ideology of the three functions of the state (legislative, executive and judicial) and the division of these among the state bodies ("the doctrine of the separation of powers").

By way of illustration I shall quote some reflections on *"what the function of an ultimate appellate court is"*: to decide the individual case or also to contribute to the making of general rules of law:

---

[1] Aubert, *Om straffens sosiale funksjon* [on the social function of punishment], pp. 2–3. Aubert builds on Merton's seminal discussion in 'Manifest and Latent Functions', cf. Merton's definition p. 105.

> "Why are certain issues reserved to the courts in our society and others left to the legislature? *What, indeed, is the function* of an ultimate appellate court? I do not doubt that English lawyers would unhesitatingly say that it is the *primary function* of the House of Lords to decide appeals, even in a sense to correct the "errors" of the lower courts, although it also has a *secondary function* as a law-making body. But who has decided that these are the primary and the secondary functions respectively? It is not part of the necessary or immutable order of things: it is, for instance quite clear that the *primary function of the Supreme Court of the United States* is not to decide disputes between litigants, but to resolve conflicts of power, and certain major issues of social policy. But in England it tends to be just assumed that the *primary function of the House of Lords* is to decide disputes" (my italics).[2]

It seems clear that the words "primary/ secondary function" in this quotation are not used in a purely descriptive sense. At the same time the words are clearly enough intended to cover certain major trends in the practice of the courts mentioned. The function terminology in the quotation thus has both descriptive and normative meaning aspects. – My impression is that the quotation is in this respect representative: It is quite usual to use function terminology as the simultaneous expression of descriptive and normative propositions.

> That side of function terminology that I have now pointed to, the systematic polysemy between the descriptive, logical and normative, is different from a couple of other sides of this terminology that have been problematised: its politically conservative tendency;[3] and its lack of application criteria, so that it may be used to explain incompatible descriptive propositions.[4]

(3) Modality terminology

By "modality terminology" I mean linguistic entities like "can/not", "must/ not", "im/possible", "un/necessary", and the like. – Modality terminology is used in the case of logical propositions ("two plus two must be four"); descriptive propositions ("if you want to pass the exam, you must read more"); normative propositions ("you must not tell lies"); and fusion of descriptive and normative propositions (lawyers' propositions de lege lata, see the examples below, cf. section II F above).

In actually occurring language and argumentation there is a tendency to choose ways of using modality terminology that conceal evaluations and choices. What form and degree of concealment are chosen varies inter alia with the area of

---

2 Atiyah, *Pragmatism and Theory in English Law*, pp. 157–58.

3 Myrdal, *An American Dilemma*, pp. 1055–57. – "While they [inter alia the word "function"] ... have been used advantageously to describe empirically observable situations, they carry within them the tendency to give a do-nothing (laissez-faire) valuation of those situations" (p. 1055; Myrdal's italics omitted); "... lead to a conservative teleology" (p. 1056).

4 Elster, *Forklaring og dialektikk* [explanation and dialectics], pp. 92–105; *Ulysses and the Sirens*, pp. 28–35. With this aspect in mind Elster terms function terminology "friksjonsløs" [frictionless], see the former work, p. 101; *Vitenskap og politikk* [science and politics], p. 19.

language and argumentation. In *lawyers' language and argumentation de lege lata* there is a tendency towards ways of use that suggest or assert logical or factual im/possibility, also in the case of evaluations and choices.[5] To illustrate this I shall mention some examples from court practice and legal literature:

In a decision that declares it punishable to drive a pleasure craft in a state of intoxication, and which justifies this with reference to the formulation in the Criminal Justice Act "the master of any ship … who … becomes intoxicated while on duty or when about to go on duty" (section 422), it says: "When one takes as a premiss that the craft is to count as a ship, there *cannot* be any doubt that the appellant's conduct took place "on duty" within the meaning of the Act" (my italics).[6] Considerations for or against letting the driving of a pleasure craft be covered do not, however, necessarily have the same weight in relation to "on duty" as in relation to "ship". Take as an example one of the considerations against, namely the consideration that citizens shall be able to foresee their legal position. This consideration has greater weight the further one moves away from a non-lawyer's understanding of the wording; and letting "on duty" cover the driving of a pleasure craft is no doubt even farther from a non-lawyer's understanding than letting "ship" cover pleasure craft. – In a decision that excludes the submission of evidence concerning discussions in Cabinet, it says: "The [Interlocutory Appeals] Committee [of the Supreme Court] considers that section 250 of the Civil Procedure Act, in view of the very special considerations that apply to meetings of the Cabinet in the transaction of its business, *must* be taken to mean that a minister's notes to Cabinet colleagues cannot be subject to the duty to produce documents. … That there are such very special considerations … *must* in the opinion of the Committee be clear" (my italics).[7]

An example with systematically broader implications is provided by court practice concerning the question of dispositivity in respect of contracts (the question of when two potentially contracting parties shall be deemed to have moved from the stage of preliminaries to that of being legally bound). One criterion that the courts often discuss here is whether the parties to a sufficient extent reached agreement on the specific terms. How judges draw this line I submit depends on fairly free evaluations and choices on their part: in particular on the consideration for the courts' ability to imply and factual possibility of implying, in a sound way, the terms necessary to fill the gaps of a contract, if such is found to exist, together with the consideration for preserving the public's confidence in the courts as being independent and impartial. Nevertheless, in drawing this line Norwegian judges most often formulate their standpoints through modal forms of expression with logical or factual colouring:

---

5 Sundby, *Om normer* [on norms], pp. 219–20.

6 *Rt. 1973/433* on p. 434 (Supreme Court; unanimous). In section II F 2 above, in my introductory remarks, I have in the indent given a brief account of this decision.

7 *Rt. 1980/711* on pp. 711–12 (Interlocutory Appeals Committee of the Supreme Court; unanimous). In section III 3.2.3 (1) above, at and in notes 15 and 16, the case material on this topic is outlined.

"Any disagreement on any point, on which no provision had been made, *would ... have had* to be resolved on the basis of law and usages in trade" (my italics).[8]

"It may well be the case that certain details would have had to be worked out in greater detail in the contract of sale that was to be drawn up, but here, in the event of disagreement between the parties, one *would have had* to build on interpretation and implication of the terms of the contract" (my italics).[9]

"I ... have reached the conclusion that ... the question of price ... *cannot* be decided by ... implication of terms."[10]

In legal literature modality terminology with logical or factual colouring is not so common as in court practice. Yet the following is not unusual:

"It *must* be a requirement that cases in public administration be dealt with in a proper manner. We *must* thus be able to set up as a general point of departure that the public administrative authorities have a duty to ensure that procedure is proper also beyond what is specified in explicit rules of procedure and concrete principles of customary law. There is not likely to be any great disagreement that the individual civil servant *must* ensure that those cases with which he deals are dealt with properly and fairly ..." (my italics; Frihagen's italics omitted).[11]

Playing on modal forms of expression with logical or factual colouring has via lawyers' language de lege lata gone over into their language *more generally*. It has, for example, gone over into the *wording of statutes*: When sections 17 and 37 of the Public Administration Act (10 February 1967) say that "The administrative body shall ensure that the case is illuminated as thoroughly as *possible* before any administrative decision is made" (my italics), the Act gives the impression of a factually cognisable boundary: between "the possible" and "the impossible". As the Act is interpreted in the literature and in practice, "possible" is, however, read as if it had said: "reasonable" taking into consideration "the manpower and resources that are available, other tasks, the importance of the case to society and the individual, the significance of the information in question for the outcome of the case, the costs of further investigations, the extent to which any parties to the case can be ordered to illuminate the facts of the case in a reliable manner, and the degree to which it may be reckoned that the party or the parties will present information in their own interest".[12]

---

8 *Rt. 1920/699* on p. 702 (Supreme Court; 6–1 decision; dissenting opinion).

9 *Rt. 1987/1205* on p. 1211 (Supreme Court; unanimous).

10 *Rt. 1992/1110* on p. 1114 (Supreme Court; unanimous). – Most often no particular justification is given for such formulations as now quoted, or the justification takes the form that the extent to which the parties reached agreement on the specific terms is used as an evidential fact for or against the parties' having intended to bind themselves; see item (6) below, where I give a more detailed account both of the courts' argumentation in the question of dispositivity in respect of contracts, and of the material on which I build.

11 Frihagen, *Forvaltningsrett* [administrative law], Vol. II, p. 15.

12 Op. cit., p. 27; cf. the discussion on pp. 21–27. Correspondingly Eckhoff/ Smith, *Forvaltningsrett*

(4) Essence terminology

A sentence like "the nature of law is to offer citizens legal safeguards" may be used to express a descriptive proposition (one claims that legal safeguards are a feature of particular existing legal systems); an analytically true proposition (one presupposes a concept of 'law' in which legal safeguards are included as a criterion); a proposition which more indeterminately purports a particularly strong necessity; or a normative proposition (one asserts that it ought to be so). Corresponding polysemy applies if one replaces the word "nature" by words such as "essence", "being", or the like, possibly reinforced with qualifiers such as "actual", "genuine", "real", "true", "rational", or the like. – Such essence terminology occurs regularly in the literature (cf. in this context also forms of expression like "la nature du droit" and "das Wesen des Rechts").

Lawyers often refer to "the natural thing"; this is particularly the case in collocations like "the natural interpretation", "the natural understanding", and the like. Such collocations are central, both in relation to the sources of abstract law ("the natural interpretation of the statute") and in relation to other dispositive acts ("the natural interpretation of the last will and testament/ promise/ contract/ individual administrative decision/ [etc.]"). Closer analysis of the individual interpretation contexts shows that expressions like "the natural interpretation", "the natural understanding", and the like, are often used with a descriptive or logical colouring, also in the case of evaluations of and choice between two or more interpretations.

(5) Theory terminology

Also *terms for more comprehensive sets of propositions* are often polysemous between the descriptive, logical and normative.

This applies to sentence forms in *everyday life*: for example to "in my view/ from my point of view ...". And it applies to terms in *academic subjects, science and philosophy*: for example to key terms like "theory", "doctrine" and "analysis".

(a) The word *"theory"* is used on the one hand of *descriptive characterisations*. This is the usual way of using it in natural science, as for example in the designation "the theory of evolution by natural selection".

On the other hand the word "theory" is also often used of *normative characterisations*: for example in collocations like "theories of justice", "theories of rationality" and "ethical theories".

In the use of collocations like those just mentioned there also tend to be, however, strong elements of descriptive propositions, in the form of presuppositions

[administrative law], p. 476. – Sundby, *Om normer* [on norms], pp. 219–20, gives numerous examples of the use of modality terminology in the language of statutes, and points to the examples' real character of weighing and balancing. Correspondingly, but more briefly, Eckhoff/ Sundby, *Rettssystemer* [legal systems], 1st ed. pp. 140–41.

about or descriptions of man and society, so that the word "theory" is used as a *common term* for descriptive and normative propositions.

> An example is: "I [have] come to pose ... radical questions about the *theory of rational choice*. How useful and fruitful is it actually? There are two reasons to be in doubt. In the first place it is clear that human beings often *act* irrationally, or on the basis of views that have come into being in an irrational way. ... In the second place the theory of rational choice cannot always tell us *how we shall act*" (my italics).[13]

The word "theory" is also used of *fusion* of descriptive and normative propositions, in that lawyers use the word also of propositions de lege lata (section II F 2 above); for example they do so in discussions about whether "viljesteori" [will theory, the subjective theory of contract], "tillitsteori" [expectation theory, a species of the objective theory of contract] or "erklæringsteori" [declaration theory, another species of the objective theory of contract] is valid contract law,[14] or about whether "regelteori" [rule theory] or "standardteori" [standard theory] gives the correct interpretation of Article 97 of the Constitution concerning retroactive statutes.[15]

In addition, lawyers use the word "theory" of *purely normative* propositions, for example when under the name of "rettssikkerhetsteorier" [theories of legal safeguards] they discuss how public administrative authorities ought to behave.[16]

(b) The word *"doctrine"* is used of descriptive propositions, normative propositions or combinations of descriptive and normative propositions. This applies completely generally, for example in the collocation "doctrine of method". And it applies more particularly, for example in the collocation "doctrine of the sources of law". – The word "doctrine" is also used of fusion of descriptive and normative propositions, in that lawyers use the word also of propositions de lege lata (section II F 2 above), for example in discussions of the "doctrine of misuse of authority".[17]

(c) The word *"analysis"* is not free of the ambiguity between the descriptive and the normative either: For example, so-called "explicative analysis" in science and philosophy, often on the pattern of or with its point of departure in Carnap's discussions of method, provides not only a description of language usage, but also normative regulation of it (sections V 3.3.1 cf. 3.3.3, below). – The word "analysis" is also used of fusion of descriptive and normative propositions, in that lawyers use the word also of propositions de lege lata (section II F 2 above). For example, under the name of "economic analysis of law" are presented not only

---

13 Elster, *Vitenskap og politikk* [science and politics], pp. 20–21; cf. Braybrooke, 'What Came to Light in the Aspen/ Cornell Colloquium on Choice and Decision', pp. 602–03, 612–13.

14 See e.g. Selvig, *Kontraktsretten* [the law of contract], pp. 542–44.

15 See e.g. Kjønstad, 'Trygderettighetenes grunnlovsvern' [constitutional protection of national insurance rights], pp. 24–30.

16 See e.g. Schartum, *Rettssikkerhet og systemutvikling i offentlig forvaltning* [legal safeguards and system development in public administration], pp. 28 et seq.

17 See e.g. Eckhoff, *Forvaltningsrett* [administrative law], 5th ed. p. 250.

descriptive propositions (descriptions of the origin of existing legal rules or predictions of the coming into being of new legal rules) and purely normative propositions (propositions about what ought to be the law), but also propositions de lege lata, with their characteristic fused descriptive and normative modality (section V 2.4 below, at and in notes 25 and 26).

(6) Relation terminology

(a) In general

I take my point of departure in the widespread formulations "X *means/ entails/ implies* ...", "It is a *result/ consequence* of x that ..." – in what follows called for the sake of brevity "the standard formulations".

Whether one presupposes that "x" stands for a word or concept, so that it is a matter of properties that by definition belong to x, or one presupposes that "x" stands for a phenomenon delimited through presupposition, so that it is a matter of a characterisation of this phenomenon, it is not possible on the basis of the wording of the standard formulations to decide whether they express *descriptive or normative* propositions. For example, this is not possible in relation to the sentence "A contract means that you must honour your promise provided the other contracting party honours his promise."[18]

The standard formulations are used a great deal in lawyers' language and argumentation de lege lata. Instead of the purely descriptive interpretation or the purely normative interpretation, a *fusion interpretation* will often be the adequate interpretation here (section II F above).

Also the words *"reason"* and *"cause"* are used of both descriptive and normative relations.[19] Examples would be: "There is reason/ cause to believe ...", "If the car would not start, then there was reason/ cause to cancel the purchase."

(b) In lawyers' application of legal rules with intention as a legally operative fact

The outlined ambiguity between descriptive and normative use of relation terms (item (a) above) is found in lawyers' language and argumentation de lege lata to a particular degree in the case of the application of legal rules with *intention as a legally operative fact*. By way of illustration I shall look at lawyers' application of the legal rules concerning the *question of dispositivity in respect of contracts* (the question of when two potentially contracting parties shall be deemed to have moved from the stage of preliminaries to that of being legally bound).

In connection with an unpublished work on the question of dispositivity in respect of contracts in Norwegian law, I went through the printed Supreme Court

---

18 For the sake of brevity I link this example only to the word "means", but it may easily be reformulated using the other relation designations mentioned by way of introduction in the present item (a).

19 O. Dahl, *Om årsaksproblemer i historisk forskning* [on causal problems in historical research], pp. 60–61, cf. 37; see also Eckhoff/ Sundby, *Rettssystemer* [legal systems], 1st ed. p. 159; 2nd ed. p. 182; *Rechtssysteme*, p. 154.

judgments concerning this question. – The arguments the Supreme Court advances, may be grouped in five main categories of typically relevant arguments: intention to enter into legal relations (what the parties actually intended with respect to binding themselves, in what follows often termed "dispositive intent" for the sake of brevity);[20] the form of the alleged contract (especially written versus oral); its content (especially to what extent the parties reached agreement on the specific terms); subsequent developments (for example the potential buyer's financing actions or the potential seller's negotiations with other persons concerning the same contractual object); and equitable considerations (for example an evaluation of the goodness of the content of the alleged contract).[21]

In nearly all of its justifications addressed to others concerning the question of dispositivity in respect of contracts, the Supreme Court asks (also) whether the potentially contracting parties "har ment å binde seg" [intended to bind themselves], and adduces the remaining arguments (also) as evidential facts in relation to this intention criterion.[22] – This way of using the typically relevant arguments is schematically represented in the first figure below.

My hypothesis is that the way in which the non-intentional arguments in fact work in the motivation process is often a different one: that they work as dispositivity criteria in their own right, in the form of factors for a value-governed weighing and balancing. – This way of using the typically relevant arguments is schematically represented in the second figure below.

---

20 When speaking about the question of dispositivity in respect of contracts, I use the word "party" in the sense of 'party to contract-preparatory acts' or 'party to a dispute about the question of dispositivity', not in the sense of 'party to a contract' (whether the person concerned is a party to a contract is precisely the question under discussion). For the sake of clarity or for stylistic reasons, in some places I also use the terms "potentially contracting parties", "potential buyer/ seller", etc.

21 An important group among the printed Supreme Court judgments concerns contracts relating to real property. See in particular the following judgments concerning purchase and sale: *Rt. 1878/486, 1878/773, 1881/72, 1882/8, 1883/597, 1892/652, 1904/633, 1907/314, 1915/441, 1917/615, 1919/28, 1920/699, 1924/1179, 1925/772, 1935/1000, 1939/496, 1940/193, 1955/719, 1959/6, 1963/234, 1964/34, 1964/1057, 1964/1260, 1971/481, 1973/1165, 1977/553, 1981/595, 1985/149, 1985/1265, 1987/1205, 1989/659, 1996/415*. See also *Rt. 1953/581, 1976/445, 1987/442* concerning leasing, and *Rt. 1992/1110, 1995/543* concerning construction contracts. – This group is important. Partly it is important because it is the numerically largest (when one categorises the existing judgments according to contractual object). And partly this group is important because negotiations in the case of contracts relating to real property most often take time and include a variety of acts on the part of the parties. Thus the grounds of judgment in these cases have to a particularly high degree contributed to creating the diversity of typically relevant arguments in the question of dispositivity, see the main text preceding the present note; and further, to a particularly high degree contributed to creating the polysemous language and argumentation structure in the question of dispositivity, see the main text in what follows.

22 The formulation "intended to bind themselves" stands here as the representative of linguistic entities that it is reasonable to interpret as expressing the intention criterion. – Some typical examples of evidential language and argumentation in relation to intention have been quoted in Eng, ' "Hva er en viljeserklæring?" ' ["what is a declaration of intent?"], pp. 38–39. See further the quotation from *Rt. 1985/1265* in section 3.3.1 (3)(b)(ii) below. This quotation also illustrates the use of the abovementioned main categories of typically relevant arguments.

THE QUESTION OF DISPOSITIVITY IN RESPECT OF CONTRACTS —
MODE OF USE$_1$ OF THE TYPICALLY RELEVANT ARGUMENTS

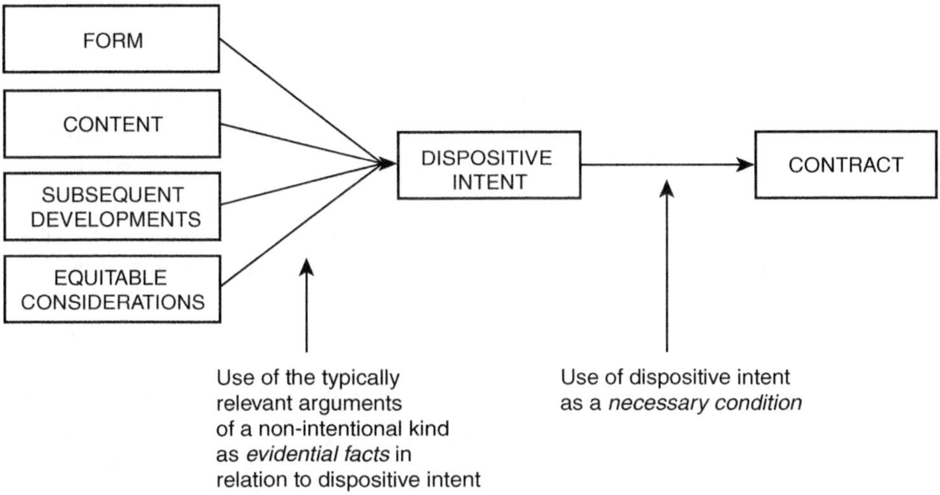

THE QUESTION OF DISPOSITIVITY IN RESPECT OF CONTRACTS —
MODE OF USE$_2$ OF THE TYPICALLY RELEVANT ARGUMENTS

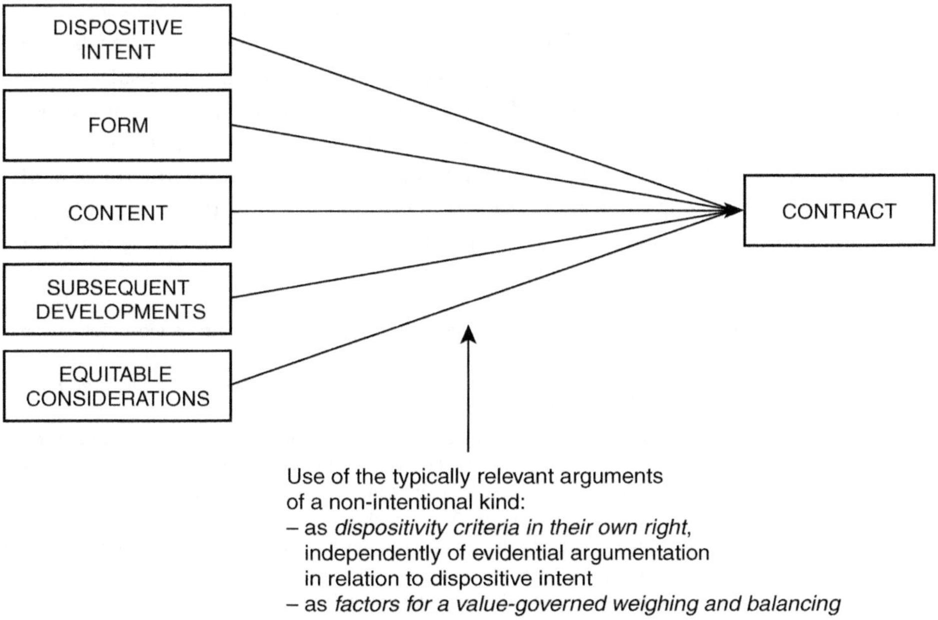

In this connection I content myself with presenting my hypothesis as a conclusion, and I shall use this conclusion to illustrate *general aspects of lawyers' discussions of intention*:[23]

The language and argumentation structure in lawyers' discussions of intention, including their use of relation terminology, makes possible a distinctive *ambiguity* in relation to the two now outlined modes of use of the typically relevant arguments: Partly there is the use of these arguments as evidential facts in relation to intention, that is to say that *descriptive* propositions are put forward, cf. mode of use_1. Partly there is the use of these arguments as criteria directly in relation to the question of whether the parties shall be deemed to have moved from the stage of preliminaries to that of being legally bound: a form of argumentation that also includes evaluations and choices, that is to say that *normative* propositions are put forward, cf. mode of use_2.[24/25]

The outlined ambiguity shows itself *in the case of* the relation terms mentioned in item (a) above, and further in the case of typical forms of expression in Norwegian court practice such as "tale for" [support], "tale mot" [go against], "trekke i retning av" [tend in the direction of], "tyde på" [suggest], "medføre" [involve], and the like. – For example, the sentence "the lack of anything in writing goes against a contract's having been established" has the ambiguity outlined. The same applies if in this sentence one replaces the words "the lack of anything in writing" by a term for one of the other typically relevant arguments, or if one replaces the formulation "goes against" by one of the other relation expressions just mentioned.

A corresponding ambiguity between descriptive and normative propositions shows itself in the case of terms for the relation between the typically relevant arguments *among themselves*. This applies for example in the case of terms like "avveining" [weighing and balancing], "skjønn" [estimation, appraisal, judgement] or "vurdering" [evaluation]. These terms are used partly of a relation between, and a co-ordinating of, the typically relevant arguments in their capacity of being evidential facts in relation to intention to enter into legal relations; and these terms are used partly of a relation between, and a co-ordinating of, the typically relevant arguments in their capacity of being criteria in the concept of

---

23 Discussions of intention in the Supreme Court, and consequently on the part of most Norwegian lawyers.

24 Here I use the term "normative proposition" in a broad sense, both of purely normative propositions and of lawyers' typically fused descriptive and normative propositions.

25 I consider it most pertinent to say that it is the language and argumentation structure in lawyers' discussions of *intention* that makes ambiguity possible in relation to the ways of using the typically relevant arguments, even though the one way of using them, use as criteria in their own right, is logically independent of discussions of intention. For in actually occurring grounds for judgment, sentences that can be interpreted as use of the arguments as criteria in their own right, lie woven into a larger pattern of evidential language and argumentation concerning dispositive intent (section 3.3.1 (3)(b)(ii) below; see also the quotation from the judgment *Rt. 1883/597* in the text at note 27 below and the analysis immediately following).

'contract', that is to say, directly in relation to the dispositivity question. – For example, the sentence "a weighing and balancing of the arguments goes against a contract's having been established" has this ambiguity.

One aspect that distinguishes criteria argumentation from assessment-of-evidence argumentation is the greater role *evaluations* play in criteria argumentation.[26] It might then be tempting to believe that words and expressions for the evaluation aspect would be suitable for distinguishing between criteria argumentation and assessment-of-evidence argumentation. But language usage does not give any sure guidance here either. – By way of illustration we can look at the use of the word *"reasonable"*. For example: "Still there is the circumstance to be noted that ... during the conversation concerned, nothing [was] mentioned about limitations with respect to the felling of timber by [the sellers], so long as they used and kept the farm; while it is indeed in the highest degree *reasonable* that something about this would have to have been provided, if a contract of sale had really been finally concluded" (my italics).[27]

In interpreting this quotation one can take one's point of departure in the *empirical regularity* that if provisions relating to important points are lacking, then most parties will not have intended to bind themselves. The absence of any provision concerning the seller's right to the felling of timber in the period between the sale and the buyer's taking over is in this case used as an *evidential fact* in support of the absence of (actual or hypothetical) intention to enter into legal relations. *Ergo*, it is "indeed in the highest degree *reasonable* that something about this would have to have been provided, if a contract of sale had really been finally concluded".

Another possibility is to take one's point of departure in the different *normative grounds* that suggest that the courts do not deem a contract to have come into being, when the parties did not to a sufficient extent reach agreement on the specific terms: in particular the consideration for the courts' ability to imply and factual possibility of implying, in a sound way, the terms necessary to fill the gaps of a contract, if such is found to exist, together with the consideration for preserving the public's confidence in the courts as being independent and impartial. The absence of any provision concerning the seller's right to the felling of timber in the period between the sale and the buyer's taking over is in this case used as a *dispositivity criterion of a non-intentional kind*, more precisely as a factor for a value-governed weighing and balancing. *Ergo*, it is "indeed in the highest degree *reasonable* that something about this would have to have been provided, if a contract of sale had really been finally concluded".

---

26 I use "criteria argumentation" also of argumentation concerning what standard of probability shall be required (burden of proof). "Greater role" refers to the fact that there is a difference, but no absolute separation between the role of evaluations in criteria argumentation and in assessment-of-evidence argumentation; see section III 3.2.3 (3) above.

27 *Rt. 1883/597* on p. 602.

3. Use of descriptive or logical modes of expression in the case of evaluations and choices

3.1. The concept. The topic: A factual tendency in the case of evaluations and choices: use of descriptive or logical modes of expression

(1) By *"use of descriptive or logical modes of expression in the case of evaluations and choices"* I mean the following situation: The sender uses formulations which interpreted on the basis of *widespread linguistic practice*[1] express descriptive or logical propositions, instead of giving an account of *his* evaluations and choices[2] (see in more detail in item (2) below on some aspects of this concept and the terminology I use). – For example: On the basis of knowledge of lawyers' language and argumentation de lege lata (language and argumentation about what the law is), including knowledge of what guidance the actually existing sources of law provide, one can quite often put forward a reasoned supposition that the lawyer's use of the descriptive formulation is not (only) governed by what facts are present, but (also) by the lawyer's evaluations and choices with respect to the reasonable, the just or other normative categories.

Use of descriptive or logical modes of expression in the case of evaluations and choices represents a more *active "flight from the normative proposition"* than those modes of expression that were discussed in section 2 above: While the latter-mentioned modes of expression objectively interpreted allow room for a normative meaning, descriptive or logical modes of expression shut a normative meaning out. – It is a matter of a *sliding scale* here. The categorisation into respectively the preceding section 2 and the present section 3 only points at two points on this scale. The reason I bring out these points is to show the possibilities of *greater or lesser linguistic distancing* from evaluations and choices, and, with this as a point of departure, to map how the possibilities are used in actually occurring language and argumentation.

In actually occurring language and argumentation in which the sender evaluates and chooses, there seems to be a *tendency not only* towards the more passive:

---

1 "Objective interpretation/ meaning"; see in more detail in section II E 2.2 above.

2 "Subjective interpretation/ meaning"; see in more detail in section II E 2.3 above.

the sender's not removing any polysemy there might be with respect to what type of proposition one is confronted with (section 2 above), *but also* (as an extension and in addition) a tendency towards the just defined and more *active*: the sender's pushing one-sidedly descriptive or logical modes of expression into the foreground.

One *symptom* of this being the case is that the sender sticks to formulations which objectively interpreted express descriptive characterisations, also when he is faced with a conflicting reality. This gives reason to suppose that the formulations subjectively interpreted express something else than descriptive characterisations: that they often express a normative characterisation, and in so doing, that they often express the sender's evaluations and choices with respect to how something shall be.[3]

Such *possible* discrepancy between objective meaning and subjective meaning creates *unclarity* about what type of proposition one shall take it that one is confronted with. It creates unclarity on the part of the *recipient* of the proposition formulation. Not seldom it also creates unclarity on the part of the *sender*: By reflecting on our own use of language we may discover that our message was not so clear as we believed. Conscious or unconscious desires concerning what something shall be like, influence our purported descriptions; we discover that we stick to formulations which objectively interpreted express descriptive characterisations, *also* when we are faced with a conflicting reality.

The more concrete *examples* in what follows will mainly be taken from lawyers' language and argumentation. However, a number of the *language and argumentation patterns* that the examples illustrate we find again in other subjects, in everyday life, in science, and in philosophy; this applies for example to persuasive definitions, absolutising of aspects, and dichotomies (section 3.2 below). Other patterns are more specific to lawyers' language and argumentation (section 3.3 below).

(2) There may be differences of opinion about how one shall formulate one's propositions when one speaks of situations in which subjective meaning moves far away from objective meaning. An example is how one shall speak of the situation in which a lawyer justifies his standpoint on a legal issue de lege lata with the formulation type "that was the legislator's intention", while the statute's wording and the travaux préparatoires may also justify another standpoint, and it is the lawyer's own evaluations that determine his choice of the one standpoint in preference to the other: (a) Shall one then say that the formulation "that was the legislator's intention" is "ambiguous" between the descriptive (objective interpretation/ meaning) and the normative (subjective interpretation/ meaning)? (b) And shall one use the expression "(subjective) meaning" at all, a way of speaking that

[3] See in more detail in section 3.2 (2) below. – For other possible interpretations, see section II E 2.2.4 (3)(a) above.

implies that the meaning of the formulation "that was the legislator's intention" may be 'that is all in all what is most reasonable and just'?

(a) I have, as is apparent from the relationship between the preceding section 2 and the present section 3, chosen to reserve the words *"ambiguity/ polysemy"* for the dimension of objective meaning. – Thus I do *not* use "ambiguity/ polysemy" of language situations in which a formulation objectively interpreted is unambiguous, at the same time as the sender uses other tenability criteria or takes into account other facts than those the objective meaning indicates. For example, I do not use "ambiguous/ polysemous" of the situation in which lawyers say "that was the legislator's intention", at the same time as the tenability criteria that the lawyer uses for his standpoint relate to values.

(b) On the other hand I have, as is apparent from item (1) above, chosen to use the expression *"(subjective) meaning"* even if the tenability criteria or facts the sender is taking into account are very different from those the objective meaning indicates. In relation to the example outlined concerning the formulation "that was the legislator's intention", I shall thus say that the subjective meaning of this formulation is a normative proposition, namely an expression of the lawyer's evaluations.

(a)↔(b) These are the structurings and namings of the material that I believe to be best suited to illuminating the topic of the present Chapter IV: forms of language and argumentation that make it unclear what type of proposition one is confronted with, with particular emphasis on the flight from the normative proposition. – I do not consider it very important, however, whether one agrees or disagrees with these definitional decisions, if one otherwise agrees with what I say, first, about the framing of the issue, and secondly, about what language and argumentation patterns actually occur and about how these patterns are used to conceal evaluations and choices (section 2 above and the present section 3).

3.2. Patterns from language and argumentation more generally

(1) Persuasive definitions and absolutisation of aspects

(2) Sticking to formulations which, objectively interpreted, express descriptive propositions, when one is confronted with a conflicting reality

(1) Persuasive definitions and absolutisation of aspects

A commonly occurring form of combination of descriptive and logical modes of expression in the case of evaluations and choices consists in persuasive definitions combined with absolutisation of aspects:

Persuasive definitions interpreted objectively and read in isolation express *descriptive* propositions (descriptive characterisations), instead of those evaluations and choices which the language user is motivated by in his setting up of the definition and which the definition is suited to transferring to the recipient.[4]

Persuasive definitions are often combined with *absolutisation of aspects*. This is so, partly directly, in that the descriptive language attire of the persuasive definition is *reinforced* with expressions like "actual", "real", "true", or the like (section II B 7.3.3 (2)(b) above); and partly more indirectly, in that the persuasive definition is included as *part of a theory* which claims that the aspect the persuasive definition seizes on, is essential.[5] – The persuasive definition thereby gives the *impression of a particular depth*, of having found its way to features of reality with a *particularly important status*. In connection with the earlier examples, may be mentioned for instance "real science", "actual norm", "true sexuality".[6] Thereby, alongside the descriptive, a *logical* proposition is also brought in: a proposition about a necessity of a *particularly strong* kind and degree, although it is unclear of what kind and degree.

(2) Sticking to formulations which, objectively interpreted, express descriptive propositions, when one is confronted with a conflicting reality

Persuasive definitions and absolutisation of aspects (item (1) above) are examples of language and argumentation patterns which by definition, or, as the case may be, in combination with commonly occurring features, entail the use of descriptive or logical modes of expression in the case of evaluations and choices; and in this respect they are examples of patterns that create lack of clarity about what type of proposition one is confronted with.

However, if one is to provide an adequate picture of the use of descriptive or logical modes of expression in the case of evaluations and choices, one cannot simply stop at language and argumentation patterns that are so *particular*; in that case one might think that the use of descriptive or logical modes of expression in the case of evaluations and choices was a well-delimited and less important phenomenon, and that on the whole our use of language, objectively interpreted, mirrored actually occurring evaluations and choices. – One must go to a higher

---

4 In section II B 7.3.1 (2) above I have given a schematic survey of the relationship between proposition types involved in persuasive definitions.

5 For example, in connection with the word "rett" [law] (or its equivalents in other languages), theories that the law is determined by the idea of law, by custom, by the interests of the ruling class, by social utility, by "das Volk", by the purpose, or the like.

6 Precisely these expressions are not found in the earlier examples. But we do find related forms of expression like "the innermost nerve in the question of the empirical content of legal science" (the first quotation in section II B 7.3.2. item (1)(a)); "the core of law" (the quotation in the same section, item (1)(b)); "real norm" (the first quotation in the same section, item (2)(a)). – See also section III 2.2.2 (3)(a) above, on how operationalisability in terms of sense-experience as a consideration in the case of the formation of concepts has been promoted through persuasive definitions of words like "meaning", "science" and "rationality", combined with absolutisation of the sense-experience aspect.

level of abstraction: to the widespread state of affairs that formulations which objectively interpreted express descriptive propositions, are stuck to by the language user *also* when the language user is confronted with a *conflicting reality*. This state of affairs is found in the case of *otherwise very different* language and argumentation patterns and in very different areas of life.

In his book *A Theory of Cognitive Dissonance* Festinger analyses phenomena that touch on the topic here. Inter alia he deals with the fact that one denies or ignores reality (subgroups of the state of affairs just mentioned in the main text above), which he sees as means to reducing what he terms "cognitive dissonance". – By the expression "cognitive dissonance" Festinger means the tension between an individual's views of reality that arises in a number of common situations: for example when one opts for an action alternative that also has disadvantages ("the car I bought does not have a powerful engine"), in preference to another that also has advantages ("the car I did not buy has a powerful engine") (Chapters 2–3); or when, as a result of the promise of a reward or the threat of punishment, one is led to perform an act that one would not otherwise have performed ("public compliance without private acceptance") (Chapters 4–5); or when one meets information ("smoking is harmful to health") contrary to the views on which one would prefer to base one's actions ("I do not harm myself") (Chapters 6–7); or when people one feels an affinity with ("we are alike") advance other views than one has oneself ("thus we are not alike") (Chapters 8–10). – In relation to such types of situation Festinger formulates a number of general hypotheses about ways in which people proceed in order to avoid cognitive dissonance, inter alia hypotheses about denying or ignoring reality (p. 265): "[E]xposure to new information which tends to increase dissonance will frequently result in misinterpretation and misperception of the new information by the person thus exposed[,] in an effort to avoid a dissonance increase."[7] – In relation to the *topic here* the emphasis is on the *relationship* between the proposition formulation that is stuck to and the denying or ignoring of reality. The latter I see as a possible *indication* that the proposition formulation which is stuck to and which objectively interpreted expresses a descriptive proposition, subjectively interpreted expresses a normative proposition;[8] see the example in the main text in what follows.

In view of the linguistic diversity of this state of affairs, it is difficult and perhaps not so interesting to map its linguistic side; the interesting *unity* that there is, seems more to lie on the *causal level*.[9] – As one, in this perspective random, *example from the linguistic side* I shall look at the *use of dichotomies*.

7 For particular applications of this general viewpoint, see pp. 6, 44–47, 135–36, 149–58, 195–96 cf. 198–200. – Compare also a number of the phenomena that one otherwise, in psychology and everyday life, speaks of as "rationalisation", "repression" or "projection".

8 Another and more unambiguous symptom of the same thing is that one, instead of denying or ignoring reality, actively tries to change it; see section II E 2.2.4 (3) above.

9 See Eng, *U/enighetsanalyse – med særlig sikte på jus og allmenn rettsteori* [analysis of dis/agreement – with particular reference to law and legal theory], section IV 4.

I have earlier discussed dichotomies in connection with criteria that are used in the setting up of and choice between normative definitions: more precisely, in connection with desires for the conceptualisation to be aesthetic (section III 2.2.6 (4)(b) above). In that context I pointed out the use of conceptual dichotomies *also* when one is confronted with a graduated reality, and assumed that the need for aesthetics was one cause.

In the present context (section IV 3) the focus has been shifted to dichotomies qua cause, more precisely qua cause of lack of clarity with respect to what type of proposition one is confronted with: When formulations which build on dichotomies and which objectively interpreted express descriptive propositions, are stuck to in the face of a graduated reality, then this may be an indication that these formulations subjectively interpreted express something else, often a normative characterisation.

For example: When lawyers structure the doctrine of the sources of law along a set of dichotomies that objectively interpreted express descriptive characterisations (see the references in notes 10–12 below), in parallel with their practising graduated transitions in their daily argumentation, then I assume this may be an indication that their sources-of-law formulations subjectively interpreted express normative characterisations: "It is perhaps not so that these dichotomies capture lawyers' argumentation de lege lata as it actually is. But lawyers' argumentation de lege lata ought to be conducted in such a way that it fits in with the dichotomies." For example: It is perhaps not so in lawyers' argumentation as it actually is, that "the wording of the statute counts most",[10] and, as an instantiation of this sentence, that the wording of the statute "takes precedence over the travaux préparatoires and precedent",[11] but it ought to be so.[12]

---

10 Boe, *Innføring i juss* [introduction to law] (1993), Vol. 1, pp. 176, 179; *Innføring i juss* (1996), pp. 184, 195.

11 Peczenik, *Juridikens metodproblem* [the problem of method in law], p. 50.

12 In section III 2.2.6 (4)(b) above I gave a more detailed survey of dichotomies in the doctrine of the sources of law. – After the quotations there I justified why I consider such dichotomies descriptively interpreted as untrue.

3.3. Patterns more specific to lawyers' language and argumentation de lege lata

3.3.1. The pervasive descriptive way of expressing oneself

(1) Overview

In lawyers' language and argumentation de lege lata there is a tension between on the one hand evaluations and choices, and on the other hand descriptive and logical modes of expression. I have earlier given an account of the element of evaluations and choices, and the resulting fused modality (section II F above, in particular section 2.1): a discussion that referred to the *level of meaning*. In what follows (the present section 3.3) I shall take a closer look at the descriptive and logical *modes of expression*.

A pervasive feature of these modes of expression objectively interpreted is that the law, both in general and as the presupposedly one right answer in the individual case, *is found in a double sense*: partly in the sense of 'already existing' and partly in the sense of 'being discovered'; both senses are in contrast to the law applier's having to contribute to creating, evaluating and choosing between several legally justifiable solutions. – With reference to a common way of putting it in Anglo-American literature on lawyers' argumentation one might here speak of "declaratory modes of expression".[13] However, the presentation in what follows will be linked to the terms "descriptive" and "logical" modes of expression, partly since the term "declaratory" is uncommon in many legal systems other than the common law systems, and partly since it is used in rather different ways. Nevertheless, in some connections I shall use the expression "*declaratory view* (of the law)" of the view that the law is found in the above-mentioned double sense.

The *main emphasis* in what follows will be on tendencies towards *descriptive* modes of expression *specific* to lawyers' language and argumentation. – When it

---

13 Eng, 'The Doctrine of Precedent in English and Norwegian Law', in particular sections 2.4.2 and 4.2.

comes to logical modes of expression there are not equally many specifically legal and interesting ones. But on the other hand logical modes of expression in language and argumentation more generally, play an important role in lawyers' language and argumentation. What follows must therefore be seen *together with* the account given in section 2 above: Lawyers weave the systematically polysemous modes of expression of a more general kind which I gave an account of there, tightly together with the more specifically legal modes of expression of which an account will be given in what follows.

Lawyers quite often say that those features of their language and argumentation which have now been outlined and which are to be treated in greater depth in what follows, are "well known". In one practically important sense this is in my view misleading (item (4) below).

(2) Ontological implications specific to lawyers' descriptive modes of expression

Lawyers' descriptive modes of expression presuppose *that* the law *is found*, in the double sense of 'already existing' and 'being discovered' (item (1) above). But these modes of expression are not necessarily bound to a special theory about *where or how* one finds the law (items (a)–(b) in what follows).

(a) In the sources-of-law dimension

Descriptive expression-elements in the sources-of-law dimension (i.e. in the generation of rules de lege lata) will typically be tied to more *time-bound ideologies* concerning the validity of law, such as principles purportedly cognised through specifically practical reason (natural law), customs (the historical school), concepts (the constructive method), social utility (teleological method, Interessenjurisprudenz, etc.), or will (will of the sovereign, will of the Führer, will of the legislator, etc.).

(b) In the subsumption dimension

Descriptive expression-elements in the subsumption dimension (i.e. in the application of the legal rule) are more *timeless*:

In relation to the *propositional content* of the norm one can say of an individual edifice that it is or is not "a building" within the meaning of the legal rules; of an individual act that it is or is not "negligent", "a cause", "a promise" within the meaning of the legal rules; of an individual contract that it has or has not been "entered into", "breached", "terminated" within the meaning of the legal rules; and so forth. – The words may be the same as in everyday life, but the criteria for their use are partly different ones.[14] As a result these modes of expression provide *new angles* on the physical and psychological world of everyday life.

---

14 Brusiin, *Über das juristische Denken*, pp. 182–85. – See in more detail in section II F 3.2.2 (1)(a) above.

The difference from the angle of everyday life stems mainly from the element of evaluations and choices in lawyers' interpretation and subsumption activity; see in more detail in section II F 3.2.2 (1)(a) above. This difference on the *level of meaning* is not in itself an obstacle to fulfilment of central political demands on the legal system: namely that lawyers' subsumptions shall be comprehensible to non-lawyers, so that non-lawyers shall be able to participate in the subsumption activity (cf. lay judges, jury), or at least shall be able to check lawyers' subsumptions (cf. the right of other people than the parties to attend court hearings). The political demands mentioned are perhaps one cause of the fact that the difference on the level of meaning is not greater.[15] – Political demands for comprehensibility, participation and checking have not, however, been able to prevent the coming into being of such descriptive and logical *modes of expression* as are the topic of the present section 3.3, cf. section 2 above, modes of expression that stand in the way of non-lawyers' comprehension of, and thereby participation in and checking of, what lawyers do. The cause is that the demand cluster 'comprehensibility, participation and checking', directs neither the only nor the strongest pressure at lawyers and the legal system.[16]

In relation to the *modality* of the norm one can say that an individual person has or does not have, or that in relation to him there exists or does not exist, for example "a right", "a claim" or "a duty". – Thus the modes of expression create notions of a *new world* of a particular kind of entities. For widespread intuitions do not permit what one speaks of as "a right", "a claim" or "a duty" to be reduced to physical or psychological facts.[17]

(3) Some descriptive modes of expression in use today

(a) In the sources-of-law dimension

In the sources-of-law dimension the descriptive tendency shows itself today particularly in the following ways:

(i) In the first place through expressions to the effect that rules and individual decisions are *determined by others* who are assumed to have *greater legitimacy* as norm-makers than the practising lawyer himself: Concerning obligation in contractual relationships one may for example say that the obligation has or has not been "entered into/ intended/ decided ... by the parties". Or the obligation may be said to follow from the wording of the statute and the travaux préparatoires, in the way the "legislator intended"; or to follow from earlier judgments, in the way the "judgment must be understood"; or from customs, in the way "people have found well founded over a long period of time".

---

15 Aubert/ Messinger, 'The Criminal and the Sick', pp. 157–58.

16 See in more detail, Eng, *U/enighetsanalyse – med særlig sikte på jus og allmenn rettsteori* [analysis of dis/agreement – with particular reference to law and legal theory], section IV 4.

17 Olivecrona, *Law as Fact*, 1st ed. pp. 12–15 (discussed in section II B 3.3.3 (2) above).

(ii) Secondly, the descriptive tendency shows itself through the *area of application of the sources of law being widened out or narrowed down*, under the semblance of necessity:

The *wording of statutes* is said to be applied "by extension", "narrowly", "by analogy", "antithetically" ("argumentum a contrario").

The *travaux préparatoires* of statutes are an important source of law. Yet the concept of 'travaux préparatoires' is vague and in any event covers very different types of statement, which the doctrine of the sources of law affords great freedom to choose between.[18]

In the case of *judicial decisions* it is not necessary to be so technical in the way one speaks as in the case of statutes ("by extension", etc.), since the precedent effect of a judgment is not linked to any particular linguistic formulation, in the way that a rule of statute law is linked to the wording of the statute. Instead one can say that the judgment is or is not "a manifestation of", "a consequence of", "an expression of", etc., the rule one wishes to accept or reject. There is, however, no general agreement among lawyers about how to identify this underlying rule; nor is there any general agreement about the presupposed premiss that every judgment is a manifestation of a general rule.[19] The *area of application* of judicial decisions as a source of law is therefore often *radically indeterminate*.

(iii) In addition to such modes of expression as are specific to the individual source of law, the descriptive tendency in the sources-of-law dimension shows itself also in modes of expression that can be applied in the case of several or all sources of law: Rules and individual decisions *are found, even if* they are not said to stem from particular other norm-makers (item (i) above), or from particular sources of law otherwise (item (ii) above). An important instance-type is *principle terminology*; for example rights and obligations in contractual relationships are said "to follow from" or "to lie in" "principles/ tenets of contract law", or the like (section 3.3.2 below).

(b) In the subsumption dimension; in particular on lawyers' evidential language and argumentation

Among descriptive modes of expression linked to the application of the legal rule, I have previously mentioned such ones as had ontological implications beyond the language of everyday life (item (2)(b) above). I refer to the examples there, which illustrated that these modes of expression are of a more timeless kind, and

---

18 See e.g. *Rt. 1973/433* (the pleasure craft judgment): travaux préparatoires of other provisions in the maritime chapter of the Criminal Justice Act which used the word "skip" [ship]; *Rt. 1975/220* (the housewife judgment): statements from the chairman of the Standing Committee on Justice and the only other member of the Storting who spoke at the meeting of the Odelsting; *Rt. 1979/1079* (the judgment concerning the right of appeal of the insane): proposed, but not yet adopted, new rule with travaux préparatoires.

19 On the first point, see Eng, 'The Doctrine of Precedent in English and Norwegian Law', section 2.4, and further sections V 2.4, 4.1 and 4.2.2, below; on the second point, see Eng, 'The Doctrine of Precedent in English and Norwegian Law', section 2.4.3.3.

that they are central in lawyers' descriptive language and argumentation patterns today too.

In addition comes a set of descriptive modes of expression without ontological implications specific to law: namely *lawyers' evidential language and argumentation*, i.e. language and argumentation directed towards the determination of facts in the individual instance.

Lawyers' evidential language and argumentation may often *appear as* being free from legal regulation, as being regulated only by common sense principles for the determination of facts, possibly with a touch of principles from the probability calculus. However, both when it comes to legal rules in general (item (i) below) and to important instance-types (item (ii) below), it is the case that the descriptive modes of expression are language attire for the lawyer's evaluations and choices.

(i) In the case of *all* legal rules the subsumption will require not only determination of what probability there is of a particular descriptive proposition's being true (assessment of evidence), but also determination of what probability shall be required (burden of proof; section III 3.2.3 (2) above). What probability shall be required is a question of law. Generating rules de lege lata about this requires evaluations and choices, just like the generating of rules de lege lata otherwise.[20]

> As an example for illustration we can take the question of irrelevant considerations as a ground of invalidity in administrative law. Going through the sources of law and concluding that the public administrative authorities' exercise of discretion may be held invalid on the ground of the public administrative authorities' taking irrelevant considerations into account, answers only some of the questions of law that arise. Other questions are *what* probability shall be required, first, for saying that irrelevant considerations *were taken into account*, and secondly, for saying that any irrelevant consideration there might be *did affect* the content of the administrative decision. The latter question may be raised partly in relation to collegiate bodies and partly in relation to the individual civil servant.
>
> I do not know of any judgment in which the Norwegian Supreme Court has said that it finds it proven *that* a civil servant did take an irrelevant consideration into account, but that the administrative decision *nevertheless* stands because the irrelevant consideration did not affect the content of the decision. Whether one should ask about effect at all in relation to the individual civil servant, and what standard of probability with respect to effect should in that case be applied, I consider to be an undetermined point in Norwegian law today. – Several considerations may *support* not asking about effect, or *support* placing a fairly strict burden of proof with respect to effect, on the public administrative authorities: Partly one may consider it worse

---

[20] Eckhoff, 'Noen ord om bevisbyrde og bevisbyrdeteorier' [some words on the burden of proof and theories of the burden of proof], p. 310: "[T]he considerations that ought to determine whether one of the parties, and if so which of them, shall bear the risk of doubt about a fact, [are] to a great extent of the same type as those considerations that form the basis of the material rules. And they are just as diverse as these"; cf. same writer, *Tvilsrisikoen* [the bearing of the risk of doubt], pp. 63, cf. 55 et seq.

to make a mistake to the disadvantage of the private individual than to the disadvantage of the public administrative authorities; partly, with a view to deterrence, one may wish to stress that irrelevant considerations cannot be tolerated; partly, with a view to preserving the private party's and the public's confidence in the public administrative authorities and the legal system, one may wish to avoid having to say: "irrelevant considerations *were* taken into account, *but* ..."; and partly one may in certain cases consider that the public administrative authorities are the more obvious party for the securing of evidence that irrelevant considerations were not taken into account. – I do not put forward any standpoint on what ought to be the rule, but use this example *as an illustration of*, first, the fact that questions of which party shall bear the burden of proof and of the appropriate standard of proof, are omnipresent; secondly, that the rules relating to these questions are often unwritten and indeterminate; and thirdly, that generating rules relating to these questions demands evaluations and choices systematically throughout.

Modes of expression such as "... is proven/ is not proven" are consequently descriptive language attire for evaluations and choices. This language attire can cover everything *from* the case in which the lawyer deems it sufficient to have a thirty per cent probability that an irrelevant consideration affected the decision made by the civil servant, so that the irrelevant consideration constitutes a ground of invalidity, *to* the case in which the lawyer does not deem it sufficient to have seventy per cent probability that the accused committed an act that constitutes murder.[21]

(ii) In the case of legal rules with *intention as a legally operative fact*, evaluations and choices are also clothed in the descriptive language attire of assessment of evidence. – An illustrative instance-type is lawyers' discussions of the question of dispositivity in respect of contracts. I refer to my earlier account of the main structure of these discussions (section 2.2 (6)(b) above).

The emphasis in this earlier account was on the fact that the language and argumentation structure in lawyers' discussions of intention makes possible an ambiguity between, on the one hand, use of the typically relevant arguments as evidential facts in relation to dispositive intent (assessment-of-evidence argumentation), and on the other hand, use of these arguments as dispositivity criteria in their own right (criteria argumentation), that is to say, an ambiguity between descriptive and normative propositions.

In the light of what has just been said about standards of probability (item (i) above), my earlier account may be supplemented: The language and argumentation structure in lawyers' discussions of intention makes possible not only a fundamental ambiguity between assessment-of-evidence argumentation and criteria argumentation, but also an ambiguity between two forms of criteria argumentation: In addition to the fact that the typically relevant

21 The percentages indicated are *metaphors* (for the range of realities that is covered by evidence terminology); an intersubjectively testable stating of figures is not possible within the framework of lawyers' evidential language and argumentation.

> arguments in the question of dispositivity are used as evidential facts in relation to dispositive intent (assessment-of-evidence argumentation) or as dispositivity criteria independently of intention (first form of criteria argumentation), these arguments are also used as criteria for what standard of probability shall be required with respect to intention (second form of criteria argumentation). For example, the form of the alleged contract, oral or written, is used not only as an evidential fact in relation to the parties' dispositive intent or as a criterion directly in relation to the question of dispositivity, but also as a criterion in relation to the question of what standard of probability shall be required with respect to the parties' dispositive intent. The judge assumes, for example, that the easier it is to get legal acceptance for an oral contract relating to real property, the less solemnly potentially contracting parties may take the forms, and the greater the number of disputes that may arise about whether a contract came into being. Given a desire to reduce the number of disputes, orality thus becomes an argument for sharpening the standard of probability to be required with respect to dispositive intent.[22]

In relation to the *present topic*, the use of more *one-sidedly* descriptive or logical modes of expression in the case of evaluations and choices, the emphasis is on the fact that in actually occurring grounds for judgment in the question of dispositivity, there is a clear tendency in the direction of evidential language and argumentation, and within this again, in the direction of advancing the typically relevant arguments as *evidential facts* (assessment-of-evidence argumentation), that is to say, in the direction of the most purely *descriptive* language and argumentation structure, the structure in which the lawyer's evaluations and choices are most consistently and effectively kept out of the linguistic expression. – The advancing of the arguments as evidential facts, combined with the tendency to conceal evaluations and choices in burden-of-proof questions (item (i) above), makes possible such forms of expression as: "Taking into account the form and content of the parties' statements, and the parties' subsequent behaviour, the court finds it proven/ does not find it proven that the parties intended to bind themselves."

By way of illustration I shall quote some central passages from the Supreme Court judgment in *Rt. 1985/1265*. This judgment is representative of the Supreme Court's language and argumentation patterns, inter alia in that the judgment uses a large part of the register offered by evidential language and argumentation. (All italics are mine, added for the purpose of emphasising the evidential language and argumentation patterns. The quotation is from the first opinion delivered; the other judges delivered concurring opinions. Instead of the parties' names I have used "B" for the alleged buyer and "S" for the alleged seller. B claimed to have purchased the property on which he had been living as a tenant for many years.):

---

22 The place of this third mode of use in relation to the other two may be indicated schematically by the replacement in the first figure in section 2.2 (6)(b) above of the formulation "use of the typically relevant arguments of a non-intentional kind as evidential facts in relation to dispositive intent" by the formulation "use of the typically relevant arguments of a non-intentional kind as criteria for the standard of evidence in relation to dispositive intent".

"The question in this case is whether there is an oral contract between [B] and [S]. Very strong *evidence* must be demanded for the Court to recognise a claim that a binding oral contract in respect of real property has come into being. ... I cannot see that [B] has to a sufficient degree satisfied the *strict standard of evidence* that applies here.

The alleged contract is said to have been entered into by [B]'s offering [S] 1.7 million kroner, with a deduction of 200,000 kroner for any money spent on maintenance and any rise in the value of the property arising from this, and by [S]'s replying "OK" to this. That such a large and valuable property as we are here concerned with should have been sold in such an informal manner, has in a high degree the *presumption against it*. In addition to this comes the fact that [B] cannot situate the formation of the contract in time more accurately than stating that it probably took place some time in the period between 8 and 10 May 1982. On [B]'s part it is ... admitted that the information that has been presented about the parties' statements in this period is not sufficient to *establish* that any contract had come into being, and that the necessary *evidence* must be sought in the subsequent circumstances.

However, I cannot on the basis of the subsequent circumstances that have been invoked, with a sufficient *degree of certainty draw the conclusion* that [S] should have bound himself to transferring title to the property to [B]. The circumstances invoked do not provide *such a clear and unambiguous picture as must be demanded* if such an obligation is to be recognised without having been expressed in writing. The *evidential factors* that [B] has adduced are essentially connected with his own *view of the matter* and how this view was expressed to others, while there is no corresponding information that [S] *saw the matter* in the same manner. ...

I also place significant weight on the fact that the parties had not discussed other central questions than the price, and that this must be seen as an *indication that* the parties had not yet bound themselves definitively. It is indeed so that I can to some extent agree with [B] that the circumstances were such that there was not the same need as otherwise for more comprehensive contractual regulation. I am here thinking in particular of the fact that [B] as tenant from 1964 was very familiar with the property and already owned livestock and equipment. In this connection it may also be mentioned that on account of [S]'s difficult financial situation it was a matter of urgency to get the farm sold, and that in such situations *it is possible* that the parties might not provide for such comprehensive contractual regulation as would otherwise be natural. Even when these circumstances are taken into account, I find it nevertheless *rather improbable* that the parties should have bound themselves after having reached agreement only on the price."[23]

In section 2.2 (6)(b) above I quoted by way of conclusion a little from *Rt. 1883/597*. Between that judgment and the one that has just been quoted here, there is a span of approximately 100 years. When it comes to dispositive intent and evidential language and argumentation in connection with this, I have not

[23] *Rt. 1985/1265* on p. 1269.

been able to trace any significant differences over time in the cases reported during this period. Inter alia I have not been able to find any evidence in the Supreme Court judgments to show that the legal criteria in the question of dispositivity in respect of contracts have undergone or are undergoing any development in the direction of becoming more "social", "societal", "realistic", or the like. The above-mentioned fundamental ambiguity in the language and argumentation structure in the question of dispositivity (between assessment-of-evidence argumentation and criteria argumentation), and the tendency in the direction of evidential language and argumentation, and within this again, in the direction of assessment-of-evidence argumentation, are *constant features* of the case material throughout this period.

> In *its* area this material consequently does not provide evidence for general cycle-theories corresponding to Llewellyn's, of alternation between "grand style" and "formal style" in the decisions of American courts,[24] or to Atiyah's, of alternation between "realism" and "formalism" in English court practice.[25] Nor does the material provide evidence for propositions limited to the law of contract, that in the interpretation of contracts the courts attach increasing weight to "the interests of society",[26] or that they have gone from "subjective interpretation" to "objective interpretation".[27]

(4) The "well known"

Many lawyers will probably say that a number of the features of lawyers' language and argumentation of which an account has now been given, represent *"well known"* facts.[28]

This is correct in the sense that a number of *writers have pointed out* that the descriptive modes of expression to a high degree represent a fiction.[29] – In the

---

[24] Llewellyn, *The Common Law Tradition*, pp. 35–45.

[25] Atiyah, *The Rise and Fall of Freedom of Contract*, pp. 660–66.

[26] Huser, *Avtaletolking* [interpretation of contracts], p. 337 at and in note 810.

[27] Compare section II B 7.2 (2) above, from after the indent and up to and including note 10.

[28] I build here in the first place on explicit statements about the "well known" in the works of central writers, see e.g. Andenæs, 'Rettsteori og rettspraksis' [jurisprudence and court practice], p. 411; Gaarder, 'Domstolene og den alminnelige rettsutvikling' [the courts and the evolution of the law], p. 225; Eckhoff, *Rettskildelære* [doctrine of the sources of law], p. 177; Brusiin, *Über das juristische Denken*, p. 201; Cross/ Harris, *Precedent in English Law*, p. 26 (cf. pp. 27–34); Simpson, 'Innovation in Nineteenth Century Contract Law', p. 247; Atiyah, *Pragmatism and Theory in English Law*, pp. 154, 160; Esser, *Vorverständnis und Methodenwahl in der Rechtsfindung*, p. 62. Secondly, I build on the fact that many lawyers today are familiar with the works mentioned in the next note (or works with corresponding content).

[29] Two approaches in the literature are central in this connection. For one thing there are the American realists' analyses and criticism of the court-based language and argumentation tradition which forms common law; on this approach, see Eckhoff, *Rettsvesen og rettsvitenskap i U.S.A* [legal practice and jurisprudence in the U.S.A], Chapter 3, in particular §§ 10 III, 11–13 and 15; Twining, *Karl Llewellyn and the Realist Movement*; Duxbury, *Patterns of American Jurisprudence*, in particular pp. 65–159. For another thing there are various writers' analyses and criticism of theories of will as a basis for law; see from Nordic literature, in particular Hägerström, *Till frågan om den objektiva*

light of this, the term "mode of expression" (polysemous, descriptive, logical) is more apt than "theory": Many lawyers might in a moment of self-reflection agree that lawyers' language and argumentation does not provide an adequate picture of how standpoints on what the law is, are actually generated in the courts, in public administration, in negotiations, etc.[30]

However, in propositions about the "well known" there often lies also the implication that the *individual lawyer can choose* to what extent he will make use of the descriptive elements, in contradistinction to expressing himself openly with respect to the choices and decisions between a number of possible solutions that must often be made. And further, as an extension of this, there is the implication that the fictive features of the pervasive descriptive modes of expression *are not particularly interesting*: For what lawyers may at any time opt out of cannot of course be bound to features peculiar to lawyers and their practice, and will therefore not be something that calls for explanation when one is specifically seeking to understand lawyers and their practice.

I consider these implications to be wrong:

(a) They *underestimate* the often compelling force of the considerations, structures and functions that trigger the use of descriptive *modes of expression*:[31] In particular they underestimate the force of the need of the individual person applying the law to disclaim responsibility;[32] the force of the need of the legal system, in particular of the courts, for confidence ("legitimacy");[33] and the force of the norms and sanctions concerning how one shall word what one says, that meet the individual lawyer.[34] – The effect of these causal factors is, I submit, that the individual lawyer is *forced* to use the descriptive modes of expression, even if he has intellectually cognised the fictive features of these modes.[35]

---

rättens begrepp. I. Viljeteorien [on the question of the concept of 'law'. I. theory of will]. – Both the approaches mentioned inspired the presentation given in Ross, *On Law and Justice*, Chapter 3 (The sources of law) and Chapter 4 (The judicial method (interpretation)). Ross' presentation had a great influence, inter alia on Eckhoff, *Rettskildelære* [doctrine of the sources of law], which in more general terms points out how lawyers' forms of expression make it possible for the evaluations and choices made by the person applying the law to be concealed (see in particular 1st ed. pp. 317–20). Since the publication of the first edition in 1971, Eckhoff's book has been a textbook for students of law (compare the final sentence of the preceding note).

30 However, the reason that I use "mode of expression" in preference to "theory" is not this one, but quite simply that the topic of the present Chapter IV is in the main our language and argumentation patterns, not our views; see section 1 above, as well as the topic specification in the headings of sections 2–3.

31 On these considerations, structures and functions, see Eng, *U/enighetsanalyse – med særlig sikte på jus og allmenn rettsteori* [analysis of dis/agreement – with particular reference to law and legal theory], section IV 4.

32 Op. cit., section IV 4.2.

33 Op. cit., section IV 4.3.

34 Op. cit., section IV 4.5 (2).

35 It is not certain that those who speak of the "well known" (see note 28 above) would disagree with what has now been said. They did not perhaps intend to express any views on the individual lawyer's freedom of choice in practice, only on the intellectual cognition. But in that case, what has been said

(b) Secondly, I assume that there is a *self-reinforcing reciprocal action* between, on the one hand, lawyers' polysemous, or one-sidedly descriptive or logical modes of expression, and on the other hand, a declaratory view of the law:

The polysemous, or one-sidedly descriptive or logical *modes of expression* confront the individual as *tradition*.[36] – This wording tradition makes it *more difficult* for the individual to have a *conceptually worked out*, stable and adequate notion of evaluations and choices; and this tradition thereby makes it *more difficult* for the individual to *formulate* the corresponding value and decision propositions, and to keep them separate from the tradition's polysemous, or one-sidedly descriptive or logical modes of expression. The wording tradition thereby contributes to establishing and reinforcing the declaratory view of the law in the individual who becomes a lawyer. – This more or less conscious view of the law contributes for its part to maintaining and further developing the use of polysemous, or one-sidedly descriptive or logical modes of expression.

(c) Further, since language is the lawyer's tool of the trade, the reciprocal action just outlined has a *potentially* strong effect. To what extent this reciprocal action *is actualised* on the part of the individual lawyer depends inter alia on personality features, such as the individual's ability and will to engage in critical reflection on his own activity, and on social factors, such as the individual's professional experience.

Here there are many forms and degrees. Generally, however, it is the case that even though this reciprocal action can in different forms and degrees drive evaluations and choices out of what is conceptually worked out, it does not remove others' expectations of and the lawyer's own wish for outcomes that are reasonable and just in a non-declaratory sense (section II F 2.1 (2) above). As a result of this the lawyer's relationship to evaluations and choices may assume *ambivalent features*: on the one hand, others' expectations of and the lawyer's own wish for outcomes that are reasonable and just in a sense that is not reduced to 'conforming with the meaning intended by the legislator', 'conforming with earlier practice', or the like, and on the other hand, a language and argumentation tradition which in different forms and degrees promotes a declaratory view of the law; on the one hand, risking oneself as a person in making value choices, and on the other hand, disclaiming responsibility through the mode of language and argumentation. – This ambivalence inheres in the lawyer's situation as a lawyer, and will thus tend to be more static and lasting than ambivalence inherent in transitional phases, such as from child to adult.

(a)↔(c) Lawyers' intellectual cognition of the fictive features of their modes of expression will in the light of this often have *limited psychological reality* in their everyday thinking.

---

here, and is treated in greater depth in the places referred to in notes 31–34 above, is an important supplement to the statements about the "well known".

36 Eng, *U/enighetsanalyse – med særlig sikte på jus og allmenn rettsteori* [analysis of dis/agreement – with particular reference to law and legal theory], section IV 4.5.

3.3.2. *On principle terminology in particular*

(1) Introduction

By *"principle terminology"* and *"principle thinking"* I mean respectively the terminology aspect and the meaning aspect of argumentation, in so far as the argumentation directly uses the word "principle", or in so far as the argumentation uses other linguistic entities, given that the linguistic entity concerned is often used in the same way as the word "principle", for example linguistic entities like "general legal tenets/ rules", "non-statutory rules/ doctrine", "legal maxims", or the like.

> Terminology is diverse. For example, one uses in the same discussion in the law of torts, social security law and insurance law, linguistic entities like "hovedårsaks*lære*" [substantial-factor *doctrine*], "betingelses*teori*" [condition *theory*], and "fordelings*prinsipp*" [distributive *principle*];[37] and in the same discussion in civil procedure, linguistic entities like *"grunn-"* [*basic*], *"grunnleggende"* [*fundamental*], *"hoved-"* [*main*], *"sentrale"* [*central*] and *"allmenne"* [*general*] principles.[38]

All according to the area of application which court practice gives a principle, we can distinguish between the following *main types* of principle terminology:

In some instances court practice makes only *unspecified* references to "unwritten/ general legal principles",[39] "general legal tenets/ rules".[40]

In so far as the area of application of a principle *is delimited*, three methods in particular are used: First, specification in terms of content, of a *particularly weighty consideration* that makes itself felt in a number of areas of law: for example "general considerations for the protection of privacy".[41] Secondly, specification of an *area* within traditional legal systematics (an area which may be more or less abstract/ concrete, wide/ narrow and in/determinate). This specification of area may be the only delimitation criterion: for example "the principles on which our administration of justice builds",[42] "general principles for the assessment of evidence",[43] "general principles for the administration of estates",[44] "general legal principles that lie at the base of our administration of criminal

---

37 Kjønstad, *Folketrygdens uførepensjon* [the national insurance disability pension], pp. 42–44.

38 Hov, *Rettergang i sivile saker* [legal procedure in civil cases], pp. 61–62.

39 *Rt. 1961/1350* (the first dentist judgment) on p. 1351; *Rt. 1983/1004* (the Børre Knudsen judgment) on pp. 1017–18.

40 *Rt. 1923-II/58* (the Irma-Mignon judgment) on p. 60; *Rt. 1973/1153* (the botulism judgment) on p. 1157; *Rt. 1977/1035* (the medical records judgment) on p. 1048; *Rt.1980/243* on p. 258.

41 *Rt. 1952/1217* on pp. 1219 et seq. (the judgment relating to the film To mistenkelige personer [two suspicious persons]; prohibition against exhibition of the film); *Rt. 1991/616* on p. 623, *1992/904* on p. 906 and *1996/1114* on pp. 1121–22 (judgments relating to exclusion of evidence in criminal cases).

42 *Rt. 1996/1315* on p. 1316.

43 *Rt. 1997/343* on p. 364.

44 *Rt. 1992/544* on p. 546.

justice",[45] "general rules in the law of contract",[46] "general principles in labour law".[47] Or the specification of area may be combined with the first-mentioned delimitation according to the content of the principle: for example "non-statutory rules concerning good faith and fair dealing in contractual relationships",[48] "a general and non-statutory duty of loyalty and fidelity in employment relationships".[49] A third delimitation method consists in bringing in a *statutory provision* in which the principle is considered to have found expression: for example "the principle in section 5 of the Sale of Goods Act",[50] "the principle in section 39 of the Contracts Act",[51] "the principle in section 41 of the Public Administration Act".[52]

In what follows I shall demonstrate *two sets of meaning aspects* of principle terminology: first, positive law aspects which tend to be advanced when lawyers reflect on principle terminology (item (2) below); secondly, natural law aspects in normal language usage among lawyers (item (3) below).

The *unity* between the two sets of meaning aspects lies in the fact that *each in its own way* provides lawyers with possibilities of formulating justifications and standpoints de lege lata *without* giving an account of the evaluations and choices that are a component in such propositions (item (4) below).

> The desire to bring into focus this unity justifies my definitions of the concepts of 'principle terminology' and 'principle thinking' (cf. first paragraph of the present item (1) for these definitions), and the joint treatment in what follows of the otherwise diverse language and argumentation phenomena that these concepts cover (cf. the examples above for illustration of the diversity). This justification also sets limits: It lies outside the present topic to adopt any standpoint on concepts of 'principle' formed with other purposes in mind.[53]

(2) Positive law aspects

Around the turn of the last century the view that principles are *simply summaries* of positively existing legal material and do not have any independent law-producing capacity, was advanced by both proponents and opponents of what was called "den konstruktive metode" [the constructive method]: The proponents put forward this view as a defence against what they perceived to be unreasonable

45 *Rt. 1984/1076* on p. 1079.

46 *Rt. 1993/954* on p. 958.

47 *Rt. 1964/1345* on p. 1346.

48 *Rt. 1984/28* on p. 34.

49 *Rt. 1990/607* on p. 614.

50 *Rt. 1923-II/329* on p. 332; *1973/1165* on p. 1175; *1978/702* on p. 708.

51 *Rt. 1963/917* on p. 921; *1983/281* on p. 284.

52 *Rt. 1990/1001* on pp. 1006–07.

53 For example a concept of 'principle' formed as an element in a theory of the system character of law, see Canaris, *Systemdenken und Systembegriff in der Jurisprudenz*, pp. 46 et seq.; or as an element in a theory of basic rights, see Alexy, *Theorie der Grundrechte*, pp. 71 et seq.; or as an element in a theory that judges enforce existing rights, see Dworkin, 'Hard Cases', pp. 82 et seq.

accusations of Begriffsjurisprudenz.[54] And the opponents put forward this view as an argument for a new way of thinking.[55] – After a relatively short time the view was advanced as apparently completely uncontroversial.[56]

As illustration of these discussions I shall quote some of Hagerup's statements:

"[T]he construction is always only a summary of individual provisions; it is not in itself a source of new provisions, which therefore have to be derived either from existing positive law or from the particular nature of the questions confronted."[57]

"... Ihering himself has ... ascribed to legal construction an exaggerated significance ... in that he actually ascribes to it a law-producing capacity. The construction can never do more than help us towards clearer insight into the legal material, insight that better equips us for the practical application of the law; and it is a methodological error ... to build a legal rule exclusively on constructive grounds, for example, to construct mortgages and other security interests as accessory security rights for claims, and to conclude therefrom that the security right ceases to apply in the event of time-barring, etc., of the claim ... The sentences that appear here as conclusions, do not follow from the construction but must be independently proven; and whether they are right will precisely be a test of the construction."[58]

"The second error, to which the constructive method has been subject, is to ascribe law-producing force to the purely formal concept deductions. This is in reality ... only the error of natural law in a new version. The concepts as such, just like economic and ethical principles or absolute categories of reason, do not possess any signifcance as a source of law outside and above the law."[59]

Today this view of principles as only summary is advanced as an apparently matter-of-course methodological point in Nordic literature.

In recent Swedish literature the doctrine of assumptions has been thoroughly discussed by Lehrberg.[60] Writing on the foundation and status of the doc-

---

54 Hagerup, 'Nogle Ord om den nyere Retsvidenskabs Karakter' [some words on the character of recent legal science], pp. 27–37, in particular p. 33; 'Ihering – Windscheid', in particular pp. 14–15; 'Nogle Ord om Forholdet mellem positiv Ret og Retsanvendelse' [some words on the relationship between positive law and application of the law], pp. 64–67.

55 Hyllested, '"Individualismen"' ["individualism"], in particular pp. 211–20; Bentzon, *Skøn og regel* [discretion and rule], p. 70.

56 Castberg, 'Den konstruktive metode' [the constructive method], in particular pp. 294–303; Lassen, 'Anmeldelse av Ö. Undén, Om panträtt i rättigheter' [review of Ö. Undén, on security interests in rights], pp. 415–17; 'Nogle Bemærkninger om Definitioner i Retsliteraturen' [some remarks on definitions in legal literature], pp. 67–68.

57 Hagerup, 'Nogle Ord om Forholdet mellem positiv Ret og Retsanvendelse' [some words on the relationship between positive law and application of the law], p. 67 in note 2.

58 Hagerup, 'Ihering – Windscheid', pp. 14–15 (Hagerup's italics and footnote omitted).

59 Hagerup, 'Nogle Ord om den nyere Retsvidenskabs Karakter' [some words on the character of recent legal science], p. 33.

60 Lehrberg, *Förutsättningsläran* [the doctrine of assumptions]; 'Förutsättningssynpunkter på köprät-

trine of assumptions, he says: "The prevailing view – to which I in principle subscribe – is ... that *the general doctrine of assumptions must not encroach upon the areas of application of the particular assumptions rules*. For example, the doctrine of assumptions cannot be applied instead of the defective goods provisions of the Sale of Goods Act" (my italics).[61]

In recent Norwegian literature Selvig writes in a general introduction to the doctrine of the sources of law in contract law: "In court practice one often sees that the court, instead of forming a rule specific for the type of contract in question, justifies its conclusion by saying that it "follows" from general rules in the law of contract. Such "general rules in the law of contract" are, however, *not normal legal rules, but formulations summarising* rules or legislative views that have *already* been recognised in most – or at any rate in many – important areas of the law of contract" (my italics; Selvig's italics omitted).[62]

(3) "Natural law" aspects[63]

(a) Generality
(b) "Law-producing capacity"
(c) The lack of authorised linguistic formulations
(d) Goodness
(e) Indeterminacy and evaluation prescription

(a) Generality

Principles will typically have a *high degree* of generality, see the examples in the introduction (item (1) above).

(b) "Law-producing capacity"

At the same time as lawyers deny the "law-producing capacity" of principles (item (2) above), they do seem, however, unwilling to abandon completely the notion of principles as *something more* than pure summaries, as having a *specific argument value*. And this often applies also to those writers who explicitly advance the view of principles as summaries. – On what basis and in what way principles are something more than pure summaries, remains unclear, however.

The following quotations may illustrate both things: partly how principles are intimated as being something more than pure summaries, and partly the unclear basis for and content of this "something more":

---

tens felbegrepp' [the concept of 'defective goods' in sale of goods law from the perspective of the doctrine of assumptions].

61 Lehrberg, 'Förutsättningssynpunkter på köprättens felbegrepp' [the concept of 'defective goods' in sale of goods law from the perspective of the doctrine of assumptions], p. 547.

62 Selvig, *Kontraktsretten* [the law of contract], p. 575; correspondingly p. 316.

63 In the heading in the text at the present note and in what follows, the term "natural law" is used as a shorthand form: positively, for those aspects of which I shall give an account in the present item (3); negatively, for a contrast to the view that principles are only summaries of positively existing legal material, see item (2) above on this view. – The quotation marks in the heading signal distance from more determinate philosophical connotations.

> "In my interpretation of the doctrine of assumptions, this derives its content ... from the particular assumptions rules, including the *provisions relating to defective goods*. For the doctrine of assumptions represents an attempt to summarise the *basic tenets of general scope that have found expression in the said particular rules*" (my italics).[64]
>
> "Such a summary [of rules or legal principles that are already recognised] may also help to resolve legal questions that have hitherto not received any clear answer in legislation or court practice. For what is the usual rule in most or the most important areas can *serve as a good guide* when, for another type of contract, there turns out to be a lack of clear rules for the resolution of the corresponding question. However, general contract law rules of this kind easily lose their significance if the distinctive nature of the contractual relationship or other circumstances mean that another rule or solution will be better suited there. ... The force of a general rule of contract law is therefore not always so great" (my italics).[65]
>
> "General rules in the law of contract have quite considerable significance for the development of the body of rules in contract law. Such general rules will have *considerable force in practice* and will be *followed by the courts* unless there are particular reasons for applying another set of rules. The consideration for consistency and harmony *suggests this*" (my italics).[66]

The *lack of clarity* concerning the argument value of principles lies on two levels:

First, does one claim that principles *ought to have* an independent argument value; that principles *do in fact have* an independent argument value for the courts; or that the courts *word what they say as if* the arguments have an independent argument value?

Secondly, given that principles are thought of as having an independent argument value, it is unclear what is the *basis* for claiming this. For in the point of departure with principles as pure summaries there lies by definition the view that they do *not* have any independent argument value. – Even a reference to consistency and harmony (see for example the final quotation in the indent above) goes *beyond* a view of principles as pure summary. For the concept of 'principle' laid down as pure summary lets it precisely remain open whether an instance that is not part of the summary is so similar in legal terms that it ought to be resolved in the same manner. – And in any case the consideration for consistency and harmony cannot provide a fully satisfactory explanation for lawyers' use of principle terminology. For by reserving this terminology for norms that are assumed to have a certain goodness in terms of content (item (d) below), lawyers demonstrate in their language and argumentation practice that they ascribe argument weight to

---

64 Lehrberg, 'Förutsättningssynpunkter på köprättens felbegrepp' [the concept of 'defective goods' in sale of goods law from the perspective of the doctrine of assumptions], p. 547.

65 Selvig, *Kontraktsretten* [law of contract], p. 316; correspondingly p. 575.

66 Op. cit., p. 575. Correspondingly Hov, *Avtalerett* [law of contract], p. 73 (on "basic principles for interpreting contracts"); *Rettergang i sivile saker* [legal procedure in civil cases], p. 62 (on "basic principles in civil procedure").

principles *also beyond* that which lies in the consideration for consistency and harmony.

The outlined lack of clarity in the *literature* reflects an ambivalence in the use of principle terminology in *concrete legal argumentation*: This terminology is used partly of pure summaries of norms. And this terminology is used partly with a "law-producing capacity", relative to the actually existing sources of law; principles are thought of not only as regulating those matters that fall under different *linguistic formulations* of the principle, but also as having an existence and sources-of-law force *beyond* these formulations.

(c) The lack of authorised linguistic formulations

The last sentence of the preceding item (b) leads over to a third meaning aspect, namely the lack of authorised linguistic formulations. The linguistic formulations of principles are not thought of as constitutive of the sources-of-law force, but more as imperfect attempts to capture the principle. According to this thinking, principles cannot be captured in any definitive linguistic formulation.

Judicial decisions as a source of law is an area in which this aspect of principle terminology is central:[67] Legal literature and practice take as their point of departure that a judgment is not a precedent for the linguistic formulations *in* the judgment, but that it is, on the other hand, a precedent for "the principle" which the judgment is *"a manifestation of", "a consequence of", "an expression of"*, or the like. – It is not unusual for the same judicial opinion to contain different linguistic formulations of the rule the judge claims to be applying, nor is it unusual for these formulations to lead to conclusions which in practice are not the same. The more such features mark an opinion and a judgment, the less the weight accorded to the text of the judgment, and the greater the weight accorded to the assumedly "underlying" principle.

In the case of *statutes* the *doctrinal starting point* is a different one. Both legal literature, and the courts in their more general statements, emphasise that the wording of the statute in itself has authority: The wording of the statute is not only presumptive evidence of, but is constitutive of what the law is. – In *actually occurring legal argumentation* there is, however, no significant difference; the courts treat the wording of statutes along the same main lines as the wording of earlier judgments:

First, the weight of the wording of the statute too is graduated: according to vagueness, polysemy, incompleteness, conflict with the wording of other statutes, etc.

Secondly, the courts have developed argumentation techniques whereby the wording of statutes too can be given the character of presumptive evidence, and correspondingly lose its independent authority. One such technique is to operate with the intention of the legislator as being what is legally constitutive, so that the wording of the statute simply becomes a piece of evidence in relation to this

67 Eng, 'The Doctrine of Precedent in English and Norwegian Law', section 2.3.

intent. Another such technique is principle terminology. Measured against an underlying principle, not only the courts' formulations, but also the wording of statutes, appear with a touch of fallibility and arbitrariness. This finds expression here too in the terminology according to which individual statutory provisions are "manifestations of", "consequences of", etc., a principle; or, as another way of expressing the same thought, the terminology according to which the principle is "embodied in", has "come to expression in", etc., a statutory provision.

Statutory provisions too can no doubt be very general, but it is not usual to speak of a principle as long as one simply keeps to the meaning content it is reasonable to say lies in the wording of the statute. The explanation for this terminology I take to lie in the said imagined existence and legal force of principles, beyond assumedly arbitrary linguistic formulations. – It is then consistent that where a rule of statute law is assumed to be applicable by analogy, so that one goes outside the rule that it is reasonable to say follows from the wording, then there is immediately room for speaking of a "principle".

(d) Goodness

A further meaning aspect of principle terminology is the goodness of principles. This aspect is different from the law-producing capacity mentioned in item (b) above. Now it is a matter of the quality of the *content* of the principle:

A rule is often termed "bad", "inexpedient", "unjust", or the like. A principle *as argument de lege lata* is seldom spoken of in such a manner; in de lege lata contexts, principle terminology is on the whole used only of those norms one considers good in terms of content. – Another matter is the fact that principles can pull in different directions, so that one must weigh them against one another in order to be able to make a concrete decision: for example, a principle of freedom of speech against a principle of the protection of privacy. – And principles that are not put forward as arguments de lege lata, for example principles in other legal systems or historically abandoned principles, are criticised in the same language as rules: for example the "inquisitorial principle".

The relationship in lawyers' thinking de lege lata between principles and other norms varies with the basis of the other norms. The assumed goodness as an aspect of principles de lege lata distinguishes principles from rules of statute law, but provides a certain *community with rules of customary law*:

In lawyers' language and argumentation the property of being good in terms of content is only to a small extent laid down as a criterion in the concept of 'statute'. This concept covers norms laid down by the Storting or in pursuance of delegation of authority by the Storting, and is thus formal. Certain constraints do no doubt lie in the Constitution and international law, but these constraints are indeterminate and the application of these constraints is to a particularly high degree determined by time and situation.

The situation is different when it comes to rules of customary law. Here lawyers seldom speak of the rule's being "bad", "inexpedient", "unjust", or the like.

A rule of customary law will, through legal methodology's criteria for customary law,[68] virtually by definition have a number of positively loaded politico-ideological properties: A rule of customary law will thus typically be considered to be good in terms of content, cf. the fact that the rule's quality in terms of content is a criterion of customary law. Further, a rule of customary law will typically be considered to have been democratically "adopted", in the sense that the number and representativity of affected persons who follow the rule is a criterion of customary law. Finally, a rule of customary law will typically be considered to have been well tested with respect to practical usability in life outside the courts, cf. the fact that the duration and frequency of the affected persons' rule-following are criteria of customary law.

In their aspect of assumed goodness, principles de lege lata are thus kindred to customary-law thinking, and somewhat contradictory to lawyers' thinking on statute law.

The joint aspect of goodness that has now been outlined opens the way for the *verbal claim, and possibly also the belief, that there is a factual connection*: What lawyers call "principles" will sometimes be suggested as having or presupposed to have a basis in custom. – A certain factual basis for this lies in the fact that principles are in some instances formed in interplay between court practice and legal literature, and, as the case may be, also in interplay with the practice of the highest state bodies, of the public administrative authorities, or of private individuals. *In so far as* this is the case, the goodness aspect of principle thinking might gain support from the above-mentioned positively loaded properties of customary law. – In many instances it is, however, clear that there is *not* any practice that can defend pointing to custom as a basis for principle thinking; see for example Rt. 1977/1035 (the medical records judgment), with its reference to "general legal tenets", where it was clear that any practice there might be went rather in the opposite direction to the conclusion of the judgment (pp. 1040, 1047–48). So in many instances the goodness aspect of principle thinking must have other sources than the above-mentioned positively loaded properties of customary law.

(e) Indeterminacy and evaluation prescription

Among other meaning aspects of principle terminology that should be mentioned are the indeterminacy of principles, and their prescribing evaluations. These properties are closely connected with two of the properties mentioned earlier: respectively the absence of an authorised linguistic formulation (item (c) above) and the emphasis on goodness in terms of content (item (d) above).

---

68 Augdahl, *Rettskilder* [sources of law], Chapters 26–29, in particular pp. 214–34; Eckhoff, *Rettskilder* [sources of law], Chapters 9–10, in particular pp. 184, 198, 219–20, 226–27; Andenæs, *Innføring i rettsstudiet* [introduction to the study of law], pp. 110–11.

(4) Unity: hiding evaluations and choices

I have now given an account of *different meaning aspects* of principle terminology in lawyers' language and argumentation: partly the doctrine's assertion that principle terminology simply *summarises* norms that lawyers *actually apply* (item (2) above); and partly the fact that principle terminology is reserved for norms with a certain *goodness*, and that these norms can *supplement or depart from* positive law (item (3) above).

How is one to explain this language usage, "illogical" as it is in terms of content; how is one to explain that the same linguistic expression is used of phenomena that in other contexts are considered as being *so* different in kind?

A mediating explanatory factor I take to lie in the *unitary function* of the positive law meaning aspect and the "natural law" meaning aspect. Principle terms are in both cases used as *names for something already existing, and existing independently of the individual language use situation*: norms in actually occurring practice among lawyers, or norms with transcendent existence and distinctive goodness. Principle terminology thereby makes it possible in both cases, in the positive law meaning aspect as well as in the "natural law" meaning aspect, for personal evaluations and choices to be clothed in the language attire of discovery and description. In this respect principle terminology is a *special instance of the pervasive descriptive modes of expression* in the case of evaluations and choices in lawyers' language and argumentation de lege lata, cf. the general discussion above (section 3.3.1).[69]

3.3.3. On linking-terms in particular

Lawyers often give their discussions de lege lata the form of definition discussions, for example discussions of "the concept of 'contract' ", "the concept of 'building' ", "the concept of 'defect' "; or more loosely, the form of discussions of what something is, for example discussions of "what is a contract?", "what is a building?", "what is a defect?".

What features of lawyers' language and argumentation *make possible* this orientation towards definitions or propositions about what something is? I shall point to what I consider to be an important explanatory factor: *mediation* through what in Nordic legal theory are called "koblingsord" [linking-terms], between on the one hand *definitions or propositions about what something is* and on the other hand *characterisations*.

By *"linking-terms"* I mean words in a certain systematising role: in lawyers' language and argumentation, words more particularly in their role of intermedi-

---

69 A unitary function of a positive law viewpoint and a "natural law" viewpoint is also emphasised by Shklar, *Legalism – Law, Morals, and Political Trials*, pp. 8–9, 12, (104–)106, 109, 129, 142–43, 156–57, and by Kaufmann, 'Durch Naturrecht und Rechtspositivismus zur juristischen Hermeneutik', pp. 82–83. However, both writers rather presuppose (postulate) this unity than provide evidence of it through analysis of actually occurring language and argumentation, which makes it difficult to assess the tenability of, and, as the case may be, to build further on, their propositions.

aries between alternative legally operative facts and cumulative legal consequences. In its capacity of being a linking-term a word has *no reference* to any thing (in the broadest sense of "thing").[70]

The question of what a word in its capacity of being a linking-term *means* in lawyers' language and argumentation can thus by definition only be answered by looking at *what legally operative facts and what legal consequences are there linked together* in the use of the term.

By way of illustration I shall take a common example in the Nordic discussion: the term "eiendomsrett" [ownership]. In its capacity of being a linking-term, the meaning of the term can be sketched as follows:

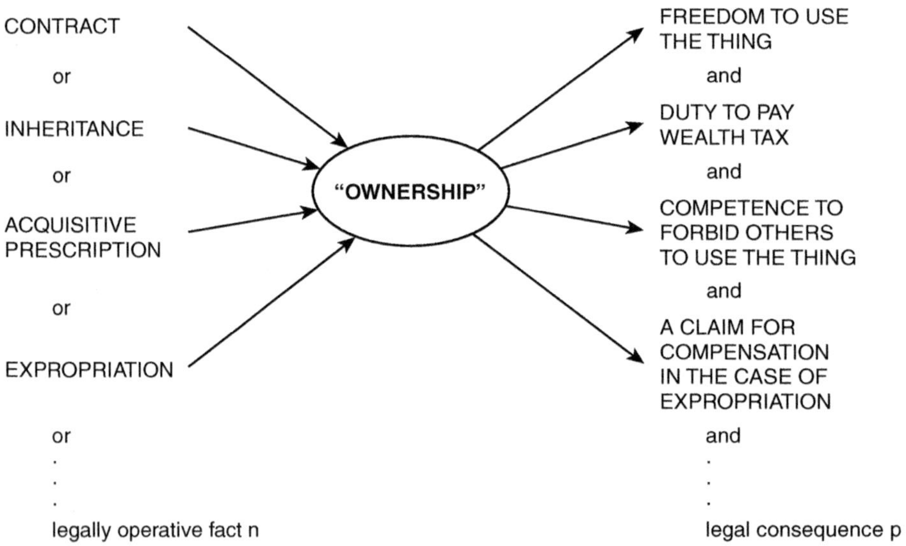

[70] The literature on linking-term interpretation in relation to lawyers' language and argumentation has gradually become extensive. – Such interpretation is explained in Ross, *On Law and Justice*, pp. 170–75; Eckhoff, *Rettskildelære* [doctrine of the sources of law], 3rd ed. pp. 39–45, in particular 43–44 (2nd ed. loc. cit.; 1st ed. pp. 25–27 and 44–51, in particular 49–50); Eckhoff/ Sundby, *Rettssystemer* [legal systems], 2nd ed. pp. 133–39 (1st ed. pp. 159–66); *Rechtssysteme*, pp. 111–17. See also Olivecrona, *Rättsordningen* [the legal system], pp. 231–32, 255–59. – A profound debate on linking-term interpretation was what is called "den nordiske rettighetsdiskusjon" [the Nordic discussion of rights] in the 1940s and 1950s, with contributions from among others Ekelöf, Strahl, Ross and Wedberg. See Sundby, 'Legal Right in Scandinavian Analyses', for a survey of this discussion, with comprehensive references to the literature. See also Eckhoff, 'Anmeldelse av Ekelöf, Valda skrifter 1942–1990' [review of Ekelöf, selected writings 1942–1990], pp. 189–90, on similarities and differences between the interpretations given by Ekelöf and Ross, two of the most central participants in the discussion. – A linking-term interpretation has also been applied in relation to the language and argumentation of psychologists and social scientists, see Eckhoff, 'Litt om det juridiske rettighetsspråk' [a little on the language of legal rights], pp. 76–77 with further references; Carnap, 'The Methodological Character of Theoretical Concepts', p. 73, cf. pp. 66–75. The discussion in the main text here is limited to lawyers' language and argumentation.

The schema represents a simplification in so far as many legally relevant matters have been omitted. Thus the absence of grounds for cessation, for example subsequent sale of the thing, has not been included. Nor have procedural conditions for instituting legal proceedings been included.[71] However, these simplifications do not affect the point that the schema is to illustrate here: the *definitional connection* between alternative legally operative facts and cumulative legal consequences.

It is this definitional connection that *makes possible the use of linking-terms*, here of "ownership". One aspect of the use of linking-terms is that it makes it possible for the person laying down or presenting the complex of rules in question to content himself with n + p sentences instead of n x p sentences.[72] Another aspect of the use of linking-terms is, however, in focus here: The use of linking-terms *makes it possible for characterisations to be expressed indirectly*, via a definition or via a proposition about what something is. To illustrate this, I shall have a look at lawyers' use of the word "contract", cf. the occurrence of this word at the top on the left in the linking-term schema above. For the sake of brevity I shall look only at indirect expression via definitions.

A descriptive definition of the word "contract" in the example above is at the same time an *indirect way* of asserting, for example, that in cases concerning whether a contract has come into being, Norwegian judges declare that the *legal-consequence side* of the linking-term schema shall take effect when and only when they deem those criteria the definition brings out, to have been satisfied. A descriptive definition of the word "contract" in the example above will thus at the same time be an indirectly expressed descriptive *characterisation*: The proposition not only describes language usage, but also (by definition, cf. the linking relationships) indirectly describes what legal rules are in fact applied.

The same goes for a normative definition of the word "contract" in the example. Such a definition will at the same time be an indirectly expressed normative *characterisation*: The proposition is not only normative with respect to language usage, but also (by definition, cf. the linking relationships) indirectly normative with respect to what legal rules ought to be applied.

---

71 There is also a simplification in that the legally operative facts have been indicated *broadly*: For one thing, on closer analysis each legally operative fact dissolves into a unity of positive and negative conditions (see e.g. the conditions that must be satisfied for a contract to be deemed to exist, section II B 3.2.2 (5)(c)(iii) above). For another thing, on closer analysis many of these conditions for their part again dissolve into a unity of weighing and balancing factors (see further concerning the contract example, section 2.2 (6)(b) above, see also section 3.3.1 (3)(b)(ii) above). – In the light of this, it would have been more apt to speak of a definitional connection between alternative "*sets* of legally operative facts" and cumulative legal consequences, but for the sake of brevity I avoid this.

72 Transition from reading the schema in the main text above *with* the term "ownership", i.e. from reading n + p sentences, to reading the schema *without* the term "ownership", i.e. to reading n x p sentences, may be seen as a *definition* of "ownership"; more particularly, it may be seen as an example of the definition method Bentham termed "paraphrasis" and which today one often terms "contextual definition"; see section II B 5.5 (2) above, at and in note 113.

Lawyers' propositions de lege lata, including their definitions, will often be neither purely descriptive nor purely normative, but have a fused descriptive and normative modality (section II F above). For the rest what has just been said applies, concerning the definition as an indirectly expressed characterisation, now with fused modality.

The use of words as linking-terms thus makes it possible for lawyers to clothe their discussions de lege lata in the language attire of discussions of definitions, or more loosely, in the language attire of discussions of what something is. – Such discussions may on the face of it seem to "hang in mid-air". The linking-term analysis demonstrates, however, the *reality basis* of the argumentation; it demonstrates the fact that, and the way in which, lawyers' discussions of definitions or of what something is, function as *indirect expressions of characterisations*: be it descriptive characterisations (propositions about what legal rules are in fact applied); normative characterisations (propositions about what legal rules ought to be applied); or fused descriptive and normative characterisations (lawyers' characterisations de lege lata).

3.3.4. Lawyers' language and argumentation de lege lata as a double abstraction: From the legal-consequence side of linking-terms. And from evaluations and choices

One key to lawyers' language and argumentation de lege lata (language and argumentation concerning what the law is) is to see that the *seemingly free-floating and interestless* definition discussions or discussions of what something is, are often language attire for characterisations concerning rights and duties (section 3.3.3 above).

Another key is to see that lawyers' *pervasive descriptive* modes of expression (sections 3.3.1–3.3.2 above) are often language attire for evaluations and choices: evaluations and choices that contribute to constituting the distinctive fused modality in lawyers' propositions de lege lata (section II F above).

For example: The sentence "Mary Smith's caravan is not (within the meaning of the Building Act) a building" expresses outside law a free-floating proposition about what something is, or, as the case may be, a descriptive definition if one includes the phrase in parenthesis. Among lawyers this sentence is, however, a normal mode of expression for a fusion of the proposition *that* the public administrative authorities ought not to be able to require building permission, lay down aesthetic requirements or in any other way invoke legal consequences of something's being a building within the meaning of the Building Act, and the proposition *that* other lawyers will probably hold the same opinion; that is to say that the sentence, as a step in lawyers' language and argumentation, expresses a characterisation with fused normative and descriptive modality.

In lawyers' language and argumentation de lege lata one thus meets a *tendency towards double abstraction*: *from* the legal-consequence side (characterisation side) of linking-terms; *and from* evaluations and choices (normativity).

This double abstraction explains how lawyers are able to express themselves as if they *are abstractly discussing and describing what something is*, while they *are distributing rights and duties* on the basis of evaluations and choices.

V

Reconstruction and redefinition: a distinct and widespread combination of the fundamental proposition types

1. 'Reconstruction and redefinition' – a concept of degree

1.1. Definition

(1) The fundamental elements of my structuring
(2) The graduatedness of the concept
(3) The complexity of the concept
(a) "Definition"
(b) "Descriptive" – "Normative"
(c) "Characterisation"
(4) Naming

(1) The fundamental elements of my structuring

A given phenomenon may logically be described from an infinite number of conceptual viewpoints (section III 2.2.4 above), and the diversity of interests that make themselves felt may in actual fact support a diversity of conceptual viewpoints' being established (section III 2.2 above). – This provides the background for reconstructions and redefinitions.

Take for example the question *"What is a legal duty?"*. Holmes answers the question as follows:

> "[A] legal duty so called is nothing but a *prediction* that if a man does or omits certain things he will be made to suffer in this or that way by judgment of the court" (my italics).[1]

Hart put a lot of work into demonstrating that such prediction analyses are not apt in relation to the essential:

> "What the external point of view, which limits itself to the observable regularities of behaviour, cannot reproduce is the way in which the rules function as rules in the lives of those who normally are the majority of society. These are the officials, lawyers, or private persons who use them, in one situation after another, as guides to the conduct of social life, as the basis for claims, demands, admissions, criticism, or punishment, viz., in all the familiar transactions of life according to rules. For them the violation of a rule is not merely a basis for the prediction that a hostile reaction will follow but a *reason* for hostility" (Hart's italics).[2]

---

[1] Holmes, 'The Path of the Law', p. 169.

[2] Hart, *The Concept of Law*, 1st ed. p. 88; 2nd ed. p. 90.

I do not believe that Holmes would have disagreed with anything that Hart says in the passage quoted. And in my opinion Hart does not have a good understanding of the relationship between Holmes' analysis and his own, cf. the fact that he substitutes his own analysis for Holmes'. The relationship between the analyses should rather be seen as a relationship between different reconstructions and redefinitions.

What I mean by "reconstruction and redefinition" I shall explain in connection with the example mentioned and the following figure:

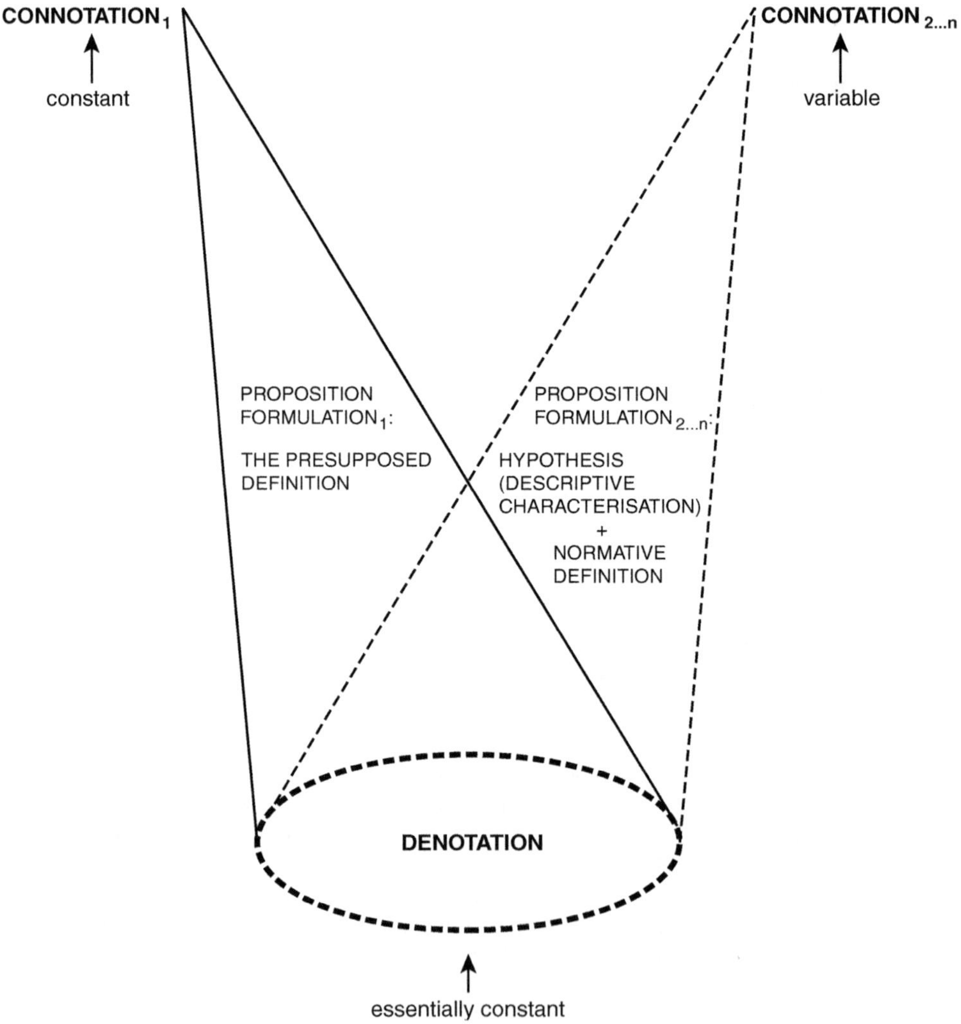

As is apparent from the figure a reconstruction and redefinition consists of *three different propositions about what something is*: a presupposed definition, a hypothesis (descriptive characterisation), and a normative definition. – Since I shall be using Holmes' relatively brief proposition formulation as an example of a reconstruction and redefinition, I must also be able to demonstrate that this formulation may reasonably be interpreted as presupposing or expressing all three propositions mentioned.

Definitional for the reconstruction and redefinition mode of analysis is in the first place the *presupposed definition*. For example, this may be a definition of "legal duty". The presupposed definition gives the *two fixed points of this mode of analysis*: For one thing, the presupposed definition gives the criteria of the concept, in our example the criteria lawyers more or less intuitively use when they take a standpoint on whether there is a legal duty (cf. "a legal duty *so called*" in the quotation from Holmes). In the figure the criteria are designated purely generally by the term *"*$connotation_1$*"*. For another, the presupposed definition gives the class of individual phenomena that have the definitional features, in our example the situations in which lawyers will say that there is a legal duty. In the figure this class is designated purely generally by the term *"denotation"*.

The definition now mentioned is the point of departure of the analysis. In the figure it finds expression schematically under the name of "proposition $formulation_1$". – This does not mean that my concept of 'reconstruction and redefinition' requires that the presupposed definition be explicitly formulated. The presupposed definition can, and will often, only be *tacitly assumed*; this is so, for example in discussions about "what is a legal duty" (or the equivalent in other languages) in which one only tacitly assumes a certain meaning of the term "legal duty", which I have the impression that Holmes and Hart do. The figure must be read with this proviso.

Definitional for the reconstruction and redefinition mode of analysis is, beside the presupposed definition, in the first place a *descriptive characterisation*: more precisely a hypothesis that the denotation of the presupposed definition has certain features.[3] – For example, it may be a hypothesis that the situations in which lawyers will say that there is a legal duty, have the feature that certain actions (breach of the duty) will probably lead to negative sanctions (cf. *"is ... a prediction"* in the quotation from Holmes), or the feature that breach of the duty is considered to be a reason for reproach (cf. Hart).

Further, it is definitional for this mode of analysis that there is a normative definition in the form of a *normative-innovative connotation specification*: more precisely a normative proposition to the effect that the features in the characterisation are to be preferred as concept criteria to the presupposed definition's concept criteria (cf. "is *nothing but*" in the quotation from Holmes). – For

[3] In the sentence at the present note and in a number of places in what follows I use "the denotation of the definition" as a shorthand form for "the denotation of the defined concept".

example, it may be a normative proposition to the effect that those criteria lawyers in their daily activity use more or less intuitively when they take a standpoint on whether there is a legal duty (the criteria in the presupposed definition: "$connotation_1$"), ought to be replaced by the criterion that certain actions (breach of the duty) will probably lead to negative sanctions (Holmes' criterion: "$connotation_2$"); or ought to be supplemented by the criterion that breach of the duty is considered to be a reason for reproach (Hart's criterion: "$connotation_3$"); or that other sides of the duty situations ought to be brought in as concept criteria (other writers' "$connotation_n$").[4]

Reconstructions and redefinitions thus say something both about *what properties what we are talking about has*, cf. the descriptive characterisation, and about *what the concept criteria for what we are talking about shall be*, cf. the normative definition. This combination of proposition types takes place more precisely through the normative definition's directly *taking over* those properties of the things that the descriptive characterisation brings out, and *"promoting"* these properties to concept criteria. – This unity of descriptive characterisation and normative definition represents the *variable of the reconstruction and redefinition mode of analysis*: a space, however modest it may be, for discovery and imagination (cf. "$connotation_{2...n}$").[5]

> I shall by way of conclusion concerning fundamental elements mention some points which, even if they are not necessary to an understanding of the conceptual fundamental structure, may shed further light on my concept of 'reconstruction and redefinition'.
>
> The presupposed definition may be stipulated (e.g. a theorist's concept of 'law') or custom-based (e.g. an everyday concept of 'law').
>
> The denotation of the presupposed definition (the denotation of the concept defined through presupposition) may be of very different kinds: physical objects; human beings; mental phenomena; linguistic meaning entities (criteria, concepts, propositions); or combinations of these or other things (e.g. situations in which one says that there is a legal duty).
>
> The denotation may be factual-existent (e.g. situations in which one has said or says that there is a legal duty), or factual-hypothetical (e.g. situations in which one will probably say that there is a legal duty).
>
> Most often the denotation will consist of a number of individual phenomena of the kind concerned (e.g. a number of individual situations in which there is said to be a legal duty: for example a number of Supreme Court judgments, cf. section 2.4 below on the reconstruction and redefinition structure in lawyers' use of judgments as a source of law). However, the denotation may also consist of only one individual instance (e.g. one situation in which there is said to be a legal duty, for example in the case of

4 When in a number of instances in what follows I speak of "normative definition" as a step in reconstructions and redefinitions, I am referring to the normative-innovative connotation specification now outlined. See also item (3)(b) below.

5 See section 4.2.2 (2) below on the urge to exercise imagination and creative power as one factor causing reconstruction and redefinition.

lawyers' disagreeing about what criteria a particular judgment shall be seen as the result of).

Those properties of the denotation phenomena that the characterisation brings out may have been found through ordinary thinking (compare the quotations from Holmes and Hart) or through more or less advanced methods for the collection and processing of data. – In whatever way they might have been found, the properties that the characterisation brings out are by definition different from the criteria of the presupposed definition (connotation$_1$). Therefore I use the term "normative-innovative" connotation specification in the case of the properties' being promoted to concept criteria (connotation$_{2...n}$). – Connotation$_2$ is of course known to the analyst (the person who reconstructs and redefines). To others connotation$_2$ may be known or unknown; the latter is the case when earlier one has not (clearly) seen these features of the phenomena.

To the extent that the sets of concept criteria are indeterminate, it may be difficult to delimit the denotation; and thus it may be difficult to decide whether the denotation is essentially kept constant or varies to a greater or lesser extent, when one goes from the presupposed set of criteria (connotation$_1$) to the new set (connotation$_{2...n}$). – Such difficulties are no objection to my concept of 'reconstruction and redefinition'. On the other hand, they represent a possible problem if one sees reconstruction and redefinition structure as a duty or an ideal (see section 4.2.2 (1) below on legal, philosophical or political reasons for sticking to a denotation).

(2) The graduatedness of the concept

It is a definitional feature of reconstruction and redefinition that all the propositions in this mode of analysis refer to *essentially the same* class of individual phenomena, namely the denotation of the presupposed definition. By the modification "essentially" I refer to the fact that sticking to the denotation is a *matter of degree*, and that I do not lay down complete correspondence as a concept criterion. – The figure in item (1) above must be read with this proviso; the circle that delimits the denotation is thus not to be seen as a sharp boundary, but as specification of an area essentially in common.

Irrespective of the degree to which the denotation is stuck to, the features of the denotation phenomena that are brought out in the different propositions of the reconstruction and redefinition mode of analysis may to a greater or lesser extent differ from one another; this means that *also difference* in the connotation dimension (connotation$_1$, connotation$_2$, connotation$_{...n}$, cf. the figure in item (1) above) is a *matter of degree*.

Against this background it is most correct to characterise my concept of 'reconstruction and redefinition' as a concept of degree; *language and argumentation may to a greater or lesser degree have reconstruction and redefinition structure*.

Many modes of analysis can be placed as *variants* of a superordinate concept of degree of this kind; i.e. as different graduated combinations of sticking to the denotation and changing the connotation. It is not possible to draw sharp boundaries between modes of analysis in this respect. Nor do I consider that this is necessary for the concept of 'reconstruction and redefinition' to be able to serve as a means to increased insight into actually occurring language and argumentation.

(3) The complexity of the concept

Such a mode of analysis as I have now defined is not amenable to being characterised sufficiently precisely only through the concept of 'definition'; within the distinction 'normative–descriptive propositions'; or only through the concept of 'characterisation'.

(a) "Definition"

It is *misleading* to term the reconstruction and redefinition mode of analysis "definition", in that this way of putting it can mislead one into thinking that it is only a question of determining the meanings of linguistic entities (determining concepts), while this mode of analysis as mentioned *also* consists of a descriptive characterisation. – The characterisation element *distinguishes* the concept of 'reconstruction and redefinition' from the concept of 'definition':

There is no *definitional connection* from defining to characterising; one can do the first without the second. In particular, one can define without at the same time implying the existence of anything falling under the concept, see for example the concepts of 'unicorn' or 'square circle'.

On the other hand, in the reconstruction and redefinition structure there is a definitional connection between defining and characterising; cf. the way in which the normative definition (the normative-innovative connotation specification) takes over and promotes to concept criteria those properties of the phenomena that the descriptive characterisation brings out. And since the characterisation will explicitly or by presupposition have to assert the existence of those phenomena that are being characterised, and, as the case may be, also of those of their properties that are brought out, there will more particularly also be a definitional connection between the normative definition and existence propositions.

> This also applies where the characterisation says that the phenomena do not have certain properties, and where this is laid down as a concept criterion. For the phenomena that are characterised negatively must by presupposition be asserted to exist.

The distinctive combination of descriptive characterisation and definition in the reconstruction and redefinition structure can contribute to explaining that in the case of many occurrences of this mode of analysis the words "theory" and "definition" are used interchangeably,[6] or the more indeterminate word "theory"

---

6 For the purpose of illustration I refer to the examples above: Hart uses inter alia the formulation "conception or theory" of Holmes' propositions about law, see *The Concept of Law*, 1st ed. p. 232; 2nd ed. p. 277. – The references to Hart in the rest of the present item (a) are to this book.

is preferred.[7] To put it more generally: The said distinctive combination can contribute to explaining that formulations concerning the status of occurrences of this mode of analysis have a distinctive duality[8] or are unclear.[9]

(b) "Descriptive" – "Normative"

When it comes to the definition part of the reconstruction and redefinition mode of analysis, it is *wrong* to term it "descriptive": Apart from lawyers' reconstructions and redefinitions de lege lata, for example in the case of reconstructions and redefinitions in other subjects or in the case of reconstructions and redefinitions in legal theory (cf. Holmes' and Hart's analyses discussed above), the definition part will have a purely normative modality. And in lawyers' reconstructions and redefinitions de lege lata, the definition part will often have a fused descriptive and normative modality. I have earlier given a thorough account of the last-mentioned modality type (section II F above). In the present discussion (Chapter V, reconstruction and redefinition) for the sake of brevity I use the word "normative" in a broad sense: both of purely normative modality and of fused descriptive and normative modality.

Further, it is in another dimension *too indeterminate* to term the definition part "normative": As is apparent from item (1) above the definition part is normative-traditional in relation to the denotation of the presupposed definition, and normative-innovative in relation to the connotation of the presupposed definition.[10]

(c) "Characterisation"

Every characterisation presupposes definition (section II A 2 (4) above). Thus the unity of presupposed definition and characterisation in the reconstruction and redefinition structure is nothing special. However, reconstruction and redefinition amounts to something more: first, that the characterisation purports to be valid for the essential part of the denotation of the presupposed concept; secondly, that those properties of the denotation that the characterisation brings out are "promoted" to concept criteria through a new definition (the normative-innovative connotation specification). – Therefore the concept of 'characterisation' is not sufficient alone, either, to give an account of the reconstruction and redefinition structure.

---

[7] Hart often uses the word "theory" of the analyses he criticises.

[8] Hart says in the preface (1st ed. p. VII; 2nd ed. p. V) that his book may be read both as "an essay in analytical jurisprudence" and as "an essay in descriptive sociology".

[9] Hart also uses the formulation "[statements] concerning the nature of law" of Holmes' propositions about law (1st ed. p. 2; 2nd ed. loc. cit.); and he characterises his own analysis by means of unclear formulations involving the words "definition" and "theory" (1st ed. p. 17; 2nd ed. loc. cit.).

[10] See sections II B 3.3.4, 4.3.3 and 8, above, on the graduated distinction between normative-traditional and normative-innovative definitions, and on the application of this distinction to the different dimensions of definitions.

(4) Naming

In naming this mode of analysis I use the word *"reconstruction"*. I do so because thought *builds with new materials*, cf. the fact that it brings out new aspects of the phenomena ("...construction"); and I do so because thought at the same time builds the *same result*, cf. that those phenomena that thought reflects on are essentially the same ("re...").

Further, in naming this mode of analysis I use the word *"redefinition"*. I do so because the materials of thought, after having been seen as properties of the phenomena and thus as elements in characterisations, are seen as concept criteria and thus as *elements in a definition* ("...definition"); and I do so because the criteria represent, in relation to other sets of criteria, a *normative-innovative* connotation specification ("re...").

1.2. The purpose of my conceptualisation: mapping (describing) what one dis/agrees about

After having demonstrated the reconstruction and redefinition structure in central parts of actually occurring language and argumentation (section 2 below), I shall compare my concept of 'reconstruction and redefinition' with some related concepts of modes of analysis (section 3 below).

This comparison will demonstrate that the concept of 'reconstruction and redefinition' has similarities with *Carnap's concepts* of 'explication' and 'rational reconstruction'. The practically most important differences spring from a *difference in interests*:

My aim is a *descriptive* one. By this I mean that I wish to construct concepts that capture a specific critically reflexive form in actually occurring language and argumentation, not to construct concepts for recommending or criticising language and argumentation (Chapter I above). – Therefore I do *not lay down definitional requirements* for exactness or fruitfulness of analyses.

Further, out of an interest in understanding what one *dis/agrees* about (Chapter I above), I wish to describe the *relationship* between different people's language and argumentation. In this perspective I consider it interesting that (sections 2–3 below) and why (section 4 below) one spends time and energy on "agreement about the denotation, but disagreement about the connotation (criteria)". – Therefore I place a *definitional emphasis* on this proposition pattern; see my definition in section 1.1 above.

2. Propositions about what legal phenomena are, interpreted as reconstructions and redefinitions

2.1. Introduction

The area of application of the concept of 'reconstruction and redefinition' is not confined to particular language and argumentation areas. However, in the present work I place the main emphasis on occurrences of the reconstruction and redefinition pattern in propositions about what legal phenomena are: partly occurrences of this pattern in propositions in legal theory (see above in section 1.1 (1); and below in sections 2.5–2.6, partly also in sections 2.2–2.3), and partly occurrences of this pattern in lawyers' propositions de lege lata (see below in section 2.4, partly also in sections 2.2–2.3).

2.2. "Løfte" [promise]; "Viljeserklæring" [declaration of intent]; "Rettshandel" [juristic act]

What are the circumstances that from a legal point of view constitute dispositive acts by which private individuals bind themselves? – This question has been discussed using varying terminology; for example it has been discussed as a question of what constitutes "løfte" [promise], "viljeserklæring" [declaration of intent] or "rettshandel" [juristic act], where these terms have been introduced as general designations for private dispositive acts.[1]

In legal literature a number of answers have been given to this question. In the present connection the interest does not, however, relate to the individual answers but to the *pattern* the answers form with respect to what one is in *agreement* about and what one is in *disagreement* about.

In many discussions of the question above the participants seem to have a *common and presupposed point of departure*, in that they on the whole seem to accept the standpoints of their respective legal systems with respect to which individual instances and instance-types constitute promises, etc.: be it standpoints in judgments or more informal standpoints of lawyers; be it standpoints on facts

[1] Eng, '"Hva er en viljeserklæring?"' ["what is a declaration of intent?"], pp. 2–3, quotes some writers' formulations of the question.

taken as established in judgments, on other actually occurring facts or on imagined examples.[2] – *Symptoms* of this acceptance of the individual outcomes of the legal system are partly that one *seldom discusses* whether a decision of an individual instance is to be considered to be right: instead one concentrates the discussion on what criteria are to be used for generating the individual instances (see the first example below); and partly that one *advances against* a conceptualisation ("theory", or the like) that it does not capture the individual instances (see the second example below).

In the present perspective this agreement about individual outcomes is an agreement about the *denotation* of concepts of 'promise', etc.; and the different features of the denotation instances that different writers bring out represent *disagreement about the connotation*. Seen in relation to one another the analyses form a reconstruction and redefinition pattern.

This pattern is to be found, for example, in the relationship between traditional analyses of the concept of 'declaration of intent' and the analyses conducted by Hägerström, Olivecrona, Ross and Karlgren.[3] The writers mentioned seem to share a tacit agreement with one another and with traditional theory of contract, with respect to what individual instances shall be deemed to fall under the concept of 'declaration of intent'; i.e. they link their analyses to a *common and presupposed denotation*.

Their disagreement about what criteria are to be used for generating the individual instances corresponds to the disagreement about what connotations are to be used in reconstructions and redefinitions, in that the individual theorist's proposal expresses a *combination* of descriptive characterisation and normative connotation specification: – The theorist's proposal is a *descriptive characterisation* in the respect that the proposal claims that the common and presupposed denotation, i.e. all declarations of intent that the legal system recognises, can or cannot have, has or does not have the features (will or other features) that are brought out. – And the proposal is a *normative regulation of the connotation* in the respect that the proposal recommends that the said features should be used or should not be used as concept criteria.

Another example is provided by the discussion around the turn of the last century concerning choice between will theory (the subjective theory of contract), expectation theory (a species of the objective theory of contract) and declaration theory (another species of the objective theory of contract). This discussion involved inter alia which of the existing theories was best suited to the corpus of

2 Only to an extremely small degree do Norwegian judges take a standpoint on other facts than those of the judgment; American judges do so to a greater degree. Such variations have little significance in relation to the present topic; they will, however, be touched on by way of delimitation in the later discussion of the judgment's constructed ratio decidendi seen as reconstruction and redefinition (section 2.4 (1) below, in the first indent).

3 Eng, '"Hva er en viljeserklæring?"' ["what is a declaration of intent?"] discusses the different sets of criteria that these writers bring out, with particular emphasis on the logical arguments against the possibility of will as a criterion that are advanced by Hägerström, Olivecrona and Ross.

reported cases. And as part of the discussion of this question it was advanced as an argument against theories, that in relation to the corpus of reported cases they could not generate those, and only those, individual instances that the courts had accepted.

> For example, Stang (who put forward a declaration theory) says in a discussion with Platou (who put forward a will theory) that even if Platou's theory "lies ... closer to reality than does the German dogma", it is "in conflict with valid law" and it "goes against *facts*, which he has not succeeded in bringing into harmony with the will dogma in a natural and logical way" (my italics).[4] He goes on: "I should have expected that Professor Platou ... would go into *Norwegian judicial practice* and seek support in it. He has not done so, however. Only occasionally does he quote a couple of judgments; but they do not support his doctrine. ... Professor Platou does not mention the many judgments I have invoked in support of the declaration theory. Thus he does not mention the Supreme Court judgment in Retstidende 1906 p. 154 that so strongly takes a standpoint in favour of the declaration theory" (my italics).[5]

Such a critique demonstrates in those participating in the discussion a presupposition of a common denotation. – And the critique demonstrates that this presupposition is normative; cf. the fact that it is considered to be a legitimate argument against a conceptualisation that it violates this presupposition. When one advances this counter-argument,[6] one at the same time demonstrates that one presupposes as the *correct* mode of analysis a *reconstruction and redefinition pattern*, i.e. a pattern in which the different sets of criteria (will, expectation and declaration theories) must be able to generate at least in the main the same class of individual phenomena in order to be able to be taken into account.

2.3. "Legalitetsprinsippet" [the principle of legality]

The difference between the traditional and the recent formulation of the principle of legality is a difference I have earlier discussed in its capacity to serve as an example of the significance of aesthetic considerations in the formation of concepts (section III 2.2.6 (3)(b) above). With reference to the earlier account of the *difference*, I shall briefly demonstrate that and in what manner the *relationship* between the propositions the formulations express, forms a reconstruction and redefinition pattern.

Through interplay between the practice of the courts and traditional theory there has come into being a relatively well-delimited *denotation* for the traditional theory's concept of 'the principle of legality': certain widely held standpoints among lawyers with respect to which individual instances and instance-types

4 Stang, 'Ord og hensigt' [words and intention], p. 661.
5 Op. cit., p. 659 in the note.
6 As e.g. Stang does in the quotations in the text at the two preceding notes.

require statutory authority.[7] – Recent theory does not appear to want to change lawyers' practice in this respect: Recent theory *presupposes* in the main the denotation in traditional theory.[8] In this respect there is *agreement*.

I see the relationship between the *criteria sets* in traditional and recent theory as the relationship between *alternative connotations* in a reconstruction and redefinition pattern, cf. the figure introduced in my general definition of 'reconstruction and redefinition' (section 1.1 (1) above): The account given of the principle of legality in *traditional theory* corresponds to *connotation$_1$*, and the account given of it in *recent theory* corresponds to *connotation$_2$*.

The *disagreement* about which set of criteria shall be used for generating the denotation instances, that of traditional or recent theory, *corresponds to* disagreement about which connotations shall be used in relation to the denotation in a reconstruction and redefinition: Recent theory presupposes in the main the denotation in traditional theory and points to particular features of this denotation. This is the element of hypothesis in the analysis: the *descriptive characterisation*. Recent theory then lays down these features as criteria in another concept of 'the principle of legality' than that in traditional theory. This is the *normative-innovative definition* (connotation specification: connotation$_2$) in the analysis.

2.4. "The constructed ratio decidendi of the judgment"

(1) The doctrine of the significance of judgments as a source of law is traditionally termed "the doctrine of precedent". A central question in the doctrine of precedent is *what a judgment is a precedent for*. The principles of the doctrine of precedent concerning the interpretation of judgments build on a presupposition of the judgment as a manifestation of a *general rule*. These principles distinguish between *three ways of generating* this general rule: the grounds explicitly stated in the judgment, also called "the stated ratio decidendi"; the grounds which the judgment can and ought to be seen as the manifestation of, but which are not

---

7 The more nuanced text in section 2.2 above, at and in note 2, applies correspondingly here.

8 Compare Eckhoff, 'Legalitetsprinsippet' [the principle of legality], pp. 233–34 in note 12 (on the relationship between traditional theory and Ross' argumentation; see in this connection section III 2.2.6 (3)(b) above, in note 80, on Ross' argumentation as part of recent theory); Eckhoff/ Smith, *Forvaltningsrett* [administrative law], p. 252 (on the relationship between traditional theory and recent theory as far as actual acts, in contrast to stipulation of norms, are concerned); Os, 'Anmeldelse av Eckhoff, Forvaltningsrett, 1st ed.' [review of Eckhoff, administrative law, 1st ed.], p. 489; Bernt, 'Legalitetsprinsippet og andre hjemmelsspørsmål i den offentlige rett – noen prinsipielle betraktninger' [the principle of legality and other authority issues in public law – some considerations of principle], p. 512 (calls the formulation in recent theory "a construction"); Boe, 'Eckhoffs/ Smiths framstilling av lovskravet i forvaltningsretten' [Eckhoff/ Smith's account of the requirement for statutory authority in administrative law], p. 156; Frihagen, *Forvaltningsrett*, Vol. II, p. 110; Revsbech, 'Anmeldelse av Eckhoff, Forvaltningsrett, 4th ed.' [review of Eckhoff, administrative law, 4th ed.], pp. 243 (bottom)–244 (top).

explicitly stated in the judgment, also called "the constructed ratio decidendi"; and the relation between the facts on which the judgment is based and the outcome of the judgment, generalised to an instance-type.[9]

Disagreement about legal rules will often be formulated or be formulatable as disagreement about the *concepts* in the rule, or alternatively, about the meanings of *words* in the formulation of the legal rule; that is to say, in both instances as disagreement about definitions.[10] Consequently lawyers will often use a judgment as an argument for the one or the other concept determination; the judgment is used as a *precedent for a definition*. For example, the judgment is used as a precedent for a definition of the concepts of 'løfte' [promise], 'viljeserklæring' [declaration of intent], 'rettshandel' [juristic act] (section 2.2 above); or 'avtale' [contract] (the present item (1), see immediately below); or other concepts, be they in private law or public law or cutting across traditional systematics, be it with a narrow or a broad area of application (item (2) below). – Thus the three above-mentioned ways of generating the general rule of the judgment will be used as three ways of generating definitions (concept criteria). In what follows I presuppose this definition and concept perspective.

Against this background I shall demonstrate that and in what manner a reconstruction and redefinition pattern shows itself in lawyers' answers to questions about what a judgment is a precedent for. The main points are apparent from the figure on p. 504, read as a parallel to the figure introduced in the general definition of 'reconstruction and redefinition' (section 1.1 (1) above). In square brackets an example to which I shall link my exposition is given in shorthand form. The example is taken from Norwegian law; however, I put forward as a working hypothesis that the main result of my analysis, the reconstruction and redefinition pattern in lawyers' discussion of what a judgment is a precedent for, is valid also for the legal systems of the other Scandinavian countries, the legal systems on the Continent and the Anglo-American legal system.

In a reconstruction and redefinition two elements are presupposed. The one element is the *denotation* of the presupposed definition. In the case of lawyers' use of judgments as arguments it is the *pairwise facts and conclusions of the existing judgments* that represent the denotation. These pairwise facts and conclusions constitute the fixed point of the analyses, the point that all constructed rationes decidendi proposed must essentially agree with. – For example, constructed rationes decidendi proposed in the case of the question of dispositivity in respect of contracts (the question of when two potentially contracting parties shall

---

[9] Fleischer, *Anvendelse og fortolkning av dommer* [application and interpretation of judgments], pp. 39–50; Eckhoff, *Rettskildelære* [doctrine of the sources of law], pp. 139–40. – For a comparison between Norwegian and English law, see Eng, 'The Doctrine of Precedent in English and Norwegian Law', sections 2.3–2.4. – In American law one most often uses the term "holding" of (large parts of) what is termed "ratio decidendi" in the present work.

[10] See sections IV 3.3.3–3.3.4 above on how use of words as linking-terms makes possible the fact that lawyers clothe their discussions of distribution of right and duty in the language of definitions.

be deemed to have moved from the stage of preliminaries to that of being legally bound) must essentially be able to generate the pairwise facts and conclusions of the existing judgments relating to this question.[11]

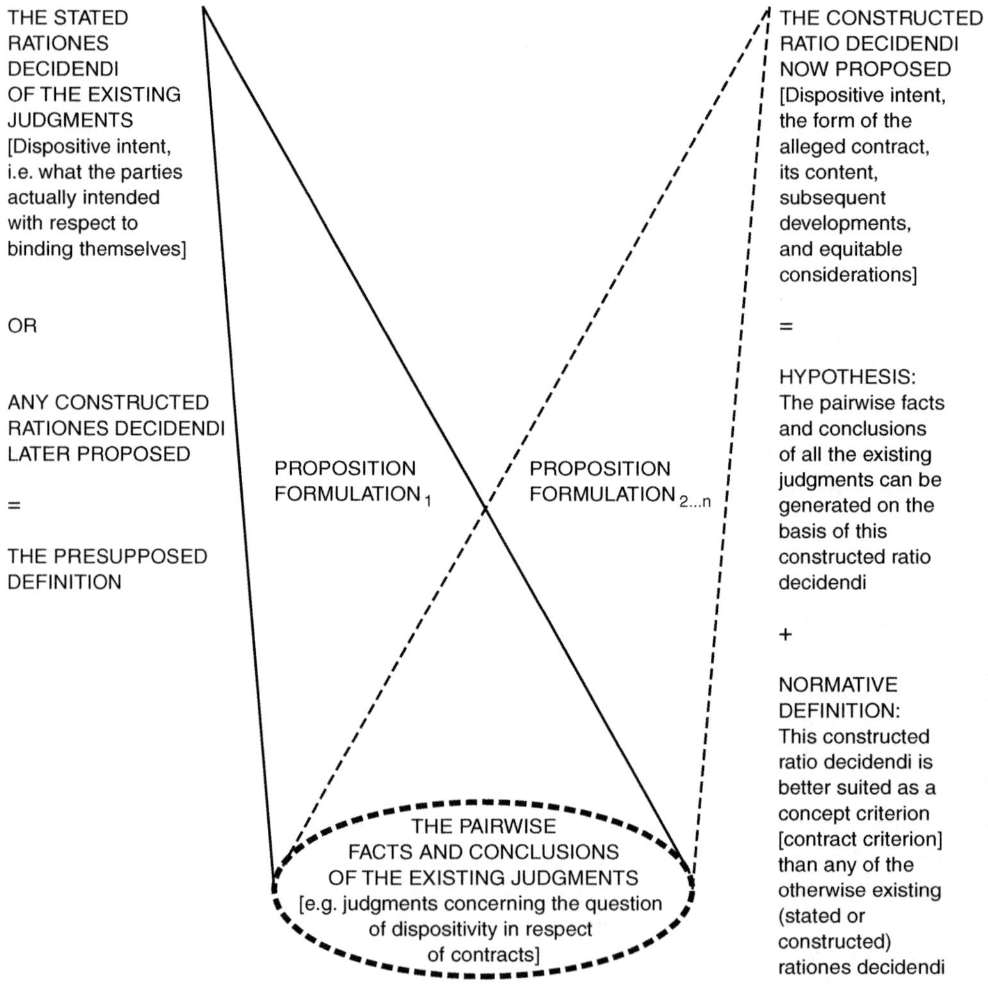

11 See section IV 2.2 (6)(b) above, in notes 21 and 22, on central judgments concerning the question of dispositivity in respect of contracts.

In order to understand the present section 2.4 it is sufficient to understand *"conclusion"* as 'standpoint on the contentions of the parties'. Since it is lawyers' language and argumentation that is being analysed, I shall however go somewhat more thoroughly into the use of this term in relation to certain points in their language usage and experience.

I use "conclusion" in the first place of those propositions that in Norwegian court practice conclude the opinion delivered by the judge sitting alone or the opinion of the first judge to deliver an opinion (or, as the case may be, the first opinion delivered within the majority of the court, if there is dissent). An example would be, in a dispute about the ownership of a piece of land: "John Brown is found in relation to Mary Smith to be the rightful owner of property x."[12] Secondly, I use "conclusion" of those propositions in which the judgment takes a standpoint on issues that must be resolved before one can reach a conclusion in the first sense. An example would be: "A binding contract had been entered into between John Brown as the buyer and Mary Smith as the seller of property x."

Norwegian judges do not to any great extent bring in *other facts than those of the judgment* as steps in their argumentation, and they to an even lesser extent take a standpoint on the legal significance of such facts. The nearest form with a certain practical significance is used as a step in the delimitation of what the judgment is a precedent for, and consists in stating that one is not taking any standpoint, for example: "I am not taking any standpoint on the issue of liability in situations in which an outside third party might have started the fire."[13] – In contrast, American judges, for example, to a greater extent bring in other facts than those of the judgment as steps in their argumentation, and they to a greater extent take a standpoint on the legal significance of such facts.[14] – I do not extend the use of the term "conclusion" to judges' standpoints of the latter kind: partly because they numerically play a minor role, and partly because they are deemed by most lawyers to be of less weight than standpoints on the facts of the judgment. If one wants to grasp lawyers' actual use of judgments as a source of law, it is therefore the concept of 'conclusion', as defined above, and the concept of 'the pairwise facts and conclusions of judgments' that are the central concepts.

The other element that is presupposed in a reconstruction and redefinition is the *connotation* of the definition: that set or those sets of criteria that have previously been put forward in generating the denotation. In the case of lawyers' use of judgments as arguments it is the *stated rationes decidendi* of the existing judgments, and any *constructed rationes decidendi later proposed*, that constitute this

---

12 In Norwegian judgments this element as a rule begins: "dom [judgment]: ...". In the Civil Procedure Act (Act No. 6 of 13 August 1915) this element is termed "domsslutning" [conclusion of judgment], see section 144 (5). It is this element in the judgment that is ascribed what in Norwegian law is called "rettskraft" [res judicata force] and, in the case of executory judgments, "tvangskraft" [enforceability].

13 *Rt. 1983/1052* on p. 1056.

14 Eisenberg, *The Nature of the Common Law*, pp. 99–103.

connotation. – For example, in the case of the question of dispositivity in respect of contracts, the courts adduce dispositive intent on the part of both parties as a contract criterion, and they adduce this criterion as a necessary condition, not as a factor to be weighed and balanced with other factors.[15]

In a reconstruction and redefinition there also lie new elements: for one thing a hypothesis (descriptive characterisation) and for another a normative definition. In the case of lawyers' use of judgments as arguments, these two propositions are expressed through the *constructed ratio decidendi now proposed*. – In the case of the question of dispositivity in respect of contracts, I assume, as previously mentioned, that judges are motivated by a diversity of contract criteria, which fall into the following main categories: dispositive intent, the form of the alleged contract, its content, subsequent developments, and equitable considerations; and that these criteria are not used as conditions but as factors to be weighed and balanced.[16] From the present perspective this is a constructed ratio decidendi.

The constructed ratio decidendi now proposed represents, first, a *hypothesis* with the following standard content: The pairwise facts and conclusions of all the existing judgments concerning the question under discussion will also be covered by this constructed ratio decidendi. That is to say: Those facts that this proposed constructed ratio decidendi singles out as legally relevant are *present* in the sets of facts of all the existing judgments concerning the question under discussion; and the facts thus singled out *can*, given lawyers' language and argumentation practice, serve as sufficient grounds for the conclusions of the existing judgments.

Secondly, the constructed ratio decidendi now proposed most often also represents a *normative-innovative definition* (connotation specification) with the following standard content: Those facts that this proposed constructed ratio decidendi singles out as legally relevant are *better suited* (section 4.1 below) as criteria for the pairwise facts and conclusions of the existing judgments than any of the previously proposed sets of criteria; they are both better suited than the stated rationes decidendi of the existing judgments, and better suited than any constructed rationes decidendi later proposed, in the literature or by other lawyers.

> A ratio decidendi *may* be constructed with a view to *pure prediction, without normative aspects*, be it prediction of what persons applying the law will support in the way of concept criteria, or more boldly, prediction of how they will subsume in given individual instances (in the latter case one must also predict something about the weight in relation to one another of all the legal criteria that might be applied to the matter). – However, it is not usual for lawyers to construct rationes decidendi with a view to pure prediction. The usual thing is instead that the construction assumes the *fused* descriptive and normative modality characteristic of lawyers propositions de lege lata

---

15 Eng, '"Hva er en viljeserklæring"' ["what is a declaration of intent?"], p. 39 (bottom); sections IV 2.2 (6)(b) and 3.3.1 (3)(b) above.

16 See in more detail in section IV 2.2 (6)(b) above.

(section II F 2 above). In the main text I use the word "normative" in a broad sense, also of these fusions (section 1.1 (3)(b) above).

The constructed rationes decidendi proposed must as mentioned be capable of generating essentially the pairwise facts and conclusions of the existing judgments: Those proposals for constructed rationes decidendi that are *not* able to account for why the conclusions of the judgments were as they were, given the facts of the judgments, are according to the doctrine of precedent deemed prima facie to have *weaker tenability* than those proposals that are able to account for the conclusions of the judgments in the light of the facts of the cases. – Thus we can say that lawyers' doctrine of precedent *"authorises" one denotation rather than another.*

(2) Reconstructions and redefinitions via the doctrine of precedent may be *more or less broadly based*:

One main group is reconstructions and redefinitions with *particular legal questions* in mind. – From private law, examples are the reconstruction and redefinition discussed in item (1) above, concerning the dispositivity dimension in the case of the concept of 'contract'; or attempts to reconstruct and redefine contractual liability for damage-causing properties of the goods sold, by means of a distinction between goods that lack properties they should have had (liability), and goods that have properties they should not have had (no liability).[17] – From tax law an example is attempts to reconstruct and redefine the debtor's tax liability in the case of waiver, time-barring or foreclosure of debt in commercial activity, by means of a distinction between the debtor's solvency (waiver, time-barring, foreclosure are taxable advantages) and the debtor's insolvency (waiver, time-barring, foreclosure are not taxable advantages).[18] – And from administrative law an example is attempts to reconstruct and redefine the boundary between the public administrative authorities' business activity and their "enkeltvedtak" [individual decisions] (cf. the statutory definition in section 2 b) cf. a) of the Public Administration Act (10 February 1967)) by means of a distinction between exchange and distribution: That the public administrative authorities choose their co-actor out of consideration for balance between the performances (exchange) may support seeing their act as a business decision. That the public administrative authorities choose their co-actor out of other considerations (in shorthand form:

---

17 Krüger, *Norsk kjøpsrett* [Norwegian sale of goods law], 2nd ed. pp. 210–11; 3rd ed. pp. 364–65, on on the one hand *Rt. 1972/1350* (seller of chicken-feed deemed contractually liable for loss of chickens caused by the fact that the feed had a lower vitamin E content than was stated in the contract) and on the other hand *Rt. 1973/1153* (seller of offal as mink fodder not deemed contractually liable for loss of mink caused by botulinus toxin in the fodder).

18 Zimmer, *Lærebok i skatterett* [textbook of tax law], 2nd ed. pp. 129–30 (127–30), on on the one hand *Rt. 1928/371, 1930/328, 1931/1250* (debtor was insolvent and the advantage was not deemed taxable), on the other hand *Rt. 1978/1001* (debtor was solvent and the advantage was deemed taxable), and as a residue, that does not lend itself to reconstruction and redefinition along this line, *Rt. 1956/1323* (debtor was solvent and the advantage was not deemed taxable). A more brief account in 3rd ed. pp. 140–41.

politically motivated distribution of the advantages) may support seeing their act as an individual decision.[19]

A second main group is reconstructions and redefinitions with whole *areas within traditional legal systematics* in mind.[20] – From private law an example is "passivitetslærer" [doctrines of laches], i.e. attempts to find criteria in common for court cases in which a right has been deemed to be lost because the holder of the right did not exercise it earlier.[21] A further example is "forutsetningslærer" [doctrines of assumptions]. These are used in particular to reconstruct and re-define outcomes concerning the legal force of contracts (promises), for example outcomes concerning transition from the stage of preliminaries to that of being legally bound, or concerning validity, interpretation, breach, etc.[22] But they are also used to reconstruct and redefine outcomes in practice concerning other questions, for example outcomes concerning condictio indebiti.[23] – And from administrative law an example is "læren om myndighetsmisbruk" [the doctrine of misuse of public administrative authority], which is used to reconstruct and redefine outcomes both concerning the traditional exercise of authority by the public administrative authorities and their business activity.[24]

A third main group is reconstructions and redefinitions cutting across and including *different areas in traditional legal systematics*. An example is law and economics.

> "[I]n a series of studies ... I and others have examined the hypothesis that the common law is *best explained* as if the judges were trying to maximize economic welfare. ... In analyzing a wide variety of legal doctrines – a few scattered *example[s]* are assumption of risk in tort law, the degrees of homi-cide, the principles of tort and contract damages, proximate cause, mistake and fraud in contract law, the principles of restitution, the doctrine of "moral consideration", the structure of property rights in water, the law of joint

19 E. Smith, 'Om fordeling av økonomiske goder i forvaltningsretten' [on distribution of economic advantages in administrative law], in particular pp. 136–38.

20 As this and the next main group illustrate, reconstruction and redefinition of a given collection of cases will often be expressed in terms of principles (section IV 3.3.2 above).

21 Arnholm, *Passivitetsvirkninger* [effects of laches], p. 113 (expresses scepticism about the pos-sibility of condensing the cases into "a single positive rule"); Knoph, *Rettslige standarder* [legal standards], p. 240 (formulates what he calls "the standard of laches in the case of subjective rights"); Augdahl, *Obligasjonsrett* [law of obligations], p. 141 (calls Knoph's proposal "a caricature of a legal rule").

22 Augdahl, *Obligasjonsrett* [law of obligations], p. 141 (cessation of right on account of laches); pp. 172–73 (breach of contract in the form of defective goods); p. 189 (termination for breach); Vinding Kruse, *Ejendomskøb* [purchase of real property], pp. 80–97 (on the concept of 'defect' in the case of purchase of real property); Ussing, *Aftaler* [contracts], pp. 457–81 (failed assumptions as a ground of discharge in the case of contractual obligations); C. Smith, *Garantikrav og garantistvern – Garantirett III* [guarantee claims and protection of the guarantor – guarantee law III], pp. 191–200 (assumptions in guarantee law). – More generally on the criteria, see Lehrberg, *Förutsättningsläran* [the doctrine of assumptions], passim.

23 Augdahl, *Obligasjonsrett* [law of obligations], p. 402.

24 Eckhoff, *Forvaltningsrett* [administrative law], 5th ed. pp. 249–63, cf. p. 319.

> tortfeasors, and the rules of salvage in admiralty law – economists and economically minded lawyers have found that the law uncannily *follows* economics" (my italics).[25]

In this passage from Posner the expressions "best explained" and "follows" are ambiguous between the relationships of cause and justification. Only the justification relationship is relevant here. – It is apparent from the context and Posner's statements otherwise that he is referring to both relationships.[26] This means that he *also* reconstructs and redefines that practice of the courts that constitutes common law: He assumes that the pairwise facts and conclusions of the existing judgments (the presupposed denotation) have the properties that are relevant according to the theory of maximisation of economic welfare (descriptive characterisation in the form of hypothesis), and that these properties are better suited as concept criteria (connotation$_{2...n}$) than those criteria that are actually stated in the existing judgments (the presupposed connotation$_1$).

2.5. "Law"

I assume that much of the discussion about "what law is", "the nature of law", or the like, can be aptly characterised as discussions with reconstruction and redefinition structure. For example, accounts such as Hägerström, *Till frågan om den objektiva rättens begrepp* [on the question of the concept of 'law']; Olivecrona, *Law as Fact*; Ross, *On Law and Justice*; Hart, *The Concept of Law*; and Eckhoff/ Sundby, *Rettssystemer* [legal systems] may in relation to many of the questions that are discussed be interpreted as having such structure.

The *phenomenon* being analysed may be the law in general or more delimited parts. For example, a discussion common to the said writers takes its starting point in the norms we call legal. On the basis of somewhat different purposes, they then put forward assertions about what constitutes the unity between these norms. – That their *answers* are different does not in any way run counter to the fact that their *modes of analysis* have important features in common: here, the features that lie in the reconstruction and redefinition structure. – For demonstration of this structure through quotations from particular discussions, I refer to the example I used for the purpose of illustration in defining 'reconstruction and redefinition' (section 1 above; the discussion between Holmes and Hart), and to section 2.6 below. In the rest of the present section 2.5 I shall give examples of another kind of evidence: statements by writers about their aims and methods that

---

[25] Posner, *The Economics of Justice*, pp. 4–5. Correspondingly in 'Some Uses and Abuses of Economics in Law', pp. 281–84, cf. p. 290; *Economic Analysis of Law*, pp. 20, 21; *The Problems of Jurisprudence*, pp. 356, 358, 361–62.

[26] See e.g. *The Economics of Justice*, p. 115: "I have tried to develop a moral theory", and "[this theory] seems to have played an important role in the growth of the common law"; *Economic Analysis of Law*, pp. 20–22; *The Problems of Jurisprudence*, p. 361: "generating both predictions and prescriptions", cf. pp. 359–61, 362–87.

indicate that the writer *himself sees* his discussion as a discussion with reconstruction and redefinition structure.

Hägerström formulates the aim of his investigation as follows:

> "In addition, the purpose is through the critical investigation to shed light on the *real nature* of law in order, in that way, to lead on to an account of that *concept* of the same that really covers *those facts one has in mind in the case of particular attempts at conceptualisation*" (my italics).27

The italicised parts of the quotation suggest the central elements in reconstructions and redefinitions: – "[T]hose facts one has in mind in the case of particular attempts at conceptualisation" designates the presupposed denotation. – "[S]hed light on the real nature of law" designates one or more descriptive characterisations in the form of assertions about what features the presupposed denotation has. – Finally, "an account of that concept ... that really covers" designates a normative-innovative definition in the form of normative regulation of the connotation, in that Hägerström would maintain that certain of the properties that he brings out in his descriptive characterisations are better suited as criteria in a concept of 'law' than those features that had been advanced in earlier literature or in everyday speech.

Olivecrona formulates his aim as follows:

> "I want to go straight to [law as fact], and treat directly the facts of social life. If in this way we get a coherent explanation, without contradictions, of *those facts which are covered by the expression "law"*, our task is fulfilled. ... The method will be simply to take up *such facts as are covered by the expression ["]rules of law["]*. No assumption is made from the beginning concerning their nature. We only use the word "law" so to say as a stick to point to the *object of the investigation*" (my italics).28

The three italicised parts of the quotation designate the first main element in reconstructions and redefinitions, the presupposed denotation. – The other elements in reconstructions and redefinitions are not directly touched upon in the passage quoted. But Olivecrona has elsewhere emphasised that the second main element, the descriptive characterisations, is one main aim: "... the aim of the book: to present an *empirical investigation* of a mass of complicated facts that one finds where one speaks of "law"" (my italics).29 – The third main element in reconstructions and redefinitions, the normative definition, is not a direct aim for Olivecrona: "I do not regard it as necessary to formulate a definition of law. A

---

27 Hägerström, *Till frågan om den objektiva rättens begrepp. I. Viljeteorien* [on the question of the concept of 'law'. I. theory of will], foreword.

28 Olivecrona, *Law as Fact*, 1st ed. pp. 25–26.

29 Olivecrona, 'Frågeställningar i rättsteorien' [problems in legal theory], p. 309. – This statement directly concerns the 2nd edition of *Law as Fact* (1971), which in many ways differs from the 1st edition. However, in relation to the question of mode of analysis that is discussed here the differences between the editions are of no significance.

description and an analysis of the facts is all that will be attempted."[30] However, if one does intend to construct a concept of 'law', I assume that Olivecrona would say that it ought to be constructed through one or more of those properties that he brings out in his descriptive characterisations, as opposed to one's constructing the concept by means of one or more of those properties that he criticises as being metaphysical, for example law as expression of will or as expression of a natural-law quality.

2.6. "Valid law"

I shall use Ross' theory of valid law as an example of a theory with reconstruction and redefinition structure; more precisely I shall show that his theory is a reconstruction and redefinition of the norms that lawyers on the whole agree are existing legal norms.

Ross' prediction theory generates essentially the *same* norms as the norms most lawyers will consider as legally existing, namely the norms that can be justified on the basis of the doctrine of the sources of law (the tenability criteria for lawyers' argumentation de lege lata). The reason for this correspondence is that Ross, when stating how one predicts what conclusion a judge will arrive at on a question of law, does not refer to the use of socio-psychological investigations, but to the doctrine of the sources of law; he does so on the basis of the premiss that the doctrine of the sources of law governs the judge's decision about what norms he shall apply.

> "In the foregoing chapter we arrived at the conclusion that the real content of the juridico-scientific assertion [that a norm] is valid law is a *prediction* to the effect that [the norm] under certain conditions will be taken as the basis for decisions in future, legal disputes. ... If, in spite of all, prediction is *possible*, it must be because the mental process by which the judge decides to base his decision on one rule rather than another is not a capricious and arbitrary matter, varying from one judge to another, but a process determined by attitudes and concepts, a *common* normative ideology, present and active in the minds of judges when they act in their capacity as judges. ... This ideology is the subject of the doctrine of the sources of law. ... [It] is the *basis* for the predictions of legal science concerning the manner in which the judges will react in the future" (my italics).[31]

The norms that can be justified on the basis of the doctrine of the sources of law thus represent a *point common* to two sets of criteria: to the doctrine of the sources of law and to Ross' prediction theory.[32] – In the present perspective and

---

30 Olivecrona, *Law as Fact*, 1st ed. p. 26.

31 Ross, *On Law and Justice*, pp. 75–76; translation slightly altered.

32 Ross himself noted this point common to the criteria constituted by the doctrine of the sources of law and to a prediction criterion, see *On Law and Justice*, p. 48. See also Strahl, 'En allmän rättslära' [a general theory of law], p. 303 (bottom); Andenæs, 'Rettsteori og rettspraksis' [jurisprudence and

in relation to the concept of 'valid law', the set of criteria constituted by the doctrine of the sources of law corresponds to *connotation*$_1$ in the reconstruction and redefinition pattern; the norms that can be justified on the basis of the doctrine of the sources of law correspond to the *denotation in common*; and Ross' prediction criterion corresponds to *connotation*$_2$.

The said premiss in Ross, that the doctrine of the sources of law governs the judge's decision about what norms he shall apply, provides (a basis for) a descriptive characterisation of the denotation, (a basis for) a *hypothesis* that the norms in the denotation have the property of motivating judges.

Ross considers this property of being motivative so important that he wishes to promote it to a criterion in lawyers' concept of the norms. His prediction theory therefore also involves a *normative-innovative definition* (connotation specification: connotation$_2$); in the place of other properties that have or could have been advanced as concept criteria, for example the property of being justifiable within the doctrine of the sources of law,[33] he puts the property of motivating the person enforcing the law.[34]

court practice], pp. 419–20; von Eyben, '"Gældende ret"' [valid law], pp. 108–09; Jørgensen, *Ret og samfund* [law and society], pp. 100–01; Stuer Lauridsen, *Studier i retspolitisk argumentation* [studies in argumentation de lege ferenda], pp. 235–37(41); *Om ret og retsvidenskab* [on law and legal science], p. 105; Eckhoff, 'Ross om rettskilder og rett' [Ross on sources of law and law], p. 210.

33 Compare section II A 5 (2)(a) above, at and in note 5. See also the quotation from Hart at the beginning of section 1.1 (1) above.

34 Ross, *On Law and Justice*, Chapter 2. Compare section II A 5 (2)(a) above, at and in note 3. See also the quotation from Holmes at the beginning of section 1.1 (1) above.

3. Comparison with some related concepts of modes of analysis

3.1. Introduction

(1) The *purpose* of the present section 3 is partly to shed light on my concept of 'reconstruction and redefinition' through pointing out similarities with and differences from other concepts of modes of analysis, and partly, to the extent that there is similarity, to demonstrate that the regularities in thought that have motivated the concept have been noticed by other writers.

A comparison demands a *yardstick*. In view of the purpose of the comparison I use the *structure of my concept of 'reconstruction and redefinition'* as the yardstick. This raises a *problem* for interpretation and comparison: My concept of 'reconstruction and redefinition' is motivated by an interest in a specific critically reflexive form in actually occurring language and argumentation (section 1.2, cf. Chapter I, above); and the concept is built up of the concepts of the fundamental proposition types of this critically reflexive form together with the distinction between the connotation and denotation of a concept. The conceptualisations with which comparison will be made in what follows spring from other interests (item (2) below); and these conceptualisations are in their construction not equally strongly oriented towards the distinctions between the fundamental proposition types, or towards the distinction between connotation and denotation. Therefore it does *not always clearly* follow from the writer's formulations whether his conceptualisation consists of definitions or characterisations, descriptive or normative; or whether his conceptualisation has any relationship to the distinction between connotation and denotation, and if so, what relationship. – I point here to this problem for interpretation and comparison, instead of constantly having to make reservations in the course of my discussions.

To facilitate matters for the reader I have grouped my individual discussions of similarities and differences essentially in the same way, see the tables of contents preceding these discussions.

(2) The *perspective and topic of the present work* – a specific critically reflexive form in actually occurring language and argumentation (Chapter I above) – often turns out to *cut across* the main direction in another writer's work. This applies in a high degree in the present section 3: When in what follows I focus on works by Carnap (section 3.3), Goodman (section 3.4) and Rawls (section 3.4), the point of contact does not lie in the main part of these works, i.e. in Carnap's formal-logically constructed languages, in Goodman's analysis of induction or in Rawls' theory of justice, but in the few pages where these writers construct concepts for critically reflexive questioning.

3.2. Næss: 'Real definition'

(1) Næss' concept of 'real definition'
(2) Some similarities and differences between Næss' concept of 'real definition' and my concept of 'reconstruction and redefinition'
- **(a) Which proposition types are combined in the concept**
- **(b) The relationship of the concept formed to the distinction between connotation and denotation. The fixed and variable points of the mode of analysis**
- **(c) Whether evaluation prescription is brought into the concept**
  - **(i) The descriptive purpose of my concept of 'reconstruction and redefinition'**
  - **(ii) My desire to avoid persuasive definitions**

(1) Næss' concept of 'real definition'

Næss establishes a concept for which he uses the terms "definition as condensed characterization" or, for the sake of brevity, "real definition". With respect to Næss' concept I refer to the quotation of Næss' definition in section II B 2.3 (1) above.

(2) Some similarities and differences between Næss' concept of 'real definition' and my concept of 'reconstruction and redefinition'

(a) Which proposition types are combined in the concept

Næss' concept of 'real definition' is *related* to my concept of 'reconstruction and redefinition', in that it captures a combination of a presupposed definition and a characterisation of the denotation of the defined concept. – In order to remind the reader of, and to exhibit, these fundamental elements, which in various combinations will crop up in what follows, I shall schematise Næss' combination. I take as a starting point the same figure that was used in the schematising of the concept of 'reconstruction and redefinition' (section 1.1 (1) above):

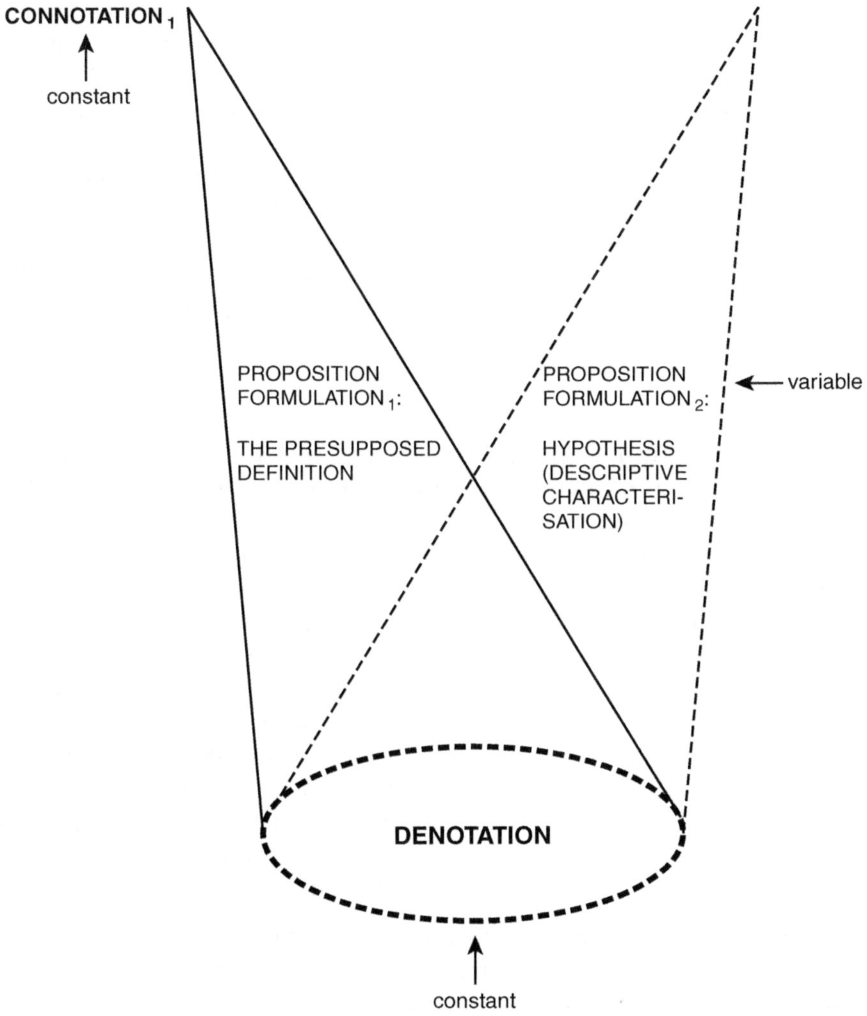

The figure illustrates that Næss' concept of 'real definition' is *less complex* than my concept of 'reconstruction and redefinition', in that Næss' concept consists of two propositions, not three: It is not a criterion in the concept of 'real definition' that those features of the denotation that the characterisation brings out are laid down as criteria in a new concept. That is to say that the third proposition in a reconstruction and redefinition, the normative definition, is not part of Næss' real definition.

Thus one can say that Næss' concept is not a concept of a *mode of analysis*, when as here one uses the term "mode of analysis" of a combination of the fundamental proposition types. For any characterisation presupposes definitions (section II A 2 (4) above), so that Næss' concept can be said to be a concept of a particular type of characterisation, i.e. a concept of a proposition type (this is the perspective in section II B 2.3 (1) above). – The reason why in the present comparison of concepts of modes of analysis I take my starting point in Næss' concept is that his concept so *explicitly and precisely seizes on elements* which many modes of analysis may be seen as being built up of, and which will be central in what follows: in the first place, the distinction between a presupposed definition and another proposition, here a characterisation; secondly, the distinction between the presupposed definition's connotation and denotation; and finally, use of this distinction for laying down a relationship between the proposition types, including the laying down of fixed and variable points in the relationship between the proposition types. – Incidentally I do not place any emphasis on whether one draws the boundary of the concept of 'mode of analysis' so that Næss' real definitions fall inside or outside.

(b) The relationship of the concept formed to the distinction between connotation and denotation. The fixed and variable points of the mode of analysis

Næss' definition of the concept of 'real definition' builds explicitly on the distinction between connotation and denotation, in that the characterisation in his proposition combination (see the figure in item (a) above) is by definition to "cover ... *all denotata* of a concept ... already introduced" (see the quotation in section II B 2.3 (1) above; my italics). However, since his proposition combination contains only one definition (item (a) above, the text immediately after the figure), Næss' concept of 'real definition' does not provide any possibility of capturing the *particular* relationship between different discussion participants consisting in their being "in agreement about the denotation, but in disagreement about the connotation (criteria)"; this relationship I wish to capture and go into more deeply with my concept of 'reconstruction and redefinition'.

(c) Whether evaluation prescription is brought into the concept

In defining my concept of 'reconstruction and redefinition' I do *not lay down requirements* for fruitfulness or brevity, as Næss does in defining his concept of 'real definition'.[1] I have two *grounds* for not laying down such requirements:[2]

(i) The descriptive purpose of my concept of 'reconstruction and redefinition'

My concept of 'reconstruction and redefinition' has been established with a view to description (section 1.2 above). This means that *brevity*[3] is inexpedient as a

[1] See the quotation in section II B 2.3 (1) above: respectively item 2 in the quotation and the note accompanying the quotation, concerning fruitfulness, and item 3 in the quotation, concerning brevity.

[2] My grounds in what follows are quite parallel to my grounds for not laying down any requirement for determinacy in the case of definition of the concepts of 'definition' and 'concept' (section II B 4.1 (3)(a) above). However, I account for my grounds here too since the parallel is not obvious in detail, and since below I shall be referring back to the present item (c).

concept criterion, since other and interesting features in the reconstruction and redefinition pattern recur in the case of both shorter and longer sequences of propositions about what something is.[4] – For the same reason, namely the descriptive aim, requirements for *fruitfulness* are inexpedient as concept criteria. True enough, fruitfulness requirements will often be considered relevant when participants in language and argumentation reflect on which of several reconstructions and redefinitions is to be preferred. Thus, views about fruitfulness requirements must be taken into consideration in description of language and argumentation. However, two points should be added here. First, the *fruitfulness requirement itself* ("what requirements ought to be laid down?") does not belong as a criterion in a concept formed with a descriptive aim: here, with the aim of demonstrating the existence and diffusion of a distinct combination of the fundamental types of proposition. Secondly, *views* about fruitfulness requirements can and ought to be taken into consideration without being laid down as a criterion in the concept of 'reconstruction and redefinition'. For fruitfulness requirements are most often implemented as factors to be weighed and balanced, and more seldom as conditions (section III 2 above). This being so, the best overview of the crucial loci at which dis/agreement occurs is provided by keeping views concerning requirements for fruitfulness outside the concept of mode of analysis, i.e. by speaking of reconstructions and redefinitions that are considered more or less fruitful, not of whether an analysis is considered sufficiently fruitful to be capable of being reckoned as a reconstruction and redefinition.

(ii) My desire to avoid persuasive definitions

Also the desire to avoid language that *conceals evaluations* and provides room for *rhetorical manipulation* goes against bringing evaluation prescriptions into the concept of mode of analysis:

When the fruitfulness criterion is kept out of the concept, one can say *: "Your reconstruction and redefinition does not contribute much." – When the fruitfulness criterion is brought into the concept, one must say **: "You have not reconstructed and redefined."

The latter form of expression (**) easily leads to a situation in which evaluations concerning what fruitfulness requirements *ought* to be demanded, are discussed in *seemingly descriptive* (i.e. in concealing) linguistic forms: "This is not a reconstruction and redefinition", "What exactly is a reconstruction and redefinition?". – The first form of expression (*) provides a more open specification of the topic, with correspondingly less room for misunderstandings and for rhetorical manipulation.[5]

---

3 A requirement for brevity is vague, but in normal language usage does not entail any evaluation prescription, and thus falls outside the topic specification in the heading of the present item (c). Out of consideration for what connections there are, however, I treat this requirement here.

4 Compare the examples in section 2 above.

5 Compare section II B 7 above, on persuasive definitions.

3.3. Carnap

3.3.1. 'Explication'

Carnap's concept of 'explication' is built up as a *two-place relation*:

The given concept (or the linguistic entity for the concept) that is to be explicated, Carnap calls *"explicandum"*. Carnap seems to require that the explicandum to a relatively high degree, but not completely, coincides with everyday language.

The new concept (or the linguistic entity for the concept) that explicates, Carnap calls *"explicatum"*. Here Carnap requires departure from everyday language and from the explicandum, if this is suggested out of certain considerations that I shall come back to.

I have grouped the further discussions as follows:

(1) Carnap's concept of 'explication'
- **(a) A couple of Carnap's examples of explication**
- **(b) The concept of 'explicandum'**
- **(c) The relation between explicandum and explicatum**

(2) Some similarities and differences between Carnap's concept of 'explication' and my concept of 'reconstruction and redefinition'
- **(a) Which proposition types are combined in the concept**
- **(b) The relationship of the concept formed to the distinction between connotation and denotation. The fixed and variable points of the mode of analysis**
- **(c) Whether evaluation prescription is brought into the concept**

(1) Carnap's concept of 'explication'

(a) A couple of Carnap's examples of explication

> "I might say, for example: "I mean by the explicandum *'salt'*, not its wide sense which it has in chemistry but its narrow sense in which it is used in the household language". This explanation is not yet an explication; the latter may be given, for instance, by the compound expression *'sodium chloride'* or the synonymous symbol *'NaCl' of the language of chemistry. ...*
>
> [I might say, for example:] "I am looking for an explication of the term *'true'*, not as used in phrases like 'a true democracy', 'a true friend', etc., but as used in everyday life, in legal proceedings, in logic, and in science, in about the sense of 'correct', 'accurate', 'veridical', 'not false', 'neither error nor lie', as applied to statements, assertions, reports, stories, etc." This explanation is not yet an explication; an explication may be given by a definition *within the framework of semantical concepts, for example, by Tarski's definition of 'true' in [Wahrheitsbegriff], ... or by D 17-1 below*" (my italics).[6]

[6] Carnap, *Logical Foundations of Probability*, pp. 4–5.

(b) The concept of 'explicandum'

As is apparent from the examples, Carnap will not accept any concept whatsoever as an *explicandum*. He distinguishes between "to make clear what is meant as the explicandum" and "[to] supply an explication". The first belongs to "the formulation of the problem", the second to "the construction of an answer".[7]

We must first "... do all we can to make at least practically clear what is meant as the explicandum".[8] When Carnap says here "all we can", this must be interpreted as "all we can *relative to everyday language* (in contrast to logic and mathematics)", and probably to a great degree also as "relative to the *use in everyday life* of everyday language (in contrast to subject-specific, scientific or philosophical variants of everyday language)". Carnap does not say this explicitly, but it follows partly from the fact that explicanda are said to be pre-scientific concepts or to belong to early stages in the development of scientific languages;[9] partly from the fact that there would be nothing left to explicate once we had used all available resources to delimit explicanda; partly from Carnap's examples of delimitation of explicanda[10] and his own practice in the case of such delimitation;[11] and partly from his general propositions about means for the delimitation:

> "An indication of the meaning [of the explicandum] with the help of some *examples* for its intended use and other examples for uses not now intended can help the understanding. An *informal explanation* in general terms may be added" (my italics).[12]

(c) The relation between explicandum and explicatum

Given that we have an explicandum that has been sufficiently clarified, the question then becomes:

> "What *kind of correspondence* is required here between the first concept, the explicandum, and the second, the explicatum?" (my italics).[13]

Carnap says in general about this:

> "[I]t is not required that an explicatum have, as nearly as possible, the same meaning as the explicandum; it should, however, correspond to the explicandum in such a way that it can be used instead of the latter."[14]

As part of a more detailed discussion of the explication relation, Carnap lays down the following four requirements the explicatum must satisfy:

---

7 Op. cit., p. 4; compare op. cit., pp. 19 et seq. and same writer, 'The Two Concepts of Probability', pp. 442 et seq. and 455 (bottom).

8 Carnap, *Logical Foundations of Probability*, p. 4.

9 Op. cit., p. 3.

10 See item (a) above; further Carnap, *Logical Foundations of Probability*, e.g. pp. 5–6, 12 and 17.

11 Carnap, 'The Two Concepts of Probability', pp. 442 et seq.; *Logical Foundations of Probability*, pp. 19 et seq.; 'The Methodological Character of Theoretical Concepts', pp. 49 et seq.

12 Carnap, *Logical Foundations of Probability*, p. 4.

13 Op. cit., p. 5.

14 Carnap, *Meaning and Necessity*, p. 8.

"1. The explicatum is to be *similar to the explicandum* in such a way that, in most cases in which the explicandum has so far been used, the explicatum can be used; however, close similarity is not required, and considerable differences are permitted.

2. The characterization of the explicatum, that is, the rules of its use (for instance, in the form of a definition), is to be given in an *exact* form, so as to introduce the explicatum into a well-connected system of scientific concepts.

3. The explicatum is to be a *fruitful* concept, that is, useful for the formulation of many universal statements (empirical laws in the case of a non-logical concept, logical theorems in the case of a logical concept).

4. The explicatum should be as *simple* as possible; this means as simple as the more important requirements (1), (2) and (3) permit" (Carnap's italics).[15]

(2) Some similarities and differences between Carnap's concept of 'explication' and my concept of 'reconstruction and redefinition'

(a) Which proposition types are combined in the concept

Carnap's concept of 'explication' is *less complex* than my concept of 'reconstruction and redefinition'. First, explications consist by definition of two definitions ("to make clear what is meant as the explicandum" and "[to] supply an explication"; see item (1)(b) above), while reconstructions and redefinitions by definition also include a characterisation. Secondly, both the definitions in an explication are normative, while reconstructions and redefinitions also include a descriptive proposition, the characterisation.

(b) The relationship of the concept formed to the distinction between connotation and denotation. The fixed and variable points of the mode of analysis

The distinction between connotation and denotation is central in my concept of 'reconstruction and redefinition'; one main purpose of this concept is to capture and go more deeply into the *particular* relationship between different discussion participants consisting in their being "in agreement about the denotation, but in disagreement about the connotation (criteria)". – Carnap's definition of the concept of 'explication' does not build explicitly on the distinction between connotation and denotation. The emphasis in Carnap's definition is on the two-place relation between explicandum and explicatum, while the emphasis in my definition of 'reconstruction and redefinition' is on the three-place relation between connotation$_1$, the denotation and connotation$_{2...n}$.

What then lies in Carnap's *requirement for similarity* between explicandum and explicatum (see the first of the requirements the explicatum must satisfy that are quoted in item (1)(c) above): Is the requirement that there be similarity of connotation, similarity of denotation, or both? – Or, to see it from the other side,

15 Carnap, *Logical Foundations of Probability*, p. 7.

the dissimilarity ("however, close similarity is not required"): Is one to tolerate dissimilarity of connotation, dissimilarity of denotation or both?

Carnap is of course aware of the significance of distinguishing between dis/similarity in the connotation dimension and dis/similarity in the denotation dimension. And if one reads Carnap's statements about similarity, and his exemplification, with one's eye on these distinctions, there is strong evidence to show that his statements refer to the denotation dimension: partly he speaks of "cases ... used", and partly his own examples demonstrate (item (1)(a) above) that he does not require any form of similarity in the connotation dimension, so that his statements about similarity cannot refer to this dimension.

With this point of departure a reasonable interpretation is that Carnap's concept of 'explication' permits *dissimilarity of connotation in full, and dissimilarity of denotation to a lesser degree*. Thus the denotation is a *more stable point* than the connotation; and *in this respect* the explication mode of analysis will have *similarity* with reconstructions and redefinitions (section 1.1 (2) above). Schematically the structural similarity can be specified as in the figure on p. 522. – The *differences* with respect to the distinction between connotation and denotation relate in this case to two points:

These differences relate partly to *how clearly the conceptualisation shall express* the distinction between dis/similarity in connotation and dis/similarity in denotation, and partly to *the degree to which the conceptualisation shall lay down as a criterion* that the denotation is essentially stuck to. – On the basis of the main aim of the present work (Chapter I above: demonstrating, and creating an awareness of, the existence, content and factual significance of a specific critically reflexive form (I 4–6), and thereby, demonstrating, and creating an awareness of, the factual significance of analysis of dis/agreement on the basis of this critically reflexive form) it is most pertinent to conceptualise the mode of analysis so that (i) the difference between dis/similarity in respectively connotation and denotation comes out clearly, and (ii) the main emphasis is on instances in which the denotation is essentially stuck to by the discussion participants: "in agreement about the denotation, but in disagreement about the connotation (criteria)" (section 1.1 (1)–(2) above). My hypothesis is that these definitional decisions constitute a concept that provides insight into central parts of actually occurring language and argumentation (section 2 above).

(c) Whether evaluation prescription is brought into the concept

Carnap lays down as definitional requirements that the explicatum is exact, fruitful and simple (see the last three requirements quoted in item (1)(c) above). The parallel in relation to my concept of 'reconstruction and redefinition' would be to lay down these requirements in relation to connotation$_{2...n}$, the normative-innovative connotation specification (see the figure in section 1.1 (1) above).

The fact that I do not lay down such requirements is for the same reasons as I advanced against corresponding requirements in the concept formed by Næss

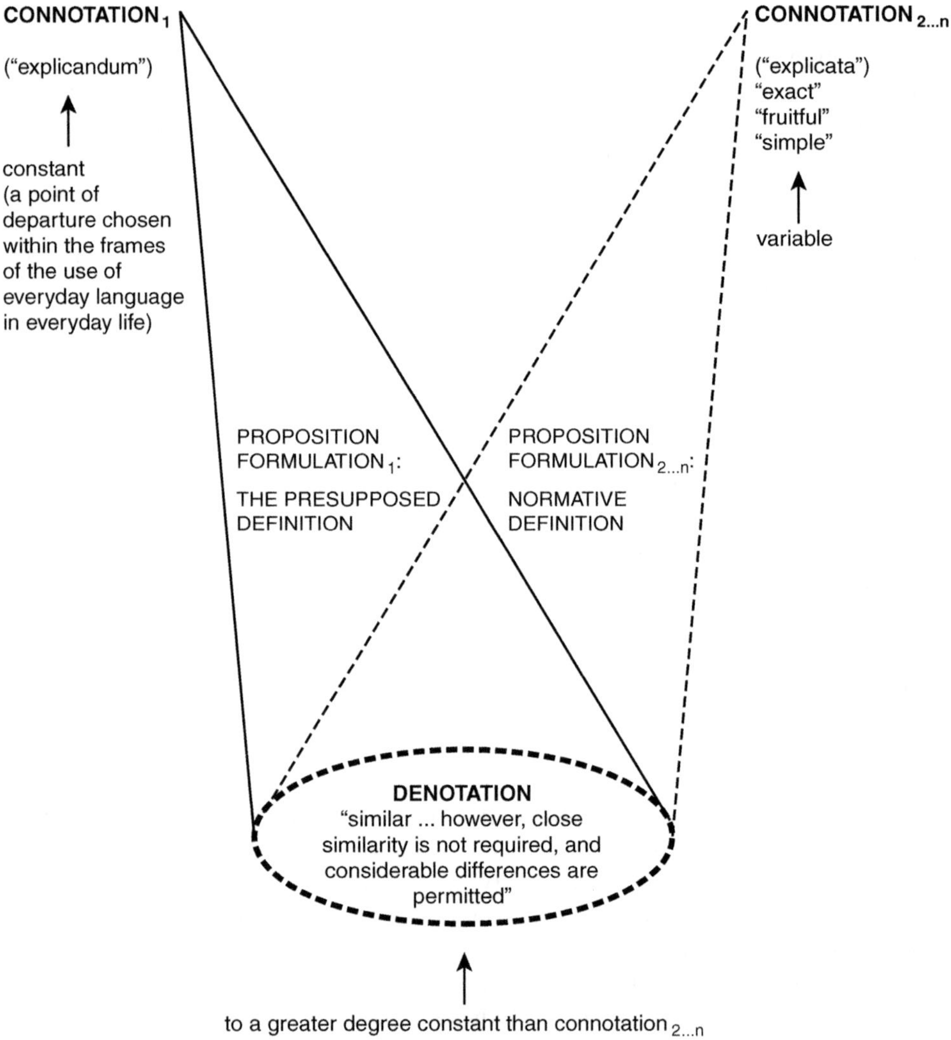

(section 3.2 (2)(c) above): in particular for the reason that the purpose of my concept of 'reconstruction and redefinition' is descriptive, not normative.

Especially for the *exactness requirement* there is the additional reason that I am in doubt whether it is at all *possible* to put it into practice in the case of *social* phenomena:

The purpose of Carnap's exactness requirement the explicatum must satisfy is determined in the following way: "exact form, *so as to* introduce the explicatum into a well-connected system of scientific concepts" (my italics). Carnap does not go explicitly into what requirements he would make of a "well-connected system of scientific concepts". However, from examples he gives, and his own works, it seems to be apparent that he is referring to *some of the most precisely developed* conceptual systems in natural science and logic/ mathematics; cf. the examples quoted in item (1)(a) above and the references there to chemistry and formal semantics, and cf. those of his works I have referred to in item (1) above in their entirety. – From this it follows that Carnap's exactness requirement is strict.[16]

I consider such an exactness requirement problematic in relation to important concepts of man and society, for example the concept of 'law'. Is it, in any reasonable sense of "same", possible to characterise legal phenomena *in the same way* as one does when one defines salt as NaCl, or in the same way as Tarski does when he defines truth, or Carnap when he defines probability? In my view the answer is in the negative.

> It is of course possible to lay down certain less strict requirements for exactness also in the case of concepts of man and society; and if one has a normative aim, i.e. if one wants to create concepts of how we ought to analyse and argue, then there may be reason to lay down such requirements. However, since the aim here is descriptive, I consequently do not build such less strict requirements either into my concept of 'reconstruction and redefinition'.

3.3.2. 'Rational reconstruction'

(1) Carnap's concept of 'rational reconstruction'

(2) Some similarities and differences between Carnap's concept of 'rational reconstruction' and my concept of 'reconstruction and redefinition'

- **(a) Which proposition types are combined in the concept. The role of characterisations**
- **(b) The relationship of the concept formed to the distinction between connotation and denotation. The fixed and variable points of the mode of analysis**
- **(c) Whether evaluation prescription is brought into the concept**

(3) Carnap's terminology

(1) Carnap's concept of 'rational reconstruction'

Carnap establishes a concept of 'rational reconstruction' with the following two *features*: first, that concepts are explicated, and secondly, that beliefs are systematised.

> "Sometimes a theory is offered as a "rational reconstruction" of a body of generally accepted but more-or-less vague beliefs. This means that the theory introduces *explicata* for the *concepts* involved in those beliefs *and* that the

[16] Perhaps a somewhat less strict requirement is expressed in Carnap, 'Replies and Systematic Expositions', pp. 935–36.

> content of the *beliefs* is represented in a *more exact and more systematic form* by statements of the theory" (my italics).[17]

For an understanding of the concept formed by Carnap it may also be illuminating to see how he talks about his mode of analysis in connection with two of his more concrete analyses, respectively a system of inductive logic and analysis of empirical concepts:

> "The system of inductive logic here proposed … is intended as a reconstruction restricted to a simple language form, of inductive thinking as customarily applied in everyday life and in science. However, it is meant not merely as an uncritical representation of customary ways of thinking with all their defects and inconsistencies, but rather as a rational, critically corrected reconstruction. It is intended to lead to results which are more systematized, more consistent, and in certain points more correct than customary ways of thinking."[18]
>
> "Inspired by Russell's description of the aim and the method of future philosophy, I made numerous attempts at analyzing concepts of ordinary language relating to things in our environment and their observable properties and relations, and at constructing definitions of these concepts with the help of symbolic logic. Although I was guided in my procedure by the psychological facts concerning the formation of concepts of material things out of perceptions, my real aim was not the description of this genetic process, but rather its rational reconstruction – i.e., a schematized description of an imaginary procedure, consisting of rationally prescribed steps, which would lead to essentially the same results as the actual psychological process."[19]

---

17 Carnap, *Logical Foundations of Probability*, p. 576.

18 Loc. cit. – In a probably corresponding meaning the terms "rational reconstruction"/ "rationale Rekonstruktion" have also been used of the relationship between everyday language and deductive logic; see Strawson, 'Carnap's Views on Constructed Systems versus Natural Languages in Analytic Philosophy', p. 503, compare *Introduction to Logical Theory*, pp. 57–58; Weinberger, *Rechtslogik*, pp. 219–20, 381.

19 Carnap, 'Intellectual Autobiography', p. 16. – The passage quoted was written in the 1960s (published in 1963), as a description of the method in *Der logische Aufbau der Welt*, written in the 1920s (published in 1928) (see also section II B 5.2 (5)(b)(i) above). In *Aufbau* itself Carnap uses the term "rationale Nachkonstruktion" of his method, see *Aufbau*, pp. 138–39, 191–92. In 1961 *Aufbau* was reprinted without any changes. In the foreword to the 1961 impression Carnap writes: "Das Hauptproblem betrifft die Möglichkeit der rationalen Nachkonstruktion von Begriffen aller Erkenntnisgebiete auf der Grundlage von Begriffen, die sich auf das unmittelbar Gegebene beziehen. Unter rationaler Nachkonstruktion ist hier das Aufsuchen neuer Bestimmungen für alte Begriffe verstanden. … Eine solche Begriffsklärung, heute oft "Explikation" genannt, …". I do not consider it necessary to take any standpoint on whether, and if so to what extent, the last passage quoted means that Carnap perceived his own ways of using on the one hand the terms "rationale Nachkonstruktion"/ "rational reconstruction" and on the other hand the term "explication" as synonymous ("his own ways of using", in contrast to others' ways of using, compare "heute oft" in the last passage quoted, and section 3.3.3 below). I consider it sufficient to state that such an interpretation would, in relation to the statements from Carnap that I build on in section 3.3.1 above and in the present section 3.3.2, be less precise *and* that the interpretation would, in relation to the topic here: to shed light on the concept of 'reconstruction and redefinition' through similarities with and differences from other concepts of modes of analysis, entail that nuances of interest were lost, see the discussions in what follows.

(2) Some similarities and differences between Carnap's concept of 'rational reconstruction' and my concept of 'reconstruction and redefinition'

(a) Which proposition types are combined in the concept. The role of characterisations

Carnap's concept of 'rational reconstruction' combines definitions and characterisations: *Definitions* in rational reconstructions are more precisely explications, cf. the criterion that rational reconstructions "introduce ... explicata for the concepts" (Carnap's definition quoted at the beginning of item (1) above). *Characterisations* in rational reconstructions relate more precisely to "a body of generally accepted but more-or-less vague beliefs"; and the characterisations "[represent] the content of the beliefs ... in a more exact and more systematic form" (same quotation).

Whether Carnap's concept also combines descriptive and normative propositions is more unclear. On the one hand, the explication element is *predominantly normative* (section 3.3.1 (2)(a) above); and the same seems to apply to the characterisation element, in that the latter purports to provide improved (alternative and more systematic) expression for given beliefs, cf. "represent ... in a more exact and more systematic form". On the other hand, purely factually such a complex mode of analysis will often bring in descriptive propositions too, for example descriptions of how, in everyday life or science, one infers from individual instances to general propositions ("inductive thinking", cf. the second quotation in item (1) above).

Thus rational reconstructions will be *more complex* than explications and *just as complex* as reconstructions and redefinitions.

Characterisations play another *role*, however, in Carnap's mode of analysis than in reconstructions and redefinitions:

A definitional feature of reconstruction and redefinition is that the normative-innovative definition *directly takes over* those properties of the denotation that the descriptive characterisation brings out, and thereby "promotes" these properties to concept criteria (section 1.1 (1) above).

In Carnap's mode of analysis *no such community of content* exists between characterisations and definitions. The characterisations function there not as preliminaries to a definition, but stand on their own feet as a systematisation of beliefs of which the defined concepts are part, for example as a systematisation of beliefs about induction. – In Carnap's rational reconstructions, characterisations thus come in in *another, more comprehensive and more indeterminate way* than in my reconstructions and redefinitions.

(b) The relationship of the concept formed to the distinction between connotation and denotation. The fixed and variable points of the mode of analysis

Carnap does not build the distinction between connotation and denotation into his concept of 'rational reconstruction'. – And it is *not possible to use the distinction* between connotation and denotation for a *systematic* analysis of the fixed and variable points of this mode of analysis, as in the case of reconstruction and redefinition:

The distinction between connotation and denotation is *only applicable in the case of* concepts/ general words and expressions, not in the case of propositions (section II A 4 above); and rational reconstructions systematise not only concepts/ the use of general words and expressions, but also propositions, cf. the fact that this mode of analysis systematises beliefs, and that beliefs are expressed through propositions (definitions, characterisations; descriptive, normative, fused propositions; analytically un/true propositions).[20]

The fact that a concept of a mode of analysis also refers to propositions does not, however, preclude a systematic analysis of the mode of analysis by means of the distinction between connotation and denotation, provided that the propositions of the mode of analysis have a *definitional or factual connection* with the connotation or denotation of concepts.

Definitions have such a definitional connection, in that we can always speak of connotation or denotation in relation to the concept defined/ the general words and expressions defined (section II A 4 above). Since explication is a definition combination, the distinction between connotation and denotation can therefore be used for analysis of the explication element in rational reconstructions (compare section 3.3.1 (2)(b) above).

Characterisations in general have no definitional or factual connection with the distinction between connotation and denotation. The question therefore becomes whether characterisations in the individual mode of analysis have a definitional or factual connection with the connotation or denotation of concepts.

In the case of reconstructions and redefinitions there is such a connection, in that the denotation of the presupposed concept is by definition a point common to the three propositions in this mode of analysis: the presupposed definition, the descriptive characterisation and the normative-innovative definition (section 1.1 (1) above).

In the case of Carnap's rational reconstructions, on the other hand, there is no definitional or factual connection between the characterisations in this mode of analysis and the connotation or denotation of concepts; the characterisations stand on their own and more indeterminate feet (item (a) above), concluding remarks).

---

20 The connection between beliefs and propositions can be made more perspicuous by one's representing beliefs in the form "Person p has the belief that ..." and substituting proposition formulations for "...".

As it is therefore not possible completely to analyse rational reconstructions by means of the distinction between connotation and denotation, it is not particularly fruitful either to *compare the fixed and variable points of the modes of analysis* by means of that distinction. – For the purpose of comparison I shall instead seize on a *structural similarity* between Carnap's combination of the fundamental proposition types and the combination in my reconstructions and redefinitions. The quotations from Carnap in what follows have been taken from the definitional propositions quoted in item (1) above.

In these quotations Carnap speaks of "a body of generally accepted but more-or-less vague beliefs", "customary ways of thinking" and "the actual psychological process" – which may be seen as a parallel to proposition formulation$_1$ and connotation$_1$ in the reconstruction and redefinition structure (see the figure in section 1.1 (1) above).

Further he speaks of the said more everyday thoughts' being "represented in a more exact and more systematic form" and "critically corrected" through rational reconstructions, and of the aim's being "a schematized description of an imaginary procedure, consisting of rationally prescribed steps" – which may be seen as a parallel to proposition formulation$_2$ and connotation$_2$ in the reconstruction and redefinition structure.

In relation to the two groups of statements that have now been mentioned, I have drawn a parallel between the connotations of concepts and (reasons for) general beliefs. In this context I call them by the common term "criteria".

Taken together, standpoints on individual instances in the case of application of general beliefs may be seen as a parallel to the denotation in the reconstruction and redefinition structure. – Standpoints on individual instances are not mentioned in the first quotation in item (1) above, but they are in the other two quotations there, cf. respectively "results which are ... in certain points more correct" and "lead to essentially the same results".

Carnap's concept of 'rational reconstruction' accordingly permits *criterion dissimilarity in full* ("represent ... in a more exact and more systematic form") and *dissimilarities in standpoints on individual instances only to a certain degree* ("lead to essentially the same results"). *In this respect* this mode of analysis has similarity with explications (section 3.3.1 (2)(b) above) and reconstructions and redefinitions (section 1.1 (2) above). – Schematically the structural similarity can be specified as in the figure on p. 528.

(c) Whether evaluation prescription is brought into the concept

Carnap has a *normative aim* with his concept of 'rational reconstruction', cf. the fact that he brings *evaluation prescriptions* into the connotation of this concept: The definitions in the rational reconstruction shall satisfy the explicatum requirements (exactness, fruitfulness, simplicity, cf. section 3.3.1 (1)(c) above), and the characterisations in it shall satisfy requirements for exactness and systematicity (item (1) above). – Since I have no normative aim with my concept of

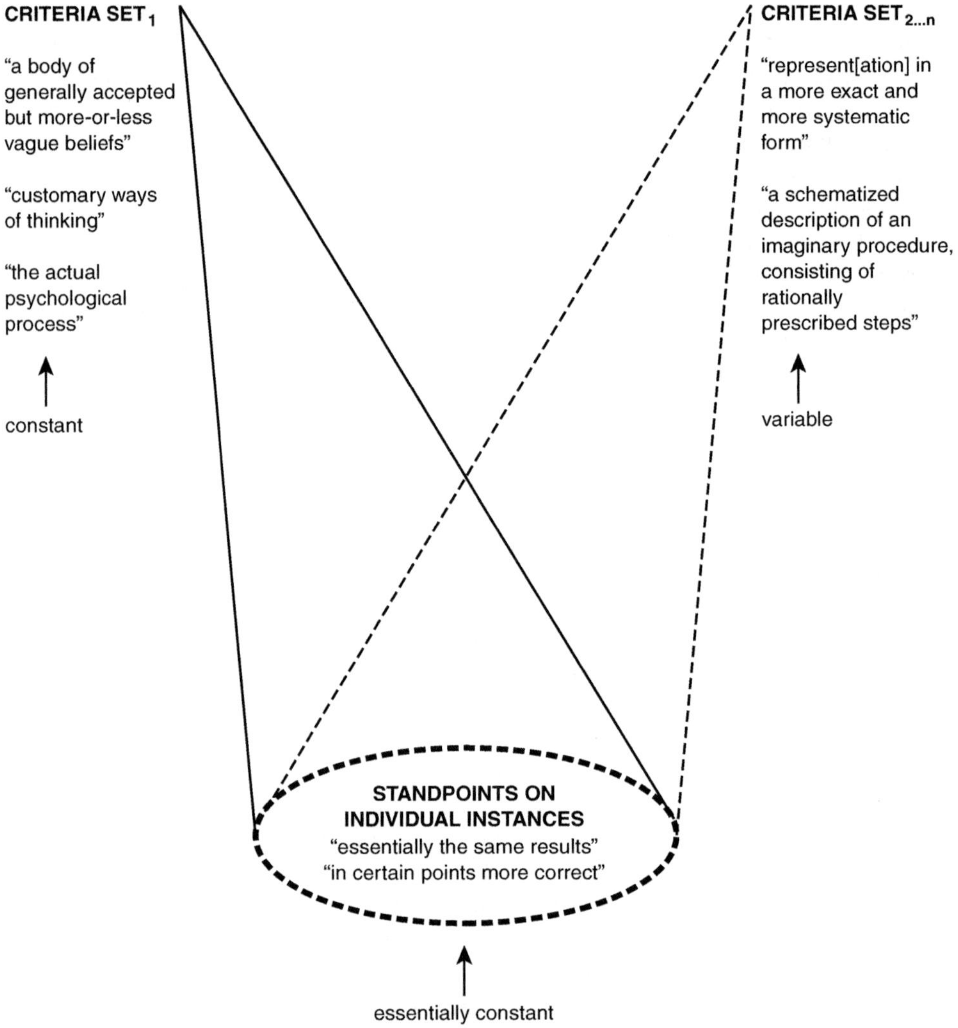

'reconstruction and redefinition', I keep evaluation prescriptions outside my conceptualisation (sections 3.2 (2)(c) and 3.3.1 (2)(c), above).

(3) Carnap's terminology

Carnap's normative aim, to conceptualise a mode of analysis that he recommends (item (2)(c) above), may also be the explanation for the *name he gives to his concept*: The qualifier "rational" is objectively speaking apt to influence, in that positive associations are attached to the word and in that these associations are transferred to what the word is used of; the word "rational" awakens an immediate intuition that one is confronted with analyses with particular epistemological solidity, in contrast to "irrational" analyses (even though Carnap does not, as far as I can see, use the term "irrational" of analyses that do not live up to his requirements, the term is psychologically natural once one has introduced the term "rational"). – Carnap's definition is thus an example of the fairly widespread use of persuasive definitions in academic literature too (sections II B 7.3.2, III 2.2.2 (3) and 2.4.2, above).

3.3.3. Others' use of Carnap's terms

Carnap's terms for modes of analysis are to a great extent also used outside the areas of science with which Carnap worked. They are used inter alia in descriptive or normative characterisations partly of *lawyers' argumentation de lege lata* (legal dogmatics) and partly of *legal theory*.

On legal dogmatics, it has been said, for example: "Explicative interpretation ... is what distinguishes ... legal dogmatics ...";[21] "[T]he proper task of legal ... dogmatics is the 'rational reconstruction' of legal materials".[22]

And on legal theory, it has been said, for example: "It is, as I see the matter, the task of legal theory to ... construct "a basic theory of law in revised form". ... The procedure in question may, as in Carnap, be called explication (or rational reconstruction) ...".[23]

Further, Carnap's terms are used in characterisations of *individual analyses*. Partly they are used in descriptive characterisations of *other writers'* analyses; as examples may be mentioned "explication" used of Hart's analysis of 'power',[24] "hypotheses about explication relationships" of Ross' analysis of 'legal rule',[25] or "rational reconstruction" of Kelsen's analysis of 'legal system'.[26] And partly they are used in statements about one's *own* analyses.[27] Such statements often

---

21 Frändberg, 'Om tolkning och förståelse' [on interpretation and understanding], p. 13.

22 MacCormick, 'Reconstruction after Deconstruction: A Response to CLS', p. 556. – Jareborg reads MacCormick's statements (also) as a description of legal dogmatics and concurs with this description: *Straffrättsideologiska fragment* [fragments of the ideology of criminal law], p. 68.

23 Frändberg, 'Till frågan om de juridiska begreppens systematik' [on the question of the systematics of legal concepts], p. 113.

24 Hacker, 'Hart's Philosophy of Law', p. 2 in note 2.

25 Ofstad, 'Om deskriptive definisjoner av begrepet rettsregel' [on descriptive definitions of the concept of 'legal rule'], p. 53, cf. p. 43.

26 Golding, 'Kelsen and the Concept of 'Legal System' ', pp. 73 et seq.

27 O. Dahl, *Om årsaksproblemer i historisk forskning* [on causal problems in historical research], p. 10 (" "eksplisering" or "transintensjonal analyse", in connection with the terminology in writers such as Rud. Carnap, Arne Næss and Harald Ofstad"), p. 42 ("eksplikative "real"-definisjoner"); Galtung, 'Expectations and Interaction Processes', pp. 225, 231–32 ("explication in Carnap's sense"); Ofstad, *An Inquiry into the Freedom of Decision*, p. 32 at and in note 3 (" 'explicatum' ... Cf. also Carnap's use ..."); Frändberg, *Om analog användning av rättsnormer* [on analogical use of legal norms], p. 4 ("rekonstruktion"), p. 9 ("rationellt analogibegrepp" [rational analogy concept]); Ullmann-Margalit, *The Emergence of Norms*, p. 1 ("rational reconstruction"); Bankowski/ MacCormick/ Summers/ Wróblewski, 'On Method and Methodology', pp. 10, 18–23 ("rational reconstruction");

combine descriptive characterisations, in the form of description of the analysis one has performed, and normative characterisations, in the form of expression of the decision one has made concerning the mode of analysis.[28]

Identity of words is just as poor a guarantee in relation to Carnap's terms as in relation to words otherwise of identity of meaning content. A writer may say explicitly that he is using the terms in another sense than Carnap. *Clues to possible difference in concepts* (including difference in definiteness of intention) are, however, more often of an indirect kind:[29] – discussion of the concepts without referring to Carnap's definitions;[30] – examples that do not harmonise well with Carnap's definitions;[31] – reference collectively to terms for modes of analysis or aspects of modes of analysis, which, in relation to the points of comparison here, are different;[32] – terminological or conceptual simplification;[33] – or combinations of Carnap's terms with one another,[34] with other writers' terms for modes of analysis,[35] or with other ordinary critically reflexive words.[36]

MacCormick, 'Foreword', pp. xiii–xiv ("rational reconstruction"); Summers/ Taruffo, 'Interpretation and Comparative Analysis', p. 463 ("rationally explicable"); Habermas, *Faktizität und Geltung*, p. 109 ("rational rekonstruieren"), p. 166 ("Bedeutungsexplikation").

28 The latter is in contrast to statements about other writers' analyses, see immediately above (at and in notes 24–26). More important, however, both in a causal perspective and in a tenability perspective, both in relation to other writers' and one's own analyses, are combinations of descriptive and normative propositions in the analyses themselves, see the main text after note 36 below.

29 Abbreviated references in what follows are to works, page references and quotations in the preceding notes in the present section 3.3.3.

30 Golding, 'Kelsen' (note 26 above), pp. 71–73; MacCormick, 'Reconstruction' (note 22 above), at and in notes 39–40; 'Foreword' (note 27 above); Bankowski/ MacCormick/ Summers/ Wróblewski, 'Method' (note 27 above).

31 Ullmann-Margalit, *Norms* (note 27 above), p. 2: "As exemplifying the practice of providing rational reconstructions in the realm of social philosophy I would regard ... Rawls's reconstruction of the just, or fair, society." As I shall later demonstrate, there are in relation to the points of comparison here important differences between Carnap's and Rawls' concepts of modes of analysis (section 3.4 below, in particular items (2)(a)–(b)).

32 O. Dahl, *Årsaksproblemer* (note 27 above): ""eksplisering" eller [or] "transintensjonal analyse""; Frändberg, 'Tolkning' (note 21 above) and 'De juridiska begreppens systematik' (note 23 above): "explikation (eller [or] rationell rekonstruktion)"; Ofstad, *Freedom of Decision* (note 27 above): "... Cf. *also* Carnap's use" (my italics); see also Ofstad, 'Begrepet rettsregel' (note 25 above), p. 43 in note 5.

33 Ayer, 'Conversation', p. 73: "[T]here is what might be called constructive analysis, as practised particularly by people like Carnap, where you don't bother so much with actual usage, or with justification, but you take some concept which is in ordinary or scientific use and redefine it in such a way as to sharpen it and perhaps make it more useful scientifically."

34 Summers/ Taruffo, 'Interpretation' (note 27 above): "rationally explicable"; Habermas, *Faktizität und Geltung*, p. 166: "Die Rekonstruktion des Rechts hat den Stellenwert einer Bedeutungsexplikation."

35 O. Dahl, *Årsaksproblemer* (note 27 above): "eksplikative "real"-definisjoner".

36 Goodman, *The Structure of Appearance*, p. xix: "logical construction", pp. xix, 385: "explicative definition", pp. 3, 385: "constructional definition"; Stegmüller, *Rationale Rekonstruktion von Wissenschaft und ihrem Wandel*, p. 23: "präzise Explikation", p. 25: "klare Rekonstruktionen"; Alexy/ Peczenik, 'The Concept of Coherence and Its Significance for Discursive Rationality', p. 135, MacCormick/ Weinberger, *An Institutional Theory of Law*, p. 42 and Peczenik, *On Law and Reason*,

One *cause* of the diverse use of Carnap's terms I take to lie in the combination of the following two factors:

First, there are *indeterminacies* on important points in the criteria for the use of the terms: indeterminacy with respect to how the concepts of 'explication' and 'rational reconstruction' relate to the distinction between connotation and denotation (sections 3.3.1 (2)(b) and 3.3.2 (2)(b), above); indeterminacy with respect to how the fundamental types of proposition may be combined (section 3.3.2 (2) (a) above); and indeterminacy as a result of evaluation prescriptions in the connotations of the concepts (sections 3.3.1 (2)(c) and 3.3.2 (2)(c), above). – These indeterminacies in the criteria give the terms "explication" and "rational reconstruction" a comprehensive and only vaguely delimited area of application. Thereby a diverse use of these terms is *made possible*.

Secondly, there is the *persuasive effect* linked to the terms: partly through Carnap's reputation, and partly through the word "rational" (section 3.3.2 (3) above). – I assume that in many connections desires to persuade (justify or recommend, to oneself or others) act as a *factor triggering* the use of Carnap's terms.

The diversity in the use of Carnap's terms illustrates the significance of continuous *critically reflexive questioning*: What proposition types, in what combinations are put forward, and what facts and criteria are thus relevant to the tenability assessment? (Chapter I above and section 4.1 below).

Keywords for modes of analysis, for example Carnap's terms, can point out a direction, but not much more, cf. above. – In my experience central parts of lawyers' argumentation de lege lata and many propositions in legal theory are *more aptly* characterised through my concept of 'reconstruction and redefinition' (section 2 above): Descriptive characterisations through adopted ways of using Carnap's terms easily become too indeterminate (the present section 3.3.3); or, if the characterisations are determinate, they easily become misleading, in that they fail to recognise the distinctive feature that the denotation is essentially kept constant (sections 1–2 above).

p. 137: "logical reconstruction", the latter work, p. 18: "precise reconstruction"; Maus, 'Freiheitsrechte und Volkssouveränität', p. 509: "kohärente Rekonstruktion".

3.4. Goodman, Rawls: 'Reflective equilibrium'

A third object of comparison for my concept of 'reconstruction and redefinition' is a set of concepts of modes of analysis originating partly in general theory of science (Goodman) and partly in ethical and political theory (Rawls and other writers).

(1) Goodman's concept. Rawls' version

(2) Some similarities and differences between the concept of 'reflective equilibrium' and my concept of 'reconstruction and redefinition'

- **(a) Which proposition types are combined in the concept**
- **(b) The relationship of the concept formed to the distinction between connotation and denotation. The fixed and variable points of the mode of analysis**
- **(c) Whether evaluation prescription is brought into the concept**

(1) Goodman's concept. Rawls' version

A fundamental contribution to the core of the concepts in question was made by Goodman in his book *Fact, Fiction, and Forecast* (first edition 1955; in the present work quotations are taken from the third edition, 1973, which in relation to the earlier editions is unchanged on the points that are relevant here). Goodman links his discussions of analysis and justification modes mainly to the question of how we justify induction and deduction, but he also links his discussions more generally to definitions.

Concerning justification for *induction* and *deduction* Goodman says:

> "How do we justify a deduction? Plainly, by showing that it conforms to the general rules of deductive inference. ... Analogously, the basic task in justifying an inductive inference is to show that it conforms to the general rules of induction. ...
>
> [O]f course, the rules themselves must eventually be justified. The validity ... depends not upon conformity to any purely arbitrary rules we may contrive, but upon conformity to valid rules. ... But how is the validity of rules to be determined? ... Principles of deductive inference are justified by their conformity with accepted deductive practice. ...
>
> This looks flagrantly *circular*. I have said that deductive inferences are justified by their conformity to valid general rules, and that general rules are justified by their conformity to valid inferences. But this circle is a *virtuous* one. The point is that rules and particular inferences alike are justified by being brought into agreement with each other. *A rule is amended if it yields an inference we are unwilling to accept; an inference is rejected if it violates a rule we are unwilling to amend* [Goodman's italics]. The process of justification is the delicate one of making *mutual adjustments* between rules

> and accepted inferences; and in the *agreement achieved* lies the only justification needed for either" (my italics unless otherwise stated).[37]

Goodman then gives the concepts outlined, 'mutual adjustments' and 'the agreement achieved', a wider area of application than simply justification of induction and deduction. He links these concepts more generally to *definitions*:

> "The task of formulating rules that define the difference between valid and invalid inductive inferences is much like the task of *defining any term with an established usage*. ... [T]he interplay ... between rules of induction and particular inductive inferences is simply an instance of this characteristic *dual adjustment* between *definition* and *usage*, whereby the usage informs the definition, which in turn guides extension of the usage" (my italics).[38]

In the given quotations from Goodman lies a good deal of material for drawing parallels with my concept of 'reconstruction and redefinition'. It is, however, reasonable to link the drawing of parallels also to Rawls' conceptualisation of mode of analysis in his book *A Theory of Justice*, which appeared in 1971; for there Rawls provides a *version*[39] *of Goodman's conceptualisation* which was to turn out to be better known than Goodman's own.

Rawls calls his version "reflective equilibrium". The function of his concept so called is to illuminate the analyses and justifications he advances for his theory of justice. Main elements in the concept are general ethical principles and concrete ethical judgements,[40] both in relation to substantial ethical questions and in relation to the deliberation situation itself.[41]

> In several later works Rawls has taken up his theory of justice for further discussion. In so doing, he has clarified and to a certain extent revised his standpoints.[42] One important clarification/ revision is that his theory is now explicitly restricted to the political domain, in contrast to more comprehensive moral theories.[43] However, Rawls has stated that he wishes to retain the concept of 'reflective equilibrium' unchanged.[44] And I cannot see, either, that the said restriction to the political domain or other clarifications/ revisions of his theory affect the concept as it was established in the first edition of *A Theory of Justice*.

---

37 Goodman, *Fact, Fiction, and Forecast*, pp. 63–64.

38 Op. cit., p. 66.

39 Rawls, *A Theory of Justice*, 1st ed. p. 20 in note 7; 2nd ed. p. 18 in note 7.

40 Op. cit., 1st ed. pp. 19–21, 46(48)–51, 577–87; 2nd ed. pp. 17–19, 40(42)–45, 506–14.

41 Op. cit., 1st ed. pp. 17–21; 2nd ed. pp. 15–19.

42 Rawls, 'Justice as Fairness: Political not Metaphysical', at and in notes 2, 20, 33; *Political Liberalism*, pp. xiv–xxx, 53 at and in note 7, 290, 371; *A Theory of Justice*, 2nd ed. pp. xii–xiii.

43 Rawls, 'Justice as Fairness: Political not Metaphysical', pp. 224–25 including note 2, 245; *Political Liberalism*, pp. xiv–xviii et passim. Rawls calls the two versions of his theory of justice "a comprehensive philosophical doctrine" and "a political conception" respectively, see *Political Liberalism*, pp. xvi, 11 et seq.

44 Rawls, 'The Independence of Moral Theory', pp. 7–8; 'Justice as Fairness: Political not Metaphysical', p. 228; *Political Liberalism*, pp. 8, 28, 45; *A Theory of Justice*, 2nd ed. pp. xii–xv, cf. pp. 17–19, 40–44, 506–14.

(2) Some similarities and differences between the concept of 'reflective equilibrium' and my concept of 'reconstruction and redefinition'

(a) Which proposition types are combined in the concept

The concept of 'reflective equilibrium' embraces descriptive and normative propositions, and definitions and characterisations. Thus a reflective language and argumentation equilibrium will be *just as complex* as a reconstruction and redefinition.

I have earlier pointed out that Carnap's concept of 'rational reconstruction' is more *indeterminate* than my concept of 'reconstruction and redefinition' with respect to the fundamental proposition types and the way in which they combine (section 3.3.2 (2)(a) above, concluding remarks). – The concept of 'reflective equilibrium' is *even more* indeterminate than Carnap's concept in this respect; it does not introduce any constraints with respect to the occurrence of the fundamental proposition types and their relationship to one another.

(b) The relationship of the concept formed to the distinction between connotation and denotation. The fixed and variable points of the mode of analysis

The indeterminacy with respect to the fundamental proposition types and their combination (item (a) above) also includes indeterminacy with respect to the distinction between connotation and denotation; this distinction is not built into the concept of 'reflective equilibrium', and it is *not possible to use the distinction* for a *systematic* analysis of the propositions in reflective equilibrium. – The reason is the same as in the case of Carnap's rational reconstructions: The distinction between connotation and denotation is only applicable in the case of concepts/ general words and expressions, not in the case of propositions; and the propositions of the mode of analysis have no systematic definitional or factual connection with the connotation or denotation of concepts (section 3.3.2 (2)(b) above).

As in the case of Carnap's rational reconstructions we must therefore use other concepts than 'connotation' and 'denotation' to identify the fixed and variable points of the mode of analysis.

I shall have recourse to the same *drawing of parallels* as in the discussion of rational reconstructions (item 3.3.2 (2)(b) above): I draw a parallel between the connotations of concepts and general views (Goodman: "rules", Rawls: "principles"). In this context I call them by the common term "criteria". Further, I draw a parallel between the denotations of concepts and standpoints on individual instances in the case of application of general views (Goodman: "particular inferences", Rawls: "judgments").

With their interplay between each other in mind Goodman terms the relationship between general view ("rule") and standpoint on the individual instance ("particular inference") "*an instance of* [the] characteristic dual adjustment between definition and usage, whereby the usage informs the definition, which in turn guides extension of the usage", see the quotation in item (1) above, in the text at note 38. – In relation to the present topic, comparison of concepts of modes of analysis with particular reference to dis/agreement analysis, I consider it important, however, to *maintain the difference* between, on the one hand, views of concepts/ general words and expressions, with their connotations and denotations, and on the other hand, views of other things than concepts/ general words and expressions, where the distinction between connotation and denotation does not apply (section 3.3.2 (2)(b) above). Otherwise the concept formed may become too loose to provide insight into actually occurring patterns (section 3.5 below). Therefore I prefer to speak of *"drawing parallels"* (and, as the case may be, of "structural similarity").

The *result* of the drawing of parallels is, however, different from the result of the drawing of parallels in the case of rational reconstructions. If we take our point of departure in reconstructions and redefinitions as a *graduated* mode of analysis and in the *extreme case* "agreement about individual instances, disagreement about criteria", then reflective language and argumentation equilibrium places itself *farther from* the extreme case than rational reconstructions:

Reconstructions and redefinitions *tend definitionally towards "agreement about individual instances, disagreement about criteria"* (section 1.1 (1)–(2) above). I have taken Carnap's statements about the concepts of 'explication' and 'rational reconstruction' to mean that these concepts have a similar structure, albeit to mean that these concepts are to a lesser degree linked to the extreme case (respectively sections 3.3.1 (2)(b) and 3.3.2 (2)(b), above). – In all these modes of analysis, standpoints on individual instances represent a relatively fixed point compared to the criteria: a point which different discussion participants are to a greater degree in agreement about or which the same discussion participant to a greater degree takes as a point of departure in new analyses. The criteria are to a greater degree the variable of the mode of analysis.

In contrast, in the case of reflective language and argumentation equilibrium, standpoints on individual instances and criteria are *to an equal degree definitionally variable*: Whether in the case of reflective disequilibrium one is to change one's standpoints on individual instances in the light of one's criteria, or whether one is to adjust one's criteria until they generate one's standpoints on individual instances, is a conceptually open question.[45]

Factually, however, a number of Rawls' analyses tend towards a reconstruction and redefinition structure, i.e. a structure in which standpoints on individual instances are given a privileged position: "In the second part I examined the sort

[45] See the references to Rawls, *A Theory of Justice*, in item (1) above, in notes 40–41: in particular 1st ed. p. 20, 2nd ed. p. 18 ("even the judgments we take provisionally as fixed points are liable to revision"); 1st ed. pp. 21 and 579, 2nd ed. pp. 19 and 507 ("justification is a matter of ... everything fitting together into one coherent view"); and 1st ed. pp. 48–49, 2nd ed. pp. 42–43.

of institutions that justice enjoins and the kinds of duties and obligations it imposes on individuals. The aim throughout was to show that the theory proposed matches the *fixed points of our considered convictions* better than other familiar doctrines ..." (my italics).[46]

(c) Whether evaluation prescription is brought into the concept
Carnap builds evaluation prescriptions into his concepts of 'explication' and 'rational reconstruction', and he states this in his definition formulations (see respectively sections 3.3.1 (2)(c) and 3.3.2 (2)(c), above).

In Goodman and Rawls it is not equally clear what role evaluations are intended to play, and in the event, what evaluations. As points of departure we can take Goodman's statement "[R]ules and particular inferences alike are justified by being brought into *agreement* with each other" (quoted in item (1) above, in the text at note 37; my italics), and Rawls' statement "Justification is a matter of ... everything fitting together into one *coherent view*" (quoted in item (2)(b) above, in note 45; my italics). – In connection with these statements it may be asked *how one decides* whether there is reflective equilibrium (sufficient "agreement" or "coherence").

Goodman and Rawls *do not say explicitly* that evaluations are to be brought into this decision. This follows, however, from the *concept of 'reflective equilibrium' otherwise*: That one shall seek to achieve reflective equilibrium in one's views is *in contrast to* one's choosing between views through arbitrary decisions ("throwing dice"). And in the alternative to arbitrary decision lies inter alia one's reflecting on what values come into play, and with what weight.

In that the concept of 'reflective equilibrium' prescribes evaluations in this way, it differs from the concept of 'reconstruction and redefinition' (sections 3.2 (2)(c) and 1.2, above) and resembles Carnap's concepts. At the same time the concept of 'reflective equilibrium' differs from Carnap's concepts in that the values are not specified and ranked (on Carnap's specification and ranking, see section 3.3.1 (1)(c) above).

3.5. The graduated transitions to significant differences

My concept of 'reconstruction and redefinition' is a concept of degree; a mode of analysis can to a *greater or lesser degree* have a reconstruction and redefinition structure (section 1.1 (2) above). There are thus graduated transitions to *such* significant differences that I would no longer call the mode of analysis "reconstruction and redefinition". – It is of little interest to lay down the boundary in general; it should be drawn with consideration for what one wishes to shed light on in the individual instance.

---

46 Op. cit., 1st ed. pp. 579–80; 2nd ed. p. 507.

A graduated concept criterion which is relevant in relation to actually occurring language and argumentation (section 2 above) and on which the main emphasis was placed in the comparison with other concepts of modes of analysis (sections 3.2–3.4 above), is whether the denotation is essentially stuck to. Many concepts of modes of analysis have a looser structure, inter alia in this dimension. – In extreme cases one forms concepts of modes of analysis *without structure*, also without structure produced by the distinctions between descriptive and normative propositions, definitions and characterisations, and connotation and denotation. In these cases the concept of a mode of analysis becomes a reference to a *conclusion*, to what one considers has the best grounds to support it. The concept does not say anything about *how* one arrives at the conclusion, about the nature or structure of the grounds. – In other cases one forms concepts of mode of analysis by means of *other distinctions* than those between descriptive and normative propositions, definitions and characterisations, or connotation and denotation. – Names with "coherence", "cohesiveness" or "integrity" (or the equivalent in other languages) as a constituent are used both of the graduatedly more structureless concepts of mode of analysis,[47] and of the graduatedly differently structured concepts of mode of analysis.[48] But one may also meet the graduatedly more structureless or differently structured concepts under the same names as the concepts discussed above.[49]

What concepts of mode of analysis *ought to be chosen* rests on what one wishes to achieve by the concept formed (section III 2 above). – A general *problem* is that the less the concepts distinguish between modes of analysis, the more unclear it becomes *what one can use the concepts for*. There are two points I should like to emphasise here.

The first point concerns concepts one uses for characterisation of *lawyers' argumentation de lege lata* or of *analyses in legal theory*: I assume that central

47 Scanlon, 'The Aims and Authority of Moral Theory', pp. 13–14: "The result … a 'method of coherence' that … amounts simply to the thesis that we should accept those principles that seem to us on reflection to be correct"; Thagard, *Coherence in Thought and Action*, pp. 41, 126.

48 With lawyers' language and argumentation in mind, see e.g. the following works (the dashes in the rest of the present note signal grouping in two main dimensions, partly from more abstract to more concrete propositions, and partly between more concrete propositions according to whether they relate to Anglo-American law (Dworkin, MacCormick), Nordic law (Bolding), or other law): – Alexy/ Peczenik, 'The Concept of Coherence and Its Significance for Discursive Rationality'; Peczenik, *On Law and Reason*, pp. 158–87; *Vad är rätt?* [what is law], pp. 571–609, 652 et seq.; see also Peczenik et al., *Juridisk argumentation* [legal argumentation], in particular Chapter 5, with further references; Peczenik, 'En förståelsesmodell för etik, rätt och argumentation' [an interpretation model for ethics, law and argumentation], pp. 32–38; – Dworkin, *Law's Empire*, pp. 225 et seq., cf. 400–07 (Dworkin uses the word "integrity" instead of "coherence"); – MacCormick, *Legal Reasoning and Legal Theory*, pp. 103–08, 119–28, 152–228; 'Coherence in Legal Justification'; – Bolding, *Juridik och samhällsdebatt* [jurisprudence and public debate], pp. 14, 18, 21, 65, 74–75, 85–86, 119.

49 Under the names of Carnap's terms, e.g. in those works of MacCormick, Golding and Bankowski/ MacCormick/ Summers/ Wróblewski mentioned in section 3.3.3 above; or under the name of Rawls' term, e.g. in the work by Scanlon mentioned in note 47 above, and in Nielsen, 'In Defense of Wide Reflective Equilibrium'.

parts of lawyers' argumentation de lege lata and many analyses in legal theory are *more aptly* characterised through my concept of 'reconstruction and redefinition' (section 2 above) than through coherence concepts (section 3.4 above and the present section 3.5). The reasons are the same as those that lead me to prefer the concept of 'reconstruction and redefinition' to adopted ways of using Carnap's terms (section 3.3.3 above, concluding remarks), but they apply even more strongly in relation to coherence concepts: Descriptive characterisations through coherence concepts easily become *too indeterminate*; or, if the characterisations are determinate, they easily become *misleading*, in that they fail to recognise the distinctive feature that lies in an interplay between definitions and characterisations, that is linked to a denotation that is essentially kept constant (sections 1–2 above). – The demonstration in this work of the existence and factual significance of reconstructions and redefinitions, just like, and more generally, the demonstration in this work of the existence and factual significance of the critically reflexive form that constitutes the perspective and topic of the work, represents a *challenge* (also) to coherence theories: A coherence theory will, other things being equal, stand stronger the more explicitly the theory relates to and is able to integrate those acts, including reconstructions and redefinitions, of which the work has demonstrated the existence and factual significance.[50]

The second point I should like to emphasise concerns concepts one uses for characterisation of *one's own mode of analysis*: Here, the less a concept distinguishes between modes of analysis, the more indeterminate it becomes what criteria are relevant to the assessment of the tenability of one's own propositions, and thus to *choice* between these and competing propositions.[51]

---

50 Compare in this connection also section II G 2 above, especially item (4)(c)(ii).

51 Eng, 'Teoristruktur og teorivalg' [theory structure and theory choice]. – Compare Peirce, 'The Fixation of Belief', p. 20: "[T]hat bad reasoning as well as good reasoning is possible ... is the foundation of the practical side of logic."

4. Tenability assessment and causal perspective

4.1. The assessment of tenability; a function of the unity of several sets of criteria

According to what criteria will the tenability of reconstructions and redefinitions be assessed, to the extent that one thinks about the question?

On this point I refer to the conclusions in Chapter III above. There criteria were mapped that are considered relevant in the setting up of and choice between propositions. As was apparent from my discussions, one uses a *diversity* of criteria in relation to *each* of the fundamental proposition types by itself. Because a reconstruction and redefinition is a *combination* of the fundamental proposition types, the diversity of relevant criteria increases correspondingly:

In the assessment of the *hypothesis* about properties of the denotation phenomena (the descriptive characterisation), one will typically take one's point of departure in the truth criterion. But other considerations too are often brought in (section III 3 above). – And in the assessment of the *normative-innovative definition* (the assessment of whether those properties that the hypothesis brings out are better suited as concept criteria than those that were used by presupposition in the delimitation of the denotation), a great diversity of criteria might be considered relevant (section III 2 above).

There is *not necessarily any logical contradiction* between different reconstructions and redefinitions: Different descriptive characterisations of the common and presupposed denotation may all be true (section III 2.2.4 above). And which of the properties the characterisations bring out are best suited in a normative-innovative connotation specification will depend on weighings and balancings within that part of the criterion diversity that is considered relevant in the individual instance (section III 2 above). – Given particular interests, one can, however, speak of *practical contradiction*, in the sense that one reconstruction and redefinition can be more suited than another to furthering these interests.

Since the unity of the descriptive characterisation and normative-innovative definition is central to reconstructions and redefinitions, the tenability of a reconstruction and redefinition will be a *function of the unity* of the tenability criteria for each of these proposition types. I have not been able to find any established patterns for this function. – To the question posed above ("according to what criteria will the tenability of reconstructions and redefinitions be assessed?") it is thus not possible to give any answer that is at one and the same time general, simple and determinate. *In general* one must content oneself with referring to the diversity of criteria that are actually in use, and more indeterminately say that the tenability is "a function of the unity" of the criteria.

> Since in the tenability assessment in relation to each of the fundamental proposition types by itself one makes use of a diversity of criteria, the same applies there: the tenability is "a function of the unity" of the typically relevant criteria. However, there is a difference of degree in the diversity that gives particular reason to emphasise the indeterminacy here, in the case of combinations of the fundamental proposition types.

In relation to *individual* reconstructions and redefinitions one can of course enquire more determinately; one can ask partly what criteria the sender of the reconstruction and redefinition had in mind, and partly what criteria particular recipients (discussion participants) used when they accepted or criticised the reconstruction and redefinition.

4.2. Causal perspective; some factors that may contribute to explaining tendencies in the direction of reconstructions and redefinitions

4.2.1. Explanation of social phenomena versus explanation of natural phenomena

When it comes to *social phenomena*, and here a good example is the law, *human (self-)consciousness* is considered to be central when the phenomena are to be explained. This is because one considers that social phenomena are a result, intended or unintended, of human acts, and that human acts are mediated via human (self-)consciousness. With these points of departure it is reasonable to assume that concepts of social phenomena, for example legal phenomena, which are to have relevance for understanding society, must have a certain connection with *human beings' perceptions of the phenomena*. It is further reasonable to assume that the connection must first and foremost be with the denotation, since one often lacks or has pretty confused perceptions of why one collects and separates the phenomena as one in fact does, i.e. of the connotation. This leads to one's considering it reasonable, in analysing concepts of social phenomena, to place the restriction on one's investigation that *denotations in everyday language are essentially to be taken as given.*

The *natural sciences*, on the other hand, are considered to be free to form concepts of the phenomena without taking into consideration the perception that the object of investigation has of itself ("the (self-)consciousness of natural objects"). There is not considered to be any reason to take human beings' perceptions of nature into consideration either, since the regularities in nature are assumed to take their course independently of human consciousness. This leads to one's not considering it justified, in analysing concepts of natural phenomena, to take connotations or denotations in everyday language as given: *Both connotations and denotations in everyday language are considered to be variables.*

The topic of the present section 4.2 is causes of the occurrence in fact of the reconstruction and redefinition pattern. The topic is no more here than otherwise in the present Chapter V arguments for or against following this pattern. Thus the main text above expresses neither concurrence with nor objection to the assumptions about social and natural phenomena that are outlined there. On the other hand the text asserts for one thing that these assumptions are widespread, and for another the fact that, and the way in which, these assumptions can thus contribute to explaining tendencies towards reconstructions and redefinitions.

4.2.2. Normatively regulated denotation

(1) The point of departure: legal, philosophical or political grounds for sticking to a denotation
(2) ... combined with requirements for innovation or an urge to exercise imagination and creative power
(3) ... combined with an urge to influence action, or a yearning for aesthetics or heuristics

(1) The point of departure: legal, philosophical or political grounds for sticking to a denotation

One cause of the occurrence of the reconstruction and redefinition pattern may be that for normative reasons the person analysing takes other people's subsumptions as given, i.e. respects the others' denotation specification and contents himself with investigating this with a view to new connotations. I shall look at three instance-types of such normative reasons: legal, philosophical and political reasons respectively.

The respect for others' denotation specification may be considered to be a *legal duty*, cf. the lawyer's duties according to the doctrine of the sources of law to build on other lawyers' views. An example is the lawyer's duty according to the doctrine of precedent to treat the pairwise facts and conclusions of judgments as a class of "brute facts", when he wants to use the judgments in justification or criticism of propositions de lege lata (section 2.4 above).

In this *authorised denotation specification* for analyses de lege lata lies a *difference* from legal theory and philosophy as a whole: The legal system neither offers nor requires any authorised establishment of the denotations of concepts like 'law', 'rule', 'right', or other basic concepts, when they are used outside the individual legal rule. Whether the analyst in legal theory or general philosophy is to take denotations as given, and if so which ones, is not regulated through methodological norms, but left to the analyst's choice. Here "choice" is not used of personal arbitrariness on a par with taste, but of the analyst's being free to follow the thought structures that he thinks have the best grounds to support them ("lead to the most tenable propositions"; compare Chapter III above); thus normative regulation takes place also in legal theory and philosophy as a whole, but now it is a question of "thought's own laws", and the research community basically leaves it to the individual to determine which ones these are.

Certain philosophical positions may, however, be seen as *parallels* to legal methodology's normative regulation of the denotation for the analysis: The duty to respect the others' denotation specification may be considered to have a basis in *reason itself*, in that one considers that a particular human cognitional faculty, often termed "intuition", stands in an epistemologically privileged position – here, in a privileged position with respect to linguistic subsumption practice.

> It is no longer usual to claim that "intuition" in the sense of *'faculty'* stands in an epistemologically privileged position.[1] On the other hand, "intuition" is quite often invoked in the sense of *'result'*, i.e. the standpoints one more or less unreflectingly has.[2] However, it is not always clear whether the latter-mentioned intuitions are put on a par with other arguments or whether they are imagined to have a particular weight.[3] And provided they are imagined to have a particular weight, then it is not always clear why. I consider it not improbable that intuitions (results) are given attention because intuition (faculty) today too, but now more unclearly, is considered to stand in an epistemologically privileged position. Nevertheless I assume that legal bases, cf. the main text above, together with political basis and empirical basis, cf. the main text in what follows, are causally the more effective today.

The respect for others' denotation specification can also be considered to have a *political* basis, in adherence by presupposition to *democracy*. – This may be so partly in the form that the reconstruction and redefinition structure is seen as being democratic to an especially high degree, *independently of* the particular concepts and views that might be part of the structure in the individual instance: democratic in relation to the *citizen* by respecting widely held views on how individual instances shall be subsumed (denotations), and democratic in relation to the *researcher* by giving him freedom to construct the sets of connotations he thinks are best, with the restriction that the criteria shall be suited to generating the widely held standpoints on individual instances. – And this may be so partly in the form that in relation to *politically controversial concepts*, for example in

[1] See e.g. Williams, *Ethics and the Limits of Philosophy*, pp. 93–94.

[2] Section 3 above; Hare, *Moral Thinking*, pp. 7, 75; Williams, *Ethics and the Limits of Philosophy*, pp. 94 et seq.; Habermas, 'Erläuterungen zur Diskursethik', pp. 125, 142, 185; MacCormick/ Weinberger, *An Institutional Theory of Law*, p. 8.

[3] See e.g. section 3.4 (2)(b) above, concluding remarks, on the fact that in his concept of 'reflective equilibrium' Rawls puts intuitions on a par with other arguments, at the same time as his factual argumentation shows signs of ascribing them particular weight.

many social contexts the concepts of 'legal rule' or 'just rule', one places *particular* weight on widely held views on how individual instances shall be subsumed (denotations).[4]

For the sake of completeness and for delimitation of the normative bases now outlined, I mention that respect for others' denotation specification is often considered to have an *empirical basis*, cf. assumptions that individual human beings have developed, or that participants in a group regularly develop, a *distinctive* "intuition". An example is the assumption that qualified and trained lawyers to a high degree adopt the same standpoint or similar standpoints in discretionary questions on which others disagree.[5]

The bases may be *combined*. For example, the lawyer who treats the pairwise facts and conclusions of judgments as an approximately fixed point[6] may be motivated partly by the *doctrine of precedent*; partly by a view that judges realise a more *general intuitive faculty* human beings possess to make the right decision when they are presented with *all* the assumedly relevant sides of an individual set of facts (something the judge and, with the exception of the parties, as a rule only

---

4 Put pointedly, but probably symptomatic of the existence of more or less conscious views of this kind, Holmes, *Natural Law*, p. 316: "Philosophy does not furnish motives, but it shows men that they are not fools for doing what they already want to do."

5 Pound, 'The Theory of Judicial Decision', p. 951; Cardozo, 'The Growth of the Law', pp. 225–26; 'The Paradoxes of Legal Science', pp. 286–87; Sundby, *Om normer* [on norms], pp. 267–68; Eckhoff, *Rettskildelære* [doctrine of the sources of law], pp. 23–24, 302–03: "[T]he trained lawyer [will] have a pretty good feeling of how much weight it is defensible to give to the various [legally relevant] arguments. And there is pretty good correspondence between different lawyers' attitudes to this. One may perhaps see it as being the case that ... the evaluation is largely governed by norms that defy formulation." – Something else than such assumption of the development of a distinctive lawyer's intuition is (i) assumption that a more general intuition comes into play, e.g. in the case of judicial decision of individual instances, compare Holmes in Lochner v. New York, 198 U.S. 45 (1905), on p. 76: "General propositions do not decide concrete cases. The decision will depend on a judgment or intuition more subtle than any articulate major premise"; and (ii) assumption that a more special intution is necessary for a good decision, e.g. for good judicial decision of individual instances, compare Knoph, *Oversikt over Norges rett* [survey of Norwegian law] p. 18: "[To be] a good judge ... it is necessary to have ... a "good iudicium", that enables the judge immediately to see the crux of a case and intuitively to seize on the right decision."

6 Compare C. Smith, *Studier i garantiretten – Garantirett II* [studies in the law of guarantees and bonds – guarantee law II], p. 13: "There is a presumption that the solution that has been adopted in a judgment is one that is good and usable in practice"; correspondingly in 'Domstolene og rettsutviklingen' [the courts and the evolution of the law], p. 313; Fleischer, *Anvendelse og fortolkning av dommer* [application and interpretation of judgments], p. 49: "[G]enerally there is a presumption that a judgment pronounced gives expression to a conclusion that is correct in practice [note with reference to the first-mentioned work by Smith] irrespective of whether the grounds might not be acceptable"; Frihagen, *Villfarelse og ugyldighet i forvaltningsretten* [mistake, misrepresentation and invalidity in administrative law], p. 191: "... the conclusions of the judgments – e.g. that the court finds for the Crown, that a fine is imposed on a man, etc., must be assumed to be good and practical solutions. However, this is not the same as assuming that the legal rules that are built on are good and practical"; correspondingly on p. 192 in note 21. See also Sandvik, *Entreprenørrisikoen* [the risk borne by the building contractor], p. 78; Austenå, *Løsningsrettigheter* [options to purchase, rights of pre-emption, etc.], p. 46.

the judge, is presented with, cf. respectively the audi alteram partem procedure and the fact that outsiders seldom follow all parts of a court case); and partly by a view that most judges, by virtue of being qualified and trained lawyers, have developed a *distinctive intuition* concerning the best relationship between the concepts in the legal rules and individual sets of facts.

My impression is that among the bases now mentioned for respecting other people's denotation specification, the legal basis is the *most effective in fact*: In their argumentation de lege lata lawyers stick to other lawyers' denotation specification to a higher degree than others stick to one another's denotation specification (sections 1–2, compare 3.3.3 concluding remarks and 3.5, above).

(2) … combined with requirements for innovation or an urge to exercise imagination and creative power

Of philosophers and scientists it is often *expected* that they shall create something *new*; and independently of what other people might expect, they may *themselves wish* to find an outlet for imagination and creative power in their work.

Expectations of innovation or an urge to exercise imagination and creative power are not in themselves causes of reconstruction and redefinition patterns. However, if the denotation is once considered normatively *locked*, cf. item (1) above, then expectations of innovation or an urge to exercise imagination and creative power will easily create a tendency towards reconstructions and redefinitions: The imagination and the creative power must in such a case seek an *outlet* in other places, typically in the construction of alternative sets of criteria for generating the given denotation.

Construction of alternative sets of criteria often takes the form of a unity of descriptive characterisation and normative definition, i.e. the variable in the reconstruction and redefinition pattern. This variable provides a space, however modest it may be, for discovery and imagination. In *law* this is one of the very few spaces for discovery and imagination – most important in practice, in the form of the doctrine of *constructed rationes decidendi* (section 2.4 above). This doctrine provides the lawyer with an opportunity to shift his thought *from* the collecting and reporting of what others have said *to* investigation of what properties previously decided individual instances had (descriptive characterisation), and *to* speculation about which of these properties may or may not be suited as concept criteria (normative definition in the form of normative-innovative connotation specification: "$\text{connotation}_{2 \ldots n}$").

(3) … combined with an urge to influence action, or a yearning for aesthetics or heuristics

I have earlier mapped criteria that are considered relevant in the setting up of and choice between normative definitions (section III 2 above). These criteria are causal factors in so far as they in fact motivate language and argumentation.

The criteria are not, however, in themselves causes of reconstruction and redefinition patterns. But they can become so, if the denotation is considered normatively locked, cf. item (1) above, in that the criteria can then provide a stimulus for a quest for new properties of the denotation phenomena (descriptive characterisation) and for deliberation of whether these properties are suited to becoming part of a new connotation (normative definition in the form of normative-innovative connotation specification: "connotation$_{2...n}$"). – This applies for example in the case of the urge to influence action (section III 2.2.5), the yearning for aesthetics (section III 2.2.6) and the desire for heuristics (section III 2.4.1).

For example, a yearning for aesthetics will, when the denotation is considered to be fixed, seek an outlet in (even) more aesthetic connotations for generating the presupposed denotation, an outlet in an (even) greater degree of simplicity, symmetry, consistency, or the like, in the concept criteria.

Taking into account the fact that the various motivating criteria are of a graduated nature and can pull in different directions, and taking into account the logically speaking infinite number of ways in which a given denotation can be generated, then there is plenty of room for that combination of agreement and disagreement that forms a reconstruction and redefinition structure ("agreement about denotation, disagreement about connotation (criteria)").

5. A more general structure

My concept of 'reconstruction and redefinition' has been built up around the distinction between the connotation and denotation of concepts. Comparison with some related concepts has shown that other writers to a lesser degree link their concepts to this distinction: In their concepts of mode of analysis, characterisations are not coupled to the distinction (section 3.3.2 (2)(b) above); or there is altogether no distinction made between definitions and characterisations (section 3.4 (2)(b) above). – Graduatedly less structured concepts of mode of analysis are accompanied by a danger that the concept formed becomes too loose in relation to interesting patterns in actually occurring language and argumentation; too many different things are treated at the same time. In extreme instances it becomes unclear what one can use the concept for (section 3.5 above).

After having now gone through the more determinate concept of 'reconstruction and redefinition', I shall, however, return to a looser conceptualisation and a previously indicated structural similarity:

The point of departure was a widening of the perspective: partly through the drawing of a parallel between, on the one hand, connotations of concepts, and on the other, criteria in general, for example justifications for why actions are right/ wrong; and partly through the drawing of a parallel between, on the one hand, denotations of concepts, and on the other, standpoints on individual instances in general, for example a standpoint on what action is right/ wrong in a particular situation. – From this widened perspective, the reconstruction and redefinition pattern is found again in the looser form "criterion dissimilarity in full and dissimilarities in standpoints on individual instances only to a certain degree": This pattern is found conceptually and factually in Carnap (section 3.3.2 (2)(b) above), and to a certain extent factually in Rawls (section 3.4 (2)(b) above, concluding remarks); and my impression is that the pattern also otherwise has a certain diffusion in philosophy and social science.

This *structural similarity* between reconstructions and redefinitions and justification patterns in a looser sense may serve as a heuristic lead to *other features in common* that are of interest. I shall point out some features in common of a psychological nature:

The structural similarity *captures a combination* of, on the one hand, acquiescence in or respect for something existing, and on the other, intellectual concern with criteria (justifications).

First, the structural similarity captures a *tendency to acquiescence in or respect for* "the bottom floor" in a given practice: concrete subsumptions in a linguistic practice or other individual actions in an extra-linguistic practice. Examples are the lawyer's acquiescence in the Supreme Court's subsumptions, or the philosopher's respect for intuitions about how individual instances should be resolved. – This provides the first fixed point of the structural similarity, the presupposed class of individual instances.

Secondly, the structural similarity captures a *tendency to dissatisfaction* with "the upper floors" in the given practice: dissatisfaction with what is perceived to be unreflected, unsystematic, or for other reasons less tenable, criteria for generating the individual instances. Examples are the lawyer's dissatisfaction with the Supreme Court's criteria, or the philosopher's dissatisfaction with the criteria "most people" give for their more intuitive standpoints on individual instances. – These criteria form the second fixed and presupposed point of the structural similarity, criteria set_1 of the analysis.

The dissatisfaction with these criteria provides a stimulus for investigation of the individual instances with a view to discovering new (other) properties of them. Further, it provides a stimulus for consideration of whether these properties are better suited to being elevated to criteria, of whether they will provide a more reflected, systematic, or for other reasons more tenable, set of criteria for generating the individual instances: for example for generating the conclusions of judgments, or for generating intuitive standpoints on individual instances. – These new sets of criteria form the variable of the structural similarity, criteria $set_{2...n}$ of the analysis.

The regularities that are brought into focus in my concept of 'reconstruction and redefinition' and in the more general structure now outlined, have no doubt been registered earlier. However, often one goes straight to, and contents oneself with, more vague intuitions, such as the metaphor "agreeing about outcomes, but disagreeing about justifications". My conceptualisation and in-depth treatment of the phenomenon of reconstruction and redefinition are thus of double value. First, they are of value by serving to create an awareness of a *distinct and widespread* combination of the fundamental types of proposition. Secondly, they are of value by laying a more precise conceptual foundation for *identifying and comparing* actually occurring modes of analysis.

In both respects my conceptualisation and in-depth treatment of the phenomenon of reconstruction and redefinition (the present Chapter V) demonstrate the *cognition value* of my concepts of proposition types (see my account of these in Chapter II above), now in their capacity of being building blocks for concepts of modes of analysis.

I↔V

Conclusion

In this work I have demonstrated the existence, content and factual significance of a relatively well-delimited critically reflexive form (section I 4), in the discussion and decision aspect (section I 4) of analysis and argumentation formulated in everyday language (section I 5), and with a certain independence (section I 6). Through this I have also demonstrated the factual significance of dis/agreement analysis on the basis of this critically reflexive form.

The work has been essentially *descriptive*. I have mapped a set of fundamental proposition types; constellations of these proposition types into regularly occurring patterns; tenability criteria that are advanced in connection with the proposition types and patterns; and underlying interests that make themselves felt and can explain the language and argumentation. I have not recommended or rejected proposition types, proposition patterns, criteria or interests.

> On certain points repetitions are necessary to a particularly high degree. The descriptive perspective is one of them, cf. the widespread propensity to interpret a writer's sentences as expressing normative propositions: as expressing rejection of or support for particular ways of acting. – The descriptive perspective has been emphasised in many ways: in headings, in introductory passages and in running text. In running text the descriptive perspective has been emphasised, for example, by linking the formulation "actually occurring" to the specific language and argumentation element that is being discussed.

I have sought to demonstrate the existence, content and factual significance of the critically reflexive form, in and through the *reader's own reality*. I have sought to do this, first, by letting the reader see the applicability of the concepts formed in this work to *his own language and argumentation*. I have sought to do this, secondly, by letting the reader see the applicability of the concepts formed in the work to the *work itself*: The critically reflexive form that is the topic of the work ("object language"), has been reflected into the work's own conceptualisations and analyses ("metalanguage"). The individual propositions and analyses in the work can be determined with respect to their kind and assessed with respect to their tenability in the same dimensions of which the work has given an account (section I 6; see for illustration, for example, section II B 9, where the work's definition theory is applied to the definitions in the theory itself).

> The fact that the propositions and analyses in the work can be determined with respect to their kind and assessed with respect to their tenability in the same *dimensions* of which the work has given an account, does not mean that the *individual concepts* that the work has established, necessarily apply. First, it is not to be taken for granted that all concepts of *points or intervals in* a dimension apply: In the modality dimension I have distinguished between descriptive, normative and fused propositions (sections II A 5; F). In this dimension the propositions in the work are descriptive or normative, never fused, cf. section II F concerning the fact that the fused modality appears to be specific to lawyers' propositions de lege lata. Secondly, it is

> not to be taken for granted that concepts of *combination of* dimensions apply: Under the name of "reconstruction and redefinition" I have introduced a concept of a distinct and widespread combination of the fundamental proposition types. None of the main analyses in the work has reconstruction and redefinition structure. For example, my definition analysis does not have such structure, since I do not take my point of departure in a presupposed denotation and say something about (the greater part of) this (sections II A 2 (1); B 2). And further, for example, my fusion analysis of propositions de lege lata does not have such structure either. True enough, in the fusion analysis I do take my point of departure in and say something about (the greater part of) a presupposed denotation, namely those propositions that lawyers call "propositions about what the law is", "propositions de lege lata", "legal dogmatic propositions" or "propositions about valid law". However, I do not lay down through a new definition (a normative-innovative connotation specification) that fused modality shall be a criterion in a concept of 'proposition de lege lata' (section II F 2.1 (1)(b)(iii)).

For the reader to cognise the existence of the critically reflexive form in his own language and argumentation, I have linked my discussions to a broad spectrum of language and argumentation phenomena: in everyday life, in politics, in law, in other subjects, in science, and in philosophy. Only in this way has it been possible to give a *representative* picture of the area of application of the critically reflexive form, i.e. a picture of the *generality* of this form (section I 5.1). – It is not possible to give an exhaustive picture. I have, however, built on the assumption that the instantiations of the critically reflexive form given in this work will awaken *recognition* in the reader, in his capacity of himself being a participant in language and argumentation; and that the instantiations of the critically reflexive form given in this work will thus initiate in the reader, in relation to the reader's own acts of language and argumentation, a process towards the cognition of the generality of the criticially reflexive form. Such recognition requires that the reader qua reader at least to a certain extent *himself* exercises the critically reflexive form (the acts presented in the present work), i.e. does not only think about the critically reflexive form, but also *through* it. Only in this way is there created for the reader qua reader an instantiation here and now of the critically reflexive form, i.e. only in this way is there created for the reader that object of comparison in relation to his language and argumentation practice otherwise that is necessary for recognition to take place. A reader who qua reader is only willing to think about the critically reflexive form, who is only willing to be an observer, a reader who qua reader is not willing also to think through the critically reflexive form, who is not willing also to be a *participant*, will thereby deprive himself of a significant part of the evidence for the generality of the critically reflexive form.

In the demonstration of the area of application of the critically reflexive form, I have throughout returned to *lawyers' language and argumentation*, including their language and argumentation *de lege lata* (language and argumentation concerning what the law is). – Seen from the point of view of the critically reflexive form, lawyers' language and argumentation de lege lata is *only one* instantiation. Seen from the point of view of lawyers, the critically reflexive form is *constitutive of their legal power of judgement*:

Unity and continuity in lawyers' language and argumentation de lege lata are created in and through a continual *definitional process*: a process with denotation specifications as an institutionalised and central means of structuring (sections II B 5.4.2; V 2.4, 4.2.2 (1)), and with connotation specifications in the form of evaluation prescription (section II B 6.1) and accompanying factors to be weighed and balanced (section II B 6.2). This definitional process is tightly interwoven with *characterisations*: via persuasive definitions (sections II B 7.3 cf. III 2.4.2), via linking-terms (section IV 3.3.3), and via reconstructions and redefinitions (sections V 2.1–2.4). In this interweaving, both elements, both definitions and characterisations, often have a *fused descriptive and normative modality* (section II F): a modality that makes it possible for even a small group of lawyers to transform their personal standpoints into law by referring to one another (sections II F 2.1 (1), (3), cf. III 2.4.2). In this process of transformation, *evaluations and choices* play a large part (section II F 2.1 (2)), and *action influencing* is an actually widespread *interest* (sections III 2.2.5, 2.4.2, 3.2.3; V 4.2.2 (3)). These evaluations, these choices and this interest in influencing action are, however, throughout *clothed in language* that is *polysemous* between the descriptive, logical and normative, or that is *one-sidedly descriptive or logical* (sections III 2.4.2; IV 3.3 cf. 2–3).

By way of introduction in the present work I emphasised that the critically reflexive form that constitutes the perspective and topic of the work, has a *certain independence* in relation to controversial philosophical, moral, legal, political or similar questions; cf. the absence of certain univocal connections between the critically reflexive form and the answers to such controversial questions (section I 6). – The *process of proceeding through* the present work to its conclusion demonstrates this independence.

The independence of the critically reflexive form, inter alia in relation to the level of fundamental philosophical positions, is another point with respect to which repetitions are necessary to a particularly high degree, cf. the widespread propensity to interpret a writer's sentences as necessarily in conformity or conflict with philosophical "...isms". – On this point, however, there are no simple keywords that can serve as reminders, in the way that, for example, "actually occurring" can serve as a reminder of the descriptive perspective. Instead, I have linked to some discussions, in the case of which I assume there may be a particular risk of misunderstanding, a reminder of or an in-depth treatment of the perspective and topic of the work (see the subject index under "independence").

My use of the means mentioned, or of other means, for the emphasising of the descriptive (first indent above) or the independent (the present indent) cannot be interpreted antithetically. They provide reminders, and, as the case may be, treatment in greater depth in a particular context, of the perspective and topic laid down by way of introduction (Chapter I). Perhaps there ought to have been more reminders. Relevant here are the two propensities of thought mentioned: to interpret a writer's sentences as expressing normative propositions, and as necessarily being in conformity or conflict with philosophical "...isms". The element of reminders of *another* perspective must inter alia rest on an estimate of readers' ability and will to follow the work on its own terms.

Now that the work is finished, there may be reason to state more precisely what the independence of the critically reflexive form *does not entail*. – Its independence does not entail that the critically reflexive form cannot be *totalised*. By "totalising" I am referring to asserting *that* the critically reflexive form is a fundamental and exhaustive rationality structure, and to justifying this assertion with *other* arguments than demonstration of the factual existence and more detailed content of the form, i.e. in other ways than in the present work. I neither assert nor deny totalising; this lies *outside* the perspective and topic of the work.

This may be illustrated by means of a *contrast* with Wittgenstein's discussions. – I use in regularly occurring critically reflexive statements (see the first and third indents above) inter alia formulations that Wittgenstein too uses (all references to him in what follows are to *Philosophische Untersuchungen*, Part I), for example "description" and "actually occurring language and argumentation" (compare section 124: "tatsächlichen Gebrauch der Sprache ... nur beschreiben") and "mapping" (compare section 122: "übersichtlichen Darstellung"). – However, the fact that totalising is not part of the perspective and topic of the present work, means that I do *not* share Wittgenstein's superordinate argumentation strategy: on the one hand of maintaining that he only demonstrates what everybody knows (compare sections 89, 109, 124, 126–29, 415), and that in philosophy one cannot say anything with another degree of necessity (compare section 599: ""Es muß sich doch so verhalten!" ist kein Satz der Philosophie. Sie stellt nur fest, was Jeder ihr zugibt"), and on the other hand of delimiting his own work against empirical problems and against science (compare section 109) and clearly purporting that his own work says something with a particularly strong ("philosophical") necessity. – The consequence of Wittgenstein's argumentation strategy is that the terms "description", "actually occurring language and argumentation" and "mapping" are ascribed a new and controversial role: to mediate between on the one hand what can be said, and on the other hand that which is truly interesting, and which cannot be said but can only be shown. The fact that totalising lies outside the perspective and topic of the present work, means that such terminology is not part of the work.

Nor does the independence of the critically reflexive form entail that the form on its own terms (without totalising pretension) is without *philosophical significance* (section I 7). – Philosophy during the last hundred years has to a great extent focused on language and argumentation. In this, as in any other perspective and topic in philosophy, *knowledge of and contact with what exists* must be assumed to have significance for the quality of philosophy. For example, I assume that the quality of philosophy depends on knowledge of *the critically reflexive form* that constitutes the perspective and topic of the present work, and as part of this, knowledge of the following features of analysis and argumentation formulated in everyday language (some of these features are mentioned above in the summary of the role they play in the constitution of lawyers' power of judgement; in what follows they are mentioned in a more general form and in the order they have in the systematic presentation in the work): – modalities, functions and means of definitions (section II B); – different dimensions in the "relationship between the descriptive and the normative" (section II B 8 with further references), and more particularly, the occurrence of the phenomenon I term "fused descriptive and normative propositions" (section II F); – criteria that are used in the setting up of and choice between normative definitions, and criteria that are used in the setting up of and choice between descriptive characterisations (Chapter III); – "the flight from the normative proposition", i.e. clothing evaluations and choices in language attire that is polysemous, or one-sidedly descriptive or logical (Chapter IV); – and how the fundamental elements of the critically reflexive form run together in certain language and argumentation patterns (Chapter V).

The present work has shown the diffusion and weight of this critically reflexive form. This diffusion and weight represent a *challenge* on the level of fundamental philosophical positions *too*. For even though I have claimed and demonstrated the absence of certain univocal connections between the critically reflexive form that the work brings into focus and the level of fundamental philosophical positions (section I 6 cf. the work as a whole), I do not claim the absence of any connection whatsoever. For one thing, absence of any connection whatsoever does not follow from the absence of certain univocal connections. For another thing, it is not very reasonable to assume absolute boundaries in thought; I have difficulty in seeing how thought might anywhere be able to escape the critically reflexive form that constitutes the perspective and topic of the present work: – By way of introduction and in relation to lawyers' propositions de lege lata I claimed that the conceptualisations in the work may be equated with a set of filters; for an apt picture of lawyers' propositions de lege lata, in contrast to an understanding of the individual aspects, one must look through several of these filters at the same time (section I 5.2). – By way of conclusion I shall as a hypothesis and in relation to language and argumentation more generally claim the same of the relationship between the perspective and topic of the work, and any other perspectives; for an apt picture of language and argumentation, one must always *also* make the perspective and topic of the present work part of one's reflections. – A philosophical position will therefore, other things being equal, *have a stronger footing* the more explicitly the position relates to and is able to integrate the acts of which the present work has demonstrated the existence and factual significance (compare section II G 2 (4)(c)(ii)).

However, the perspective and topic of the work, the critically reflexive form that has been discussed, is given *less attention* than the existence and factual significance of this form would suggest. Neither in literature within general or legal philosophy, nor in any other literature have I been able to find any analysis of this form along the lines in the present work: no nuanced and coherent conceptual model for mapping the critically reflexive form, with accompanying demonstration of – the reality basis of the concepts – the internal coherence of the form (its system character and dynamics) – the independence of the form – and the factual significance of the form: what acts take place, and in what connections and for what language users these acts are significant. – In philosophy and logic the emphasis is more on totalising or idealising perspectives (see for example section II B 2.2). In psychology and sociology descriptive perspectives are no doubt adopted, but seldom in the form of mappings in the dimension of dis/agreement and tenability. *In theoretical respects* the critically reflexive form leads a *shadow existence*.

With the present work, and not until this, a *necessary condition* has come into being for discussion of what more nuanced connections might exist between the critically reflexive form that the work brings into focus and the level of fundamental philosophical positions: namely the condition that one *first* systematically maps the critically reflexive form. In this respect the work has a derived value.

In addition, the work has intrinsic value: In the title of the work I see the work as the analysis of dis/agreement. Since the topic is our own acts, viz. language and argumentation, the work can also be seen as *self-cognition*. The work has demonstrated acts we perform in our capacity of being participants in analysis and argumentation formulated in everyday language: be it in everyday life, in politics, in law, in other subjects, in science, or in philosophy. The work has demonstrated how in these different areas, in and through our own practice, we constitute and uphold the critically reflexive form that has determined the perspective and topic of the work. – With the present work we no longer relate blindly to a form in language and argumentation in and through which significant acts take place: a form at the core of our power of judgement.

Literature referred to

AARNIO, Aulis. See Aarnio/ Alexy/ Peczenik; Peczenik/ Aarnio/ Bergholtz

AARNIO, Aulis/ ALEXY, Robert/ PECZENIK, Aleksander. 'The Foundation of Legal Reasoning'. (1981) 12 *Rechtstheorie*, pp. 133–58, 257–79, 423–48.

ABELSON, Raziel. 'Definition'. In: P. Edwards (ed.), *Encyclopedia of Philosophy*, Vol. 2, pp. 314–24. New York: Macmillan and The Free Press – London: Collier Macmillan. 1967.

ADORNO, T. W./ FRENKEL-BRUNSWIK, E./ LEVINSON, D. J./ SANFORD, R. Nevitt. *The Authoritarian Personality* [1950]. Abridged ed. [1982]. New York – London: W. W. Norton. 1993.

AHLANDER, Björn. *Är juridiken en vetenskap?* [is law a science?]. Stockholm: Hugo Geber. 1950.

AJDUKIEWICZ, Kazimierz. 'Three Concepts of Definition'. (1958) 1 *Logique et Analyse*, pp. 115–26.

ALEXY, Robert. *Theorie der juristischen Argumentation* [1978]. Frankfurt a.M.: Suhrkamp. 1983.

———. *Theorie der Grundrechte* [1985]. Frankfurt a.M.: Suhrkamp. 1986.

———. 'On the Structure of Legal Principles'. (2000) 13 *Ratio Juris*, pp. 294–304.

———. See also Aarnio/ Alexy/ Peczenik; Alexy/ Peczenik

ALEXY, Robert/ PECZENIK, Aleksander. 'The Concept of Coherence and Its Significance for Discursive Rationality'. (1990) 3 *Ratio Juris*, pp. 130–47.

ALMÉN, Tore/ EKLUND, Rudolf. *Lagen om avtal och andra rättshandlingar på förmögenhetsrättens område* [the Act concerning contracts and other juristic acts in the area of law relating to obligations and property]. 9th ed. by T. Nordström. Stockholm: Norstedt & Söner. 1968.

ALSTON, Philip. 'No Right to Complain About Being Poor: The Need for an Optional Protocol to the Economic Rights Covenant'. In: A. Eide/ J. Helgesen (eds.), *The Future of Human Rights Protection in a Changing World: Essays in Honour of Torkel Opsahl*, pp. 79–100. Oslo: Universitetsforlaget. 1991.

ALSTON, William P. *Philosophy of Language*. Englewood Cliffs, New Jersey: Prentice-Hall. 1964.

ANDENÆS, Johs. 'Rettsteori og rettspraksis' [jurisprudence and court practice]. Here cited from: *Avhandlinger og foredrag*, pp. 408–24. Oslo: Universitetsforlaget. 1962.

———. Andenæs, *Statsforfatningen i Norge* [constitution of Norway]. 7th ed. Oslo: Tano. 1990.

———. *Innføring i rettsstudiet* [introduction to the study of law]. 4th ed. Oslo: Grøndahl Dreyer. 1994.

———. *Alminnelig strafferett* [general criminal law]. 4th ed. Oslo: Universitetsforlaget. 1997.

———. *Norsk straffeprosess* [Norwegian criminal procedure], Vol. 1. 2nd ed. Oslo: Universitetsforlaget. 1994.

———. See also Andenæs/ Kvamme

ANDENÆS, Johs./ KVAMME, Helge. 'Om grunner til uenighet om rettsspørsmål' [on grounds for disagreement on questions of law]. In: K.S. Selmer (Chief ed.), *Nordisk gjenklang*, Festschrift for Carl Jacob Arnholm, pp. 19–44. Oslo: Johan Grundt Tanum. 1969.

ANDENÆS, Mads. 'Tolking av lover med både strafferettslige og sivilrettslige sanksjoner – belyst ved tre av dem' [interpretation of statutes with both criminal law and civil law sanctions – illuminated by three of them]. *Lov og Rett*, 1983, pp. 163–99.

ANDERSSON, Jan/ FURBERG, Mats. *Språk och påverkan* [language and influence]. 8th ed. [1984]. Stockholm: Thales. 1991.

ANSCOMBE, G. E. M. *Intention*. Oxford: Basil Blackwell. 1957.

ARENDT, Hannah. *Eichmann in Jerusalem – A Report on the Banality of Evil*. Revised and enlarged ed. with a new Postscript [1965]. Harmondsworth: Penguin Books. 1994.

ARIANSEN, Per. *Miljøfilosofi* [philosophy of the environment]. Oslo: Universitetsforlaget. 1992.

ARNHOLM, Carl Jacob. *Passivitetsvirkninger* [effects of laches]. Oslo: Johan Grundt Tanum. 1932.

———. 'Fra avtalerettens arbeidsområder' [from the research areas of the law of contract]. *Tidsskrift for Rettsvitenskap*, 1946, pp. 314–32.

———. 'Omkring rettshandelsteorien' [concerning the theory of juristic acts]. *Tidsskrift for Rettsvitenskap*, 1948, pp. 368–431.

———. *Alminnelig avtalerett* [general law of contract]. Oslo: Johan Grundt Tanum. 1949.

———. 'Noen metodologiske betraktninger' [some methodological considerations]. *Svensk Juristtidning*, 1952, pp. 505–23.

———. 'Fra rettens grunnproblemer' [on some fundamental problems of law]. (Review of A. Ross, *Om ret og retfærdighed*). *Tidsskrift for Rettsvitenskap*, 1954, pp. 113–76.

———. 'En håndbok i obligasjonsrett' [a handbook on the law of obligations]. (Review of K. Rodhe, *Obligationsrätt*). *Tidsskrift for Rettsvitenskap*, 1958, pp. 124–42.

———. *Privatrett II: Avtaler* [private law II: contracts]. Oslo: Johan Grundt Tanum. 1964.

———. *Lærebok i avtalerett* [textbook of contract law]. Oslo: Johan Grundt Tanum. 1969.

———. *Arveretten* [law of succession]. Oslo: Tanum – Norli. 1974.

ARNOLD, Thurman. *The Symbols of Government* [1935]. New York – Burlingame: Harcourt, Brace & World. Harbinger Books ed. 1962.

ASCHEHOUG, Torkel. *Norges nuværende Statsforfatning* [the present constitution of Norway], Vol. 2. 2nd ed. Christiania: H. Aschehoug. 1892.

ASTRUP HOEL, G. *Den moderne retsmetode* [the modern legal method]. Oslo: Gyldendal. 1925.

ATIYAH, P. S. *The Rise and Fall of Freedom of Contract*. Oxford: Clarendon. 1979.

———. *Pragmatism and Theory in English Law*. London: Stevens & Sons. 1987.

AUBERT, Vilhelm. 'Logisk analyse og sosiologi i rettsvitenskapen' [logical analysis and sociology in legal science]. *Svensk Juristtidning*, 1952, pp. 524–39.

———. *Om straffens sosiale funksjon* [on the social function of punishment] [1954]. Oslo: Universitetsforlaget. 1979.

———. 'Predictability in Life and in Science' [1961]. In: *The Hidden Society*, pp. 116–36. New York: Bedminster Press. 1965.

———. *Sosiologi* [sociology]. Oslo: Universitetsforlaget. 1964.

———. *Rettens sosiale funksjon* [the social function of law]. Oslo, etc.: Universitetsforlaget. 1976.

———. 'Om relationerna mellan juridiska och sociologiska begrepp' [on the relations between legal and social concepts]. In: U. Bondeson (ed.), *Rationalitet i rättssystemet*, pp. 58–83. Stockholm: LiberFörlag, Jurist- och Samhällsvetareförbundets Förlag. 1979.

———. *Sosiologi 1. Sosialt samspill* [sociology 1. social interaction]. Oslo: Universitetsforlaget. 1979.

———. *Rettssosiologi* [sociology of law]. Oslo, etc.: Universitetsforlaget. 1982.

———. See also Aubert/ Eckhoff/ Sveri; Aubert/ Messinger

AUBERT, V./ ECKHOFF, T./ SVERI, K. *En lov i søkelyset* [a statute under the searchlight]. Oslo: Universitetsforlaget. 1952.

AUBERT, Vilhelm/ MESSINGER, Sheldon L. 'The Criminal and the Sick'. (1958) 1 *Inquiry*, pp. 137–60.

AUGDAHL, Per. *Rettskilder* [sources of law]. 3rd ed. Oslo: Aschehoug. 1973.

———. *Den norske obligasjonsretts almindelige del* [the Norwegian law of obligations, general part]. 5th ed. Oslo: Aschehoug (W. Nygaard). 1978.

———. See also Augdahl/ Hambro

AUGDAHL, Per/ HAMBRO, Peter. *Arveloven med kommentarer* [the Inheritance Act with commentary]. Oslo: Aschehoug. 1985.

AUSTENÅ, Torgeir. *Løsningsrettigheter* [options to purchase, rights of pre-emption, etc.]. Place of publication not specified. Universitetsforlaget. 1976.

AUSTIN, John. *The Province of Jurisprudence Determined* [1832]. London: Weidenfeld and Nicolson. Library of Ideas. 1971 [1955].

AUSTIN, John L. 'The Meaning of a Word' . In: *Philosophical Papers*, pp. 23–43. Oxford: Clarendon. 1961.

———. 'Other Minds' [1946]. Here cited from *Philosophical Papers*, pp. 44–84.

———. 'A Plea for Excuses' [1956]. Here cited from *Philosophical Papers*, pp. 123–52.

———. *Sense and Sensibilia*. Oxford: Clarendon. 1962.

———. *How to do things with Words* [1962]. "Reprinted from corrected sheets of the 1963 reprint". Oxford: Clarendon. 1965.

AYER, Alfred J. *Language, Truth and Logic*. 2nd ed. 1946. Harmondsworth etc.: Penguin Books. Pelican Book ed. 1971.

———. 'The Vienna Circle'. In: G. Ryle (ed.), *The Revolution in Philosophy*, pp. 70–87. London: Macmillan. 1956.

———. 'Logical Positivism, Editor's Introduction'. In: A. J. Ayer (ed.), *Logical Positivism*, pp. 3–28. New York: The Free Press. 1959.

———. *Wittgenstein*. London: Weidenfeld and Nicolson. 1985.

———. 'Conversation'. In: B. Magee, *Modern British Philosophy*, pp. 67–87. Oxford – New York: Oxford University Press. 1986.

BAKER, G. P./ HACKER, P. M. S. *Wittgenstein: Meaning and Understanding. Essays on the Philosophical Investigations*. Oxford: Basil Blackwell. 1983.

BAMBROUGH, Renford. 'Universals and Family Resemblances' [1960–61 LXI Proceedings of the Aristotelian Society]. Here cited from: G. Pitcher (ed.), *Wittgenstein, The Philosophical Investigations: A Collection of Critical Essays*, pp. 186–204. New York: Doubleday, Anchor Books. 1966.

BANKOWSKI, Z./ MACCORMICK, D. N./ SUMMERS, R. S./ WRÓBLEWSKI, J. 'On Method and Methodology'. In: D. N. MacCormick/ R. S. Summers (eds.), *Interpreting Statutes*, pp. 9–27. Aldershot etc.: Dartmouth. 1991.

BATESON, Gregory. *Steps to an Ecology of Mind* [1972]. Northvale, New Jersey – London: Jason Aronson. 1987.

BENEDICT, Ruth. *Patterns of Culture* [1934]. New York: Penguin Books. Pelican Book ed. 1946.

BENTHAM, Jeremy. *A Fragment on Government* [1776]. Here cited from: W. Harrison (ed.), A Fragment on Government and An Introduction to the Principles of Morals and Legislation, pp. 1–112. Oxford: Basil Blackwell. 1948.

———. *Of Laws in General*. J. H. Burns (General ed.), The Collected Works of Jeremy Bentham, Vol. III: ed. by H. L. A. Hart. London: University of London, The Athlone Press. 1970.

———. *Essay on Logic*. J. Bowring (ed.), The Works of Jeremy Bentham, Vol. VIII, pp. 213–93. Edinburgh: William Tait. 1843.

———. *The Theory of Fictions*. A selection made by C. K. Ogden from J. Bowring (ed.), The Works of Jeremy Bentham. Printed in: C. K. Ogden, *Bentham's Theory of Fictions*. London: Kegan Paul, Trench, Trubner. 1932.

BENTZON, Viggo. *Retskilderne* [the sources of law]. Vol. 1–3. Copenhagen: G. E. C. Gad. 1900, 1905, 1907.

———. *Skøn og regel* [discretion and rule]. Copenhagen: Københavns Universitet. 1914.

——. 'Retskildeproblemet' [the sources-of-law problem]. *Svensk Juristtidning*, 1929, pp. 524–40.

BERGH, Trond/ HANISCH, Tore J. *Vitenskap og politikk, linjer i norsk sosialøkonomi gjennom 150 år* [science and politics, trends in Norwegian economics over 150 years].Oslo: Aschehoug. 1984.

BERGHOLTZ, Gunnar. See Peczenik/ Aarnio/ Bergholtz

BERGMAN, Sigurd. 'Bör naturen tillerkännas rättigheter?' [ought Nature to be accorded rights?]. *Retfærd*, 1993, pp. 22–36.

BERNT, Jan Fridthjof. 'Legalitetsprinsippet og andre hjemmelsspørsmål i den offentlige rett – noen prinsipielle betraktninger' [the principle of legality and other authority issues in public law – some considerations of principle]. In: A. Bratholm/ N. Christie/ T. Opsahl (eds.), *Lov og frihet*, Festschrift for Johs. Andenæs, pp. 509–26. Oslo: Universitetsforlaget. 1982.

——. See also Doublet/ Bernt

BLOOR, David. *Wittgenstein: A Social Theory of Knowledge*. London – Basingstoke: Macmillan. 1983.

BOE, Erik. Boe, 'Eckhoffs/ Smiths framstilling av lovskravet i forvaltningsretten' [Eckhoff/ Smith's account of the requirement for statutory authority in administrative law]. *Jussens Venner*, 1983, pp. 151–73.

——. 'Utvikling i lovers form og innhold – en utfordring til rettsvitenskapen' [development in the form and content of statutes – a challenge to legal science]. *Tidsskrift for Rettsvitenskap*, 1987, pp. 651–77.

——. 'Utviklingslinjer i forvaltningsretten' [lines of development in administrative law]. *Lov og Rett*, 1989, pp. 51–72.

——. 'Fusadommen i forvaltningsrettslig og rettsteoretisk perspektiv' [the Fusa judgment in the perspectives of administrative law and legal theory]. *Lov og Rett*, 1991, pp. 323–46.

——. *Innføring i juss* [introduction to law]. Vol. 1–2. Oslo: Tano. 1993.

——. 'Domstolskontroll med forvaltningen' [judicial review of public administrative action]. *Lov og Rett*, 1994, pp. 323–48.

——. *Innføring i juss* [introduction to law]. Oslo: Tano Aschehoug. 1996.

BOK, Sissela. *Lying* [1978]. London etc.: Quartet Books. 1980.

BOLDING, Per Olof. *Juridik och samhällsdebatt* [jurisprudence and public debate]. Stockholm: Almqvist & Wiksell/ Gebers. 1968.

BOLZANO, Bernard. *Grundlegung der Logik. Ausgewählte Paragraphen aus der Wissenschaftslehre, Band I–II*. Hamburg: Felix Meiner. 1963.

BOYLE, Alan E. 'International Law and the Protection of the Global Atmosphere: Concepts, Categories and Principles'. In: R. Churchill/ D. Freestone (eds.), *International Law and Global Climate Change*, pp. 7–19. London etc.: Graham & Trotham/ Martinus Nijhoff. 1991.

BRAITHWAITE, R. B. 'Verbal Ambiguity and Philosophical Analysis'. (1927–28) XXVIII *Proceedings of the Aristotelian Society*, pp. 135–54.

BRATHOLM, Anders. 'Den straffeprosessuelle betydning av at et bevis er skaffet til veie på ulovlig måte' [the criminal procedural significance of the fact that a piece of evidence has been obtained in an unlawful manner]. *Tidsskrift for Rettsvitenskap*, 1959, pp. 109–32.

———. See also Bratholm/ Hov

BRATHOLM, Anders/ HOV, Jo. *Sivil rettergang* [civil proceedings]. Oslo etc.: Universitetsforlaget. 1973.

BRAYBROOKE, David. 'What Came to Light in the Aspen/ Cornell Colloquium on Choice and Decision'. In: M. Black (ed.), *Problems of Choice and Decision*, pp. 600–27. Ithaca, New York: Cornell University – Aspen, Colorado: Aspen Institute for Humanistic Studies. 1975.

BRIDGMAN, P. W. *The Logic of Modern Physics* [1927]. New York: Macmillan. 1960.

———. *Reflections of a Physicist*. New York: Philosophical Library. 1950.

———. 'The Operational Aspect of Meaning'. (1950–51) VIII *Synthese*, pp. 251–59.

BRUSIIN, Otto. *Über das juristische Denken* [1951]. Here cited from: *Der Mensch und Sein Recht: Ausgewählte rechtstheoretische Schriften*, pp. 132–264. Berlin: Duncker & Humblot. 1990.

BUGGE, Hans Chr. 'Rio-konferansen i rettslig lys' [the Rio conference in a legal light]. *Lov og Rett*, 1993, pp. 469–85.

———. ' "Bærekraftig utvikling" og andre aktuelle perspektiver i miljøretten' ["sustainable development" and other current perspectives in environmental law]. *Lov og Rett*, 1993, pp. 485–98.

CANARIS, Claus-Wilhelm. *Systemdenken und Systembegriff in der Jurisprudenz*. Berlin: Duncker & Humblot. 1969.

CARDOZO, Benjamin Nathan. 'The Nature of the Judicial Process' [1921]. Here cited from: M. E. Hall (ed.), *Selected Writings of B. N. Cardozo*, pp. 107–84. New York: Fallon Law Book Company. 1947

———. 'The Growth of the Law' [1924]. Here cited from *Selected Writings of B. N. Cardozo*, pp. 185–250.

———. 'The Paradoxes of Legal Science' [1928]. Here cited from *Selected Writings of B. N. Cardozo*, pp. 251–337.

CARNAP, Rudolf. *Der logische Aufbau der Welt* [1928]. Hamburg: Felix Meiner. 1966.

———. 'Formal and Factual Science'. [1935]. Here cited from: H. Feigl/ M. Brodbeck (eds.), *Readings in the Philosophy of Science*, pp. 123–28. New York: Appleton-Century-Crofts. 1953.

———. 'Testability and Meaning'. (1936) 3 *Philosophy of Science*, pp. 419–71; (1937) 4 pp. 1–40.

———. 'The Interpretation of Physics' [1939]. Here cited from *Readings in the Philosophy of Science*, pp. 309–18.

———. 'The Two Concepts of Probability' [1945]. Here cited from *Readings in the Philosophy of Science*, pp. 438–55.

——. *Logical Foundations of Probability*. Chicago: University of Chicago Press. 1950.

——. 'Empiricism, Semantics, and Ontology' [1950]. Her cited from: *Meaning and Necessity*, Supplement, pp. 205–21.

——. *Meaning and Necessity*. 2nd and enlarged ed. Chicago – London: University of Chicago Press. Phoenix Books. 1956.

——. 'The Methodological Character of Theoretical Concepts'. In: H. Feigl/ M. Scriven (eds.), *Minnesota Studies in the Philosophy of Science*, Vol. I, pp. 38–76. Minneapolis: University of Minnesota Press. 1956.

——. 'Intellectual Biography'. In: P.A. Schilpp (ed.), *The Library of Living Philosophers Vol. XI: The Philosophy of Rudolf Carnap*, pp. 3–84. La Salle, Illinois: Open Court – London: Cambridge University Press. 1963.

——. 'Replies and Systematic Expositions'. In: *The Library of Living Philosophers Vol. XI: The Philosophy of Rudolf Carnap*, pp. 859–1013.

——. See also Neurath/ Hahn/ Carnap

CASTBERG, Frede. 'Hvilke statsviljesytringer maa avgives i lovs form?' [which utterances of the will of the state must be issued in statutory form?]. *Norsk Retstidende*, 1918, pp. 721–30.

——. 'Den konstruktive metode' [the constructive method]. *Tidsskrift for Rettsvitenskap*, 1922, pp. 294–317.

——. *Norges statsforfatning* [constitution of Norway], Vol. I–II. 3rd ed. Oslo: Universitetsforlaget. 1964.

CAVELL, Stanley. 'Must We Mean What We Say?'. In: *Must we mean what we say? A Book of Essays* [1969], pp 1–43. Cambridge etc.: Cambridge University Press. 1976.

CHOMSKY, Noam. *Rules and Representations*. Oxford: Basil Blackwell. 1980.

CHOPRA, Sudhir K. See D'Amato/ Chopra

CHRISTENSEN, Anna. 'Förutsättningar och misstag' [assumptions and mistakes]. *Tidsskrift for Rettsvitenskap*, 1973, pp. 311–40.

——. 'Kvinnorätten och lagpositivismen' [women's law and legal positivism]. *Retfærd*, 1986, pp. 88–96.

CICERO. *Brutus*. Loeb Classical Library, transl. by G.L. Hendrickson [1939]. Revised ed. London: William Heinemann – Cambridge, Mass.: Harvard University Press. 1962.

CLAUSEWITZ, Karl von. *Vom Kriege* [1832]. Frankfurt a.M. – Berlin: Ullstein. 1991.

COHEN, Felix S. 'Transcendental Nonsense and the Functional Approach'. (1935) 35 *Columbia Law Review*, pp. 809–49.

COHEN, Stephen F. *Bukharin and the Bolshevik Revolution. A Political Biography* [1973]. London: Wildwood House. 1974.

COLLINGWOOD, R.G. 'Modern Politics'. In: *Essays in Political Philosophy* [1989], pp. 177–86. Oxford: Clarendon. Paperback edition. 1995.

CONQUEST, Robert. *The Great Terror*. London – Melbourne: Macmillan. 1968.

CROSS, Rupert. *Statutory Interpretation*. 2nd ed. by J. Bell/ G. Engle. London: Butterworths. 1987.

———. See also Cross/ Harris

CROSS, Rupert/ HARRIS, J. W. *Precedent in English Law*. 4th ed. Oxford: Clarendon. 1991.

DAHL, Hans Fredrik. 'Obituary of Jens Arup Seip'. *Dagbladet*, 9. September 1992.

DAHL, Ottar. *Om årsaksproblemer i historisk forskning* [on causal problems in historical research]. Oslo: Universitetsforlaget. 1956.

DAHL, Tove Stang. *Women's Law: An Introduction to Feminist Jurisprudence*. Oslo: Norwegian University Press. 1987.

———. 'Kvinnerett – en rettsvitenskapelig fornyelse' [women's law – a renewal of legal science]. *Jussens Venner*, 1985, pp. 65–78.

DAHLØ, Ingrid. See Lydersen/ Dahlø

D'AMATO, Anthony/ CHOPRA, Sudhir K. 'Whales: Their Emerging Right to Live'. (1991) 85 *The American Journal of International Law*, pp. 21–62.

DAVIDSON, Donald. 'A Nice Derangement of Epitaphs'. In: E. LePore (ed.), *Truth and Interpretation: Perspectives on the Philosophy of Donald Davidson*, pp. 433–46. Oxford: Basil Blackwell. 1986.

DELEUZE, Gilles/ GUATTARI, Felix. *Qu'est-ce que la philosophie?* Paris: Minuit. 1991.

DOSTOYEVSKY, Fyodor. *The Brothers Karamazov* [1879–80]. Harmondsworth: Penguin Books. 1993.

DOUBLET, David/ BERNT, Jan Fridthjof. *Retten og vitenskapen* [the law and science]. 2nd ed. Bergen: Alma Mater. 1993.

DRURY, Maurice O'Connor. *The Danger of Words* [1973]. Here cited from: *The Danger of Words and writings on Wittgenstein*. Bristol: Thoemmes Press. 1996.

DUBISLAV, Walter. *Die Definition*. "Unveränderter Nachdruck der dritten völlig umgearbeiteten und erweiterten Aufl. von 1931". Hamburg: Felix Meiner. 1981.

DUXBURY, Neil. *Patterns of American Jurisprudence* [1995]. Paperback ed. "with corrections". Oxford: Clarendon. 1997.

DWORKIN, Ronald. 'The Model of Rules I' [1967]. Here cited from: *Taking Rights Seriously* [1977, 1978], pp. 14–45. London: Duckworth. 1987.

———. 'The Model of Rules II' [1972]. Here cited from *Taking Rights Seriously*, pp. 46–80.

———. 'Constitutional Cases' [1972]. Here cited from *Taking Rights Seriously*, pp. 131–49.

———. 'Hard Cases' [1975]. Here cited from *Taking Rights Seriously*, pp. 81–130.

———. 'A Reply to Critics' [1978]. In: *Taking Rights Seriously*, pp. 291–368.

———. *Law's Empire*. London: Fontana Press. 1986.

EAMES, Elizabeth R. 'A. J. Ayer's Philosophical Method'. In: L. E. Hahn (ed.), *The Library of Living Philosophers Vol. XXI: The Philosophy of A. J. Ayer*, pp. 157–74. La Salle, Illinois: Open Court. 1992.

ECKHOFF, Torstein. *Tvilsrisikoen* [the bearing of the risk of doubt]. Oslo: Johan Grundt Tanum. 1943.

———. 'Noen ord om bevisbyrde og bevisbyrdeteorier' [some words on the burden of proof and theories of the burden of proof]. *Tidsskrift for Rettsvitenskap*, 1949, pp. 298–320.

———. 'En bok om bevisbyrden' [a book on the burden of proof]. *Tidsskrift for Rettsvitenskap*, 1952, pp. 28–37.

———. *Rettsvesen og rettsvitenskap i U.S.A.* [legal system and legal science in the U.S.A.]. Oslo: Akademisk forlag. 1953.

———. 'Legalitetsprinsippet' [the principle of legality]. *Tidsskrift for Rettsvitenskap*, 1963, pp. 225–85.

———. 'Litt om det juridiske rettighetsspråk' [a little on the language of legal rights]. In: M. Blegvad, et al. (eds.), *Festskrift til Alf Ross*, pp. 63–78. Copenhagen: Juristforbundets forlag. 1969.

———. *Rettskildelære* [doctrine of the sources of law]. 1st ed. Oslo: Johan Grundt Tanum. 1971. 2nd ed. Oslo: Tano. 1987. 3rd ed. Oslo: Tano. 1993. – Unless otherwise stated, references are to the 3rd ed.

———. 'Juss og samfunnsforskning' [law and social research] [1972]. Here cited from: *Retten og samfunnet*, pp. 317–32. Oslo: Tanum – Norli. 1976.

———. 'Feed back i rettstenkning og rettssystemer' [feedback in legal thinking and legal systems]. *Tidskrift utg. av Juridiska Föreningen i Finland*, 1976, pp. 68–79.

———. *Forvaltningsrett* [administrative law]. Oslo: Tano. 1st to 5th eds. 1978, 1982, 1989, 1992 and 1994 respectively. 5th ed. by E. Smith. See also Eckhoff/ Smith.

———. 'Retningslinjer og "tumregler"' [guidelines and "rules of thumb"]. *Tidsskrift for Rettsvitenskap*, 1980, pp. 145–63.

———. 'Kan elver og skoger ha rettigheter?' [can rivers and forests have rights?]. *Hefte for kritisk Juss*, 1980, pp. 2–5.

———. 'Almenprevensjon og forvaltningslovgivning' [general deterrence and public administrative legislation]. In: A. Bratholm/ N. Christie/ T. Opsahl (eds.), *Lov og frihet*, Festschrift for Johs. Andenæs, pp. 99–112. Oslo: Universitetsforlaget. 1982.

———. *Statens styringsmuligheter, særlig i ressurs- og miljøspørsmål* [the state's possibilities of governing, with special reference to questions of resources and the environment]. Oslo: Tanum – Norli. 1983.

———. 'Ross om rettskilder og rett' [Ross on sources of law and law]. *Tidsskrift for Rettsvitenskap*, 1987, pp. 197–213.

———. 'Rett, moral og politikk' [law, morals and politics]. In: *Juss, moral og politikk*, pp. 9–25. Oslo: Universitetsforlaget. 1989.

———. 'Anmeldelse av Ekelöf, Valda skrifter 1942–1990' [review of Ekelöf, selected writings 1942–1990]. *Juridisk Tidskrift*, 1992–93, pp. 184–90.

———. See also Aubert/ Eckhoff/ Sveri; Eckhoff/ Smith; Eckhoff/ Sundby

ECKHOFF, Torstein/ SMITH, Eivind. *Forvaltningsrett* [administrative law]. 6th ed. Oslo: Tano Aschehoug. 1997.

ECKHOFF, Torstein/ SUNDBY, Nils Kristian. 'Om selvrefererende lover' [on self-referring statutes]. *Tidsskrift for Rettsvitenskap*, 1974, pp. 34–61.

———. 'The Notion of Basic Norm(s) in Jurisprudence'. (1975) 19 *Scandinavian Studies in Law*, pp. 123–51.

———. *Rettssystemer* [legal systems]. 1st ed. Oslo: Tanum-Norli. 1976. 2nd ed. Oslo: Tano. 1991. – Unless otherwise stated, references are to the 2nd ed.

———. *Rechtssysteme*. Berlin: Duncker & Humblot. 1988.

EISENBERG, Melvin A. *The Nature of the Common Law*. Cambridge, Mass. – London: Harvard University Press. 1988.

EKELÖF, Per Olof. 'Juridisk slutledning och terminologi' [legal inference and terminology]. *Tidsskrift for Rettsvitenskap*, 1945, pp. 211–72.

———. 'Är den juridiska doktrinen en teknik eller en vetenskap?' [is legal doctrine a technique or a science?] [1951]. Here cited from: *Valda skrifter 1942–1990, De Lege, Juridiska fakulteten i Uppsala, Årsbok, 1991*, pp. 91–126. Uppsala: Iustus. 1991.

———. *Processuella grundbegrepp och allmänna processprinciper* [fundamental procedural concepts and general procedural principles]. Stockholm: Norstedt & Söner. 1956.

EKLUND, Rudolf. See Almén/ Eklund

ELSTER, Jon. *Forklaring og dialektikk* [explanation and dialectics]. Oslo: Pax. 1979.

———. *Ulysses and the Sirens*. Cambridge etc.: Cambridge University Press – Paris: Maison des Sciences de l'Homme. 1979.

———. *Vitenskap og politikk* [science and politics]. Oslo: Universitetsforlaget. 1989.

———. See also Føllesdal/ Walløe/ Elster

ENG, Svein. Eng, 'Sondringen mellom regler og retningslinjer' [the distinction between rules and guidelines]. In: N. Christie et al. (eds.), ... *den urett som ikke rammer deg selv*, Festschrift for Anders Bratholm, pp. 473–83. Oslo: Universitetsforlaget. 1990.

———. 'Begrepene 'kompetanse' og 'gyldighet' i juridisk argumentasjon' [the concepts of 'competence' and 'validity' in legal argumentation]. *Tidsskrift for Rettsvitenskap*, 1990, pp. 625–71.

———. 'Noen synspunkter på en teori om etikk, rett og erkjennelse' [some views on a theory of ethics, law and cognition]. *Tidsskrift for Rettsvitenskap*, 1991, pp. 279–305.

———. 'Teoristruktur og teorivalg' [theory structure and theory choice]. *Tidsskrift for Rettsvitenskap*, 1992, pp. 496–504.

———. '"Hva er en viljeserklæring?" Er det logisk umulig at disposisjonsvilje er begrepsmessig kjennetegn ved privatrettslig disposisjon?' ["what is a declaration of intent?" Is it logically impossible for the will to exercise competence to be part of the concept of 'juristic act' in private law?]. *Svensk Juristtidning*, 1993, pp. 1–42.

———. 'The Doctrine of Precedent in English and Norwegian Law – Some Common and Specific Features' [1993]. *Scandinavian Studies in Law*, Vol. 39: International Aspects, pp. 275–324.

———. *U/enighetsanalyse – med særlig sikte på jus og allmenn rettsteori* [analysis of dis/agreement – with particular reference to law and legal theory]. Oslo: Universitetsforlaget. 1998.

ENGISCH, Karl. *Die Idee der Konkretisierung in Recht und Rechtswissenschaft unserer Zeit*. 2nd ed. Heidelberg: Carl Winter. 1968.

———. *Einführung in das juristische Denken*. 7th ed. Stuttgart etc.: W. Kohlhammer. 1977.

ESKELAND, Ståle. *Fangerett* [prisoners' law]. Oslo: Tano. 1989.

———. See also Eskeland/ Syse

ESKELAND, Ståle/ SYSE, Aslak. 'Sosialrett i en innstramningstid' [social welfare law in a time of cut-backs]. *Aftenposten*, 19. March 1993.

ESSER, Josef. *Vorverständnis und Methodenwahl in der Rechtsfindung*. 2nd ed. Frankfurt a.M.: Athenäum. 1972.

ESSLER, Wilhelm K. *Wissenschaftstheorie I: Definition und Reduktion*. Freiburg – Munich: Karl Alber. 1970.

EYBEN, W. E. von. '"Gældende ret"' [valid law]. In: M. Blegvad, et al. (eds.), *Festskrift til Alf Ross*, pp. 97–112. Copenhagen: Juristforbundets forlag. 1969.

———. *Juridisk grundbog, Bind 1: Retskilderne* [basic manual of law, vol. 1: the sources of law]. 5th ed. Copenhagen: Jurist- og Økonomforbundet. 1991.

FEIGL, Herbert. 'Some Major Issues and Developments in the Philosophy of Science of Logical Empiricism'. In: H. Feigl/ M. Scriven (eds.), *Minnesota Studies in the Philosophy of Science*, Vol. I, pp. 3–37. Minneapolis: University of Minnesota Press. 1956.

———. 'The Wiener Kreis in America'. In: D. Fleming/ B. Bailyn (eds.), *Perspectives in American History, Vol. II. The Intellectual Migration: Europe and America, 1930–1960*, pp. 630–73. Cambridge, Mass.: Charles Warren Center for Studies in American History. 1968.

———. 'The Origin and Spirit of Logical Positivism'. In: P. Achenstein/ S.F. Barker (eds.), *The Legacy of Logical Positivism*, pp. 3–24. Baltimore: Johns Hopkins Press. 1969.

FINSTAD, Liv. 'Forord' [foreword]. In: M. Stoppard, *Erotiske gleder*, p. 5. Oslo: Gyldendal. 1992.

FISCH, M. H. 'Justice Holmes, the Prediction Theory of Law, and Pragmatism'. (1942) XXXIX *Journal of Philosophy*, pp. 85–97.

FLEISCHER, Carl A. *Anvendelse og fortolkning av dommer* [application and interpretation of judgments] [1965]. Oslo etc.: Universitetsforlaget. 1981.

———. *Grunnlovens grenser* [the limits of the Constitution]. Oslo: Universitetsforlaget. 1968.

———. *Rettskilder* [sources of law]. Oslo: Ad Notam Gyldendal. 1995.

FODOR, Jerry A. 'On Knowing What We Would Say' [1964]. Here cited from: J.F. Rosenberg/ C. Travis (eds.), *Readings in the Philosophy of Language*, pp. 126–36. Englewood Cliffs, New Jersey: Prentice-Hall. 1971.

FOGELIN, Robert J. *Wittgenstein*. 2nd ed. London – New York: Routledge & Kegan Paul. 1987.

FONER, Eric. *The Story of American Freedom* [1998]. London: Macmillan. 2000.

FOOT, Philippa. 'Morality and Art'. (1970) LVI *Proceedings of the British Academy*, pp. 131–44.

FRANK, Jerome. *Law and the Modern Mind* [1930]. 6th printing, with its own Preface [1949]. New York: Doubleday, Anchor Books. 1963.

———. *Courts on Trial. Myth and Reality in American Justice*. Princeton, New Jersey: Princeton University Press. 1949.

FRANKFURTER, Felix. *The Public and Its Government*. New Haven: Yale University Press. 1930.

FREESTONE, David. 'The Precautionary Principle'. In: R. Churchill/ D. Freestone (eds.), *International Law and Global Climate Change*, pp. 21–39. London etc.: Graham & Trotham/ Martinus Nijhoff. 1991.

FREGE, Gottlob. *The Foundations of Arithmetic* [1884]. Transl. by J. L. Austin. 2nd and revised ed. [1953]. Oxford: Basil Blackwell. 1980.

———. 'On Sense and Meaning' [1892]. Here cited from: P. Geach/ M. Black (eds.), *Translations from the Philosophical Writings of Gottlob Frege*, 3rd ed., pp. 56–78 (in earlier editions printed under the title 'On Sense and Reference'). Oxford: Basil Blackwell. 1980.

———. 'Frege on Definitions – I' [excerpt from Grundgesetze der Arithmetik, Vol. II, 1903]. In: *Translations from the Philosophical Writings of Gottlob Frege*, pp. 139–52.

FRENKEL-BRUNSWIK, Else. See Adorno/ Frenkel-Brunswik/ Levinson/ Sanford

FREUD, Anna. *Normality and Pathology in Childhood*. New York: International Universities Press. 1965.

FREUD, Sigmund. *Die Traumdeutung* [1900]. Here cited from: *Freud – Studienausgabe* in ten volumes [1969–75], Vol. II, 9th and revised printing. Frankfurt a.M.: S. Fischer Verlag. Year of publication not specified. Printed in 1994.

———. 'Das Unbewußte' [1915]. Here cited from *Freud – Studienausgabe*, Vol. III, 7th and revised printing, pp. 125–62.

———. *Vorlesungen zur Einführung in die Psychoanalyse* [1916–17]. Here cited from *Freud – Studienausgabe*, Vol. I, 12th and revised printing, pp. 37–445.

———. *Abriß der Psychoanalyse* [1940]. Frankfurt a.M.: Fischer Taschenbuch. 1953.

FRIHAGEN, Arvid. *Villfarelse og ugyldighet i forvaltningsretten* [mistake, misrepresentation and invalidity in administrative law]. Oslo etc.: Universitetsforlaget. 1966.

———. *Forvaltningsloven – kommentarutgave* [the Public Administration Act – a commentary]. Vol. 1. 2nd ed. Oslo: Forlaget A. Frihagen. 1986.

———. *Forvaltningsrett* [administrative law]. Vol. I. Oslo: Forlaget A. Frihagen. 1991. Vol. II. Bergen: Forlaget A. Frihagen. 1992.

FRISCH, Ragnar. 'Skillet mellom sak og vurdering' [the distinction between fact and evaluation]. In: R. Frisch/ W. Keilhau/ I. Wedervang, *Plan til en økonomisk strukturoversikt for Norge*, pp. 7–12. Oslo: Fabritius & Sønners Boktrykkeri. 1936.

FRÄNDBERG, Åke. *Om analog användning av rättsnormer* [on analogical use of legal norms]. Stockholm: Norstedt & Söner. 1973.

———. 'Till frågan om de juridiska begreppens systematik' [on the question of the systematics of legal concepts]. *Tidsskrift for Rettsvitenskap*, 1985, pp. 79–116.

———. 'Om tolkning och förståelse' [on interpretation and understanding]. (1985–86) 26 *Kungl. Vetenskapssamhällets i Uppsala Årsbok*, pp. 5–19.

FURBERG, Mats. *Saying and Meaning. A Main Theme in J. L. Austin's Philosophy*. Oxford: Basil Blackwell. 1971.

———. See also Andersson/ Furberg

FØLLESDAL, Dagfinn: 'Den moderne positivisme og dens kritikere' [modern positivism and its critics]. In: *Symposia Universitatis Upsaliensis Annum Quingentesimum Celebrantis 4: Livsåskådningsforskning*, pp. 93-133. Uppsala: Acta Universitatis Upsaliensis. 1977.

———. See also Føllesdal/ Walløe/ Elster

FØLLESDAL, Dagfinn/ WALLØE, Lars/ ELSTER, Jon. *Argumentasjonsteori, språk og vitenskapsfilosofi* [argumentation theory, language and the philosophy of science]. 6th ed. Oslo: Universitetsforlaget. 1996.

FØRDE, Olav Helge. See Søgaard/ Førde

GABRIEL, Gottfried. *Definitionen und Interessen: Über die praktischen Grundlagen der Definitionslehre*. Stuttgart: Frommann. 1972.

GALLIE, W. B. 'Essentially Contested Concepts'. (1955–56) LVI *Proceedings of the Aristotelian Society*, pp. 167–98.

GALTUNG, Johan. 'Expectations and Interaction Processes'. (1959) 2 *Inquiry*, pp. 213–34.

———. 'Deductive Thinking and Political Practice. An Essay on Teutonic Intellectual Style'. In: *Papers on Methodology*, pp. 194–209. Copenhagen: Ejlers. 1979.

GEERTZ, Clifford. 'Common Sense as a Cultural System' [1975]. Here cited from: *Local Knowledge* [1983], pp. 73–93. London: Fontana Press. 1993.

GOFFMAN, Erving. *The Presentation of Self in Everyday Life* [1959]. Harmondsworth etc.: Penguin Books. Pelican Book ed. 1971.

———. *Asylums* [1961]. Harmondsworth etc.: Penguin Books. Pelican Book ed. 1968.

———. *Stigma* [1963]. Harmondsworth: Penguin Books. 1990.

GOLDING, M. P. 'Kelsen and the Concept of 'Legal System' ' [1961]. Here cited from: R. S. Summers (ed.), *More Essays in Legal Philosophy*, pp. 69–100. Berkeley – Los Angeles: University of California Press. 1971.

GOODMAN, Nelson. *The Structure of Appearance*. 2nd ed. Indianapolis etc.: Bobbs-Merrill. 1966.

———. *Fact, Fiction, and Forecast.* 3rd ed. Indianapolis – New York: Bobbs-Merrill. 1973.

———. 'The Significance of Der logische Aufbau der Welt'. In: P.A. Schilpp (ed.), *The Library of Living Philosophers Vol. XI: The Philosophy of Rudolf Carnap*, pp. 545–58. La Salle, Illinois: Open Court – London: Cambridge University Press. 1963.

———. 'Science and Simplicity' [1963]. Here cited from: *Problems and Projects*, pp. 337–46. Indianapolis – New York: Bobbs-Merrill. 1972.

———. 'When Is Art?'. In: *Ways of Worldmaking*, pp. 57–70. Hassocks, Sussex: Harvester Press. 1978.

GOUTAL, Jean Louis. 'Characteristics of Judicial Style in France, Britain and the U.S.A.'. (1976) 24 *The American Journal of Comparative Law*, pp. 43–72.

GRAVER, Hans Petter. *Materiell forvaltningsrett* [substantive administrative law]. Oslo: Universitetsforlaget. 1996.

GRAY, John Chipman. *The Nature and Sources of the Law*. 2nd and revised ed. by R. Gray [1921]. Boston: Beacon Press. 1963.

GREENAWALT, Kent. *Law and Objectivity* [1992]. New York – Oxford: Oxford University Press. 1995.

GRICE, H. P./ STRAWSON, P. F. 'In Defense of a Dogma'. (1956) 65 *Philosophical Review*, pp. 141–58.

GROSS, Richard D. *Psychology: The Science of Mind and Behaviour*. 2nd ed. London: Hodder & Stoughton. 1992.

GUATTARI, Felix. See Deleuze/ Guattari

GULLVÅG, Ingemund. 'Carnap, Innledning' [Carnap, introduction]. In: I. Gullvåg (ed.), *Carnap*, pp. 11–82. Oslo: Pax. 1968.

———. 'Arne Næss og Oslo-skolen i norsk filosofi' [Arne Næss and the Oslo School in Norwegian Philosophy]. In: I. Bostad (ed.), *Filosofi på norsk I*, pp. 99–133. Oslo: Pax. 1995.

GUYER, Paul. 'The Possibility of the Categorical Imperative' [1995]. Here cited from: P. Guyer (ed.), *Kant's Groundwork of the Metaphysics of Morals: Critical Essays*, pp. 215–46. Lanham etc.: Rowman & Littlefield. 1998.

Gyldendals fremmedordbok [Gyldendal's dictionary of foreign words]. 13th ed. Oslo: Gyldendal. 1974.

GÖDEL, Kurt. 'Russel's Mathematical Logic'. In: P. A. Schilpp (ed.), *The Library of Living Philosophers Vol. V: The Philosophy of Bertrand Russell* [1944], pp. 124–53. New York etc.: Harper & Row. Torchbook ed. 1963.

GAARDER, Karsten. 'Domstolene og den alminnelige rettsutvikling' [the courts and the evolution of the law]. In: G. Nissen/ F. Hiorthøy/ K. Gaarder, *Den dømmende makt*, pp. 223–90. Oslo: Universitetsforlaget. 1967.

———. *Innføring i internasjonal privatrett* [introduction to international private law]. 2nd ed. [1990]. Oslo: Universitetsforlaget. 1993.

HABERMAS, Jürgen. 'Wahrheitstheorien'. In: H. Fahrenbach (ed.), *Wirklichkeit und Reflexion,* Festschrift for W. Schulz, pp. 211–65. Pfullingen: Neske. 1973.

———. 'Diskursethik – Notizen zu einem Begründungsprogramm'. In: *Moralbewußtsein und kommunikatives Handeln*, pp. 53–125. Frankfurt a.M.: Suhrkamp. 1983.

———. 'Erläuterungen zur Diskursethik'. In: *Erläuterungen zur Diskursethik*, pp. 119–226. Frankfurt a.M.: Suhrkamp. 1991.

———. *Faktizität und Geltung: Beiträge zur Diskurstheorie des Rechts und des demokratischen Rechtsstaats*. "4., durchgesehene und um Nachwort und Literaturverzeichnis erweiterte Aufl." Frankfurt a.M.: Suhrkamp. 1994.

HACKER, P. M. S. 'Hart's Philosophy of Law'. In: P.M.S. Hacker/ J. Raz (eds.), *Law, Morality, Society*, pp. 1–25. Oxford: Clarendon. 1977.

———. See also Baker/ Hacker

HAGERUP, Francis. 'Nogle Ord om den nyere Retsvidenskabs Karakter' [some words on the character of recent legal science]. *Tidsskrift for Rettsvitenskap*, 1888, pp. 1–58.

———. 'Ihering – Windscheid. En litterær Karakteristikk' [Ihering – Windscheid. A literary characterisation]. *Tidsskrift for Rettsvitenskap*, 1893, pp. 1–26.

———. 'Anmeldelse av Fredrik Stang, Innledning til formueretten' [review of Fredrik Stang, introduction to the law of obligations and property]. *Tidsskrift for Rettsvitenskap*, 1912, pp. 177–202.

———. 'Nogle Ord om Forholdet mellem positiv Ret og Retsanvendelse' [some words on the relationship between positive law and application of the law]. *Tidsskrift for Rettsvitenskap*, 1915, pp. 16–77.

———. 'Til Retsbegrebets Bestemmelse' [on the determination of the concept of 'law']. *Tidsskrift for Rettsvitenskap*, 1915, pp. 297–314.

———. *Retsencyclopædi* [encyclopaedia of law]. 3rd ed. Oslo: Aschehoug (W. Nygaard). 1931.

HAHN, Hans. See Neurath/ Hahn/ Carnap

HALL, Roland. 'Excluders'. (1959–60) 20 *Analysis*, pp. 1–7.

HAMBRO, Peter. See Augdahl/ Hambro

HANISCH, Tore J. See Bergh/ Hanisch

HARE, R. M. *The Language of Morals* [1952]. "Reprinted from corrected sheets of the first edition". Oxford: Clarendon. 1961.

———. *Freedom and Reason* [1963]. Oxford: Oxford University Press. Paperback ed. 1965.

———. *Moral Thinking: Its Levels, Method, and Point*. Oxford: Clarendon. 1981.

HARRIS, J. W. *Legal Philosophies*. London: Butterworths. 1980.

———. See also Cross/ Harris

HART, H. L. A. 'The Ascription of Responsibility and Rights' [1948–49 XLIX Proceedings of the Aristotelian Society]. Here cited from: A. G. N. Flew (ed.), *Logic and Language*, First Series [1951], pp. 145–66. Oxford: Basil Blackwell. 1978.

———. 'Definition and Theory in Jurisprudence'. (1954) 70 The Law Quarterly Review, pp. 37–60.

———. 'Scandinavian Realism' [1959]. Here cited from: *Essays in Jurisprudence and Philosophy*, pp. 161–69. Oxford: Clarendon. 1983.

———. *The Concept of Law*. – 1st ed. Oxford: Clarendon. 1961. Here cited from: Reprint with Corrections. 1975 [1970]. – 2nd ed. (p. vii: "unchanged, except for minor corrections"), with a Postscript. Oxford: Clarendon. 1994.

HEDENIUS, Ingemar. *Om rätt och moral* [on law and morals]. Stockholm: Tidens förlag. 1941.

HEGEL, G. W. F. *Grundlinien der Philosophie des Rechts* [1821]. Frankfurt a.M.: Suhrkamp. 1976.

HEIDER, Fritz. *The Psychology of Interpersonal Relations* [1958]. New York: John Wiley & Sons. Science Edition. 1967.

HEISENBERG, Werner. *Der Teil und das Ganze: Gespräche im Umkreis der Atomphysik*. Munich: R. Piper. 1969.

HELLNER, Jan. 'Positivism och metod inom rättsvetenskapen' [positivism and method in legal science]. In: Å. Frändberg/ U. Göranson/ T. Håstad (eds.), *Festskrift till Stig Strömholm*, pp. 351–73. Uppsala: Iustus. 1997.

HELSET, Per. 'Innledning til rettskildelæren' [introduction to the doctrine of the sources of law]. *Jussens Venner*, 1986, pp. 261–96.

HEMPEL, Carl G. 'Geometry and Empirical Science' [1945]. Here cited from: J. R. Newman (ed.), *The World of Mathematics*, Vol. III, pp. 1635–46. New York: Simon and Schuster. 1956.

———. 'Empiricist Criteria of Cognitive Significance: Problems and Changes' [1950, 1951]. Here cited from: *Aspects of Scientific Explanation And Other Essays in the Philosophy of Science*, pp. 101–19. New York: The Free Press – London: Collier-Macmillan. 1965.

———. 'A Logical Appraisal of Operationism' [1954]. Here cited from *Aspects of Scientific Explanation And Other Essays in the Philosophy of Science*, pp. 123–33.

HOHFELD, Wesley Newcomb. *Fundamental Legal Conceptions as Applied in Judicial Reasoning* [1919]. New Haven – London: Yale University Press. 1964.

HOLMES, Oliver Wendell. 'The Path of the Law' [1897]. Here cited from: *Collected Legal Papers*, pp. 167–202. London: Constable. 1920.

———. 'Natural Law' [1918]. Here cited from *Collected Legal Papers*, pp. 310–16.

HOMANS, George C. *The Human Group* [1951]. London: Routledge & Kegan Paul. 1975.

HONKASALO, Brynolf. 'Nulla Poena Sine Lege'. In: Förhandlingarna å det sjuttonde nordiska juristmötet (1937), Bilag II. Helsinki: Lokalstyrelsen i Finland. 1938.

HORNEY, Karen. *The Neurotic Personality of Our Time* [1937]. New York – London: W. W. Norton. Year of publication not specified.

———. *New Ways in Psychoanalysis* [1939]. New York – London: W. W. Norton. Year of publication not specified.

HOSPERS, John. *An Introduction to Philosophical Analysis*. 2nd ed. [1967]. London: Routledge & Kegan Paul. Paperback ed. 1973.

HOV, Jo. *Avtalerett* [law of contract]. 3rd ed. Oslo: Papinian. 1993.
———. *Rettergang i sivile saker* [legal procedure in civil cases]. 2nd ed. Oslo: Papinian. 1994.
———. See also Bratholm/ Hov
HULL, Clark L. 'Quantitative Aspects of the Evolution of Concepts'. (1920) XXVIII *Psychological Monographs*, no. 1.
HUME, David. *A Treatise of Human Nature* [1739–40]. Ed. by L. A. Selby-Bigge; 2nd ed. by P. H. Nidditch [1978]. Oxford: Clarendon. 1981.
HURLEY, Susan. 'Objectivity and Disagreement'. In: T. Honderich (ed.), *Morality and Objectivity: A Tribute to J. L. Mackie*, pp. 54–97. London etc.: Routledge & Kegan Paul. 1985.
HUSER, Kristian. *Avtaletolking* [interpretation of contracts]. Bergen etc.: Universitetsforlaget. 1983.
———. *Avtalesensur* [policing contracts]. Bergen: Publisher not specified. 1984.
HYLLESTED, E. ' "Individualismen." Nogle Bemærkninger om juridisk metode' ["individualism." some remarks on legal method]. *Tidsskrift for Rettsvitenskap*, 1910, pp. 211–54.
HÄGERSTRÖM, Axel. *Till frågan om den objektiva rättens begrepp. I. Viljeteorien* [on the question of the concept of 'law'. I. theory of will]. Uppsala: Akademiska Bokhandeln – Leipzig: Otto Harrassowitz. 1917.
———. 'Om moraliska föreställningars sanning' [on the truth of moral notions] [1911]. Here cited from: *Socialfilosofiska uppsatser*, pp. 35–57. Stockholm: Orion/ Bonniers. 1966.
HAAVELMO, Trygve. *Samfunn, styring og velferd* [society, governance and welfare]. Memorandum from the Department of Economics, University of Oslo. 1976.
IBSEN, Henrik. *The Wild Duck* [1884]. Here cited from: *Hedda Gabler and Other Plays*. Harmondsworth: Penguin Books. 1961.
IHERING, Rudolph. *Geist des römischen Rechts*. 2. Theil, 2. Abtheilung. Leipzig: Breitkopf und Härtel. 1858.
ILLUM, Knud. *Lov og ret* [law and justice]. Copenhagen: Nyt Nordisk Forlag. 1945.
JANIK, Allan/ TOULMIN, Stephen. *Wittgenstein's Vienna*. New York: Simon and Schuster. 1973.
JAREBORG, Nils. *Begrepp och brottbeskrivning* [concepts and the description of criminal offences]. Stockholm: Norstedt & Söner. 1974.
———. 'Regler och riktlinjer' [rules and guidelines]. *Tidsskrift for Rettsvitenskap*, 1979, pp. 385–410.
———. 'Regler och riktlinjer – en replik' [rules and guidelines – a rejoinder]. *Tidsskrift for Rettsvitenskap*, 1981, pp. 436–44.
———. *Straffrättsideologiska fragment* [fragments of the ideology of criminal law]. Uppsala: Iustus. 1992.
JEBENS, Sverre E. 'Opplesning av vitneforklaringer' [the reading out of testimony]. *Lov og Rett*, 1993, 87–108.

JENNINGS, Robert/ WATTS, Arthur (eds.). *Oppenheim's International Law.* 9th ed. Vol. I. Harlow, Essex: Longman. 1992.

JOHANSEN, Leif. 'Spillteori som grunnlag for samfunnsanalyse' [game theory as a basis for analysis of society]. *Sosiologi idag*, 1975, pp. 3–21.

JOHNSEN, Dag. 'Anmeldelse av N. Kr. Sundby, Om normer' [review of N. Kr. Sundby, on norms]. *Norsk Filosofisk Tidsskrift*, 1976, pp. 167–70.

JOHNSON, Mark. See Lakoff/ Johnson

JØRGENSEN, Stig. 'Typologi og realisme' [typology and realism]. In: K.S. Selmer (Chief ed.), *Nordisk gjenklang*, Festschrift for Carl Jacob Arnholm, pp. 143–63. Oslo: Johan Grundt Tanum. 1969.

——. *Ret og samfund* [law and society]. Copenhagen: Berlingske forlag. 1970.

KANT, Immanuel. *Von der Form der Sinnen- und Verstandeswelt und ihren Gründen* [1770]. Wiesbaden: Insel Verlag. 1958.

——. *Kritik der reinen Vernuft.* A = 1st ed. [1781], B = 2nd ed. [1787]. Stuttgart: Philipp Reclam jun. 1966.

——. *Grundlegung zur Metaphysik der Sitten* [1785]. Hamburg: Felix Meiner. 1965.

——. 'Über ein vermeintes Recht, aus Menschenliebe zu lügen' [1797]. Here cited from: Kleinere Schriften zur Geschichtsphilosophie, Ethik und Politik, pp. 199–206. Hamburg: Felix Meiner. 1973.

KARLGREN, Hjalmar. 'Några spörsmål i anslutning till 8 § Avtalslagen' [some questions in connection with section 8 of the Contracts Act]. In: *Studier i allmän avtalsrätt*, pp. 3–146. Lund: Håkan Ohlssons Boktryckeri. 1935.

KAUFMANN, Arthur: *Analogie und "Natur der Sache". Zugleich ein Beitrag zur Lehre vom Typus.* 2nd ed. Heidelberg: Decker & C. F. Müller. 1982.

——. 'Über den Zirkelschluß in der Rechtsfindung' [1973]. Here cited from: *Beiträge zur Juristischen Hermeneutik*, pp. 65–77. Köln etc.: Carl Heymann. 1984.

——. 'Durch Naturrecht und Rechtspositivismus zur juristischen Hermeneutik' [1975]. Here cited from *Beiträge zur Juristischen Hermeneutik*, pp. 79–88.

KELSEN, Hans. *Reine Rechtslehre.* – 1st ed. Leipzig and Vienna: Franz Deuticke. 1934. Here cited from: Neudruck. Aalen: Scientia Verlag. 1985. – 2nd ed. ("vollständig neu bearbeitete und erweiterte Auflage"). Vienna: Franz Deuticke. 1960. – Unless otherwise stated, references are to the 2nd ed.

——. 'Die Entstehung des Kausalgesetzes aus dem Vergeltungsprinzip'. (1939–40) 8 *Erkenntnis*, pp. 69–130.

KENNY, Anthony. *Will, Freedom and Power.* Oxford: Basil Blackwell. 1975.

KJØNSTAD, Asbjørn. *Rett til helsehjelp og sosiale tjenester* [the right to health care and social services]. Oslo: Ad Notam. 1990.

——. *Innføring i trygderett* [introduction to social security law]. 2nd ed. Oslo: Tano. 1991.

——. *Folketrygdens uførepensjon* [the national insurance disability pension]. 2nd ed. Oslo: Universitetsforlaget. 1992.

———. 'Pasientrettighetenes framvekst' [the growth of patients' rights]. In: A. Kjønstad/ A. Syse (eds.), *Helseprioriteringer og pasientrettigheter*, pp. 189–276. Place of publication not specified. Ad Notam Gyldendal. 1992.

———. 'Trygderettighetenes grunnlovsvern' [constitutional protection of national insurance rights]. In: A. Kjønstad (ed.), *Trygderettighetenes grunnlovsvern*, pp. 9–106. Place of publication not specified. Ad Notam Gyldendal. 1994.

———. See also Kjønstad/ Syse

KJØNSTAD, Asbjørn/ SYSE, Aslak. 'Pasientrettigheter i Norge – framvekst og utviklingsmuligheter' [patients' rights in Norway – growth and possibilities for development]. *Lov og Rett*, 1993, pp. 387–405.

———. *Velferdsrett* [welfare law]. Oslo: Ad Notam Gyldendal. 1997.

KNOPH, Ragnar. *Hensiktens betydning for grensen mellem rett og urett* [the significance of intent for the boundary between the lawful and the unlawful]. Kristiania: Olaf Norli. 1921.

———. 'Nogen ord om dommerens stilling til kutymene' [some words on the position and attitude of the judge in relation to usages in trade]. *Norsk Retstidende*, 1923, pp. 305–18.

———. *Oversikt over Norges rett* [survey of Norwegian law]. 3rd ed. by S. Grette. Oslo: Nationaltrykkeriet. 1949.

———. *Rettslige standarder* [legal standards]. Oslo: Grøndahl & Søn. 1939.

KOESTLER, Arthur. *Darkness at Noon* [1940]. London etc.: Vintage. 1994.

KRUSE, A. Vinding, *Ejendomskøb* [purchase of real property]. 6th ed. Copenhagen: Jurist- og Økonomforbundets Forlag. 1992.

KRÜGER, Kai. *Norsk kjøpsrett* [Norwegian sale of goods law]. 2nd ed. Bergen etc.: Universitetsforlaget. 1977. 3rd ed. Bergen: Alma Mater. 1991.

———. *Norsk kontraktsrett* [Norwegian law of contract]. Bergen: Alma Mater. 1989.

KVAMME, Helge. See Andenæs/ Kvamme

LAKOFF, George/ JOHNSON, Mark. *Metaphors We Live by*. Chicago – London: University of Chicago Press. 1980.

LANGER, Susanne K. *Philosophy in a New Key*. 3rd ed. [1957]. Cambridge, Mass.: Harvard University Press. 1980.

LARENZ, Karl. *Methodenlehre der Rechtswissenschaft*. 6th ed. Berlin etc.: Springer-Verlag. 1991.

LASSEN, Jul. Lassen, 'Anmeldelse av Ö. Undén, Om panträtt i rättigheter' [review of Ö. Undén, on security interests in rights]. *Svensk Juristtidning*, 1916, pp. 415–18.

———. 'Nogle Bemærkninger om Definitioner i Retsliteraturen' [some remarks on definitions in legal literature] [1921]. Here cited from: F. Dahl (ed.), *Udvalgte Afhandlinger*, pp. 59–72. Copenhagen: Gad. 1924.

LAURIDSEN, Preben Stuer. *Studier i retspolitisk argumentation* [studies in argumentation de lege ferenda]. Copenhagen: Juristforbundets forlag. 1974.

———. *Om ret og retsvidenskab* [on law and legal science]. Place of publication not specified. Gyldendal. 1992.

LEHRBERG, Bert. *Förutsättningsläran* [the doctrine of assumptions]. Uppsala: Iustus. 1989.

———. 'Förutsättningssynpunkter på köprättens felbegrepp' [assumptions perspectives on the concept of 'defective goods' in sale of goods law]. *Svensk Juristtidning*, 1990, pp. 543–65.

LEMMON, E. J. 'Sentences, Statements and Propositions'. In: B. Williams/ A. Montefiore (eds.), *British Analytical Philosophy* [1966], 3rd impression, "with corrections", pp. 87–107. London: Routledge & Kegan Paul – New York: The Humanities Press. 1971.

LEVINSON, Daniel J. See Adorno/ Frenkel-Brunswik/ Levinson/ Sanford

LEWIS, C. S. *Studies in Words*. Cambridge: Cambridge University Press. 1960.

LLEWELLYN, Karl N. *The Bramble Bush* [1930]. New York: Oceana Publications. 1960.

———. 'A Realistic Jurisprudence – The Next Step' [1930]. Here cited from: *Jurisprudence – Realism in Theory and Practice*, pp. 3–41. Chicago: University of Chicago Press. 1962.

———. 'On the Good, the True, the Beautiful, in Law' [1942]. Here cited from *Jurisprudence – Realism in Theory and Practice*, pp. 167–213.

———. *The Common Law Tradition: Deciding Appeals*. Boston – Toronto: Little, Brown. 1960.

LORD MORAN. See Moran

LOVIBOND, Sabina. *Realism and Imagination in Ethics*. Oxford: Basil Blackwell. 1983.

LUHMANN, Niklas. *Rechtssoziologie*. "2., erweiterte Auflage". Opladen: Westdeutscher Verlag. 1983.

———. *Soziale Systeme: Grundriß einer allgemeinen Theorie* [1984]. Frankfurt a.M.: Suhrkamp. 1987.

———. *Das Recht der Gesellschaft*. Frankfurt a.M.: Suhrkamp. 1993.

LUKES, Steven. *Power: A Radical View*. London – Basingstoke: Macmillan. 1974.

LYDERSEN, Aksel/ DAHLØ, Ingrid. 'Refleksjoner over arbeid med teknisk terminologi' [reflections on work on technical terminology]. In: L. Mæhle/ E. Lundeby/ O. Grønvik (eds.), *Fornying og tradisjon – språkvern og språkrøkt 1972–1988*, pp. 90–100. Oslo: Norsk Språkråd/ Cappelen. 1987.

LYONS, John. *Semantics*. Vol. 1–2. Cambridge: Cambridge University Press. 1977.

———. *Language and Linguistics: An Introduction*. Cambridge etc.: Cambridge University Press. 1981.

MACCORMICK, [D.] Neil. *Legal Reasoning and Legal Theory*. Oxford: Clarendon. 1978

———. 'Reconstruction after Deconstruction: A Response to CLS'. (1990) 10 *Oxford Journal of Legal Studies*, pp. 539–58.

———. 'Coherence in Legal Justification'. In: *De Lege, Juridiska fakulteten i Uppsala, Årsbok, 1992*, pp. 311–30. Uppsala: Iustus. 1992.

———. 'Foreword'. In: Reprint of *Legal Reasoning and Legal Theory*, pp. ix–xvi. Oxford: Clarendon. 1994.

———. See also Bankowski/ MacCormick/ Summers/ Wróblewski; MacCormick/ Summers; MacCormick/ Weinberger

MACCORMICK, D. Neil/ SUMMERS, Robert S. (eds.). *Interpreting Precedents: A Comparative Study*. Aldershot etc.: Ashgate – Dartmouth. 1997.

MACCORMICK, [D.] Neil/ WEINBERGER, Ota. *An Institutional Theory of Law*. Dordrecht etc.: D. Reidel. 1986.

MADSEN, K. B. *Psykologiens historie* [history of psychology]. Oslo: Gyldendal. 1972.

MALT, Gert Fredrik. 'Svake normer' [weak norms]. *Tidsskrift for Rettsvitenskap*, 1986, pp. 167–91.

———. 'To glemte linjer i tradisjonell rettsfinningslære' [two forgotten lines in the traditional doctrine of finding law]. *Tidsskrift for Rettsvitenskap*, 1992, pp. 48–83.

MARC-WOGAU, Konrad. 'Definisjon' [definition]. In: K. Marc-Wogau, *Filosofisk leksikon*, Norwegian ed. by E. Dalseth, pp. 36–37. Place of publication not specified. Fabritius & Sønner. 1969.

MARGALIT, Avishai. 'Open Texture'. In: A. Margalit (ed.), *Meaning and Use*, pp. 141–52. Dordrecht etc.: D. Reidel – Jerusalem: Magnes Press. 1979.

MAUS, Ingeborg. 'Freiheitsrechte und Volkssouveränität'. (1995) 26 *Rechtstheorie*, pp. 507–62.

MCDOWELL, John. *Mind and World*. Cambridge, Mass. – London: Harvard University Press. 1994.

MCGINN, Colin. *Wittgenstein on Meaning* [1984]. Oxford – New York: Basil Blackwell. 1987.

MEAD, George H. *Mind, Self, and Society* [1934]. The Works of G. H. Mead, Vol. 1. Chicago – London: University of Chicago Press. Phoenix ed. Year of publication not specified.

MEDVEDEV, Roy A. *Nikolai Bukharin – The Last Years*. New York – London: W. W. Norton. 1980.

———. *Let History Judge – The Origins and Consequences of Stalinism*. Revised and expanded ed. Oxford – New York: Oxford University Press. 1989.

MERTON, Robert K. 'Manifest and Latent Functions'. In: *Social Theory and Social Structure*, pp. 73–138. Enlarged ed. New York: The Free Press – London: Collier Macmillan. 1968.

MESSINGER, Sheldon L. See Aubert/ Messinger

MILL, John Suart. *A System of Logic*. 8th ed. [1872]. London: Longmans, Green, and Co. People's Ed. 1884.

MONK, Ray. *Ludwig Wittgenstein: The Duty of Genius* [1990]. London: Vintage. 1991.

———. *Bertrand Russell: The Spirit of Solitude* [1996]. London: Vintage. 1997.

MOORE, George Edward. 'A Defence of Common Sense' [1925]. Here cited from: T. Baldwin (ed.), *G. E. Moore: Selected Writings*, pp. 106–33. London – New York: Routledge. 1993.

———. 'Proof of an External World' [1939]. Here cited from *G. E. Moore: Selected Writings*, pp. 147–70.

———. 'Certainty' [1951]. Here cited from *G. E. Moore: Selected Writings*, pp. 171–96.

———.'Hume's Theory Examined' [1953]. Here cited from *G. E. Moore: Selected Writings*, pp. 59–78.

MORAN, LORD. *The Anatomy of Courage*. London: Constable. 1945.

MORGENSTIERNE, Bredo. *Lærebok i den norske statsforfatningsret* [textbook of Norwegian constitutional law], Vol. 2. 3rd ed. Oslo: O. Christiansens Boktrykkeri. 1927.

MYRDAL, Gunnar. *An American Dilemma* [1944]. New York etc.: Harper & Row. Torchbook ed. 1969.

———. *The Political Element in the Development of Economic Theory* [1953]. London: Routledge & Kegan Paul. 1971.

———. *Value in Social Theory*. London: Routledge & Kegan Paul. 1958.

NAGEL, Thomas. *Mortal Questions*. Cambridge etc.: Cambridge University Press. 1979.

NENT [the national committee on research ethics for natural science and technology], *Føre-var prinsippet: mellom forskning og politikk* [the precautionary principle: between research and politics]. Oslo: NENT Publication No 11. 1997.

NEURATH, Otto/ HAHN, Hans/ CARNAP, Rudolf. *Wissenschaftliche Weltauffassung: der Wiener Kreis* [1929]. Here cited from: Otto Neurath, *Empiricism and Sociology*, pp. 299–318. Dordrecht – Boston: D. Reidel. 1973.

NIELSEN, Kai. 'In Defense of Wide Reflective Equilibrium'. In: D. Odegard (ed.), *Ethics and Justification*, pp. 19–37. Edmonton, Alberta: Academic Printing and Publishing. 1988.

NIETZSCHE, Friedrich. *Zur Genealogie der Moral* [1887]. Here cited from: Karl Schlechta (ed.), Werke in drei Bänden, Band II, pp. 761–900. Munich: Carl Hanser Verlag. 1966.

Norsk riksmålsordbok [Norwegian Riksmål dictionary]. 2nd ed. Oslo: Kunnskapsforlaget 1983.

NÆSS, Arne. *"Truth" as Conceived by Those who are not Professional Philosophers*. Oslo: Det Norske Vitenskaps-Akademi. 1938.

———. 'Elementære analytiske undersøkelser' [elementary analytical investigations]. In: S. Holm (ed.), *Filosofiske problemer*, No. 1, pp. 1–39. Oslo: Skrivemaskinstua. 1944.

———. 'Finnes det objektive normer?' [are there objective norms?]. *Norsk pedagogisk årbok*, 1946–47, pp. 189–205.

———. *Interpretation and Preciseness*. Oslo: Det Norske Vitenskaps-Akademi. 1953.

———. *An Empirical Study of the Expressions "True", "Perfectly Certain" and "Extremely Probable"*. Oslo: Det Norske Vitenskaps-Akademi. 1953.

———. *Democracy, Ideology and Objectivity*. Oslo: Oslo University Press – Oxford: Basil Blackwell. 1956.

———. 'Do we know that Basic Norms cannot be True or False?'. (1959) 25 *Theoria*, pp. 31–53.

———. *En del elementære logiske emner* [some elementary topics in logic]. 9th ed. Oslo – Bergen: Universitetsforlaget. 1961.

———. 'We still do [not] know that Norms cannot be True or False'. (1962) 28 *Theoria*, pp. 205–09.

———. *Logikk og metodelære* [logic and methodology]. 2nd ed. Oslo: Universitetsforlaget. 1966.

———. *Scepticism.*Oslo: Universitetsforlaget. 1968.

———. *Hvilken verden er den virkelige?* [which world is the real one?]. Oslo etc.: Universitetsforlaget. 1969.

———. *The Pluralist and Possibilist Aspect of the Scientific Enterprise*. Oslo: Universitetsforlaget – London: Allen & Unwin. 1972.

———. 'Ayer on Metaphysics, a Critical Commentary by a Kind of Metaphysician'. In: L. E. Hahn (ed.), *The Library of Living Philosophers Vol. XXI: The Philosophy of A. J. Ayer*, pp. 329–40. La Salle, Illinois: Open Court. 1992.

———. 'Equality, Sameness, and Rights'. In: G. Sessions (ed.), *Deep Ecology for the Twenty-first Century*, pp. 222–24. Boston – London: Shambhala. 1995.

———. 'Self-realization: An Ecological Approach to Being in the World'. In: *Deep Ecology for the Twenty-first Century*, pp. 225–39.

O'FALLON, James M. 'Adjudication and Contested Concepts: The Case of Equal Protection'. (1979) 54 *New York University Law Review*, pp. 19–82.

OFSTAD, Harald. *Alf Ross's begrepsbestemmelse av begrepet 'rettsregel'* [Alf Ross' determination of the concept of 'legal rule']. Oslo: Skrivemaskinstua. 1949.

———. 'The Descriptive Definition of the Concept 'Legal Norm' proposed by Hans Kelsen'. (1950) 16 *Theoria*, pp. 118–51, 211–46.

———. 'Om deskriptive definisjoner av begrepet rettsregel' [on descriptive definitions of the concept of 'legal rule']. *Tidsskrift for Rettsvitenskap*, 1952, pp. 38–83.

———. 'The Functions of Moral Philosophy'. (1958) 1 *Inquiry*, pp. 35–71.

———. *An Inquiry into the Freedom of Decision*. Oslo: Norwegian Universities Press – London: George Allen & Unwin. 1961.

OGDEN, C. K./ RICHARDS, I. A. *The Meaning of Meaning*. 10th ed. [1949]. London: Routledge & Kegan Paul. 1972.

OLIVECRONA, Karl. *Law as Fact*. 1st ed. Copenhagen: E. Munksgaard – London: H. Milford. 1939.

———. *Rättsordningen* [the legal system]. 2nd ed. Lund: LiberLäromedel. 1976.

———. 'Frågeställningar i rättsteorien' [problems in legal theory]. *Tidsskrift for Rettsvitenskap*, 1973, pp. 308–10.

O'NEILL, Onora. 'Universal Laws and Ends-in-Themselves' [1989]. Here cited from: *Constructions of Reason: Explorations of Kant's Practical Philosophy*, pp. 126–44. Cambridge etc.: Cambridge University Press. 1989.

OPPENHEIM, L. See Jennings/ Watts

OPSAHL, Torkel. 'An Inquiry into the Meaning and Function of Legal Definitions' [1957]. Here cited from: *Law and Equality: Selected Articles on Human Rights*, pp. 657–74. Oslo: Ad notam Gyldendal. 1996.

ORWELL, George. 'Arthur Koestler' [1946]. Here cited from: *The Penguin Essays of George Orwell*, pp. 274–84. Harmondsworth etc.: Penguing Books. 1984.

OS, Audvar. 'Anmeldelse av Eckhoff, Forvaltningsrett, 1st ed.' [review of Eckhoff, administrative law, 1st ed.]. *Lov og Rett*, 1980, pp. 488–92.

Oxford Dictionary, The Concise. 8th ed. Oxford: Clarendon. 1990.

PALME, Olof. *Politikk – det er å ville noe* [politics – that is the will to achieve something]. Oslo: Tiden. 1970.

PARKINSON, G. H. R. 'Introduction'. In: G. H. R. Parkinson (ed.), *The Theory of Meaning* [1968], pp. 1–14. Oxford: Oxford University press. 1978.

PARSONS, Talcott. *The Social System* [1951]. New York: The Free Press – London: Collier Macmillan. Paperback ed. 1964.

———. 'Definitions of Health and Illness in the Light of American Values and Social Structure' [1958]. Here cited from: Social Structure and Personality, pp. 257–91. New York: The Free Press – London: Collier Macmillan. 1964.

PASSMORE, John. *Philosophical Reasoning*. 2nd ed. London: Duckworth. 1970.

PATTERSON, Edwin. *Jurisprudence*. Brooklyn: Foundation Press. 1953.

PEARS, David. *Wittgenstein*. London: Fontana/ Collins. 1971.

———. *The False Prison: A Study of the Development of Wittgenstein's Philosophy*. Vol. I. Oxford: Clarendon. 1987.

PECZENIK, Aleksander. *Juridikens metodproblem* [the problem of method in law]. Stockholm: Almqvist & Wiksell. 1974.

———. *Rättsnormer* [legal norms]. Stockholm: Norstedts. 1987.

———. *On Law and Reason*. Dordrecht etc.: Kluwer. 1989.

———. 'En förståelsesmodell för etik, rätt och argumentation' [an interpretation model for ethics, law and argumentation]. *Tidsskrift for Rettsvitenskap*, 1992, pp. 20–47.

———. *Vad är rätt?* [what is law?]. Stockholm: Norstedts Juridik. 1995.

———. See also Aarnio/ Alexy/ Peczenik; Alexy/ Peczenik; Peczenik/ Aarnio/ Bergholtz; Peczenik/ Schött

PECZENIK, Aleksander, with the assistance of AARNIO, Aulis and BERGHOLTZ, Gunnar (Peczenik et al). *Juridisk argumentation – en lärobok i allmän rättslära* [legal argumentation – a textbook of legal theory]. Stockholm: Norstedts. 1990.

PECZENIK, Aleksander/ SCHÖTT, Roland. 'Juridisk konservatism' [legal conservatism]. *Svensk Juristtidning*, 1993, pp. 709–34.

PEIRCE, Charles S. 'The Fixation of Belief' [1877]. Here cited from: J. Buchler (ed.), *Philosophical Writings of Peirce*, pp. 5–22. New York: Dover Publications. 1955.

———. 'How to Make Our Ideas Clear' [1878]. Here cited from *Philosophical Writings of Peirce*, pp. 23–41.

PETERSEN, Hanne. *Informel ret på kvindearbejdspladser – en retsteoretisk og empirisk analyse* [informal law in women's workplaces – a legal-theoretical and empirical analysis]. Copenhagen: Akademisk forlag. 1991.

PHILIP, Allan. *Dansk international privat- og processret* [Danish international private and procedural law]. 3rd ed. Copenhagen: Juristforbundets forlag. 1976.

POPPER, Karl R. 'What is Dialectic?' [1940]. Here cited from: *Conjectures and Refutations*, 4th ed., pp. 312–35. London and Henley: Routledge & Kegan Paul. 1972.

———. *The Open Society and Its Enemies*, Vol. 2. 5th and revised ed. [1966]. London and Henley: Routledge & Kegan Paul. 1980.

———. *Unended Quest*. Fourth Impression, with corrections. Place of publication not specified. Fontana/ Collins. 1978.

———. *Logic of Scientific Discovery*; a transl. of *Logik der Forschung*, Vienna, 1935. 10th and revised impression [1980]. London etc.: Hutchinson. 1987.

POSNER, Richard A. 'Some Uses and Abuses of Economics in Law'. (1979) 46 *University of Chicago Law Review*, pp. 281–306.

———. *The Economics of Justice*. Cambridge, Mass. – London: Harvard University Press. 1981.

———. *Economic Analysis of Law*. 3rd ed. Boston – Toronto: Little, Brown and Company. 1986.

———. *The Problems of Jurisprudence*. Cambridge, Mass. – London: Harvard University Press. 1990.

———. *Cardozo: A Study in Reputation*. Chicago – London: University of Chicago Press. 1990.

POUND, Roscoe. 'The Theory of Judicial Decision'. (1923) 36 *Harvard Law Review*, pp. 641–62, 802–25, 940–59.

———. *An Introduction to the Philosophy of Law*. Revised ed. [1954]. New Haven – London: Yale University Press. 1988.

QUINE, W.V. 'Truth by Convention' [1935]. Here cited from: *The Ways of Paradox and other Essays*, revised and enlarged ed., pp. 77–106. Cambridge, Mass. – London: Harvard University Press. 1976.

———. 'On What There Is' [1948]. Here cited from: *From a Logical Point of View*, 2nd and revised ed., pp. 1–19. New York: Harper & Row. 1961.

———. 'Two Dogmas of Empiricism' [1951]. Here cited from *From a Logical Point of View*, pp. 20–46.

———. *Mathematical Logic*. Revised ed. [1951]. New York – Evanston: Harper & Row. 1962.

———. *Word and Object*. Cambridge, Mass.: M.I.T. Press. 1960.

———. 'Necessary Truth' [1963]. Here cited from *The Ways of Paradox and other Essays*, pp. 68–76.

———. 'Carnap and Logical Truth'. In: P.A. Schilpp (ed.), *The Library of Living Philosophers Vol. XI: The Philosophy of Rudolf Carnap*, pp. 385–406. La Salle, Illinois: Open Court – London: Cambridge University Press. 1963.

———. 'Epistemology Naturalized'. In: *Ontological Relativity and Other Essays*, pp. 69–90. New York – London: Columbia University Press. 1969.

———. 'Vagaries of Definition' [1972]. Here cited from *The Ways of Paradox and other Essays*, pp. 50–55.

———. *The Roots of Reference*. La Salle, Illinois: Open Court. 1973.

———. 'Goodman's Ways of Worldmaking' [1978]. Here cited from: *Theories and Things*, pp. 96–99. Cambridge, Mass. – London: Belknap Press. 1981.

———. 'Things and Their Place in Theories' [1980]. Here cited from *Theories and Things*, pp. 1–23.

———. 'Reply to Herbert G. Bohnert'. In: L. E. Hahn/ P. A. Schilpp (eds.), *The Library of Living Philosophers Vol. XVIII: The Philosophy of W. V. Quine*, pp. 93–95. La Salle, Illinois: Open Court. 1986.

———. 'Reply to Ulrich Gähde and Wolfgang Stegmüller'. In *The Library of Living Philosophers Vol. XVIII: The Philosophy of W. V. Quine*, pp. 137–38.

———. 'Reply to Geoffrey Hellman'. In *The Library of Living Philosophers Vol. XVIII: The Philosophy of W. V. Quine*, pp. 206–08.

RADBRUCH, Gustav. *Rechtsphilosophie*. "6. Auflage", by E. Wolf. Stuttgart: K. F. Koehler. 1963.

RADZINSKY, Edvard. *Stalin*. New York etc.: Doubleday. 1996.

RAWLS, John. *A Theory of Justice*. 1st ed. [1971]. Oxford etc.: Oxford University Press. 1973. 2nd ed. ("revised edition"). Cambridge, Mass.: Belknap Press. 1999.

———. 'The Independence of Moral Theory'. (1974–75) 48 *Proceedings and Adresses of the American Philosophical Association*, pp. 5–22.

———. 'Justice as Fairness: Political not Metaphysical'. (1985) 14 *Philosophy & Public Affairs*, pp. 223–51.

———. *Political Liberalism*. New York: Columbia University Press. 1993.

RAZ, Joseph. 'Legal Principles and the Limits of Law'. (1972) 81 *Yale Law Journal*, pp. 823–54.

———. *The Concept of a Legal System*. 2nd ed. Oxford: Clarendon. 1980.

———. *The Morality of Freedom*. Oxford etc.: Oxford University Press. 1986.

REGAN, Tom. *The Case for Animal Rights* [1984]. London – New York: Routledge. 1988.

REHBINDER, Eckard. 'The Precautionary Principle in an International Perspective'. In: E.M. Basse (ed.), *Miljørettens grundspørgsmål*, pp. 91–105. Copenhagen: G. E. C. Gad. 1994.

REVSBECH, Karsten. 'Anmeldelse av Eckhoff, Forvaltningsrett, 4th ed.' [review of Eckhoff, administrative law, 4th ed.]. *Tidsskrift for Rettsvitenskap*, 1994, pp. 240–54.

RICHARDS, I. A. See Ogden/ Richards

RICKERT, Heinrich. *Zur Lehre von der Definition*. 3rd and revised printing. Tübingen: J. C. B. Mohr (Paul Siebeck). 1929.

ROBINSON, Richard. *Plato's Earlier Dialectic* [1941]. 2nd ed. [1953]. Oxford: Clarendon. 1970.

———. *Definition*. Oxford: Clarendon. 1950.

———. *An Atheist's Values*. Oxford: Clarendon. 1964.

RODHE, Knut. 'Om gränserna för lagstiftarens makt på civilrättens område' [on the limits of the legislator's power in the area of civil law]. *Ekonomen*, 1944, pp. 96–106.

———. *Obligationsrätt* [law of obligations]. Stockholm: Norstedt & Söner. 1956.

———. 'Beskrivning – prognos – rekommendation[.] En trosbekännelse' [description – prognosis – recommendation. A confession of faith]. *Juridisk Tidskrift*, 1996–97, pp. 1–4.

ROMMETVEIT, Ragnar. *Social Norms and Roles*. Oslo: Akademisk forlag. 1953.

———. *Språk, tanke og kommunikasjon* [language, thought and communication]. Oslo, etc.: Universitetsforlaget. 1972.

RORTY, Richard. 'Two Retrospective Essays'. In: R. Rorty (ed.), *The Linguistic Turn*, pp. 361–74. Chicago – London: University of Chicago Press. 1992.

ROSENBERG, Jay F./ TRAVIS, Charles. 'Readings in the Philosophy of Language, Editors' Chapter Introduction'. In: J.F. Rosenberg/ C. Travis (eds.), *Readings in the Philosophy of Language*, pp. 391–94. Englewood Cliffs, New Jersey: Prentice-Hall. 1971.

ROSS, Alf. *Kritik der sogenannten praktischen Erkenntnis*. Copenhagen: Levin & Munksgaard – Leipzig: Felix Meiner. 1933.

———. *Om ret og retfærdighed* [1953]. Copenhagen: Nyt Nordisk Forlag. 1971.

———. *On Law and Justice*. London: Stevens & Sons. 1958.

———. 'Om begreberne "stat" og "statsorgan" i statsforfatningsretten' [on the concepts of 'state' and 'state body' in constitutional law]. *Tidsskrift for Rettsvitenskap*, 1958, pp. 106–23.

———. 'Friheds- og ejendomskriteriet' [the freedom and property criterion] [1957]. Here cited from: Statsretlige studier, pp. 71–124. Copenhagen: Nyt Nordisk Forlag. 1959.

———. *Hvorfor demokrati?* [why democracy?]. 2nd ed. Copenhagen: Nyt Nordisk Forlag. 1967.

———. *Directives and Norms*. London: Routledge & Kegan Paul. 1968.

———. *Lærebog i folkeret* [textbook of international law]. 5th ed. Copenhagen: Nyt Nordisk Forlag. 1980.

———. *Dansk Statsforfatningsret* [Danish constitutional law], Vol. I. 3rd ed. by O. Espersen. Copenhagen: Nyt Nordisk Forlag. 1980.

ROSSVÆR, Viggo. 'Transcendentale problemstillinger i moderne filosofi' [transcendental problems in modern philosophy]. *Norsk Filosofisk Tidsskrift*, 1972, pp. 105–16.

RUSSELL, Bertrand. 'On Denoting'. (1905) 14 *Mind*, pp. 479–93.

———. *Our Knowledge of the External World* [1914]. London – New York: Routledge. 1993.

———. *Introduction to Mathematical Philosophy*. London: George Allen & Unwin. 1919.

———. See also Whitehead/ Russel

RÜTHERS, Bernd. *Die Unbegrenzte Auslegung. Zum Wandel der Privatrechtsordnung im Nationalsozialismus*. Tübingen: J. C. B. Mohr. 1968.

———. *Entartetes Recht. Rechtslehren und Kronjuristen im Dritten Reich*. "2., verbesserte Auflage." München: C. H. Beck. 1989.

RYCROFT, Charles. 'An Enquiry into the Function of Words in the Psycho-Analytical Situation'. (1958) 39 *The International Journal of Psycho-Analysis*, pp. 408–15.

RYLE, Gilbert. 'Philosophical Arguments' [1945]. Here cited from: *Collected Papers, Vol. II: Collected Essays 1929–1968*, pp. 194–211. London: Hutchinson. 1971.

———. 'Ordinary Language' [1953]. Here cited from *Collected Papers, Vol. II: Collected Essays 1929–1968*, pp. 301–18.

———. See also Ayer

RØSTAD, Helge. 'Lovprinsippet i strafferetten' [the principle of statutory authority in criminal law]. In: *Innkast i straffefeltet*, pp. 65–87. Oslo: Universitetsforlaget. 1993.

SANDVIK, Tore. *Entreprenørrisikoen* [the risk borne by the building contractor]. Oslo: Johan Grundt Tanum. 1966.

SANFORD, R. Nevitt. See Adorno/ Frenkel-Brunswik/ Levinson/ Sanford

SAPIR, Edward. 'Cultural Anthropology and Social Psychology'. (1932) 27 *Journal of Abnormal and Social Psychology*, pp. 229–42.

SCANLON, T. M. 'The Aims and Authority of Moral Theory'. (1992) 12 *Oxford Journal of Legal Studies*, pp. 1–23.

SCHARTUM, Dag Wiese. *Rettssikkerhet og systemutvikling i offentlig forvaltning* [legal safeguards and system development in public administration]. Oslo: Universitetsforlaget. 1989.

SCHAUER, Frederick. *Playing by the Rules. A Philosophical Examination of Rule-Based Decision-Making in Law and in Life*. Oxford: Clarendon. 1991.

SCHEEL, Herman. 'Om Rettens Grund som Udgangspunkt for Læren om Retskilderne' [on the foundation of law as a point of departure for the doctrine of the sources of law]. *Tidsskrift for Rettsvitenskap*, 1907, pp. 249–62.

SCHJELDERUP, Harald. 'Filosofiens vesen' [the essence of philosophy] [1922]. Here cited from: A. Ås (ed.), *Forskerferd i sinnets dybder*, pp. 47–57. Oslo: Gyldendal. 1965.

SCHLICK, Moritz. 'Meaning and Verification' [1936]. Here cited from: H. Feigl/ W. Sellars (eds.), *Readings in Philosophical Analysis*, pp. 146–70. California: Ridgeview Publishing. 1949.

SCHOPENHAUER, Arthur. 'Zur Rechtslehre und Politik'. In: *Parerga und Paralipomena: Kleine philosophische Schriften* [1851]. Here cited from: *Werke in zehn Bänden*, Band IX, pp. 261–89. Zürich: Diogenes. 1977.

SCHÖTT, Roland. See Peczenik/ Schött

SCRUTON, Roger. *Art and Imagination: A Study in the Philosophy of Mind* [1974]. London etc.: Routledge & Kegan Paul. 1982.

SEARLE, John R. *Speech Acts*. Cambridge: Cambridge University Press. 1969.

———. 'A Taxonomy of Illocutionary Acts' [1975]. Here cited from: *Expression and Meaning*, pp. 1–29. Cambridge etc.: Cambridge University Press. 1979.

———. 'Indirect Speech Acts' [1975]. Here cited from *Expression and Meaning*, pp. 30–57.

———. 'Literal Meaning' [1978]. Here cited from *Expression and Meaning*, pp. 117–36.

———. 'Metaphor' [1979]. Here cited from *Expression and Meaning*, pp. 76–116.

———. *The Construction of Social Reality* [1995]. Harmondsworth: Penguin Books. 1996.

SEIP, Jens Arup. *Et regime foran undergangen* [1945]. Oslo: Gyldendal. 1965.

———. *Utsikt over Norges historie* [survey of Norwegian history]. Oslo: Gyldendal. First Part, 1974; Second Part, 1981.

———. 'Det 19. århundres norske byråkrati belyst gjennom moderne forvaltningsteori' [the 19th century's Norwegian bureaucracy illuminated through modern administrative theory].[1965]. Here cited from: *Problemer og metode i historieforskningen*, pp. 159–71. Oslo: Gyldendal. 1983.

———. ' "Ekte" og "uekte" vurderinger i historieforskningen' [genuine and spurious evaluations in historical research] [1967]. Here cited from *Problemer og metode i historieforskningen*, pp. 184–89.

———. 'Modellenes tyranni' [the tyranny of models] [1975]. Here cited from *Problemer og metode i historieforskningen*, pp. 199–227.

SELVIG, Erling. *Kontraktsretten* [law of contract]. In: B. Stuevold Lassen (ed.), *Knophs oversikt over Norges rett*, 10. ed., pp. 298–647. Oslo: Universitetsforlaget. 1993.

SHARPE, Ella Freeman. 'Psycho-Physical Problems Revealed in Language: an Examination of Metaphor' [1940]. Here cited from: *Collected Papers on Psycho-Analysis* [1950], pp. 155–69. London: Hogarth Press and The Institute of Psycho-Analysis. 1978.

———. 'A Note on "the Magic of Names" ' [1946]. Here cited from *Collected Papers on Psycho-Analysis*, pp. 107–08.

SHEPPARD, Anne. *Aesthetics*. Oxford – New York: Oxford University Press. 1987.

SHKLAR, Judith N. *Legalism – Law, Morals, and Political Trials* [1964]. Cambridge Mass. – London: Harvard University Press. 1986.

SIMPSON, A. W. B. 'The Common Law and Legal Theory'. In: A. W. B. Simpson (ed.), *Oxford Essays in Jurisprudence*, 2nd Series, pp. 77–99. Oxford: Clarendon. 1973.

———. 'Innovation in Nineteenth Century Contract Law'. (1975) 91 *Law Quarterly Review*, pp. 247–78.

SMITH, Adam. *The Theory of Moral Sentiments* [1759]. Oxford: Clarendon. 1976.

SMITH, Carsten. *Studier i garantiretten – Garantirett II* [studies in the law of guarantees and bonds – guarantee law II]. Oslo: Universitetsforlaget. 1963.

———. 'Domstolene og rettsutviklingen' [the courts and the evolution of the law]. *Lov og Rett*, 1975, pp. 292–319.

———. *Garantikrav og garantistvern – Garantirett III* [guarantee claims and protection of the guarantor – guarantee law III]. 2nd ed. Oslo: Universitetsforlaget. 1981.

SMITH, Eivind. 'Om fordeling av økonomiske goder i forvaltningsretten' [on distribution of economic advantages in administrative law]. *Jussens Venner*, 1978, pp. 115–46.

———. 'Legalitetsprinsippets hjemmelskrav og subjekter' [the principle of legality's requirement for legal authority, and its subjects]. *Tidsskrift for Rettsvitenskap*, 1978, pp. 655–91.

———. See also Eckhoff/ Smith

SOLZHENITSYN, Alexander. *The Gulag Archipelago*. Part I [1973]. London: Collins/ Fontana. 1974.

STANG, Fredrik. 'Ord og hensigt' [words and intention]. *Norsk Retstidende*, 1911, pp. 657–67.

———. 'Om rettsvidenskap' [on legal science]. *Tidsskrift for Rettsvitenskap*, 1933, pp. 118–34.

———. *Innledning til formueretten* [introduction to the law of obligations and property]. 3rd ed. Oslo: Aschehoug (W. Nygaard). 1935.

STANG DAHL. See Dahl

STEGMÜLLER, Wolfgang. *Rationale Rekonstruktion von Wissenschaft und ihrem Wandel*. Stuttgart: Philipp Reclam jun. 1979.

STEIN, Peter. 'Elegance in Law' [1961]. Here cited from: *The Character and Influence of the Roman Civil Law: Historical Essays*, pp. 3–17. London – Ronceverte: Hambledon Press. 1988.

STENIUS, Erik. *Wittgenstein's Tractatus* [1960]. Reprint. Westport, Connecticut: Greenwood Press. 1981.

———. 'The Concepts 'Analytic' and 'Synthetic' '. In: R.E. Olson/ A.M. Paul (eds.), *Contemporary Philosophy in Scandinavia*, pp. 57–76. Baltimore – London: Johns Hopkins Press. 1972.

STEVENSON, Charles L. 'The Emotive Meaning of Ethical Terms' [1937]. Here cited from: *Facts and Values*, pp. 10–31. New Haven – London: Yale University Press. 1963.

———. 'Persuasive Definitions' [1938]. Here cited from *Facts and Values*, pp. 32–54.

———. *Ethics and Language*. New Haven – London: Yale University Press. 1944.

STIGEN, Anfinn (ed.). *Betydning og mening, handling og ytring* [signification and meaning, action and utterance]. Oslo: Universitetsforlaget. 1967.

———. *Generasjoner i norsk filosofi* [generations of Norwegian philosophy]. Oslo: Gyldendal. 1973.

STOLLEIS, Michael. 'Gemeinschaft und Volksgemeinschaft. Zur juristischen Terminologie im Nationalsozialismus' [1972]. Here cited from: *Recht im Unrecht: Studien zur Rechtsgeschichte des Nationalsozialismus*, pp. 94–125. Frankfurt a.M.: Suhrkamp. 1994.

STONE, Christopher D. 'Should Trees Have Standing – Toward Legal Rights for Natural Objects'. (1972) 45 *Southern California Law Review*, pp. 450–501.

———. *Should Trees Have Standing – Toward Legal Rights for Natural Objects*. Los Altos, California: William Kaufmann. 1974.

STORHEIM, Eivind. 'Innledning' [introduction]. In: E. Storheim (ed.), *Kant: Morallov og frihet*, pp. XI–XXVII. Oslo: Gyldendal. 1970.

STRAHL, Ivar. 'En allmän rättslära' [a general theory of law]. *Svensk Juristtidning*, 1955, pp. 289–315.

STRAWSON, Peter F. *Introduction to Logical Theory* [1952]. London: Methuen. University Paperbacks. 1963.

———. 'Carnap's Views on Constructed Systems versus Natural Languages in Analytic Philosophy'. In: P.A. Schilpp (ed.), *The Library of Living Philosophers Vol. XI: The Philosophy of Rudolf Carnap*, pp. 503–18. La Salle, Illinois: Open Court – London: Cambridge University Press. 1963.

———. See also Grice/ Strawson

STRÖMBERG, Tore. *Inledning till den allmänna rättsläran* [introduction to legal theory]. 8th ed. Lund: Studentlitteratur. 1981.

———. *Rättsordningens byggstenar* [the building bricks of the legal system]. Lund: Studentlitteratur. 1988

———. 'Hur gick det för kvalifikationsnormerna?' [what happened to the qualification norms?]. *Tidsskrift for Rettsvitenskap*, 1991, pp. 42–49.

STRÖMHOLM, Stig. *Rätt, rättskällor och rättstillämpning* [law, sources of law and application of the law]. 5th ed. Stockholm: Norstedts Juridik. 1996.

STUER LAURIDSEN. See Lauridsen

SUMMERS, Robert S. 'Legal Philosophy Today – An Introduction'. In: R. S. Summers (ed.), *Essays in Legal Philosophy* [1968], pp. 1–21. Berkeley – Los Angeles: University of California Press. 1976.

———. '"Good Faith" in General Contract Law and the Sales Provisions of the Uniform Commercial Code'. (1968) 54 *Virginia Law Review*, pp. 195–267.

———. 'The General Duty of Good Faith – Its Recognition and Conceptualization'. (1982) 67 *Cornell Law Review*, pp. 810–35.

———. *Instrumentalism and American Legal Theory*. Ithaca – London: Cornell University Press. 1982.

———. See also Bankowski/ MacCormick/ Summers/ Wróblewski; MacCormick/ Summers; Summers/ Taruffo

SUMMERS, Robert S./ TARUFFO, Michele. 'Interpretation and Comparative Analysis'. In: D. N. MacCormick/ R. S. Summers (eds.), *Interpreting Statutes*, pp. 461–510. Aldershot etc.: Dartmouth. 1991.

SUNDBY, Nils Kristian. 'Legal Right in Scandinavian Analyses'. (1968) 13 *Natural Law Forum*, pp. 72–107.

———. *Om normer* [on norms]. Oslo: Universitetsforlaget. 1974.

———. 'Kritisk juss: hva er det?' [critical law: what is that?]. *Jussens Venner*, 1975, pp. 115–32.

———. 'Strafferetten og dens begrensninger' [criminal law and its limitations]. *Lov og Rett*, 1976, pp. 51–91.

———. See also Eckhoff/ Sundby

SVERI, Knut. See Aubert/ Eckhoff/ Sveri

SYSE, Aslak. See Eskeland/ Syse; Kjønstad/ Syse

SZASZ, Thomas S. 'The Myth of Mental Illness'. (1960) 15 *American Psychologist*, pp. 113–18.

———. *The Myth of Mental Illness*. 2nd ed. London: Paladin. 1972.

SØGAARD, Anne J./ FØRDE, Olav Helge. 'Jo mer helse, jo mindre trivsel' [the more health, the less enjoyment]. *Aftenposten*, 9. October 1992.

TARUFFO, Michele. See Summers/ Taruffo

THAGARD, Paul. *Coherence in Thought and Action*. Cambridge, Mass. – London: MIT Press. 2000.

THORNSTEDT, Hans. 'Legalitet och teleologisk metod i straffrätten' [legality and teleological method in criminal law]. In: *Festskrift tillägnad Nils Herlitz* (ed. not specified), pp. 319–68. Stockholm: Norstedt & Söner. 1955.

TOULMIN, Stephen. See Janik/ Toulmin

TRANØY, Knut Erik. ' 'Ought' implies 'Can': A Bridge from Fact to Norm?'. Part I. (1972) XIV *Ratio*, pp. 116–30.

———. 'The Ideology of Scientific and Scholarly Conduct'. In: R.E. Olson/ A.M. Paul (eds.), *Contemporary Philosophy in Scandinavia*, pp. 331–49. Baltimore – London: Johns Hopkins Press. 1972.

———. 'The Foundations of Cognitive Activity: An Historical and Systematic Sketch'. (1976) 19 *Inquiry*, pp. 131–50.

———. 'Anmeldelse av N. Kr. Sundby, Om normer' [review of N. Kr. Sundby, on norms]. *Lov og Rett*, 1976, pp. 475–79.

———. 'Vitenskap og etikk, sannheten som verdi' [science and ethics, the truth as a value]. In: T. Støren (ed.), *Ikke-kristen etikk*, pp. 120–29. Oslo: Gyldendal. 1981.

———. *Vitenskapen – samfunnsmakt og livsform* [science – a power in society and a way of life]. Oslo etc.: Universitetsforlaget. 1986.

TRAVIS, Charles. See Rosenberg/ Travis

TUCKER, Robert C. *Stalin in Power: The Revolution From Above, 1928–41* [1990]. New York – London: W. W. Norton. 1992.

TUGENDHAT, Ernst. *Vorlesungen zur Einführung in die sprachanalytische Philosophie* [1976]. Frankfurt a.M.: Suhrkamp. 1979.

TWINING, William. *Karl Llewellyn and the Realist Movement* [1973]. Reprint with Postscript. London: Weidenfeld and Nicolson. 1985.

ULLMANN, Stephen. *The Principles of Semantics*. 2nd ed. [1957]. Oxford: Basil Blackwell – Glasgow: Jackson. 1963.

ULLMANN-MARGALIT, Edna. *The Emergence of Norms*. Oxford: Clarendon. 1977.

URMSON, J. O. 'Polymorphous Concepts'. In: O.P. Wood/ G. Pitcher (eds.), *Ryle: A Collection of Critical Essays*, pp. 249–66. London: Macmillan. 1971.

USSING, Henry. *Obligationsretten, almindelig del* [the law of obligations, general part]. 4th ed. New printing, revised by A. Vinding Kruse. Copenhagen: Juristforbundets forlag. 1967.

———. *Aftaler* [contracts]. 3rd ed. [1950]. Copenhagen: Juristforbundets forlag. 1974.

VAHLÉN, Lennart. *Formkravet vid fastighetsköp* [the form requirement in the case of the purchase of real estate]. Stockholm: Nordiska Bokhandeln. 1951.

———. 'Bör förutsättningsläran avskaffas?' [ought the doctrine of assumptions to be abolished?]. *Tidsskrift for Rettsvitenskap*, 1953, pp. 393–409.

VINDING KRUSE. See Kruse

VOLKOGONOV, Dmitri. *Stalin – Triumph and Tragedy* [1989]. Rocklin, California: Prima Publishing. 1992.

VON EYBEN. See Eyben

VON WRIGHT. See Wright

WAHRIG, Gerhard. *Deutsches Wörterbuch*. Munich: Mosaik Verlag. 1986.

WAISMANN, Friedrich. 'Verifiability' [1945]. Here cited from: A. G. N. Flew (ed.), *Logic and Language*, First Series [1951], pp. 117–44. Oxford: Basil Blackwell. 1978.

———. *Ludwig Wittgenstein and the Vienna Circle*. Oxford: Basil Blackwell. 1979.

WALLØE, Lars. See Føllesdal/ Walløe/ Elster

WEAVER, Richard M. *The Ethics of Rhetoric*. Chicago: Henry Regnery. 1953.

WEBER, Max. 'Die "Objektivität" sozialwissenschaftlicher und sozialpolitischer Erkenntnis' [1904]. Here cited from: J. Winckelmann (ed.), *Gesammelte Aufsätze zur Wissenschaftslehre*, 4th and revised printing, pp. 146–214. Tübingen: J. C. B. Mohr (Paul Siebeck). 1973.

———. 'R. Stammlers "Überwindung" der materialistischen Geschichtsauffassung' [1907]. Here cited from *Gesammelte Aufsätze zur Wissenschaftslehre*, pp. 291–359.

———. 'Über einige Kategorien der verstehenden Soziologie' [1913]. Here cited from *Gesammelte Aufsätze zur Wissenschaftslehre*, pp. 427–74.

———. *Wirtschaft und Gesellschaft*. "5., revidierte Auflage", by J. Winckelmann. Tübingen: J. C. B. Mohr (Paul Siebeck). 1972.

WEINBERGER, Ota. *Rechtslogik*. 2nd ed. Berlin: Duncker & Humblot. 1989.

WEITZ, Morris. 'Open Concepts'. *Revue Internationale de Philosophie*, 1972, pp. 86–110.

WELLS, Michael. 'French and American Judicial Opinions'. (1994) 19 *Yale Journal of International Law*, pp. 81–133.

WHITEHEAD, Alfred North/ RUSSELL, Bertrand. *Principia Mathematica*, 2nd ed., Vol. I [1925]. Cambridge: Cambridge University Press. 1950.

WHORF, Benjamin Lee. *Language, Thought, and Reality*. Cambridge, Mass.: M.I.T. Press. 1967.

WILLIAMS, Bernard. *Ethics and the Limits of Philosophy*. London: Fontana Press/ Collins. 1985.

WILLIAMS, Glanville. 'Language and the Law' I–V. (1945) 61 *The Law Quarterly Review*, pp. 71–86, 179–95, 293–303, 384–406; (1946) 62, pp. 387–406.

WILSON, Edmund. *To the Finland Station* [1940]. New York: Noonday Press. 1972.

WISDOM, John. 'Philosophy, Metaphysics and Psycho-Analysis'. In: *Philosophy and Psycho-Analysis*, pp. 248–82. Oxford: Basil Blackwell. 1953.

———. 'G. E. Moore'. (1958–59) 19 *Analysis*, pp. 49–53.

WITTGENSTEIN, Ludwig. *Tractatus Logico-Philosophicus*. Transl. by C. K. Ogden [1922]. London etc.: Routledge & Kegan Paul. 1981.

———. *Philosophische Untersuchungen* [1953]. Frankfurt a.M.: Suhrkamp. 1982.

———. *Bemerkungen über die Farben* [1977]. Frankfurt a.M.: Suhrkamp. 1984.

———. *Zettel*. Revised ed. 1979. Frankfurt a.M.: Suhrkamp. 1984.

WORLD COMMISSION ON THE ENVIRONMENT AND DEVELOPMENT. *Our Common Future*. Oxford – New York: Oxford University Press. 1987.

WREDE, R. A. *Lagen om rättshandlingar på förmögenhetsrättens område* [the Act concerning juristic acts in the area of law relating to obligations and property]. 2nd ed. Helsinki: Söderström. 1949.

WRIGHT, Georg Henrik von. 'Form and Content in Logic' [1949]. Here cited from: *Logical Studies*, pp. 1–21. London: Routledge & Kegan Paul. 1957.

———. *The Varieties of Goodness*. London: Routledge & Kegan Paul – New York: The Humanities press. 1963.

———. *Norm and Action* [1963]. London and Henley: Routledge & Kegan Paul. 1977.

———. *Myten om framsteget* [the myth of progress]. Stockholm: Albert Bonnier. 1993.

———. 'Value, Norm, and Action in My Philosophical Writings'. In: G. Meggle (ed.), *Actions, Norms, Values: Discussions with Georg Henrik von Wright*, pp. 11–33. Berlin – New York: Walter de Gruyter. 1999.

WRÓBLEWSKI, J. See Bankowski/ MacCormick/ Summers/ Wróblewski

YOUNG-BRUEHL, Elisabeth. *Hannah Arendt*. New Haven – London: Yale University Press. 1982.

ZAPFFE, Peter Wessel. 'Den sidste Messias' [the last Messiah] [1933]. Here cited from: *Essays*, pp. 15–28. Place of publication not specified. Aventura Forlag. 1992.

———. *Indføring i litterær Dramaturgi* [introduction to literary dramaturgy]. Oslo – Bergen: Universitetsforlaget. 1961.

ZIFF, Paul. *Semantic Analysis* [1960]. Ithaca and London: Cornell University Press. Cornell Paperbacks. 1967.

ZIMMER, Frederik. *Lærebok i skatterett* [textbook of tax law]. 2nd and 3rd eds. Oslo: Tano. 1995 and 1997 respectively.

ZIPPELIUS, Reinhold. *Das Wesen des Rechts*. 4th ed. Munich: C. H. Beck. 1978.

ØSTERBERG, Dag. *Forståelsesformer* [forms of understanding] [1966]. Oslo: Pax. 1972.

ØSTERUD, Øyvind. 'Er nasjonalstaten foreldet?' [is the national state a thing of the past?]. *Nytt Norsk Tidsskrift*, 1992, pp. 351–64.

———. *Hva er nasjonalisme?* [what is nationalism?]. Oslo: Universitetsforlaget. 1994.

AALL, Jørgen. *Rettergang og menneskerettigheter* [legal proceedings and human rights]. Bergen: Universitetsforlaget. 1995.

AARBAKKE, Magnus. 'Harmonisering av rettskilder' [harmonisation of sources of law]. *Tidsskrift for Rettsvitenskap*, 1966, pp. 499–518.

———. *Skatt på inntekt* [tax on income]. 3rd ed. Part 1. Oslo etc.: Universitetsforlaget. 1973.

———. 'Aksjetegning. Ugyldighet, mislighold og ansvar' [subscription of shares. Invalidity, breach of contract and liability]. *Tidsskrift for Rettsvitenskap*, 1989, pp. 333–58.

Index of authors

Index of subjects

The following index is particularly directed at topics, words and contexts that cannot be immediately read out of the table of contents. Basically subentries have been organised alphabetically; however in some instances they have been organised according to other principles (e.g. logical order, proximity in substance matter, or relative importance).

Abbreviations	def	definition (in the same sense as in the present work, including inter alia both decision propositions concerning one's own use of language and descriptive propositions concerning other people's use of language)
	w.f.ref.	with further references
	n	only or in the main in a note (where a topic is treated in both text and note, the latter is not specially indicated)
	v	in contrast to (versus)

GPSR Compliance

The European Union's (EU) General Product Safety Regulation (GPSR) is a set of rules that requires consumer products to be safe and our obligations to ensure this.

If you have any concerns about our products, you can contact us on ProductSafety@springernature.com

In case Publisher is established outside the EU, the EU authorized representative is:

Springer Nature Customer Service Center GmbH
Europaplatz 3
69115 Heidelberg, Germany

Batch number: 10823951

Printed by Printforce, the Netherlands